BREAKING IN, BREAKING OUT

BREAKING IN, BREAKING OUT

AN AUTOBIOGRAPHY BY
NICHOLAS MONSARRAT

WILLIAM MORROW & COMPANY, INC., NEW YORK 1971

To the next generation

OF MOLLY:

JENIFER GREEN
JEREMY PROCTOR
SUSAN PROCTOR

OF FELICITY:

GILES ARMSTRONG
JUDITH ARMSTRONG
KAREN ARMSTRONG
PIERS ARMSTRONG
MEG ARMSTRONG

OF DENYS:

GILLIAN PETERSEN

AND OF ME:

MAX MONSARRAT
MARC MONSARRAT
ANTHONY MONSARRAT

with love and good luck

FOREWORD

I planned this book backwards, and I can hear the acid voice of Ivor Chippe, my favourite critic, saying: "You don't need to tell us that." Yet it is true, and important.

I wanted to write a story never shared, in full, with anyone. Starting with the year of "Now," I went further and further back, on an entirely novel voyage of discovery, until I reached the year of "Then"; and "Then" was a full half-century ago, the small moment of innocence which is surely guaranteed by the fact of being one year old.

I was going to tell my story in decades—or rather, with a decade between each section; and the book was to have been called *Take It in Tens*. But the ten-year span proved intractable, and impossible to obey. The gaps were too great; between eleven years old and twenty-one years old, for example, the formative years are crucial; between forty-one and fifty-one they are, thank God, still formative. So I changed the focus, halved the height of the jumps, threw away less and remembered more, and brought the intervals down to five.

A five-year period, I learned long ago at school, was called, in Latin, a *lustrum;* the antique Roman word (from *luere,* to wash) described an act of purification after the taking of the quinquennial census.

Well, I surely hope so.

N.M.

CONTENTS

Photographs appear between pages 256 and 257. Unless otherwise specified, they are from the author's private collection.

"This is the state of man: today he puts forth
The tender leaves of hopes; tomorrow blossoms,
And bears his blushing honours thick upon him;
The third day comes a frost, a killing frost,
And when he thinks, good easy man, full surely
His greatness is a-ripening, nips his root,
And then he falls, as I do."

SHAKESPEARE, *KING HENRY THE EIGHTH*

ONE

—◦◦◦—

1911

THE LAST OF THE EDWARDIANS

IT WAS, AND IS, a tall house, the house where I was born; not bad-looking, in a formal sort of way, though its colour is no pleasure to classify—something between battleship-grey and institution-ochre. It stood, and stands, in a row of eight other tall houses, in a street of eighty-eight tall houses, which was, and is, Rodney Street in Liverpool.

Our house was Number 11. Number 9, next door, boasted a pale blue plaque recording that Arthur Hugh Clough, poet, had lived there some seventy years earlier. There was nothing on Number 11 save a modest brass plate which said: "Mr. K. W. Monsarrat, F.R.C.S." My father.

He is ninety-three as I write this sentence; in 1911, when I was one, he was thirty-nine; Dean of the Faculty of Medicine at Liverpool University, consulting surgeon, lecturer on operative surgery at the Northern Hospital. (When it came my turn to be thirty-nine, I was head of the British Information Service in South Africa. I think my father wins that particular contest.) But this was why we lived in Rodney Street, which was, and is, all doctors; it is the Harley Street of Liverpool—though, in those days of no-nonsense, northern pride, we would probably have called Harley Street the Rodney Street of London.

I had been born the previous year, on 22 March 1910, which made me, technically, an Edwardian, since the last of our Merry Monarchs did not die until May of that year. I was also a Tolstoyan,* sharing the same world with that superb artist for more

---

* My other contemporaries included Rodin, Florence Nightingale, and Joshua Slocum. But my father could beat that, any day of any year; he was able to claim Brahms, Tennyson, Disraeli, Gladstone (born at 62 Rodney Street), Sir Henry Irving, Napoleon III, Zola, Melville, Trollope, and Garibaldi. Most enviable of all, he was nine years old when Nelson's daughter Horatia died.

than seven months. It is a pity that one cannot know of these rare privileges at the time.

The Edwardian angle was never to be important, not even in anecdotage, but something else was: the fact that, owing to a long-standing caprice of my mother, my birth had been registered in the wrong name.

For certain interior reasons, Mother had always favoured a fancier spelling of our surname, which was sufficiently odd in any case; there was, she assured me many years later, a French nobleman, the Marquis de Montserrat, who was "definitely related," and that was the way she was going to spell it, "whatever your father says."

So there my birth-certificate lies, and will lie forever, recording my name as "Montserrat" in plain, unvarnished misinformation, although my father, and his before him, and all the family trees ever climbed by the inquisitive, had never wavered from "Monsarrat."

It was to be a recurring embarrassment later on; first, at boarding-school, when my parents' letters were addressed to two different versions of me; then when I wanted to take the scholarship examination for Winchester, and to have my own passport, and to go to Cambridge; then when I joined the Navy, and had to prove, to the satisfaction of their Lordships of the Admiralty (with all the preoccupations of Dunkirk on their minds), that I was actually the man I claimed to be.

It popped up once again when I was offered a job, which had some security aspects, in the British Information Service; and last of all, when I wanted to emigrate to Canada.

Even marriages were made more difficult; and as for divorces . . . I never quite got over this feeling of being, officially, a marked man. Indeed (to quote, for the first time, the chap who puts in all the bad jokes), birth-marked.

However, all this, on the second morning of spring, 1910, was still in the delicious, folded future; all I had to worry about, on that day, was the business of staying alive, at a time when my expectation of life was forty-four years (it would now be sixty-eight), and the infant mortality rate one hundred fifty per thousand (now down to under twenty). But I survived; and after the birth came the registration (all wrong), and after the registration the christening—very much all right, with a big flock of well-heeled relatives and, as godfather, an uncle who subsequently became Archbishop of New Zealand.

I was christened round the corner and down the street, at St. Luke's Church, a solid grey-black monument to Christian piety which, thirty years later, I was to watch being pounded to death in the merciless Liverpool blitz of 1941.

The selection of names must have sparked some far-ranging family reminiscence, as well as certain foreboding thoughts on the theme: "What will he be when he grows up?" All the choices were wide open.

My father (Keith) was a surgeon; my grandfather (Henry) a country clergyman in Westmorland; my great-grandfather (Mark) a wine-merchant in Dublin; my great-great-grandfather (Nicholas) a wine-grower in the Midi; and *his* father (Jean, b. 1693) a notary of the village of Rocquecourbe, which is near Castres, which is near Toulouse in the district of Tarn. Castres had been a famous Huguenot stronghold in the sixteenth century, but my prudent forebears seemed to have kept clear of that.

On the maternal side, things were also prudent, as well as being rather more prosperous. My other grandfather, a man of Victorian consequence, dealt in leather, in the largest possible way; and leather made him, successively, the chairman (for twenty-three years) of the Electricity Committee of the City of Nottingham, Lord Mayor of that same city, and, like Falstaff, a solid knight (Sir John Turney, Kt.) under that all-embracing, all-forgiving banner, "For political and public services."

If I had been able to raise my head, in the domed, doomed magnificence of St. Luke's, I would have heard that I was being christened Nicholas John Turney Monsarrat; Nicholas for the old paternal ancestor, and John Turney for more practical considerations (which didn't actually work out). But it was reported that I slept placidly, not yet knowing what I had to live up to.

Now, at long last, I was one year old, and picking up a few of the facts; walking possibly, talking certainly, and—with shining blue eyes and long golden curls—a child so beautiful that people cried as they looked at me, convinced that I could not live. (Let us forgive a mother's reminiscent bias; indeed, let us honour it.)

I had an elder brother, Toby, and two sisters, Molly and Felicity; I was the youngest of the batch, and people had to be nice to me, and not make a fuss if I bothered them or took their toys. . . . It was a strong position, and no doubt fully exploited.

The nursery was dark, because it was at the top of the tall house; and Liverpool skies, on most days of the year, put a lowering lead umbrella over the whole city. There was a daily outing; myself heavily veiled in the custom of the time, the nurse pushing my pram, Toby and my sisters slogging manfully along behind, for the five solid miles to Prince's Park and back again. There was a summer trip to the seaside, to Trearddur Bay in North Wales, where my father had just built a house; but I did not yet know about that, nor how much I would come to love this particular corner of the world.

There were certain slogans to make me eat. "Bite for King George!" the nurse would say, as she rammed the stuff into my mouth; and "Down the red lane!" for the next installment. There were impertinent games with my toes ("This little piggy went to market"), and the beginning of a vast indoctrination of nursery rhymes, never afterwards forgotten; Little Boy Blue, Pat-a-Cake Pat-a-Cake Baker's Man, Fee Fi Fo Fum, Old King Cole Was a Merry Old Soul.

Indeed, in this, the downy innocence of the world, while gentle Jesus, meek and mild, looked upon this little child, and outside, a viable motor-car had just been invented, my nursery stage was already crowded with a whole gallery of eccentrics. A cow jumped over the moon. A goosey-gander wandered upstairs and downstairs. There was a crooked man who walked a crooked mile. Cock-a-doodle-doo, one dame had lost her shoe, while a second, older woman lived in another one, with all those children. Four-and-twenty blackbirds were baked in a pie. My bonnie lay over the ocean. A mouse ran up the clock. The little dog laughed to see such fun.

There was even a man in the moon!

SIX

1916

THROUGH SIX-YEAR-OLD EYES, the tall house in Rodney Street had now taken on definite shape.

It was tall, because it was narrow—only one room thick all the way through—and because of all the things that had to go on inside it. On the ground floor was the consulting-room, from which we were totally barred; though a sneaky visitor, in off-duty hours when its owner was at the hospital, or in the very early morning, could find there all the mysteries of my father's trade.

Behind this focal point was the waiting-room for the patients, which also doubled as the dining-room at night, when the magazines were cleared away, and the chairs brought up to the table again. I don't know what happened at lunch-time. Perhaps 1 P.M. to 2 was kept free of sufferers.

Beyond that was a kitchen with a vast coal range, and the serried instruments of cookery, and a succession of bad-tempered people who told you to leave things alone, but who would, if you put on the right face, usually come across with a slice of bread-and-syrup or a hunk of yesterday's cold suet pudding.

That was the end of the ground floor, and perhaps the best end, since I could not remember when I was not absolutely ravenous.

Above this street-level mixture of professional and domestic skills, our family took over completely. Steep stairs led up to the drawing-room, another place, of some elegance, which was labelled "By invitation only"; then there were more stairs, steeper still, with a wooden gate across the top which only my elder sister Molly knew how to unlatch; stairs which climbed up to the gas-lit, window-barred nurseries—one for day, one for night—where we spent perhaps twenty-one hours out of every twenty-four.

By day, the main nursery was mortally cold; the rattling windows let in a ferocious draft which seemed to have come straight off the Irish Sea; the scuttles of coal had to be carried up three flights of stairs, and since the under-nursemaid was often at war with the housemaid, each disdaining this low-class haulage job, the fire suffered, and we with it.

It was no better in the night nursery, and at night it was worse. This was a low-ceilinged, shadowy room, into which the moon peered in cold, eerie inspection; and above it, right under the rafters, was the attic. We all knew the attic, and we tried not to think about it; it was almost pitch-dark, and intensely forbidding, with a cistern which never stopped gurgling to itself, musty domed trunks which might have held *anything,* boards that creaked without reason, ghosts which had no other place to live.

I never visited it, even by daylight, except on a dare; and every night-time, as I lay in my bed, wearing my "scrum-cap" because my ears stuck out like jug-handles, yet still able to hear the creaks and the groans and the mad laughter up above, it was like having all the characters out of all the most terrifying books staring through the ceiling at me, waiting for closed eyes to give them a chance to drop down.

I could even believe that there was a giant up there, who roared out "Fee, fi, fo, fum!" as he smelled the blood of an Englishman.

It compelled me, very early on, to demand a night-light, and to scream my head off until I got one. Servants slept up there; I thought they were very brave, even the ones I didn't like: too brave for me to copy, braver than I would ever be, even if, as was freely forecast, I grew up and joined the Navy and was immediately made an admiral.

Every night, until I obeyed the Sandman and fell asleep, under the strange shadows moving to and fro across the ceiling, and the awful things going on just above that, I wished I could be far, far below, safely down where the coal was stored, with the cook, in the basement.

The wish did not escape anyone's notice.

"Cowardy cowardy custard!" chanted my sisters, at least once a day, taking it in turns, like small antiphonal witches, to push home the poisoned dart. "He has to have a night-light!"

"Just like a baby!"

"Crying!"

"I might have to get up in the night," I would counter feebly.

"You ought to go before you go to bed."

We were always "going," it seemed to me; the inquisitive

"Have you been?" seemed to be the first question that occurred to anyone, as soon as they saw me. It was part of the nursery discipline, administered by a succession of nurses, mostly middle-aged, and good-hearted, and good-tempered too. There were other disciplines; by now I knew very well what it meant to be naughty, because this invariably brought, with no delay at all, a short sharp belt on the behind—which was called, technically, the "sit-upon," and was very rude.

It was from nurses, mostly, that I had so far learned; and the result was a jumbled storehouse of myth, proverb, caution, and fantasy, which, like that prompt smack on the bottom, never did anyone a lick of harm.

But, by 1916, the nursery was no longer the only learning-ground. Already I was going to school. For those days, this was a little early; but I had become (according to contemporary account) "such a little pest" that the longer I could be kept out of the house, the better. (Let us forgive, once again, a mother's natural bias. But it was true that the phrase "as good as gold" did not exactly ring in my ears all day long.) Anyway, there I was, with crested cap and bulging satchel, commuting daily by tram between Rodney Street and St. Christopher's, Linnet Lane.

I thought it was a wonderful idea. I was fed up with girls, in the form of older sisters, already; this was my first big chance to meet sensible people, many of them six years old.

St. Christopher's School for Boys was a substantial private house, converted to its present use by knocking down a few walls and painting all the others in that gruesome shade of chocolate-brown which resisted, equally, the passage of time, male children, and all advancement in interior decoration. It was a matriarchal establishment, which did not worry me, since I took all my orders from women anyway; all the teachers, and even the gardener, were female, and at the top of this formidable heap were the two co-owners and principals, Miss Smith and Miss Nellie. It took me almost two years to discover that Miss Nellie was actually Miss Nellie Smith, younger sister of the one we called Miss Smith, who was indubitably the boss. It was not important, since we were in permanent awe of both of them; it was just an early example of that capacity for getting people's names wrong which has plagued me ever since.

Side by side with my crouched companions, I learned the letters, and then the numbers; I learned to spell, and to read, and to write, all with a healthy exercise of effort, compressed beneath a small yet furrowed brow. By all accounts, the process has been altered, restored, improved, and re-altered, many times since then; and I do not know whether the experiments have turned out better, or worse, or just the same as in more simple days.

Long division loomed ahead, like some forbidding peak which had to be scaled because, like Mount Everest, it was there. I could also tell the time, which was useful, though it cancelled out one prime excuse for never being on hand when I was wanted. I won a prize "for good progress in drawing," and a citation for being the best-behaved boy at lunch-time. I would hate to think what the worst-behaved boy was allowed to get away with.

But since I had learned to read, I put it to increasing use at home; and the books were the hand-me-down classics of the time— *The Tinder Box*, and Brer Fox and Brer Rabbit of *Uncle Remus* (it took me approximately thirty years to discover that "Brer" was a slip-shod Americanism for "Brother"), and all the gallery of Beatrix Potter's kindly creatures—Flopsy Bunny, Mrs. Tittle-mouse, Peter Rabbit, Squirrel Nutkin, Jemima Puddleduck, Mrs. Tiggy-Winkle—and that much less kindly cast from *Struwwel-peter*: Little Johnny Head-in-Air, Little something Suck-a-Thumb, Shock-headed Peter—and, to bring me back to safe English ground, the staunch quartet of Rat, Mole, Badger, and Toad in *The Wind in the Willows*.

I loved or feared them all, and scooped them up, again and again, from the newly discovered printed page. But, being lazy already, and of course exhausted by successive hard days at St. Christopher's, I preferred to be read to, rather than to read; by Felicity if necessary, by Mother if possible. Molly was always too busy, and Denys, the new younger brother, aged two, was natu-rally hopeless.

The family was really taking shape now, more than school, more than the tall house, more than anything.

Toby, the eldest, had died and gone straight to heaven, after falling from the steepest of all the rocks that lined our summer beach at Trearddur Bay. He had been replaced, the following year, by a new member, of the vintage of 1914, called Denys.

I have often wished, without intrusion, to know the real reason why Denys was conceived, as he must have been, within a short month after Toby's death; whether in sorrow, or in duty, or in protest against the rage of heaven, or in the relief of tenderness after bitter loss, or to complete a four-square family pattern (two boys, two girls, two sides to the world's original question), or to draw together a pair of grief-stricken people, or to fill an empty cot or an empty heart or an empty head, or, mundanely, because he would have popped up anyway.

I never asked, nor could have asked, my mother or my father for the private replies of fifty years ago. Even now, I can hear the sharp voice of far-off reproof saying, with more than the usual bite: *"Curiosity killed the cat."* Yet the question remains—intriguing, possibly very moving, important in the sense that all questions of human motive are important; and I mourn the fact that I shall never find out, nor cease to wonder, why one son should so promptly replace another.

Anyway, there he was, the child of hazard, love, or calculation, my younger brother, Denys Keith Turney Monsarrat.

Felicity was eight, dark and pretty, slightly rebellious, usually in trouble—a nice sister to have. Molly was much older—sixteen —and almost out of our nursery ken; going to dances, rolling bandages at the Red Cross, dressing up fit to kill when we went to church on Sunday. But on week-days we were all rigged out alike, in sailor suits of purest white, correct in every naval detail, from the caps with "H.M.S. Dreadnought" on the ribbons down to the lanyards and boatswain's pipes round our stiff little necks; and in this splendid get-up we would, at least once a week, parade solemnly up and down Bold Street, in line abreast, insistently saluting every officer in sight.

Even at a time of fierce and universal patriotism, this must have seemed an excessive expression of it. But we loved every minute; and even if we had not, it would not have made any difference. For the author of this, as of everything else in our lives, was Mother.

She was an attractive woman; tall, fair, slim, well-connected, likely to be rich one day—in fact, very much of a catch for the struggling young surgeon, just out of Edinburgh University, which my father had been in 1898. We loved her very much, we feared her also; she was very strict, immensely strong-willed, some-times harsh, but never (at this stage) unfair.

She was many good things, and some bad—though of course we would not, then, have dreamed of passing any such judgment. She was Mother, and that was all, and more than enough for a quartet of children, ranging in age from sixteen to two, who—whether they were up in the nursery or down in the drawing-room—were being brought up to do exactly what they were told, with the rules all fixed and the latitude for free-will pared down to vanishing-point.

All this time, there was one person missing, and one person missed. It was, of course, our father.

He had gone off to the war in 1914, as punctual as Denys was to be in 1939, and a shade more prompt than myself in 1940 (though I had what I thought was a good excuse). He was then forty-two, and might well have stayed at home, lecturing at the university and the Northern Hospital, or operating on the enor-mous throng of "wounded soldiers" who were now beginning to be carried back from the slaughter, or simply consolidating what had already become a thriving surgical and consultative practice.

But he belonged to a Territorial regiment, which must have imposed some rules, and he was also a man of devotion and duty, which imposed the most compelling rules of all. So he went to war, as a captain and very soon as a major, in the Royal Army Medical Corps; first to France, and then to a strange-sounding place called Salonika.

Marshalling my lead soldiers, I could play games with an extra sense of urgency, and still enjoy using the troops of an even more glamorous era—shining Lancers on horseback, bearded Cossacks, scarlet Spahis with gleaming white gaiters, the actual Fortress of Sevastopol crumbling before ancient field-guns (now up-dated to "French 75's").

In terms of manpower, the new dull khaki jobs, up against this sort of thing, didn't look at all like winning the war. But of course they would! That was one grown-up promise which could never be broken.

There was something worthwhile nearly every day. We had that smart naval rig-out for showing off. Brave military bands still stamped up and down the streets, calling the laggards to arms. Someone invented a new game, which also made use of contemporary history; at a given signal, one child would cry "Russia!," another "Prussia!," and a third "Austria!" The result, we believed, sounded like a gigantic concerted sneeze.

Nothing spoiled the war, the newest of all games. There was no suffering or slaughter in Liverpool, no thunder of guns along Rodney Street; no hint at all that Britain was now pouring out the blood, treasure, and manhood of an entire generation—of a generation no longer entire.

Vaguely, up in the nursery, we were afraid that our father "might not come back" (we had picked this up from somewhere); but not coming back was still something like missing a train— there would be another one along later, and he with it, and all the family would be together again.

Only the wounded soldiers, limping and stumbling about in their bright uniforms, or sitting glumly on the park benches, offered proof that there was something else to war besides glamour, and brass bands, and smart salutes for towering officers. But for us, "wounded soldier" was only a phrase, never a gross fact; the colours they wore were so fresh and pretty that one could not really see them as sad.

Molly was always rolling bandages, and these were the people the bandages were for. Sometimes they had a sore leg (this was the nursery gloss), and if it really hurt, the King would give them a medal, and everything would be all right. And of course, wounded soldiers never cried, and ate up all their tapioca pudding. . . .

Perhaps food was the only thing which came near to spoiling the war.

It was very dull, and there wasn't enough of it; we were always hungry, and yet had great difficulty in getting down the nursery stodge which was all that wartime rationing allowed; the grey potatoes, eternal rice-pudding, watery cod-fish, bread with almost no butter, and no jam at all. (All the jam—indeed, all the favourite items—were said to be "going to the front." I had visions of hordes of greedy soldiers gulping down *my* jam and *my* treacle tart and *my* apple dumplings; it was a painful test of patriotism.)

I suppose it couldn't be helped; food *was* scarce, rationing was rationing, and the authorities had better things to do than tempt little boys to finish their noon-day dinners. But I think the "home front" was considerably neglected, on this occasion; there was no idea, in that mid-war year, of any kind of a balanced diet for growing children, and certainly none of the measured governmental hand-outs of orange juice and cod-liver-oil and black-currant extract which, in exactly parallel circumstances twenty-five years later, so bolstered my eldest son (b. 1942) that he grew up to be six-foot-three and a formidable boxer.

Now, we suffered under a different system of priorities. There were "munitions," and then "war loan," and then the "land army," and then "Your King and Country Want YOU!" (YOU was always a grown-up.) There were lots of other things; somewhere at the tail-end of the procession, my mealtimes came under brusque official scrutiny, and were, it seemed, deliberately downgraded to dry rice-pudding and emaciated prunes.

Prunes were one item never in short supply—I could well imagine the soldiers not liking *them*. They were worse than parsnips. But when we were bold enough to protest, we got nowhere. "They're good for the complexion," said Mother, without any qualification except sometimes to add, absent-mindedly: "Have you been yet?"

So prunes it was, by the bowl-full, and tears and howls and sulks, and dark subversive thoughts about what *I* would do when *I* was grown up.

Two things were certain. I would be a sailor, and I would have lots to eat.

Mother was away from home for most of every day. She had a job—which for women was very rare at that time, and for married women almost unthinkable. But this was "war work," which had passed the stage of being *chic* and was becoming a matter of genuine importance. She was working in the Department of Censorship, which for some reason had a substantial branch office in Liverpool, and presumably scrutinized all mail going overseas through this particular exit.

Without undue emphasis, it must be said that opening other people's letters, reading them, and snipping out the bits which threatened public security, was a job with particular appeal for a great many women. I am sure that Mother enjoyed it, though she was professionally tight-lipped about the whole thing.

"Did you catch any spies?" we used to ask her, at the day's end. Up in the nursery, we would have been answered with a tart: "Ask me no questions, and I'll tell you no lies." Down in the drawing-room, the brush-off was more aloof. "Sit up straight," we were commanded. "Don't ask so many questions. Let me see your nails."

We were sure that she was only being modest. She could catch us doing *anything*.

But a great deal of 1916 was, for us, much the same as any other year. The weeks went by, not too exciting, not too dull. Presently it was the turn of the year, and then July, and we began to cross the days off the calendar. The third week of July meant our annual progress to the seaside—the summer house at Trearddur Bay, the high peak of our delight, the place which nothing marred, where everything was wonderful.

Trearddur was a seaside village, tucked away near Holyhead at the very tip of North Wales. To make the 150-mile journey there involved us all in tremendous preparations which must have taken weeks to organize, and driven Mother nearly to distraction. Those attic trunks, of fantastic size with domed roofs, had to be packed; wicker baskets took the overflow of sun-bonnets and sand-shoes. One parent, four children, two nursemaids, and a cook had to be moved from A to B, with all the attendant dangers of lost luggage, straying children, and people-who-were-nasty-in-railway-carriages.

But we always got there: somehow, we always got to Trearddur Bay, and that made up for everything. For we loved that place: and year after year, right up to the end, we loved it more. It changed, it grew, it was built up and overrun: people died or stayed away, other people crowded in, chucked their weight about, imported an alien smartness: it never made any difference. I went there—we all went there, except Molly—every summer of my life from 1910 to 1939. It took a second war to break this cherished routine: I know that Denys, like myself, was happier during the summers he spent there than at any other time of his life.

The journey down was all excitement: the drive to Central Station in a cavalcade of three four-wheel cabs, the railway noise, the recurrent crises, the rattle and slop of the sterilized milk can, the chaos at Chester. But then came the best part of the journey —hard-boiled eggs for lunch, the bridge over the Menai Straits with the stone lions at each end, the first sight of Holyhead Mountain. No wonder one of us was always sick before the train drew in.

And after Holyhead came the most intoxicating part of all— the four-mile drive in the wagonette to Trearddur Bay.

The horses, promoted from the plow, trotted decorously, and walked up all the hills. They smelled strongly and wonderfully. They *always* relieved themselves on the journey. It was magnificently, fascinatingly rude; we never knew if we ought to watch. Felicity, at that time an excessively ladylike child, in frilly clothes and a huge ribboned sun-hat, would turn away and look at the scenery. I would not.

The luggage followed us home by farm-cart. This cart, and the wagonette, belonged to Edward Williams, the farmer who supplied us with the milk and butter and who looked after the house during the winter. Edward, his wife, and his four sons (the whole family dressed in the same heavy dark corduroy) were an essential part of Trearddur Bay: in those early days, when there were only seven visitors' houses in the whole district, one had need of a solid background such as they provided, to ensure food supplies, deal with transport problems, and act as allies in what was, to some degree, a wild foreign country.

It was Edward who drove the wagonette. In our children's eyes he could have no dizzier claim to distinction.

A long steep hill led down into Trearddur Bay: at the top of it the horses were reined in and the brake clapped on; then we descended gingerly, feeling our way into this uncertain country. But as the slope died, our familiarity grew: we were reaching home ground now, where shopping and walks and loitering on wet days made us citizens.

And so at last to Hafod, the curling drive, and tea.

Hafod . . . In Welsh the name means Summer House: to us it meant a whole horizon of delight, bound up with summer and the sea and sunshine. The house, built by my father in 1908 as the seventh in Trearddur Bay, was small: a pebble-dash bungalow, in fact, with three bedrooms, a nursery, and an attic for the servants, reached by a step-ladder from the kitchen. There was, of course, no telephone, and no lighting except oil-lamps.

Water was drawn from the garden well, a much-publicized danger spot covered with a slab of slate; the haunt of frogs, which swam round and round hopelessly, and of a curious hollow echo. At the back of the house was an earth-closet, of what must have been, in those days, a very superior design. Its "cistern" was daily filled with loose soil dug from the garden: when the plug was pulled, a miniature landslide did its duty; and one of Edward's strapping sons emptied the bucket over the garden wall every morning.

But no domestic crudity could rob Hafod of its real glory—the spot where it was built. In 1908 there was still the whole coast to choose from: the corner where the house was set remains, to this day, the most enchanting of all. It was high up on the very edge of the sea, the last heather slope before the granite outcrop which plunged down to water-level: below us the Irish Sea washed and thundered, rolling into the arm of a bay whose rocky outline —at high tide, at low, in flat calm or under the shock and surge of a south-westerly gale—was more precious and familiar to us than anything else in our lives.

In all our later journeying, there was no "view" we knew and loved so much as the one from the windows of Hafod. It had everything: a fringe of sea-pinks at the edge of the garden, a glint of sunshine on wet rocks, a triangle of sea, and far away, a mile off-shore, the single dark spot—Oyster Rock—which bore so sinister a reputation for wrecking ships and drowning men, but which completed this lovely pattern in the only way conceivable.

Year after year we returned to this view, and learned its outline afresh: it never failed either the eye or the heart, it was something we carried with us out of our childhood, to balance and sweeten the ugly adult world.

Probably we did not sleep, for a long time, that first night: there was the noise of the sea almost under our window, the funny smells and the new shadows, the tremendous excitement of being down at Trearddur again, and all the joys of tomorrow.

They were simple joys, for many years to come: even to the grown-ups, Trearddur Bay offered a life untouched by 1916's modest "civilization," a life which did not take on the smallest sophistication till more than a decade later. As yet there was not even the beginning of what was later the whole point of Trearddur Bay—the thriving sailing club which we built up, with its fifty-odd class racing boats, its three races a week, its continuous year-after-year rivalry and notable comradeship.

Now, if one took to the ocean at all, one "boated" with the lobster-fishermen or hired a dinghy by the hour from the Trearddur Bay Hotel.

On special occasions there would be formal tea-parties, usually at the Cottles' or the Buckleys', who both had large families of four or five children. Sunday morning meant a family procession to church, which at that time was a corrugated iron hut so small that an overflow of worshippers always collected on the grass outside, stood up for the hymns, and knelt, somewhat self-consciously, when "Let us pray" came faintly through the church door.

We were all dressed in our best on these occasions, gloves included: Felicity and I were bored, but Molly, a holy child, chanted vigorously and frowned when we fidgeted. Mother held our hands in her lap during the sermon, which was never less than half an hour: then (as it seemed) we paid a penny to get out, and were free for the beach once more.

That was the Trearddur Bay we loved. It had its share of trial and anguish, like everywhere else; but here these scars were so much easier to forget. Trearddur was the unfailing salve for everything: eating our breakfast porridge out of the blue bowls, each day lay before us with the same infinite promise as yesterday.

The shadow of Toby's death was gone, and he of course was almost forgotten; who could remember another person, even a brother, for three years? We knew that he was buried across the moors, in Rhoscolyn churchyard, which could just be seen on the far horizon; and once a year we walked, or drove in the trap (which Mother liked to call the "governess cart"), to lay flowers on the small grave.

But that was all. Denys had taken Toby's place; the quota was full again, and death did not belong to the nursery, nor to

Trearddur Bay, nor to our heartless enjoyment of the sun and the sand and the clear blue water.

We still had a little bit of the war with us, in a rather dramatic form: a daily flight of airships—large dirigibles, shining and silvery in the sun, very exciting, very beautiful.

They often flew directly over Hafod; we would see them first as a gleaming dot in the sky, then as a widening circle; and then the huge bulk was superbly poised overhead. We would all wave, and sometimes a tiny helmeted figure would wave back, and then steer out to sea, peering and hovering, on guard against the lurking enemy. We were always hoping that one of them would "loop the loop," but it never happened.

What these patrols were looking for was U-boats, which were wicked, and not at all like our own brave submarines. And of course airships were not in the least like Zeppelins, which sneaked up in the dark and killed people, and dropped German spies dressed as nuns (you could actually see their boots!).

But this was not really Trearddur. Trearddur was paddling at the water's edge, and "popping" seaweed, and munching biscuits with sand all over them, and, for Denys, not catching cold (though in brilliant sunshine) in his relaxed seaside rig of "binder" (a kind of cholera-belt for the mid-section), a pair of combinations, a two-piece romper, socks and sandals, and a vast floppy sunbonnet. The sea air could be treacherous.

Trearddur was our young fisherman friend, Llewellyn, squatting on the foreshore sorting out his catch of lobsters and crab, and, one memorable day, dissecting for bait a huge dog-fish which was beginning to smell to heaven.

Trearddur was shrimping, and having to ask Felicity to take them out of the net (she was the brave one, I the squeamish). Trearddur was building battlemented sand-castles with sea-shell décor, and making tunnels and slopes and spiral ramps deep inside them, so that a golf ball could roll all the way down from the top to the bottom.

Trearddur was playing hop-scotch on the sand, and shouting "I'm the king of the castle. Get down, you dirty rascal!" and climbing rocks ("Not too high!") and playing Grandmother's Steps and stump cricket and rounders. Trearddur was grown-ups getting tired so easily that it was astonishing; quite suddenly they said: "I've got a bone in my leg," and flopped down exhausted, and even went to sleep!

Thus we played out our cherished summer, while the season swung and changed, almost without our knowing it. The yearly shoals of mackerel came and went in the bay; the blackberries darkened and then were no more; soon even the early morning mushrooms had all been picked. Already we tried *not* to count the days, but nothing could stop the end of September looming up, and that was the signal to go.

The thing to look forward to now, and the last significant date of 1916, was Christmas.

For this festival, we made another journey, of even more consequence: across country to Gedling House, near Nottingham, the handsome lair of that superior grandfather, Sir John Turney.

It was a family gathering—*all* the family; and there was no doubt who was in charge of it, and who counted the assembled heads. For children and grown-ups alike, Grandfather was a formidable figure; and for children especially, the nearest thing to God we were likely to meet on a very long day's march.

He was old, he was fierce, he had a long white beard and a shock of white hair, he had lots of money; the combination left no loophole for irreverence or for anything except good behaviour and discreetly lowered voices. But we still enjoyed those Christmas visits.

About Gedling, that year, there were two unusual things: sledging in the snow, the first substantial snow we had ever seen, with Denys, who had now usurped my position as everybody's favourite and whose fair curls and attractive face might have been invented to grace just such a party as this; and the fact that, while *romping* (that terrible word), I jogged Grandfather's elbow as he was signing some enormously important papers, and was in disgrace for over four days.

The rest was a medley of crowds of people, a tall house with unexpected rooms which I had forgotten were there, and a giant Christmas tree round which the "estate children" gathered on Christmas afternoon, for such heart-warming presents as mufflers, woollen gloves, and bars of soap.

We had had our own presents earlier. The pride of my personal loot was a "pop-gun" which fired a cork bullet. Officially, the cork had to be tied by a piece of string to the muzzle. But when I had coaxed the string into breaking, it was a much better weapon.

As in the drawing-room sessions at home, the children were expected to do their share of entertainment. All the cousins, just like us, came up with some sort of an act; one of them actually did conjuring tricks, involving strings of coloured flags and disappearing coins, with a degree of sophistication which was a sensational advance on anything we could do.

I was still stuck with my only party-piece, a song called "Dance for your Daddy, my Little Laddie"; like some old-time vaudeville act which had lasted far beyond its allotted span, there was still a sentimental demand for it. But Molly had some new songs, hot off the "sheet-music" stand.

"We don't want to lose you, but we think you ought to go," she piped up, looking innocently round a group of male relatives, some of whom were of ideal military age. And there was "Keep the Home Fires Burning," a brand-new hit by I. Novello. This seemed to be more acceptable, perhaps particularly to Grandfather, who was currently amassing a fortune by curing the leather which made the boots which shod the brave lads over there. He was keeping the home fires burning, without a doubt.

Christmas week itself involved a lot of church-going, as well as family prayers, carol services, a formal call from the bishop (smart buttoned gaiters, and a top hat with black strings attached to it), and whispered devotional talks from a relative who was, I realize now, slightly cracked in several directions. Already I was not too happy in this area; it was not the boredom (though church services were then *very* long), so much as the number of words and phrases which I did not understand.

Not yet was the language splendid and memorable, as it later came to be; now it was simply a puzzle.

But to balance this holy confusion, in fact to drive it out of mind altogether, there was the last treat of the Gedling visit, and of the year; the pantomime in Nottingham, on the night after Christmas.

Everyone went to this; Grandfather took a whole row at the theater, and sat in the middle of it like a benign ring-master.

This time, even *I* was allowed to go, on condition that I was tremendously good for at least forty-eight hours beforehand, and that I had a solid sleep in the afternoon. I *was* tremendously good, and, though sleepless with anticipation, I screwed my eyes shut till they hurt.

By the time we reached the bright splendour of the theater, things were so pent up with excitement that I had to be rushed into the building at a fast trot. But I made it. Nothing was going to spoil my chances that night.

It was a "real" pantomime, the first (and the last) I ever saw, full of incomprehensible characters like Harlequin and Columbine, a dog with a ruff round its neck called Toby, Pantaloon, Clown, red-hot pokers galore, and many a string of outsize sausages to drive the dog Toby wild. I couldn't make head or tail of it, but it never ceased to be wonderful; the most beautiful, strange, and glittering evening of my life so far.

ELEVEN

1921

DEAR MOTHER,
I AM THE SCHOOL LIBERIAN

N OW WE LIVED IN THE COUNTRY, in a wonderful new house
called Melbreck. It was at Allerton, about ten miles outside
Liverpool.

Melbreck was the perfect place for children: a big, old-fashioned rambling house, with a large garden, set in what was then
the heart of the country. With its long corridors, wide curving
staircases, and at least twenty rooms, it must have been a housemaid's nightmare. But it had all the elbow-room we craved; and
the nursery wing, well isolated from the fastidious grown-ups,
with rooms to be alone in, rooms where we could make any
amount of mess, rooms where we could kick up all the noise we
chose without someone knocking on the wall, was almost ideal.

It had one drawback, this isolation, from which we suffered
later: the fact that our nurses could, and did, give free expression
to whatever sort of cruelty or malice made the most appeal to
them, without any supervision from our parents. But this was
not the strongest memory of Melbreck, nor anything like it.

We were each given a small patch of garden to ourselves, to
develop our talents, if any, and to keep us from damaging the
main section. Mine grew, obligingly, wild strawberries: Denys
raised a fine crop of nasturtiums: Felicity favoured more dramatic
items such as mignonette and virginia stock. On an appointed
day, we submitted our efforts to a "garden competition." Mother
was the judge: the prize was a shilling, and the contest fierce.

Already we had a well-developed commercial sense. Indeed,
when my father promised to double any sum I deposited in the
Post Office Savings Bank, I used to borrow Denys' pocket-money,
bank it, draw the parental bonus, repay Denys, and be left with
a clear hundred percent profit, as well as a reputation for thrift.
This ingenious fraud was discovered before very long; some
innocent comment by Denys started a probe. But I still kept the
money.

There was a dairy-farm next door to Melbreck: a good place to wander into when we were bored with our own domain. It belonged to a man called Steele, a tough, red-faced farmer whose corduroy coat and leather gaiters could hardly have been more authentic.

Hygienic regulations governing the purity of milk could not, in those days, have been very strict; the "shippon" where the cows were stalled was the dirtiest place I had ever seen; and when the wind was in the wrong quarter the smell of it could permeate all Melbreck. But we did not mind; Steele was a great friend, and made us free of his house and farmyard; we learned how to milk cows, and watched him killing pigs; and the slices of bread-and-dripping which were always available in the kitchen were a valuable addition to our austere nursery diet.

Except for Molly, we all still went for a daily afternoon walk; and now we were all on foot. As at Rodney Street, there was one basic route, into Allerton: it led past Steele's dairy, past the rectory where lurked a formidable man by the name of Canon Gibson-Smith, past the convalescent home with its long line of blue-uniformed "wounded soldiers" who, after three years of peace, still leaned over the wall and talked to the passers-by; past Allerton Church, and into the village itself. Here the trams started, the Liverpool trams which we boarded when, once or twice a week, we went shopping with Mother "down-town."

We were certainly better off at Melbreck than in Rodney Street; the air was freer, the ground softer, the space (for children) seemingly endless. But in spite of the garden attractions, we were not absolutely dedicated to the open air. We used to spend a lot of time in the kitchen, always scrounging for food, and enjoying also the cooking smells and the warmth that came from the vast black range which burned day and night.

There was always a hissing kettle on top, and things being boiled up to make soup, and a batch of scones gently browning, and an iron cauldron of porridge which was left to steam and bubble all night, and a rack of the "potato cakes" which were the cook's favourite, and ours too.

The table in the middle had been scrubbed till its very ribs showed through; the enormous Welsh dresser was loaded with plates and soup-tureens and sauceboats and meat-platters. In the corner cupboard, there was soft soap, like axle grease, in tins; and Old Dutch Cleanser, and bars of yellow Monkey Brand, and Blanco and boot-polish and floor-wax and gritty knife powder.

We loved the kitchen, because there was always something happening there. Twice a year a black-faced man, cheerful, grinning, yet strangely unpopular, took possession of it, and, using wonderful instruments, brought cascades of soot down the chimney and (to some extent) into a bulging sack. "That sweep!" said the cook sourly. "I'd like to sweep *him!*" Twice an hour, it sometimes seemed, one of the bells on the "bell board" jangled and quivered as the squeaking wires were pulled from above.

But we were not too popular around the kitchen quarters, and before long we would be chased out again; indeed, if we ever stayed indoors too long we were called "frowsty cats" and given a lecture on the virtues of cold fresh air. Then it was back to the garden, and playing hide-and-seek round the pergola (another unpopular move, since it menaced the climbing plants), and watching the London trains go by over the kitchen-garden wall, and getting in Gresty the gardener's way as he mowed the lawn or coaxed the green-fly off the rose-leaves with a rabbit's-fur brush, or marked out the tennis-court with a rickety travelling whitewash pot.

When sated with this kind of civilization we retreated to one of the "caves" we had built in the shrubbery, of branches and cardboard boxes and string, and there pretended to be Indians, or trappers, or brave men climbing Everest.

Mostly we pretended to be people in books, like the Swiss Family Robinson or the Last of the Mohicans. We were all mad about reading.

In the nursery bookcase was a jumble of books for all ages and both sexes: my own collection, Molly's old school stories, Felicity's Girl-Guide sagas. I read all of them, without distinction; I often read by candle-light till nearly midnight, when a stern nurse or a prowling parent would still be answered with "Just another page," or even "Just another sentence."

We were now seeing more of our parents, especially Mother, in a slight lowering of the formal barrier between grown-ups and children: the drawing-room hour had been stretched into a more frequent series of contacts. We sometimes had our tea with Mother, and after tea were allowed to play the gramophone, an entirely novel instrument whose open-mouthed horn was, she complained, "simply a dust-trap."

Another "great treat" which I was less sure about was "going down to dessert"—that is, joining our parents at the end of their dinner and eating an apple or a pear or an orange in their company. It seemed very sophisticated, and it was nice to stay up late; but the call was for absolutely perfect behaviour, which was no sort of treat at all.

I felt the same way about "middle-day dinner" on Sunday, which saw the whole family round the dining-room table in an ordeal even more lengthy. This had the added hazard of a choice of cutlery. But the ritual food was so magnificent, and so much better than anything we ever got in the nursery, that I was prepared to chance it. Roast sirloin of beef, plumped-up Yorkshire pudding, golden roast potatoes, and a vast juicy apple-pie with an egg-cup in the middle to take the strain—for this, I was ready to try *really* hard, and to accept almost any criticism.

Our father presided, and carved with great precision and a certain flourish, as a distinguished surgeon should. He knew I liked the "under-cut," which was in short supply, and I always got some. I was the senior son, after all.

But, on these and all other occasions, it was Mother I watched and listened to most closely. The motive was probably self-interest, or even self-defense; it just didn't do to get on her wrong side, as Felicity, in a series of repeated clashes, scarcely any of them her fault, was currently finding out. Denys was still "the baby," and seemed immune from trouble; I was somewhere in between, the elder son who had to turn out right. I wasn't going to get caught in the wrong corner of this particular triangle.

So I watched her, in small things and in great.

She was always busy; there was a big house to run, and she ran it on a tight rein, and still had lots of time to read the Light Romances then popular. She had—she must have had—a great vitality. It outlasted every day; and each night, every piece of furniture in every downstairs room was covered with its own particular patterned dust-sheet. This was the last task of her long routine, and gave the rooms an air of ghostly abandonment which only vanished with the morning sun.

But she was never too busy to miss anything *we* might be doing, when in public view. In all our dealings with Mother, we had to be very careful. To "behave" was the household watchword; and if we didn't behave, we were sharply reminded of it. What would do for "common children" would not do for us.

There was one rebuke, much used, which covered nearly everything; and this was "Don't be affected." It implied showing off; and showing off involved almost all the things one did on impulse: talking too loudly, not talking loudly enough ("It's rude to whisper"), pulling a face, playing up to visitors, laughing in a way Mother did not like, running into the room, slamming the door going out, walking with too much bravado, dragging the feet, answering back at times of crisis, or repeating nursery jokes and catchwords in the wrong part of the house.

All these things earned a steely glance from behind her pince-nez, and "Don't be so affected" from a firm-edged tongue. If we hung back in company, we were labelled "Slow Coach"; if we overdid the social graces, the charge was "Clever Dick"—an early forerunner of Smart Alec. Sometimes the frontier of good behaviour extended to unusual areas. We always had to answer when we were called. But: "Never answer when you're in the lavatory," said Mother. "It's rude."

It was one more thing to remember; and this was a list which could never grow shorter. The list was not even static, like the Ten Commandments; it grew, it covered entire walls within our bulging heads; there were days when it seemed that it could never be mastered, not even by the best-behaved boy in Liverpool, a boy on positively pre-birthday behaviour, which everyone knew had to be flawless.

But we did our best; and, on a day-to-day basis, the best must have been just good enough. Our rewards were still rare; to "behave" was not to be exceptional, it was to be normal. (This was "Virtue is its own reward," in the meanest possible disguise.) Rewards always came like bonus dividends, as "surprises."

In this area, especially, we learned not to nag for things, whether they were toys or treats or something (like speedometers for our bicycles) which other children had and we did not. Nagging defeated its own purpose; it set up a pattern of denial which often even a grown-up found it impossible to reverse. So when we asked the "Can I?" question—or rather the "May I?" question, thus avoiding an even prompter refusal—we asked it once, and then perhaps once more; if the answer was no, that was the end of that.

The best answer of all was "Presently," a truly magic word. If Mother said "Presently," we knew three things immediately: that the object in view was worthwhile, that it needed a little thought on her part, but that we would definitely get it. This was one of her unbreakable rules, and both sides knew it. We had only to raise a wail of "But you said *presently!*" to be sure of success.

Of course, we had to be telling the truth. That was another unbreakable rule; and if one rule could be more unbreakable than another, this was it. There were "fibs" (forgivable), and there were lies. All the evasions which really mattered were lies.

Obviously, Mother was being professionally stern with us, and perhaps it was the best thing for her to be, at this formative moment of preparation for the stern world in front of us. And we were not alone, in this sharp pattern of discipline. She was being stern with some other people too, as we were beginning to notice.

She had just started her life-long contest with domestic help, a contest which began as a search for the ideal staff of servants, degenerated swiftly into an automatic rejection of all candidates after a maximum period of three months, and left her, at the end of a full quarter-century of turmoil, disenchanted, absolutely impossible to please, and of course servantless.

Already we were seeing a procession of young and old women, from cooks to housemaids, who came into the house bright-faced and willing, survived a short endurance test compounded of critical stares, continual correction, and occasional ferocious bullying, worked a final disconcerting month "under notice," and then left (as they used to say, in citing an example of the figure of speech known as a *zeugma*) in tears and a hansom cab.

Mother talked of them as "dome-sticks" (though she pronounced *"Pas devant la domestique"* with embarrassing clarity), or sometimes, not altogether jokingly, as "menials." There were many ways in which they could displease. There were many reasons for abrupt dismissal.

For good or ill, the nursery wing was the center of action at home; and though (being now at boarding school) I only spent four months of the year there, it was still a potent focus of family life. In the "day nursery," we ate our meals, spent the evenings and the wet days, had our quarrels, and suffered our punishments; down the corridor was the bedroom I shared with Denys, and Felicity's room—Molly had been promoted to the grown-up part of the house; and, still farther down, the bathroom with the magnificent mahogany-encased bath, the toga-sized towels, and the mat known to us affectionately as TAM THAB.

One floor below the day nursery was a large bare vault called the Billiard Room, which had a raised dais at one end, essential for staging the frequent plays put on by the Melbreck Theater Company—us.

This was our world. It had room for everything, except the blessing of being alone and escaping notice.

The good plain fare which was our normal lot in the nursery took a great deal of getting down. It built bones, we were assured, and was good for the teeth, and made our hair curl, and turned us into big boys or girls; against these undoubted long-term benefits, the fact remained that the food was dull.

There was never a fair proportion of the things we liked, such as ice-cream and toad-in-the-hole, and there was a permanent over-load of unpopular items. Among these latter were certain vege-tables which my father and Gresty grew in perpetual, overwhelming profusion, and which we all loathed. An endless surging wave of parsnips, Brussels sprouts, and Jerusalem artichokes topped this list.

At nearly every mealtime, there were battles, there were pun-ishments, there were appeals to reason and humanitarianism. "Remember the starving Russians" had now taken the place of the wartime "Remember the starving Belgians," since the Russians were now enduring a post-revolutionary famine of horrible pro-portions, and we were meant to feel glad and grateful for the blessings of our abundance, and to finish off the current plateful of mashed turnips, without any more nonsense.

It was difficult to feel glad and grateful for Brussels sprouts, or porridge with lumps in it, or brown bread, or rice pudding. Rice pudding always had a skin on top of it. The skin was part of the pudding, and had to be eaten; if not, it came back for the next meal. The prospect of cold rice pudding for tea had to be weighed against its disgusting nature then and there, when it was hot.

Such dilemmas often took a tearful time to resolve, and time, under nursery discipline, had its own iron grip.

The silly part was that, however much trouble and grief we had in forcing down spoons-ful of such prime non-favourites as damsons or junket, we were always hungry about an hour afterwards. Indeed, we were ravenous nearly all the time, and particularly so at 10 A.M., 2:30, and 5.

We begged for food at the kitchen door; we hung around Mrs. Gresty, licking our lips, until for very shame she had to give us one of her rough-and-ready hand-outs—a treacle sandwich, or thick slices of bread-and-dripping speckled with those delicious patches of blood.

"Is this cupboard love?" she used to ask, and we always assured her: "No!" We were telling the absolute truth. This was real love.

At times of denial or interior crisis, we were driven to foraging in the dust-bins; stealing from the chickens, munching potato peelings, draining ancient jam-jars and syrup tins of their last drop of sweetness.

For this alone, we should have died like flies. But nothing of the sort happened. I have never really believed in the hygienic handling of food since those days: since the first time I bit into a discarded hunk of corned beef, and enjoyed it to the last strand of gristle, and survived.

When we were not hungry, we were ill.

"Feeling poorly," it was called in the nursery, and "seedy" in the drawing-room. Either way, it soon became enjoyable, since everyone was sorry for us, and our odious nursemaid Fanny was neutralized, and we were spoiled and comforted and cosseted, and we realized that we had at last succeeded in attracting attention which was neither critical nor punitive. At such times, Mother especially was wonderful.

Usually the trouble was a cold, or a cough, or a badly skinned leg or arm; in due succession, it was chicken-pox, and mumps, and adenoids-and-tonsils, and measles. For run-of-the-mill complaints, the remedies were also run-of-the-mill; but the mill then was on the old-fashioned side of this particular stream.

For me, there was only one doctor, even though he was not allowed to treat us, and this was my father. From a very early age, however, we had been cautioned firmly and continually against ever referring to him as "Dr. Monsarrat."

"He is a surgeon," Mother told us. "It is *quite* different. He is Mr." So Mr. he was, and now he was back with us, at the head of the table and the head of the house.

We still did not see a great deal of him; at this stage he was phenomenally busy, building up a vast surgical and consulting practice, as well as lecturing at the university, teaching at the Northern Hospital, and overseeing his own nursing home. He was out of the house very early, and back very late. Only on Sundays was he really there, for all of us to see and to admire.

He was now nearly fifty, though we did not know it at the time; in those days, children knew nothing of their parents' ages, and would never have dreamed of asking. He was tall and dark, with a bristly moustache; he had beautiful hands, and a grip of exceptional strength, useful for the control of boys under punishment, essential (in a secondary sort of way) for surgical proficiency.

Among the strange debris in the Melbreck attic, ranging from dome-topped trunks to dressmakers' "forms" which I was later to recognize as voluptuous, there was a sword and a German helmet, to remind us how brave he had been in the war. Now, back from mysterious Salonika, he was deeply engaged in something which made him almost as remote.

But for a short part of every day, I at least was in touch. There had grown up a tradition that I could watch him shaving; and this I always did, fascinated by the whole complex of equipment and operation—the shaving-mug full of hot water, the soap in the circular wooden bowl, the lathering, the "stropping" and wielding of a long-handled, long-bladed razor which I was on no account to touch, the "shaving papers" on which the razor was periodically wiped.

As he shaved, he sang; and it was always the same song, about the brave little cabin-boy who volunteered to sink the Spanish enemee, and how he was cheated out of his just reward by the wicked captain, and how he swam round and round, and called: "Oh shipmates, help me up, for I'm drifting with the tide!" but on the deck he died, and—

They left him in the Lowland, Lowland, Lowland,
They left him in the Lowland Sea.

It was just about the saddest thing I had ever heard; but it was a
good story, and I loved it.

It was my father who, at the beginning of every term, managed
to find time to drive me back to school, across the Wirral Penin-
sula to the address which headed all my letters home—The Leas,
Hoylake, Cheshire.

It was not easy to be happy there, or even to feel safe. The Leas
was a much, much tougher place than St. Christopher's had ever
been. I had been a boarder there since I was seven, and I knew.

It was, and is, a tall house, the house where I was taught; a
grey-brown, pebble-dashed building, three stories high plus an
attic, under a steep-sloping red-tiled roof. It had more than a
hundred windows; most of them were kept permanently open,
since it was then believed that warmth and comfort sapped the
character (hot baths had brought down the Roman Empire, after
all) and that austerity was the only thing to endow superior boys
with characteristics of manliness and leadership.

The Leas was therefore chillingly cold throughout the spring
and autumn, and murderously so during the winter, when we
grew accustomed to breaking the ice on our wash-basins in the
early morning. We shivered; our tiny hands were frozen; we
thrashed our arms about in the effort to keep warm. Our noses
ran continually; "You've got a dew-drop" was the commonest
winter-time greeting.

Agonizing chilblains kept us scratching for hours. Colds and
coughs abounded. Delicate boys spent weeks in the sickroom,
hovering, we believed, between life and death. It was true that
we never lost a boy, during the whole time I was there. *But it
could have happened.*

The entire place was cold, and drafty, and parts of it were dour
indeed. There was one exception, one warm spot in the midst of
this howling wilderness; this was the Hall, a sort of miniature
town-meeting-place, surrounded by notice boards on which all
the good and bad news appeared—appointments to the Second
XI, failure in examinations, lost and found notices. Its chief and
most blessed feature was a large open fire-place, protected by a

massive iron guard, which did in fact give out heat over a restricted area.

But a position anywhere near this haven was reserved for the
biggest boys. I was not a big boy, and therefore kept my place
in the outer ring, hoping that a little warmth would occasionally
seep past the massive bodies of people who were two or even
three years older than I.

From this point of ground-zero (or a little above), the hint of
comfort gave way to Arctic zones of austerity. There was the
adjacent dining-room, with its twelve long tables covered with
blue oil-cloth, its wooden benches on which we sat bolt upright
("No slouching there!") to eat, and its single comfortable chair
at the head of each table, where presided the master who carved
the joint, ladled out the vegetables (watched by covetous eyes),
and kept a sharp watch for breaches of good behaviour.

The reaction to the latter was the curt order: "Go to the pigs'
table!" a sort of wooden flap attached to the wall in one corner
of the room at which one had to eat standing up, with one's
face turned away from decent company.

There always seemed to be someone standing there; and occasionally it was myself. I used to stretch out for the salt, whereas
the proper drill was to say "Salt, please," and wait for it to be
passed, even if it was smack in front of one's plate.

"At home, *everyone* has their own salt-cellar," I used to boast,
by way of justification. But it did not do me any good. "Sent to
the pigs' table!" they used to answer, and then, in chorus: "Oink,
oink!"

Down the corridor from the dining-room were the class-rooms,
each for ten or twelve boys. Here the desks were joined in pairs,
their tops ink-stained and heavily notched with carved initials,
assorted patterns, rude words, and plain destructive knife-work.
Here we sat on two-seater benches, and shared an ink-well with
our partner, and elbowed each other unceasingly. Here, before
each class, we perched on the lukewarm water pipes, unfreezing
our bottoms until the look-out called "Cavee!," and there was a
stampede for our proper places.

One of these class-rooms housed the school museum, and to
the dry pervasive odour of chalk was added a secondary smell,
which we took to be antiquity. It rose from such items as an

albatross, a stuffed crocodile, two capercaillie ("shot by the headmaster"), a python skin, a bow-and-arrow from some nameless
jungle, some pieces of flint bravely labelled "Ancient Implements,"
and a South Carolina cotton pod. There was also an old, old armadillo, yellow and scaly, covered with bristles which it was beginning to shed.

Forty-five years later, that old, old armadillo was still there,
now approaching total baldness but otherwise unmarked by time.

Next came the gymnasium, where we climbed ropes and vaulted
horses and swung hand-over-hand along horizontal ladders, like
Tarzan himself. Discipline here was maintained by a Regimental
Sergeant-Major, known as "The Sergeant," a most formidable
figure in a shiny blue serge uniform, with a row of medals dating
from the Afghan Wars, and a pointed and waxed moustache,
which he kept pointed and waxed by material from its most convenient source—his ears.

The Sergeant taught boxing, which was still listed as "the manly
art of self-defense"; but the manly art, thank goodness, was not
compulsory, and one could climb ropes and twirl Indian clubs
instead. He also kept an eye on our private lockers, which lined
the gymnasium, and from which things were occasionally filched
—but things so ripe for stealing, such as chocolate and cake, that
we thought far less of this crime than did anyone in authority.

The importance of food to desperate boys was never really
appreciated by the enemy.

Farther on, in cold outer space, were the changing-rooms,
where we each had a pair of numbered pegs for our football or
cricket clothes. There were rows of brown earthenware wash-
basins, for removing the main marks of strife, and in the middle
a large tiled footbath with a bench across the middle. Here we
sat like senators, retailing the latest gossip and soaking our
football-filthy feet; and (not too much like senators) comparing
various samples of what we called "toe-jam," to exclamations of
"Phew! What a niff!"

The lavatories—"the bogs," in our own language—with their
coarse scrubbed wooden seats, completed this section of the school,
which was in a perpetual state of sloshing water, uproar, moist
footprints, and the flicking of bare posterior flesh with wet towels.

Upstairs were the dormitories, for anything from six to eleven boys, except for a superior one called the "Long Dorm," which had eighteen occupants and an elected parliament of its own, given to voting on group punishment for our own range of crimes, principally sneaking and "sucking up." Our beds were narrow; a cross-lacing of wire took the place of springs, and on this the minimal mattresses sagged like sheets of cardboard.

Above each bed was a tiny foot-square cupboard in which we kept our modest toiletries; and above that, those ever-open windows, through which the wind from across the Sands of Dee sighed and whistled and chilled our sleeping blood.

There were three baths to each bathroom, and on the door was posted the bath-list, intricately timed to allow seven minutes per bath per boy, in six shifts.

That was all, inside the solid cold shell of The Leas. Outside, sixteen acres of grounds included a seven-hole golf course, a shooting range, a squash court, and a swimming pool, as well as the various pitches on which we performed our feats of skill and endurance.

The fees for all this were one hundred and twenty pounds a year. There were special terms for brothers.

The actual word *brother* was for some reason taboo. One spoke of "my major" or "my minor," for elder or younger relatives. Spurned even more scornfully were the tender terms *mother* and *father*. These had now become mater and pater or, collectively, "my people."

Sisters were never even mentioned. I lived in constant terror that someone would find out what my sister was called. Nicholas itself was bad enough, and never never *never* to be written on envelopes. But Felicity . . .

Sitting above us all the time, like a thick layer of crust on an ill-mixed loaf, was the Staff, the people who ruled our lives for two-thirds of every year. It was obvious that their standards were high, although we didn't know it at the time; we just thought they were impossible. But we had to be made to work and to behave, and both were clearly being well taken care of.

In all their dealings with us, there was one kind of discipline which was happily absent, and this was sarcasm, that unfair,

unanswerable weapon which is often more wounding than anything dreamed up by armourers. Instead, we groaned as we
wrote out our "impots," sometimes in a fair round hand on the
blackboard, which had to be covered with "I must not talk in
class," or "I must hang up my clothes."

Later on, it was Latin verse which had to be transcribed, over
and over again, or even Greek hexameters. But by that time we
had learned, for the most part, how to avoid this kind of punishment; we had finally picked up some common sense, or at least
the appearance of it.

Serious breaches of discipline were dealt with by caning, which
was very rare, and thought to be rather disgraceful, and was
administered by the headmaster only, after a terrific, tear-jerking
lecture on the evils of evil.

My "best friend" was caned for spitting in someone else's mug
of tea (I don't know why he was my best friend). Another culprit
ran amuck and kicked the matron, and a third spirited an air-gun
out of the shooting-range and started knocking off sparrows just
outside a fully populated gymnasium. These three were the only
memorable cases during my six years at The Leas. No one was
expelled, though it was whispered that not too long ago a boy
had actually hanged himself (or, according to other accounts,
starved himself to death), rather than face his parents after his
expulsion for some crime unknown.

Caning, the most serious punishment within our own experience, was administered with a two-foot ruler on the bottom;
and the bottom, after its chrysalis stages as the sit-upon and the
bum, was now officially the arse.

Into this sea of troubles, where everyone, it seemed, was a
foot taller than myself, I had been thrust at the age of seven.
Now, four years later, under-sized, puzzled, and afraid, I was
still trying to stay afloat.

I was very small for my age, as was freely pointed out several
times a day. I was known as a "shrimp," or, even less flatteringly,
as a "squit." My first nickname was The Rat, and then, for some
reason, it was changed to Lime-Juice, after a well-known brand
of this product which came from Montserrat Island in the West
Indies.

At school, everyone had a nickname; it was not a sign of popularity, as grown-ups always maintained (even to the extent of inventing one for themselves), but simply a local habit. One boy who, because of some spastic condition, walked with a curious galloping, head-tossing motion was nicknamed Neddy; we used to jump on his back and ride him round the gym, goading him on with the spikes of cricket-stumps.

Another, who had the misfortune to be sent to school on his first day wearing long black stockings instead of the normal short grey ones, never lost the nickname Girlie, which followed him like a curse until he left. Serve him right, we thought as we cat-called. His people should have known better. They must be a *very* common family.

Nicknames were only labels, usually of derision, and you were very lucky if you managed to escape with something neutral.

The Leas was at that time an exclusively northern school; we were mostly from Liverpool and Manchester, and the flat Lancashire accent, adenoidal and endearing, was practically universal —so much so that one never knew one had an "accent," that most shaming thing in all England, until one went to school somewhere else.

We all dressed alike, in the "school uniform" of grey flannel suit (short trousers for the young ones, longs for the old), striped tie, and a dark blue cap with a light blue Maltese cross. On Sundays we wore Eton jackets (called, in a whisper, "bum freezers"), wide white stiff collars, and what must have been very small top hats; and in this confining rig we spent a confining day.

Whenever one appeared in a new suit, one was pinched severely on the upper arm by everybody one met—only one pinch to each customer, it was true, but this still involved eighty separate assaults, most of them ill-natured. It was the first of many small brutalities which seemed at the time enormous, and which, in fear and occasional terror, one had to take for granted.

The ganging-up was flagrant and merciless; all that one could hope for was that before too long the heat of the fire might be directed elsewhere, and one could join the gang, the baying throng, oneself. But that was sometimes a far-off prospect of relief. "Hack his shins!" they called out, in rising chorus, and set to work to do so. "Turf him out! Let's have a Rat hunt!" The torment did not stop at night; caught unawares, one could be jumped on in bed, suffocated with pillows, pummelled all over, and generally left for dead.

To complain (it was the same at home, in the nursery) would have been unthinkable; this was "sneaking," the prime crime, and it invited reprisals which would *never* cease, which would be revived the next term, and the next. To cry was "blubbing," a mistake equally awful and memorable. To fight back (as was occasionally done) would have been very brave, and yet for me it would have been hopeless.

I was not brave, I was too small, I was a squit, and squits were scarcely God's creatures at all.

But presently I achieved something which began to keep this horrid world at bay, which none of my companions could ever spoil; a status involving both a private joy and some degree of public security. I was made school librarian; and, with the job, I had a cast-iron retreat, not to be breached by the boldest barbarian who might, for several reasons, be after my blood.

The library was housed in one of the larger class-rooms; it had long glass-protected shelves, reading tables, and the best thing of all—the rule of silence. "NO TALKING, NO RAGGING OF ANY KIND," said the blessed notice which summed up my letters of *marque;* under this banner, I thrived and was at peace. I spent hours in the library, much more than the small job demanded. "They" could not get at me here, they could not even talk to me except about books. Here I was safe, and irreproachably so.

There was not very much for the librarian to do. I unlocked the shelves at the appointed times, wrote down the names of the borrowers and the books they borrowed, and upheld the silence rule, backed by the real authority, Mr. Sutton, the classics master, who had only to growl to be obeyed. In between times, I devoured my own wares.

It was a boys' library, with undertones of things we *might* want to know about, as soon as we got some sense into our heads; but these guide-lines to the future could not match the excitement which was available to us, at this moment. Rider Haggard was the man, these days; such books as *She,* and *Allan Quatermain,* and *King Solomon's Mines* (Gagool, the terrifying witch, haunted many a dream) were, to use a librarian's phrase, always in brisk demand.

Vice Versa gave us hope that one day, with the aid of magic, we might turn the tables on the adult world. *Tarzan and the Jewels of Opah* promised us superhuman powers, if we could only pass safely into the jungle.

But the real heavyweights of my collection were the bound volumes of *Punch,* dating back to the 1880's, which filled a whole book-case. Their dark and musty bindings made them look very dull; but inside, they were not dull at all. In fact, they were fascinating.

The jokes were really very good, and the drawings, old-fashioned and painstaking, invited hours of close inspection.

I think I took all my social convictions from *Punch*; and they were to last a very long time. *Punch* made it clear, beyond a doubt, that all the lower orders were laughable, particularly when they made grammatical mistakes; that workmen were lazy, drunken, and dirty; that the children of the poor ("urchins"), who rang front door bells and ran away, and shouted "Yah!," thumb-to-nose, when rebuked, were to be absolutely shunned; that servants were unreliable, and (when "under notice") disgracefully impertinent; and that newly rich men like *Punch's* favourite, "Sir Midas," inevitably made absurd social blunders which betrayed their horrid origin.

All these views clearly coincided with Mother's, so that there was no home-and-school conflict here.

The recurring "Look it up!" command from Mr. Sutton was the best thing he could ever have said to me, though I didn't appreciate this to begin with, and found it irksome to move over to the dictionary or the encyclopedia, in order to ferret out something which Mr. Sutton could perfectly well have told me himself. But from being a bore it grew into a habit, and then into a pleasure; and this of course was real education (from *e-*, out, and *ducere,* to lead; I lead out, I bring out, develop, from latent or potential existence).

Thus I entertained myself, safely, innocently, and in the end profitably. Being school librarian involved writing the "Library Notes" for the school magazine, *The Leasian,* at the end of term;

and since this marked my very first time in print, the impulse
to immortalize cannot be resisted.

LIBRARY NOTES

Books have been taken out in quite large numbers during
the term. There has been a great run on Sapper's *Bulldog
Drummond* and *The Black Gang.* Books by Rider Haggard
have been widely read, and some by Dumas have been taken
out by several of the senior boys. It is interesting to note how
the Tarzan books, by Burroughs, which used to be very popular, have entirely fallen out of favour. *The Child's Treasure
House,* the bound *Punches,* and the four big volumes of *The
History of the World,* the latter, alas,* being rather the worse
for wear, are always in demand.

N.J.T.M.

I loved the library, and the job of running it, for dozens of
different reasons. When I moved elsewhere, *The Leasian* said:
"As librarian, we shall miss him greatly." It was a generous verdict,
and entirely mutual.

In one other area I also had *expertise,* grudgingly admitted by
all. I knew *everything* about motor-cycles.

I don't remember what had originally sparked this wild enthusiasm, but I know what sustained it; the gleaming splendour
of Mr. Sutton's Indian, which spent the day outside the gym, and
the arrival each week of my real bible, a magazine called *The
Motor Cycle.*

The Indian could be gazed at, and smelled, though never
touched or mounted; *The Motor Cycle* was devoured with enormous, unfailing appetite. It was a big thick magazine; for 2d. a
week, it was extraordinarily good value; it told you all you wanted
to know, and at crucial times like the Motor Cycle Show or the
Tourist Trophy races in the Isle of Man, it was deliriously detailed.

With its help, I had come to know my hobby from stem to
stern. I knew all the makes by sight, and what they cost, and what

* Note the early use of "alas."

extra equipment could go with them—leg-shields, saddle-bags, Bosch magnetos, Lucas ("King of the Road") lighting—and the pros and cons of belt-drive versus chain-drive.

I followed the "reliability trials," and the hill climbs, and the racing results; in the world of motor-cycling, this was a great duelling period, Douglas against Norton, and all enthusiasts took sides, as in the Swan pen against the Waterman.

This was the year that I invented the automatic gear-change, and though I make no substantial claim against Borg-Warner, I *was* there, many a year ahead of their chief designer, who was almost certainly a grown-up. My model, for which I drew endless pages of diagrams, involved a thing called a "governor," of a type to be found on most stationary engines. The invention still needs diagrams to make it absolutely clear.

When the machine was in low gear, the engine speed was normal (Fig. 1, next page). Then you accelerated. As the engine speed rose (Fig. 2), the balls of the governor (I'm sorry; there is no other way of expressing it) flew outwards, thus (a) lifting the collar, the ratchet, and the gear-lever, and so (b) changing gear. The engine speed then dropped (Fig. 3), the balls resumed their normal position, and the falling collar lowered the attached ratchet down one notch. You were now in second gear, and ready to repeat the process (Fig. 4).

You could have as many gears as you liked, depending on the number of teeth to the ratchet. The teeth only pivoted one way; they could lift, but they couldn't push down.

By this time I was absolutely convinced that I was on to something fantastic; that I would almost immediately be famous, and never be short of money again. I worked on the ideas, modifications, and sketches until I had perfected everything, with no possible loopholes for failure. Then I fair-copied the diagrams, added the words "Not to Scale," and presented the whole thing to Mr. Sutton.

I had caught him on a normal day; he was ferocious, short-tempered, and very busy. He probably thought that I had come to him with some mundane problem concerning the Ablative Absolute, and he was not too pleased when there landed on his desk, already littered with twelve terrible essays on "How Shall I Spend My Summer Holiday?," the blue-prints of an invention

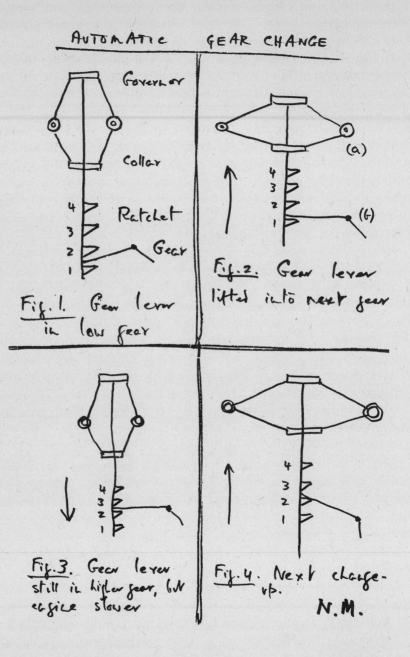

AUTOMATIC   GEAR CHANGE

Governor

Collar

Ratchet

Gear

Fig. 1. Gear lever in low gear

(a)

(b)

Fig. 2. Gear lever lifted into next gear

Fig. 3. Gear lever still in lower gear, but engine slower

Fig. 4. Next change-up.

N.M.

with which I was going to revolutionize the entire car and motor-cycle industry.

But he was a fellow motor-cyclist, after all, and he did not demolish me there and then. When he had completed his lecture on concentration, discipline, and waste of valuable time, he did actually examine my drawings, while I held my breath.

First he frowned, but then he was always frowning; anything else would have meant that he wasn't paying attention. Then he took out a blue pencil, and I caught my breath again. *He was going to come in as a partner.* Sutton and Monsarrat? Monsarrat and Sutton? The Sutton-Monsarrat Automatic Gear Company? Then he said, with a sigh—and even his sighs were still pretty fierce: "No, no, no."

It was not nearly enough for me, even in triplicate. "Please, sir?"

"How do you get back into low gear?"

I had been ready for this question—or rather, not ready for it at all. "I'm going to invent that as well, sir. This part is just for changing-up."

He frowned again. "Then there's the clutch. What about the clutch?"

"I'm going to do that, as soon as I do the changing-down invention."

"You're going to be busy, aren't you?" he said, still looking down at my drawings.

"I don't mind, sir."

"Well, I do!" he roared out suddenly. His timing was always good. "You have *work* to do! Weeks and months of *work*! This stuff is—" he swept the papers away from him, like dead leaves, "—just fooling about!" I must have looked very crestfallen, because he said: "Oh, for heaven's sake take off that sick-face!"

It was the first time I had heard him using our own slang, and I could have wished for a happier occasion. But obscurely I appreciated the effort. It represented a kind of very short slim olive branch, and I reacted to it.

"Sorry, sir," I said, humble and hopeful.

"I should think so," he answered promptly. "This thing—" he jabbed a thumb at the scattered sheets, "—is quite ingenious. But it won't work as it is, and it probably won't work in the future, whatever you do to it. And in the meantime—" the word *work* must have touched a near-the-surface nerve, because he raised his voice again, "—you've got better things to do! Haven't you?"

"Yes, sir."

"Well, get on with it! Do them!"

"Yes, sir."

He looked at me under his fierce curling eyebrows. "What does ingenious mean?"

"I don't know, sir."

"Look it up! And write the answer at the end of your English *précis,* in case I forget."

It was Latin, of course; everything was Latin. It meant "clever at contriving," from *ingenium,* cleverness. I duly appended this information at the end of the next day's offering. Mr. Sutton gave me an alpha minus for the *précis,* but after "ingenious" he scribbled: "Distinguish from ingenuous."

I distinguished, with the side-by-side sample sentences which I knew he would demand if I did not produce them in the first place.

"The invention needed an *ingenious* (clever) brain," I wrote, rather daring and fed-up. "The boy was *ingenuous* (frank, artless) when he showed it to people."

There was no official reaction to this transparent piece of cheek, very much to my relief. But it was the end of the exchange, and of the Monsarrat automatic gear system, which is now standard (with certain broad modifications) on a million new cars every month.

I had one other enthusiasm, during that summer term. This was running.

I was still very small, and therefore, in self-defense, I worked hard to develop a turn of speed which would take me out of danger. Often it did so; it also brought me some silver medals, and a thin residue of fame. For my age, I was the fastest boy in the school, both on the flat and over the jumps; at the Junior Sports, I won both the hundred yards and the hurdles.

I was only second in the high jump, but this, as everyone knows, is just a knack.

For all my time at The Leas, I was in sharp, continual competition with a boy called Marchant, nicknamed the March Hare because it was supposed he could run rather fast. But that was just propaganda. I almost always beat him.

Now at last (and never more welcome) it was the end of July, the last week before we broke up for the holidays.

The sports were settled, the deadly cricket matches which lasted the whole afternoon were all over; the nervous horror of the Parents' Match (for which my father kept solemnly promising me to volunteer, but was always, thank heavens, too busy) had been disposed of.

Empty trunks began to pile up in one corner of the gym, ready for Lum-Lum's (the matron's) monumental task of packing. I set to work rounding up all my library books, and threatening to fine anyone who did not deliver on time.

Choosing a good day and a safe tide, school and staff together went on the annual Hilbre Picnic, involving a long hike across the Sands of Dee to Hilbre Island. To reach this rock outpost, which housed the Wirral lifeboat station, we plodded across reputed quicksands (they had been left wet by the receding tide); once on Hilbre, we were treated to a paddle or a bathe, a little crab-chasing, a little rock scramble, and a tour of the lifeboat house.

After that, we demolished mounds of sandy sandwiches and bottles of fizzy lemonade which had glass marbles as stoppers, and plodded back home again, a few minutes (we liked to think) ahead of the incoming, racing tide, which on a good day (it was said) could go faster than a galloping horse.

Back at The Leas, we started singing our going-home song:

> This time next week,
> Where shall we be?
> Not in this academee!
> No more Latin, no more Greek,
> No more cane to make you squeak.
> No more mutton, no more stew,
> No more beef to make you spew.

It contained a gross element of exaggeration, appropriate to boys who would be off the hook in a matter of hours.

On the last night, there was a school concert. This featured piano duets by promising pupils, and a funny monologue, incorporating the names of all the boys who were leaving, from old Mr. Hadley. Mr. Sutton sang "Drake's Drum," in a thunderous bass; and one of the boys' mothers let fly with "Cherry Ripe." As she hit the high note of "Ripe *I-I-I* cry!" I thanked all the gods in the world that my own mother could not sing.

Finally there was a rendering of "Strawberry Fair" by the sixth form. I did not like the sixth form, and was delighted that they had to sing "Ri-fol, ri-fol, toll-de-riddle-i-do" like a lot of chumps.

Then, next morning, we were free. Station buses came, and taxi-cabs for richer boys, and a Daimler for Monsarrat, and something else very superior for Laird, small scion of Cammell Lairds, the shipbuilders. The pile of trunks and tuck-boxes in the drive dwindled and sank to nothing. We did not stay long enough to hear utter peace and silence descend upon The Leas, but, at a guess, it must have been wonderful.

It was wonderful for me, too. This had been a dreadful term, and now it was past, and I had won through to the hols, which meant Trearddur Bay again.

Trearddur Bay was growing, in just the way I would have chosen if, at the age of eleven, I could have relished the past, commanded the present, and foreseen the future.

I thought everything was wonderful, and, as far as Trearddur was concerned, I kept on thinking this for another twenty years. Possessed by that special, careless enchantment in which happiness, sunshine, and the teeming edge of the sea were blended into the warmest of warm welcomes, I loved it without reserve.

From being the seventh house to be built in the bay, Hafod now stood near the top of a long and growing list. The growth had been by rumour, by word of mouth, by wise selection; the same people, coming back year after year, brought their friends with them, tipped off relatives who were certain to enjoy the same kind of relaxation, and spread the word that here, above all other places, people would find the simple holiday ease they were looking for.

Of the earlier days at Hafod, it is the evenings I remember best. Almost always we spent the evenings quietly in the sitting-room at home. This very comfortable room, made up from two rooms of the old Hafod, had been furnished with great care by Mother; in the yellow lamplight (so far, only our exotic neighbours, the Graysons of Ravenspoint, had electric light) the old oak furniture and the pewter on the Welsh dresser gave back to us a warm twinkling glow.

We would all be there except Denys, who still kept early hours; our father writing in the armchair by the fireplace, Mother sewing opposite him, Molly laying out the cards for Patience, Felicity and I playing Ludo or reading, chin on hand, at the center table, under the hanging lamp with the fly-papers clipped to its base. We both read a good deal, even at Trearddur Bay, drawing our books from the nursery library, a haphazard collection replenished chiefly by visitors' rejects; we found them sufficiently interesting to be read over and over again, year after year.

Throughout the evening we sucked sweets continuously. At nine o'clock, tea would be brought in, and a big tin of biscuits, including the sugar-topped ones with animals on them, known as "Playmates," which had supplanted "squashed flies" in favouritism. Then, very soon afterwards, Mother would say thoughtfully: "Children . . ." which was the warning shot for Felicity and me to start packing things up.

We said goodnight, took a candle from the hall table, washed ourselves free of sand and the stickiness of sea-water, and went soberly to bed. Felicity slept on the ground floor: I shared an upstairs room, fitted with two bunks, with Denys. Sometimes he was still awake when I came up, and we would talk—we were far better friends at Trearddur Bay than anywhere else.

Before blowing out the candle I would draw back the curtain and look out of the dormer-window. The starlight was bright on the water: if the moon were full I could see all the gleaming rocks right out to the point and even distinguish, because I *knew* it was there, the black outline of Oyster Rock caught in the silver moon-track. Save for the restlessness of the waves climbing the rocks and falling back again, the night was still, and very quiet.

Everything was very quiet, both by night and by day; and for this reason, for this single year, Trearddur Bay had begun to go a little sour. There was one basic denial at the root of this feeling, this first-time irritation.

We wanted to sail. Everyone else was sailing; the newly formed Trearddur Bay Sailing Club ran two races a week, as well as a two-day regatta in mid-August which saw the whole circle of the bay alive with big and little craft. The Buckleys had a boat. So did the Dales. The Munros had two, the Smellies had *four* (Mr. Smellie was the commodore of the club). What about the Monsarrats?

We were much too young, we were told. I did my best to refute this. Peter Munro was the same age as I was, and he sailed every week. Then there was the cost. How much did these sailing-boats cost?

I didn't know, but I very soon found out. An Insect Class boat (one sail) cost forty-five pounds. A Myth Class model (two sails, beautiful red ones) cost sixty pounds. They were made by Dickie, of Bangor. They had fitted floor-boards, and mahogany gunwales. They were clinker-built.

"Sixty pounds," said my father, in a sixty-pound voice. "Do you realize that that's more than I charge to take out an appendix?"

It did sound an awful lot of money, put like that. But dash it all! think of the Daimler. . . . So how about a sailing-boat? *Please,* how about a sailing-boat?

My father said that he would think about it. Mother said the same; she did not even say "Presently," which was ominous. It was clear that we would have to wait, at least for another year, and meanwhile our entire lives were slipping away, and everyone else was sailing, and we were still splashing about in a rowing boat, like *infants*. It was too awful.

Yet we had to put up with it, and try our best to enjoy ourselves, though burning with that particular, piercing resentment felt by under-privileged children. All I could do was to get as near as I could to the lucky sailors—the little boy on the edge of the big-boy gang, hungry for a nod, a single word, the magic of a beckoning finger.

There was one memorable oddment of that year—memorable for at least the next thirty years, when it finally slipped into its appointed slot. I had been walking back from the beach with my father, one evening after two days of very rough weather, which had brought rumours of a wreck off South Stack lighthouse. I happened to look back at the bay, as we climbed the hill towards Hafod.

The waves were still running high, and the sun, low on the western horizon, was just catching their curling tops, so that when they broke into thunderous foam the change from dark green, sullen water to creamy spume was shot through with a dazzling yellow glow.

It was beautiful, even to a small boy who thought the promised supper of fish-cakes and blackberry pudding likely to be the most beautiful thing of all, and I said so.

My father, perhaps thinking of split ships and drowned sailors, was not at all impressed. He answered me with two sentences which were to have the longest echo of any other words I ever heard: "The sea isn't beautiful. It is cruel."

Back to Liverpool; back to the city rhythm, the shopping for school, and (sad, sad, sad) The Leas, Hoylake, Cheshire, again.

I was growing a little, even though the growth was exceptionally modest, like progressing from Size 0 to Size ½; thus the autumn term meant new suits, new socks, new shirts, new shoes, a new rain-coat—new everything. This in turn demanded lots of shopping trips, down-town into Liverpool; they were the very last fun of the holidays, and precious pearls on that account.

There couldn't be many boys at The Leas, I kept on thinking, with warm self-esteem, whose mothers were able to buy everything in sight at a place like Cooper's, whose parcels were brought home in a Daimler, and who had a lovely eleven o'clock gorge at Troxler's as a matter of course, every time they went into town.

We were privileged, obviously, but we did not mind that at all, and were indeed often proud of it. It was simply because our father was so clever. . . .

The poverty and the misery of post-war England, which could later be established as facts, were grounded in things which we only heard about very vaguely. We could not know, and we certainly could never have understood, the sour feeling of let-down after the war, the conviction that the brave glitter and the binding ties had been some kind of a swindle.

The huge fact of Victory must have been the most grisly joke of all, because it had melted into thin air while the winners were looking the other way. Something had gone wrong, for millions of people; they had been defeated after all, just like the Germans. It turned out that everybody had lost, except the people who were on top; and they—surprise! surprise!—were exactly the same people as before.

But for us, all this really was unknown, and its many causes very vague in our minds. Though we were encouraged to read the newspapers, both at school and at home, it was a sketchy operation; the "Pip, Squeak, and Wilfred" cartoons which had just started in the *Daily Mirror* were much more interesting than anything to be found on the front page, and the *Liverpool Post* looked too solid and grown-up to be anything except boring.

Yet we did take in, more or less, the Coal Strike, which went on and on, for more than three months, because the miners wouldn't give in. We knew that there were lots of unemployed, nearly two million—there had been a riot in Liverpool about it; and even when the dole was raised from eighteen shillings a week to twenty, it didn't seem to make any difference.

There was a sort of war going on with Ireland, which wanted to be free ("They don't know when they're well off," said Mother). It was the Sinn Fein against the Black and Tans; the Sinn Fein pulled men out of their beds and shot them; they blew up troop trains, and ambushed people, and kidnapped them; they even started fires in Liverpool, where there was a "Roger Casement" club, which for some reason was thought to be particularly disgraceful.

There was a sad story, and some awful pictures, of an airship called the R.38, which broke in two and fell in flames into the River Humber; some of the people got out, but forty-six were killed. There was a terrible famine in Russia, with "acres of dead and dying"; it was brought home to us because there were "Save the Children" funds all over England, and we gave some of our pocket-money, more or less spontaneously, to help the Liverpool one. There was something called the Yellow Peril, but we were not asked to do anything about that.

A Member of Parliament called Horatio Bottomley (who had a magazine which was banned at Melbreck, *John Bull*) got into all sorts of trouble with his Victory Bond Club; they couldn't find the account books, which had been sent to Paris, and the judge said it was the "grossest irregularity." Another man called Sir Thomas Beecham, the one who made the pills, told the bankruptcy courts that he had lost more than two million pounds trying to put on operas in England.

A much worse man, a Frenchman called Landru (or sometimes "Bluebeard"), was found to have murdered fifteen women. He really gave himself away because he was so mean; he used to sell their hair and false teeth.

Lloyd George, who had won the war, was still Prime Minister, and still determined to "Make Germany Pay!" There was going to be something called the Geddes Axe, which would cut down money. Caruso (we had his gramophone record) died. Princess Mary got engaged to Viscount Lascelles. It was a love match.

And that, for us, was that; a year's news, good and bad, from a world we didn't really know anything about.

As far as those unemployed were concerned, we only knew what we overheard, the snapshot verdicts of the time—that they were lazy and "work-shy," that they were ungrateful, that if you gave them a house with a bath they put coal in it. It was impossible to care very much, because we never heard anyone talking who really did care.

The poor were always *they,* the miners were they, the Russians were they, whether starving or not; in Rodney Street, even dentists were they, because they weren't really doctors at all. The idea of one England was as remote as the idea of one world, one universe.

Round us were people who were different. Further on were other, lesser nations who couldn't really be trusted. Above us were the remote stars, and the admired, unwanted moon.

We, the children of Melbreck, were all right. We were part of a Liverpool family, prosperous, solid, and (if we had known the word) smug; cushioned for ever in the bountiful feather-bed of the upper middle class.

Things were much better that Christmas term.

Certain awful boys had left—and I hoped were getting absolutely *squashed* at their new schools. I was allowed to give up riding, which I loathed, after the first week, when I fell off going over a jump, and was lucky enough to chip a cartilage in my knee.

"It was terribly high," I wrote to Mother, while convalescing. *"Worse than Becher's Brook!"* My report struck the right note; the famous Grand National jump was always killing horses and maiming men. Mother ordered that this exercise should cease forthwith.

All that term I wore, as a badge of honour, an elastic surgical support round my knee. It was the only one in the whole school.

Finally, we were now playing my favourite game, soccer, and I was making good at it. I had been given my Second XI colours, playing center-half—a "key position," as Mr. Craig the games-master pointed out. People were less inclined to bully members of the Second XI; the chances of our winning against other schools might be endangered. And these "away matches" were always fun, since they included not only a bus trip, and the game itself, but a whopping tea afterwards, and a chance to sample someone else's food.

There was a tradition that boys at other schools were very badly behaved, and we watched their table-manners carefully. But their food, we were ready to admit, was always much better than ours.

As team-members, we told each other that we were in "strict training," and gave up a certain small percentage of sweets and chocolate. We practiced shooting at goal, every evening until the light faded. We shouted "Buck up!" if anyone lagged. We compared our leg muscles, and the scars and bruises on our hacked shins, and were proud of them all.

In the realm of athletics (as I then saw it), there was one thing I was slightly ashamed of. Bigger boys could make "tents" under the bed-clothes, and they demonstrated this prowess freely. It was a complete mystery to me why it should ever happen, and to what purpose, but I did my best, since some of the top athletes were involved.

Each night, striving for results, I thought and thought; but nothing happened. I just couldn't make a tent. It was clear that I would have to work on it in the holidays, like a lot of other things.

I had one other worry. The Winchester entrance exam was

looming over the horizon; I was due to take it next year, and the extra coaching for it was now becoming intensive. By way of long-range preparation, old Mr. Hadley let me see some of the papers which had been set in past years. They were absolutely terrifying.

But it was no use arguing. All the masters—Mr. Barr, Mr. Dealtry, Mr. Hadley, and Mr. Sutton—were all quite determined about Winchester. My father was the same, and so was my godfather, the Bishop of Carlisle.

SIXTEEN

1926

A SEASON IN HELL

I THOUGHT WINCHESTER WAS AN AWFUL PLACE, and I still do.
It might only have been my own house, which had a reputation for vicious cruelty unmatched among the other nine. It might
have been simply that the time I was there coincided with a certain disgusting peak of bullying and tyranny. It might have been
my own fault—in the sense that I was a misfit or a fool or a born
loser.

But the fact remained that most of the five years I spent at
Winchester were a never-to-be-forgotten ordeal, with fear, unrelenting worry, and a persistent unhappiness at its core.

Things must now have changed for the better; there could be
no other way for them to go. Indeed, contemporaries of mine
who have sons there maintain that it is now "a very happy place"
—a phrase which, in 1926, could only have been used with the
most grisly kind of sarcasm.

I hope this is true, anyway. The idea of any boy going through
the same brutal mill of the nineteen-twenties is still enough to
turn the stomach.

It was all wrong. Winchester should have been wonderful.
It had absolutely everything, as befitted a school founded in
the very dawn of Western learning.* It had some of the most
beautiful buildings in the whole world. There was the original
College itself, built in 1393; the small chapel called "Chantry," a
cloistered jewel of 1445; and my own favourite, the rose-brick
beauty, designed by Wren, which we knew as "School" and which,
dating from 1687, was, by our reckoning, rather a latecomer on
the scene.

Here they all were, these superb gems of architecture maintained with a loving, five-hundred-year-old piety and pride. Here

* In 1382, by William of Wykeham, as "a school of seventy poor and needy
scholars and clerks, living college-wise." The latter construction is thus sancti-
fied, history-wise.

was I, privileged by history and the cherished art of putting one stone upon another, admitted to the freedom of an academic grove which had been a reverent home of scholarship and teaching when Henry V was a boy.

Yet here was I, beset by a daily, barbarous cruelty which seemed to be accepted at every level, and which (in the last analysis) must have had the blind-eye sanction of authority.

I had been enormously proud of getting into Winchester, and so was everyone else connected with the enterprise. I could still remember Mr. Sutton, the prime begetter, shouting "No!" when I told him the terrific news, and then pumping my hand up and down in an astounding display of congratulation, which made me think, for a brief moment, that I really had been rather clever.

At any time during the last three years, I would readily have changed places with anyone—the man who cleaned the shoes, the pantry boy, the snivelling child who ran errands for School Shop— *anyone* who was not trapped in this wretched door-less cage.

It was twice as awful as The Leas and St. Christopher's put together.

The trouble was bullying, both official and lay, which was a sport so popular that it occupied a large part of our waking hours, and much of our dreams.

There was absolutely nothing that we would not do to each other, from picking a private quarrel to organizing a merciless "hunt," from throwing someone's hat into the furnace (it was a special crime, worth a minimum of three strokes of the ash-plant, not to wear a straw hat out of doors) to pouring a traditional mixture of ink, glue, and Eno's Fruit Salts over the books, papers, and personal trifles on any neighbouring desk.

The tormenting never stopped. It began on the first day of term, and ended on the last, when one might still find one's trunk tossed outside the back door and up-ended into the gutter.

Within this wide bracket, which ranged from stinging mockery to the crudest of violence, we lived our little lives. All the time, we still had to cope with a load of enormously difficult work, which started at seven-thirty every morning and finished at ten o'clock at night.

Too old to cry, too small to hit back, too out-numbered to do anything, the chosen targets, of which I was one for at least two years, were left to sweat, to hide, and (until one forgot all faith) sometimes to pray.

I can remember, with horrid clarity, the names, faces, and habits of all the notable bullies of that day, just as I can remember the swindlers and liars, the mean men or violent women who, at one time or another, have added flavour to the stock-pot of the past.

They must have stayed in the memory because of a scar, big or little; because of what they were able to do, whether it was to spoil a day or a decade, or to poison hope, or to astonish in love, or to betray charity and trust.

I can also remember how, when we all grew a little older, and I a little bigger, these savage school faces softened to an occasional wintry smile, how their owners tried to pretend that none of the past had ever really happened. . . . I would not name them now; they were too awful. Most of them were called Smith, anyway. But it is good to think that they are now beginning to die off.

There were other terrors, besides cruelty and spite.

There were endless rules about things which did not matter at all; about the number of coat-buttons one might leave undone (depending on the number of years one had been at the school); about the courtyards and the exact pieces of lawn on which one must not tread; about the styles of clothes (like double-breasted waistcoats) one could not wear, the colours of shoes and ties and socks which were not permitted.

There was that pressure of work, which was real and unrelenting. Being "Up to Books" at seven-thirty meant getting out of bed at six forty-five to run the prefects' baths and call out the time for luckier late risers. After the first three-quarter-hour session of work there was a chapel service every day; and only then came breakfast, the prelude to the day's real routine.

There was the daily bout of compulsory exercise, called "Ekker." If you were not playing football or cricket, you had to run a mile, or play fives or squash-rackets for a certain length of time, or do something convincing in the gymnasium, or row a boat. If you failed to do one of these things, you were "oiling off ekker," and that was bad trouble.

There was, at any time of any day, from early morn till bedtime, the curse of "sweating," which was the Winchester term for fagging. At any moment, one of the six house-prefects would bawl out: "Here!" and all the juniors had to rush towards him; the last man to arrive got the job, which could be anything from making toast to pressing trousers, from turning on baths to cleaning Officers' Training Corps uniforms, from fetching coal to scraping mud off football boots.

On Sundays the prefects were not allowed to shout "Here!" The thundering rush of feet, the crash of bodies against the door, were thought unsuitable for a day of worship and contemplation. So they shouted "Junior!" or "Jun. man!" instead. Jun. man was me, for a whole year of Sundays.

If you did anything wrong, you were beaten. If you were slow in answering, you were beaten. If you forgot anything, you were beaten. If you hadn't been beaten for some time, you were beaten.

There was the everlasting, stupid tyranny, which affected me most of all, of not being allowed to "sport a line."

"Sporting a line" meant walking three abreast, on the many-times-a-day journey from the house where one prepared one's work to the school where one displayed it—or from anywhere to anywhere, for that matter. Walking in threes was not allowed until one had been at Winchester for two years. Walking alone was absolutely forbidden.

Thus one was under compulsion to walk in pairs, with one's own contemporaries, between the ages of thirteen and fifteen. It happened that this was, for me, a mathematical impossibility.

There were five men (Winchester did not use the word *boy*) in my term; for students of precise actuarial detail, we were called Whitley, Davis, Baird-Smith, Watt, and Monsarrat. Since I had only just scraped through that Entrance Examination, I was the ordained jun. man, starting in a lower form than anyone else.

On any public excursion which called for the pairing system, we were therefore bound to split up as (1) Whitley and Davis, and (2) Baird-Smith and Watt. A child could do this particular piece of arithmetic, and this child was left with the answer. It omitted (3) Monsarrat, eternally unpaired—like some loathèd, party-less M.P., like the bereaved half of twins, like the shirt man's one remaining eye.

It was *my* unique problem, and it cropped up several times a day. It gave me a choice, a miserable choice, of latching on to a pair of more privileged, older men, which was very unpopular and somewhat suspect; or waiting until the last moment, and then running solo all the way; or of hoping that one member of some other junior pair would fall ill, or drop dead, and thus create a vacancy.

Of all the idiotic forms of social exclusion, this, the earliest, was the most cruel and the most embarrassing. It was an extraordinary fact that there was literally no one to whom I could say, in all humility: "There are five men in my year. The four senior ones make up two pairs. I am left out. What shall I do?"

Any prefect worth his salt would be bound to answer: "That's your problem," and beat me if I did not find the solution.

If I had ever appealed to the Housemaster (an unthinkable idea), he would doubtless have ruled that such dilemmas were good for the soul.

I had to find my own answer. Usually it was by last-minute running. Otherwise there wasn't one, and I could only wait for the customary night-time vengeance.

Beating was the handsome perquisite of the prefects, and could involve anything from three to six strokes. Even through day clothes, it drew blood, and it was meant to.

If one ran into a bad patch, which sometimes happened, its effect could be harsh indeed. One man, a year ahead of me, was beaten three times in a single week, for a total of eleven strokes. At the end of this exercise, his back was a bloody criss-cross of scars which would not have disgraced a naval flogging in the mutinous year of 1797.

I had plenty of my own wounds to show. From being a squit, I was now a "loather"—the generic term for the man at the bottom of the heap. Loathers could only be beaten—there was no other cure for their condition.

Wild ideas of running away ("tolling abs" was the technical term), of going to the police, of demanding to see a doctor, were always spinning round inside my head at these times. But it was hopeless. It was unthinkable. Nothing could possibly happen; I would simply be sent back again, and then absolutely *murdered*, by each prefect in turn.

All that one was left with were the very stripes of Christ, and an un-Christian intention to hit back, as soon as one had the power, as soon as one was a prefect oneself.

I was never made a prefect, thank heaven—which was the best thing that ever happened to me at Winchester. The non-prefecture cancelled an important link, between wild rage and the power to work it off on other people.

Prefects! . . . They were the giants, the elected giants, in those days, and their prerogative of giant-hood was established very early. Even at Winchester, it was heavily weighted in favour of brawn; athletes were known to be natural leaders, their sterling characters forged and tempered on the playing field; scholars deserved credit for hard work and the urge to learn, but a clever boy could never really match a gifted cricketer, in terms of public esteem.

By contrast, non-athletes and non-scholars were chained to the galleys for ever, and they knew it—very early, also—and so did everyone else.

What a lot of rubbish this proved to be. I have not kept track of all the dazzling characters who were with me at Winchester— it is difficult to keep track of anonymity; but of my own near and exact contemporaries in the house, of all these phenomenal athletes, paragons of personality, born captains of men and of me, I do know a little.

They pose few problems in the Tables of Precedence. One is a stockbroker, one a bank executive, three are solicitors, two are gallantly dead, one is an educational publisher, and the last is secretary to a Deaf Aid society.

These are all honourable goals, particularly death; but heavens above! these people were then marked out as gods, with matching powers of good and evil. They were the future molders of the race, the glittering stars of our fixed firmament. Now they are where they are, fixed as ever, but fixed like dusty glass eyes, like old prawns in aspic.

They had their good times, bright and early in life, at my expense. Then, I thought that the luckiest men in the world were these proud possessors of the keys of our kingdom, and I was deeply envious. But I was wrong; and it now comes out as a very easy equation:

If Pride $+$ Envy $= x$, then $x =$ Error.

I was still on the small side, though doing my best, with Indian club, chest-expander, dumb-bell, and press-up to improve on this. Starting again, as a "new man," at Winchester, had been a salutary surprise; from being a soccer and running star at The Leas, I had once more reverted to being a nervous nothing.

There was, I discovered, nothing so ex as an ex-star. I had even stopped being any good at football. Everyone else now seemed so enormous, so determined, so full of "character." I had lost my character, somewhere between Lancashire and Hampshire. I was "windy." It was another bad start.

I doubled that bad start, as usual, in the realm of work. A very clever boy at The Leas, I was just run-of-the-mill among this real competition; having found that out, I lost scholastic heart straight away. It was as if I had shot my bolt, just getting into the place, and needed a prolonged convalescence to put me on my feet again.

I grew lazy, and stayed lazy, for far too long; for more than a year, in fact, until an interview with the terrifying headmaster, and an explicit threat of expulsion, brought a swift reversal.

Though I wanted, more than anything else in the world, to escape, I did not want to be expelled. I began to work like a badger.

The effect of a few well-chosen words from a man who went on to be, first, Chaplain to the King, and then Bishop of Winchester, was suitably miraculous. The following term, I "raised books" (won the top prize) and was moved up a notch; the term after that, I was placed second even in the new form. But there was a limit to miracles, even from this source. Once more, I ran out of juice, slacked off, and stayed that way until the end.

There was a certain sneaky logic on my side. Statistics showed that as soon as you were a two-year-man, you were pretty well a fixture; Winchester was stuck with you, and you with it. I was, at long last, a two-year-man. I also had a newly discovered poet to back me up in this policy decision, W. H. Davies (officially recommended), whose couplet:

A poor life this if, full of care,
We have no time to stand and stare,

echoed my mood exactly.

As the girl said, it was a long time coming.

If anyone finds it hard to believe, in this more liberal age, that a boy could reach the age of sixteen without ever having had an orgasm, without even knowing what an orgasm was, nor how to produce one, then I can appreciate their disbelief. Indeed, I am now inclined to share it. But *then*, this primal innocence was a fact.

The experience had not yet been mine, and I didn't know how to make it happen, and I didn't really know what was supposed to happen, anyway.

It was true that I could now make tents—in fact, it sometimes seemed that I could not stop making tents; and tents were obviously connected with this thing that everyone else was talking about, and laughing about, and which sparked those unending, incomprehensible stories. But within the tent, absolutely nothing happened.

I didn't know why or why not, nor how or how not. Like any disappointed Arab, I presently folded my tent and silently stole away. I just couldn't puzzle it out at all.

I did my very best. I listened carefully to every confidential word, though still far from understanding what people were talking about. I longed to join in, since whatever this exact sport was, it was very highly spoken of. But I still did not know what sport, nor why, nor how.

It had become a thoroughly confused world, and the distant past was really no help in the urgent present. A classical education only made matters worse.

There were all those things which the gods and goddesses did to each other, or were annoyed about when mortals joined in the fun. There was Leda and the swan. There was Europa and the bull. There was Hera, seduced by a cloud, and Zeus, who did it disguised as a shower of gold. But what did Zeus actually do, and why?

He ravished her, the book said. Very well—what did ravish mean? The dictionary told me that it meant "to carry away a woman by force, sometimes implying subsequent violation." Violation was "defilement of chastity," or, on a softer note, "flagrant disregard of some standard of conduct," or alternatively, "rape."

Rape was, once again, "violation or ravishment." It was also "the common turnip." Neither of these took me very far along the road of discovery.

Then there was *Venus and Adonis,* a reading treat highly recommended throughout the house. At some sort of a climax in this story, Venus fell down, and Adonis fell on top of her, and then it said:

> Now is she in the very lists of love,
> Her champion mounted for the hot encounter.

What was all the excitement? It sounded to me like a very ordinary fight. *What did it mean?*

I got it at last, though it was only by accident. But for the very first time in my life, "accident" meant something good.

It happened on a warm, sleepy, sensuous, summer afternoon, a rare kind of afternoon in England, perfect for watching other people play cricket, and for falling asleep as the dull game languished and died. I was not watching cricket, because I had work to do.

There was some sort of inquisitive examination, or other classical hurdle, coming up over the horizon, and I was not entirely ready for it. That afternoon, therefore, found me lying on the lawn in the Housemaster's garden, made available to studious boys who found it hard to work in a noisy Hall, where the gramophone was inevitably booming out the close-harmony offerings of the Mills Brothers.

I was reading, for profit rather than pleasure, the *Metamorphoses* of Ovid.

I lay face downwards, book on grass, chin on hands; it was bad for the eyesight, they always said, but ideal for the lazier kind of student. A certain crowding sensation at the groin was nothing new. It was always happening, and I still didn't know why. I accepted it, like an inverse law of gravity. This was just an apple that went the other way.

The word *puella,* the pretty word for "girl," came into view on the printed page. It set me dreaming.

Puella. . . . The warm sun filtered down through the branches. *Puella.* . . . The throaty blackbirds were singing, and the thrushes with them. *Puella.* The earth was warm, and hard, and up-bearing. *Puella,* girl, *puellae,* girls. Somewhere far away a lawn-mower was purring, rhythmical as the rise and fall of a sleeper's breast. *Puella,* girl, *puellae,* girls, soft gentle girls.

Presently I became aware that something else was happening, under the tree in the garden, under me.

It was a mounting pleasure such as I had never known before, a tide coming steadily in, a wave which must surely break. I moved slightly, already astonished, and aah! that was really something, that was an extra pulse with honey under it, pushing it upwards.

I moved again, testing, exploring, because I had enjoyed it so much the last time, and quickly it was aah! again, somewhere near the crest of that breaking wave.

Puellae, girls. Me, it, the hard earth. The horizon began to swim, and I with it. I seemed to be balanced on some magical seesaw; a touch one way, and it began to lift crazily, a touch the other, and it fell back into a throbbing pause, waiting for that next, most beautiful high-rising.

I was already panting. The ground beneath me was hard as a rock, soft as a pillow under my loins. Make it last, don't make it last. Break the wave now, hold the wave for one more surge. Then suddenly it was no longer for me to choose. I was climbing and drowning at the same exquisite moment.

There was a last, gulping onslaught of pain and joy; the rim of the round world went red, and then I was left with my receding tide; shaking, shattered, drained—and at last a man.

Certain sucking spasms continued, unnerving me: I was scared enough already. Even now, I was not yet sure what had happened; I thought it might have been a heart attack. . . . When I stood up at last, my head was still spinning, and all my limbs heavy as lead.

Then, just as suddenly as I had been puzzled, suddenly I was not. *I knew.* It couldn't be anything else. It was a Biblical friend, the sin of Onan. It was what another boy in the house had called, inelegantly, a honeymoon in the hand—and now I understood *that,* as well.

I scanned the rows of windows anxiously, alert (much too late) for spies who might have been watching me. But there was no one in view. Presently I took to masturbation, on the most strenuous scale. I don't think I could have stood Winchester, without this self-signed, shop-soiled, essential exit-permit. It kept me sane rather than drove me mad, it promoted no other drive save straightforward sexual ambition, and it disappeared, along with many another habit, as soon as it was replaced by something better.

The summer was still, and always, Trearddur time. All other places, by comparison, were never more than Grade Two. And Trearddur Bay itself had been wildly up-graded. We now had our own sailing-boat.

She had started life, the year before, as "our" sailing-boat; but I soon disposed of the cosy fiction that the boat belonged to the whole family equally. Denys was much too young to get a fair share, and Felicity of course was "only a girl"; who else but I could possibly be trusted to look after the boat properly, and above all to race her?

I had been able, within a fortnight, to stake a claim which quickly assumed the status of a vested interest.

The boat had the unlikely name of *Ptah;* she belonged to the fourteen-foot Myth Class, named for such "myths" as Neptune (Roman god of the sea), Zephyr (the West Wind), and Lachmi (origin untraceable). Ptah had been an Egyptian god who assumed human form and thereafter fashioned the world (or the other way about). His name also occurred here and there in a dynasty of Egyptian kings; cf., as Mr. Sutton would have insisted, Merneptah, well-known son of Rameses II.

To me, *Ptah* was the goddess.

I fell truly in love with her from the moment she was delivered, glistening new, literally as smart as paint, from Dickie's Yard in Bangor; and I looked after her with the sort of jealous care which Mother bestowed on her collection of Victorian china dogs. All the Myth Class had bright, turkey-red sails, white hulls, and were painted either blue, red, or green underwater; they looked exceedingly handsome, and we all thought the world of them.

They were also tough and seaworthy; we were, in fact, the smallest class which was allowed to sail in open water, the boats junior to us (the "Insects") being locked into the Big Bay unless the weather was mild as milk.

Peter Munro had taught me the basics of sailing, in his twelve-foot boat *Hornet,* the star of the Insect Class; now Nigel Wood had taken over, continuing, as far as discipline was concerned, the best tradition of St. Christopher's, The Leas, and Winchester, except that he did not actually beat me when I made a mistake. Nigel was much more than my crew; he was, in those days, the mainspring of *Ptah.*

He taught me with remarkable patience, which only occasionally—say, once or twice a race—overflowed into despair or bad temper. He explained the trickiness of the tides, he settled our course, he decided when to change tacks and when to hang on and take a chance for the next mark.

It was under his firm and unrelaxed tuition that, the first year of my racing career, I earned my first headline in the *Holyhead Mail*—"Schoolboy of Fifteen Wins Regatta Cup." Nigel had won it, of course; all I had to do was to follow his directions and suffer, in silence, the cascades of invective which greeted any lapse.

I could remember every detail of that race, a tense, sweatily nervous affair in which we scraped home, by a boat's length, from the queen of the Myth Class, Dorothy Evans in *Zephyr.* It was the first time *Zephyr* had been beaten for three years. I felt quite ready to die happy, my life's work accomplished before I was sixteen.

Now, down in Porth Diana, it was an active and cheerful scene. All around us, the sails were going up; the line of eighteen-foot half-raters—*Valmai, Dunlin, Kittiwake, Seamew, Shearwater*—which were due to start ahead of us, slipped their moorings one by one and left the bay by the narrow northern channel which led to the starting-line.

As we hoisted our own bright red sails, they made a splash of colour in the sunshine; the slapping, fluttering sound of the wind catching them was the most familiar and significant of all the preliminaries.

Nigel and I worked in silence, on a routine already so assured that we could have done it blindfolded; he bailed and sponged out, and then hoisted the jib, while I saw to the set of the mainsail, shipped the rudder, and lowered the center-board. Often we would be in a hurry; the time-gun which gave us half an hour would sound, before we were anything like ready, and we still had to sail round to the Big Bay and the starting-line.

The boat rocked as we plunged about in a frenzy of hoisting, tightening, untangling, bailing, coaxing ropes through blocks, and putting the oars out in case we had to row round. (By the rules, we had to be clear of our moorings before the five-minute gun was fired.) Getting from Porth Diana to the Big Bay could, in bad weather, be a ticklish operation; it meant going out into the open part of the bay, where the sea was worst, and making a sharp alteration of course in a patch of broken water.

It was a favourite place for capsizing; *Ptah* was once dismasted there during a bad squall—a trying and (it might be added) very expensive occasion.

But usually, as we came round into the Big Bay and made for the starting-line, the half-raters would just be shaping up for their own start, a quarter of an hour before ours. We kept well out of their way; they had considerable advantage in weight, age, and bad language. While we were waiting for them to get clear we hung about, talking to each other, perhaps lowering and resetting a sail, chivvying the twelve-footers out of our neighbourhood, and watching the crowds on the headland.

The races were started from the club flag-staff, set on a small stone terrace overlooking the bay; round about it, the grass slope and the rocks were always crowded—this was a community occasion which everyone attended throughout the season.

We would pick out Mother and Felicity and Denys, and they would wave to us; other spectators would accept and return various signals, of derision or of good-will; then the ten-minute gun would go, Nigel would set the stop-watch, and we would edge over towards the position we had chosen for our starting run.

This was the most exciting part, which often sparked a tremendous tension; the race could be lost or won in the next ten minutes. The ideal to aim at was to be crossing the line, at full speed, well clear of everyone else, precisely as the starting-gun fired; out of the two dozen starts I had made so far, very few—well, none—had fitted this pattern exactly.

To begin with, everyone else had the same idea, and hung about in roughly the same place behind the line; we were coming to know each other's tactics by heart, and only very rarely was it possible to fool the fleet with an individual effort while pretending to do something quite different.

The enterprise could be further messed up by over-eagerness, by bad judgment of distance, and by loose time-keeping. It was really no wonder that into those few minutes before the start was concentrated a singular blend of chicanery and bad temper.

Between the ten-minute and the five-minute guns, we dawdled, as discreetly as possible. While I kept *Ptah* cross-tacking, well off the wind, about fifty yards from the line, Nigel gave me a running commentary on what the rest of the field was doing; it was a measure of our nervous tension at this moment that our language, usually sedate, now plumbed the depths of the picturesque.

From the shore, the binoculars began to be trained on us; it was now, I knew, that Mother was starting to say, in a carrying voice: "What *is* Nicholas doing? He'll be left behind! Can't he see that?" while Felicity, blindly loyal, countered with: "I think he's doing it on purpose." She was occasionally right.

The five-minute gun sounded loud and clear, and Blue Peter and our course-flags were broken out at the flag-staff. Nigel now began to count off the half-minutes for me. From this moment on there was a continuous cross-talk in the boat, jerky, nervous, and varying from qualified optimism to wild despair. My grip on the tiller became painfully fierce; whether the sun shone or the rain was pouring down, I always began to sweat freely.

Nigel, stop-watch in hand, crouched in the thwarts. "Four and a half minutes. . . . Keep her moving."

"Jib in a little!"

"Jib's all right. . . . Better start to edge over now."

"This——wind is shifting!"

"Just keep her full," Nigel snapped back. "Four minutes."

"Blast! We're too near already. Slack off jib! Push the gaff over."

"Don't lose way, or you'll be stuck. . . . Three and a half. . . . *Zephyr* coming up astern."

"Whereabouts?" (I was not allowed to look behind me.) "God damn this wind! It's all over the——place!"

"Dead astern of you. She can't get to windward if you keep pointed up. . . . Three minutes."

"In a little, in a little! I'll luff up. . . . Where are the others?"

"Look ahead," ordered Nigel. "Don't worry about them. Just sail your boat!"

"But where are they?"

"*Zephyr*'s in the wind, astern. . . . Two and a half. . . . *Neptune* passing her. . . . Falling back again. . . . *Lachmi* well back. . . . *Watch that luff!* . . . Two minutes."

"Where's *Zephyr* now?"

"Right on our——tail. . . . Moving across to port. . . . She'll blanket us in a minute. . . . Better go for it now."

"It's too soon."

"One and a half. . . . *Zephyr*'s level now. . . . Point up, you bloody fool!"

"I can't go any higher. It's this——wind, fluking all over the place. Jib in!"

"Jib taut. . . . Sit to leeward a little—no, sit still, for Christ's sake! One minute."

"We're going too fast! We'll be recalled!"

"Three-quarters. Keep her moving."

"Where's *Zephyr*?"

"Dropping back. . . . We're all right like this. . . . Half a minute."

The quartet of red sails suddenly began to move all together, crowding down on to the line. The ripples chattered against our hulls, the wakes spread green and white astern of us. We were committed.

"Give me the seconds. . . . In jib a little."

"Twenty-five."

"In a bit more."

"All taut. . . . Twenty seconds. . . . *Neptune* slipping your stern to leeward. . . . Go for it now!"

"All right. Haul everything!"

"Fifteen. . . . *Zephyr* coming up fast. . . . Just on your quarter."

"The jib's flapping, blast it!" I was in anguish.

"Can't get it any tighter. . . . You're too close. . . . Sail her off a little. . . . Ten seconds!"

"Hell, now we're going too fast! Where's *Zephyr*?"

"Overlapping you. . . . Don't bother about her. . . . Luff up a little. . . . Six."

"She's going to blanket me. We'll be over before the gun."

"No, we won't. . . . Four. . . . Hold on, it's O.K. . . . Three."

"Slack jib! We'll have to bear away. . . . There's no——room!"

"Two. . . . One. . . . Gun!"

No gun.

"Christ, what's happened?" I jerked the tiller uselessly. "It's that ——stop-watch! There's no room to go about. We'll have to—"

BANG!

"Haul in!" shouted Nigel. "Hell, what a swinish start! We're dead in the water! I *told* you to keep her moving! Pull in that main sheet! Sit out! *Zephyr!* If you bear down on us—"

After that, the race itself sometimes seemed rather tame. All starts were like that, unless we made some hopeless mistake and were right out of the running. Nigel and I, and later on Denys and Felicity, must have expended more nervous energy in that fifty-yard section of the Big Bay than anywhere else in the world.

In Myth Class racing, we were sent three times round a course of about three miles; a long leg to seaward, a broad reach across the mouth of Trearddur Bay, and a run home. Sometimes it was as smooth as glass, and we had to spend hours trying to stem the tide round the Porth Diana mark, while *Neptune*'s gramophone played "Blue Skies, Why Am I Blue?" and *Ptah,* creeping away into a corner, started that unscrupulous (and later outlawed) method of propulsion known as "tiller-waggling."

Sometimes it was gloriously and appallingly rough (after all, this was no pond, it was the open Irish Sea), and we would rocket round the course, two reefs down and half full of water, while on shore our relatives clasped their hands and besieged the Officer-of-the-day with demands that the "No Race" gun be fired forthwith, and the Recall flag hoisted.

All sorts of funny things happened to the Officer-of-the-day, from accusations of nepotism to charges that he had deliberately tried to wound a dog with the starting-gun. Once, when I took on the job, and hoisted, in error, a course-flag which sent the little Insects round the full outside course in particularly foul weather, I was called a murderer and someone tried to hit me with an umbrella.

The Insect Class, naturally, loved it. It was their first breath of freedom for years.

Very occasionally I won a race, even against the redoubtable *Zephyr;* mostly I was second or third—fourth and last place being reserved for the Buckleys' boat, that mysterious *Lachmi,* which over the years proved to be a real brute, and might have been permanently towing a bucket over the stern, as far as her speed was concerned.

There were golden days, and bad days; dew on the grass in a calm dawn, crashing seas on the rocks below Hafod; sun warming the deep red tiles of the *loggia,* salt spray on the sitting-room windows; clear water with dark fish swimming, and the sandy, gritty, boiling turmoil of the Big Bay under attack by storm.

This was Trearddur, wonderful Trearddur, better and better every year, because there was more to see, more to feel, more to want.

There was always tomorrow, always sailing and people and regular jokes, and little sisters who this year had become girls—until suddenly our time ran out like the swift ebb-tide, and there was no tomorrow left; only today, when we had to haul *Ptah* up onto the beach, and stow the oars and spars and sails in the garage, where they must face the bitter winter by themselves.

We had finished third in the season's cup standings. It was not good enough; but no one could really beat *Zephyr,* and Mr. Harvey, who sailed *Neptune,* was *old.* . . . He had a daughter *older than me.* . . . We had beaten *Lachmi* by miles.

Wonderful Trearddur Bay. . . . When the sad September date arrived, we packed our trunks, and said goodbye, and went back home to Liverpool.

Though Liverpool was still home, home was now somewhere else. We had moved again, exchanging Melbreck, in Allerton, for another big house four miles nearer town. This was No. 10, Holmfield Road, in a fortified suburb with the unmelodious name of Aigburth.

I think we had moved because Allerton was beginning to spoil; like many another outlying community, it was no longer in the country. The Liverpool tram-lines had crept outwards like lengthening claws, creating and feeding a vast new sprawling development all round the city center; the houses which came with it had seeped up to the very doors of Melbreck, east from Allerton and west from Garston, leaving us as the lone "big house" in a lapping sea of little ones.

They were not very nice houses, Mother said, which meant that they were owned by not very nice people.

Since we could not move farther out, because my father had to work in Liverpool, we moved farther in, into a solid enclave which still had plenty of protection. We were not "cutting down," Mother assured us, using a favourite phrase which she applied to any family which had over-reached itself and had been compelled to back away from the competition. (Whenever she said: *"They're cutting down!"* we knew that the people involved were absolutely doomed, as if by a mortal disease. Sometimes she added: "They were waiting for dead men's shoes," which seemed equally contemptible.)

The Monsarrats were not cutting down. In fact, they were enjoying the reverse process.

Holmfield was the sort of house you lived in, in Liverpool, if you had earned a good deal of money and expected, at the least, to hang on to it. All round us, at decent intervals marked by fat sandstone walls, were solid properties of the same standing. The house was as big as Melbreck, but far better built and planned; a four-square, chunky edifice whose chief feature, a panelled drawing-room extending into a leafy "conservatory," was gracefully proportioned, and as rarely used as a working-class "front parlour."

It had a four-acre garden, with plenty of fruit- and rose-trees as well as wild corners which invited solitude; greenhouses for tomatoes, "frames" for marrows and cucumbers, and stabling for six horses, three cars, or any single child who wanted to keep out of sight. At the farthest end, a grove of huge elms stood guard over a deep sandstone quarry, which my father had turned into the largest rock-garden I ever saw in my life.

When we took over, the place was somewhat neglected. But Gresty, who had come with us from Melbreck, and his eldest son Sam, soon caught up and made a success of it.

Success was, undoubtedly, the Holmfield keynote. My father had now emerged as a substantial man, though substance was, I imagine, the very last consideration which drove him to work so hard and with such brilliant concentration. The material results, however, were the ones most pleasing to us. There was about the household that air of solid comfort and achievement which children, the world's most ruthless snobs, find so agreeable.

The tennis parties, the three cars, the sewing-maid tucked away in an upper room; the ordering-by-telephone, the chauffeur touching his cap, the generous pocket-money; the cellar of champagne and claret and port, the dressing for dinner, the decanter going round (though not yet for me)—all these were, for provincial sons and daughters, the real hall-mark of achievement.

The sons and daughters must now have become an expensive item. Molly was still in the thick of successive Liverpool "seasons"; Felicity was at a finishing school in Paris, and would shortly have to "come out" with a suitable bang; I was at Winchester, and Denys at the Dragon School in Oxford. Thus we were four substantial liabilities, and likely to remain so until the girls got married and the boys faced the competitive world on their own.

All this rested upon my father's brain and hands; and it was our loss that we saw very little of him throughout these crowded years, when his work and his reputation increased so enormously. I was proud of him, by instinct (and perhaps, here and there, for the right reasons), and I watched him as far as I could, just as I used to watch Mother. But my father was a hard man to watch.

He left the house early, at least an hour before his lazy elder son came down for breakfast (to eggs now tepid, in spite of the "egg-cosy"); he returned for dinner, which was a session shared, and then he withdrew into his study, and settled down, in absolute solitude, to work or to read or to think. This was the limit of our contact, and it had to last until the following evening.

To fill in the gaps called for long-term, slow observation, laced with guess-work. But I had still been able to compile a modest catalogue of fact.

I knew how old he was, because I looked it up in *Who's Who*— and how proud (and astonished) I had been to find him there. He was fifty-four!—and that was astonishing, too. It sounded so ancient.

I knew, because I had sneaked an unauthorized look at some papers on his desk, that he was coming up for election to the General Medical Council, the medical governing body of the entire British Isles.

I knew that he worked very hard, because it was obvious; and that he spent the morning at his nursing-home, or at the Northern Hospital, or at the University—or all three: his afternoons in his consulting-room: and some part of some days of the week at the cottage hospital at Neston, across the Mersey. I realized that he must be tired after all this, and that this was why we didn't see him in he evenings, when he wanted to be alone, if only to take a nap or write letters or read *The Lancet*.

I knew (or perhaps guessed) that he wanted one of us to be a doctor: preferably myself, the elder son, the natural heir of the pride and satisfaction he found in his profession. Sometimes he took me with him on his morning hospital round; it was our joint misfortune that these visits had an effect quite different from what he might have hoped.

I found them horrible, in a way which was to return in full force later on, when I had my own share of bandaging and stanching wounds and stitching-up to do. Now, the astringent hospital smells and the occasional moving sights—the sunken faces of tubercular patients, the screens round the condemned bed, the children pale and withered as dead flowers—were enough to convince me that I would never be any good at my father's job.

But these "rounds" were not wasted. From them, I came to learn what people thought about him, at the Northern. Everyone —the nurses, the young doctors trailing him, the patients—all had much the same look on their faces. They trusted him, they admired him, and some of them thought he was wonderful.

I knew that he had one hobby or even addiction, which was rather out of character—the stock-market. I suppose that he had to do something with all those piles of money he was making, but even I knew the difference, in quality, between solid British Consols and flighty things like tobacco shares or copper mines, and I was surprised that such wagering could interest him.

But obviously it did. Once, when I was roaming round his consulting-room, waiting for Mother to pick me up, he showed me some share certificates which had just arrived in the post. They were headed "Baird Television."

"Do you know what that is?" he asked, pointing to the second word.

I said no, I did not. I had never heard of it. I didn't even know how to pronounce it.

He explained. It was an idea, a new invention, like the wireless, only with moving pictures as well as sound. It might well take the place of "listening in"—the current and universal craze. He sounded so enthusiastic that I felt I should show some interest.

"What's Baird?" I asked.

"He's the man who invented it. Or rather—" my father was always precise "—he is in the process of inventing it. This is only the beginning. He has actually sent pictures over several miles. Now he is trying to improve the reception, and of course the range."

"But will it really work?"

"I believe that it will."

John Logie Baird never actually made it to the top, though his "invention," in an altered form, certainly did; and thus my father never made a million pounds out of Baird Television. But I came to realize, later on, that anyone who, born in 1872, invested money in television in 1926, had a degree of business acumen and imagination which, as far as I am concerned, has skipped a generation.

At long last, romance blossomed for Holmfield, and for us. It was not exactly a rush job. First, Molly "had an understanding," as Mother was finally brought to admit, or was "walking out," according to the cook. Then she was officially engaged (sensation). Then the date had been set! Then we had an actual wedding in the house!

The winner (or victim, or insidious snake, according to whose side you were on) was a young man named Philip Proctor, whose father was a director of Dunlop's, and who worked in the same concern. We liked him very much, and the preliminaries had been given our tactful co-operation (our idea of tact being to blurt out "Excuse me a minute!" and bolt from the room as soon as he arrived, leaving Molly with a clear field. "But what do they want to *do?*" Denys used to ask, as I hustled him from the morning-room. "They want to talk," I told him. "Oh," said Denys; "you mean, tell each other jokes?" I was left to wonder what sort of a place the Dragon School was).

Philip had set off for Canada immediately the engagement was announced, to put in some time at the Dunlop factory there. As soon as he came back, the show was on.

It was our first involvement with a wedding, and we made the most of it. Felicity, of course, was a bridesmaid, in powder-blue; I was an usher, wearing my first morning coat and a racy-looking pearl-grey stock; Denys was a page in "court dress," and undoubtedly stole the show. The wedding had all the traditional trimmings: a marquee to ruin the lawn, a detective behind the arras, hired menservants who failed to give the illusion of permanent employment, lovely food, and lashings of champagne.

I had started the year as a two-year-man; now I was a three-year-man, which meant that I could not be beaten (except by the Headmaster, for some grave crime which fell short of expulsion); that I could wear a double-breasted waistcoat, and the flaring trousers called Oxford Bags (up to twenty-four inches round the bottom of the leg); and that I could not only walk boldly across Flint Court, but actually stand on it and talk to other people.

I began to coast, rather agreeably: not too much work, not too much ekker. I wasn't going to be a prefect—the places were all filled, even at this early stage. I wasn't going to be a football star, scoring all five goals against the Corinthians, nor a cricket hero, acknowledging with a touch of the cap the applause which greeted my century in the Eton Match. Though I had stroked my boat into the final of the Senior Fours, we had been solidly defeated, so I wasn't going to be a rowing hero, either.

I might (and subsequently did) run just fast enough to represent Winchester against the Achilles Club.

But that was the limit of my prospects; there would be no significant promotion, and no dramatic defeat, unless I got drunk, assaulted a master, or opted for sodomy.

With none of these ambitions, I decided that I could take it easy, for the rest of my time at school. This still water had come too late for true content, but it was welcome nonetheless.

Three-year-men were allowed to wind up the hard-driven H.M.V. gramophone in Hall, and play their own choice of records; I made the most of this privilege. It was the time of the Two Black Crows, with their slow-talking, lunatic dialogue ("I can play anything on this trumpet!" "You can't play piano on it, you can't do that."); of Waring's Pennsylvanians, and "Ukulele Lady," and Whispering Jack Smith, and "If you Knew Susie"

(Like I Know Susie), and "I Miss My Swiss," and "Horsey, Keep Your Tail Up, Keep the Sun Out of My Eyes."

I loved them all, and played them until they were ruined.

I was freer outside the house also. I could now "sport a line," or walk solo if I chose, or even step out with a man from another house, without shame. But for the most part I tacked on to my other term-mates, John Baird-Smith and Andy Watt. It was a singular relief not to have to hope that one of them would drop dead, leaving me with a surviving partner.

John Baird-Smith was becoming a good friend. He was a tall, red-headed, angular Scottish boy, the son of a Glasgow solicitor.

"My father's a W.S.," John had announced proudly, at our first meeting; and his tone of voice when he found that he had to translate this for me (it meant "Writer to the Signet," a high legal caste in Scotland), indicated that I should have known it all along.

We had enjoyed some good holidays together: a camping trip on the Solway Firth, a walking tour in the Lakes. Still concealed in the future was a gruesome occasion when I stayed in his house for a superior Christmas ball and, unaware of the potency of Scotch whisky, passed out in cold collapse for the first and the last time of my life.

It was with John Baird-Smith and Andy Watt that I took "London Leave" that term, and went up to town, with official permission, to see, for the first time, what London had to offer.

We prepared very carefully for this excursion, which broke new ground. I was from Liverpool, John from Glasgow, Andy from Edinburgh; and though the other two had passed through London on their way to and from school, they had not spent any time there. I had never been nearer to it than Didcot Junction, on my way south. We were all determined to make a strong impression.

This involved, for me, shaving for the first time, with my newest purchase, a Rolls razor, which was a sort of cross between an old-fashioned cut-throat and the new-fangled Gillette. I cut myself on the chin—but then I had expected to—and stanched the wound with a styptic pencil and some cotton wool. Then I put on a heavily striped shirt, a stiff white collar, and my light grey herring-bone suit.

"You were quite wrong," I was told later by a superior boy,

whose father was in the Foreign Office. "Don't you know?—you should *never* wear tweeds in a capital city."

I had not known this, so I was not unhappy. Indeed, I was very proud of the total effect. I crowned it with pale grey spats and a curly-brimmed Homburg hat (just like Rod la Rocque) and, thus lavishly equipped, joined the others for the journey up to town. They both looked equally smart, except that John Baird-Smith had got one big step ahead of us with a tightly rolled silk umbrella.

Our time in London was limited, since we had to be back before midnight on the last available train; the most we could take in was lunch, a theater *matinée,* a cinema straight afterwards, and a very quick meal before dashing down to Waterloo Station.

It was a tight program, but then we went through a tight program every day of our lives. This was one we could enjoy.

On the way from Waterloo to Piccadilly we played a beard-spotting game which was then universal. It consisted of calling out "Beaver!" whenever one saw a man with a beard, and "King Beaver!" (two points) if the beard covered his tie. No longer a secret from its victims, it was slowly but surely driving beards off the streets of Great Britain.

We lunched at Simpson's in the Strand, where the gorgeous roast beef came to the table-side on a great silver-domed trolley, and was carved into wide dripping slices by a fat man in a chef's hat. If you knew what was what, you tipped this talented man a shilling.

We lunched better than we had ever done before, washed it all down with tankards of draft Bass, topped it off with a little ripe Stilton, and then, inhaling deeply and blowing down our nostrils, enjoyed our cigarettes.

These were something very special. They could not be mere Virginians—if one offered someone a Virginian cigarette, one always had to say: "Sorry—only a gasper." We all smoked an exotic brand called Eram Khayyam, more on the strength of the advertising than anything else. This promised a great deal more than straight tobacco.

Eram Khayyam (it said) were perfumed with amber, and tipped with Cork, Gold, Mauve Silk, Red Silk, and Rose Petals. They were "specially prepared for the Princes and Potentates of India";

and when you smoked them, mysterious visions and eastern charms were revealed. They cost a shilling for a box of ten, and definitely tasted different from other cigarettes.

Thus inspired, we presently strolled along the Strand to the nearby theater; somewhat cross-eyed, leering at every woman we passed, and whispering to each other: "Did you notice? She was loitering! She's a whore!"

We had debated for the best part of a month what show we wanted to see in London. It was a choice between a musical comedy and a funny play; we did not really consider buying tickets for anything "serious," even though *Easy Virtue* sounded a tempting idea, and *White Cargo* was said to be very hot stuff.

There was a tremendous list of musical comedies. There was the new C. B. Cochran revue, with Hermione Baddeley and Massine; and an American importation, *Wildflower,* which Oscar Hammerstein (we saw his name on lots of records) had written. There was *Sunny,* with Elsie Randolph and Jack Buchanan, and the glamorous June (the subject of many a rude pun) in *Mercenary Mary.*

Rose Marie was still running at Drury Lane, after years and years; and there was another possibility, said to be very daring: *Blackbirds,* with Florence Mills.

There were not too many funny plays; it really boiled down to *The Farmer's Wife,* which had also been running for years, and Noel Coward's *Hay Fever,* with Marie Tempest. We decided that our best bet was the latest of the "Aldwych farces"; and this was the one we had settled on. It was called *Rookery Nook,* by the man who wrote them all, Ben Travers.

This was the first time, of course, that I had been to the Aldwych Theatre, and the first time I had set eyes on the two famous principals, Ralph Lynn and Tom Walls. They, and *Rookery Nook,* made up the funniest show I had ever seen in my life.

Ralph Lynn was a cheerful, toothy idiot, Tom Walls a lewd man-of-the-world; and backing them up was a glorious trio—a nervous, egg-bald man called Robertson Hare, a rasping washerwoman type, Mary Brough, and a beautiful young girl named Winifred Shotter.

It didn't have any plot—or rather, it had so much plot that

I lost track of it very early on. But the jokes . . . I laughed so hard that half-way through I had a severe wrestling-match with my lunch, and had to go out at the interval for some fresh air.

But I recovered, and came back for the second half. I think I would have come back anyway. The jokes were even funnier, and Winifred Shotter even more alluring. When we finally emerged into the five o'clock sunshine, blinking like surprised owls, there wasn't any doubt in our minds that *Rookery Nook* could never be matched.

We sped along to our cinema, which was *Beau Geste,* with a story so exciting, and characters so noble and self-sacrificing, that we could only glow with pride as the tricolour waved over the beleaguered fort, and the treacherous Bedouin bit the sand under murderous fire. It was wonderful to know that, if the worst came to the worst, the Foreign Legion would always have a place for us.

After that, it was time for Lyons Corner House, and a gulped supper of sausage, egg, and bacon on top of a toasted crumpet. Then we caught our train at Waterloo, and flopped down exhausted, and dozed our way back to Winchester.

The return journey was bound to be an anti-climax; we were bound to feel let-down and discontented, as the lights of the train flickered through a chalk cutting, the badge of Hampshire, and we knew that we were close to captivity again. Why did we have to go back? Why could we not live in London, men-of-the-world like Tom Walls, and have days like this every day of the week? . . . But we *had* had a terrific time; no one could take that away.

I decided that I would think about Winifred Shotter that night, and for many more nights. She was much too good to waste. It was said that if you were a Guards officer and wanted to marry an actress, you had to "send in your papers." For Winifred Shotter, I would have sent in my papers, any time.

After this burst of speed, I settled back into the slouch position. But I worked a little for my own advancement. This was the year that I invented perpetual motion.

It was much simpler than my automatic gear change, with fewer moving parts. It consisted of a revolving arm which ran down one hill and then up another, propelled first by gravity and then by a heavy rotating flywheel which maintained the necessary momentum until it topped the next rise. It was so simple that it seemed incredible to me that no one had thought of it before.

As I had done with Mr. Sutton, I made out a couple of diagrams (see page 102), tidied them up, and presented them to authority. This time it was to Mr. Brown, who taught us the kind of mathematics which I was slowly ceasing to master: advanced algebra (just comprehensible), logarithms (receding out of my grasp), and differential calculus, which had been a complete mystery from the moment I read even its definition: "A method of calculating the infinitesimal differences between consecutive values of continuously varying quantities, and their rate of change."

Mr. Brown was a tall yellowish man, remote and subdued, with a soft voice and a gentle disposition: a type so very rare at Winchester that he was one of my favourites. Indeed, we all liked him, because though he could not communicate his enthusiasm he showed that it was there, and we sympathized. We did realize that, for him, the word "isosceles" was not ridiculous; rather was it music. We did understand that if the square on the hypotenuse had *not* been equal to the sum of the squares on the other two sides, the bottom would have fallen out of his world.

When I approached him, he did not roar at me, like Mr. Sutton; he was not the roaring kind. But his verdict was the same. He examined my sketches with care, nodded his head once, shook it once, and then said: "No, I'm afraid not."

I respected his opinion, because he actually wrote some of our mathematical text-books. But it was still possible that he could be wrong.

"Sir, why wouldn't it work?"

"Friction."

I waited for more; but it seemed that this was not only the first word but the last one as well: a word so powerful that it could destroy inventions and dash all hopes.

Suddenly he was smiling at me; he smiled much more than he frowned, which was one reason why we tried to understand what he was teaching us.

"Don't be too depressed," he said. "They've been chasing this dream for at least two thousand years."

"Sir, what else have they tried?"

Nice as he was, he had given me enough of his time.

1. PERPETUAL MOTION: TOP VIEW.

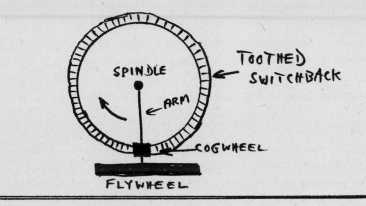

SPINDLE

TOOTHED SWITCHBACK

ARM

COGWHEEL.

FLYWHEEL

2. PERPETUAL MOTION: SIDE VIEW

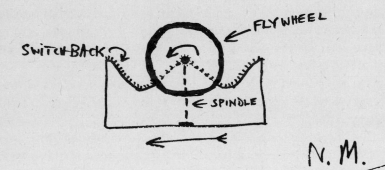

FLYWHEEL

SWITCHBACK

SPINDLE

N. M.

"There's an interesting article in the *Encyclopaedia Britannica*," he answered, becoming grey and rather remote again. "I can recommend it."

I read the article, and it *was* interesting. People in search of this goal had certainly tried everything: pendulums in vacuums, self-driving water-wheels, magnets which drew metal balls up slopes and then dropped them down again, and wet sponges making use of capillary attraction.

It seemed to me that I had come just as close to it as anyone else. But we had all been brought down, apparently, by the first and second laws of thermodynamics. In the circumstances, it was an honourable defeat.

With eight church services a week, and evening prayers in Hall every night, we heard a great deal of the Bible, and of the Book of Common Prayer, Hymns A. & M., and the Psalms.

The language being so wonderful to hear and to remember, it should have been wonderful also as the prelude to my Confirmation, which was now upon me. But it did not work that way. Confirmation did not take.

I knew exactly what I was expecting, because I had been encouraged to expect it. It was going to be something like whatever happened to Saul on the road to Damascus—a shaft of light from heaven, or some kind of a thunderbolt which, if it had been strong enough to turn Saul into St. Paul, must surely bring me grace, and purity, and freedom from sin.

As soon as the hands of the Bishop of Winchester touched my head, everything would be different. I would very likely decide to take Holy Orders.

It would be high time. Already I had an overload of sin. Even if everything came to a dead stop now, and they closed the books, I would go straight to hell, because of the sin of Onan. This had become more than a habit. Even when I was too lazy to practice it, a technical lapse (called, accurately enough, a wet dream, or, in text-book formality, a nocturnal emission) was likely to put me in the wrong column, for yet another night.

There were lots of other debit items. Cool calculation (and this was the time for it, perhaps the last time) told me that I committed at least five of the Seven Deadly Sins, every time the clock went round twenty-four hours; they were Envy, Sloth, Wrath, Gluttony, and Lust, and there couldn't be any argument about them.

Confirmation had to be the key to my release, Confirmation must really get me out of this.

I really worked hard for it. I was sure that I was ready. I had enormous, humble hopes of its effect. But it still did not take. Nothing happened to me. I did not feel any better after it, nor any worse. The laying of hands upon my compulsorily greaseless hair brought no message, struck no spark, cured no evil.

I was terribly disappointed, and sure that it must be my fault, but there it was. I was not going to be a clergyman, nor a monk, nor even a boy without sin or stain.

This year had had the same rise and fall, the same rhythm, as all the other years. Far back in memory, there had been the last Christmas-time, and school at the new year, and the journey home for Easter; then it was school again, and blessed Trearddur Bay again, and home again, and school again. But now the year's tide was running in, at full flood, for the last time. Now it was Christmas again, and Christmas with a difference.

Suddenly the festival had grown up, just as I had. I was nearly seventeen, and so was everyone else who was worth anything at all. It had brought a very big change. The change was labelled *"Vive la différence,"* the new catch-phrase which at last I understood. The change was girls.

Mother called them all "she-males," which made them sound rather unattractive; I knew for a fact that they *were* attractive, and to me (as I reported to Denys) they were either ripping, or stunning, or top-hole. They now wore skirts just at the level of the knee, and beneath that they wore "undies." I had not seen any undies yet, except hanging on the fire-guard at Holmfield, which didn't count at all. I was very keen to see some undies in action, but it was still only a faraway ambition, like driving a three-liter Bentley or growing a moustache. It was something to think about.

The girls' hair was short—either bobbed, or shingled, or bingled, or Eton-cropped. A couple of years earlier it had been a family sensation, attended by tears all round, when Molly cut off her golden tresses; but now, when Felicity did the same thing, it was hardly noticed at all. "Woman's crowning glory" was not mentioned any more, even in fun.

Everyone was cropping their hair, copying the Bright Young Things, a race of super-girls who lived in London and spent all their time at Tango Teas.

I wasn't sure that I could cope with super-girls yet, but it would not be long, because I had made a very interesting discovery. Girls, who hadn't seemed at all interested before, actually liked hugging and kissing; they enjoyed hugging on the dance-floor, which was almost legal, and kissing behind doors and out of sight behind the banisters, which was a more serious step.

I had thought that this was only a vague hope of my own. But no! It was theirs as well!—or, to be accurate, it was the hope of most of them. They really liked it, especially when they didn't have to commit themselves.

Actual kissing was a commitment; but hugging while the band played was a shared secret, a dividend which need not be declared, which wasn't even acknowledged. When girls were dancing, they liked to be held as tightly as possible, and squeezed and maneuvered and pushed against; and, as far as I was concerned, this was better than all the books and advertisements ever written, better than *The Song of Solomon,* better than anything.

It was real. You could actually feel it, and then use it. I had discovered this, all by myself, at Christmas dances.

Felicity and I went to lots of dances at Christmas; this was Liverpool's prime social season, and the private "hop" was a favourite Liverpool entertainment for its sons and daughters. Sometimes we attended five or even six of them during a busy week. They were now much more sophisticated, as we were ourselves. I had achieved my first dinner-jacket, and Felicity was definitely "out." Denys, at the age of twelve, had to be excluded from functions which now lasted from eight o'clock until one in the morning.

The routine was well established. We would change before dinner, eat a hurried and rather nervous meal in advance of the rest of the family, and then be driven in the Daimler to whatever solid house was the scene of that night's party. On the way there, I would invariably have an attack of stage-fright, and would always say: "It's sure to be awful. Why do we go to these things?"

Felicity, with far more reason (as a girl) to be worried about propping the wall with an empty program, would sweetly bolster my morale. "Don't be silly, Nicholas," she would say. "You know you're going to enjoy it." Of course she was right. I always did.

As we turned into the front drive she would straighten my tie and tell me if my hair was tidy. In turn, I would tell her, as a loyal brother, that she looked all right. Once inside, we would automatically separate, though I was prepared to help out if she were partnerless for more than one dance. This very rarely happened. She was a pretty girl, a good dancer, and, once out of Mother's grasp, had a touch of "fastness," not enough to get herself talked about but sufficient to keep the boys guessing and hoping.

Whatever house we were going to, the same maid always opened the front door. She was supplied by the catering firm which everyone patronized; she had become an old friend, adroit with hairpins for Felicity and advance information on the refreshment menu for me. Her presence there, in starched apron and frilly cap, and her welcoming smile, were guarantees that this party was going to be the sort we were used to; no better, and no worse.

She would greet us, as she had done the previous night and would doubtless do again tomorrow; passing through the hall decorated with paper streamers, Japanese lanterns, and a bunch of mistletoe, Felicity would be led away to one bedroom and I to another. A quick glance at the number of coats and hats already piled on the bed would tell me whether I had to loiter—brushing my hair, even taking the enormous chance of re-tying my tie—or to hurry.

All these Liverpool dances conformed to an agreed pattern; we knew it by heart, we liked it, we felt at ease and safe from surprises. Just inside the doorway of the "dance-room" (usually a drawing-room gutted of furniture), the floor of which had been freshly sprinkled with rosin, our host and hostess stood, flanked by those members of their family who were of dancing age. We greeted them formally, delivered our parents' good wishes, and took a program from a silver tray on a side table.

Boys had blue programs, girls had pink. The problem now was to fill them, with the right number of "duty dances" and (as far as I was concerned) the maximum amount of hot stuff.

About twenty minutes were taken up with this preliminary skirmish, the most important of the evening. Felicity, of course, had to wait with a brave smile for things to develop; but after I had booked the required dance with the daughter of the house, I was free to forage at will, keeping an eye on the door, working out the diminishing odds, and trying to achieve the impossible— a full program which still left room for last-minute favourites.

It was always a great mistake to lose one's nerve, in fear of loneliness, and give away precious dances to plain, available girls, when a little patience, a little fortitude, would see the arrival of some really desirable candidate whom one supposed had not been invited.

It was the saddest of all moments when one had to tell such a late-coming star: "I'm awfully sorry—I'm full."

In making out our programs, we still used the formula: "May I have the pleasure of a dance?" Three dances was the outside limit to claim from any one partner; the supper-dance, which involved leading the girl into the dining-room, waiting on her, and talking to her for at least half an hour, went if possible to the one you loved the best of all.

When most of the programs were full, the five-piece band would produce a roll of drums and a cymbal-clash, and then lead off with a slow fox-trot.

The dances themselves were now much more sophisticated. Sir Roger de Coverley was absolutely out, as outmoded as the Highland Schottische and the gallop. Now we performed to the fox-trot, the one-step ("Slow, slow, quick-quick, slow"), the two-step, and the waltz. The tango was not yet featured. It was a dance for foreigners, and for Bright Young Things; not for Liverpool, not for us.

I usually had that first fox-trot with Felicity. Subsequent dances were separated by ten-minute "intervals," which we spent sitting on the stairs, two-by-two up to the next landing, and making uneasy conversation with our partners. It was important to work out some sort of technique for this, to save time and trouble and to avoid awkward silences. Ten minutes could be a very long time.

I had perfected two lines; the first began: "What a pretty dress —did you make it yourself?" which led either to hurt denials and a review of Bold Street shops, or to compliments on cleverness, other home interests ("Do you knit much?") and such safe harbours as stamp-collecting and poker-work.

The second was more direct, and had to do with contrasting hair-styles (the details eavesdropped from Molly and Felicity). It seemed that there were now things called "kiss-curls," the mention of which was good for a fiery glance and a meaning smile. It could become agreeably personal, or it could peter out into some very small talk indeed, about hairdressers and Amami Night shampoos.

Whichever way it went, one had to endure until the music struck up again. About the fourth or fifth dance, there would probably be ice-cream or iced coffee available, to ease the parched throat. There was nothing else to drink before supper, unless the host, who had withdrawn early into his study, beckoned you in to inquire after your father and, being rather vague about your exact age, offered a well-diluted whisky and soda.

Sometimes he would ask, in a furtive whisper: "Do you know your geography?" I made a fool of myself, the first time this happened, and both of us were terribly embarrassed. All he meant was, did I know the way to the lavatory?

Since the same catering company "did" for all of us, the supper menu at private dances could be accurately forecast, within very narrow limits. We worked our way through cold consommé, chicken or lobster patty, cold turkey and salad, and a choice of ice-cream, trifle, meringues, fruit salad, and jelly—a very adequate spread. The basic drink was always claret-cup, served from a bowl with a silver ladle. I suppose it would have been theoretically possible to drink enough to get intoxicated (the new word was "blotto") but I never saw it happen to anyone, and it did not happen to me, even after two glasses. I must have, I decided, a very strong head.

Nor did it ever seem necessary. These evenings needed no such help to make them very worth while. We were young, active, talkative enough, sometimes in love; the girls in their flowered dresses and puffed sleeves were mostly pretty, mostly desirable; fun and laughter came as easily as breathing, as easily as sex, which was all round us, all the time—secret, unadmitted, universal.

It seemed, that Christmas, that I had joined another confederate club, which everyone had known about but me.

The end of the dance always came as a surprise; it seemed impossible that time could have flooded by so quickly. The band, fortified by glasses of beer discreetly planted beneath their chairs, would usually oblige with one or two extras; then they played "Auld Lang Syne," then "God Save the King," and that was all. Cars were announced; cups of chicken soup were handed round to warm us for the journey home; and after formal goodbyes, for which we had been intensively coached by our parents, we took our leave.

It would have been inconceivable either to see a girl home, or to have delayed her departure in any way. Such a thing was possible after an evening at the Adelphi Hotel, which was the most advanced form of social intercourse in those days. But a private party really ended when the clock struck one, and I don't think any of us, even the boldest, expected otherwise.

We had to make the most of our time while the fun was on, and the girls were still within reach. Actual kissing was dangerous, because there were so many people "keeping an eye on us"; and, being so sinful, it was best done in the dark, and the dark was hard to find, and the girls difficult to lure there anyway.

Once, on the drive home after a dance, Felicity reproved me. She said: "You've got some lipstick on your chin," and while I set to work to wipe it off (Mother would be waiting up for us, and Mother didn't know anything at all about this), Felicity went on: "You really shouldn't do it, Nicholas. You don't know what it's like for the girl. It can put her head in an absolute whirl!"

I was delighted to hear this; it was very encouraging news. I was so delighted that I never thought to ask Felicity how she knew.

That was a wonderful holiday. I got some actual money as well as ordinary presents. And at last, sex had been put into Christmas. Thus hallowed, it must be there to stay. . . . With lively appetite, with a defiant swish of the tail, I looked forward to New Year's Eve, when there was going to be another terrific dance, and Sonia would be there, and Joan and Alice, and the bad old year would go out in one big roaring rush—*just—like—that*.

TWENTY-ONE

1931

EXIT THE
DOUBLE-BREASTED FUNSTER

GENTIL-JONES, AS USUAL, was wandering round my rooms, picking things up, turning them over, reading them if they had print on them, and sniffing at them (for some reason) if they were made of wood. He often did this, and I did not mind. In fact, I was always flattered by the exploration.

By his standards, I had very few possessions, and they sometimes seemed rather dull. Also, as well as being a familiar friend, Gentil-Jones was a viscount; and this year (like last year, and the year before) I was very fond of noblemen.

Making his rounds, he very rarely said anything; he was not inquisitive, merely alive (in a negative sort of way) to the fact that other people's rooms had other people's things in them. I had once seen him wandering along the coat-racks at the Devonshire Club, looking at the initials in other people's bowler hats.

Now, he examined books and gramophone records, ornaments, bottles, and invitations. Then his eye was caught by a tailor's label. His head on one side, he asked:

"Why do you live in Liverpool?"

It was the first time he had ever asked me this, and I looked at him in surprise. I wished that I had a satisfactory answer—satisfactory to the world of Gentil-Jones. . . . G.J. was tall, strongly built, patrician in a way which was instantly recognizable. His family, though now metropolitan, was rooted in the Welsh Marches, and there was sometimes in his voice a faint echo of their music.

He enjoyed life, because he did not have to worry about it; I enjoyed life because I had been made free of it, for the very first time. He had a moustache like the Laughing Cavalier, while I had one like Ronald Colman. Girls came down from London to see him, and sometimes stayed the night. No one, as yet, had come down specially to see me.

He was a Hunt Ball man, a house-party man. He had been at

Eton, for the maximum number of terms. He played polo, and was a great point-to-point rider. He usually wore a "hacking jacket" with leather-padded elbows.

When we went to Newmarket, all the bookmakers knew who he was, and called out: "What's it to be, my lord?" as soon as he drew near.

One day he would be an earl, and I would probably still be tied to Liverpool.

After a moment I answered: "Well, I was born there. My father practices there." I felt bound to add: "He's on the General Medical Council."

It still sounded like another world; and even more so when Gentil-Jones said: "It must be very convenient for the Grand National."

The clock on the tower of Trinity Chapel struck the half hour —a mid-morning half hour, either ten or eleven. Then all the other clocks in Cambridge had the same idea, and the soft May morning air was filled with their various chimes, high and low, which could not be discordant because they were as old and mellow as the time they told.

They drew me—partly because I wanted to be drawn, turning my back on Liverpool—to the open lattice of the big bow window, and thus to my favourite view.

It was a short perspective, since my second-floor rooms in Whewell's Court stared slap into the eye of Trinity Great Gate, twenty yards away. But what more could one ask than rose-brick towers and a Gothic archway, built when Henry VIII was still married to his first wife? I had never grown tired of this view, and I would not have swapped it for the Acropolis itself.

There was nothing else to be seen except the crazy-patterned roofs of Trinity Street, and nothing to hear except the bells and the endless snore of the traffic below. But I didn't want anything else. This was *my* view and *my* college and *my* Great Gate, and I loved them all dearly.

Behind me, Gentil-Jones suddenly said: "Poetry!" It was a rather unlikely word, and I turned.

"What?"

He held up the book he had been looking at. I recognized it from its cover, even before he said: "It's called *The Wild Party*."

"I got it yesterday."

"What's it about?"

"Oh, you know—good old sex. It's American. He puts his hand under her dress and onto one of her breasts. They're just going to get down to it when he's shot by the husband, and the police arrive."

"Hard cheese. . . . Where's that bit?"

"Page seventy-four."

He leafed over the pages, and read in silence. After a moment: "I rather like that," he said judiciously. He adjusted his trousers without pretense. "One misses a good deal in university life, don't you think?"

"I thought that you *didn't* miss it."

"Oh, well. . . ." He grinned at me. "That's what I hear about you."

"I do my best."

That wasn't true. Though I was twenty-one, I still hadn't done my best. But I had cultivated a different legend, for quite a long time, and it had stuck.

Gentil-Jones closed the book. "I'd hate to get shot while I was doing that. . . . I'm thirsty, if it's all the same to you."

"Horse's Neck?"

"Very good idea."

The brandy-and-ginger-ale mixture was our favourite mid-morning tipple; it was thought to be a sovereign cure for the hangovers which we sometimes had and always claimed. I was pouring out two Horse's Necks, and adding the lemon peel, when some steps sounded on the stairs below.

One could hear people climbing up to my rooms from quite a long way off, since the approach was by a spiral stone staircase which set up a wonderful, ringing, hollow echo inside its massive turret. This was occasionally useful, when I really had to work, or if I had seen, wandering across from Great Gate, a man I did not particularly want to talk to, and thought he might be on his way up.

Then, the solid oak door could be firmly bolted, and after a little hammering and shouting, people went away.

The steps drew nearer; they were signalling two visitors, plodding upwards in uneven rhythm. A voice said: "Why does he

have to live up this *mountain?*" and another, equally short of
breath, answered: "Perhaps he doesn't like Mahommed." Silly,
but not too bad for eleven in the morning. . . . I poured two
more drinks, having recognized the voices, and called downstairs:

"Nobody here! Go to hell! Frig off!"

Just outside the door, Julian Syme said: "I didn't know the
Archbishop of Canterbury was in town."

Julian was one of that breed of young men whose labels changed
from season to season; at the moment they were called "nancy-
boys." But he did not bother any of us, and we were all very fond
of him; he could be very funny, very articulate, very loyal, and
he dressed exquisitely.

This morning he wore a tightly tailored black suit, a flowered
silk waistcoat, a contrasting foulard tie, and little pointed boots.
It would be enough to get him chi-iked, where'er he walked, on
any street in Cambridge; but we put up with that, as he did, and
even defended him against insult and violence.

For us, he was a sort of club mascot; for us, he was not just a
nancy, he was Julian Syme, our odd friend who had happened to
grow up like this—like a beautiful child with six toes, like a blue
carnation. We were sure that one day, in one way or another,
he would be famous, because he was the sort of person who deserved it.

I had the same unspecified understanding with him as we all
had. I did not want him, and he (I was sure) did not want me.
He had plenty of other friends.

As soon as he came in, we went through our traditional minuet
of greeting:

"Mr. Syme, as I live and die!"

"Stap me vitals! Mr. Monsarrat!"

"Vastly gratified!"

"Hugely diverted!"

"Will you take wine with me, sir?"

"With all me heart and soul!"

I bowed. "Your devoted servant."

"Your most obleeged!"

Then I gave him his Horse's Neck.

We had barely finished with this nonsense when the second

visitor, toiling to the top of the ladder like any other British workman, came into view at the head of the spiral staircase. He was another double-barrelled friend, George Clay-Clarke, the nearest approach to a "hearty" who could be included in our visiting-list.

George was a reassuring bullock of a man, built on that four-square, chunky design which had enabled Stonehenge to last so long. He was a rowing blue, and the particular star of the Third Trinity boat, which we hoped would regain its head-of-the-river position, in about a month's time. (Third Trinity was not our third-best eight; it was a private establishment, a club-within-a-boatclub reserved for Old Etonians, and, in a lower tone of voice, for people who had been at Westminster.) George arrived puffing and blowing, and I was left to wonder how a man who could row like hell-fire for more than twenty minutes could make such heavy weather of two flights of stairs.

However, that was his problem, not mine. . . . George was not a real hearty, not what we called an "oik"; not the kind who wore a college scarf, and puffed a colossal pipe, and shouted "Wotcher!" to other hearties across Great Court; not the kind who made miserable the lives of people like Julian Syme, de-bagging them at will, throwing them into fountains any time after ten o'clock at night.

He was just George Clay-Clarke, a kind of animal Rock of Gibraltar, who could not help his muscle-bound solidity any more than Julian Syme could help his quick-silver gait.

George was a cousin of Gentil-Jones, and thus approved; and if snobbery was an element in this approval, then snobbery was approved also.

Like Gentil-Jones, he was wearing a hacking jacket, though his was fashioned from a hound's-tooth check which could almost be heard baying for blood. (I could never have worn it myself; it was as much as I could do to get away with my pepper-and-salt plus-fours.) Like Julian, he said: "Hallo, G.J.," as soon as he caught sight of Gentil-Jones.

Gentil-Jones had two Christian names; but one was Ianto and the other Peregrine.

George Clay-Clarke took the proffered drink immediately, and then, just as immediately, handed it back.

"Thanks, old man," he said. "But I'd better stick to beer. God, I was pissed as a newt last night!"

"I thought you were meant to be in training," I said, as I unscrewed a bottle of the preferred local brew, Tolly's Light Ale, and poured him a glass.

"Oh, I am," George assured me. "But we're allowed beer." He gulped thirstily at his drink, and then quoted the advertising slogan: " 'Work takes it out of a man. Beer puts it back.' Though I'm never quite sure what 'it' is. But even the chaplain says it's all right."

"He would," said Julian Syme waspishly. "Thank God I'm an atheist!"

"What's it like, being an atheist?"

Julian gave me his innocent smile. *"Divine!"*

We settled down to the customary, hazy hour-before-lunch, which had been a cherished feature of our lives for at least two years.

The talk was not so deep as a well, but it would serve, since it was all we wanted at that particular moment. The deeper thoughts were for the darker hours, when the tongue loosened with the collar and tie, when the hair was let down, and the Dutch uncles started to wag their warning fingers.

We had plenty of those sessions, too; but this one was pre-lunch, pre-lunch on a morning in May, when (in spite of those Tripos exams looming on the near horizon) every dawn was fresh, every "good remark" wildly funny, and every man in view a firm friend. Presently I looked at the clock, and saw that it was half-past one already; and as I did so, Gentil-Jones suddenly said: "Lunch-time," and stood up.

We were all ready to leave, as soon as he said it. Sometimes it puzzled me, this odd aspect of leadership: how when one man said "Lunch-time," everyone stood up, and when another man said it, though just as loudly, no one even heard him. If I had said "Lunch-time," there might have been a reasonably prompt drift towards the door, because I was the host; but not for any other reason.

Already I was beginning to record a small series of messages here: they told me that I would never be an earl, that I would always be a surgeon's son from Liverpool; that the hymn which proclaimed: "He made them high and lowly, and ordered their estate," was absolutely true; that my estate had been ordered, even thus early, and a pattern printed which might well last the rest of my life.

But the best message of all was that none of this really mattered, because I was happy: happy with a whole collection of things which had come my way during the last three years, especially happy to have moved from Rodney Street to a set of rooms over-looking Trinity Great Gate, with viscounts and rowing blues and poker parties and honours degrees (if I managed to get one) as a natural part of the decoration. All I had to do was keep it up.

At home, Mother sometimes asked me: "Are you sure you're in the right set?"

The true answer was probably "No," for some rather subtle reasons. But I always said "Yes," and meant it.

I collected my gown, as did the others, and lowered myself gently down the spiral staircase, suddenly hungry for a large lunch in Hall.

We straggled and even weaved our way across Trinity Street, under the noble arch of the gateway, past the indulgent, top-hatted porters, and then across Great Court itself.

I had thought this splendid, the very first time I saw it, when I came up for a preliminary interview with my tutor-to-be; and during the past three years it had, if anything, grown in mag-nificence. There was something about its combination of rose brick, ancient weathered stone, trim green lawns, and the superb edifice of the fountain in the middle, which instantly smote the eye, and captured it for ever.

Great Court was huge, and it had to be, to contain all its splendour.

We made our slow way across, past some familiar figures: the Master himself, Sir J. J. Thomson, his hands clasped behind him, resting on his laurels after discovering both the electron and the isotope, stalking to and fro like—well, like a stork; and then two grey old dons, whom we called Null and Void, pacing the lawn outside Chapel.

There were other, anonymous passers-by: first-year men coming down the steps from Hall (how early some people ate their lunch, we thought); a kitchen porter carrying on his head a tray laden

with silver-topped dishes, for somebody's lunch-party in his rooms;
beefy men in scarves and white rowing shorts, on their way to
the river; a crocodile of little boys being chivvied into Chapel for
choir-practice; some tourists with cameras, and a forgetful undergraduate smoking a cigarette, who was promptly yanked into the
porters' lodge, where he would be relieved of the customary fine
of six shillings and eightpence.

At a very sedate pace, we made it up the steps on the farther
side of Great Court, and so into Hall.

Hall had always been a good match for my other favourite, the
building we called "School," by Christopher Wren, at Winchester.
Under a soaring roof, which at night was lost in its own shadows,
the room recalled some old picture of a giant baronial dining-hall;
from the high table at the head, the dons could look down upon
what must have seemed like acres of their retinue, sitting in long
ranks at the massive oak tables.

From the walls, the stern or benign portraits of past Masters
and Fellows gazed down on us, spanning the centuries from the
collar-and-tie days of the twentieth to the ruffs and laces of the
sixteenth; in the very center, a glittering portrait of our founder,
in the prime of his lusty manhood, told us exactly what the
Flemish painter Hans Ewouts saw in the face and bearing of
Henry VIII, across the width of a room at Whitehall Palace.

The red roses and the lion *passant gardant* of Tudor England
which made up the college crest decorated the panelled walls;
they seemed easier to live up to than the motto, *Virtus Vera
Nobilitas,* virtue is the true nobility, which was not, for us, a
thought we lived by, every day of the week.

The food was very good (three courses for lunch, five for dinner); and the two bottles of hock which today were shared between
the four of us provided the easiest of all drinks to swallow. We
were waited on hand and foot, as was everyone else; but Gentil-
Jones, perhaps, drew to our corner of the long central table that
special, adroit deference which was the spoiled privilege of the day.

We played poker-dice for the wine, though discreetly; there
must surely be some ancient statute which forbade scholars to
resort to gaming at table. I sighed as I lost the final round; two
bottles of hock, even 1926 Liebfraumilch, cost twelve shillings,

and already, at the end of my third year, there stretched behind and in front of me a vast series of such bills which would, within a month, all have to be confessed to my father.

It was nearly three o'clock by the time we had scooped up the last chalky crumbs of the Stilton, and drained the second glass of port, and decided that lunch was ended. Slightly over-fed, definitely muzzy, well contented, we made for the door; a turn to the right would lead us to another Wren masterpiece, the Neville's Court library, a turn to the left offered us Great Court again, and the somnolent sunshine of a May afternoon.

We set the correct course, and presently were standing in the shadow of Great Gate, making up our tattered minds what to do next.

"A flick," said Julian Syme. He was an even greater devotee of the cinema than I was. "Who's for the flicks?"

"I forget what's on," I said.

He would have been ashamed not to know the answers. "They're all talkies. Ben Lyon in *Hell's Angels*. It's got that girl Jean Harlow in it."

"She looks an absolute rasper!"

"If you like that sort of thing. . . . Laura la Plante, your statuesque friend—" (I was a Laura la Plante partisan, Julian was not) "—in some dreary drama thing which doesn't matter. She suffers *all* the time. Paul Lukas in the one about the super-butler. I wouldn't mind seeing that again. When he's asked who he goes to bed with, he says: 'Oh, mostly the upper servants. Sometimes a governess at Christmas.' Rather sweet. . . . So take your choice."

"It's a terrible thing to have to say," said Clay-Clarke, "but I've got a boat at four."

"Rowing?" said Julian, as if he could hardly believe his ears.

"No, no. The *Mauretania*."

"Silly old coot. . . . Nick?"

"Well," I said, considering. I knew what I ought to do, I knew what I wanted to do. Only one of them was tempting. Then, across the hazy width of Great Court, I caught sight of a small figure standing outside a doorway. It was Mr. Duff, my supervisor in the Law Tripos, the man who kept my nose as close to the grindstone as was safe for such a prominent feature. He was a fellow Old Wykehamist, but this had not led to any particular admiration on his part.

It was now less than a month to the last examination of all, the second part of the Tripos, on which our degrees would stand or fall. Mr. Duff recalled this painful fact, just by standing still about a hundred yards away.

"I'm sorry, old man," I answered. "I *must* work."

"It's too late."

"Don't *say* that!"

Gentil-Jones remarked: "I think I'm going to work, too."

That settled it, as usual. "All right," said Julian. "Honest toil it is. . . . I'll see you tonight, anyway. What time is this glorious blind?"

"Half-past eight," answered G.J. "Meet in my rooms at eight. I've asked everybody else. We can crack the first bottle there."

"Wizard," said Julian, and turned to go. *"Arrivederci!"* he added, and gave us a playful wave. *Exit Ariel,* I thought, as he sped off down Trinity Street on nimble feet. I had no doubt that he was going to the flicks anyway.

Clay-Clarke was sitting astride his bicycle, his long legs easily reaching the ground on either side. But he did not seem too comfortable in this position, and kept shifting cautiously.

"My bottom's absolutely raw," he complained. "I don't *want* to row."

Gentil-Jones laughed. "Too late, old boy. You've made yourself indispensable."

"Gertcher!" said Clay-Clarke, with the authentic hearty ring, and cranked his squeaking machine, and took off across the cobblestones, tacking manfully like a sailor on horseback.

"Come with me to Pratt's," said G.J. "I feel like a new suit. Then we really will work."

Naturally enough, I went with him.

By the time we emerged once more into the bustle of Trinity Street, it was getting on for four o'clock, and we were both entirely exhausted. We stood in the middle of the pavement, under the warm sunshine, our knees slack, considering the future. Ordinary people walked round us, or even crossed the street, without protest. We were undergraduates.

"We ought to work," said Gentil-Jones. "What about it?"

"How do you feel?" I asked him.

"Tight as a tick," said G.J. candidly. "But it will pass."

The air was hazy, soporific, benign. Summer heat rose from the stone beneath our feet, and shimmered gently, confusing the eyesight; small seams of tar were bubbling in the roadway. A car hooted as it went past, and I waved, not knowing to whom. It was obvious that our rooms—any rooms, anywhere indoors—would be unbearably hot. Then I had a better idea.

"Do you have to write an essay?" I asked him. "Or is it just reading?"

"Reading. The decline of secular puritanism during the last years of the Interregnum, 1649 to 1660. That's Oliver Cromwell, in case you don't know."

"How did secular puritanism decline?"

"They started doing it in the streets again."

"Oh." Maybe I should have been studying History instead of Law. "Well, I want to read as well. Why don't we take a punt, and work on the river?"

Gentil-Jones rocked back on his heels. "Brilliant!" he exclaimed, and added a current catch-phrase: "Ah, if you could only cook!"

The Backs—part of the scholars' domain of Cambridge, fronting the waterway which was, for the most part, the River Cam—were always beautiful, and particularly so on this hot May afternoon. Gentil-Jones lay in the bows, cushioned like a Rajah, while I punted slowly between green lawns, and under noble trees, and past the magnificence of Trinity Hall, and Clare, and King's College chapel.

We passed beneath the complex wooden bridge, reputedly designed by Sir Isaac Newton, a Fellow of our own college; a bridge which, it was rumoured, was a structure so subtly balanced that it needed no nail, peg, or fastening to support it: so balanced, indeed, that when later experts in architecture took it apart to see how it worked, they could not put it together again, and had to use nails, pegs, and fastenings by the bag-ful, to keep it from collapsing.

Whether true or not, this was a story which suited us very well, because it involved the foolishness of authority.

We floated gently onwards, towards Grantchester. Punting was easy, except in the funny papers: a deep thrust, a turn of the wrist to free the pole from the mud, a long swing forward while the water dribbled and splashed back again, another stroke, and progress was assured.

It was not even energetic, unless one was showing off; and, when it took one past such noble monuments to building as King's College, and Queens', and Peterhouse, it was the only way to travel.

There was very little traffic, and not a girl to be seen anywhere. I often wondered about this, and I wonder about it now. There never seemed to be any available girls at Cambridge, except for those forbidding "undergraduettes" of Girton and Newnham; there were no girls looking helpless in canoes, no girls sitting alone in cinemas, certainly no girls walking about the streets at night.

It was always said that, in this area, the University authorities had absolute control, and that the police gladly co-operated: that there was no such thing as a brothel within fifty miles, because the University said "No": that unattached girls who could not explain their presence in Cambridge to a grim-faced board of discipline were simply told to move on: that suspected street-walkers were run out of town, as soon as the next day dawned.

It was difficult to tell if this were true, because I was not an expert. I still did not know what a brothel looked like, far less how it was operated; I *thought* I could distinguish a prostitute from a respectable married woman, but only because the prostitute stared you straight in the eye, whereas the married woman hurried past, looking fixedly at the pavement.

It was certainly true (because it had happened to men I knew) that if you walked more than fifty yards at night, down any street in Cambridge, with a girl, there would be a sudden surging of top-hats all round you as soon as you reached the next lamplight, and one of the disciplinary "bull-dogs," his hand on your arm, would say: "Will you kindly speak to the Proctor, sir? And you too, madam?"

It was also a fact that the "dancing-school" which I had attended, for social purposes, in my second year, had disappeared without trace between one term and another, and the two rather

pretty girls on whom I was basing my hopes of emancipation—
either one of them would do—were seen no more.

At any rate, there were now no girls in sight on the Backs.
Bereft by my sensual daydream, not caring very much either
way, I decided that I had punted long enough, and turned towards
the bank. Gentil-Jones and I only had each other, and one of us
seemed to be asleep.

I brought the punt to a slow halt, under a willow tree trailing
its slender fingers in the water, and plunged the pole in, upright,
to keep us anchored. As I did so, G.J. opened his eyes.

"Well done," he said. "You're improving."

I flopped down at my end of the boat, and lay back. It was
utterly peaceful and still; it was hazy, lazy, dreamy, just as the
last three perfect years had been. The ripple of water running
against the bows was like the sound of a lute among the reeds.

"Work," I said, and took up my book.

"I think I'll have a little nap before I start," said G.J., smiling
gently, and closed his eyes.

"Very wise."

The sun was warm, the willow green, the water soft and lapping. With a sigh, I set to work to refresh my memory on the
manumission of slaves, under Roman Law, in the fourth century
A.D., and presently I, too, smiled and nodded and drifted off into
sleep.

Gentil-Jones' rooms in Great Court, on the ground floor and
almost opposite the fountain, were very elegant.

In contrast with most rooms in college, which seemed to be
repositories for massive Victorian furniture set against a backdrop of beige paint, his had been newly furnished throughout
when he moved in. "My mother came up, and did the whole
thing," he once told me, rather apologetically; but one could
only be respectful about the result. It was really very distinguished;
and the number of undergraduates who had a Countess as their
interior decorator was small indeed.

His surroundings were as much like a London drawing-room,
and as little like rooms in college, as they could possibly be.
There was none of the usual undergraduate gear on display; the
squash racket, the gun-case, the fly-rod, and the golf-clubs were

all somewhere, but they were kept out of sight, like G.J.'s gramo-phone records, and his magnificent set of ivory poker chips. And as for a chest-expander or a bar-bell. . . .

Silk, brocade, and things with tassels on them were much in evidence; the pale grey carpet on the floor would, in my own home, have been out of bounds for family use. A marble-topped "smoking table" displayed a jar of Balkan Sobranie pipe-tobacco, cigarettes by Le Roith, and two brands of cigars. (It was here that I had begun my life-long love-affair with *Romeo y Julieta*.) Nineteenth-century sporting prints decorated the walls—scenes of straight-armed prize fighters, and horses not touching the ground. In the place of honour over the mantelpiece was an earlier *tableau*, the cautionary sixth scene from Hogarth's *A Harlot's Progress*.

The room always seemed impeccably clean and tidy, at any hour of the day or night, since G.J. retained one of the college menservants, known to us as "gyps," to look after him.

It was here that the members of the Lucullus Club were as-sembling, ready for the last dinner of the summer term. Like the room, we were very elegant.

The Lucullus had no premises; it was a dining club, restricted to its eight founding members. We had taken the name, not be-cause Lucullus was a greedy old man but because he did serve, by all the reliable accounts of 65 B.C., splendid meals, and was also (so said the Encyclopedia) "hospitable to scholars." We held two dinners each term, and for these occasions wore the special club uniform, consisting of a silk dinner-jacket, bottle-green with paler facings, and a waistcoat, also of silk, with a repeated *motif* of what looked like scarlet—well, scarlet apexes.

This splendid rig had cost each of us twelve pounds, and had been designed by Julian Syme, who claimed that the apexes were larks' tongues.

There were no club rules, except to dress up and enjoy the best possible dinner, six times a year; though Clay-Clarke had once suggested that we adopt a rule which he swore was on the books of one of his father's clubs: "Members shall not relieve themselves in the umbrella-stand during the asparagus season."

It was a haphazard membership, brought together, during our second year, at a poker party, when we had all felt completely ravenous at one o'clock in the morning, and all I had to offer was stale brown bread and cheese-rinds, and somebody had asked: "Why don't we have a proper dinner beforehand?"

We tried that "proper dinner" once, and it was not a success; the meal was excellent, but the poker, starting at 10 P.M., was a shambles, with people mistaking two queens and two jacks for four kings, and betting accordingly, and becoming liable to fall off their chairs when disaster struck.

Thereafter we kept the two things apart; we were Lucullans twice a term, and felt no need to be anything else afterwards, and certainly not players of poker, which could be organized on any other day of the week.

Besides the four of us who had been in my rooms that morning, we had Frank Oppenheimer, a South African, one of the two sons of Sir Ernest Oppenheimer, who was reputed to own all the gold *and* all the diamonds in that well-endowed country; and Tom Fenwick, a young don of the utmost charm, who was only a couple of years older than us but was already lecturing on economics.

It was considered good insurance to include a don in our company, in case we made too much noise or broke an important window. But we would have included him anyway.

Then there was another lord, John Acheson, President of Trinity Athletic Club, who had been running, consistently, just a little bit faster than myself for the past three years; and a magnificent "blood" of a man, Oliver Bertram, who owned a most glamorous Mercedes-Benz racing car, the kind with three silver-plated exhaust pipes curling like snakes out of one side of the bonnet.

He drove regularly at Brooklands; and I had once put the Mercedes through a dozen laps there, while Oliver crouched by my side, listening to the roar of the engine and shouting churlish remarks about the tappets.

Thus the Lucullus Club had two noblemen, one pansy, one hearty oarsman, one don, one embryo racing motorist, one future mining magnate, and me. I sometimes wondered how I was categorized myself; but after the third drink, it never seemed to matter.

We were having the first of those drinks now. It was the current version of the cocktail, a gin-and-it—the "it" being sweet Italian vermouth. We were being served with Jeeves-like solemnity by Preston, G.J.'s gyp, the kind of man I would never be able to afford, whose chief testing-time was on an evening such as this.

The gramophone was playing a record by that splendidly named couple, Stephane Grappelly and Django Reinhardt, who were the stars of a band with an equally dramatic label, the Quintet of the Hot Club de France. But good as the Hot Club was, it faded into the background before very long, as the room filled up with richly garbed Lucullans, and the drink began to flow, and the talk with it.

After two hours' sleep, a hot bath, and a leisurely change of clothes, I felt as fresh as paint. There was some added excitement this evening because it would be our very last dinner, and probably the end of the Lucullus Club, unless Tom Fenwick, the only survivor who was not going down for good, managed to keep it going. Perhaps, I thought, he would like to buy, second-hand, seven green-silk dinner-jackets, as a basis for revival.

After tonight, also, I really was going to work.

Snatches of other people's conversation rose to the surface, like mysterious bubbles in a pond. "He's a terrible womanizer," said George Clay-Clarke, and I wondered whom he was talking about. "It was a bagatelle, old boy," said someone else, and I would like to have known what had been a bagatelle, which was our current slang for something very easy to do. "He went arse over tip into the river," announced Oliver Bertram; "I laughed like a drain!" I wished I had been there, to laugh at whoever it was.

Tom Fenwick also looked round the room, his eyes sharp, his lively face without expression. Then he said: "I don't think we'll be seeing this sort of thing much longer—or perhaps ever again. Delightful though it is, we shall be saying goodbye to it, before very long."

"Now, why on earth?"

"Because we can't afford it," he answered promptly. "No one can afford it. No *university* can afford it, really. They need the space for something better. Playing is great fun—" he was smiling now, "I found it great fun myself, only two or three years ago—

but playing is getting terribly out of date. Like a lot of other things."

I took my fifth drink from Preston's tray as he passed. "What sort of other things?"

But Tom hadn't heard me, or he wanted to pursue his own line of thought. "We're living in the past," he said. "We've been living in the past for years. In a way, we're still living on our Victorian fat, and it's disappearing much too quickly. Sooner or later we're going to wake up, and find that there isn't any left. You know what's been happening in America?"

"Well, sort of."

"They've been having an economic blizzard there," he said, because he understood that I didn't really know at all. "It's been going on for nearly two years, and strong as they are—because they *are* strong, and they're going to be *the* nation, whether we like it or not—they're having a very hard time getting through. Now it's coming our way, and I'm not sure that we're really strong enough to get through it ourselves."

"America *the* nation?" This was an entirely new idea, and I didn't believe a word of it. "But we're still—I mean, it's impossible."

"It is not."

"But it's so *sad!*"

"It's rather exciting, as well," he said. "Among a great many other things, it means that *this*—" he gestured round the room, "—will have to fade away. It means that before long, people will actually have to work when they get to Cambridge. *If* they get to Cambridge."

"What—*everybody?*"

"Yes, everybody." He smiled again. "Incidentally, how's your own work going?"

"Pretty well, I think."

"Your name came up when I was talking to Mr. Duff, the other day."

"What did he say?"

"Oh, he was just talking about degrees, and the Tripos examination."

A small cold breeze seemed to be blowing round the back of my neck. But: "Tell me," I said. "I feel strong enough."

"He seemed to think," said Tom Fenwick, "that in your case it might involve some degree of luck."

I opened my mouth to answer, but was forestalled by a tremendous, ear-splitting blast on a hunting horn. In the ensuing silence, Gentil-Jones, the author of the uproar, announced: "Gentlemen, I don't want to hurry you, but the soup will be getting cold."

"It *is* cold," said the voice of Julian Syme, who planned our menus.

"Then it will be getting warm. We'd better drink up."

I did not drink up, but put my glass down, half empty, instead. This was not because of what Tom Fenwick had said (though it was all rather discouraging), but because of some advice my father had given me when I first came up to Cambridge—about the only advice I had remembered.

"Never finish a drink if you don't really want it," he had counselled me. "It doesn't prove anything. In particular, it doesn't prove that you're a man. You can be more of a *man* if you know when you've had enough, and leave it."

I decided that four and a half gins-and-its was, in this case, enough. There was still sherry, white wine, red wine, and port to come, in the very near future.

We spilled out into Great Court, and set course for the opposite side, where owing to a convenient wangle of Tom Fenwick's we had a private room for our dinner. The eight of us, strung out, made up a small wavering procession.

"This really is great fun," said Julian Syme, stepping jauntily by my side. "Quite a little hunger march!"

An hour later, awash with port, bemused by cigar smoke, happy as the tongues of larks, we finished signing each other's menus, scrawled the last affectionate or obscene message on the inside page, declared the dinner at an end, and flowed out into Great Court again.

It was a beautiful night; even if it had been snowing it would have been a beautiful night. But this night was warm, and benevolent, with a cloudless sky and a moon like an unblemished Stilton cheese adrift in limbo above our heads.

We savoured it in silence, not shouting, nor singing, nor being sick in corners. It was only hearties who did these things; it was only hearties, also, who fell down, roaring with laughter, in Trinity Street, and widdled against lamp-posts and pillar-boxes, and generally gave drunkenness and debauchery a bad name.

We were Lucullans, going home after our last club dinner. Our preoccupation was to walk straight, and not to be sick. Smitten by fresh air, we did not find either of these things easy. They needed concentration, and two or even three years' practice. But we had these allies, and this was the moment when they counted.

Great Court on such a night was wonderfully attractive, fit to make you cry.

It was lamp-lit, of course; the pools of yellow light on the cobbled walks were separated by chasms of shadow, broken here and there by orange rectangles, which were the curtained windows of the studious. This was Winchester again, with the same aura of antiquity and learning; but now it was benign, with no harsh reality lying in wait for us, next morning or next term.

Nothing spoiled it, nothing threatened; and that cautionary motto which had faced us in Winchester "School"—*Aut disce, aut discede. Manet sors tertia—caedi,* which we had speedily learned to translate as "Either learn, or leave. Your third choice is to be beaten"—was unthinkable here, and by comparison monstrous.

Even at eleven o'clock of a fine night, there was still movement as well as calm stillness. Porters in top-hats bore messages from staircase to staircase, men wandered in through Great Gate after an evening at the flicks or in some other college, dons in cap and gown paced up and down, disputing like the most ancient Schoolmen in the world.

In the very center of this oasis, which much love and gentleness had fashioned, as well as the cutting edge of intellect, the tall restless fountain splashed and chattered. But it did not intrude. Instead, it bound the whole thing together, in a pattern which, after four hallowed centuries, was going to last a minimum of four centuries more.

Walking by my side, George Clay-Clarke, who seemed to be at odds with his balance, swayed slightly from the true and cannoned into me. It was alarming, like being nudged by the leaning tower of Pisa, and I had to exercise great care to stay on my feet.

"Sorry, old boy," he said. "Trod on a bad cobblestone." He paused, his head in the air, to consider the situation. "What a lot of stars," he said. "Find me a good one, and then I can steer."

I found him the North Star, from long practice. "North Star," I said, and pointed. "Over that chimney."

I was trying to find Sirius for him, Sirius my favourite star, the Dog Star of wandering mariners, when there were some noisy interruptions nearby.

I had been hearing them for some time, without paying any attention; they were the customary noises of someone being toppled into the fountain. Or rather, of someone not being toppled into the fountain, because in Trinity this was extremely difficult to do, and involved the hoisting of a struggling man at least ten feet into the air, and then over the lip and into the water. The victim had to either be very weak, or very drunk, or very willing.

In the half-darkness, I watched such a man, more agile than most, escaping his captors and speeding away into the night. He seemed to have no trousers on. Hearties. . . . There were whoops as they lost him, and fresh whoops as they caught sight of our party. (Our dinner-jackets tended to reflect the light, and even to increase it.) They descended upon us in a body. There were about ten of them, noisy, bunched together, determined on execution of some kind.

The Lucullus Club, in very loose order, was nearing G.J.'s rooms again. George and I, the worst stragglers, were a little way away, and clear of the trouble. We could have remained so. But George did not see this as a moment for prudence, which I might have done myself.

"Rally round, old boy!" he commanded sharply. "Give her ten!"

He seemed suddenly not to be drunk at all.

We came up at a fast trot, to meet an ugly scene indeed.

The Lucullans, wending their careful way home, had become spread out; to a distant eye, we might have been a body of eight moving figures, all in the same funny-looking uniform, but we were not compact enough for the sort of onslaught which a dozen determined men, robbed of one prey and hungry for another, could bring to bear.

When George and I caught up, a kind of cutting-out maneuver

had taken place; and the strangers—they were rugger players, judging by their strenuous oaths and cries of "Scrum down, Trinity!"—had managed to corner Julian Syme.

"It's Syme the slime!" they cried, backing him against a wall. "Don't let him get away!"

"Bloody pansy!"

"Lay him out!"

"Jesus, what a get-up!"

"Let's de-bag him!"

"Let's give him a bath!"

Julian's coat had already been ripped up and draped over his head, by the time we arrived.

The other Lucullans, walking ahead, had been taken by surprise; but now they turned and came to the rescue. I noticed, out of the corner of my eye, that Tom Fenwick stayed in the background; this was not cowardice, I knew well, but official prudence. Tom would intervene if it became necessary, but in the meantime this was not something for a don, however junior, to get involved in.

The rest of us had no such inhibitions.

We waded in. If these people, who must be absolute oiks, were in the mood for exercise, then so were we. George Clay-Clarke, looking about nine feet tall in the lamplight, caught one man a back-handed clout which seemed to knock him senseless; Oliver Bertram, who had been a boxer before he took to motor-racing, laid about him manfully. Gentil-Jones selected his target with fastidious care, and brought him low with a shrewd, ungentlemanly kick in the groin.

Even I—only a runner, after all—picked the smallest opponent in sight and, using some well-developed weight-lifting muscles, got a very unfair grip on the nape of his neck and bashed his head against a wall. Then George came up to the man who was holding on to Julian Syme, and without hesitation dealt him a ferocious blow on the top of his head.

The man, who was no weakling, turned to meet the attack. His ox-like face, sweaty and tough, betrayed an honest surprise. He said: "What the hell!" and then, recognizing his assailant, essayed a smile. "Wotcher, George!" he said. "What's your trouble?"

He got no "Wotcher!" in return. "Let go," said George in a rasping voice. "Let go, and beat it!"

"Hell, it was only a joke," said the man. But he did let go, and fell back, while the rest of his clan, now at bay, stood round looking silly and undecided. "Don't take it so seriously, for God's sake!"

My own enemy, still caught in a horrid grip (my nails were rather long), gave a squeal, wrestled himself free, and turned to look at me.

"Oh, it's you," he said, with great contempt. He then swung on his heel and walked away, leaving me unsure whether I had won or lost.

Julian freed his head from the ruined dinner-jacket, and retreated unsteadily into G.J.'s rooms.

"That's all," said Gentil-Jones curtly. "The party's over."

As if to confirm this, an anonymous voice in the dark outer ring said: "This is all bloody silly. Let's go and beat up old Charles."

"Charles!" said another voice. "*He* won't mind!"

They then dispersed, in bad order. At one moment they had been there, menacing and brutal; the next, they were gone, tacking away across Great Court, and singing *"Oh dear, what can the matter be? Three old ladies locked in the lavatory,"* in vague dispirited voices.

Left in possession of the field, we trooped into Gentil-Jones' rooms, feeling in very good form indeed.

Inside, Julian Syme, looking pale unto death, was enthroned on a sofa, with Preston the gyp dabbing at his forehead, which someone or something had scratched. His coat lay in rumpled ruin at his feet. But he was not at all distressed—or rather, he was resisting distress with that special brittle flippancy which meant (as he had once phrased it to me, on a similar occasion) that he was "struck to the heart." The foolish expression, and the way he mouthed it, showed that he had in fact been truly hurt.

"Such high spirits!" he said, in his own high voice, as we gathered round him. "What funny people one meets at this university!"

"Are you all right, Julian?" asked Gentil-Jones, looking down at him.

"Right as a trivet," answered Julian, "whatever a trivet may be. I picture it with rather *long* ears, don't you? Dear Preston has been a positive *angel* of mercy!" He winced as Preston, a small bald man with the grim look of long servitude, probed a little deeper with a blood-stained sponge. "Thank you all so much for the rescue."

"It was a pleasure," said Oliver Bertram, and I was sure that he meant it. He was sucking his knuckles, which must have made contact with something harder than mere flesh. "We won't be seeing that bunch of bastards again."

I went across to the sideboard, feeling the need for a whisky and soda, and was followed by Frank Oppenheimer.

"Who *were* those people?" he asked, sounding rather shocked.

I gave the names of the men I had recognized, and added, on a virtuous note: "I suppose they've got nothing better to do. But they really should have grown out of that sort of thing by now. Thank God it doesn't happen very often."

"Once is too much," said Frank. "They ought to be put in jail."

He spoke as a man who could put people in jail, if they didn't behave themselves perfectly.

I poured out our drinks. Julian was still holding court on the sofa, but now he was not doing so well. I could hear his voice getting higher and higher, more and more shrill, as his jokes and comments grew wilder. It was only a matter of minutes before the thin shell of his self-control suddenly cracked, and I heard and saw him call out:

"Oh, Christ! Why does this always happen to *me?*"

He was actually crying: the tears glittered on his eyelids as he threw his head back and rocked it from side to side. He then turned a remarkable shade of green, jumped up, and bolted for the nearest door, which was the one leading into G.J.'s bedroom.

G.J. said calmly: "Preston," but he need not have given this warning; Preston was already following the casualty, at a pace almost as swift. Unfortunate sounds of upheaval were heard, before he was able to close the door.

It should have been very sad, but in fact it was a relief; we had won our battle, not lost it, and Julian always passed out for one reason or another, and it had been a terrific dinner anyway, and now we were thirsty. We settled down to the whisky with a will; and when presently Preston came out again, and said to Gentil-Jones, with that clear disapproval which just stopped short of mutiny: "He's been sick, my lord, and now he's asleep," he was hardly heard.

G.J. answered: "Good," and Oliver said: "Poor little sod," and that was Julian's epitaph for this evening—an evening which was still ours.

We went back to the bottle, and the delights of argument and fooling with words. On the gramophone, Frank Crumit sang "There Once Was a Gay Caballero," and the violent saga of Abdul A-Bul-Bul Amir and Ivan Skivisky Skivar. We harmonized in company—not loudly, just melodiously. When the clock finally began to strike twelve, and I had to leave them, in order to reach Whewell's Court before the strokes ceased, the party was still in top gear.

As I left, Frank Oppenheimer called out: "Don't forget, if you're ever passing through Johannesburg—" and someone else said: "Keep right on going!" G.J. said: "See you at half-past seven," and then I was outside in the silent darkness, and alone.

A promising, and indeed an urgent daydream was interrupted by a thunderous knocking on my outer door.

I did not stir, but lay prone and still, not even bothering to wonder who it could be, at such a ridiculous hour. Let them just go away. . . . But though the knocking ceased, the intrusion did not. I must have forgotten to bolt the door the night before, because almost immediately I heard it open. There were footsteps, and then Gentil-Jones' voice:

"Are you ready?"

I had forgotten all about it, all about the trip to London.

G.J.'s head came round the door, inquiring but not at all hesitant. He was looking too damned healthy altogether. "Oh, for God's sake!" he exclaimed. "You're not even up yet!"

I blinked the eye which was nearest to him. "I must have overslept," I said, mumbling authentically. "What time is it?"

"Half-past seven. Come on, Nick—we're meant to be on the road!"

I groaned, and it was not too difficult to do so. I still had a solid residue of headache; I wanted to go to London, but I knew that I shouldn't; I had been interrupted in a private pleasure which might not recur that day with quite the same insistence. I groaned again, rolling my eyes like Othello himself, and said: "Sorry, G.J. One hell of a hangover. . . . What time is it?"

"I told you. It's half-past seven. We arranged all this last night —don't you remember? We're going up to town for the day."

"Of course I remember. Engraved on my heart. Just give me a minute."

"How do you feel?"

"With my middle finger."

I turned over, in time to meet his expression of distaste.

"It's a bit early in the morning," he said, "for one of those fragrant jokes. How do you feel, actually? You look like death warmed up."

"I'm pretty well clapped," I told him. "That was a hell of a party."

"It was yesterday. Do get a move on, old boy. We've still got to saddle up the car. I wanted to be in town by nine."

It was not convenient for me to get out of bed at that moment, and so I temporized.

"Be an angel, G.J."

"What sort of an angel?"

"Make me an oyster. Make *us* oysters. Then we'll both feel better."

"I don't need to feel better. I've been up since six o'clock." But though Gentil-Jones could command, he could also be commanded. It had always been a nice balance between us, and it tilted gently, once again. He sighed his agreement. "All right. But don't frig about. Get up, get dressed. Where are the eggs?"

"Somewhere."

"Thanks a lot. What do you want me to do? Rob a nest?"

I concentrated, as best I could, and the result was not too bad. "The eggs are in the what-not by the sink. Worcester sauce on the side-board. Salt and pepper likewise. Glasses—glasses— well, you know what glasses look like."

He left me, and after a moment I got up and started to shave, as quickly as possible. My face in the flawed glass of the mirror was not encouraging; G.J.'s traditional phrase, "Like death warmed up," seemed, in the cold light of day, to be a generous verdict. But I did the best I could, only cutting myself once, only misjudging the symmetry of my moustache by a retrievable quarter of an inch, and then I slapped on some Larola, originally purloined from Mother and now a permanent feature of my *toilette*.

I had already started dressing when G.J. appeared with the prairie oyster, snug in its champagne glass.

"Try this," he said. "The egg didn't *seem* to be fertile."

With difficulty, I dismissed that particular picture. "Thanks. This should put some lead in the pencil."

"I don't think that's your trouble."

The concoction went down, as it always did, on a hit-or-miss journey. The raw yolk of the egg made a very large mouthful, the Worcester sauce was hot and potent on the back of the throat. I waited for that crucial moment, while the interior chemist decided whether to accept or reject; but God and his chemist were with me, and the oyster found a comfortable bed again. G.J., who had been watching me, said: "Well done," and walked out into the sitting-room, while I went on with my dressing.

I could hear him wandering about, making his usual exploration. Presently he called out:

"What's the starboard tack?"

"What?"

"What does 'on the starboard tack' mean?"

"Oh." With a little effort, I deduced that he was reading from the Trearddur Bay Sailing Club fixture-list, which incorporated some of the basic rules of racing. "It means, when the wind is coming from the right-hand side."

I went on dressing, in my smartest town suit, the double-breasted kind that G.J. was wearing himself. I was hoping that he would turn to the right page in the booklet, the one that I secretly gloried in. But his next question showed that he had been sidetracked.

"Your boat is called *Ptah*," he announced. "Now what on earth does that mean?"

"He was an Egyptian god."

"Never heard of him. . . . Who's D. K. T. Monsarrat?"

"That's my brother. Younger brother."

"Where's he?"

"Haileybury."

After another pause: "His boat is called *Clytie*," said G.J. "You people certainly choose some funny names. Who was Clytie?"

"A sea nymph."

"Did she ever have a go with Ptah?"

I was knotting my tie, and nearly ready. "I would imagine so. They all did it, all the time."

"Two boats in one family," said Gentil-Jones, still pursuing his researches. "Isn't that a bit extravagant?"

I laughed. "My dear old boy, you could get about forty of those boats for the price of one Bentley."

"That would be ostentatious." Then suddenly he found what I had been hoping he would find. "Good God, you're the secretary of this club!"

"Yes." I could have matched his surprise, a couple of years earlier. "In fact, you're reading one of my books."

"You mean, you wrote all this?"

"Well, I dished it up."

"Secretary. . . ." He really did sound impressed. "You should have told us. We'd have given you a party."

Fully clothed at last, I walked through into the sitting-room. "We have enough parties, as it is," I said. "How was that for quick dressing?"

"Pretty good. You're an hour late, that's all." He put the club booklet back on the mantelpiece, and then indicated, in a rather off-hand way, a suitcase standing in the middle of the floor. "I'm taking my dinner jacket, in case we get held up. You'd better bring yours."

"But I thought we were coming back here, in time for dinner."

"Well, you never know. We *could* have dinner in town, and then start back afterwards. I mean, it could happen like that. Otherwise it's hardly worth the trip, is it?"

"But I've got to work, damn it!"

"Dinner in town, dinner in Hall—what difference does it make?"

The omens were not good. "Just about five hours, if we're lucky." But it never took me long to weaken, and I weakened now. "All right," I said. "I'll take mine, just to be on the safe side. But let's make an effort. We really ought to try to get back."

"Oh, we'll try, all right," said G.J. "This is just *in case*." Having won his point, he became energetic. "Come on—five minutes to pack, and then we'll get going. I've put the car in Jesus Lane."

"Very wise." Jesus Lane was round the corner and out of sight of Great Gate, and of the spying porters whose duty it was to report such early stirrings. I went back into the bedroom, and started packing my evening clothes. I was going to ask G.J. why we needed dinner-jackets, if it was just to be a quick dinner in town, but then I remember that this would be a Liverpool sort of question, and I kept silence.

If you were in London, and your name was Gentil-Jones, you dressed for dinner, and that was that. It was a mistake even to mention it.

Of course, this whole excursion was now a good deal more complicated than I had been counting on. . . . I felt guilty, and therefore bad-tempered, as we slipped out of the back of Whewell's Court and made for his car. But the mood did not last. It was a wonderful morning, and, as soon as we were on the road, a wonderful way of spending it.

"Good morning, Hooper," said G.J., as the butler swung back the massive front door. "I meant to telephone, but I didn't have time."

"It is no matter, my lord," answered Hooper, who, I felt, would have been impeccably dressed and manifestly alert if we had arrived at three o'clock in the morning instead of nine-thirty. He was a small, plump, very nice old man who had endeared himself to me, on a previous occasion, by offering me a pinkish, chalky draft, an obvious charm for my hangover, with the words: "This will ward off your heavy cold, sir."

He had bowed to G.J. as he opened the door, and now he bowed to me, a secondary, controlled sort of bow which indicated that, though not one of the family, I was entitled to cross the threshold. Then he asked: "Have you breakfasted, my lord?"

"No," said G.J. "That's what we want, first of all. Is anyone at home?"

"No, my lord. His lordship is in Scotland."

"Fishing?"

"I could not say, my lord. . . . Her ladyship is still in Italy."

"Oh." Gentil-Jones gave a slight shrug, compounded (it seemed to me, guessing as usual) of all sorts of things—indifference, disappointment, resignation, non-surprise. "Well anyway, we've just come up for the day. Let's have breakfast, to start with. Then I've got to go out again. Are there any kippers?"

"Yes, my lord."

"Lots of kippers."

Later, over the toast and marmalade in the long panelled dining-room, G.J., who had been silent and intent while he was eating, suddenly said: "I'm sorry my people aren't here. Particularly Daddy. He likes you. He once said a very funny thing about you."

"What was that?" It was odd to hear one of the premier earls of England, whose title had been first conferred by James II, labelled "Daddy," just like my own father. But it was the verdict that I wanted to have.

"He said you were good for me." G.J. wiped his mouth free of toast-crumbs, and grinned amiably. "I don't know what the hell he meant by that. I don't mind saying, I bloody nearly threw up on the spot."

"Good Lord!" I said, really surprised. "I wouldn't blame you."

"Of course he gets tight awfully easily."

This was the very reverse of the truth, and we both knew it; it was probably some sort of cover-up for embarrassment, or for what G.J. was really thinking—not about me, but about his parents. I was beginning to wonder over this, when G.J., perhaps catching my thought, said: "I'm sorry Mummy's away, too. . . . She's been in Italy since January. . . . I might as well tell you, there's a bit of a sickness going on."

"What sort of?"

"Oh, you know. They've just stopped liking each other. Isn't it childish, at their age? That's why I'm here, really. It's sort of— oh, you know, scouting round and then taking sides."

I was astounded, and appalled. It was all very well for G.J. to sound so sophisticated, but this sort of thing, to my mind, was nothing short of an earthquake. Fancy having to take sides between your father and your mother. . . . I could not even imagine what this might entail for Gentil-Jones.

Would it mean living with one or the other of his parents? Not getting any money from one of them, if he chose wrong? *Giving evidence?* Though shaken by the possibilities, and intensely curious, I could not bring myself to ask for details; in this solid and splendid house, which seemed to stand for rock-like stability, for the very shield of honour (there was a photograph of the King and Queen in one of the other rooms, signed "George R," "Mary R," in actual violet ink), the idea of divorce, or of any other kind of dissolution, was truly shocking.

I said: "I'm awfully sorry," and did not know what else to say.

Luckily G.J., after this rare degree of confidence, steered quickly away from it again. "Oh well—easy come, as the girl said to the bishop. Have you had enough to eat?"

"More than."

"Those are terrific kippers, don't you think? We have a mad relative in Yarmouth who sends them down by goods train, in absolute shoals. By the end of September, this side of Belgrave Square smells worse than Billingsgate. We once had a complaint from Buck House."

I did not believe him, but it had made a welcome transition from the horrid subject which had peeped out from behind the curtain.

"What does one say when the King complains?"

"Sorry, *sire.*"

Somewhere above us in the lofty house a melodious clock struck the hour, and G.J. looked at his watch.

"Ten o'clock. I must hie me hence."

"Whence?" I realized that this was wrong. "Correction. Whither?"

"Thither," said Gentil-Jones, and smiled. "By God, I think I'm still a bit bottled. . . . To some awful slum in the City. And then back to Cavendish Square. After that, you and I have a luncheon appointment. How about half-past twelve?"

"Any time you like. Where will that be?"

"At the Buttery. I'll tell Hooper to arrange a table. All right?"

"Perfect."

When he was gone, I took it very easy. After a much more luxurious bath than I could ever get in Trinity, and a spell under a "sun lamp" (something I had never seen before) in one of the dressing-rooms, I came downstairs again. In the drawing-room, the black-and-gold escritoire beckoned me, as it had often done before.

It bore a lavish supply of note-paper, smooth as glass, blue as heaven, elegantly lettered with the minimal address: "Belgrave Square, S.W." The embossed coronet, on both paper and envelope, made absolutely sure that there need be no mistaking where they actually came from.

I wrote brief, gay notes to Mother, and to Felicity, and to three girls who loved me, and to another girl in America who, alas, did not. (But now she would see what sort of a man she had spurned.) Basically, I was only trying to give these correspondents pleasure.

Punctually at eleven-fifteen, just when I was feeling in the mood, Hooper came in with a bounteous silver tray bearing smoked salmon, pickled walnuts, stuffed black olives, toast, chopped onions, a generous scoop of caviar, and half a bottle of champagne in a delicately fluted cooler. He was smiling, as well he might be.

"His lordship asked me to say that you should keep up your strength."

How could I ever leave this charmed paradise, and seek my seedy fortune elsewhere?

The Berkeley Buttery was crammed, as it always was. It was *the* place to go nowadays, and it looked like it, and the people who were already crowding the cream-and-gold ante-room when I arrived, punctually at half-past twelve, looked like it too.

Discarding my bowler-hat, lemon-yellow gloves, and gold-headed Malacca cane, I sought the eye of the head-waiter. I was shy, as usual, but I knew that my passport was a good one.

"I am lunching with Lord Gentil-Jones," I told him, as soon as I had nailed him down.

"Oh yes, sir." His eyes, which had lacked luster when they first fell on me, now brightened perceptibly. "I have a window table for three."

"For three?"

"Yes, sir. And I have a table for you in here as well." ("Here" was the ante-room, where all the greeting and drinking was going on.) He motioned me forwards. "This way. His lordship's other guest has just arrived."

His lordship's other guest was a stunning girl with the brightest blonde hair I had ever seen, the largest grey eyes, and the widest mouth. She was dressed in black, as was almost the entire female population of the Berkeley; but her get-up was much enlivened by a fox fur, a hat with a pink veil, and some truly gorgeous pearls. ("Dripping with pearls," we used to say. She was dripping with pearls.) She sat on a sofa at a corner table, showing the utmost disdain for her surroundings and a generous amount of leg.

I thought: "Ho, ho, ho!" and assumed my very best leer. But she soon took care of all that.

"Hallo," she said, as I made my appearance. "I'm Millicent Strang. You must be Nick something."

I introduced myself more formally, as I deserved.

"That's the one," said the girl. "I've heard about you. You're G.J.'s little chum at Cambridge."

I did not care for "little chum" very much, but it was not possible to argue the point. I sat down on one of the spindly chairs, saw that she had not yet had a drink, and asked: "Would you care for a cocktail?"

She was examining me, with a cool, indifferent look which I was sure was taking in everything—my grey double-breasted suit, my black Oxford brogues, my silk socks with the "clocks" on the ankles, and my Old Wykehamist tie, secured by a gold tie-pin which linked the two wings of my collar. This urban *ensemble* was the very best that I could do, and hitherto I had been proud of it. Now, Millicent Strang made it seem only passable, just by looking at it with uncommitted eyes.

"What would you recommend?" she asked.

"A side-car?"

She shrugged those beautiful shoulders. "If you like."

Since I adored side-cars, which were so much more than a cocktail, something like a friendly flash of lightning—an insidious blend of brandy, Cointreau, and lemon-juice—I could not imagine anyone being so neutral towards them. But I ordered two, nonetheless, from the alert waiter, snapped open my gold cigarette-case (twenty-first birthday present, engine-turned, monogrammed), lit her Egyptian cigarette, and set out to entertain her.

I wished that I knew how old she was, but I wasn't any good

at that sort of guessing. She looked like a true woman of the world, and above all an absolute pippin.

I also prayed very ardently that G.J. would not fail to join us. Side-cars cost half-a-crown each, and the minimum lunch in the Berkeley Buttery cost God-knew-what. I had two pounds, and some silver, and that was the lot.

It soon became obvious that I was not entertaining her at all. Either she was waiting for G.J., and only for G.J., and was bored by the idea of spending any time on me; or she had taken an actual dislike to me; or she had written me off, on hearsay, as some sort of provincial rubbish, bound to be picked up in a college as large as Trinity.

It came as a great relief when G.J. strode in, shed his accessories, and crossed the ante-room towards us.

He waved to several friends on the way, and was unmistakably stared at. He was looking very smart and assured, and wore a dark red carnation in his lapel, as I did—there had been two of them waiting for us on the hall table, straight after breakfast. When he sat down beside Millicent Strang, he beamed at both of us, obviously in much better spirits. Then he gave her thigh a lingering squeeze, in a way which, about fifteen minutes earlier, I would have offered big money to essay, and then said to me: "Has she been behaving herself?"

"Almost excessively well," I answered. It was the nearest I could come to stating my point of view. "I think she's been waiting for the Prince."

G.J. gave me a very close look, and then relaxed, as if satisfied with something he saw, or did not see, in my face. "That's funnier than you think," he said. He suddenly laughed, loud enough, in spite of the chatter and the constant movement, for people at nearby tables to turn and look at him. "In fact, a damned sight funnier. . . . What are you drinking?"

"Side-cars."

"Super! Let's have three more."

Later, over a terrific lunch (asparagus, trout in aspic, and strawberries and cream, which were still wildly out of season), G.J. himself brought up the afternoon, and how we should spend it.

"Come to a flick with us," he suggested to Millicent. "Or come back and have tea at the house."

She looked very sad. "My darling, I'd give the *earth,* but I just can't. I've got one of those awful bun-fights, a sort of *post-mortem* on last night, with all the mothers being acid about everything. *Grisly!* And the *chaps* who come to those things. . . . Debs' delights—my God! I'll give you three guesses, which one of them we call Lord Acne."

G.J. laughed. "Poor old Flopsy."

"Right! Will you be doing that sort of thing, when you come down?"

"As little as I can," announced G.J.

Millicent sighed. "You're so lucky. We're in *irons.*"

"Well, let's think about dinner, then," said G.J. "Will they let you off for that?"

"Oh yes." She smiled warmly. "Mummy approves of you."

"I should bloody well think so," said G.J., and there was a thoughtful, slightly loaded pause, which delighted me. That was the way to talk to this girl. Then he went on: "All right. I'll pick you up about eight. We'll go to Quag's."

I chipped in: "It'll have to be a pretty quick meal."

G.J. turned. "Oh, I forgot to tell you," he said, cool and careless. "I may have to stay the night."

I had a sudden, dismaying sense of having been betrayed—or, at least, of having been lured into something which I thought we had agreed was out of the question. First we had been driving up to London for the inside of a day, and going back for dinner so that we could work; then it was to be dinner in town, but definitely a return straight afterwards; now it was this. Why couldn't G.J. have told me what he was planning, in the first place? . . . He must have seen some of this in my face, because he went on: "My people may be coming back tomorrow. Daddy, anyway. I *would* like to see him."

I found that I couldn't argue with this, and perhaps it would not be too long before I believed it.

"Well, I'll have to get back, anyway," I said. "The way we arranged it originally. If I don't do some reading, I just won't be able to cope with that exam."

"But it only means a few more hours. Why don't you stay over yourself? We can have our party, and then if I have to stay, you can take the breakfast train back."

Millicent Strang, once again, was looking from G.J. to myself, ready to play her part as soon as she had decided which part it should be. Finally she said: "Of course, if he *wants* to get back—"

I stayed as long as I could, for all sorts of reasons, and it turned out to be a little too long.

I was very fond of Quag's, the most alluring of all the night-haunts. It was only a superior cellar, really, though beautifully tricked out, with a dance-floor (as they were fond of pointing out in the *Bystander*) "about the size of a pocket handkerchief"; but the band was terrific, the food wonderful, and the people obviously from the topmost drawer.

It was always difficult to get a table there, even at early dinner-time; yet once you had one, and had surrendered to the noise and the crush and the elegant air of misbehaviour, the evening was made.

I enjoyed myself thoroughly, from the very beginning; and all the time I was able to think that I was only doing this for G.J., to save him from the clutches of a designing female—as I had now categorized her. It was a great pleasure; and when I danced with the designing female, I was able to hold her at a cold arm's length, like Sir Lancelot in the early stages, and think: "You have this alluring body, but you are *only a trap!* I just know!"

"There's Prince George," she murmured at one point, and turned a creamy naked shoulder towards the willowy young man nearby. What a hope!

We dined very well, teeing-off with snails, one of our latest addictions, and moving on to a concoction of veal which seemed to have some fantastic oddments tucked away inside it. We drank plenty of champagne. "Let's have some fizz," said G.J., as soon as he sat down, and passed the massive wine-list over to me. "You choose," he said. He had always thought that I had some pretensions to wine-knowledge, and perhaps he was taking care to include me in the party. "Pol Roger '21," I told the *sommelier*, and G.J. nodded, adding: "We'll start with a magnum."

There was not a great deal of the magnum left by the time I said goodbye to them. But it was also much too near ten o'clock. "Liverpool Street station!" I called to the taxi-driver, as I emerged from Quag's at a brisk pace, and added, just like George Raft: "Drive like hell!"

I was unencumbered, since G.J. would be bringing my suitcase back next morning. But even with a good taxi, and everything on my side, I still missed the train. It was an inexorable ten-fourteen by the station clock when we whipped down the slope to the entrance, and another fatal minute later when I came up against the closed platform barrier, and saw the red tail-light disappearing round the bend of the track.

The 10:12 to Cambridge was gone forever.

Through the bars, the ticket-collector peered at me, a not-too-rare exhibit in the zoo world of passengers. "Bad luck, sir," he said, with that slight air of satisfaction appropriate to the moment.

"Thank you," I answered. "I must have cut it too fine. . . . It doesn't really matter." But it did.

I turned away again, aware that rather a lot of people were staring at me; and perhaps the sight of a man sprinting madly up to a platform barrier in a top hat, with a scarlet-lined cloak streaming behind him in the wind, was a bit odd. Resisting the temptation to shout "Curses!" and twirl my moustache, I walked slowly back towards the cab-rank outside.

Between Pol Roger and this sudden burst of exercise, my head was spinning slightly. But it suddenly seemed very important to get back to Cambridge that night, and by the proper time. There was still more than ninety minutes to go. It could be done, with a little luck.

The usual line of taxis was waiting at the curb, and a knot of drivers at the head of it, gossiping. They broke off to watch me as I came up.

"I want to drive to Cambridge," I announced. "It's about fifty miles. Anybody like to take me?"

There was a very prompt "Not me!" from one of the younger drivers, and some head-shaking from the others. A second man said: "I'm off at twelve," and another: "Too far—all that way back." Was this the spirit which had made England great? I was about to offer them double fare, without even knowing what the single fare would be, when another man came out of the shadows and joined the group.

"What's up?" he asked.

"Gent wants to go to Cambridge."

"Cambridge Circus?"

"Nah! Cambridge College."

The newcomer sucked his teeth. "Must be a hundred miles."

"Fifty-four," I said. "What about it?"

"All right," he answered, surprisingly. "I'm game."

He did not look game at all; he was an oldish, snivelling man in a greasy brown top-coat, his wisp of a moustache walking a sad spectrum from nicotine-orange to graveyard-grey. His taxi, half-way down the line, was even less encouraging. It was an ancient, raddled brute, the kind one always avoided if there was anything better in sight. But he seemed to be the only volunteer, and so I echoed his "All right," and stepped in.

The journey swallowed three full hours, and it was nearly half-past one before I was deposited, practically lifeless, outside the barred oaken door of Whewell's Court. The meter showed that I owed 32s. 6d. for this forlorn caper; since I did not have enough money, I had to borrow from the porter, which ended all thoughts of sliding into college unnoticed. It was almost impossible to climb into Whewell's Court anyway. But a London taxi ticking away at the curb was the clinching evidence of misdemeanour.

"I'll have to report this, sir," said the porter, with a certain relish, sounding rather like the ticket-collector at Liverpool Street. He had been woken up, when he might have been dozing comfortably; but now he had not been woken up for nothing.

Alone in my room, staring at the wall, with all the champagne a vanished memory, I thought of that smooth ennobled bastard Gentil-Jones, still clipping Millicent Strang to his bosom in the warm twilight of Quaglino's. It wasn't fair. . . . Somehow, G.J. was absolutely certain to get away with it, while here was I, chilled to the bone, and two pounds the poorer, and yet another lost day nearer to the Tripos, and in deep trouble with authority. It wasn't fair!

"I understand," said Mr. Duff, putting the tips of his fingers together and sighting me carefully along this convenient level, "that you have been gated for a fortnight."

"Yes, sir."

It did not seem necessary to add that I had also been substantially fined, which hurt even more than being restricted to college after the hours of darkness. In fact, there had been, as I had feared, more than a bit of a sickness; the Senior Proctor was not in the least amused by my story, and made the fact plain in a bleak interview. "Hard cheese, old boy," said G.J., to whom nothing at all had happened, when I told him about it. "Millicent *said* you'd miss that train."

"In the circumstances," Mr. Duff went on, "I consider it an excellent idea. I don't think you can afford *any* distractions, at this moment."

I liked Mr. Duff, a small, kind-hearted, yet authoritarian man who had been at Winchester about a decade before me; and even when he took this strong line, with myself carpeted in his study, I still liked him. We had once skated together on the Backs, frozen over for the first time within memory; we had even waltzed, like the show-offs one saw on the Pathé Pictorial news-reels; and he had invited me, afterwards, to a noble tea of muffins, crumpets, and honey-in-the-comb.

We got on very well, apart from work. But as my supervisor, he had to make it clear that here the ice was much thinner; and though he gave my awful essays on Civil Law as much attention as if they had been the reputable product of scholarship, he withheld his approval very consistently indeed.

In the world of law, I had already slipped some way down the scale. At the beginning, I was going to be a barrister; I was thus enrolled at the Inner Temple, and "ate my dinners" there on all the necessary occasions, as part of their strange, tribal initiation dance. These nights were always very formal; while the Benchers reigned at the High Table, people like myself sat in serried ranks below them, going through the motions of ceremony, hoping not to attract attention.

We sat at the long tables in groups of four, all scared to death of doing the wrong thing; there was an intricate bit of nonsense over passing the sherry decanter, and another with the claret, and another with the port. It was not enough to know that these should always move clockwise; they also had to cut across the table at a precise moment, so that the supply did not pass from the control of those entitled to it.

Apart from these hazards, the dinners were very long and very good. Like "belonging" to Trinity, belonging to the Inner Temple brought its own secret satisfaction. But at the end of the exercise, I had failed my Bar exams.

This was a great disappointment; it meant that never would I be a brilliant barrister: never a man like Norman Birkett, now making himself a resounding reputation in such gory productions as the murder trial of Rouse; never a man whose cross-examination could bring the most brazen criminal to a stammering halt in the witness-box.

Now, even if I passed the Cambridge Tripos, I would only be a solicitor; and later, perhaps, a partner in my uncle Thornton Simpson's firm in Nottingham. It was all right, but it was not glory. . . . The question already was, was I going to pass?

I had only just scraped through the first part of the Tripos, earning (as Mr. Duff had not failed to point out) the lowest number of marks (three hundred out of nine hundred) which would satisfy the examiners. The final test, on which all depended, was now a short three weeks ahead.

Mr. Duff was echoing my day-dream. "You have to work," he told me. "You have to work as hard as you possibly can, for the next three weeks. You have to work *flat out*." He spoke this strange Americanism with such care that I wondered where he had heard it. Perhaps he liked films, just as much as I did. . . .

"Is that understood?"

"Yes, sir."

"Whether you are gated or not," he said, driving the point home with precise blows, "is neither here nor there. You should confine yourself to college in any case. You should concentrate on *catching up*."

"Yes, sir," I said again. He really was very fierce today.

"Otherwise. . . ." But he did not proceed with "otherwise." Instead, he tapped with his finger my latest treatise, a hurried, messy review of a question originally propounded to me as: "*N. kills his baby under the delusion that it is a rabbit. Discuss.*"

"I do not think," he began, "that you have entirely grasped—"

I really did work very hard for those last three weeks; the prospect of leaving Cambridge without a degree was really too disgraceful to think about. This was now crucial. . . . I read and read and read, until my eyes seemed to project on bloodshot stalks; I refused all invitations, gave up poker, cut down on the cinema, belatedly talked to known scholars who were sure to get Firsts, and told everyone else to go to hell.

The subsequent examination was dreadful. Even as I glanced swiftly through the paper (*"Eight questions* and no more should be attempted") I knew that I was doomed. These were all things which I had "done," yet I could not remember a shred of information about any of them.

Suddenly it was May Week, and Cambridge was full of girls.

It was as if all the rules had been cancelled at sunrise, as if the Senior Proctor had taken down his "Strictly Monastic" notices and posted others which read: "Nymphs and Shepherds—Come This Way!" From Petty Cury to Jesus Lane, from Christ's Piece to Maid's Causeway, the girls blossomed for us, more richly than the gardens of Kew in spring.

Gentil-Jones was staging the party, as usual; and when I reached his rooms, resplendent in tails, wearing an ultra-fashionable black-buttoned white waistcoat, the high-class uproar was in full swing. Just audible was the gramophone, with Ted Lewis beating out "The Sunny Side of the Street" in throaty invitation; the rest was crowds, voices, laughter, raised glasses, lowered eyelids, love, and urgency.

It *was* the sunny side of the street, just for that single moment. This was the beginning of the last triumphant fling. The exams were over, for good or ill; and as long as we did not know the results, we could still hope, and bask in freedom. Everything else was over; there was nothing now to do except to kiss Cambridge good-bye, with all the love and warmth which had been three years a-growing.

Even rowing, the crux of May Week, was over, with Third Trinity, which had crashed from Head-of-the-River to fifth place the previous year, only just managing to hang on to this forlorn demotion. But George Clay-Clarke, who was the first person I saw, did not seem to mind.

"Bad luck, George," I said, as soon as I was within earshot.

"You can't have been watching," he answered cheerfully. "It was *bloody* bad rowing."

Preston maneuvered his way towards me, with a magnificent array of champagne glasses and a full bottle. I took the offering, quaffed it liberally, and then looked round the room. The Lucullus Club was well represented—and that was another thing which was gone forever. But to hell with the Lucullus Club tonight! "Here's metal more attractive," Hamlet had once said, being rude to his mother. The precious metal was now in full display.

"What a lot of pretty girls," I said. "Aren't you glad you're out of training?"

"*They* are glad," he answered imperiously. Then, with his vast forearm, he gave me a nudge, rather like a swinging lunge from an iron bar. "Have you seen the one over there?"

I turned to look at the girl he indicated, on the other side of the room; and by God it was Winifred Shotter!

She was instantly recognized; no one else looked as alluring as that. . . . It was a long time since I had first seen her, in *Rookery Nook;* but since then she had been on view in all the Aldwych farces, an unbroken run of hits—*Thark, Thunder, A Cup of Kindness, Turkey Time*—which had established her as the absolute darling of the light-comedy stage.

She had dark curly hair, and dimples, and a beautiful figure. Elevated by champagne, galvanized by memory, I said "Goodbye, George," and was swiftly by her side.

She was talking to Frank Oppenheimer; but all the diamonds in Africa were not going to stand in my way.

Close to, she was all that I had imagined: very pretty, exceedingly feminine, with a merry face which, of course, masked deeper, stronger, more fundamental urges. . . . My first actress. . . . Frank faded out, like the nice chap he was, while I set to work to charm this ravishing creature towards the life she really deserved.

Amazingly, she did not seem to take me very seriously. When I asked, in my most intent manner: "Do you mind if I smoke?" she answered: "I don't mind if you burn," and went off into a peal of laughter so ringing that heads turned all over the room. This was probably good for my reputation, but for self-advancement—no. We talked like this for quite a long time. It was unusual to have someone else making the jokes. She really was extremely attractive, but I could see why she specialized in comedies. Such merriment. . . .

Preston approached us. He was so much at ease, so serene in spite of all the press and scurry, that I suspected he had been making sure that none of the champagne was corked. This was confirmed when, after refilling our glasses, he said confidentially to Winifred Shotter: "Strongest man in the University, madam."

"Goodness!" she exclaimed, when Preston was gone. "How much do you pay *him?*"

It was not very encouraging. "Nothing at all," I answered rather stiffly.

"Well, you should," she said promptly. "Lots of people would be *terribly* impressed!"

I felt that I was losing ground, and soon I had lost it all. Before long there was a small uproar near the door, which resolved itself into Julian Syme, slightly cross-eyed already, negotiating the entrance. He tripped over the rug, and nearly fell, which caused a sudden silence; he could then be heard singing "Wassail, wassail, all over the floor!" in a touching contralto. After that he smiled at the assembled company, and announced: "Yes, I am here. But no formality, please."

Winifred Shotter, laughing harder than ever, asked: "Who's that *sweet* little man?"

"Julian Syme," I answered. "You wouldn't like him."

"I love them," she said elliptically. "Do bring him over."

I caught Julian's eye, and beckoned him. He arrived almost at a run, gave Winifred Shotter a smacking kiss on the cheek, and said: "You mustn't mind me, dear—I'm just an old Roman gladiola."

Soon they were deep in conversation about her ear-rings. Before long I faded out, excluded, mortally offended. My first actress. . . .

But things did go much better, a little later on. I actually stole someone else's girl, and kept her to myself, all through a delicious night.

The Trinity May Week Ball was always a great occasion—the biggest and best of them, like the college itself. This year they had sold something like two thousand tickets, and to accommodate this throng the place had been wonderfully disorganized, with marquees in two of the courts, a giant drink-and-buffet-supper operation going full out, and covered passageways leading from the college down to the river bank.

On the river, a free punt service for ticket-holders offered a voyage which started under flickering Chinese lanterns and could end anywhere—in the outer darkness, in secret stretches of the Backs, in delirious triumphs.

Ambrose, the topmost Mayfair orchestra leader, gave us smooth music; Trinity gave us a superb setting; the girls gave us energy and ambition. By eleven o'clock the rising tempo was plain for all to feel.

By eleven o'clock, however, I was still lonely. I was nominally in Gentil-Jones' party, but Gentil-Jones' party, haphazardly planned, consisted of twelve men and seven girls, and for some reason I was constantly out-maneuvered. I did dance a few times, but the music —"Putting on the Ritz," "Moaning Low," "In the Still of the Night"—was about all that I enjoyed; the girls always seemed to be on their way to another rendezvous, and my darling Winifred Shotter still maintained such a mood of laughing non-involvement that I knew I would have to settle for being a respectful admirer, practically a tourist, after all.

This was not what I wanted, on my next-to-last night at Cambridge. Then I saw what I did want, and after that, everything went just right, just like a fairy-tale.

It was of course a girl, a tallish blonde girl, slim as a wand, very pretty in that sunburned sort of way which, I realized, made the current peaches-and-cream fad look more like curds and whey. She was standing alone by one of the champagne buffet-tables, in a sheath-like red dress which also made a sharp focus of colour in the paler world around her.

I had been watching her for rather a long time, wondering at her solitude; pretty girls were two a penny that night, but none of them was unemployed, and this one was something more than pretty.

It was a night for daring deeds, a night when there was nothing to lose. I picked up a spare glass of champagne, and sidled over. "Can I help you?" I asked. "You look a little stranded."

She turned, smiling, without hesitation. "I'm not stranded," she said, "so much as stood up." It was a new expression to me, but her accent explained it: a soft American drawl, unexpected, distinctly exciting. I had met another American girl in Brittany, a couple of summers ago, and the voice of this one recalled the voice of the other. "My partner seems to have faded out."

"How silly of him." I held out the champagne glass. "I brought this for you."

"Well, aren't you cute?" She took it, again without hesitation. Our fingers touched briefly, as they were meant to. "I really do have a partner. But he went to get some cigarettes."

"When was that?" I asked, producing my own cigarettes with a flourish.

"About two dances back. . . . Confidentially, I don't think he's going to last out the evening."

"Confidentially," I told her, "I don't give a damn."

We got on very well, over that glass of champagne. Her name was Christabel something—I never did get the full label; I wrote it down on the back of my program, and then lost the program some time between midnight and dawn. She actually lived in Washington, but was now in London, where her father was somebody in the American Embassy. It was all very glamorous.

We danced, to an insistent tune called "Stevedore Stomp." Christabel certainly knew how to dance, especially to a tune like this. When we slacked off a little, she clung to me in a very liberal sort of way; she had a most delicious figure—soft and yielding where it should be so, firm and muscled where this was a help. She had no hesitation in letting her cheek nestle close to mine as we circled—which was also something entirely new. All sorts of people I knew kept looking at us, and then muttering something to their partners. It was doing me a great deal of good.

At the end of the long dance, Ambrose's band struck up a fanfare, ending with a resounding crash on the cymbals, and he announced: "Twelve o'clock! The witching hour! First call for supper!"

"Are you hungry?" I asked her.

"Not yet. Do I get another chance?"

I consulted my program. "We can have supper now, or at one o'clock, or at two."

"Sure they won't run out of food?"

"This is Trinity College, Cambridge."

"Pardon me. . . ." Christabel looked around the dance-floor, now emptying rapidly. "That sounds swell. But I'm only playing hooky, you know. I do have this man. Sooner or later he's going to show up."

It was time to strike. "Come back and see my rooms, and then we'll dance again, and then we'll eat."

"O.K. But I *will* have to keep a lookout for him."

"Oh, quite. We might go on the river, too."

"You're driving."

She used all sorts of new expressions, exciting, like passwords heard for the first time. I loved her already.

Halfway up my spiral staircase, she turned, pretending to need a rest, and let me catch up with her. Then she slid down into my arms; the red dress blurred with the sunburned skin, and then with the offered mouth. When we kissed, her response was so frank and free that I wanted to go to America tomorrow. That must be the country. . . . It was the first time I had ever kissed anyone on a spiral staircase. I could feel her legs clinging to mine, and they were long and slim, like the rest of her.

We went on up to my room, and had a drink, and played a record ("Mood Indigo"), and lay entwined on the sofa for nearly an hour. I did not really know what to do, so I didn't do anything. This was a very strange girl to me—so lovely, so ready. . . . Girls weren't really meant to be like that. . . . And then she might have a baby. . . . Dishevelled, appeased in one way, unappeased in others, I said, in the end: "We ought to go back," and she answered: "O.K.," without demur.

She did not sound surprised. She did not sound anything special. She was there, and I was there, and we had kissed long and closely, and we were not technically lovers, and that was the way it was.

That was the way it was, all that night and all the early morning. When we got back we danced again, to a silly tune called "Cooking Breakfast for the One I Love," and another much better one called "Crying for the Carolines"; then it was two o'clock, and we found that we were ravenous, and we were just in time for the last session of supper—lobster, chicken, ice-cream, God knows what—and we sat and ate and talked about everything. I wanted to be a writer, like Somerset Maugham, she wanted to go on the stage, like Katharine Cornell. We were sure that we would both succeed.

She was still flawlessly lovely, and cunning in her glances, and seemed intent only on me. Her partner never came back, and indeed was never heard of again. I had not really believed in him, any more than I believed in this moment, this night, and her frank willingness to please.

We danced a third time, tightly clipped, alone in a throng of other couples slowly circling. The mood was now dreamy; we were moving towards the formal end of the night. Then, when the music died, in favour of "D'ye Ken John Peel" and "Auld Lang Syne," I said: "How about the river?" and she answered "Yes," and we went down to the wooden quay where the punts were waiting for the last mariners. It was half-past four; pale light was already beginning to show above the enormous trees on the Backs.

I still did not know what to do, except to keep this thing going forever, never to finish it, never to win, never to be defeated. In a backwater, I moored the punt, and slipped down beside her, and then on top of her. She did not seem to mind. She did not seem to mind anything. When I was tender, so was she; when the mood was fierce, so was hers. We did all things short of the last thing.

If she would have allowed this, I did not realize it. If she was surprised, I did not know that either. She was American, and candid, and wildly beautiful, and she kissed me like a hungry angel, and when prompted held me like a glove.

Suddenly, when I turned over, it was full daylight. I took the punt on up to Grantchester, where we had a ham-and-egg breakfast in a meadow—still talking, still in love with each other; and then I punted gently back again, while Christabel first trailed her fingers in the water, and then slept, lying at my feet, curled up like a slim animal, under the warming sun.

We landed below Trinity, as the clock struck eight. There were a few other couples like ourselves, still entranced; and men wearing blazers over their white ties and waistcoats, wandering in a private daze; and people sweeping up the tangled streamers and dead balloons, and goodly citizens going to work.

We walked slowly back into Great Court, hand in hand, fingers entwined, more fresh than such tired daisies had any right to be. We kissed in the shadow of the fountain—and that was a first and last time, too.

"No one is ever going to believe this," said Christabel.

I did not really know what she meant, but it did not matter. "Let's have breakfast," I said.

"We had that."

"Let's have it again. We'll have breakfast with Lord Gentil-Jones."

"We certainly haven't had *that*."

G.J.'s front door was open, and I led the way in, while Christabel followed. She glanced at herself in the mirror over the mantelpiece, and touched her hair, and smoothed her red dress. She was looking a great deal better than I was. She was looking wonderful.

The bedroom door was firmly shut, and I knocked on it, loudly.

"Are you sure this is O.K.?" asked Christabel, turning at the noise.

"Of course. He won't mind. He's a friend of mine."

"Maybe he has another friend."

"Good heavens!" I exclaimed. "In college?"

She said again: "No one will ever believe this."

Of course G.J. was asleep, and of course he was alone. But he rallied himself, and put on a magnificent brocade dressing-gown, and came out to greet us.

"Now what have you two been doing?" he asked, when he had blinked his way to full consciousness.

"Nothing at all," I said.

"I didn't ask you."

"Nothing at all," said Christabel. "Didn't you know? The English are terribly reserved."

G.J. rubbed his face, not for the first time. He had been looking awful, as I probably did myself; but quickly he was getting into shape again.

"I thought he might have lost his head," he said to Christabel, and then to me: "You have just a *trace* of lipstick on your collar. And I still don't like that *bloody* waistcoat. And there's just a little champagne left."

We had black velvets, and after that a colossal mushroom omelette, and sausages, and great strips of grilled bacon. Then other people began to come in: dopey, happy, talkative, nursing their hangovers like egg-shells, admitting to folly, disclaiming all knowledge.

I looked across at Christabel, enthroned on the sofa; beautiful, a little tired now, but still my love, my secret servitor. Perhaps, if I had played my cards right. . . . She winked at me, and blew me a kiss from the palm of her hand; and the champagne flowed again, and the music of the clarinet began to weave within the voices of my friends; and that, before another sun-down, was the end of Cambridge, and of a thousand other things besides.

Liverpool seemed incredibly dull and drab and defeating, like thin sleet after warm sunshine; and Holmfield, though solid and comfortable, not much more than a station hotel where one waited for the next slow train to the next slow town. I mooned about the house, with (as Mother put it) nothing to do and all day to do it in; finding everything pointless, and probably seeming pretty pointless myself.

I was destitute, as usual, but this was the least of it. I was also cornered at last.

My father was becoming a figure very remote from us all. He worked all day, harder than ever; and in the evenings he retired to his study, either to read (he had become an admirer of Joseph Conrad, and collected the first editions of all his books), or to write (he had already had two volumes of poetry published, and was now engaged on an enormous tome in which science and philosophy were blended into one impressive enigma).

In fact, he had retreated into a private shell, in search of whatever he could not find outside it: a retreat which I did not fully understand till many years later, when my own turn came.

Mother had developed a habit of referring to him as "O.F." It was short for "Our Father," and the allusion was Biblical. This was the only reference she ever made to the fact of his withdrawal, and it was not intended to be sympathetic.

For me, he was a formidable figure, though respected beyond question because he worked so hard and took care of so many things. I could not help realizing that, as a family, we were a worrisome lot, even though I felt, at the same time, that it was his job to worry about his own children. There was already a catch-phrase, popular among my discontented contemporaries: "I didn't ask to be born." Since we were here, without having been given the choice, we felt that we were owed a living, and that it ought to be a good one.

In my pursuit of trying to make it a very good one indeed, I had run deep into debt, for the third time in three years; and this was the inevitable subject of a post-mortem about three weeks after I came down from Cambridge, when the forgotten bills began rolling in.

In his study, after dinner, my father was precise, orderly, and courteous, as he always was; but I could see that he was also annoyed, by what must have seemed something like a simple confidence trick. He had let me have a generous allowance at Cambridge, based on my tutor's estimate of what a young man should be given if his father did not have to worry too much about money; but every year so far, my father had had to come to the rescue.

Now, at the end of my third and last year, the final reckoning was at hand, and it must have been startling.

"I've added all these up," he said, tapping the pile of bills on his desk. "Do you know how much they come to?"

"Not really," I said, though I had a very good idea.

He gave me the enormous total figure. He was frowning, as he had every right to do. "Do you realize that this is more than your allowance for the whole year? Are you in a position to pay it?"

"No. As a matter of fact, I'm a little overdrawn at the bank."

"How much?"

"About five pounds."

He made another note on the pad in front of him. Then: "But this is exactly why I gave you an allowance," he said. "So that you could pay your way. All these bills—" he tapped the horrid pile again, and then began to leaf through them one by one, labelling them as he went along, "there's a tailor—a wine merchant —cigars—books—records—sports outfitter—even your bills for meals at Trinity—and what's the Forum Club?"

"Just a club."

"You owe them eight pounds," he said curtly. "It says 'Account rendered.' What does that mean?"

"Oh, meals and things, I suppose." I was turning sulky, and I knew it was wrong, and I couldn't help it.

"For all those swells you call your friends?"

"I suppose so." No one used the word *swells* any more. It was like saying "In full fig" for evening dress, or "It's bad form," or "That cock won't fight," or "I've got a bone to pick with you." Our real language was so different. "I'm awfully sorry about it," I said, because I really was sorry—sorry for discovery, sorry that I was being hauled over the coals like this. "I honestly thought I would have enough money."

"How could you? You haven't nearly enough money. In fact, you haven't any money, have you? I really would like to know what you've done with it all."

It was almost impossible to say in detail, except that the money was gone. "I just spent it, I'm afraid," I said.

"You know that you were meant to spend it on these bills."

This was perfectly true, and I wished that he would not harp on it.

"I hope this is all," he said finally, when he realized that I had nothing more to say.

"Well, not exactly," I told him. This was the moment I had been dreading.

He raised his eyes, to look at me across the desk. The silence, in the book-lined room with the clock ticking on the mantelpiece and the gas-fire gently burbling to itself, was very oppressive.

"What does that mean? How much do you actually owe? Apart from all these bills, and your overdraft?"

"I owe someone else twenty pounds."

"Who?"

"A man called Gentil-Jones. You know—Lord Gentil-Jones. I told you about him."

"You told me about *him*," answered my father ironically. "Another of your swells. . . . What do you owe him twenty pounds for?"

What did I owe G.J. twenty pounds for? For small borrowings: for my May Week ball ticket; for shares of bills in Cambridge and London when I had no ready money; for bets on horses, and my railway-fare home to Liverpool, and half-bottles of champagne at Newmarket. We had fixed the whole thing at twenty pounds, and I had said: "I'll send you a check as soon as I get home."

Twenty pounds was nothing like what I really owed him, even in money, and we both knew it; but G.J. did not mind, because he had no great expectations of me, and I could not argue about it, because I was not in a position to pay him back any more.

If my father had known the full details, he would have called it sponging.

"It was just for little things," I said.

I could never have explained just how big some of the things had been.

A stern lecture followed, a very stern lecture indeed; but I was so tremendously relieved, now that all the secrets were out and I need not feel guilty any more, that I gave it less attention than it deserved. It was only a definitive, up-to-date version of what I had heard many times before.

I had reached the age of responsibility. I was now twenty-one. I was starting work in a couple of months. What would happen then, if I didn't keep exact accounts, if I spent money which didn't really belong to me? And *was* I going to work properly, at last? I had only just got my law degree, a degree hardly worthy of Cambridge, much less of Winchester. I had wasted all the fees paid to the Inner Temple. Would I now waste the fees which had established me as an articled clerk in my uncle's office?

I let the very reasonable words flow over me, while I day-dreamed, chiefly about the fact of being twenty-one, which had been the occasion of a terrific party at the Adelphi. A gold cigarette case had marked it, and lots of champagne, and a wild-eyed argument which led me to break off one engagement and get deeply entangled in another, even more binding and sacred and alluring.

It had wilted to nothing since then; but *that* night, it had been an eternal vow, with pleasing undertones of what Mother meant by "liberties."

My father was still talking, in his patient, well-modulated, authoritative voice. He was explaining, not for the first time nor the tenth, about the important difference between debit and credit, and how one kept track of this in a ruled account book which must be written up ("Posted," he called it) at the end of each day. Otherwise. . . .

I knew all about otherwise. Otherwise really boiled down to this sort of session, which was actually quite tolerable once it had been faced. In fact, it was nothing at all to pay, when weighed against all the fun which the prodigal son had managed to have before he came down to the husks.

My father finally undertook the whole weight of my debts, of course, and bailed me out again. I was very relieved, and therefore happy, but a little resentful at the same time. I had not asked to be sent to Cambridge. . . . What I did not know until later was that he himself was terribly worried about money, at that very moment. He was heavily committed in the stock-market, and it was 1931.

"What did O.F. want you for?" Mother asked me, as soon as I came back.

"Oh, it was just about money."

"Have you spent all your allowance?"

"Pretty well."

We were in the sitting-room, waiting for the silver kettle atop its ornate spirit lamp to come to the boil, for our half-past nine tea. Felicity was sewing, her face pale and withdrawn. I was already crunching shortbread biscuits, full of the pleasures of confession and absolution.

"Would you like to go down to Trearddur?" asked Mother suddenly.

We both looked up. "When?" It was only the seventh of July.

"In about a week, if you like. We could open the house early."

"What about Denys?" asked Felicity. Denys was stuck at Haileybury till they broke up, in about three weeks.

"He can go straight there."

I had never heard a better idea. Trearddur Bay seemed more than ever a wonderful prospect. I had hundreds of things to do, as secretary, which could only be settled on the spot, with plenty of spare time to deal with them properly. And this would be my last full summer, the last real roll of the wave. After that, a holiday would mean a single wretched fortnight, just like people in offices.

"That would be absolutely super," I said.

"We can have a really long holiday," said Mother, echoing my thoughts, "before you start work. O.F. can come down later."

When I inherited the job of secretary of the sailing club from Peter Munro, he sent me a long, not too formal memorandum on all the things I would have to take care of, from the beginning of the season till the end. The range had grown, because the sailing club itself had grown.

From those small beginnings of ten years earlier, when we were still paddling mutinously round the bay in our rowing boat, the club had sprouted so vigorously that it had become the focal point of Trearddur Bay. Now it claimed our whole attention; and all sorts of yearly rituals had developed round it.

We cruised in company up and down the coast, to Holyhead or to Rhoscolyn; we organized sailing picnics, when the whole fleet, fifty sail strong, bore down upon Coppermine Bay, and there landed in a great wave of gramophones, girls, picnic-baskets, Thermos flasks, bottles, shrimping nets, fishing rods, and bathing dresses. We staged swimming and rowing regattas, nautical parties, and lectures on "How to Win." All these things bound us together in a lively routine, of which racing was the climax.

Mad sailors all, we raced three days a week, rain or shine, in dead calm or cracking wind; and as the number of boats increased, and the new stars left the nursery and challenged the Old Guard (anyone over eighteen), the competition grew really tough. There were now eight half-raters, thirteen Myth Class, and twenty Insects, as well as certain unclassifiable craft built before racing itself was invented; the mooring problems which resulted were only solved by depositing the whole thing (for some reason) in the lap of the Board of Trade, which promptly batted it back to the Trearddur Bay Sailing Club, designating us as the sole authority for "Pleasure Boat Accommodation."

It did not give us any more room; but at least, when someone complained, the Sailing Committee could answer: "Your application for mooring facilities in the north-east channel must be rejected on the grounds that it would impede navigation and might become a hazard to coastwise shipping. By order, the President of the Board of Trade."

They might argue with me, but not with something which was practically a Cabinet decision.

There was never much argument, in any case; sailing was too much fun, Trearddur was too wonderful to spoil, people were too good-humoured to bear grudges or gang up into cliques.

This was not a good season for *Ptah* and me; already, both of us were growing old, and the prized trophies were beginning to elude us. *Ptah,* having won the Regatta Cup three times in six years, could no longer really keep up with the fleet; the fleet had grown from four boats to thirteen, half of them brand-new, and new boats, with taut flat sails, polished hulls, and timbers without an extra ounce of water to pull them down, were proving very fierce competition. The freshly risen stars were also from Hafod, but they were now Denys, and *Clytie.*

Clytie, as I had told Gentil-Jones, was a water nymph who, because of unrequited love for Apollo the sun-god, was changed into a sunflower, and turned her adoring face towards the sun all day and every day. It was a touching little story, and of course a great comfort to me when *Clytie* led *Ptah* all round the course, as she usually did, and romped home the winner.

Denys had become an excellent sailor, and a very good racing skipper indeed; he had that tough and tender hand on the tiller which was unmistakable, which could never be learned, although almost everything else about sailing could be learned, if the apprenticeship were long and hard enough.

He won two out of the three available cups this year, while the Hon. Sec., beset by problems of state, finished in the ruck. It was partly the march of time, partly the spark which comes from nowhere and glows at will. From being a despised younger brother, Denys was now giving a neat new twist to the tortoise-and-hare story by turning himself into the hare halfway through the race.

Things I had had to sweat for, or had never won, were coming to him rather easily. Girls looked his way as readily as mine; silver cups fell into his lap with a monotonous clang. And while our friend Llewellyn the fisherman, now about forty-five, had only succeeded old Robert as club boatman when the latter retired, with no particular grace, at an age somewhere between seventy-five and eighty, Denys achieved a quicker inheritance. He took over from me as secretary immediately my three-year term was up.

The faint aura of nepotism which surrounded this appointment did not survive for long. He was streets ahead of any other competitor; even as a brother, I would have had to vote for him.

He was seventeen now, taller than I, good-looking, supple, and fundamentally self-sufficient. He played rugger for Haileybury, in the lonely and exposed position of full-back. Soon he was going to Queen's College (we never went to the same establishments, by popular request: for The Leas, Winchester, and Cambridge, he substituted the Dragon School, Haileybury, and Oxford). To my father's great satisfaction, he was planning to try for a medical degree.

Away from racing, away from its stresses and disappointments, this was a golden summer indeed.

Neither Denys nor I needed any special excuse to enjoy sailing; if there were no race to win or to lose, it was still just as much fun to hoist sail, maneuver out of Porth Diana, and set course up or down the coast, under the simple label of "exploring."

We had the freedom of a lovely coastline, which we came to know in exact detail; the main arm of the bay, about seven miles across, was cut up into countless beaches and inlets, where a small boat, prudently handled and creeping in slowly with a watchful look-out in the bows, could penetrate at will. This sort of voyage, good for our inshore navigation, good for practice in the simple exercise of getting in and out of trouble, was enough for a whole day of delight.

The sunlight on our bright red sails, the wheeling seabirds, the wash and suck of the tide, the awesome silences as we were blanketed by towering cliffs—all these combined to give us the sharpest of pleasures, piercing the heart with the sudden knowledge of what it was really like to be in love with sailing.

There was one place to avoid, one stretch of coastline to which we gave a wide berth, at least when we were in an open boat. The farthermost arm of the bay, near South Stack lighthouse, was made up of a line of steep cliffs, stretching westwards till they fell away to the sea level. But this was not the end of the rock-formation; the line continued underwater, in the form of a mile-long ledge over which the flood tide roared like a torrent.

The result was a series of vicious over-falls, and a square mile of broken water in which no undecked boat could survive. We knew it as The Race; its evil reputation was well grounded. Except for its counterpart at the other end of Britain—the Pentland Firth between the Orkneys and the mainland, where wind meets waves in wild collision—it remains the most wicked stretch of water I have ever seen.

Denys and I sailed through it half a dozen times, in borrowed half-raters, on our way to Holyhead for the regatta there; a half-rater, with its enclosed decks and long counter, was reasonably safe from being swamped, if the crew sat outboard and used their hunched bodies as a shield against the breaking waves. The worst one could get was a soaking wet bottom.

But it was still a memorable experience to go smoking through with the tide, the last outcrop of cliff a few feet from our hull, and the jumble of broken water coming at us from all angles. Wind and tide together, we must have been going all of fifteen knots; there was nothing to do, once one was committed to The Race, but to sit tight and take whatever came.

There was always an odd and sinister moment of calm in the middle, when the tide-rip was carrying the boat along faster than the wind could drive it, and the sails flapped in idleness. That was the only section which could actually be described as dangerous; with no effective steerage-way, one could do nothing to avoid the breakers or to meet them at a safe angle. We always used to get drenched on this tormented passage; but to come out on the other side, into water suddenly still, was a real breakthrough, a signal for smiling relief.

On the one occasion when we sailed round to Holyhead in *Ptah*, we kept well away from The Race, and did not close the coast again till we were level with the lighthouse, a mile or so to the north. Even so, it was exciting enough, with the tide still fierce and the water still troubled. There was a knot of sight-seers, collected on the South Stack headland, staring down at what must have looked like a David-and-Goliath act—a fourteen-foot dinghy, about the size of a cork, shooting past them under the shadows of the cliff.

Denys, catching sight of them, waved and grinned. Then he felt the need for something more. "Look at that little boat, Auntie!" he mimicked, in his most foolish voice. "There ought to be a law!" I was too busy with bailing to do more than tell him to look where he was going.

But nearer home, within the bay, there were plenty of simpler ways to enjoy ourselves. One of the high spots of the year was still the mackerel season, when the shoals came in and every boat in the club turned out to have a try for them. We used to jog along slowly, under jib alone, trailing three or four lines with silver spinners attached. A swirl of water, with the seagulls screaming and swooping round it, was the tell-tale mark; as fast as the lines were unreeled the gleaming fish darted for them and were hauled in.

The Lancasters took the all-time record catch, a hundred and eight mackerel in an hour; normally we would be content with a couple of dozen—at such times of glut they were rather hard to give away. Grilled within half an hour of being caught, they made the best of all breakfasts.

There were always other harvests to be gathered, to vary this menu: prawns, and pink crab, and lobsters, and sea-trout. This year, someone had the idea that the Oyster Rock, off the coast opposite Hafod, must have been given its name for a good reason, and that there might in fact be a forgotten oyster-bed at its base. Llewellyn had unearthed an old oyster dredge, which seemed to bear out this theory; and we decided to put it to the test.

Twenty strong men were co-opted, with promises of rich shares in the spoil; we re-launched the old lifeboat which was used for laying the racing marks, and toiled all the way out to the rock— not less than seven miles. It was very hot work, and hotter still when we shot the trawl and began to tow it along the sea-bed. We kept up our spirits by visualizing that evening's dinner, which was now almost certain to start with at least two dozen Trearddur Bay Natives apiece, that delicacy which had so charmed the Roman legions, and before them the Druids. . . .

We collected almost everything in that trawl except oysters;

there were starfish, crabs, some unidentifiable bones, a lot of empty mussel-shells, and tons and tons of seaweed. Hauling in this marine rubbish was a very heavy job; at least fifteen of us had to tail onto the rope, and it came in a foot at a time, wet and slimy.

It was strange to circle the rock, black and dripping at half-tide, and to remember the many ships, particularly in the old sailing days, which had struck there in thick weather or under a fatal weight of wind, and had slid down to their graves. It gave a sinister and speculative turn to the job of examining the trawl when we got it in-board; in my mind's eye the wet, gleaming skull which might break surface ("Those are pearls that were his eyes"), and come in over the gunwale, was very real.

It did not happen; nor did we bring up anything which gave us the smallest clue as to why it had ever been called Oyster Rock. But we had plenty of time to theorize, on that very long row home. No one said anything about their first course for dinner that night. Ours was sardines.

Every promising young man who came to Nottingham for any reason at all found his way, if he could, to Edgmont. It had everything which anxious mothers hoped for: respectability, strict rules, a certain *esprit de corps,* and an iron hand at the helm. It stood, symbolically, on the highest point in Nottingham, at the top of the Derby Road. It was a tall house, or rather a clump of tall houses, since it was actually four late Victorian dwellings congealed into one, which resulted in a number of different floor-levels and a slightly disjointed air.

The rooms were lofty, with ornamental ceilings and threatening chandeliers; they were comfortably carpeted on the ground-floor, a little austere on the first and second, and frigid at the top, where the carpeting gave place to linoleum and worn boards. It reminded me all the time of Rodney Street, which had had this same system of hierarchy, as well as the same cutting drafts; downstairs was for grown-up show, upstairs was where the children (in this case the poorer inmates) made the best of their meager seniority, in circumstances reduced to the bare essentials.

Edgmont was home for forty-six people, headed by Mr. Marshall, an ancient grey fixture who was reputed to be the oldest practicing solicitor in Nottingham and District. There were newcomers like myself, who hoped they would not be there for long; and "permanents" like Miss Pycroft, who had been there for twenty-two years, and who played "Silver Threads Among the Gold" on the piano, calling out: "Come on, everyone—dance!" before settling down to Pelman Patience as the customers melted from the lounge.

There were people going bald, and working very hard to disguise it; people going broke, quite shamelessly; the young hopefuls and the old failures, the bright-eyed and the bleary, and the soggy suet puddings in between. There were malcontents like Henry Usborne, and prudent planners like Norman Pearson. There were two nubile girls, one almost pretty, one not absolutely hideous, whom desperate young men might just have brought themselves to woo, if the girls had not given out that they were practically engaged, and so been free to look around for more promising material.

Ruling this assorted family (just like Mother, which made another link with Rodney Street), was that strong hand on the helm, the owner and operator, Mrs. Pierce.

Mrs. Pierce had been running Edgmont for more than thirty years. First it had been her family home, then it had been her inherited white elephant, now it was her living, and (with forty-six people paying an average of four pounds a week) a very good one. She was strong-willed, capable, and despotic: quite an old lady now, dressed in shiny black with lace trimmings, armoured about with a breast-plate of cameo brooches: quite an old lady, but more than a match for any young whipper-snapper, just down from Cambridge, who might think himself too good for his new surroundings.

"A decayed gentlewoman," Mother had once called her, but Mother had been wrong. There was no trace of decay here; this was part of the authentic backbone of England, the no-nonsense landlady who gave full value for money, and expected in return to be paid on the nail.

Mrs. Pierce expected some other things too, and she got them all. The rules of the house were inviolable. There was to be no noise after ten o'clock. There was to be no gambling except with counters, no rowdiness, no excessive drinking at any time. No one was to be more than ten minutes late for meals: breakfast was sharp at eight o'clock, lunch at one, dinner at seven, Sunday supper (cold beef, pickles, and cheese) at six forty-five, and if you went over the deadline you went hungry as well.

Above all, there was to be no "nonsense"—which meant no girls being sneaked in by one of the four back doors after night-fall, and never, never, never any internal slippered traffic between bedroom and bedroom.

The rambling, rickety establishment was in fact very well run; though there was plenty to laugh at, there was plenty to be grateful for, and to admire. Edgmont was a Nottingham institution: like the vanishing lace trade, like Turney Brothers (which was the style of my grandfather's leather works), like the annual Goose Fair at Michaelmas.

Sometimes, it was true, the hot water ran out unreasonably early; sometimes the meals went on and on, complicated by an inexorable five-course pattern which wended all the way from Brown Windsor soup to silver-papered cheese. They were further slowed by a lack of competent staff which Mother would have recognized, and an eccentric senior parlourmaid called Vera, whose monologues were freely imitated.

"You can have chicken, roast beef, or cold tongue," she would say. "Well, the roast beef is off, really—and Mr. Marshall took the last chicken, so it's tongue and potatoes, isn't it?—roast, boiled, or mashed—oh no, the roast went off with the beef, it's tongue and mashed, cauliflower or greens, it might just be greens by now, will you be having rhubarb tart or jelly, they want to know in the kitchen so they can divvy up the pastry."

If one arrived at the very last moment, not having heard the gong (which seemed to summon every other inmate at a speed matching those well-remembered wolves-on-the-fold), and if one answered, as I sometimes did, "Oh, anything will do," Vera used to snap back: "Well, that's not very nice, is it?" and the service would be slower than ever, and I would play with one of the monumental cruets until I knocked it over, and everyone turned to stare.

I sat at a center table, together with seven other young men whose professions ranged from Articled Clerk (myself) to Junior Quantity Surveyor. Older, more favoured guests sat at small tables for two. They included a married couple of so forlorn an appearance that they must in truth have been in mourning for their lives: a couple who, in the whole of the eighteen months I spent at Edgmont, were never seen to exchange either a word or a look.

Sometimes I liked the place, because it was all new, and intermittently funny in a grisly kind of way. Sometimes I was optimistic about it, because I could not possibly be staying there very long, and then discontented, because I could not see how I was going to escape.

But mostly I was resigned, since it was beginning to dawn on me that perhaps this was all I was worth, and that life could go on like this forever, until I was as old as Mr. Marshall, that oldest of all practicing solicitors, the figure of fun without the fun, the old dead man among the live young ones who, in all probability, were simply studying to be old and dead themselves.

My bedroom was on the ground floor, though in an unfashionable area which overlooked a narrow back street lined with garages and iron railings. It had a ceiling which almost disappeared into the shadows, like most of the other rooms; a vast marble mantelpiece above a black-leaded grate garnished with crinkly green paper; flaking plaster, chocolate-brown paint, and a single overhead lamp, to which I had rigged an ingenious gadget, of string and staples, so that I could switch it off when I was in bed.

By this uncertain light, coming from entirely the wrong angle, I read myself to sleep each night. Trying to improve my taste, or to impress Nottingham, or both, I had begun to branch out from Dornford Yates and Denis Mackail. I had recently finished George Moore's *Héloïse and Abélard,* which as well as being a classic was definitely hot stuff, within the meaning of the phrase.

Now I was plowing my way, a little self-consciously but with actual, tangible pleasure, through Marcel Proust's enormous multivolume novel, *Remembrance of Things Past.* I was already up to Volume Two, in the translation by Scott-Moncrieff (ex-Winchester, of course); he had called it *Within a Budding Grove,* but I still thought that its proper title, *A l'Ombre des Jeunes Filles en Fleurs,* was one of the most beautiful phrases in any language.

That was the world for me . . . Proust lived and wrote, it was said, in a silent, cork-lined room, totally removed from the rude world, surrounded only by the exquisite and the rare. I envied him, sometimes, above all other mortals; and when I stopped reading, and clicked off my light, and began to drift into sleep, I longed to have just such another room as Proust.

It would be elegant, and private, and sound-proofed against the throng. Perhaps there might be a girl as well, who could make as much noise as she liked.

That should be my world, the world of luxury and soft-footed service: the world of Odette and Albertine, of the Baron de Charlus and the Duchesse de Guermantes. But it was not going to be so. Tomorrow, I knew, just before I began to dream about it, I would still be prisoned in my own world: the world of Nottingham, beige wallpaper, porridge, trams, and Messrs. Acton, Marriott & Simpson, Solrs.

Since it was downhill all the way, and the grinding trams, worse even than Liverpool's, were always crammed to the rafters, I walked to work in the mornings. The journey was about a mile, and it gave me, whether I wanted it or not, a good cross-section of Nottingham: down Derby Road, lined with the cheap and tawdry furniture shops which for some reason took pride in announcing "No Connection with the Establishment Next Door!" through a cavernous cut devoted to warehouses and the backs of red-brick tenements; and out onto the broad breathing lung of the Market Square.

The streets were grimy, the pavement hard as rock, the work-bound faces morose and resigned. Such was Nottingham on a typical Saturday morning, weary to death of its long week, but looking forward (after a brief respite involving a "half-day," a football match, a beery pub-crawl, Saturday night's ritual coupling, and a desolate Sunday with the kids and the wireless and the papers), to nothing more beckoning than another week just like it.

This must be life, I thought, as I plodded along, past paper-sellers and bleary-eyed shop assistants rolling up their shutters: past the cut-price tailor who advertised "Genuine Misfits": through the jostling ranks of wage-earners marching and counter-marching, grey as the murky skies, like extras in some smudgy crowd scene. This must be life, not only in Nottingham, but life anywhere, for anyone caught in the trap of circumstance.

I turned the corner of King Street, caught the eye (for the

hundredth time) of the pretty girl in the bookshop, crossed the road, and climbed the worn, abrasive stone steps to the place I always thought of (because that was the way I signed my lowly letters) as A. M. & S.

The legal life, I had found, was dusty all over; it bred old paper, and old paper bred dust, and dust bred dusty old solicitors, and dusty young ones like myself. A. M. & S. was housed on one side of a shadowy corridor which had not seen the sun since the roof was first put on, a hundred years earlier; we lived and worked in tall brown rooms with tall brown windows, through which we had a craned-neck glimpse of shop-fronts, chimney pots, and above them a bar of wan light which was the actual sky.

The best office, the one on the Market Square corner, was occupied by the only surviving partner, my uncle Thornton Simpson (both Acton and Marriott had long ago gone to dust themselves). But his office was just the same as ours: dominated by a desk piled high with papers, and lined with black tin boxes, stacked to the roof, with such compelling labels as "Dankworth Deceased" and "Exors of Sir Jos. Drumhalloran."

Untidy by day, the rooms were set sketchily to rights at night, when the cleaners, advancing from office to office, emptied the ashtrays and briefly rearranged the dust.

I shared an office with the same ceiling-high lining of tin boxes, a colossal eight-foot-square desk, and the other articled clerk, Philip Jones.

I had come to know that desk very well, whether I was crouched over it like a shackled galley slave, or had set my feet on it like a tea-time lord of creation. It had a scored, ink-stained leather top; but the top was rarely to be seen, since it was never clear of paper-work and (I knew already) never would be.

I seemed to live and work, elbow deep in legal junk. There were dog-eared volumes on Company Law and Trust Accounts: piles of title deeds with beautiful brittle seals: stacks of draft memoranda and schedules of real property, bound with pink ribbon: great mounds of Completion Statements (which was our polite word for bills): easements, liens, and attachments: ancient mortgages with curling parchment edges: wills, codicils, probates, depositions, deeds of assignment, contracts, rental agreements, and acres of those interminable "conveyances" prefaced by the Gothic phrase which, after only two months, was already enough to set me screaming: "THIS INDENTURE WITNESSETH."

I had come to know that desk, and its burden, very well indeed; it was the lurching galley which, however hard the slave tugged and sweated and groaned, would never stem the tide. I had come to know Philip Jones very well too; and he, frankly, had proved to be my saviour.

He was a tall, solid, square young man, rather like George Clay-Clarke only with brains: a little older than I, and just completing his three-year articles with A. M. & S. He seemed to know so much about the law that I realized that I would never catch up; he knew the right book to pull from the shelf, the right form to fill in, the right kind of draft to present to my uncle, the right way of doing everything.

Hopes that I would one day be a partner seemed to evaporate, whenever I watched Philip at work; it was obvious that he would be promoted years before my name even came into the conversation. In terms of merit, it would be no race.

Yet the possibility that I might have some sort of family pull must have occurred to him. In the circumstances, the fact that, even at this stage, he went out of his way to help me, do almost all my work, cover up my mistakes, conceal my absences, explain away my hangovers as sudden feverish colds, and generally take the load from my worthless back, was proof of something more than good fellowship.

Years later, when I heard that he had abandoned first the law and then the Colonial Information Service, taken Holy Orders, and settled most happily as the chaplain of an inter-racial student hostel in London, it only confirmed what I had suspected, almost from the first moment I met him. The man was a saint, as well as a wise and patient counsellor. He was the first saint I had met, and he could not have arrived at a better time.

The trouble, for me, was that the office was so dull. Work, after Cambridge, would have been awful anyway; but this brand of work was murder. A. M. & S., a solid safe firm with an admirable reputation, trod the very middle of the legal road. There were no court appearances, no drama, no chasing of ambulances to find out who had been foully wronged; there were no libel suits, no criminals running in and out, trying to raise bail or beat the rope, no cunning traps for blackmailers; no divorce, rape, civil insurrection, paternity suit, nor piracy—none of the things which had made law at Cambridge a tolerable study.

All we did, virtually, was to draw people's wills, and put them into effect when they died; and, along the rest of life's highway, help them to buy or sell their houses, form small companies, raise mortgages, and collect debts, using the statutory form of stern letter.

Who could enjoy this? Who could like the customers?—the watchful widows less than grief-stricken, the beefy speculative builders talking about land values in their flat Midland accents: the people who wanted to add codicils to their wills, leaving the set of ivory elephants (free of legacy duty) to a life-long companion in token of their esteem?

Who could enjoy making out those damned bills, listing all the letters at 6s. 8d. each, the consultations at 13s. 4d., the sundries including search-fees, the apportionment of the water-rate on date of completion, the settlement of an outstanding claim for damage to property due to cess-pool seepage?

Who could really write, with a straight face: "To ringing you up on the telephone and learning you were out: 6s. 8d."?

This was why I needed Philip: because I could not get myself involved and interested, yet the work had to be done, somehow, by someone. He might not have been interested himself; perhaps he was as bored as I was; but at least he was utterly competent and dependable, whereas I was neither, and we both knew it, and we had agreed, tacitly, to keep it a secret.

It was all so dull. Nothing ever happened. The most exciting thing that winter was the arrival (after what I knew was a full year's debate, close comparison of different makes, and lengthy negotiations over the value of the old model) of a new typewriter for the outer office. But when we had all admired it, and tapped its space-bar, and ting-ed its bell, we all went back to work, and I went back to an incomprehensible tome labelled "Book-keeping and Trust Accounts."

There were still lots more exams on my horizon. Trust Accounts were part of them, and there I was heavily bogged down already. Soon I must be in the thick of Criminal Law again, and

the Law of Torts, and the sacred Law of Property. I had the
deepest foreboding that this was going to be like the Bar exams
all over again: I wasn't going to pass. Yet I *had* to pass, if I was
ever going to be a solicitor. . . . It was much too early to be so
completely fed up, to have lost all hope. But already I knew that
this job was not for me, and never would be.

So, behind a fortification of law books, in the forlorn hope of
rescue, I was writing a novel. (Philip knew all about that, too.) It
was a very advanced story, about a young man and a girl who, on
the eve of parting forever (she was going to marry somebody else),
spent one last perfect day together, culminating in a fiery heap on
the sofa (wide and deep).

I was being spurred on, apart from anything else, by the appearance of a new phenomenon, the universal best-seller which
everyone bought in droves and talked about all the time—J. B.
Priestley had just published two in quick succession, *The Good
Companions* and *Angel Pavement*, which gave all us writers a
mark to shoot at; and by the news that Felicity (Felicity!) had
actually had a book accepted, and that after some changes it was
going to be published.*

It was only about a troop of Girl Guides camping out at Trearddur Bay, but damn it all! she was likely to be in print before I
was!

By the time I arrived at the office, this Saturday morning, Philip
was already at his desk. He always was. There might come a day
when I would be sitting there, head dutifully bowed over a sheet
of draft paper, mulling over some knotty point concerning the
rights of the second mortgagee, as Philip came into view; but it
had never happened yet.

This morning, as usual, he was hard at work, smoking his pipe,
wielding his neat gold pencil. He was conservatively dressed in
very dark grey, which meant that he looked like a partner already.
I had taken the Saturday license to wear flannels and a "rough
coat," and looked like an undergraduate. Once again, it was no
race.

He bade me good morning, searched me unobtrusively for

* *The Oakhill Guide Company,* by Felicity Keith (Blackie, 1933).

signs of excess or debauchery, found that there were none, and said, "Your uncle was asking after your grandfather."

"Oh God. . . ." It was Saturday, and I was even less enthralled by the Estate of Sir John Turney, Deceased, than on any other day of the week. "It's coming along all right. . . . Why can't people just turn up their toes and die? Why do they have to leave wills?"

"To save other people trouble." He smiled. "It may not seem like that to you, at the moment."

He was right, I thought, as I sat down on my side of the loaded desk: Sir John Turney, Deceased, had meant nothing but trouble from the outset; for me, he was even more alive now, even more formidable, than he had been in the old days at Gedling. He had died about four years previously, and probate had been disposed of; but there were still all sorts of loose ends to be tied up, and each winter the accounting of his estate had to be brought up to date.

It had been the first file to land on my desk, together with the humble task of getting out that year's preliminary figures for the executors. It involved much more money than I would ever have at my command: six surviving children, and twenty grand-children: investments, mortgages, income distribution to bene-ficiaries, market value of stocks and shares, bank charges, advances to legatees in anticipation. . . . The file was on my desk now— or rather, the cavalcade of files, since they had multiplied till they could no longer be carried by one man with two strong arms.

I was in the thick of calculation. I hardly understood any of it. I kept pushing it away, and substituting easier things like drafting waivers of the right of Ancient Lights, or reading the paper, or writing one of my own paragraphs, or doing nothing. But some-where in the very near future, I would have to produce the results of my researches.

When I had told Philip that they were "coming along all right," this was fiction more imaginative than anything I could concoct in secret. They were not coming along at all. They were hope-lessly stalled, somewhere between ignorance, confusion, and sloth.

I settled down to work, and the morning ground its way on, leaden-footed, almost immovable. At one point I found myself

writing the name "Ada Marguerite Turney Monsarrat," and
then realized, with a certain shock, that this was Mother. It was
odd to discover how much she had got from the estate, and actually to write the figure down. Such riches! . . . It gave me a
sense of management, of behind-the-scenes power. But there was
no doubt that I would rather have had the money.

Silence reigned. Philip puffed at his pipe, I shuffled my papers,
asked an occasional question, and received, always, a concise, detailed answer. The rain which had been threatening now dripped
steadily down the window panes, changing King Street into a sad,
spectral blur. Tea arrived, dark brown, acid, brewed and served
by one of our two typists. One of them was young and pretty, one
was not. This morning it was the latter. The tea was always the
same.

At half-past eleven there was a slow shuffling step outside, and
the cashier, the office early-bird, asked if we had anything to be
put in the safe. He was a very old, very pale man with dropsy;
he had been there in the days of Acton and Marriott; in fact,
some said that he had been there when Mr. Acton himself was
an articled clerk, which placed him on a misty pedestal indeed.
He spent most of his day crouched before the fire in his office,
rubbing his bony bloodless hands together with a dry rustling
sound. I liked him, and he was always kind to me. He also had
the right idea about Saturday mornings—that they should end as
early as possible.

I had nothing for him, and told him so; Philip merely said "Not
yet," a dusty answer for a dusty old man who wanted to go home.
Then there was a much firmer tread in the corridor, and my
uncle came in.

I had grown fond of him in the last few weeks, because he was
another person who was kind to me, and if he was regretting his
bargain in taking me on as an articled clerk, he had never yet
showed it. He was about sixty: red-faced, rather stout, stooping
when he walked, just as he stooped over his desk. He could be
firm, and sometimes fierce; he could pick out a mistake in the
twinkling of a rather cold blue eye, and jab his fore-finger down
on it, and draw his breath, and say (much like Mr. Sutton): "No,
no, no!"

It seemed to me already that he knew every conceivable thing about being a solicitor. Philip said that he was "highly competent"—which was the same verdict, but spoken with an authority I would never have.

He was wearing light-brown plus-fours, his own Saturday morning rig, and he shook his head as he motioned towards the rain on the windows.

"There goes my golf," he said. But that was all, as far as this topic was concerned; he was still in his office, the office he undoubtedly loved and firmly controlled, and it had all the priorities. He looked down at my side of the desk. "What are you on now?" he asked.

"The Turney estate, sir," I said. I called him "sir" once every day, for our mutual comfort.

"Oh yes. . . ." It wasn't really a matter of "Oh yes" at all; the Turney estate was in the forefront of his mind, he had not forgotten it for a moment, and he knew that if I wasn't working on it, then I ought to be. "How is it going?"

"All right. I was hoping to bring it in next week."

"Have you finished the schedule of investments?"

"Well—"

"I was just going to check the figures," Philip interposed, admirably prompt.

"I wanted Nicholas to deal with this," said my uncle rather testily.

"Oh, he is," answered Philip, who was really quite brave. "But I was working on them last year. That's the only reason."

"H'm. . . ." Uncle Thornton opened his mouth to say something else, but then thought better of it—or not enough of it to make it worthwhile. "Well, I'm off," he said. "Have a good weekend."

"Did I really finish the schedule of investments?" I asked, as his footsteps died away down the corridor.

"Well, let's say it *is* finished."

"Thank you very much."

"Prego," answered Philip, who was planning to spend his holidays in Italy next year and was, typically, already learning the language.

I did a little more work, but the spur of my uncle's presence, the necessary discipline, was gone. Next week would be early enough, to clear up this damned mess. . . . The town-hall clock boomed out midday, and I glanced at my watch. Then I leaned back, and stretched.

"All right," said Philip, without looking up. "They're open."

"Why don't you come with me?"

But Philip never came with me, even on Saturday mornings. He would be there in the office for another half hour at least. He would be the last to leave, and his side of our desk would be clear when he did so.

No race, no race. . . . Five minutes later I was in the bar of the Black Boy Hotel, one elbow on the counter, watching the frothy draft bitter spill over the lip of my glass mug as it poured from the spigot.

The bar was already full—full of the same people as on any other weekend, the people I loathed, and would soon resemble. They were rugger players, mostly, and golfers, and Saturday cinema-goers; professional Romeos getting up their nerve, dull boors, noisy blockheads, brave spirits who were daring to be late for family lunch. They wore checks which were just wrong, pork-pie hats with feathers stuck in the band, wide green trousers, near-Harrovian ties, and yellow camel-hair coats with the collars turned up.

They were hearties in another version—provincial hearties, a little louder and cruder, and even more bone-headed, than the cheerful dolts of Cambridge. Having a lot of Nottingham relatives who had a lot of Nottingham friends, I had quickly been accepted as one of the gang.

These good fellows, having wolfed down ham sandwiches and hard-boiled eggs along with their cascades of beer, would leave at two o'clock, *en route* for various sports; I would have to take off earlier, in time for Edgmont's punctual lunch. But they would all be back again at six; if not at the Black Boy, then the Flying Horse, or the murky inn, dating from the time of the Crusades, called The Trip to Jerusalem. I would often be back myself, on these Saturday night swills. There was nothing else to do, and I was drawn to this sort of thing by a kind of mud-wallowing despair.

The bar would grow raucous as the hours went by, and heady with smoke and sweat and competitive beery gulpings—the true test of manhood. At the end we would bid each other long, maudlin good-nights on the street corner, and I would catch my tram back to Edgmont, and fall into bed like a sodden sack.

Sunday was for recovery. On Monday, at noon, we would all meet again, and compare stories and facial blemishes (either "shag-spots" or "grog-blossoms"), and announce, over and over again: "God, I was tight on Saturday!"

The dreary year was running out, and certain very dreary things were limping along with it. On one of those Saturday night jaunts I got into some spectacular trouble at the local Palais de Danse, in company with one of Nottingham's bright sparks, Tom Forman, whose family owned the city's only newspaper. Tom was another man who had been at Cambridge at the same time as I; he was a great friend of Malcolm Lowry, who was now, he told me, trying to get an advance of one hundred pounds for *Ultramarine,* instead of an offered fifty pounds.

Tom Forman was, at the moment, somewhat at a loose end, though he was much better equipped than I to fill in his spare time. He had a beautiful, low-slung little car called an M.G. Magnette, and a two-seater, open-to-the-breezes Gypsy Moth airplane in which he gave me four flying lessons, before we decided that this branch of science was beyond me. He was like Gentil-Jones in some ways, and he had the same sort of effect on me; he communicated a taste for extravagance which I could not afford, he got me into debt by the innocent fact of seeming to like my company, and he made me thoroughly discontented with my low estate.

At the Palais de Danse we became involved in a ferocious argument with some other young men, less refined, over one of the "dancing partners," who sat in a pen in one corner of the ballroom and waited for custom. Intent on this, the prettiest of the girls, Tom and I had invested in a long roll of sixpenny tickets, and expected to be able to monopolize this charmer for at least an hour. However, a jealous suitor, backed up by his friends, started to pick a quarrel with this arrangement.

One thing led to another. Tom was very strong, and gallant in a piratical sort of way; I was rather inebriated. Before long there was a scuffle and, with my ally temporarily out of action, a bullet-headed opportunist seized me by the lapels of my coat and butted me violently in the mouth.

It stunned me, gave me a brilliant black eye, and also broke a front tooth. Tom and I were then thrown out of the place, with instructions never to return again. Until I was able to make repairs, in three or four days, I looked very unlike a promising young solicitor, and had to stay immured at Edgmont, with yet another feverish cold.

It gave me plenty of leisure for a good wallow in self-pity. This time last year, I thought, as I nursed my wounds and smarted from the dentist's drill, things had looked a great deal better. This time last year there had been no work to do, because there were at least two terms before I had to take the Tripos seriously. This time last year we had stayed up all night, playing poker, in order to go duck-shooting at dawn, in the Norfolk marshes so near to the King's estate at Sandringham that it was probably *lèse majesté* as well as poaching. (But G.J. had reassured us: "Oh no, he won't mind a bit. He's some sort of cousin.")

This time last year, we had made one of our swift excursions to London, and there, cheered on by a frieze of what we then called "princely dames," staged a leap-frog race all the way round Belgrave Square, from G.J.'s front door to the very pillars of the Marquess of Londonderry's corner mansion, while the indulgent police did nothing but grin.

Now all I had was Nottingham, and a black eye and half a waggling front tooth. All I had was regular weekend boozing, and trying to keep up the interest on a crippling loan of £15, and writing a letter of apology to the manager of the Nottingham Palais for thus tarnishing his premises.

England seemed to be going to the dogs at about the same pace as I. That autumn, we had actually allowed Gandhi, a funny little chap in a bath-robe who had been making all sorts of trouble in India, to come to London and ask for independence. And then—the most hair-raising as well as the most disgraceful event of all—two ships of the Royal Navy had mutinied at the naval base at Invergordon!

The Labour people (cocky as ever, even though the election had cut them down from 287 seats to 52, which showed what they were really worth)—Labour said it was all due to "Admiralty

meanness and incompetence," which was obviously absurd. It
boiled down to the fact that some sailors, chiefly in the battleship
Rodney, refused duty because their pay had been cut. Well,
wasn't that just too bad. . . . Lots of people had to take pay-cuts.
I had taken one myself.

Apparently there was one awkward moment when the *Rodney,*
flag-ship of the Atlantic Fleet, actually couldn't put to sea, because the chaps wouldn't come out on deck. But of course it all
petered out in the end, as it was bound to, and they got busy on
applying a little discipline again. Twenty-four of the leading bol-
shies were dismissed the service. The fact that, after an inquiry,
the pay-cuts were restored didn't make much difference. It was a
pretty humiliating episode, and took a lot of getting over. The
Morning Post was especially angry about it.

There was a phrase in one of the papers (not the *Post,* of course)
which did, for some reason, stick in my mind. When a sailor from
the *Rodney* was asked by a reporter what it was all about, he was
said to have answered ("bitterly"):

"My wife had to sell her wedding ring to make do last week.
That's what it's all about!"

But that couldn't really be true, otherwise something would
obviously have been done about it long ago. . . . I went back
to reading of the secure world of Marcel Proust, as an antidote to
any disquiet. I read Hemingway's *A Farewell to Arms,* the first
war book I had ever come across, and thought it was wonderful.
(It was also about defeat, but defeat in battle, not by going on
strike!)

I read C. E. Montague's *The Name of Action,* and remembered
that the title was from *Hamlet* (almost everything memorable
seemed to come from *Hamlet*), when in a mood of dark despair
he said:

> And enterprises of great pitch and moment,
> With this regard their currents turn awry,
> And lose the name of action.

Skulking in my Edgmont bedroom, averting my battered face
from the inquisitive throng at dinner, mourning the bright past,
seeing nothing in the future but drabness and dust and defeat,
I knew that this was exactly what was happening to me.

Somehow I *must* change *everything!*

I must have a girl, really have her, absolutely naked, in bed, no fooling.

I must write a book.

I must get away.

TWENTY-SIX

1936

GONE AWAY!

VERY OCCASIONALLY WE SLEPT THREE IN A BED, because Francesca, the other girl, who had been at school with Jo, sometimes quarrelled with the young man whom she referred to as "my friend," and returned in a rage to camp out with us: because there was only one bed, and Francesca on these occasions (when she stopped being angry, and had drunk her Ovaltine) was sad and bereaved, and needed company, and liked to watch us, or listen to us, or even ask us if all was going well.

When this happened, we called Francesca our chaperone, and made her cook breakfast next morning. But mostly Jo and I were alone, and rapturously so.

She was exactly tailored for this rapture, in many more ways than one. Jo was a comely orphan with left-wing convictions and a little money of her own, which took care of the daylight hours; she was also good-looking, with a wide mouth and a lovely strong body—a real blonde, blonde all over, which took care of all the rest. She was a virgin, which put me off at first, when the subject came up for discussion; I had only had one other virgin, and one was enough. I knew that they were likely to be a trial and a trouble and a damned nuisance.

But Jo was none of these things, when the moment arrived. She gave it all generously, as if grateful to me for the shedding of this burden: as if the words "A time to every purpose under the sun: a time to embrace, and a time to refrain from embracing" were at last making sense.

She had said, somewhere in the middle of that night: "You know, I always hoped that it would be a doctor. Because he'd know what to do, and he wouldn't mind seeing me naked." We presently agreed that it didn't have to be a doctor.

"That night" had been the night that King George died, the twentieth of January, 1936; and though he did not die till nearly midnight, there had been an earlier bulletin which gently yet stonily sealed off hope: "The King's life is moving peacefully towards its close." Thus, that night I had been sad, because though I was now a convinced republican, this was the man who had ruled me, and all England, since the first year of my life, and it was the end of a long epoch.

I was so sad that I would have preferred not to keep our date, not to take Jo home to my lair in Hampstead, not to be the executioner. But it turned out that I was not too sad after all, and the night went as I had planned it—as we had both planned it—and we had lived together faithfully and happily from that moment onwards.

There had been one single pause in that happiness, very early on—in fact, five nights after "that night"—when I left her about midnight, and took the bus down to the Embankment, and joined the queue outside Westminster Hall, waiting to file past the King's bier as he lay in state.

Jo had not wanted me to go; she was as fierce a socialist as I, and rather more consistent. She made it very clear that on this particular night I ought to be quite happy, lying in a state with her. I had said: "But we'll do it again as soon as I get back," and she had answered: "Like hell we will!"

On that cracked note we had parted—she to the bathroom, I to the solemn, somber magnificence of the place where George the Fifth, by the Grace of God, of Great Britain, Ireland, and the British Dominions beyond the Seas, King, Emperor of India, Defender of the Faith (the elaboration of GEORGIVS V DEI GRA: BRITT: OMN: REX FID: DEF: IND: IMP: which we read on every coin we handled)—where this benevolent and faithful man had now set up his immortal rest.

Part of me felt, with Jo, that it was all a lot of nonsense; part of me, the most private part of all, was moved almost to tears by a family loss which could not be retrieved.

This had become the whole mood of England. It was something rather dangerous to joke about. Black ties and black arm-bands sprouted overnight; theaters and cinemas were closed, the B.B.C. went into its "solemn music" routine which one could grimace at, but never really criticize. A new film of George Formby's called *Where's George?* had the bad luck to have its general distribution scheduled for this very week; it had to be cancelled, and the film was never heard of again. The popular advertisement for Lyons' Corner Houses—"Where's George? Gone to Lyonch!" also disappeared without trace.

It was this sense of old-fashioned propriety, thought to have been outgrown, which had made me join the pilgrimage and the queue, that cold January night on the Embankment.

I reached the tail-end of the procession at 1 A.M. It was then a little over a mile long (by day it had been nearly three miles, across the Thames and back again) and ten people deep—a winding column of whom most were silent and all dead-tired; the score of policemen who brought up the rear stood within a few yards of the Tate Gallery, their faces half-shadowed by the overhead lamps, their waterproof capes gleaming in the drizzle.

For a long time we did not move at all, and leaning against the stone embankment I could stare down at the river and its wavering lights, and listen to the water; the tide was flowing swiftly, so that the swirl of current round the piers of Lambeth Bridge was clearly visible. It made me think of another man sadly dead— Frank Oppenheimer, drowned by night the previous spring at Madeira. Street traffic had long ago died away to nothing, and save for a low murmur of voices, swelling and diminishing like distant surf, the only sound came from the chiming clocks and the trains across the river.

Soon we began to move, a few steps forward at a time; in the crowd, quiet and orderly, there was no pushing for places, only a common fellowship. Too closely packed to see the people ahead, we could note, every now and then, their long shadows on the roadway giving a surge forward: and then we ourselves would get ready to gain a little ground, thankful for the relief of movement. It was two o'clock before we came level with Lambeth Bridge.

Here there was more activity: hawkers sold chocolate and the early morning papers, St. John Ambulance men busied themselves with those on whom the strain was beginning to tell. Many policemen now marshalled us: by our side the huge face of Thames House rose up, staring through rows and rows of sightless windows at this invasion from the shadows. As the rain stopped it grew colder; coat collars were raised, and the thin wasted lad next to me began to tremble.

"Perishin', ain't it?" he mumbled. "But I'll stay, any road." He had never seen the King, he told me in a spurt of confidence; and now his chance was suddenly taken away from him, and he was trying to make up for it.

The procession moved on afresh, step by step. Three o'clock saw us level with the House of Lords; slowly we passed King Richard's statue, edging forward, shuffling over the pavement, creeping past one buttress after another, growing more awakened and perhaps more nervous. And then, almost unexpectedly, we mounted the steps, and stood at last within the threshold of Westminster Hall.

We would not be there for more than thirty seconds. . . . As soon as I could I looked upwards, trying to take in at one glance the essentials of the scene; but there could be no detailed impression, only a sense of solemn loveliness which fitted the moment in every single respect.

There was nothing wanting in that picture—the motionless quartet of black bearskins, the frail old Yeomen of the Guard, the purple-draped coffin on its dais, the glittering of the crown amid the flowers, the tide of mourners approaching and receding, and lastly the great arched roof overhead: fashioned with sure craftsmanship, thick with shadows, the finest canopy that king or commoner ever had.

I took a second's pause at the outgoing doorway I felt the instinct if not the wish to pray; and then I was outside again under the stars, trying to fit new words to old thoughts, and radical rebellion to a royal moment.

The moment was half-past three o'clock, as the great booming overhead presently told me.

I did not get back to Hampstead until dawn. I felt drained and dog-tired; it did not seem possible that I could make love to Jo, even if she asked me to—though I was very ready to say I was sorry for leaving her, that it was just a hangover from the past, that it would never happen again. . . . But she had other ideas— two other ideas.

She bounded out of bed as soon as I shut the door behind me, and rushed into my arms as if I had been away for months. I discovered a taste of salt on her cheeks. She had been crying.

"I'm sorry," she declared, between kisses. "Darling, I'm *so* sorry. I was a beast! I'll never do that again. I promise!"

"It doesn't matter," I said, moved for the second time that night. "It was mostly my fault. I shouldn't have left you. But I just had to."

"You can leave me any time," she assured me, "as long as you rush back immediately. Did you have a nice time? Would you like some tea? I've had the kettle boiling for *two* hours!"

We had our tea, lying on the bed, holding hands, entwining legs. The daylight was now coming in strongly through the curtain, but it was still, we were inferring, last night. Jo undressed me, rather skillfully ("I took the nursing course at school") and it soon became obvious that I was not really tired at all; and so she slipped down beside me, and presently her nipples came out to play, and all was one again.

We had moved into a small two-roomed flat in Churton Street, behind Victoria Station; and there we played house very agreeably, on Jo's money and my promises (and hopes) that I would pay the rent as soon as I had another book published. It was an old grimy building on an old grimy street; beneath us was a boot-repair shop, and one of those family-run grocers' which seemed to stay open twenty-four hours a day, ready with anything at any time, from the last of the milk to a hunk of salami, from cheese to pickled walnuts.

The flat was cheap, because the neighbourhood was cheap. Churton Street was in Pimlico, and we were thus Pimlicans, as were nearly all our friends, holding the kind of fierce local loyalty which the Bloomsbury-ites of an earlier generation, and the children of Chelsea in a later, brought to their own private village.

Pimlicans met, as often as they could afford it, in the Café Royal—not the smart part, which we vaguely despised, but the lower end of the downstairs concourse, surrounded by its mirrors and red velvet and gilded cornices, a decor which had remained happily unaltered since the Nineties. We spent hours there, after concerts or film shows or the ballet or political meetings, and we did not have to go broke in the process. A tall glass of Pilsener cost 1s. 1d., and could be made to last a very long time.

Inside the Café Royal there was warmth and companionship and love and scandal; outside was the whole of London—its plays, its ballet at Covent Garden and the Alhambra, its Promenade Concerts by Sir Henry Wood, its "classic" film shows, its throngs of different people with different ideas. Nothing in London cost very much, if you knew how to go about it. We were poor, and proud of it, and proud of this city, which could give us so much.

It was all still heaping and swelling and happening to me, in magic abundance: the discovery of all the worthwhile things— music, ballet, opera, books, sex, sober drinking, fierce and compassionate politics. It had come very late, of course; I was twenty-six, and should have won the freedom of this city many years earlier. But it seemed that the blessed process might well go on forever.

I was still falling in love with music: starting, by accident, with Brahms' First Symphony, going on to Beethoven, and the Mozart piano concertos, and Chopin when the mood was tender, and then back to the pure fountain of Bach. I had, at home, an E.M.G. gramophone, with a huge, ugly, dominating horn, and a special snipper for sharpening the bamboo needles—incredibly antiquated now, but producing music of marvellous tone and purity, bringing the piano of Horowitz, or the oboe of Léon Goossens, or the Léner String Quartet, into my very room.

With its aid I learned all the lineaments of my new love; and I was wonderfully helped by the Promenade Concerts, for which we always scraped together enough money for subscribers' tickets, and which seemed the best bargain in the kingdom.

Night after night, during the season, we would stand stock-still in the central bear-pit of Queen's Hall, and listen, and learn, and love.

It was another part of the freedom. And behind it all, round it all, I had friends who were actually doing things—or if not doing them, then talking about them and spurring me on to do them myself; and I also had Jo, who made loving sense of the whole new world.

The first year after I said goodbye to Nottingham, I had published a novel, and two articles in the *Yachting World;* the year after that, another novel, nine pieces for the *Yachting World,* and twelve for a new entertainment magazine called *London Week.*

Now, in the spring of 1936, I had a third novel half finished, and had sold another article to the *Yachting World,* and seven more to *London Week.*

I had also written a play, which was going the rounds of half-a-dozen managements in London, via that essential go-between in every writer's life, an agent.

My agent (still the same firm, thirty-two years and one amalgamation later) sold those first two novels to Hurst and Blackett for thirty pounds each, and thus made six pounds out of me in two years. I can only speak for my side of the transaction when I say that this was the best investment I ever made; and later on, when that three pounds a year grew to nearer five thousand pounds, I still could not grudge a penny of the money.

Agents, for their ten percent, do everything—everything a writer cannot afford the time to worry about: contracts, negotiations, accounting, arranging translations and serials and film-rights and radio adaptations.

My own firm, for their ten percent, looked after all these things admirably. But in 1936 most of them—nearly all of them—were still in the far future. Then, I had only managed to make a tiny dent in the world of literature: with *Think of Tomorrow* in 1934, for which the *Liverpool Post,* God bless it, gave me my most favourable review ("A very notable first novel: Mr. Monsarrat should go far"), and *At First Sight* (1935) which they scaled down to "Very readable."

But reviews, good or bad, did not really matter. I was in print at last—and in the whole of my life so far there had been no thrill to compare with holding in my hand, on my twenty-fourth birthday, my first "author's copy" of *Think of Tomorrow:* 288 pages, Crown 8vo, black with gold lettering, 7s. 6d. net.

Both the novels retailed everything I knew about the pangs of love at the age of twenty-three or -four, and thus they sank without trace, even in Boots' Library. No one, alas, bought either of them; as yet, nobody had ever heard of me.

My dreams of rocketing to fame overnight had sadly evaporated; it was going to need something else besides blinding literary skill. I often envied, in this connection, a thriller-writer called Agatha Christie who, when relatively unknown (or at least, a bad third to Dorothy Sayers and Ngaio Marsh), had mysteriously disappeared just after her new novel was published, leaving behind her a motor-car, complete with what could have been blood-stains, abandoned on the edge of a quarry ("Missing Author Sensation: Foul Play Suspected").

After a nationwide hunt, and false clues galore, she was found a week later staying at a hotel in Harrogate, under a different name, a victim of amnesia. Her new book, called *The Murder of Roger Ackroyd,* which included a character who also disappeared, was a prompt best-seller; and after that Agatha Christie had never looked back. If only I could have a stroke of luck like that!

The articles I wrote for the *Yachting World* were meant to be funny, ringing the changes on that handful of basic jokes (tumbling overboard, catching pneumonia, getting cracked on the head by the boom) with which I had tried to break into *Punch,* four years earlier. (The first one had earned me my very first check, for £1 8s. 6d., on 9 February 1934—another red-letter day.) The stuff for *London Week,* my principal life-belt, was mostly short paragraphs and fillers. They earned shillings rather than pounds. However, they all added up; and shillings were now what I lived on.

London Week was the lively brain-child of Richard Usborne, brother of Henry, whom I had known at Nottingham. It had been launched in 1935, as a sort of miniature *New Yorker,* covering the whole range of London entertainment, from jazz to the Royal Academy, with short articles on anything else which might be going on; and we all tried to write like the *New Yorker*—witty, cynical, sharp-pointed prose, which would prick the bubble of the established world without disturbing the advertisers.

There was to be no religion, sex, politics, or rudeness to celebrities. We were not to write the sort of reviews which might affect the allocation of press passes. Otherwise, the entire oyster was ours.

I was free-lancing for them, like all the other riff-raff: only Dick Usborne and a couple of other executive types drew salaries (as much as six pounds a week; a fabulous wage). One of my chief assignments was to go round all the principal restaurants and the newly-opened "Road Houses"—I covered eight of these, from the Ace of Spades on the Kingston By-pass to the Spider's Web somewhere near Watford—eat a previously negotiated free meal, and write up the merits of the establishment in terms suitable to such an arrangement.

Never had such delicious meals been served in such gorgeous surroundings, either before or since.

In between times I did whatever seemed a good idea at the moment, whatever might be salable later, and then wrote it up, and hoped that it would somehow stick. I joined a flight from Croydon, on one of the earliest night-time sight-seeing trips—"See London lit up—£1," and flew round and round Piccadilly Circus for an hour. I got on board one of the old-style sprit sail barges taking part in the Medway Barge Race, and had a wonderful briny voyage out to the Nore Lightship, and made over two pounds on the deal.

I joined the May Day March, an annual Labour Party classic —I would have joined it anyway—and (even though I carried one stave of a banner proclaiming "VICKERS—MERCHANTS OF DEATH!") managed so to purge the day of politics that even *London Week* accepted my account of it. I wrote bits of verse, at a shilling a line, and a sad piece about a pavement artist who ran out of yellow chalk while drawing a portrait of Christ, so that the halo looked like a tattered bowler hat, and got him into all sorts of trouble.

I wrote another sad piece about the King's lying-in-state, but it never appeared—washed away by tears, no doubt. I wrote about the ballet, and the Changing of the Guard, and the old lunatic professor who lectured on shorthand in Hyde Park, and the muddy Thames at low tide, and proof-reading, and furious lying mothers protecting their young in the juvenile court. I wrote about everything that came along.

It was a way of scratching a living. It was good training for my trade, a good apprenticeship in learning to write about anything, and if necessary nothing. It was wildly exciting all the time. Even rejection slips had their own special professional glamour.

Much to my relief, *London Week* somehow managed to stay alive. Indeed, it is still alive, though under another label adopted some years later—*What's On?* At one point it was salvaged, or at least reorganized, by a man called Edward Martell, an energetic, impressive, rather sinister young man who "took things in hand" on a whirlwind basis, starting with our accounting system and

moving outwards into the realm of office overheads and typewriter ribbons.

He was only sinister, of course, because he had an absolute
command of the principle of profit and loss, and knew for certain
which one of these was to be preferred. This seemed to me, in
those days, a terrible thing to worry about. But I was not at all
surprised to identify him, later, as the Managing Editor of *Burke's
Peerage*, which may safely be classified as a no-nonsense publication.

I stayed alive also, just like *London Week;* but however hard
I tried, I could never quite do it by writing alone. When the time
came to add up the accounts of 1936, my third year of free-lance
sweating, I found that, with three articles for the *Yachting World,*
twenty assorted bits-and-pieces for *London Week,* and one other
slice of luck, I had still only made a total of £72 3s. 6d.

It worked out at just under twenty-eight shillings a week, almost
the same as the dole, and not enough to keep the holes out of my
shoes as I walked about the town. But I had a lot of help, a lot
of precious and powerful allies never to be repaid, never to be
forgotten.

I had Jo, who believed in me, in spite of torrents of evidence
to the contrary. I had the Proctors (the London-based family of
Philip Proctor, who had married Molly): a family of veritable
angels who fed me when I was hungry, bought me clothes when
my own became too wretched and too frayed at the sleeves and
the turn-ups, stuck one-pound notes in the pockets of my overcoat
whenever I came to dinner, and three times took me ski-ing at
Adelboden, because they thought I might be lonely at Christmas.

I had Norman Pearson, now graduated from Boots' Cash Chem-
ists in Nottingham to an infinitely imposing firm called Borax
Consolidated in London: Norman, who lived in splendour in
Queen's Gate, and remained a staunch right-winger, and eyed my
Pimlican friends as if they were part of Rag Week; but who still
invited me to his parties, and had not flinched from introducing
me to the most beautiful and glamorous young woman in all London—Vivien Leigh.

Vivien was just spreading her wings after an explosive debut
in *The Mask of Virtue,* when the critics ran out of adjectives long
before the public tired of adoration. I was one of the public. I

had really written my play for her to star in, but this could never happen. Her theatrical future had swiftly been sewn up, for at least the next two years.

I had Lyons' Corner House, mecca of the poor (though they might not quite appreciate that label): Lyon's Corner House at Marble Arch, where daily, from eleven o'clock till three, they served a meal called "Brunch," consisting of sausage, egg, bacon, potatoes, a small cutlet, and a fried tomato. It cost 1s. 10d. altogether, and it was the best money's worth, and sometimes the most crucial bargain, in the whole city.

I had a small allowance—two pounds a week—from my loyal father, who was now living happily in another part of the town, in circumstances which, initially, had come as the biggest shock of our lives so far.

It had happened in 1932, when without forewarning, without danger signals, without a prior clue of any sort, our parents had separated. This shattering turn of events coincided with my father's retirement from active practice, at the age of sixty; and it was (though this took me some years to work out) the end-result of that gradual withdrawal—to his study, to his books, to his writing and thinking—which was becoming evident while I was at Cambridge.

We were invited, by Mother, to choose one side or the other; but this I found absolutely impossible. We had not been brought up even to talk about this sort of thing, much less do anything about it. I could see what she wanted and expected; I could see, more and more, what he had lacked, for a very long time. He had the brains, and the studious application; she had the lively appetite for *trivia*. She also had to cope with the sad non sequitur of being a wife outdistanced, and a mother whose children, if they had not actually flown the coop, were already fledged as the next batch of adults.

I came to see all these things, in the end, including the pattern of disengagement which I had copied, exactly, when I turned my back on Nottingham and holed up in my own secret shell. If you had things to do, you had to do them, even though it left in your train a lot of sad, surprised, or resentful people. There were no clear-cut rights or wrongs, no absolutes; the bitterness of desertion had to be weighed against the arid actuality of life with a stranger.

Men worked, and women wept. It could be the other way about. If either side could prove themselves to be "in the right," it was still an empty solace, like being "in the right" when you were also the captain of a sunk ship, or were dead at the wheel of your car.

After the first astonishment, I made my own withdrawal, and in the process I summoned up a few professional, cold-blooded adjectives. Mother was silly, vain, snobbish, warm-hearted, generous and much loved; my father was cool, preoccupied, immensely well-read, ruthless about his privacy—and also much loved. No magic wand was going to bring these two breeds of cat together again. In the meantime, I had my own troubles, and my own pleasures as well.

Felicity, naturally, emerged as the angel in all this turmoil. It was she who stayed at Mother's side, when she might have got married or taken a job; it was she who, forgetting the strife and the nail-marks of the past, gave Mother the only permanence of the rest of her life.

They had stayed on at Trearddur Bay, for one terrible, mournful, bitter winter, in hiding from "the disgrace"; then Mother moved back to Nottingham, and took Felicity with her, and settled down again in Sir John Turney country, surrounded by sympathetic relatives.

But she could not "settle down." She bought a run-down house, improved it, made a small gem of it—and then, after a bare two years, sold it and bought another. She was to do this five times in twelve years, in a wretched, restless progress which, obviously, would never really have an end.

At the moment, she was installed in a handsome, solid farmhouse, on the ancient Fosse Way between Nottingham and Newark. In a year, she had done wonders with it, and when I went up there, that spring, I told her so. But already the symptoms of "moving on somewhere else" were in sight.

"Oh, I don't know about *staying* here," she said. She was looking round the sitting-room, which had a vast stone fireplace with an oak beam across the top, hung with the shining horse-brasses which were her new enthusiasm. "It's still not quite what I want."

"But it's just right."

She shrugged. "It's so poky."

Perhaps she was still in mourning for Holmfield, or for Melbreck, or even for Gedling House.

Felicity was there, of course, the permanent companion, the peace-maker, the loving and giving daughter of duty; and Denys also. Denys had fallen on evil days, compared with the "might have been" of a few years back. He had gone up to Queen's College, Oxford, intent on a medical degree, and then something went wrong straight away.

He failed his first examinations, and came down after two years, degreeless and half-defeated already; now he had a rotten run-of-the-mill job with a firm of dental mechanics in Nottingham, and lived at home, and played football brilliantly, and was just starting (I could not help but notice) to adorn quite naturally the dreary, beery rugger crowd I had known too well in my own time.

It was as if some interior spring had already begun to give way, too far and much too early. It was sad, it was a great waste; but once again I had my own troubles, my own niche to carve; I really could not get involved. . . . In selfish relief, I went back to London as soon as I could: back to work, back to music, back to the delicious thread of sexual certainty which was summed up in the name "Jo"; back to another true love, politics.

Socialism was the only answer. We all knew that for certain.

I had come late to this conviction, slow to the scene of protest; even then, people usually "went bolshy" at the age of nineteen or twenty, while later on, when government by student became the vogue, the mid-teens were not too early to take in hand the reorganization of the entire globe. But my conversion (there could be no other word) had been delayed, by accident of birth, by prejudice, by lazy thinking, by the skull I was born with; not until I was twenty-three, and clear of Nottingham, did the bolt strike. But when it struck, it struck for life.

Invergordon had started me thinking; Invergordon, that uncomfortable, fantastic naval mutiny which had then seemed as incredible as a man running up a wall. But incredible or not, it had happened; the story had a beginning, a middle, and an end;

and the end did not explain the beginning, which had—which must have had—the same seeds of quiet desperation as had driven me to walk off my own job and out into the free air.

I could not forget that sad picture of a wife selling her wedding ring to buy food, while the sailor husband, ordered away on a spring cruise, smarting under a surprise pay-cut, was expected to obey orders and leave her to it. There was something wrong here, even for someone who had always expected sailors to obey orders, as part of the natural law.

I started to think, and then to question, and then to read, and then to look about me.

The reading was solid: dull at first, and then inspiring, and then, it seemed, conclusive. I read H. G. Wells' *The Work, Wealth and Happiness of Mankind,* and a novel of Richard Aldington's called *All Men Are Enemies,* which derided the established world in a way exactly suited to my own discontent. I changed my newspaper, leaving behind forever the *Morning Post* and taking the *News Chronicle* and the *Week-End Review* as my twin bibles, fountains of the gospel truth. I read Bernard Shaw, and listened to him instead of laughing at him. I read John Strachey, and Palme Dutt, and Harold Laski.

I began to use my eyes, as soon as I was broke and lonely in London; and it became obvious that other people who were really poor—not those like myself who could cheat, who could in the last resort go back to the bosom of a rich family, or take hand-outs from kindly relatives—that the really poor, clinging to the most meager existence with their raw finger-nails, were not lazy, or work-shy, or "ungrateful," as Mother used to declare.

They had been disadvantaged, and degraded, by a system which needed repair, or even upheaval, to set it to rights. The repairs would never come from the Conservatives, who liked things the way they were, with cheap labour and a line of unemployed at the gates. Repairs could only come from the Left Wing, where revolt was stirring, where want and poverty were bitterly understood, where stories of food being burned, or wheat plowed into the ground, or fish thrown back in the sea, in the interest of "price maintenance," were a wicked caricature of a world of plenty, and a perfect illustration of Proudhon's "Property is theft."

It took me a long time to get the picture; it took disillusion-ment, and the cruel figure of two million men out of work, and frustration, and the shedding of many skins, thick and thin. But in the end I got it, and I kept it forever. It was an indescribable moment: it was the light from heaven which St. Paul saw on the road to Damascus, the touch of divine magic which I had missed, and mourned, at my confirmation.

All the world was wrong. But it could be put right! At last there was something I could believe!

At last we could all believe—for I had friends now who felt the same way as I did, staunch brothers and very welcome sisters who knew the pass-word and shared the secret. Part of the secret was contempt; another part was charity, and another, hope. First we had to turn the whole rotten world upside down; but when we had done that, the right-side-up would be fair and bright and promising, and on it, Reason and Justice and Brotherhood would all be enthroned. How could anyone with sixpennyworth of brain argue about that, or fail to see it? . . .

At last we could believe. We could believe in all generous ideas, just as other people believed in the spectrum. Our choosing had to be nimble; good deeds and bad were being flung in our direction every day, every hour. There was a fire in England, and in Europe, swiftly lighting, swiftly catching; and it was being fed and stoked by experts who could be fools and knaves at the same time.

One thing was certain. They could not possibly be men of good will, like us.

Who remembers now the old fights? Who remembers the Peace Pledge, when a million signatures (including mine) on a pacifist manifesto made the Government think twice about its wavering support of the League of Nations? Who remembers the treacher-ous sell-out of the Hoare-Laval pact? The pepper scandal? The income tax soaring to 4s. 9d. in the £1, for hated rearmament? The budget leakage, which proved beyond doubt that business-men were a bunch of bastards, crooked enough to corrupt even an honest Labour man like Mr. J. H. Thomas?

Who remembers, now, the atrocious unemployment of the Thirties, when an area like the Rhondda Valley could have seventy-five percent of its population out of work, some of them for six or even eight years, with a cold-blooded Means Test to keep them in line?

The stale old quarrels have all gone to dust, like the people, like the problems, like the sparks they drew from anyone who was aware and hopeful. But *then,* they were real, and bitter, and as sharply felt as daggers. The Angry Young had something to be angry about.

There was misery, and want, and indifference, and corruption in England; and outside, there was one war coming to an end, in the most odious circumstances: another, with appalling civil butchery, brewing in Spain: and a third, which was to be the worst of all, just below the pitch-black horizon in Germany.

The war which was coming to an end was the war of Mussolini's Italy against Abyssinia, a wicked, one-sided slaughter which could best be summed up as Lions 10, Christians nil.

It had started in October of the previous year, as a piece of raw aggression designed, like many another overseas adventure, to shift the limelight from chaos at home to glory on a foreign field. It was a contest brutally unequal, from the start: a "civilized" nation against a pastoral survival: guns against spears, bombs and poison-gas against flocks and herds. For once, it pricked the conscience of the world; and the world reacted with a new idea, a single tender shoot of idealism and hope.

Spurred on by evidence of ruthless slaughter, roused by Italian bombing of both the Swedish and the British Red Cross units, fifty-two nations were slowly cajoled into line, and then into voting to apply sanctions against the aggressor.

It would have worked, if it had been done determinedly; even after the Hoare-Laval pact, a proposal for the partition of Abyssinia, with Italy rewarded by a vast share of the spoil, it could still have been made a shining example of majority pressure on minority crime. But those sanctions were never honestly applied, even though our own Government had just won an election on a pledge to uphold the Covenant of the League.

The Suez Canal, which might have been closed, continued to serve as a waterway for the aggressor; and oil sanctions, which could have been decisive, were voted down. In fact, both Britain and America continued to supply oil to Italy throughout the campaign.

The half-hearted reality of the whole-hearted dream meant that the dream was doomed—a dream, said the *Daily Mail,* of "screaming sanctioneers" at a time when "the nation has had enough of Geneva, which it regards as a nest of intrigues, international humbug, and chicanery of every kind." (The Fascists put it more bluntly: their slogan "Mind Britain's Business!" seemed to be chalked up all over London.) In the event, nothing much was done, and nothing *could* be done, either at Geneva, which was hamstrung, or at home, where the Government had a solid, sheep-voting majority of nearly two hundred and fifty, and could not be budged.

The rest of the world stood by, slack-handed, while the Abyssinians fought our battle with spears and even bows-and-arrows, and shook their fists against the metal falling from the sky, and died for a promise which had been a lie from the very beginning.

There was nothing which even Pimlicans could do, except to rage at cowardice and treachery, and become set in a pattern of revolt which did not reach its full flower for another ten years. At the moment, all we could do was to be anti—anti all the things which disgraced the name of honour, all the people who were calling the tune, all the ideas which were setting this atrocious pattern. Savage politics, sullen hatred were all we had to feed on.

We were anti-Conservative, because Conservatives seemed to be the chief villains, because in spite of expressions of horror over what Italy was doing, they made a social darling of dear Dino Grandi, the Italian Ambassador with the virile black beard and the charming manners.

We were anti-British Empire, which appeared to be a sentimental racket run by the same lot.

We were anti-Big Business—again, the same lot—because it was obvious that our whole world was organized and manipulated by beefy red-faced company directors who were making big money out of rearmament, while grudging the miserably small money which went to the small people.

We were anti-Royalty, because this was another piece of sentiment which was part of the same swindle. The King was "all right," but the people round him—the duchesses and debs and flunkeys, the Master of the Horse and the Women of the Bedchamber, the Gentleman Usher of the Black Rod and Rouge Dragon Pursuivant—seemed to be standing in the way of everything worthwhile. There was too much adulation, too much nonsense and snobbery, too much semi-hysterical clap-trap about the simple fact of monarchy.

The headline in an Oxford Labour paper, when Edward VIII succeeded to the throne, seemed to us to put things in truer perspective. It was: "Magdalen Man Makes Good."

We were anti-Religion, which was the same trick done in a different uniform, with hell-fire for dessert. In church, they prayed: "Give us peace *in our time,* oh Lord," which was only another way of saying: "Anything for a quiet life." In Italy, especially, the men of God seemed particularly loathsome, veritable hounds of heaven. They blessed the guns, and absolved the soldiers from all wrong-doing in their sacred cause. No Italian soldier left his native land, *en route* for murder, without a comforting pat on the head, and a swig of Christ's blood to put him in good heart.

At no time during a base regime did the Pope, the seventy-five-year-old ex-Cardinal Ratti, say a single word against Mussolini, or fascism, or this gross example of its progress.

Could one imagine Jesus Christ giving His benediction to the troops setting out for Abyssinia?—blessing the bombers, and the canisters of mustard gas? Would He not rather have been with the Abyssinians, waving their spears against the hideous sky which was now falling on them? Would He really have seen the war (in the words of the *Tribuna,* on the day when Italian war-widows donated their wedding rings to the state) as "the answer of nuptial, prolific, family, and Catholic Italy to the Masonic-plutocratic-Bolshevist-protestant plot of the egoist and Malthusian peoples"?

Pimlicans were anti-Italy, which went without saying; but we were also anti-German, the other half of the Fascist rotten apple, because the Germans were "starting it all over again." German troops were now back in the Rhineland, in defiance of the Versailles Treaty; and Hitler, after ruling uneasily for three years, had just won a resounding, landslide victory in the elections, and on the theme of *"Ein Reich, ein Volk, ein Führer,"* now led a unified nation, and cast baleful eyes on Danzig, on Austria, on "living space," and on the colonies which Germany deserved and would somehow win.

The Germans were on the march once more, mixing threats with tearful appeals, the pounding fist with the bended knee. Ribbentrop, their Ambassador in London, had become, like Count Grandi, the sweetheart of the upper crust. Mr. Chamberlain had "affirmed his personal belief in the sincerity of Herr Hitler's appeal for a negotiated peace." Our own personal belief was something different, but we could not get the floor to say so.

We were anti-Fascist, and especially anti-Fascist at home, where vicious Jew-baiting in the East End, violence by black-shirted men and women "stewards" at Fascist meetings, and a general feeling that the police consistently sided with Oswald Mosley's bully-boys, were poisoning all politics. There was a strong undercurrent of fear and menace, typified by the small-type advertisements for the S.S.-Jaguar motor-car: "FASCISTS NEED FAST CARS."

Anyone who even breathed an opinion contrary to ours was a crypto-Fascist, or, as we called it, a "crypto." Winston Churchill, though he was plugging away all the time at the need to resist Hitler, was a terrible crypto, because he still voted with the Conservatives.

Above all, we were anti-war, anti-recruiting, anti-uniforms, anti-militarism. War was *the* evil, and soldiers, sailors, and airmen *the* bloody fools. Only pacifists, spurning khaki and either shade of blue, were good enough, generous enough, and nice enough to run the world.

As pacifists, as left-wingers, as Pimlicans, we carried two banners and shouted two slogans. The first was: "STOP FASCIST AGGRESSION!" and the second: "REARMAMENT MEANS WAR!" Anyone who did not subscribe to both of these, with equal fervour, was just a crypto.

I carried such a banner, on the May Day March to Hyde Park.

I marched between Jo and Francesca, and we certainly had the prettiest girls in our column-of-route. The other stave of my banner was held by Francesca's young man, a tall, bearded, rather detached Pimlican who was always called Drainpipe, for reasons lost in some schoolboy past which I had not shared. Drainpipe wrote poetry by day, and made love to Francesca at night, and that was all I knew about him. But he was a good, dependable man with a banner.

We both had to be dependable, since there was a brisk wind whipping along the Bayswater Road which, as we neared Hyde Park, attacked our "VICKERS—MERCHANTS OF DEATH!" emblem as if with high explosive. Yet it was a good day, and a brave day, nonetheless. The sun shone brightly, the drum-and-fife band just ahead of us kept up a lilting beat, the mounted policeman who rode at our side seemed actually to be one of us, instead of one of them.

But this view was not everybody's. "Bloody cossacks!" said Francesca, loud enough to be heard, when the policeman's horse brushed against a weaving marcher who might or might not have been drunk. She was in a bad temper. Drainpipe had done something wrong the previous night—or had not done anything, which was infinitely worse. (The story was not clear, and Drainpipe was keeping his own counsel.) The policeman, who looked as much like a brutal cossack as Don Quixote on a mule, stared straight ahead of him.

I found myself wondering if he had his own troubles, just like me: saddle sores, or major and minor debts, or a sergeant forever sitting on his neck, or a nagging wife who waited for him at home, in curlers and a Jaeger dressing-gown, ready to ask where he had been all day, why it was always him that had to do the overtime, why he didn't stick up for himself, just for a change. . . . It was possible that the policeman actually was one of us, after all.

We had been joined, at various check-points along the route, by other contingents from other parts of London; and our column was a mile long, with thickened ranks and waving banners, by the time we reached Marble Arch. Here, to a vast concourse standing silent, or surging towards the platform, or sitting on the grass nursing their sore feet, Harry Pollitt made a good fighting speech, from his hard-line communist viewpoint, and then Attlee, the slightly forlorn leader of the Labour rump-opposition in Parliament, gave us his contribution.

They were both of them good, but their message was the same: all the news was bad. Over great tracts of Europe, the Fascists were on the march, and war preparations multiplied, and the forces of evil prospered, while the Government did nothing but "deplore" it (using Mr. Anthony Eden as chorus-master), and freedom went by default. It could have been put in a single sentence: our side was losing.

We scarcely needed the day's headlines to confirm this. The Abyssinian war was just about lost. Addis Ababa was on the verge of falling; Emperor Haile Selassie was ready for flight. Hitler, sniffing blood, was getting ready to strike—no one knew where, but he had plenty of choice. In Spain, a Fascist revolt was brewing, and must before long plunge the country into misery and bloodshed.

There was nothing to be done on our side, because we had no weapons, and not enough people who gave a damn what happened, as long as it did not spoil the long weekend. We were like the Abyssinians: we had our wretched crooked spears, while the other side had all the weight of armour and all the big battalions, and could get away with murder.

Even at home, Mosley's boys had come out with a brand-new uniform, jack-boots and all, and strutted like fighting-cocks, while the Jew-boys and Red rowdies (that was us) jeered feebly and then slunk away.

It was enough to make one sick, and, on that bright May afternoon, it suddenly made me sick. It was like Nottingham all over again: I felt that I had to get away, and breathe some better air. Forty-eight hours later, this was exactly what happened.

Jo's only living relative, an aunt in North Wales, fell ill, and had to be visited, and looked after. I could not go to Wales with her, for reasons of propriety. Instead, I bade her a temporary goodbye, and went for a wonderful walk, across the Pyrenees.

In Pamplona, as my money was about to run out, and it was clear that I must go home and earn or borrow some more, instead of moving on to Madrid, a fantastic page was turned. At the Post Office, there was a cable among my letters, from my agent in London. It was short, and sweet indeed: PLAY ACCEPTED. JULY PRODUCTION WITH GREER GARSON. RETURN SOONEST.

The play was called *The Visitor,* and it was my very first effort. It had its roots in the redemption of man, and its head firmly clamped in the clouds. It was all about a poor young socialist playwright who was picked up by the beautiful daughter of a stockbroker in Hyde Park (she had just quarrelled with her fiancé) and brought home to stay until his play could be produced.

After he had converted the entire household to socialism, his play was a flop, and he walked out into the night again, insulting his benefactors, taking a final snap at the hands that fed him, and intent only on commercial success. ("He showed his hairy heel, didn't he?" remarked my father.) The girl married the steady fiancé after all.

The play had some good lines, and the profound misconceptions on which it was based (e.g., that you have only to tell a London stockbroker that he is a social parasite in order to have him hang his head and repent overnight) enshrined some of my dearest convictions. It also had some very good people in the cast.

The fact that Greer Garson was going to be the star was a tremendous stroke of luck. She had then just sky-rocketed onto the West End stage, as Vivien Leigh had done, a little time before; she was young, beautiful, talented, and glamorous—*the* name of that year. She must have seen something in *The Visitor,* even if it was only impudence, because she could have had her pick of half-a-dozen other plays; and as soon as she was signed up, the money, the theater, and the rest of the casting all fell into line, almost automatically.

Money sprouted on trees; the theater—Daly's, in Leicester Square—was ours for as long as we wanted it; and the cast-list was a very respectable sample of London's current "safe name" players. Aubrey Dexter was the long-suffering father, and Guy Middleton the patient fiancé. Margaret Scudamore played the mother, with all the authority of a long West End career, capped by the fact that she was also the actual mother of Michael Redgrave.

As the red-blooded radical interloper, the "visitor" of the title, we had a Dutch actor called Louis Borell, who had made a sudden name for himself as an imported "leading man," with threatening sexual overtones, and looked like a winner in every sense of the word.

Louis had only one greeting, for any woman between the ages of twenty and ninety. *"Ich küss' die Hand,"* he would murmur, and bow low, and nuzzle like a browsing goat. "He kisses their hands right up to the elbow!" complained Aubrey Dexter, who was regretfully past the age for such outlandish goings-on. "You can see them *quivering!*"

I was only envious. Louis Borell—a blond European menace, beautifully groomed, insidious and appealing, fluent in the whole language of love—was all that I hoped to be. He was also just the kind of man we needed, to make the "visitor" come to convincing life.

I met them all, as soon as I came hot-foot back to London, and after that there began a very exciting six weeks of rehearsal. To me, it was all new: the whole world of the theater, fantastically enclosed and self-regarding, was wildly exciting from the first moment I set foot in it. I could never quite get used to the behind-the-scenes sweat which produced the elegant, effortless spectacle on stage; and the daily crises, the quarrels, the spiteful feuds, the male and female bitchiness, the universal, meaningless *"Darling!,"* the life-long friendships which could be shattered by a chance word during the lunch-time break—all these made up a brand-new set of tribal customs, undreamt-of, scarcely credible, like making love with a giant clam, or eating with the feet.

I could never get used to being suddenly important: to being waylaid by actors who wanted to say it this way instead of that way: to calls for two extra lines of dialogue, preferably brilliant, while the stage waited, and the man checking the bulbs in the footlights broke off to listen for the unborn gem.

When Greer Garson said: "Darling, please help me," I would have died to do so. When Margaret Scudamore, a stately old treasure, asked: "Nicholas, do you really think—" I was ready to re-think the entire play, for her alone. When Guy Middleton protested: "Good God, old boy, I can't be such a bloody fool as *that!*" it was an enormous pleasure to convince him that he could.

I had never been anything before. Suddenly I was The Author, the manipulator of all these charming, talented lunatics. There had been nothing to match this power to move, since I had first told Jo to lie back, and had stroked and coaxed and spread her into the ready attitude of love.

Jo, unfairly, was rather forgotten in all this whirl of fortune.

She was the background; down-stage and center (I had picked up the jargon very quickly) was my cast, and surrounding the cast was a whole new world of glamorous, brittle make-believe. I lunched at the Ivy, and at Rules' in Maiden Lane, and at Quo Vadis. I had free tickets to see other people's plays. I met players who had so far only been names: Diana Churchill, in the ever-running *The Dominant Sex,* and Rex Harrison, now charming the whole town in another boundless success, *French Without Tears.*

I stared enviously at Noel Coward and Ivor Novello, who never wrote anything less than rousing hits; and yearningly at Peggy Ashcroft, an exquisite young woman who, playing opposite John Gielgud and Edith Evans in *The Seagull,* made the very stage glow where'er she walked.

But it was with his own leading lady that The Author, traditionally, fell in love.

The attachment was not mutual, and thus remained in eclipse, which was just as well, since I had squandered nearly all my advance royalties from the play, and, penniless again, could scarcely have bought her a cup of coffee to cement our union. But who could *not* have fallen in love with Greer Garson, at such a moment of time? She was a most beautiful girl, as all the world knows, with splendid red hair, a pale skin, and a generous sense of humour. She had brains as well—and it seems idiotic to speak of her in the past, since she had, even then, made plans to be immortal.

Once, when we were sitting in the Savoy Gardens, near the river-bank, enjoying the lunch-time sun before we went back to slavery on the stage at Daly's, she said, out of the blue: "I'm *not* going to grow old gracefully. I'm going to stay like this till I'm sixty: then I'll go into retreat for a couple of months, and press a button, and suddenly reappear as an old woman with blue hair."

When I said that I wanted to be there to see it, she smiled, and shook her head, and answered: "This is our time."

Our time was innocent, as her answer was innocent. She knew that I was ready to adore her, that I was broke, that one day I would make, with luck, another small chunk of money, and spend it on some other girl. She was a realist, a lovely young prodigy a hundred years older than I would ever be.

She had toiled in repertory theater for years, as I had toiled in free-lance writing. She had played bits, just as I had written bits. But in the process she had learned all, and I had learned nothing—nothing but how to make more mistakes, dream fruitlessly, and zigzag between the "Yes" of bright hope and the absolute "No" of defeat.

A few days before the opening, she said: "If this play doesn't work, write another one, straight away." Typically, I only heard half of this. "Oh, I'll write lots more plays," I assured her. "But only if you'll be in them."

"Any time," she answered. But already, like any other actress, she had taken off on a private voyage, with no room for passengers. "In the last act, when Louis jumps on the table, don't you think I would say—"

The play took shape, the excitement mounted, the first night drew near. We had costume rehearsals, and lighting rehearsals, and a flurry of last-minute changes. There was the name, *The Visitor,* on all the posters; there was *my* name outside the theater, and photographs of the cast, and an open window at the box-office.

Suddenly a line of "sandwich-men" was shuffling down Regent Street, their message proclaiming: "Tonight at 8:15. *The Visitor,* by Nicholas Monsarrat," repeating the notice which had appeared in all the morning papers, from *The Times* to the *News Chronicle.* The show was on, and I was in raptures, and sick with nervousness at the same time. It was essential for *The Visitor* to be a roaring success.

I arrived, dressed as the author (white tie and tails) at the somewhat absurd hour of six o'clock. The stage-door-keeper, an old unruffled man who had seen 'em come and seen 'em go, for the last quarter-century, greeted me between bites from an enormous cheese sandwich.

"Well," he said, "you're not going to miss 'God Save The King,' are you?" Then he handed me a bunch of telegrams, mostly from loyal relatives, said: "Good luck, sir," and went back to his supper. I envied him, as I used to envy the boot-boy at Winchester.

He was safely out of the line of fire, he didn't have my worries. . . .

I wandered about, first through the deserted dressing-rooms, smelling of sweat and powder and stale grease-paint, and then on stage, where the set ("A Drawing-room in Park Lane") stood waiting for the action. It was empty, like the dressing-rooms, save for two men checking the essential props ('Cigarette-box —right! Table-lighter—right! Flowers on mantelpiece—right! Whisky decanter and six glasses—right!"). They nodded to me, but I was far from being an essential prop, and they went back to their job without comment, while I stepped down into the auditorium.

The dust-sheets still covered the rows of seats, and the whole place looked like a grey-white desert. In the foyer, a vast pile of programs, newly delivered, was stacked on a side table, and I picked one up, with a rare feeling of accomplishment. I still could not get over *"The Visitor,* by Nicholas Monsarrat." . . . I read the program from cover to cover, advertisements and all. Stalls, 12s. 6d. Dress Circle, 10s. 6d. Gallery, 1s. 6d. Cigarettes by Abdullah. This theater is disinfected throughout with Jeyes' Fluid. An evening gown from Debenham and Freebody cost eight and a half guineas. Size forty-eight and over, one guinea extra.

People began to arrive, and Daly's Theatre warmed to sudden, nervous, overwhelming life.

I had once thought that nothing could ever match the excitement of holding in my hand the first copy of *Think of Tomorrow,* hot from the printer, a couple of years earlier; but this night topped everything. I was twenty-six, and this was my first play, and it was opening in the West End, and people were actually trooping in to see it. . . .

Backstage, the cast were busy making up. There were kisses, and handshakes, and best wishes, but everyone concerned seemed excruciatingly calm. Aubrey Dexter was applying eye-shadow with a hand as steady as Gibraltar. Louis Borell's dressing-room was full of old women, cooing like contented doves. Guy Middleton said: "It simply can't miss, old boy!" Greer Garson, absolutely lovely in the green evening dress she wore for the first act, thanked me for my flowers, and gave me a kiss for luck—our first and (to be entirely accurate) our last as well.

When I wandered onto the stage, and peeped through the curtain, there was my father, bless him, sitting bang in the middle of the stalls, reading the program as attentively as I had done myself.

All the family was there, though it was not exactly a close reunion. Mother and Felicity had one of the stage boxes, and Denys was in the dress circle, with Meryl Wardle, the girl he was to marry three years later. Jo, Francesca, and Drainpipe, wearing clothes for which they must have ransacked all Pimlico, were near my father in the stalls. They had not been introduced.

The orchestra began to tune up, and I sped back to the lavatory.

It went off perfectly, that whole evening. There were no missed cues, no fluffs, no dry-ups, no awkward pauses. People laughed in most of the right places, and none of the wrong ones. When the final curtain rang down, there was more than enough applause to justify the author's coming out of hiding (behind his mother, at the back of the stage box), and making a modest speech. Greer was wonderful, Louis made the female half of the audience sigh throughout, Guy Middleton almost deserved to win.

I was wringing wet, and wildly happy. *The Visitor* had come to stay, and I had done it all, with my little eye and my little typewriter.

Next morning, reaction set in, and continued for the rest of the week, prompted by small houses, and notices which were quotable but not really compelling. The reviews were mixed— really mixed, not just plainly awful. They ranged from James Agate's forthright opening sentence "This is a silly little play about a half-wit" to the *Sunday Dispatch*'s "I hope this play is a success. It should be."

The *Daily Telegraph* said it had "a certain engaging freshness." The *Observer* said that the author "has theatre sense and the courage of his romantic convictions." The *Morning Post* said he had "undoubted promise as well as ambition." The *Daily Mail* conceded that "the play was well received." Everyone agreed that Greer Garson was terrific.

Nobody came to see it.

The theater, lavishly "papered," always looked full (not for us that terrible verdict: "Even the hospital nurses won't use the free tickets") but the actual paying customers were few. There were all sorts of excuses. The weather was too hot. People were worrying about Spain, and the Fascists, and the unemployed, and the attack on the King in Hyde Park. We had some serious opposition from established favourites like *Night Must Fall* and *Tonight at 8:30*. But the hateful, unarguable fact was that receipts fell off, until we were not even averaging fifty pounds a night.

Though we stumbled hopefully on for three weeks, *The Visitor* never looked like a winner. Presently it languished, and died.

The fact that Daly's began to die with it, and was pulled down and replaced by Warner's Cinema, and that Greer Garson very soon left the stage forever, to be seen next in M.G.M.'s *Goodbye, Mr. Chips,* could hardly be laid at my door. But I was bitterly disappointed. It had all been wonderfully exciting, and the play *had* been produced; yet it was a failure instead of a success. Hungry for money, thirsty for fame, I could no more endure public failure on the stage than some feeble private shortcoming in bed.

I walked and hitch-hiked all the way to Trearddur Bay that summer, sweating out a certain sad dissatisfaction with every single thing in life, muttering *"Time is the dog which barks us all to hell"* at intervals. For the most part, this was proving rather a good year; but one could not dress up *The Visitor* as anything less than a defeat. I didn't want to write another play; I wanted to lick my wounds, and finish the novel I was working on, and sail, alone, as much as I could. Trearddur Bay was the only place to make for.

It was wonderful, as usual, though some important rules were now changed. My "summer girl," just married, was not there, and could never be counted on again; and Hafod itself was not there either—Mother had sold it, straight after "the separation," and we had lost all our rights to this heavenly corner of the coast.

Instead, we camped out at a local farmhouse, which was shabby and cramped, but had one prime blessing—a daily supply of delicious Welsh farm butter, fresh and moist from the churn, rich enough to be sloshed onto scones or soda-bread, and eaten without anything else to help it down. It was butter to be remembered for years afterwards, when the same honoured name was used for the oily, chemicalized substitute, laced with preservative, frozen and stockpiled for at least two years, which took its place.

For the rest, nothing of Trearddur was altered, and nothing lost. Denys had the edge in racing, but I did not mind that; I thought that he deserved it. (It was good to hear, in the same way, that Peter Scott, a Cambridge friend, had won a bronze medal, sailing at the Olympics.) The sun shone, the fair weather made one forget the bad, the creamy wake which spread out astern of *Ptah* as she wandered up and down the coast was a clean, dependable pattern in a troublesome world.

There were some girls, but nothing to cast a shadow on the record-books; if I wanted anyone, it was Jo, and, she away, I settled for innocence.

When I had finished the book,* and perfected my sun-tan, and loitered till the summer's end, I strapped my pack on my shoulders, feeling much better after this swim in quiet waters, and went back to London, and to life.

Everything was on in London: it was as rich a world as ever, even for poor people, since there was a fraternity of the poor and the loving which served as a pass-word, taking the place of money. Somehow, seats could always be wangled, and free passes slipped from hand to hand; there was always a friend of a friend who knew the producer, or the first violin, or the theater-manager, and knew also how to strike the hidden vein of tickets which penniless Pimlicans had to have.

I got back in time to see the last few performances of the Ballets Russes de Monte Carlo, at Covent Garden, which for me was my favourite entertainment in the whole world.

There was no trouble about tickets here; seats in the gallery (five towering stories up) cost two shillings, and if this meant queueing for six hours to get anywhere near the front, then we were more than ready to do so. (*Balletomanes* was the new word for such enthusiasts: that was us, every night of the week.) The distinguished company was headed by Massine, Danilova, and Lichine; and there was a trio of what we called the "little girls"— Baronova, Toumanova, and Riabouchinska—who, night after night, drove us all wild with delight.

Then, as now, it was almost impossible to describe ballet in

* *The Whipping Boy* (Jarrolds, 1937, Pan Books, 1969).

words, just as one ran into a word-block with music itself. It was easy enough to swap jargon about *jeté* and *entrechat* and *fouetté,* in the same way as one reeled off *legato* and *rallentando* and *con amore.* But these were only words, bare of feeling; one needed actual pictures—pictures in the eye and the ear—to communicate to another person what music really meant.

The delight, like the delight of sex, had to remain private. There were no words for an orgasm; there were no words for certain moments in *Les Sylphides,* or *Lac des Cygnes,* or *Petrushka.*

One could only say: I *love* that passage, or I *love* the moment when—. So it was with a ballet like *Le Beau Danube,* with Massine heel-clicking as the proud Hussar, and the gorgeous Riabouchinska as the pure patrician innocent who overcame the shop-soiled wiles of Danilova. So it was with *La Boutique Fantasque,* with its sad toys and happy ending. So it was with Schumann's *Carnaval,* and its gentle, heart-rending moment of appeal, which the program-notes could only label lamely as "Chiarina, in in a mask, enters. . . ." So it was with *Symphonie Fantastique,* the "Episodes in the life of an artist," to which Berlioz gave his masterly music, and Leonide Massine the tremendous complement of his own art.

It was a beautiful ballet in itself, and it gave me a precious cross-reference to the music of Berlioz as well. Until then, I had sworn that, except for Brahms, no one later than Chopin could ever seduce me. But *Symphonie Fantastique* was in some ways a "visual" symphony, as well as all the rest. It conjured up pictures, and it needed pictures: pictures of happiness, in the waltz theme of the ballroom: gruesome pictures like the Procession to the Scaffold, with that hideous double bounce of the guillotined head at the end; eerie and wicked pictures like the Witches' Sabbath, "scored for clarinet and broomstick" (and how I wished I had said that, instead of Donald Tovey).

There were two other "symphony ballets" that year: *Choreartium,* which was Brahms' Fourth, and *Les Présages,* the Fifth Symphony of Tchaikowsky. They were not all that I came to see and hear; I still retained the softest spot in my whole heart for the finale of *Le Beau Danube,* when it all came out right, and the grand chain of dancers circled and surged and leaped, as the music itself leaped, to prove the triumph of love over base intrigue.

But suddenly to "see" a symphony, as well as hear it, was not only a delight; it was another notch on the gun-handle of knowing, another gain, another area of awareness won, another dividend from this overflowing world of miracles.

Some people kept lists of women. I kept a list of such discoveries in pleasure, a list of newly charted blessings. It was at least as long as other men's boasted weapons, and, fresh each day, it could never fail me.

There was one other oddment, scarcely over the horizon, in this unfolding reconnaissance. Drainpipe had a rich cousin who made bathroom taps, by the thousand, every day of his life; he was referred to, rudely, as the Lavatory Man, and the Lavatory Man actually owned a television set. Occasionally we used to drop in to watch this unheard-of marvel; the flickering pictures, the real people and real sounds coming out of this deadwood box, were new enough to seem absolutely miraculous.

It was another invention made especially for me, like all the other prime discoveries of the last twenty-six years. My father's nominee, John Logie Baird, was still prominent in the television contest, though the Marconi system was coming to be preferred; in any case, there were now regular B.B.C. broadcasts from Alexandra Palace—mostly of tap-dancers and cabaret shows—to be picked up, if, like the Lavatory Man, one owned one of these rare machines.

I once drove out to Alexandra Palace with Greer Garson, and there, on exhibition, was Baird's original television set, described (even by the inventor) as being made of "bits of old bicycle, cocoa-tins, magic lantern lenses, sealing-wax, and string," at a total cost of 7s. 8d. But the thing worked, and no later refinement could add to the basic, astonishing feat of sending invisible pictures flying through the air, and into the window, and then out of the front of the set itself.

I had escorted Greer so that she could perform in the very first play ever presented in this medium—an adaptation of James Elroy Flecker's *Hassan,* with Greer, as Yasmin, looking as if she could indeed spark the despairing words of Hassan's appeal:

Shine down thy love, O burning bright!
for one night or the other night
Will come the Gardener in white
and gathered flowers are dead, Yasmin!

It was most strange that they should choose Flecker for a trial of such unearthly magic. In *To a Poet, a Thousand Years Hence,* he had once written:

I send my soul through time and space
To greet you. You will understand.

Exactly.

Politics, and what was happening in politics, and in war, which was their natural extension, were making us all restless as well as angry. The Abyssinian invasion had ended disgracefully, with the capital in flames and the Emperor, scarred by mustard gas, fleeing to England, there to find a cool official welcome, and a curious shuffling diversion of his arrival procession via the back streets of Waterloo, by-passing the crowds waiting to cheer him.

After that, Collective Security was simply a matter for the undertakers, who sprang to their shovels with a will.

Already there was another war to play with, and, if you were interested in that sort of market, to bet on. The civil war in Spain was now raging, with all the barbarous cruelty with which brother could fall upon brother. It had been set off by simultaneous "garrison uprisings," the army against the Republican Government, in Madrid, Seville, Cadiz, Saragossa, Cordoba, and Malaga: a synchronization which, whatever one thought of the motives, said a good deal for the army's communications.

Madrid had been bombed, and (as the rebels advanced) the government evacuated to Barcelona; now massacre and counter-massacre, red terror and black murder, and a senseless rage had taken possession of both sides. Hostages were shot, prisoners thrown into wells; one could match a crucified priest with a castrated village mayor, any hour of the day. In the headline war, "RED BEAUTY QUEEN TORTURES 28 NUNS" could be trumped by "FASCISTS TOSS HAND-GRENADES INTO HOSPITAL BEDS."

"Non-intervention" was the official watchword in England, even though both Germany and Italy were sending arms and troops to help General Franco, and Russia was replying with aid for the other side. A merry "Irish Brigade" set off from Dublin to do battle for Holy Church, finding themselves in the same nest as the much less merry Moorish troops whom Franco reimported (after three hundred years) to slice up some of the ingredients for this stew.

Faces missing in Pimlico meant that certain of the inhabitants had also taken off (instead of just talking about it, like the rest of us) to join the astonishingly mixed bag—socialists, communists, anarchists, republicans, syndicalists, trades-union stalwarts, and plain democrats—which backed and fought for the lawful government of Spain.

But Spain was a losing battlefield, as far as our side was concerned, though we did not accept this, even when four columns of the enemy were at the very gates of Madrid, and the murderous siege began, and Franco, coining a brand-new phrase, boasted of a "Fifth Column" within the city, waiting to rise up in revolt. We did not accept, either, that all this brutish blood-letting was only a dress rehearsal, and Spain a cheap testing-ground for new weapons, new techniques, even new colours of uniform.

We thought that the chief, most blatant interventionists, the Germans and Italians, really cared about Spain. We could not know that the Germans, particularly, were only practicing, and that any populated battle-ground would have served. Hitler had received the message, loud and clear, from what had happened when Italy attacked Abyssinia: that the rest of the world was selfish and preoccupied, that a man with a mission could get away with murder, provided it was swift and brutal enough, and he called it something else.

His "volunteer" troops in Spain were nicknamed, with loathsome cynicism, *"Moros Rubios"*—Blond Moors. They too were only practicing.

We were worrying about the humanities; about his Jew-hating aide, Julius Streicher, who proclaimed: "There is only one answer to the Jewish question: Extirpation!" We should have worried more about other things: about Hitler's carefully balanced growling, screaming, and begging for "living-space," for colonies, for Germany's just rights; about his Ambassador to Britain, Herr von Ribbentrop, ladling out the champagne at Carlton House

Terrace and turning the fat heads of diplomatic London with strange alarming talk of a Jewish-bolshevist plot against Europe.

We were confused; Hitler was not. We were worrying about political morality; he was concerned with weapons, strength, allies, neutrals, and exact timing. We knew that Europe was going to hell, and we were angry with our Conservatives for doing no more than make formal noises of disapproval.

It was the wrong thing to be angry about, and anger was the wrong reaction anyway. Winston Churchill, as it turned out, had the right reaction: Arm with all speed, look to your moat, jump the gun if you have to. But Churchill—damn it!—was such a crypto.

I was nearest to communism at this time, like nearly all my friends. As politics grew more savage still, we longed for action, even while we shunned it. The Labour Party—*our* party—was doing nothing; and as well as being ineffective, it was so damned *dull.* Churchill, for once, had been dead right when he said, of a prominent Labour politician: "He uses every cliché except 'Please adjust your dress before leaving.' " *

More than ever, the Fascists seemed to have the initiative, holding their disciplined meetings, getting away with Jew-baiting marches into the East End of London, snarling their song: *"Yids, Yids, we've got to get rid of the Yids!"* as they swung along to victory. England had its Oswald Mosley, and France its Colonel de la Rocque, leading the *Croix de Feu.* Belgian Fascists rallied to Léon Degrelle. All we had in Pimlico was Mr. Attlee, and a Labour Party which seemed to have lost its mainspring somewhere on the way.

On the Left, only the Communists seemed militant, and ready to fight this declared enemy. I very nearly joined them—they used to hand out membership leaflets at the Friends of the Soviet Union film shows, and it would have been very easy to sign up. But something always put me off—the people, or their fatuous slogans, or the fact that I simply did not believe in the idea of using force to advance an idea. If the idea were any good, it would advance by its own momentum.

I used to tune in, late at night, to Radio Barcelona, the anti-

* Notice displayed in (male) public lavatories. There were other cautionary advertisements for, or rather against, venereal disease.

Franco station: the thin, fading, faraway call-sign: *"E-A-Jota-Uno.*
. . . Here is news from the front,"* made the small hours, when
England was asleep, come vividly and painfully alive. Since the
station invited listeners to send in their comments, and report the
sort of reception they were getting, I wrote a couple of times,
and got answers back again.

The answering letters, innocuous enough ("Dear Comrade,
Thank you for your interest. We are pleased at good reception.
Arriba España!"), had always been opened, somewhere between
Barcelona and London, and then resealed, without subterfuge.
Perversely, I hoped this meant I had qualified for my own secu-
rity file, with black marks on it already.

If I did not fight, at least I could suffer social stigma; because,
when all the weighing-up was done, and all the horrors had cancelled each other out, the wrong people were winning in Spain,
and might win forever; and it seemed much more important to
be counted, publicly, on the losing side than to be neutral and
safe.

The hunger marchers from Jarrow, the Tyneside ship-building
town still plagued by vicious unemployment, were with us again.
They had marched their three hundred miles, in straggling ranks,
in twenty-seven days; they were fed, and sheltered, and had their
socks darned, and were offered money wherever they passed, all
the way down the spine of England, in villages, in grimy towns,
in neat "garden city" suburbs—a heartening display of sympathy
which really did make one feel that, in this country at least, the
idea of One World had made a tiny beginning.

I was one of the "marshals" for the last ten miles before the
arrival in Hyde Park, a job which involved nothing more than
wandering up and down the ranks with a red arm-band to prove
my importance, and a certain dividend of personal good-will from
the London crowds—something else I did not really deserve. It
was pouring with rain nearly all the time; occasionally, as we
trudged southwards down the Edgware Road, I shared an old
Army ground-sheet, and some spirited conversation, with the
Jarrow M.P., the diminutive, red-headed, tireless Ellen Wilkin-
son, who had marched two hundred miles with them, and would
still have been ready to take on Stanley Baldwin in single combat
at the end of the journey.

They had a very warm welcome in London also, from the most unexpected people—from cinema managers who offered free tickets, from Conservative borough councils who made all sorts of accommodation available, from prim men with rolled umbrellas who thrust one-pound notes into the collecting boxes, as furtively as if they had actually been petty thieves.

But when all was over, and the last speech made, the marchers just went home again by train, with nothing except florid promises of "sympathetic and active consideration" to show for their sweat and sore feet; and I went home also, under the drab and weeping November skies, to my own warm nest.

The march, I felt, hadn't done any good, because it wouldn't change anything. The brief spark of brotherhood, the welcome warm enough to make the eyelids prick, would not last out the weekend. Tomorrow London would be the same, and the world would be the same—and Jo and I were just as bad as anyone else, because we had carved out our own secure haven for ourselves alone, as selfishly as any company director and his strapped-up, purse-proud, sniffy wife, and there we lived in a loving harmony which we did not deserve.

There had been a derisive phrase in a recent *New Statesman* book-review, of some tender-hearted pinkish philanthropist: "He can't forgive himself for not being an unemployed cotton-operative on the dole." I felt exactly like that: guilty, convicted of happiness in a world of misery, and damned glad of it.

But at home in Churton Street, there was worse to come, and I swallowed it with never a gulp.

We went to bed as soon as I got in, because I had been away nearly two days, and that was the way we still felt about separation, short or long. But later on the post arrived, and Jo padded out into the hall to pick up the letters (we had agreed from the start that men got much more tired than women), and brought back some news.

"How lovely!" she exclaimed (and I could have said that to her, too). "Aunt Margaret left me her motor-car."

"Oh." I had been hoping for money, but there were some other claimants who must have been preferred. However, a car was a car. "When do you get it?"

"Now, if I like." She sat down on the edge of the bed, and

started to quote from the letter. "It's from old What's-his-name—one of the executors." She began to mimic old What's-his-name, who seemed to have a lemon stuck up his nose. " 'Though in a technical sense we cannot transfer ownership until probate is obtained'—what's that mean?"

I explained about probate.

" '—until probate is obtained,' " Jo continued, " 'yet since the car is eating its head off in the stables—' "

"Are you sure about this?" I interrupted.

"The garage *was* the stables," she explained. "It only has hens now." She went back to the letter. "Well, anyway—blah, blah, blah—I can use the car now, if I want to. It's free of duty—that's good, isn't it? But I have to sign a form that I'll pay the legacy duty if the estate is bankrupt. What does *that* mean?"

"Nothing. What sort of car is it?"

"That's the silly part," answered Jo. She looked up at me and smiled suddenly; she meant, really, that it was I who was silly about cars, and that she forgave me in advance. "It's a Rolls-Royce."

Jo had been right to smile; I came to life as if a trumpet had sounded. "A *Rolls!* What sort of Rolls? Is it an old one?"

"Quite old."

"But what does it look like? Have you actually seen it?"

"Oh, yes. I walked round it when I was getting the wheelbarrow."

"Well?"

But Jo wasn't much help. "It has very big lamps," she said finally.

"They all do!"

"Then that's all right, then." But she was not as indifferent as she seemed. "Darling, I know you'll love it. So let's celebrate! Let's drive somewhere—the Continent, somewhere like that."

"I can't afford it. I'm down to the bones of my arse again."

"Don't be so ——ing crude!" said Jo crisply. Then she tried a more gentle approach. "It needn't cost much. I've got fifteen pounds, anyway."

"We can't drive round Europe with a Rolls and fifteen pounds."

"Why not? We can stay at awful hotels. And we could practically live in the car, if we had to."

We argued the point for a while. The temptation was strong indeed.

"All right," I said, before very long. "I could raise about seven pounds. That makes twenty-two. We can go quite a long way for that."

"I want to go to Budapest."

"Why not?"

"Shall we take the others with us?"

That meant Francesca and Drainpipe.

"No."

I had a good reason for this prompt refusal. Francesca was always cross with me these days; she wanted me to marry Jo, and she suspected that I was moving further away from it instead of nearer to it. This was almost a policy decision. I kept remembering something my father had said to me, years ago, in oblique reference to the fact that I was always getting engaged to unlikely candidates.

"In the medical profession," he had told me carefully, "we know that when a man gets married, he is quite useless, as far as his job is concerned, for about two years. After that, he gets over it, and goes back to serious work again."

I had been shocked, even then, by this dismissal of women as frivolous *impedimenta,* who had to be "got over" before one's life could settle down again to the essentials. When the time came, I wanted it to be quite the reverse: I *wanted* marriage to make me "quite useless," in exactly the sense my father meant it. I was determined to become tied, and dedicated, and entranced, and preoccupied with sex as the natural end of every day, and love as the focus of all.

I did not want to tire of the girl, and then go back to the typewriter. I wanted to tire of the typewriter, and go back to the girl, who would make sense of this exhaustion, and repair it, and cancel it all out, and send me back to the typewriter again like a bird taking wing in the morning.

This would never be true with Jo, I knew already. I loved her, and often longed for her; I was sure that I would do so for quite a long time yet. But, sadly, there would come a day—and that was the day I hoped would never dawn—when I finally got married.

So I said "No," aloud, to Francesca's coming with us, and "No," under my breath, to marriage at this moment. But I certainly said "Yes," with rare and selfish pleasure, to the Rolls, and to "driving somewhere" with Jo, and to Budapest on the blue, blue Danube as our distant goal.

The car, when we went to fetch it from North Wales, turned out to be a superb forty/fifty horsepower Phantom, about ten years old. It had only done twenty-six thousand miles, which in Rolls-Royce language meant that it had still hardly been run in. It was one of the new "owner-driver" models, which in turn ensured that the front seat was just as comfortable as the back, and that we were sumptuously sheltered from the wind and the rain.

This chariot made an enormous sensation in Pimlico, where cars tended to be smaller, or non-existent; even the Lavatory Man only had a Lagonda. When the day came, we left London in high style, with promises to Francesca and Drainpipe to meet them in Paris for Christmas. We carried a tent, and a Primus stove, and lots of tins of pork-and-beans. We had twenty-two pounds, and a car worth about two thousand pounds.

I felt guilty about the Rolls, and the Jarrow marchers, and the feeling of escape, until we drove off the boat at Calais. But there, the rattling cobblestones and the "driving on the wrong side" through roads lined with marching poplars, were twin signals of basic change; and after that we had a wonderful time.

There was a fantastic sense of freedom in beginning to wander at will, steering anywhere we chose to point that distinguished Rolls radiator. We did not like the way the world was going; but in the meantime, this charmed corner of it was ours, and we could take the best of it, instead of fearing the worst—a habit which had been poisoning the last few months.

I think we both had the idea that, with all that was going on, and all that threatened, this might be for us a sort of "last round-up" of Europe before the roof fell in, and we made the most of our chance.

We skirted Paris, because we planned to come back there later on, and drove straight for Austria instead. Our route took us through Strasbourg, and across the Rhine, and through the silent brooding pines of the Black Forest, and then deep into Southern Germany. The main stop was Munich—a city of grim foreboding for Pimlicans, because it was here that Hitler had started his thrust for power, and here—if the hordes of clumping, jack-booted S.A. men thronging the streets, and the hateful chalked *"Juden Raus!"* signs,* were anything to go by—that this power was now flowering rankly.

It was here that, with absolutely no personal justification, I was especially proud of the lordly Rolls, which made even the long-nosed black Mercedes in which the party elite roared through the streets seem vulgar and intrusive. There had been reports, a month or so earlier, of a vast national savings-scheme towards the buying, by every German adult, of a "People's Car"—literally a *"Volks Wagen,"* which would give them all the freedom of the great open road.

Volkswagens, so it was said, were to come off the assembly line by the million in the very near future, as a reward for all faithful supporters who kept up their payments for the next few years. . . . It sounded like a swindle; but the *Volkswagen* had become an article of belief, like Hitlerism, like "the myth of the Good Jew," like Germany's destiny, like millions of marching feet treading down all opposition.

I had a vision of *Volkswagens* swarming all over the Rolls, like rats or fleas. Let them just try it. . . . It was a relief to cross into Austria, still "the other Germany" where they remained sane and happy and liberal; and it was a special delight to come back to Salzburg.

I had been there, for the Festival, the year before, and I had a wonderful set of twenty-four photographs of Toscanini conducting at the *Festspielhaus,* and a souvenir program of *Jedermann,* to prove it. But the Festival of this year was long over; Toscanini was gone, and Lotte Lehmann, and Bruno Walter, and all the other stars which made this firmament glow, year after year. We were too late for music, and too late for me to wear my *Lederhosen,* the romantic leather shorts which I had carefully cherished and carefully brought back with me. I did try once, but when my knees began to turn blue I knew that the *Lederhosen* season was over. The prudent natives knew this already, and were now muffled up in cloaks.

---

* "Jews Get Out!" Sometimes even more curtly scrawled as "J ↓ ."

Yet Salzburg itself, and the mountain-like country round about
it—the Salzkammergut—was magnificently rewarding. Here we
really did wander, and waste time, and squander our Schillings.
Here was a paradise hardly to be imagined in England, hardly
in the same world as begrimèd Pimlico. Here were small gems of
villages like Fuschl and St. Gilgen: toy lakes like the Mondsee
(a "moon-lake" indeed) with toy ferry boats threading to and fro
across them: mountains forever capped with snow, water forever
emerald or blue, a sky forever pure.

Here was the famous White Horse Inn at St. Wolfgang: free
of tourists, and now just an inn, a simple haven where we could
sit on the terrace, and drink Niersteiner, and watch the funny
little trains chuffing along the edge of the lake, stopping hopefully
at each *Strandbad* to pick up swimmers who had left weeks before.

Here we gathered wild strawberries, and wandered into tiny
churches so incredibly baroque that they seemed top-heavy, like
a mad chef's wedding-cake. Here we camped out, deep in the
mountain shadows which curtained the lake as soon as the sun
went down. Here we slept in the Rolls, and, as Jo said, "christened it."

Here she said to me, brewing coarse-ground coffee on the
Primus: "Why can't we live like this forever?" and I answered:
"This may not last forever"—a sad thought for a happy morning,
but prompted by the fact that yesterday, for the first time, in
answer to our friendly country greeting of *"Grüss Gott,"* the passing young man had countered with *"Heil!"* and marched past us
without another word.

It had been like a drop of poison in clear and sunny water, a
single dark drop, strong enough to infect the whole source.

We counted our money, and moved on.

Vienna was next: noble Vienna, lively Vienna, cynical and
faded Vienna, which had seen history come and go, and never
been a penny the better for it since 1815, when the Congress
danced there to celebrate the fall of Napoleon, under the crocodile eyes of Metternich and Talleyrand. We stayed at an out-of-
the-way hotel which was just like Vienna itself: it was still elegant, but had seen better days, it was out-of-date and did not care
a rap, it must assuredly be pulled down before very long. Our
room was lofty, and hung with magnificent, tattered brocade; the

bed was like a fat gondola, the lift a gilded cage which responded, very slowly, very gently, with certain interior groans, to a tug on the worn rope.

It all reminded me, irresistibly, of another delightful old ruin— the Cavendish Hotel in London, presided over by Rosa Lewis, reputed friend of royalty and undoubted mistress of her present domain. The Cavendish had the same air of inevitable, regal decay. I had only been there once, with Gentil-Jones; he had said, "Let's go and see old Rosa," at eleven o'clock one bright morning, and we had made our way by musty corridors into a sort of Edwardian parlour, so crammed with photographs that there was scarcely room for people.

A champagne party was in progress; everyone seemed to be an Old Etonian except myself and Rosa Lewis, who did not need to be anything but a fabled beauty now more at home in a twilight room. An hour later, there was some question of a bill. "I'll sign for this, Rosa," said G.J. readily. "You have, dear," said Mrs. Lewis, and that was that. One early look from those sharp, knowing, bewrinkled eyes had told her that, as a champagne-party-giver, I could be counted out.

But in Vienna, at this other ruined resting-place, I was much more of a star. When the Rolls drew up outside, the ancient liveried porter had stared at it entranced, swept off his braided cap, and said: *"Jawohl, Herr Baron!"* When the time came to pay my bill, it was made out to *"Der Hochwohlgeborene* Herr Monsarrat"*—*"Highly born," the nearest I had come to such an accolade in twenty-six years.

It was very easy to behave like tourists in Vienna, and we did so. We ate cream pastries at Sacher's, and *Wienerschnitzel* at a café-restaurant in the Prater, and were scorned for drinking beer instead of champagne at the Femina nightclub. We wandered about, under the linden trees, and round the Ringstrasse, and within the Stephans-Kirche, and out to Schönbrunn, the Imperial Summer Palace, where the overload of golden salons and towering mirrors and spidery candelabra had their own exotic beauty, and history still lived vividly, even though caged in a museum.

It might have been last summer that the Emperor Franz-Josef brought his bride, the fabulously beautiful Elizabeth of Bavaria, to this enchanted palace, and then so bored her that they had agreed on a polite but scandalous separation; it might have been yesterday that here he was mourning his only son, the suicide of Mayerling, in secret, savage despair.

The living Viennese were not so savage, nor so sad; they were in that grey area in between—mostly poor, and no longer proud, and waiting to be rescued from the bondage which history had clamped upon their necks. If it had to be Hitler who rescued them, then let it be Hitler. . . . The signs of poverty were everywhere: in the hordes of women—young and thinly pretty, old and ugly and bone-weary—patrolling the pavements as if they were being paid by the mile; in the beggars on the street corners, in the hopeless eyes of men who had lost the spark or never known that it existed.

Beggars plagued all the outdoor cafés, and the front of the sleek Bristol Hotel, at any hour of the day or night, hawking matches or postcards or wretched pen-and-ink sketches. One never had to wait long before a hand came out, and snatched the scraps of food from a deserted table; and above the hand would be a glimpse of a pinched student face, or behind it an old man's body in tailored rags—all that remained of a genteel or even a noble past.

Though it was nearly a generation after the defeat of 1918, the defeat was still going on, and Vienna summed it up, with its upper crust of the affluent, and its vast hopeless jumble of dispossessed below.

I wanted to tell everybody that Jo and I were not rich, nor even solvent most of the time; I wanted to stand on a table and shout that none of this mess was our fault—or, if it *was* our fault, then we were desperately sorry for it, and we would revoke the whole Treaty of Versailles, and share our last crust of bread with the bitterly poor, in order to prove it. But of course we sat apart, and were condemned. We were tourists, lounging on the terrace of the Imperial, gorged enough to leave rolls of bread half-eaten. We were "they."

Soon it was time to leave; our money really was running out— and I wished I could have stood up and cited this also. Taking the road eastwards towards Budapest, I remarked: "Well, I think we did just about everything."

"Yes," Jo said, rather flatly.

"I should really have sat under a tree and written a couple of short stories. There's a wonderful title for them."

"Tales from the Vienna woods," she interrupted, on the same note.

"Oh."

"Sometimes I can hear your jokes coming."

We then had a rousing quarrel. It had happened two or three times on the trip so far; travel in a car was always crowded, even in a car like this opulent barge, and we had been at very close quarters for nearly a thousand miles. This time she was in a bad mood because of Vienna, which on balance had been depressing; at other times it had started with keeping her waiting, or browsing too long through a wine-list, or leaving things behind when I packed, or (once) running out of petrol on a road which could be seen to stretch, naked as an egg, to the farthest horizon on either side.

At such moments her face would turn stormy, and remain so, and I knew I was in for one of those cold nights; Jo would give up as Passion's Plaything and revert to the Spirit of Apathy (non-speaking part), for which King Lear had the perfect and grisly phrase—

Whose face between her forks presages snow,

and neither double bed nor winning ways nor humble penitence would cure it, but only time, the great healer.

Today, thank God, it was cured, ahead of time, by Budapest.

We had decided, even before we set out from England, that Budapest was going to be the high point of our travels; and when it turned out exactly so, we were inclined to congratulate ourselves just as much as Hungary. The approach was all that we had hoped: past vineyards, and villages with fierce inhabitants ("Magyars," we assured each other: "Just look at their moustaches!"), and rolling farm-land which stretched away out of sight, and flat deserted plains on which something was moving all the time—and the something was herd after herd of wild horses, their manes streaming out in the wind, galloping to keep pace with us.

We bought a loaf of bread and some goat's-milk cheese, thick and sour as lemon-curd, and stopped to have lunch on the river-bank; afterwards I washed the car in the Danube itself, which, as had been apparent in Vienna, was not blue at all, but a pale cloudy grey. ("After the christening, the baptism," I said; but she was not yet in the mood for jokes—even jokes as good as this.) Then we followed the Danube into the city, and found that it split Budapest in two—Buda on one side, Pest on the other; one was old and sleepy, the other sprawled and milled about like Liverpool itself. But it was not really like Liverpool. It was beautiful.

If we had had any money, we would have splurged it all on staying at the magnificent Dunapalota; since we had hardly any, we drove round and round until we found a district where they did not know a Rolls-Royce from a surplus Army tank, and, with signs and smiles, booked a hotel room at the equivalent of five shillings a day.

This was our base, and a good one too, because it was near the quays, the favourite strolling place for half the town; and we could sit drinking sleepy Hungarian wine, or the fierce liqueur known as *Barack,* and watch the people, and accept the lovely setting of this city.

Across the river there was a hill with a castle on top; we never climbed that hill, but just sat and stared at it, day after day, knowing that this was what it was there for. On one of these days, a tall bold man wearing a white raincoat with buttoned epaulettes slung across his shoulders, the arms hanging down like empty scabbards, tried to pick up Jo while I was buying a newspaper. I could not blame him; her bright blonde hair and glowing face had turned a hundred heads already.

I had visions of being challenged to a duel, of a heavy stitched-leather glove dealing me a stinging slap across the cheek. But when I came up to them, frowning, the man only glanced at his watch, and bowed, and walked away again, his empty sleeves swinging jauntily as he moved.

"Who was that?" I asked.

"My lover."

"That swine!"

"He was awfully polite. He *murmured.*"

"Probably indigestion."

Indigestion was on our minds. We seemed to be living on goulash, and chicken showered with paprika, and dumplings. If we had stayed much longer, we would have been goulash and dumplings through and through. But when we counted our money again, we found that we had three pounds left.

The weather had turned cold, anyway, and it was time to go. Money made it quite a race—money against miles.

The money, or rather the Rolls, won this gallop, though it was a near thing. Cold winds, and a hint of snow, chased us onwards as we left Hungary, and crossed all of Austria from Styria to the Tyrol, and bit off a small slice of Italy, and began to weave through the Swiss Alpine passes.

We had money for our bare outlay on petrol and food, and nothing else; the bitter cold nights we spent in the tent, or curled up in the back of the car, which retained just enough engine-heat to let us get to sleep in peace. But we faced each morning chilled to the bone, stiff as old scarecrows; if the sun did not shine, we were doomed to shiver through half a day of misery.

Making love, we found, was no cure for winter's edge. One gained on the swings, and then lost it again on the roundabouts, which lasted longer.

The snow began to come down, in good earnest, as we left Switzerland; if we had stayed a week later, many of the passes behind us might have been cut, leaving us very much the orphans of this storm. (I had visions of wintering seven thousand feet up the St. Gotthard Pass, on one of its ferocious hairpin bends, selling bits of the Rolls for firewood.) But the whole nightmare journey was exhilarating, and fiercely funny, and always worth doing.

Sometimes, also, it was quite maddening, as when we arrived south of Dijon, in the heart of the Burgundy district, and wished to pay our sentimental respects to Nuits St. Georges (all we were able to pay), and had to drive, entirely penniless, through a whole wine-list of towns and villages—Chambertin, Vougeot, Meursault, Beaune—whose names cried out for flagons, and a few francs to fill them.

We had no francs now. We had a full tank of petrol ("Take care of your horse first," the riding-master at The Leas used to command us), and nothing else at all except a sponge-bag half full of small change—German and Austrian pfennigs, Swiss francs, Italian lire, and Hungarian pengös. It might come to about fifteen shillings altogether.

I tried to turn this treasure into French francs at a bank in Dijon, but met with an aloof refusal, and a glance at the sponge-bag which could have frozen the St. Gotthard for the rest of the winter. Astonished glances followed me as I retreated, furious, to the Rolls, and got in, and drove away with this ravishing *poule de luxe*. . . . Then we quartered Dijon, looking for our last resort, a *mont-de-piété*.

Anyone who has ever tried to pawn fifteen shillings' worth of copper coinage, from four or five foreign countries, in one of the more prudent parts of France, will have learned many things in the process, and above all humility. But I persevered, against shameful odds. We had nothing else to pledge, except a brooch of Jo's and my own wristwatch, neither of which we wanted to leave behind, like the dishonoured dead, in France.

I sold our life savings in the end, though at a severe loss. But at least we had enough for one single small meal. We made it an early lunch, not having dined the previous night, and set off on the last lap.

From Dijon to Paris is about one hundred sixty miles. I drove them with exceptional care; if anything went wrong—if we ruffled a single chicken's feather, or were stopped for speeding, or even touched a farm-cart, or needed the smallest repair—we were doomed.

"What happens if we have a puncture?" Jo asked me at one point.

I had been thinking along the same lines, remembering that the spare wheel had been patched and repatched already.

"There'll be a bang," I answered, "and then a sort of hissing noise, and one side will go down, and I shall stop the car."

"All right," said Jo. "I just wanted to know."

But we made it, beset by worry and an aching hunger, by late evening—and there had been no better moment than to see the lights of *La Ville Lumière* in the far distance, and to approach them gradually, and cross to the Left Bank, and drive at last into the garish, beloved harbour of the Boulevard du Montparnasse.

We reached our favourite crossroads, where it meets another broad avenue, the Boulevard Raspail, and parked the car outside the Rotonde (one could get away with a lot in a Rolls-Royce). We tumbled out, stiff and cold, broke and utterly famished—and

there behind a glass partition were Francesca and Drainpipe, like
the King and Queen of Carnival, inclining their heads graciously
as a huge fluffy Spanish omelette was presented for their inspection.

Their eyes were alight, their cutlery poised. But they had no
chance against us.

We had a lot of catching up to do, apart from eating, and the
first item of news was the most astonishing. They were still crying
the evening papers outside the Rotonde, and I heard something which sounded like *"Roi d'Angleterre"* and then the word
"Boulogne." My mouth full of the last of the Brie, I asked:
"What's all this? A state visit?"

"State nothing!" answered Francesca promptly. "Haven't you
heard? He abdicated."

"What?"

"Two days ago. He's on his way to Austria, to stay with one
of your Rothschild pals."

"What?" This time it was Jo, as astonished as I was. We hadn't
heard a single word of this. "But what happened?"

"He abdicated," said Francesca again. It was, once more, a
shattering word. " 'I cannot carry on without the help and support
of the woman I love.' " This sounded like a direct quotation,
though in an unfriendly voice. "So Baldwin and his herd of cattle
ganged up on him, and out he went. He did a farewell broadcast.
The announcer said: 'His Royal Highness, Prince Edward,' instead of calling him the King, and that was that."

"But *who?*"

"Mrs. Simpson." Francesca looked at me pityingly; she had
been annoyed about the omelette, and was determined to work
her way back, until she was at least three eggs ahead. "You *are*
out of touch, aren't you?"

"Good Lord!"

We had heard the usual gossip about this affair; I had once
even discussed it with Mother, who had said: "Mark my words—
it will *burn itself out!*" and had then gone through the Royal
Garden Party number of the *Tatler*, picking out some "really
nice girls" who would be much more suitable as royal brides. As
far back as June, there had been a complaint in the Commons

about the bits which were being snipped out of *Time* magazine before it was put on sale; the inference was that *Time* was being censored because it was saying rude things about the King, who didn't behave like that at all.

Then there had been his summer cruise in Lady Yule's yacht, the *Nahlin,* and occasional photographs of the "royal party" bathing on the Dalmatian coast—a royal party which always seemed to include a good-looking, dark-haired woman of whom knowing Pimlicans said: "That's her. That's Mrs. Simpson." You could almost hear those "S's" exploding all over the Café Royal.

But it was still only gossip, and remarkably uninformed. In spite of what we were told later about the torrent of spicy items which had appeared in other papers, all the way round the world, there was not a single word about it, in a single British newspaper, until the story broke.

Francesca and Drainpipe had only arrived in Paris that morning. Naturally they knew all about everything.

"Some bishop started the ball rolling," Francesca told us. "The Bishop of Bradford. He gave the King a ripe ticking-off in a sermon. Said he wished he showed more signs of spiritual grace." She smirked. "Of course we all agreed with *that*. It was the *one* thing missing."

Drainpipe, the only poet I knew who read *The Times,* took up the tale, on a more objective note. "Then the newspapers got busy. They were a bit late, but they soon caught up. It was like knocking away the last wedge when they launch a ship." With a delicate wave of his hand, he knocked away that last wedge, and we saw the vast bulk begin to slide. "Columns and columns about it, and a leader every day. Especially *The Times. The Times* said—" he changed his voice to a suitably portentous note "—'Such a marriage would deeply offend and perplex large numbers of His Majesty's subjects.'"

Drainpipe was wearing a workman's blue blouse, tied with rope round his waist and buttoned up to his beard; it was really very odd to hear such majestic elocution proceeding from this raffish source. But in fact we were an odd quartet altogether. Francesca wore a kind of smock made of red sacking and fringed with beads, Jo the flowered dirndl which she had bought in Salzburg. I, having felt the cold this many a long day and night, was dressed for foul-weather sailing. The corduroys were particularly serviceable, and the knitted muffler authentic.

I could hear, somewhere, the voice of that correct Winchester man reproving me: "Don't you know?—you should never wear tweeds in a capital city." . . . Yet we were still His Majesty's loyal subjects.

"But didn't anyone think it was a good idea?" I asked. "What about all the other papers?"

"Just what you'd expect from that bunch of lackeys," said Francesca, who often used conventional Communist jargon to make a point.

"You mean, they supported the King?"

"No, I *don't* mean that!" She glared at me. "I mean, they stood up for the established order. They closed ranks, like a lot of stupid policemen. Rally round the flag, boys, and to hell with private enterprise!" She sounded a bit confused: I guessed suddenly that the whole country had been confused in the same way, and that an awful lot of slogans had been turned upside down to prove an awful lot of arguments. "They said he had to marry a princess, or not at all," Francesca went on. "No commoners need apply. And no Americans, ever!"

"I thought you didn't like Americans."

"This is different."

"What about the *News Chronicle?*"

"That bourgeois rag! . . . They took the morganatic marriage line. He could marry her, but she wasn't to be Queen. Baldwin soon put a stop to that. He said there was no precedent for that sort of thing, and he wasn't going to start one now. Then Churchill made a sort of try in the House for a King's party, to back him up whatever he did."

"Good old Churchill!" At a first glance I was on the King's side in this, because it sounded as if the Church of England had started it, and Baldwin of course was absolutely hopeless. There must have been a great deal of snobbery and social pressure involved, too.

"Rubbish," said Francesca. "It was just the usual crypto maneuver. Anyway, Churchill got shouted down, and after that the King hadn't anyone left on his side."

"Poor old Pragga Wagga."

"What?"

I felt myself blushing. "Sorry. A bit of old-time slang. It means Prince of Wales."

"Good God!"

I tried to turn the fire. "What do the French think about all this?"

"They think it's *merveilleux,*" said Francesca spitefully. "Giving up all for love! Ooh la *la!*" She shot me a meaning look. "They think *everyone* should give up *everything* to marry the one they love."

"They don't do anything of the sort," I answered crossly. "They think of the money first, and then love as a dividend. They're realists."

"Reminds me of a chap I know."

"Oh, do shut up, Francesca," said Jo loyally. "It's not like that at all."

"I think," said Drainpipe, who had been blowing smoke-rings, through what smelled like a wet Gauloise cigarette, with such concentration that I knew he had not missed a word, "I think that Baldwin did pretty well, if we can bear to admit it. It was a hell of a choice to have to make. On balance, I'm afraid he was dead right all the time."

"The King was doing pretty well, too," I objected. "After all, he *had* a social conscience. He did visit the distressed areas, and say that something had to be done about them."

"Bloody nice of him," said Francesca. "Oh God, what does all this matter, anyway? What does it matter which particular puppet is the King or the Queen? It's the *system* that's all wrong! And think of all the other rotten things in the world that are a million times more important. Think of Spain. Think of Madrid! It's on its last legs already. That swine Franco has got within ten miles of it! If something doesn't happen soon—"

We began to talk about Spain instead of the King. The vast clatter and bustle in the Rotonde, the roar of voices, the smoke, the mirrors which reflected an endless series of people talking, people moving in and out, people smiling and frowning and quarelling and kissing, seemed to prove beyond doubt that there were indeed a million things going on in the world, and that we were right in the middle of them.

The lights of Paris outside, twinkling, changing, beckoning, were all part of this restless beating pulse. Only the rain, falling gently, gleaming on the hood of the Rolls, seemed like a static element. It fell on Paris, it fell on Liverpool, it fell, probably, on Vienna and Budapest. It was doubtless falling on Madrid, at this very moment. Rain, rain, go to Spain. . . . She wore a wreath of roses round her tum-te-tum-te-tum. . . . I had drunk more than enough Pernod already—and that was something else which was going to be a static element, if I could possibly organize it.

We had no problems of our own to plague us: we seemed to have shed the lot as soon as we arrived in Paris. Drainpipe was momentarily rich, having sold a couple of long poems (one about Spain, the other about eagles) to the *Atlantic Monthly,* which paid cash on the nail, at rates which seemed to us fantastic. Within two or three days, my own advance royalty for *The Whipping Boy* came through from London—and there was I, rich as well, with thousands of francs burning thousands of holes in my corduroys.

Best of all, we had a borrowed flat, just off the Boulevard Raspail, with a glimpse of the Luxembourg Gardens across a forest of chimney pots; and we could all live there for nothing at all, at least until the new year.

The flat had only one bedroom, and we took forty-eight-hour turns at this—Francesca and Drainpipe for two days, Jo and I for the next two. The losers had to pool their amorous secrets, if they wished, upon the sofa in the sitting-room. But since the bathroom was on the opposite side of the apartment, and there was a good deal of traffic to and fro, the cautionary "Wait for the bed!" presently became a catch-phrase, and we settled for rationed ecstasy.

We took all our meals out, from *café complet* onwards (we actually found a place where they served Swiss cherry jam at no extra charge). Francesca never soiled her fingers with a single dish (housekeeping, she declared, was *bourgeois,* and that was that), and Jo, though a dear girl, had never developed her cooking skills beyond what might be called *Cordon Brun.* But who could complain, when all the back-street restaurants of Paris were within touching distance, and their meals were so cheap and so delicious, and one could window-shop, comparing the menus displayed outside to the nearest *centime* and the nearest pat of butter, and make of eating, like *pointillisme,* the most exact art of all?

The four cafés which stood sentinel at our crossroads—the Rotonde, the Dôme, the Coupole, and the Select—loomed very large in the pattern of our lives. There was a huge floating clientele, ourselves among it, which made daily and nightly rounds of these four ports-of-call; and there was always one which was more in favour than any other, for no reason at all except the sort of reason which must prompt a school of minnows to turn left into one bay rather than right into another.

We would patronize the Rotonde, which was our favourite, and then suddenly the Rotonde would be almost deserted, as if it had a plague cross nailed over the entrance, and we could look across the street in perplexity, and there would be the Coupole, crammed with all our friends, packed to the roof-tops, turning away the tourists with scarcely a civil word. . . . Drainpipe had a theory, ingenious but unprovable, that the four cafés had a working arrangement which allowed each of them to take a rest in turn; when the Select, for example, had had enough of its crowded hour, it would allow its service to slacken off, and the waiters to become flat-footed and morose; whereupon the Dôme would spring into favour, and everyone would flock there, and proclaim to all the world that the Dôme was the only place where one met *anyone.*

Whichever one it was, we went there to talk, and we spent hours of every day at this exercise. We talked of everything under the sun; sex and politics, music and the theater, writing and painting, sex and politics again. Magic and deplorable opinions attained the scope and status of Holy Writ; the world was reorganized, the arts transformed, and sex itself re-invented, every time a bus went by, or a pretty girl turned our heads.

Zest and appetite ruled everything we did and said. Life-long love-affairs—with Kafka, with Kierkegaard, with Georges Duhamel and Major C. H. Douglas—were passionately declared, and bonded with drafts of *champagne nature.* Slanders flew from side to side; reputations were destroyed between one cigarette and another; political creeds spouted from the top of a *carafe de blanc,* and had taken full charge of the entire globe by the time the bottom had been sighted.

We listened raptly to each other, but no one else paid us the least attention. No one interviewed us, or sought our opinions; no one thrust a tape-recorder under our chin, inviting our pronouncements and embalming them for posterity; no one clamoured to put us on television, as the authentic Voice of Youth, before which the rest of the world must shut up, and faint dead away.

We were like the young of all the world, since the world began. We were dissatisfied; we complained, criticized, pontificated, prophesied. Everything was wrong; things could not go on like this; the universe was rightly doomed; war was on the way; freedom was denied, greed and lust for power still ruled our lives shamelessly.

We talked, and no one listened. We talked more wildly, more freely, because we were sure that this wild freedom could not last forever, or even for much longer. There had been a Lost Generation from the last war; now there was a Doomed Generation, waiting like dumb oxen for the next one, and that Doomed Generation was us.

No one listened to us, no one made notes, no one paid any attention. We were youth, subservient youth, silly and harebrained and wise and disregarded. The day might come when we would be listened to, or our children might be listened to—and that, though we did not know it and would have cried to hear it, would not be a specially good day, nor a specially bad day; just a day like any other day, like Judgment Day, like Mother's Day, like Monday Tuesday Wednesday.

Meanwhile we made love as lions, and slept as lambs, safe in our private certainty that all this could somehow be made to last forever; that we had discovered a delicious, mysterious balance of love and hate, hard work and good luck; that somewhere between "Stop Hitler now!" and "Refuse to fight," between "I love you" and "I must write," the children of innocence and hope would survive, and prosper, and laugh much more than they would cry.

We had not asked to be born, but how glad we were!

THIRTY-ONE

1941

IT WAS CRUEL

1.

WHO REMEMBERS THE OLD FIGHTS? Who wants to? Who really remembers the bomb that took the house next door, the charnel tanks cremated in choking sand, the hideous night-sky over Berlin, the convoy so mauled that it seemed to be bleeding to death? Who really cares—not in boozy annual reunion, but with deep feeling, and sorrow, and the rare edge of triumph?

I used to talk about the war at sea, for a year or so afterwards; and then it became a bore, and peacetime grew exciting and much more important. I wrote about it twenty years ago, but not again. Yet even now, a great wheeling quarter-century later, it is still vivid, still awful, still a scar of sorts, however handsomely healed.

It is still, in memory, a wild excitement as well, a testing-time never to be matched until the last enemy comes calling again. So there must be a place for it in the life-and-times; a small place, but still to be filled with the taste and smell, the sight and sound, of men trying to kill each other, or to save each other, or to run away and hide from both endeavours.

I kept the middle watch, all that year of 1941; one of the tied tenantry of a corvette's open bridge, along with two look-outs, a helmsman, and a messenger; on guard, sometimes for seventeen days on end, from twelve o'clock until four, A.M. and P.M., in the black box of night or the wine of clear sunlight; to and fro across the Atlantic or down to Gibraltar, zigzagging endlessly at slow convoy speed—which was six and a half knots.

A corvette, if harried by the Chief Stoker, might well provoke its push-pull engine up to a shuddering fourteen knots; but we never did fourteen, unless we were chasing a U-boat contact or, blessedly, slipping home for a boiler-clean and the five days' leave which went with it.

On our escort job, we had to match the speed of the slowest member, like a House of Lords procession; and some of the ancient crocodiles in our charge drifted along like seaweed on the tide, as if their very barnacles were asleep.

At the beginning, even a slow old ship, a creeping convoy, a cottonwool fog, a whole night at action stations, a week of merciless weather, had been exciting; the novelty had been all. Now we were getting into the second year of it, and nothing was new any more. It was merely the longest sweat of our lives. No optimism touched our ship, nor any other, so far as we could tell; no one now sang that 1939 fool's favourite, "We'll Hang Out the Washing on the Siegfried Line"; no one whistled "Run, Rabbit, Run" while contemplating the bust of Hitler.

Already, in dull endurance, we were thinking of ourselves as "hanging on." If we had known that this grotesque Allemande was to continue, with increasing fury, with the flow of blood beginning to match the tidal sea, for nearly four years more, we might well have had some perilous second thoughts.

My father had once said, of his old, wicked, gory Salonika war: "All I could think of, at the time, was keeping going when we were all dog-tired." Now there was another war, and this time it was mine instead of his. But the deadly weariness, shot through with fear, was the very same.

I had gone to my war as a gentleman should (in 1940), by answering an advertisement in *The Times,* which invited "Gentlemen with yachting experience" to apply for commissions as Temporary Probationary Sub-Lieutenants in the Royal Naval Volunteer Reserve.

My father had cut out the advertisement and sent it to me (I was still loyally bound to the *News Chronicle,* and would not have been seen dead with *The Times,* even as bedclothes in Hyde Park); and after thinking it over I sent in my application. Apart from yachting experience, which I could reasonably claim, the time was ripe, in many other ways.

Our trouble, in early 1940, was inaction—inaction, doubt, and dismay.

So far I had spent seven months, from the day before the first day of the war, in suspended valour: first as a humble stretcher-party driver, and later as the boss, of an Air Raid Precautions depot in Harley Street. Taking this non-combatant job had been a matter of conviction. Though we were at war with Germany, I was still an ardent pacifist, war or no war, and this, I decided, was as far as I could go.

It did not seem at all shameful, nor cowardly. At that time, we were all certain that London, at least, would be bombed and burned to cinders, on the first evening of Day One, and that we, as well as succouring the wounded, would be catching the bombs with our bare hands.

Yet nothing at all had happened, for weeks and then for months. In Harley Street we had nothing to do but splint and bandage each other, diagnose and treat suspected epilepsy (piece of wood between the teeth), build practice-scaffolding to prop up tottering buildings, and queue up at the canteen (run at first by comedian Douglas Byng) for tea, hot saveloys, and egg-and-chips. After a few months of this, total boredom had set in.

This wasn't what we had volunteered for, even at £2 18s. 5d. a week. What was the point of it, if no one was going to drop any bombs? And what had gone wrong with the war outside Harley Street?

So far there had been complete stalemate on the Continent, where by rights all the men-at-arms ought to be cutting each other to ribbons, and all the battle honours should be adding up to total annihilation of the hated Hun. As a matter of sad fact, it seemed that we hadn't the strength even to march up to the Siegfried Line, much less use it for our laundry.

In a London strangely empty of children, who had been issued with miniature gas-masks and re-christened "evacuees," we had come to call this puzzled trance the phoney war. But that was a blinkered verdict. It wasn't in the least phoney for other people. What had "gone wrong" with our war had in truth gone wrong for most of the rest of Europe.

The Soviet-German pact, the crudest piece of dog-mathematics in modern diplomacy, had taken care of Hitler's back door. Italy was now preparing to come in on the German side. Russia had jumped on the Finns with both her iron-shod boots and ground the tiny nation into the snow. We could do nothing about that, even if we had wanted to. Hitler then overran Poland in about three weeks, occupied Denmark without a cross word on either side, and invaded Norway.

It could not be disguised, even from idle, yawning, strategically-minded stretcher-bearers, that everyone in the war was doing something useful or valiant except us, the stock-still British; and among "us" was me, and I was as bad as anyone. The only action I had seen so far was to assume the uniform of a St. John Ambulance Brigade sergeant, and "line the route" on the Horse Guards Parade for the triumphant march of the crews of H.M.S. *Exeter* and *Ajax,* on their return from sinking the pocket battleship *Graf Spee.* Armed with iodine and sal volatile, I was there in case any ladies fainted.

Other events now marched on with gruesome speed; they were no longer a joke, or good for a Windmill Theatre song-title, or even "part of our overall plan." While I had been waiting to hear whether I had answered that R.N.V.R. advertisement correctly, Hitler swallowed Holland and Belgium; while I was still under training at H.M.S. *King Alfred,* learning how to salute and how to respond in a seamanlike manner to the Loyal Toast (don't stand up), and studying an ambiguous manual called *Street Fighting for Junior Officers,* France collapsed and Dunkirk happened.

The suggestion made at the time, that the only way out of our grim plight was to appoint the Duke of Gloucester as Supreme Allied Commander-in-Chief ("He would rally the whole nation!"), seemed to hint that we were still not taking this very seriously. But *I* was serious enough, because I had now turned my full somersault, shedding ideals like post-nuptial confetti.

Drunk or sober, sad or boastful, I could bring it down to one simple equation, in three sentences. Pacifism was useless in wartime. Once the thing started, you had to win it as Nelson or Wellington, and then, if you chose, begin all over again as Jesus Christ. *Ergo* (Lat., therefore) *everyone* must get into the fight.

So now, after the months of waiting and the years of nothing much, I was a naval officer, just the way Mother had planned it, back in 1918. But it was only just: my rung on this ladder scarcely cleared the ground. Starting life as a Temporary Probationary Sub-Lieutenant, at an income bracket of £20 a month, I had now come up to Lieutenant (£26 a month, plus £2 6s. 6d. hard-lying money); and I was earning it as a watch-keeping officer in a corvette plying the North Atlantic.

It really was a somersault, and I knew it even then. Discipline, order, a sense of hierarchy and service—all the Winchester virtues or constraints had come flooding back again, as good as new after more than a decade in the attic of derision.

As well as being scared to death a lot of the time, and unspeakably tired always, I was also very proud.

There was a catch-phrase on board, "A corvette would roll on wet grass"; and its ring of truth had swiftly turned sour indeed.. Corvettes were abominable ships to live in, in any kind of weather; already cramped, wet, noisy, crowded, and starkly uncomfortable, they pitched and rolled and swung, with a brutal persistence, as long as any breeze blew.

To fight in, with any kind of spirit, they were worst of all. The first enemy and the last, the eternal bully, was the atrocious sea; and when we had come to terms with that, we still had to tackle the men who were trying to burn us, or maim us, or blow us up, or hunt us down, and strangle us with the sea's own noose.

Our personal shield, our own tin lifeboat, was H.M.S. *Campanula*, the eighteenth corvette out of many hundreds soon to be built in a crash program designed to meet the swift and violent threat to our convoys, the early prime thrust of the enemy. Even in the slow-starting first month of the war, we had lost 41 merchant ships; in the first year, this had swelled to the fearsome total of 617.

Campanula was Clyde-built, which meant, in those days, that she was as sound as salt; but her size—203 feet long, 900 tons— and her design—an old-fashioned whaler-type hull, with a well-deck often awash with tons of sluicing sea-water—could not make her anything but a storm-tossed lemon, as far as the North Atlantic was concerned. By some ludicrous stroke of policy, all corvettes bore the names of gentle and delicate flowers; in *Campanula*'s escort group there were also *Bluebell, Zinnia, Hyacinth, Aubretia, Convolvulus,* and *Coreopsis* (the latter ship was to be met again, years later, in extraordinary circumstances).

Some names, it was obvious, were preferable to others; we would rather have had our own, even with its elective pronunciation, than *Wallflower,* or *Periwinkle,* or *Daffodil,* or *Meadow-sweet* (their Lordships of the Admiralty, with man-of-the-world delicacy, had excluded *Pansy* from the list of possibles).

But the ships, however prettily christened, were all the same: bare platforms for a four-inch pop-gun and a huge clutch of depth-charges, and wallowing cages for eighty-eight men, subjected to every kind of insult from the sea, surviving, with a dull endurance which for the rest of our lives we were to find incredible, a world of shock, fatigue, crude violence, and grinding anxiety.

Dr. Samuel Johnson, that quarrelsome old landsman, gave it as his view that "Being in a ship is being in a jail, with the chance of being drowned"; and, substituting the word *probability* for *chance,* the two-hundred-year-old verdict must stand, as far as a minor ship-of-war in our wringing wet corner of the world was concerned. There was one other item which Dr. Johnson would doubtless have appreciated: our jail would not keep still.

On the job of convoy escort we simply had to point ourselves in the right direction—due west for the New World, and after that due east for the battered Old—and then get going; convoys, at this crucial moment of the war, when an average of three precious ships a day were being sunk, and yet supplies had to be brought in to keep the island fighting, to keep the island fed, to let the island survive at all—convoys could not wait upon the weather.

We had to bash our way through, and come home with what-ever we had left—a percentage of the stake-money, in terms of blood and treasure, men and ships: a percentage, like a fuel-oil return, of strength remaining: a percentage of spirit for the next time.

During the first few convoys, in mid-1940, when our officer-complement had been set by a short-handed Admiralty as a Cap-tain, a First Lieutenant, and two green-as-grass Sub-Lieutenants, we had to keep watch-and-watch at sea—four hours on, four hours off, for day after day until the voyage was over, which could be more than a fortnight later.

It meant that sleep was sliced up desperately small, and often cherished sleep itself would not come to a fluttering brain or a fearful man; or else it was shattered by those hateful clanging bells which, drilling the thin skull, yanked us up to action stations and the astonishment of smoke and flame, and then to sunk ships, half-drowned survivors, and dead men leaking their loathsome salad-dressing of blood and oil into our virgin scuppers.

After about six months of that watch-and-watch nonsense, it had become obvious that we were likely to drop dead ourselves if we had to go on with it. Representations were made, throughout our harassed fleet; some kind soul in the Admiralty did a little sum and came up with the right answer; and presently we were given, first one and then two more officers.

After that, we spent four hours on watch and eight hours off; and even though we lived like pigs, three in a two-berth cabin and the fourth man in a hammock in the pantry, at least (apart from occasional whole nights at action stations) we got the sleep which was our nearly crying need. But the job itself remained awful.

The nights, of course, were worst of all: the nights when anything, no matter how murderous or vile, could always happen; when even without the jostling of the enemy we stood our watch under sentence of misery, clamped to a wing of the open bridge (made of canvas laced to the stanchions), taking the worst of the wind and spray upon a very tired body, and keeping station on the nearest ship in the convoy, an only friend who was never more than a now-and-then black specter in a howling grey gloom.

For our own protection, we did the best we could. Like all the others—and we certainly knew each other's wardrobes, in that mean slit of a cabin—I wore two vests, thick long pants, third-best uniform trousers, big clumping sea-boots, a sweater and a fisherman's jersey, a duffle coat, a towel and a woollen scarf round my neck, sheepskin gloves from blessed South Africa, and a Balaclava helmet also donated by faraway, loving hands.

By now I had, in addition, a long curly beard. It took care, at least, of half the face. And who wanted to shave, in this wilderness? We weren't *going* anywhere.

Strait-jacketed in this clownish rig, one endured the cumulative blows of a four-hour watch. In bad weather—North Atlantic winter weather—great icy dollops of salt water found their way everywhere: down the neck, up the wrists, into the trouser-legs and sea-boots. I used to stand there like a sodden automaton, ducking behind the canvas "dodger" as every second wave sent spray scudding over the compass house; and then I straightened up to face once more, with eyes raw and salt-caked and streaming, the horrid enmity of the sea. Twice already, in my middle watch, we had had the windows up on the bridge smashed in, by a giant sea which curled up and broke right on top of them.

Mere armoured glass could give up; the man standing in front of it could not.

He had to stay where he was, an amateur Ahab defying the screeching elements, and do three things: run his watch properly, cherish the ship and its ninety-strong boxed cargo of wakeful or sleeping men, and—without benefit of radar, a blessing still unborn as far as corvettes were concerned—maintain station as a link in the escort screen.

We were the smallest warships on convoy escort in the North Atlantic, the armed trawlers being gradually phased out after the wicked winter of 1940; and we were very proud of the fact. We were also very glad to give up and go home again, after our own eternal pasting by the elements.

The first shore-light we saw at night, when nearing home, was likely to be a dearly loved friend on the island of Inishtrahull, off Northern Ireland; it would arc across the black horizon like the promise of Christmas. Our first daylight landfall would be the fair coast of Scotland, running down to the Mull of Galloway. Near land, the porpoises and the seagulls played sea-games round the ship; the porpoises seemed to be racing us home with great laughing leaps, the seagulls criss-crossed to and fro under our stem, skimming close, planing upwards suddenly if they met another player coming round the other way.

Presently we would be under the lee of the Isle of Man, and there the sea gave up. From the bridge one noticed the first patch of drying deck below. It spread outwards; it meant peace. Then the Bar Light Vessel, guarding the approach to Liverpool, loomed up like a rusty-red signpost to our haven.

It was the prelude to a whole range of delights about to be showered on us: sliding through the dock gates towards our berth, getting the first heaving-line ashore, then the head-rope, then the stern-wire: ringing off the engines—their first respite for perhaps four hundred hours: the curious warm silence which fell on the ship as the mail came on board and was doled out: the first guaranteed night in port, first drink, first undressing for a fortnight, first bath, first good sleep.

The trouble was that this blessed peace never lasted beyond a bare twelve hours. Even in our home port, safely buttoned to the dockside, we had very little rest during those five-day spells in harbour.

A duck-sized warship such as the one we were blessed with still needed a lot of day-to-day thought and care, to keep her (in the naval phrase which was now an oppressive part of my life) on the top line. First—because we might have to go out again in a hurry—we had to be refilled with everything we had spent on the last brave voyage, which meant making requisitions for, and then taking delivery of, a steady stream of crates, boxes, parcels, drums, and wicker baskets which flowed up the gangway in tidal tribute from the Department of Naval Stores.

There were the consumables we lived by—the bread which lasted five days before it had to be soaked in milk and water, heated up again, and thus "reconstructed"; the fresh vegetables which lasted a week, the tinned stew which lasted forever, the choice cuts of meat which finished up as a tired frieze of cinders on the galley stove, the rum with the colour of Nelson's blood and the taste of sweet fire itself.

There were tons of fuel oil with that hateful acrid stink which filled the clean sea air every time a ship in convoy was lost; now it poured on board through filthy gurgling hose-pipes which fouled everything they touched. There were the depth-charges which we had dropped so sourly, and the anti-aircraft ammunition we had merrily and futilely tossed into the air.

There were the medical stores—splints, and bandages, and morphia under my own lock-and-key, and contraceptives which were called "condoms" (issued free to all comers), and the wretched little tubes of tannic acid which melted into a man's face like raindrops on the crust of a burned-up desert.

There was gin for the wardroom (2½d. a tot), and mile after mile of toilet paper for everyone, and "b'osun's stores" (paint, wire rope, scrubbing brushes, canvas buckets, Lysol, beeswax for splices), and duty-free cigarettes, and the suggestive-looking roll of pipe-fill known as "prick tobacco"—a corruption of *perique,* which first saw the light of day in far-off Louisiana.

While all this to-and-fro was going on, and the stuff was being counted, and signed for, and stowed away, we had to clean up the terrible mess left by the sea—all the soaked bedding, smashed benches, weeping rivets, bent stanchions, ruined carpets, scarred paintwork, and hammocks which had burst their lashings and spilled their innocent cargo on to the iron deck.

While all *this* was going on, we, the expendable lieutenants R.N.V.R., took turn-about as Officer-of-the-day, a twenty-four-hour duty which made us the target for every bad-tempered sally issuing from the captain's cabin, and every other stupid or laughable crisis which might blow up from anywhere else. All that happened to the O.O.D. was inevitable, unavoidable, to be borne with the dumb-ox patience which was the very fabric of war.

He had to be on tap all the time, like an over-exploited butler —indeed, a very stupid butler who had signed an acre of small print without bothering to read it. The "day" started at 5:30, with a call (now known more accurately as a "shake") from the quartermaster, a cup of tea, a quick shave and dress; and the first action was at 6 A.M., when one had to take "Hands Fall In—Wash Down," involving a cold windswept deck, the bleak charms of a Liverpool dawn, and a guarded stare at a muster of nineteen seamen who, shivering in their working rig, stared reproachfully back.

At this first grisly encounter, the day's work was doled out and then supervised: hosing down, scrubbing decks, storing, painting, practicing lifeboat drill, and depth-charge loading drill, and gundrill, and fire-drill, and damage-control drill, and the drill for throwing overboard all the Confidential Books when the ship was judged to be sinking.

There were times when I knew that if I had been ordered to drill for oil, I would have started to rig a derrick, without further question.

The long day ended at 2300 (the hour of 11 P.M. had vanished with the civilized past) when the last of the liberty-men stumbled down the quay, stumbled up the gangway, arranged themselves in a tousled wavering line, and were, after scrutiny, allowed to go below. This inspection was not an item of vile slave-tyranny. Mild drunkenness did not matter; but incapacity—i.e., falling headlong down a twelve-foot ladder and earning a broken neck at the bottom—was too expensive to be allowed, if a searching glance could take care of it.

The Officer-of-the-day had done his job if the ship settled down peacefully by midnight. He had failed if someone got hurt in a fight, or hurt himself on his way to sleep. There were marginal areas, often summed up in certain formal charges to be preferred next morning: "Able Seaman Briginshaw did create vandalism in the galley," or "Did urinate in the stokers' messdeck," or (a charming phrase) "Did poke bravado at his superior." Any of this meant that the O.O.D.'s searching glance had not been searching enough.

The light at the top of the gangway was not always good.

Between that five-thirty shake and the respite of midnight (though if the ship was at anchor out in the stream, one would be standing an anchor-watch on the bridge for the rest of the night, or, for that matter, one might be in charge of dusk-till-dawn fire-watching, since Merseyside was taking a recurrent pasting from the Luftwaffe all through the early months of 1941)— before the respite came at midnight, one was a natural dog's-body, a true beck-and-call-boy.

Tending the shore wires, calling taxis, pouring drinks for visitors and often signing for them, keeping an eye on men working aloft, watching the gangway in case an admiral turned up— the poor butler never had a moment to himself. *Campanula* also had to take her turn as Guard Corvette—which was not some noble task of watch-and-ward while the rest of the fleet slept, but meant supplying quay-sentries, and berthing parties for incoming ships, and a signal link for all ships in harbour; keeping the dockside clear of anything which might get in the way of the cranes— for, if thwarted, the dockers could get terribly angry, and lay down their tools, and (choosing the moment carefully) march off to the nearest pub a convenient space before it closed; and seeing that the rubbish of half-a-dozen ships was properly disposed of, and that no vulgar fish-heads, pigs' entrails, nor chicken feathers sullied the sweet waters of the River Mersey.

It was the Officer-of-the-day of the Guard Corvette who bore the brunt of this manly housekeeping. But in H.M.S. *Campanula,* whether she was Guard Corvette or not, he also had one more hazard to put up with.

It could come, at any moment, in the form of a brawling voice which rang out with a particular, raucous, prison clang: "Monsarrat! I'm going ashore!"

Or: "Monsarrat!" (I had never realized that my name could sound so like the bark of an Alsatian.) "Where's that bloody steward?"

Or: "Monsarrat! That stern-wire's slack again! Hop to it!"

Or: "Monsarrat! There's too much noise over my cabin!"

Or, on one memorable occasion: *"Monsarrat! I've been calling you for ten minutes!"*

"Sorry, sir. I was in the lavatory."

"Don't go to the lavatory! Bake it!"

This was our captain, on whom my present peace of mind and future prospects entirely depended.

One thing we all had to do, as soon as we came back to harbour, was to catch up with the latest amendments and additions to our twin bibles, *King's Regulations & Admiralty Instructions* and *Admiralty Fleet Orders,* which contained page after page of directives on anything under the sun or moon.

K.R. & A.I. and A.F.O.s, as we called them, had to be watched very carefully; they could trip you up if neglected, or you could miss some tiny crumb of comfort which might later make life bearable. Chart corrections came into the same category, and had to be dealt with on an immediate basis, for obvious reasons: it was a finicky chore, rather hard on the patience and the eyesight: corrections to depth-of-water soundings (now who, unluckily stuck on the putty, had found *that* out?), altering buoys from "Flashing three every half-minute" to "Flashing two every ten," and wreck buoys, wreck buoys, wreck buoys all over.

The other task, exclusively for me, was to catch up with fourteen days' weight of the ship's correspondence.

Just as I was in the Navy because I had raced a fourteen-foot dinghy from the age of fifteen, and crewed in boats as big as four tons, so I was the Correspondence Officer because I had written four novels and a play.

It was a painstaking, dreary job which regularly dropped into

The Turney family, about 1895.
Sir John and Lady Turney,
with future uncles and aunts.
Mother at back on the left.

Mother, newly married, 1898.

Porth Diana,
Trearddur Bay, 1926.
Ptah setting sail (lower
right); Ravenspoint on
the horizon above her.

The magnificent
Daimler.

Right The family at
Trearddur Bay, 1919.

The wartime nursery,
1916. Denys on the right.

My father,
off to the war, 1914.

The Halliday Portraits
(*by Edward I. Halliday,
P.R.B.A., R.P.*)

Molly in 1926.

Felicity in 1927.

Denys in 1929.

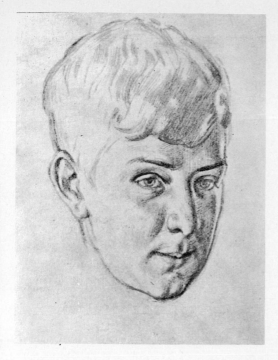

My father in 1932.

N.M. (*by Edward I. Halliday*), 1929.

Great Court, Trinity College, Cambridge. Left to right: Chapel, Fountain, Great Gate. (*Stearn, Cambridge*)

A Street in Dresden, 1930.
N.M., Frank Lucas,
Karl Fastenau.

The first advertisement
. . . and the second
(with colouring matter added).

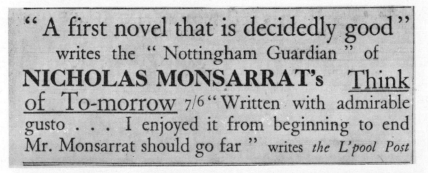

" A first novel that is decidedly good "
writes the " Nottingham Guardian " of
NICHOLAS MONSARRAT's Think
of To-morrow 7/6 " Written with admirable
gusto . . . I enjoyed it from beginning to end
Mr. Monsarrat should go far " writes *the L'pool Post*

At First Sight
by NICHOLAS MONSARRAT

With a subtle and witty pen the author has given us a compelling love story
set in the gay cosmopolitan French watering place of Dinard; handsome gigolos,
faded aristocrats, and venturesome gamblers and romantic tourists add colour
to a delightful novel. By the author of " Think of To-morrow." *(Friday)* 7/6

HURST & BLACKETT

Then a soldier:
my brother Denys in 1941.

General Smuts, Prime
Minister of South Africa, at the
summit of Table Mountain.

Eileen and Max
at the war's end.

The well-dressed naval officer.
Left, in theory
(*Edwin Hadley, Nottingham*)

... and right, in practice. (*Lt.-Comdr.
R. F. J. Maberley, R.N.V.R.*)

Corvette, with Christmas icing. (*Imperial War Museum*)

H.M.S. *Campanula* on wet grass. (*News Chronicle*)

Into exile. Seretse Khama and escort waiting for the plane to take him out of Bechuanaland. Commissioner McKenzie on left. (*J. J. Wesselo, Johannesburg*)

After a short drought the rains came.

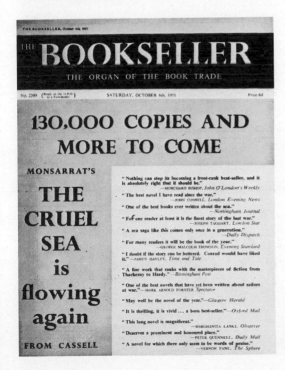

H.M.S. *Compass Rose,* ex-*Coreopsis,* steams into the limelight. (The Cruel Sea—*a Michael Balcon Production*)

Jack Hawkins on the bridge. (The Cruel Sea— *a Michael Balcon Production*)

The first of the XK Jaguars reaches Johannesburg.

Arriving for the New York premiere.

In darkest northern Quebec. Caricature by Bob Hyndman.
(*Reproduced by kind permission of Mr. Robert Hyndman*)

Anthony, Marc, and shaggy dog (aged 2, 3, and 13).
(*Capital Press Service*)

"Stone House," Aylmer Road, Province of Quebec.
(*Newton Photographic Associates Ltd.*)

Three jolly sailormen: Max, N.M.,
and Commodore J. P. Dobson,
C.B.E., D.S.C., R.D., R.N.R.,
on board the *Empress of Scotland*.
(*Canadian Pacific Railway*)

The first Continental Bentley, in Rockcliffe Park, Ottawa. (*Newton Photographic Associates Ltd.*)

Winning smiles. *Valhalla* coming home, wringing wet, after retaining the Windmill Point Shield, 1956.

my lap at the very moment when all I wanted to do was sleep. I answered letters, and filled in forms, and typed out requests for more of this and not so much of that. I checked through the Stores Lists and made out all those interminable requisitions needed to top the ship up again for the next convoy.

I prepared memoranda on lice infestation (known below stairs as "mechanized dandruff") and the possible advantages of using wrapped bread. I gave my considered judgment (or rather, the captain's considered judgment) on the most acceptable kind of "ship's comforts" (South African sheepskin jerkins *marvellous,* knitted Balaclava helmets not too popular—they got wet and stayed wet).

When my eyelids began to droop, I would give up, and stick on a few "Official Paid" stamps, and consign the batch to the postman. But there would be another batch tomorrow. And I still had to make out a return of defaulters and their crimes ("Did abandon his post as bridge-messenger without reporting to the Officer-of-the-watch, contrary to good order and naval discipline" —i.e., the poor bastard was seasick) during the past fourteen days at sea.

There was only one sure cure for seasickness, some hard-hearted fellow once told a sufferer: go and sit under a tree.

There were other jobs assigned to me, and there was often a good enough reason for this—or, at least, some kind of eerie logic to back up the choice.

I was the Censoring Officer. I took Divisions on Sunday (the naval version of Church Parade), and read the service. I was also appointed the ship's Medical Officer within a few hours of reporting on board. This was the worst of all my jobs, the most moving, the most ugly, the most calculated to make me wish that I could revert to an innocent child again.

At first it meant nothing much. But then *Campanula* went to sea, and then to war, and then to violence and bloodshed; and after that my patients were all survivors from ships torpedoed in convoy, and the worst horror-film of my life began.

I got used to it in the end, but if anyone had told me, when I first answered that *Times* advertisement for gentlemen with yachting experience, that as a result I would soon be stitching up a gashed throat without benefit of anesthetics, or trying to coax a dangling eyeball back into its socket; or if I had known that a man with a deep stomach wound, spread-eagled on what seemed like the very rack of Christ, could actually *smell* so awful, like an opened drain, I might well have kept my yachting experience as secret as the grave, and settled for the Army Pay Corps, or for prison, or for shameful defeat itself.

First, mine was butcher's work, and then, all too often, dustman's. To tidy up my medical practice, and because it was probably all my fault anyway, I was assigned to take charge of all burials, and to see the bodies—noted in the log, with raw finality, as "Discharged Dead"—tipped over the side for their long dive.

I came to know that burial service by heart. I could easily have closed the book on *"Man that is born of woman hath but a short time to live, and is full of misery,"* and run right on through the "Stop engines" signal to the bridge, and *"We therefore commit his body to the deep,"* and finished strongly on *"Blessed are the dead which die in the Lord; even so, said the Spirit, for they rest from their labours,"* without a written word to help me.

But I did read from the text, for fear of making a mistake, and also because the words were so beautiful, and deserved this reverence. Yet true feeling—loss, bereavement, a sense of wastage and futility, even with men who were all strangers, who might never have drawn a living breath on board our ship—true feeling had itself wasted away to cold routine, to nothing.

Sometimes I felt that it would never return, even at the grave of my father, or my wife, or my son if I ever had a son.

Just as with my crude doctoring, so with this allied task: one grew hardened to it; it was almost in the realm of paperwork—the most important thing was that the figures should add up correctly at the end of the voyage, and that the Coxswain's "victualling sheets," swelled by these chance visitors, should be shown to have been diminished by the moment of this leave-taking. A tidy disposal was all.

Finally, to round off the long list of things I was doing to bring the Germans to their knees, I was the Depth-Charge Control Officer: not the skillful fellow who operated our asdic set * to

---

* This was our U-boat search weapon, christened from "Allied Submarine Detection Investigation Committee." The Americans preferred to call theirs "Sonar," and so in the end did we.

decide when the depth-charges should be dropped, but the man who actually rolled them over the stern or splayed them out from the throwers; and that job, at last, suited me fine.

As a lapsed pacifist, I was still glad that I didn't have to fire guns, which could shed blood and were terribly noisy anyway (even our modest four-inch peashooter, which was boldly dated 1913). Depth-charges were quite different, as all the world knew. They didn't really kill people; they just sank U-boats, metal objects which were trying to kill *us*. The convention that whereas we had submarines (noble and skillful), the hated Hun actually used U-boats (wicked and treacherous), was still a persistent gloss on history, continued from 1914.

Depth-charges exploded with satisfying violence, an almighty WHOOMP! which shattered the surface of the sea, brought the middle depths to the boil, and, when adroitly used in coastal waters, could supply all hands with a prime fish dinner. The D.C. Control Officer had an inevitable link with the Correspondence Officer. I had to keep an individual case-history of every single one under my charge—or rather, of the numbered detonator-pistols which set them off: the date they were fired, the depth setting, the type of pattern, and the performance. Then the empty boxes, all of them also listed in detail, had to be returned to Naval Armaments.

It might not do any damage, I sometimes thought, as I cast my mighty missile into the sea; but by God I had its right number!

So Monsarrat—sailor, surgeon, scribe, and sexton, all wrapped up in one harassed parcel, tied with the tarry twine of naval discipline—so I confronted the enemy. Or rather, all the enemies. First there was the sea, undeniably hostile. Then there were the Germans, violently and successfully so. Then—not last at all, often near the top of my private list—there were the people who were supposed to be on my side: certain of my shipmates and superiors, the small string of putrid albatross which never left my neck.

Who remembers the old fights?—not with humour, but with the blood-chilling anger which they provoked at the time? *Campanula* was a miserable ship in which to serve, under the discipline and submission to which I had sworn; and I used to curse the day, and the stroke of ugly luck, and the very admiral who had assigned me to her odious wardroom. Now, like love or acne, it does not matter. But then it was awful—a Winchester afloat, a jail swine-fevered forever; and to this horrid coop I was committed, without a single idea in my head of how to get out.

The last convoy of March was one of the most terrible so far, completing the toll of an awful month which had started with the loss of twenty-nine ships *in one week;* from the atrocious weather, and then from the enemy, we took such a mauling that my private graph (Are we winning? Are we losing? How will it all end? Watch this space!) made its steepest nose-dive of the war, far below the horizon of hope. A scudding wind was bashing us against the pier as we began to make ready for sea; the familiar summons in the familiar accent: "Hands to stations for leaving harbour! Special sea-duty-men—close up!" sounded like the chaplain's call for a dawn hanging.

There were snowflakes in the navigation lights as we went down river. They swirled against us, and then with us; they were very beautiful, a sort of magic—for who but God or the Officer-of-the-watch could command red snowflakes, and green snowflakes, and then red snowflakes again, as if performing some gigantic con-juring trick with a child's chemistry set? But for sailors who had given up the wonders of nature for the duration, the foreboding trick was only a trick.

So it turned out. The wind was westerly, hard westerly, as we butted our way outwards from the Bar Light Vessel into the Irish Sea, and set course for Chicken Rock, off the Isle of Man. We had twenty ships under our wing, the Liverpool portion of the west-bound convoy; and for many long hours we cherished them, and chivvied them, and joked with them, and told them to make less smoke and crack on more speed. Then, rounding the last light of England, we turned north, and began to roll and shudder in good earnest.

Very slowly we drew past places which we only knew as labels, the names of lighthouses and headlands and forbidding cliffs; places we would never visit, places we might never see again. But we had learned them all by heart now, as one must come to know a necklace of significant stones; the pretty names alternated with the rough ones—Mull of Galloway, Mull of Kintyre, Islay, Skerryvore, Tiree, and Muck; and then, after a distant glimpse of two truly strange retreats—the Sound of Eigg and the Sound of Rum— we went rolling rolling rolling up through the Minches, with more names to ring more bells.

This was our own branch line on our own suburban spur: Barra Head, Eriskay, Benbecula, Dunvegan, Shiant, Stornoway, Point of Stoer, Butt of Lewis, and the fearful Cape Wrath. On passage, we picked up ships like anticipant girls—some of them very old girls; gradually we drew together a vast acreage of sixty-five merchantmen which, with us, was trying for the tenth or the twentieth or the fiftieth time the fearsome passage from the old world to the new.

Cape Wrath was our last sight of land; its grim outline, thrashed by centuries of giant rollers, blurred and blasted by spray, faded astern as we turned north-west again for Iceland, and into the teeth of an Atlantic gale, enough (said our Leading Signalman, a noted phrase-maker) to blow the balls off a bull.

The convoy was in fighting shape now, in spite of all the elements against it: a huge blunt fortress of ships, ranged in eight columns and more than two miles wide from flank to flank: with six scurrying corvettes as outriders, and an elegant old V & W destroyer * to keep the whole thing in line. The fact that the convoy stayed resolutely in this pattern was something I never ceased to marvel at, and to admire.

In the next six howling days and nights, with visibility anything from poor to nothing at all, it still remained a convoy: keeping good station, preserving discipline and order, turning when it was ordered to turn, showing no lights, making no betraying smoke. These were men, it should be remembered, whose first instinct on sighting another ship was to keep as far away from it as possible: to whom collision was the ultimate disaster; who truly hated such close company.

And yet, in this awful weather, which made a big ship almost unmanageable, and a small ship a wildly bucking hazard, they still agreed to crowd together and to obey the rules; and on the bridge of the Commodore's ship the man in total charge was

---

* So christened because of their names: *Wolverine, Walker, Vanoc, Vortigern*, etc. They were designed, and some of them saw service, in 1917.

probably a retired admiral, not less than sixty-five years old, who had left a Sussex garden or a Chelsea flat or a fireside of grand-children to take on this grinding sea-duty again.*

I could never forget, and I did not forget now, that while we took pride in our little blue suits and little brass buttons and little bits of gold braid, and zigzagged about and turned on a sixpence and dashed off towards the nearest horizon, there were other sailors—thousands of them—who had to stay faithfully in convoy, and keep their unwieldy ships in line, even in this wallowing turmoil; who trusted us to guard them while they plodded onwards at a speed grotesquely less than their best; whose ships were often *the* target—slow-moving, slow-turning, large, violently inflammable.

Yet, when one met them ashore, elbow-to-elbow in a dockside pub, they were quiet men in quiet shabby suits, in whose quiet voices the enormous tensions of this shared ordeal could not even be guessed at.

Our battering continued, for watch after watch and day after day; *Campanula* had deteriorated to her usual ugly shambles, with water sloshing about in the mess-decks, and one of the wardroom armchairs thrown against a bulkhead and smashed to splinters. The food had gone the same way as the ship; for three days we had been reduced to a changeless menu, at all meals, of tea, soup, and corned-beef sandwiches. Nothing more ambitious could be made to stay in or on the galley stove.

There was one comforting thought, to help the eternal strain and tiredness; it was too rough for U-boats, which would have given up the hopeless task of taking aim, and be comfortably riding this out, in the still calm of six fathoms down.

But there was another thought, not so comforting, which went with this, as the ship took her endless punishment, and successive tons of sea-water came roaring over the fo'c'sle and thudded down on to the well-deck. If it was too rough for U-boats, might it not be too rough for us? Small ships, hammered too fiercely, rolling too far under a solid top-weight of water, could sometimes lose

---

* Among their honoured ranks was the man with the longest name in the Navy List: Admiral the Hon. Sir Reginald Aylmer Ranfurly Plunkett-Ernle-Erle-Drax. He was a sprightly sixty-three when he took on the job.

their stability, and the heart that went with it, and give up altogether.

Within sight of Iceland it was bitterly cold ("Brass monkey weather," said the Leading Signalman, whose mind seemed focused on one tender area of suffering). The black forbidding land loomed up briefly, and was lost in the scud again; later on, high above it, in one clear patch of night, a fantastic spread of northern lights, changing shape and colour every second, flickering ten miles high in tongues of cold flame, gave the scene a fearful beauty.

We shed a few ships for Reykjavik, and wished above everything that we could have been one of them—anything for peace, anything for a dry ship and a deep sleep—and then we turned southwards again, groaning and labouring, for our meeting with the east-bound convoy, the one we were, at long last, to take home with us.

Luck, and naval navigation, and skillful planning by slide-rule men on those faraway east and western shores, gave us a perfect rendezvous—correct to within five miles, in an ocean which held thirty-one million square miles of salt water, all of it in total disorder. The change-over was without dramatics: we gave them our lot, and took over theirs, and then settled down in station again.

But turning in the teeth of this gale, bringing the ship round with agonizing slowness, wallowing helplessly in a long succession of huge wave-troughs, and then starting to run before a wicked following sea which often lifted our stern higher than the top of our funnel—that set the pattern for another two long days of torture.

Running before a wind so strong was hell for everyone, not least for the arm-weary helmsmen, who had to wrestle with a ship which simply would not keep in one straight line. We yawed wildly from side to side, and buried our nose deep into grey-green water, and shouldered that off, and then felt a fresh blow of malice, an iron thudding as the next huge wave crested without warning and broke over our stern.

Sometimes, for a treacherous change, the sea seemed to explode under our bows: an enormous pile-up of water would collect itself, and come to the boil, and hiss, and roar, and then burst outwards with a hammer-blow and a mad phosphorescent smother of foam. After forty-eight hours of this, the wind unbelievably took on an extra edge of frenzy, and the wise Commodore signalled us all to heave-to—which meant turning our raw faces into the storm again, with the same painful slowness, and settling down with the wind on the port bow, and the bare revs to give us steerage-way and keep us balanced there.

Sadly, despairingly, we had turned our backs on home, and were going the wrong way. But at least we were doing it very slowly; and perhaps the whole ocean itself, under this violent attack, was moving eastwards for England, taking us with it as it went.

We were imprisoned thus for a day and a night, and then, at the second dawn, there came a sudden lull. Our world fell silent; the rigging and the signal halyards and the funnel-guys gave up their screaming, and slatted idly in the sulky air; the waves no longer broke, but butted us, and each other, with lumpish ill-humour. While it lasted, we waited in this stillness, suspecting it, uneasy at such swift respite.

It might mean peace at last, or else this was the eye of the storm, only waiting to spring another trap.

The battered convoy, seizing the chance, drew its ranks together, came quickly round, and headed eastwards with hopeful readiness; and then, with no more notice than a distant sighing, the wind itself whipped round, and picked up its surging strength, and began to blow savagely against us again. It was now a northeast gale, straight from Siberia; the other side of this treacherous coin; and there was now a vile cross sea, baffling, coming at us from all angles, to make it viler still.

But this, it turned out, was only a quick, two-day piece of spite; presently, after a pitch-black howling night, it really did ease off, and once more we pulled ourselves together, coaxed the convoy into tight shape again, and set a fair course for home. It was the sixteenth day already, and we were still in twenty-five degrees West, a thousand miles from safety; and very soon, as if to make the point beyond doubt, the radio began to chatter, and from Commander-in-Chief, Western Approaches, using his magic box in faraway, much-loved Liverpool, the first U-boat reports began to arrive.

In the better weather, they had come up for air, and for us.

It was an established sequence: the wolf-pack pattern which the Germans were now bringing to a grisly peak of efficiency. One U-boat must have spotted us (the convoy had made quite a lot of smoke when it put on speed again, and in clear weather smoke could be seen from fifty miles away). He had called up all his chums, strategically placed across a hundred miles of the known convoy tracks, and waiting for this sighting report; and within twenty-four hours, as the diligent Admiralty signalled, there were "up to seven U-boats in your area."

The familiar sick feeling took hold of *Campanula*—or at least it took hold of me, a good average coward, and I did not mind owning to it. The odds were rough indeed; if we had had double the number of escorts, seven U-boats could always get through the screen. All it needed was for two of them to show themselves, or make some kind of diversion (firing a distress rocket was a favourite) ahead and astern of the convoy; corvettes had to be sent away to investigate; the convoy's flanks were thus left with gaps literally a mile wide, and through these the other U-boats slid, and went to work.

It was a middle watch attack, as usual, starting with an under-water thud reported by a stunned asdic operator, and then a huge sheet of flame, topped by acrid smoke billowing black against the stars on the far side of the convoy. It could only be an oil-tanker. . . . I pressed the alarm-bell for action stations, but already I could hear sea-boots, of men in a hurry, men in fear or expecta-tion, drumming and echoing along the iron decks. It was not a night for sleeping.

It was in fact the start of a desperate, three-day, running fight with the enemy, during which we lost eleven ships and got noth-ing in return. I do not want to fight it again. But there were certain highlights, or lowlights, or moments of special ugliness and terror: successful snapshots in the odious album of war, the ones that came out, and because of their quality stayed out, and have never faded.

These did not always happen when "Darken ship" was piped: when the deadlights were dropped and screwed home over the portholes, and canvas screens were rigged across all entrances, and the wheelhouse shutters were put up: when no single chink of light showed, and we settled down to wait for the first blood of the night.

One torpedo scored a hit in broad daylight, on what must have been an ammunition ship; we had noticed her earlier, because she carried a packed deck-cargo of armoured cars and medium tanks, and aircraft with folded-back wings, stuck on to the upper deck like presents on a Christmas tree.

She went up with a great roar, disintegrating from end to end at a single stroke; and after that her place in the convoy was marked only by huge spray-filled splashes as that precious deck-cargo fell back into the sea, item by item.

The U-boats sank two more tankers, to add to the first victim. They were only small ones, but death in burning oil must always be just about the same size.

Not all the news was awful. We had an old friend with us, a big bluff tanker called *Narragansett Bay* which we had escorted many times before. The U-boats got the ship ahead of her, and the ship astern, but they didn't get her.*

While we were collecting the aftermath of this considerable mess, just after dawn, a Sunderland flying-boat (known to us as a steam chicken) flew over on its patrol. She signalled, on her Aldis lamp: "What happened?" The captain was fed up, as usual, with other people's stupidities, and for once I didn't blame him. He sent back: "Everything," and we got on with the task of tidying up a most squalid corner of the sea.

We had with us what was known as a CAM-ship, the initials standing for Catapult Aircraft Merchant: an ordinary freighter, but specially equipped to launch a Hurricane fighter-plane from a monstrous steam-catapult on the fo'c'sle. When the pilot had finished his job, he ditched his aircraft and parachuted down; it was an expensive, even madcap exercise, but it was aimed at doing something about a new breed of German reconnaissance plane called a Focke-Wulf (at least, some called them that) which was currently plaguing our convoys.

One of them was plaguing us now; the Hurricane took off in

---

* Not till nearly four years later, when in the last months of the war she went up in flames. I was in mourning that day.

a cloud of steam and a whirl of salty spray, chased its quarry and lost it, and the R.A.F. pilot then jumped, according to the drill. But a cross-wind carried him into the middle of the convoy, which could not stop for such heroics; and while we waited astern to pick him up, his parachute got entangled in the propellers of a small, intent, persevering merchant ship which also could not leave its station, nor alter course, nor slacken speed, nor cut him loose; and he was towed away to a dog's death—but slowly.

The third night was the worst; we lost five good ships, and uncounted men, and we never came to grips with a single one of the enemy. Struck with the guilt of sailors who should have done much better, who should have warded off at least some part of this slaughter, we did the only thing left to us—stopped engines, and waited, dead in the water, to pick up survivors.

We were not the only dead in the water. By the light from a ship burning handily nearby—which incidentally gave *Campanula* a wonderful silhouette for any marksman in the outer ring—we could see the usual rubbish of disaster: crates, planks, balks of timber, coal-dust, doors, rope-ends, a dead cat, odd bits of clothing, empty life-rafts, and wallowing corpses—all floating in inch-thick stinking oil, all part of the wrecked jumble-sale which was the only souvenir of a wrecked ship.

But presently it became the familiar seascape with figures. Men lived here. There was a lifeboat coming towards us, with creaking oars; there were dozens of little lights clustered together—the small bulbs, clipped to life-jackets, which gave men still swimming their only chance of being seen in time for rescue.

There were the sounds of men thrashing about in desperate terror; shouts of "Don't go away!" shouts of "Help me!" shouts of "Christ!" There were the other sounds, of men dying, cold to the bone but still showing a last hot anguish for life; and the particular throaty gurgle of men swallowing oil instead of air, and trying to cough it up through a scalding gullet, and failing, and giving up life instead.

We did the best we could. Among the lolling dead who drifted alongside and were hauled in with the rest, there was one extraordinary object: like a dummy figure, like a caricature of a man, grossly swollen, with a great pink face which, by the light of a torch, might have been part of some obscene carnival.

Staring down at it, I had visions of a new weapon, a decoy-man which, like a decoy-duck, lured others to their doom. Still slow in the uptake, I called down to the leading seaman clinging to the foot of the scrambling net, who was trying to get a line round this bobbing balloon: "What on earth is it?"

He looked up at me. His face in the torch-light was the colour of putty. Then he was sick. Then he called back: "It's an old one."

We did the best we could, on that night as on the other nights. We picked up a total of one hundred eighty survivors in the three-day action; the crowding, and the stench of oil all over the ship, the groaning and the retching, the patient agony and the trembling terror, gave *Campanula* a foretaste of the very marrow of hell. There were twelve Norwegians and Danes and Poles, some bare-footed, some in rags of uniform, quartered in the wardroom; one hundred sixty-eight Malays and Chinese and Indians in the crammed messdecks. "There's a big raffle on, sir," said my friend the Leading Signalman, who was helping me. "First fifty winners get to the heads."

It was worth a thin laugh, but not much more. I was a busy man, on that last night; and I was down in the messdecks myself, seeing how the poor lived, ten feet below the waterline, ten feet from the barest chance of safety. It had been crowded enough with eighty-eight of our own crew; now, with another one hundred sixty-eight men added, it was chaos.

The survivors filled every available space: asleep on the steel deck, on benches, against bulkheads: sitting at tables with their heads between their hands: talking, shivering, wolfing food, staring at nothing. Some of them were half-naked, wrapped in blankets; some had wretched little cardboard suitcases clutched between their knees. There were puzzled black features, pinched yellow ones, bleary white masks, oil-streaked blurs of the human face.

There were men praying, and weeping, and laughing on a cracked note of hysteria, and crooning as they cradled their dead friends; and other men struck dumb, but screaming with their eyes.

This was my surgery, on that busy night. Here were the men waiting to be helped, and other men waiting to be buried.

I did the best I could, with the Coxswain to bear a hand, and the Leading Signalman to hold the first-aid kit, and a telegraphist who had once been a vet to give me a second opinion. But how did one set a broken thigh, when this, wrenched askew by the strongest muscle in the body, simply would not come straight again? How did one tell a burned man, while staring straight into his jellied eyes, that he would be feeling better soon? What did one do for the tortured lascar with the mortal oil seeping down into his gut? Say "Choke up, chicken!" like my mother before me?

Often I willed such men to die, even while I tended them; and sometimes they agreed. The sound of their dying was not so wide as a church door, nor so deep as a well, but by God it was enough, it would serve. Yet when the longed-for silence did fall, when they became acquainted with death, that was the worst moment of all.

Then, sometimes, the whole awful picture blurred to nothing, as compassion, the enemy of manhood, came flooding in uncontrollably. Then the Coxswain would say: "Your eyes are running, sir. Must be the smoke. I'll wipe them off."

He wiped them off, while men, like death, looked stolidly on. He knew all about my running eyes; otherwise the cotton-waste would not have been so handy.

One of my father's odd bits of old wartime slang had been to say, when a man was killed in the trenches, that he had become "a landowner in France." Now, in my turn, I could greatly improve on this; the moment had come when I could confer on these lost warriors the vast freehold of the Atlantic.

I was unspeakably tired as I stood balanced on the swaying quarterdeck in that pale and miserable dawn, and prepared to wind up my accounts. My face was stiff with cold; my sea-boots had leaked a clammy mixture of God-knows-what which I could feel between my toes; there was blood on the sleeves of my duffle coat, and my hands were begrimed with oil. I had been up all night, and we had been at action stations for nearly all the past seventy-two hours. I felt light-headed, and realized I was vulnerable.

I cut the service as short as I could, knowing, as soon as I had stumbled over the "Off caps!" order, that the performance would not be too good. Fancifully, I seemed to hear a spectral voice, borne on the mourning wind, echoing its complaint about

Ophelia's "Maimèd rites"; calling me a churlish priest; asking me "What ceremony else?"

Just for once, I did feel that burial as a loss, as a truly sad moment. I *did* want some ceremony else, not for the dead but for the living, for the small bunch of bedraggled survivors, and our own burial party, who had come aft for the committal.

I wanted—God! how I wanted—to say something true about the grey anonymous canvas oblongs ranged at my feet: how they had been sailors like us, how lonely and cold was their grave, how it could happen to any of us at any moment, how it was a waste and yet a hopeful payment, how I wanted us all to remember this, because, because . . .

But there was really no time; and probably the words would not have come to a stumbling tongue, in any case. I might have managed "Dry sorrow drinks my blood," and then turned away in fresh tears. That was no way to behave, even in this watery desert.

So I cut it short, and at an early moment they were tipped over, and slipped down into the great shroud of the sea: the final act of a short, bad play which had started lyrically enough with:

> Oh shipmates, help me up!
> For I'm drifting with the tide,
> And I'm sinking in the Lowland sea,

and ended now with this sullen splash.

But it was still the cleanest burial of all—and even at that moment I remembered a slightly drunken conversation, years earlier, with a man belonging to the Imperial War Graves Commission, who had just come back from Flanders. He had been busy transferring World War I bodies from a small cemetery to a larger one, in the interest of economizing on real estate, and to appease the French.

"There are never any coffins left, *as such*," he had told me, importantly. "No uniforms either. Just a skeleton, and some buttons, and the socks. Always the socks."

Always the socks. . . . I put on my cap, saluted, and turned away, and climbed up to the bridge to enter my own graveyard item in the deck-log. Then I went below to the messdecks. There were so many things to do, at the dawn of another day, and I had to be on watch again at noon.

But nothing lasted forever, not even murder at sea. It was the R.A.F. who eventually came to our rescue, not for the first time; they sent out two of their new flying-boats, called Catalinas, and then two more, on a round-the-clock search-and-strike patrol which really worked. The planes kept the U-boats below the surface by day, and scared them down again with flares at night; gradually the convoy was able to draw ahead, and slip out of danger.

Catalinas were remarkably graceful in flight, and remarkably hardworking also; some of these patrols lasted up to seventeen hours, which was a lot of time to spend flying round a bunch of matelots who couldn't look after themselves. We blessed them as we made our escape, and plodded slowly home with what we had left.

This was quite a lot of ships, in fact, though it hadn't felt like it while the convoy was taking its thrashing; we still had fifty-four deep-laden merchantmen on our books, and as we led the Liverpool portion up river we began to feel happier. There was something about this safely delivered consignment, steaming slowly in line ahead up the muddy Mersey River, which was exciting and satisfying, in spite of past miseries.

We had been brothers-in-arms for so long, across a thousand miles of wicked ocean; there were gaps, of course, and some sad backward glances at the losers, but there were plenty of winners also, full of arms, full of food, full of all the things so badly needed, and here they were, coming into harbour like champions.

The finish did not seem too tame, nor too depressing. It was even, on a minor key, triumphant. There was still this solid array of ships; there were our one hundred eighty survivors, now crowding the rails and looking at the shore-line as if it were part of Eden instead of the distant prospect of Bootle. I had not killed too many men. And we still had, somewhere down the queue, the good old *Narragansett Bay*.

The finish was enlivened by an incident which was not tame at all. Steaming past the Bar Light Vessel, we touched off a magnetic mine, and this could really be called a near-miss; it exploded with a shattering bang and a huge column of dirty water, about thirty yards astern of us. There was no damage, except to our nerves; but we reported it swiftly to the shore signal-station, in case it was one of a cluster.

Perhaps we made it sound worse than it was. Their immediate acknowledgment came in the form of the most heartless signal ever to reach us from Western Approaches Command. It was the simple directive:

"Do not sink in the swept channel."

Campanula scraped the knuckle of the dock as we came into harbour, and it was my fault; in charge on the quarterdeck, I misunderstood one of those mysterious whistle-blasts, and held on to the back-spring too long. The ship lost a bit of paint, and I some poise. *"Monsarrat!"* came the expected roar from the bridge. "What the hell are you playing at?"

But he could not really harm me now. We were due for a boiler-clean, and at last it was my turn for leave—five days of blissful relief from the violence of all my enemies. This could not be stolen from me either: not without an injustice so barbarous that even my fellow-officers would have to take note of it.

2.

I had got married on 7 September 1939, four days after war broke out, as a matter of clear necessity (though this should not be mis-construed: our son was not born till 1942). But the enormous confusion and uncertainty dictated by war, the severance of so many accustomed ties, the massive breaking of rules, all seemed to make such a step inevitable; a loving marriage was the answer, the anchor, the rock, restoring the comfort and security which war was robbing from almost every other nest.

Her name was Eileen Rowland; we had been engaged for about six months, in the face of tepid enthusiasm on the part of her parents. I was manifestly a poor prospect, a cul-de-sac in the tun-nel of love; her mother took a dim view of my inward nature ("Bolshy!") and my outward appearance, especially my only pair of shoes, which were of grey suede scuffed down to the bone.

Her father was dubious about my financial prospects, candidly admitted to be nil.

Since he headed a company which made such a large proportion of the world's abrasive instruments that they could call themselves, accurately, Universal Grinding Wheels, with a factory about half a mile long to be seen as one's train drew into Stafford station, he was uniquely qualified to judge this particular field.

But I liked him, and he was always nice to me, though I was aware all the time that he could tell a fortune-hunter at a very considerable distance, just as Eileen's mother could spot an "actor fellow," as I had promptly been labelled, the moment he slid his dusty boots on to the high-gloss drawing-room parquet.

However, the fearful deed had been done, at Marylebone Town Hall (best man, senior witness, and champagne pourer, old friend Norman Pearson from darkest Nottingham); and we had set up house in a tiny flat in Church Street, Kensington, conveniently sited over a grocer's shop (London flats were very easy to pick up, at that doubtful moment of history). We lived frugally on my stretcher-bearer's pay of £2 18s. 5d. a week, plus Eileen's dowry of £1 a week from her parents. Since my working hours were twelve on and twelve off, changing to night-duty every other month, married life was disjointed; but we were very happy, independent at last while conducting some singularly tight housekeeping based on a black japanned money-box with seven labelled divisions: Rent, Coal, Food, Gas, Electricity, Sundries, and, unbelievably, Savings (2s. 6d. a week).

Marriage had seemed important when it happened, under the first impact of war. Now, two and a half years later, it had become essential, involving reason itself. I knew already (and it did not need blood, squalor, nor the miserable pricks of authority to drive the point home), that I would never survive this particular prison sentence without her; and the debt remained, never to be repaid, long after the war was won and the tender magic had been swallowed by it, or destroyed by me, or lost in a post-war, duller-than-dull detergent wash.

Women, I found, were marvellous at war—in their bravery, their disguise of emotion, their careful ignoring of time. They could fashion out of mundane sticks and stones a center of warmth and peace, giving it their whole care although they knew, better than anyone, that it could only be enjoyed for a short while. This they maintained secure, against all the aching odds, under the very shadow of dispersal. They spent themselves to the limit while one was there, knowing that the next zero-hour, the next circle of the clock, meant bankrupt solitude again.

War was inevitably a matter of saying goodbye, usually in grisly circumstances: on black winter mornings, in grimy railway stations, outside dock-gates in the rain. It was made more grisly still, for both of us, by knowing exactly what lay in store as soon as the bell tolled: I was headed for my particular menu of cold, exhaustion, boredom, and fear, while she went back to her empty lair, to find, on the mat, a fresh sheaf of directives from the Ministry of Food. But we had managed to give this whole process a lift by renting a small cottage in Gateacre, a village just outside Liverpool, and there setting up house.

It was only a bungalow, as shabby, run-down, and drafty as a bottom-of-the-garden shack; but it was the rock-cave I had to have, and Eileen swiftly fashioned it into a longed-for home. I had already invested in a motor-cycle, a 2½ horsepower Frances-Barnett, as a means of getting about when public transport was curtailed or, under threat of an air-raid, had given up altogether; and this was my home-coming chariot, my link between Albert Dock in the gruesome heart of Liverpool and the rustic solitude waiting for me outside.

We did nothing at all in that funny little house, except eat and sleep and make love and, as far as I was concerned, uncoil the fearful spring which a seventeen-day convoy could tighten almost beyond endurance. We had one prime blessing, a treasured gramophone which I had bought second-hand, for thirteen pounds, on the first day of the war, as a gesture in the face of all that was plaguing us, or was going to, and on this we listened, with deep content, to our music: Mozart piano concertos, Beethoven quartets, the simple rites of Telemann and Purcell. I read *War and Peace,* the current target of all those who had never managed to buckle down to it, and after that *Crime and Punishment,* and then, with a backward glance, *Remembrance of Things Past* again, and then the doyen of all the great novels, *Vanity Fair.* Eileen knitted *matinée* jackets for her pregnant friends, while I wore slippers for sixteen hours a day.

We ate with relish, occasionally with elegance. But some of our meals were spare indeed, and guiltily enjoyed. What we were swallowing was not food but coupons, the rarest of all the war-time treasures. The ration-book was the real required reading, not a lot of rubbishy old novels; and coping with this drab, day-to-day puzzle was now her destiny, whether I was there or not.

I came back from one precious leave to find, on board *Campanula,* a superior break in the clouds. Suddenly I had an ally, someone I could talk to; instead of the zoo-like grunting and snuffling which had ruled us so far, actual sentences were now to be heard, with verbs and all.

My rescuer was a man called Jim Harmsworth—or, more correctly, Lieutenant St. J. B. V. Harmsworth, R.N.V.R., a Dead-End Kid like myself (there were an awful lot of lieutenants R.N.V.R. in the Navy, chained forever to their oars), whose cheerful disposition did much to dispel the gloom of our non-advancement as well as the sub-zero temperature of *Campanula* herself. He had been a barrister, and hoped one day to return to practice "when all this inconvenience is over."

Sometimes he mentioned, without emphasis, "my cousin Esmond." As a small ex-snob from Liverpool, I was very impressed. Cousin Esmond was Lord Rothermere, a man of such power and prestige in Fleet Street that his principal toy, the *Daily Mail,* had no need to be either consistent, accurate, or discerning. It was simply successful.

Jim Harmsworth, as well as his distinguished name, had the added glamour of having been torpedoed, in an armed merchant cruiser called *Patroclus* which went to the bottom off Bloody Foreland in November 1940.

"Oh, I simply swam about," he said, when questioned about this. "There were various people looking after us, and they came round to me before too long. But I may say that Bloody Foreland was christened with tolerable accuracy. Quite apart from the snow, the water was *extremely* cold."

He had also established, though God knows how, that *Patroclus* had been sunk by U.99, under the command of one of the three top German aces, Captain Kretschmer. Kretschmer had been taken prisoner, after finally losing his U-boat, about a month earlier, and was now languishing on the Isle of Man.

"I must confess that I opened a bottle of fizz when I heard about it," was Jim's comment on this. "And I did *not* remember him at Christmas."

At that moment of history he had grown a large red beard,* though the effect was appealing rather than imposing, like a Father Christmas known to be only Daddy after all. As an officer, he was easy-going, and famous on board as an undeniably soft touch, from the disciplinary point of view.

Once, when an infuriated "Hostilities Only" able-seaman, hauled before him by the hard-breathing Coxswain, burst out in a sudden snarl of revolt: "Well, I'm buggered if I'm going to be buggered about by a silly old bugger like this bugger here!" Jim's comment was: "You are in some danger of becoming monotonous."

I was glad to note, many years later when he was a magistrate at Great Marlborough Street Police Court, and dealing with a substantial traffic in student protest, that things had tightened up considerably in this area.

Liverpool was now, more than ever, a sailors' town; night after night, month after month, sailors by the tens of thousands, from a dozen escort groups and a hundred merchant ships, came rolling ashore, intent on drinks and girls and perhaps a good brisk fight at closing-time; and the fact that these licensed marauders, turning the place upside down, were still welcomed and forgiven by the sober inhabitants, made me more sure than ever that the city of my birth had a special quality, a special spirit, which nothing was going to quench: not the weather, not the Germans, not even us.

It was wonderful to walk down *Campanula*'s steep gangway, free of the farmyard at last, and traverse the jetty on my faithful Frances-Barnett: past the nose-catching dockside lavatory where, I knew, a shaky hand had chalked the inscription which had so

---

* Our entire wardroom, save for the captain, was now heavily bearded. A *News Chronicle* photographer who made a trip with us observed, on first seeing us: "Christ, that's quite a crop of horticulture you've got there!" We were glad he was so seasick.

delighted me at the age of thirteen: "This is where the knobs hang out"; past the indulgent customs men (indulgent over a pot of jam or a tin of corned beef, not at all indulgent about cigarettes or anything in a bottle); past the tall policeman who always said: "Enjoy yourself, lads!" and out on to the wide cobbled freedom of Pier Head.

Ashore, we left the salt grime behind, and wore spotless suits of warranted, superfine, No. 1 doe-skin, and high-gloss ankle boots from Gieves, and pigskin gloves, and, by edict, the prime nuisance of the war, our gas-masks. The target was always the Adelphi Hotel, that splendid monument to heavyweight Edwardian charm, built when no one would dream of using a brick where a stone would do, or a stone when a slab of mottled marble was just the ticket.

This was the mecca where, ten years earlier, I had daily surrendered my bowler-hat and gold-topped Malacca cane, and taken Afternoon Tea in the lounge. Now, as we went through the revolving door in search of the same sort of gilded relaxation, it was marvellous to find the welcome as assured as ever.

There, *en route* for Gateacre, and peace, and Eileen's blessed cooking, and the first appetizing meal of the day, we besieged the American bar and got mildly plastered. There we gazed longingly at the permanent frieze of beautiful Wrens, though (even if we had not both been happily married) these flowers were not for us to pick; they were reserved for the base staff, against whom we would never have stood a chance.

These insidious shore-types were *there,* while we were not; they could lay a long-term siege while we had a bare three or four days to complete the mating dance; they could creep adroitly back into bed while we crept past the Mull of Kintyre.

There I once saw Vivien Leigh, more ravishing than ever, walking through to the grill room for an early dinner before she went on stage and entertained the troops. She gave me a wave and a gorgeous smile; then she turned back to her escort. He was a Rear-Admiral. What a hope!

There we once saw Mr. Winston Churchill, who had come north to cheer the city up after a bad blitz. He wore his Trinity House uniform, and looked like a good, dependable, sea-faring man; he also looked a very rock of confidence. Crossing the foyer, he gave us a beam and a victory sign, and we, having rocketed straight out of the bar, returned him an identical salute.

At that moment, I felt the same warm uplift as did the rest of the Western world whenever they caught sight of this lion among men, or heard his rallying snarl on the radio. In spite of firm principles, I could even forgive him his awful remark, when goaded in the House of Commons by Aneurin Bevan (whom he labelled "a squalid nuisance"): "I am told that one cannot get into the underground shelters because of the Socialist sewer rats who are there already."

Conservative or not, he was the man we had to have, and even a brief glimpse was enough to prove it.

There, one evening, Jim Harmsworth and I caught a German spy.

We had stayed longer than usual in the bar; Eileen had somehow procured—probably from her parents, who lived in the country and had access to all sorts of rarities—an actual whole ham; and to this unheard-of luxury, which might never come our way again, she wanted to give the sort of preparation and the scrupulous cooking which it deserved. We were not expected until nine.

We stood up at the American Bar counter, surveying the agreeable scene with tolerant good humour. Presently a voice at my side said: "Have you lads just come in?"

I turned on one elbow. It was a stranger in a dark suit, a small fifty-ish man with a lean face and friendly eyes. He looked all right—not a nuisance, not a homosexual. I did not mind the direct approach; I did not mind us being addressed as "lads"; at that stage, I did not mind anything.

"No," I answered. "As a matter of fact we've been here quite a long time."

The man smiled, with great good humour. "I mean, just in from your convoy?"

"Oh. Yes, we got in a couple of days ago."

"Rough trip?"

"Not too bad."

At my back Jim Harmsworth, like me at peace with all the world, asked: "Who's your friend?"

The stranger, changing places adroitly, stepped round until he stood between us. He murmured a name which I did not catch, and then said: "How about a drink?"

We were not in the mood to say no; and as far as I was concerned, gin-and-tonic at Adelphi shore-prices did not suit my lieutenant's scale of pay. Before long, we were a companionable trio. But there was no doubt that the third man was inquisitive.

"I work down at Gladstone Dock," he told us presently. "See a lot of you chaps coming in and out. What are you in? Destroyers?"

"Corvettes," I said.

"What are they like to live in?"

"Awful."

"But you get quite a long time in harbour, don't you?"

"Four or five days."

"Then I suppose you'll be off pretty soon."

I was about to say "Tuesday," and then I thought: "No, damn it—I'm not supposed to say that," and I answered instead: "It all depends."

He seemed to switch subjects very quickly. We turned—*he* turned—to ship repairs ("Of course, I'm interested, working at Gladstone"), and how well they were being done, and what the Liverpool dockers were like, and all the new kinds of equipment coming in.

It must have been at exactly the same moment that Jim and I, exchanging alert glances, decided that this man was an obvious German spy, and that we were being tempted into gross indiscretion. The moment was when the stranger asked: "I suppose you've got huff-duff?"

"Yes," said Jim, after a thoughtful pause. "We had it for lunch."

There was a merry laugh. "You know what I mean. HF/DF. Those bloody great aerials. I think I've seen one or two of the corvettes fitted with them. It must be a great help. *If* it works."

"Why shouldn't it work? What are you hinting at?"

The man, meeting Jim's keen and formidable glance, seemed to back away. That in itself was suspicious. . . . "Well, it's new, isn't it?"

"But what does HF/DF *do*?" I thought this question of mine was a very clever ploy; it switched the ball right back into his court, putting him in danger of betraying himself. Jim and I could certainly take care of this.

"I'm not an expert," the stranger countered. "I leave that to you chaps. Some sort of direction-finding, I suppose."

"Talking of that," said Jim, "I really must go and wash my hands. Then we must be off."

"So early?"

"In point of fact it is late."

"Come back and have another drink."

"I would prefer not."

Jim could be very stiff when he cared to, and this was one occasion. The man reacted:

"Well, you needn't be like that about it!"

Gone was our warm friendship; vanished the easy masculine companionship of the past hour. We were practically declared enemies; this was almost certainly one of the people on the warning posters; tittle-tattle might easily have lost this battle if we had not been so prudent, so vigilant.

"As a matter of fact," said Jim, "I don't like your attitude."

"I don't know what you're talking about! I haven't got an attitude!"

"That's what we don't like." It was my turn for the brilliant, telling dialogue. "Confidentially, do you think we're winning the war?"

"How should I know?"

"Ah! Alarm and despondency!"

"If I were you," said Jim, with enormous emphasis, "I should be extremely careful in the future."

We then roared away into the black of night on the Frances-Barnett. Our headlight with its slotted cardboard cover was masked down to nothing: Jim swayed to and fro on the pillion-seat: the red beard and the black streamed in the wind, while the road curved and dipped, and the front forks wobbled like a pair of jellied eels, and God spared us. Shouting above the up-roar, we decided that we had been more than a match for that insidious, traitorous swine.

Looking back on it, it seemed likely that the man was either a natural gossip, or a lonely character who actually did know a thing or two about our ships, or else one of our own security

officers, trying to find out whether careless talk had infected the
Navy, and if so, how deeply. I chose the latter, and I would have
dearly loved to have read the transcription.

Though full of patriotic resolve, we did not report the encounter ourselves. Eileen's glazed ham, adorned with hoarded
sugar and inherited cloves, was much too good to spoil; and next
morning, as on every other next morning, things seemed quite
different, as soberly explainable as the sunrise.

There was one special reason why it was so good to be back in
Liverpool. The war had, by fantastic chance, brought us all back
to our native city, to flog our guts out at a crucial moment in its
history: the "all" being my father, my brother Denys, and myself.

My father, who was now well into his seventieth year, had assumed a dull title (Group Officer, Emergency Medical Service)
and an appallingly demanding job: the disposition of all wartime
casualties, over a large area, from the first bang to the last dismissal to the grave.

This was at a time when Lancashire, whether from its own
air-raids, or from hospital trains from other harder-pressed areas,
or hospital ships from thousands of miles away, was at the
receiving-end of a steady, mounting tide of sick, broken, half-
dead or wholly dead fellow-citizens.

He discharged this task throughout the war, for six years on
end, working through the boredom and pettiness of the waiting
period, the fearsome casualties of the Liverpool blitz, and the gross
seepage of wounded and dying from the new fronts in France,
Africa, Italy, the Atlantic, and France again. It was the compassionate crown of a lifetime of looking after the wounds of other
people.

I found, on one occasion at least, that he could still find the
patience to look after my own.

I had told him, between one convoy and another, how awful
I found my absurd appointment as Medical Officer in *Campanula*;
how it sickened me, how I hated and feared it, how it was the one
thing about the Navy which I was not sure I could stand.

"If it is any comfort to you," he answered, in a memorable
lecture, "I felt exactly the same way when I was approximately
the same age as you—and don't forget, this was my chosen profes-

sion, the way I was going to earn my living and spend the rest of my life. I can tell you *now*" (did he think I had suddenly grown up?) "that the prospect appalled me. The worst moment was here in Liverpool, at the Northern Hospital.

"I was on duty in the casualty department, and my very first job was to be called down to the docks, in the ambulance, to do something about a stevedore who had been caught by a cargo-sling. The hook had gone through his mouth, and come out just below one eye. He was still hanging from it when I got there. I had once seen a fish like that—foul-hooked, we called it—but that was all. . . . Try to remember that these are only bodies, like your own; they are human, they are sad in suffering, but they are *material*."

He said "material" in a very special way, as a tailor might say "cloth," or an artist "paint"; it was clear that he had come to work unconcernedly with such material; he had touched it, shaped it, used it, liked it, perhaps honoured it; but above all he knew it, and he wanted me to know it too.

"Try to remember," he said again, "crude as the idea may seem, that a piece of the human body is like a piece of raw steak. You are not shocked by cutting up a raw steak. Do not be shocked by raw human flesh. Be gentle, be precise, be ruthless if you have to, but do not be sick."

I was still sick, now and again, but at the worst times I could always think of that cargo-sling, and know that I was not alone.

My brother Denys, in contrast with my father's dedicated life-time, had now achieved, at the age of twenty-seven, the first worthwhile job ever to come his way. Things had gone wrong for Denys, rather too early on the private road of life. A failure at Oxford had been succeeded by a futureless job in Nottingham. From this, glorious war had rescued him, as it rescued a melancholy and shameful proportion of young men caught in the same trap, the gross human swindle which was the fag-end of the Thirties.

He had joined up straight away, enlisting as a private in the Royal Artillery; as with my father, twenty-five years earlier, he was that sort of young man. The dead-end job, the lapse of promise, might have had something to do with it; but I think he could claim to have seen the thing more closely and urgently than I did, from the very beginning.

As I clung to the rags of pacifism, and fooled around as the man in charge of a stretcher-party depot which was not to be put to the test until a year later, Denys was already sweating away in khaki, and learning a really effective, professional job.

We had only met once, during that suspended period, when we foregathered in Nottingham for Felicity's wedding to a solicitor, Hilary Armstrong, who was also a newly minted soldier. Denys looked tough and competent, with, already, a Lance-Bombardier's stripe on his sleeve; technically I outranked him, in the foreboding black uniform of a St. John Ambulance Brigade sergeant.

When we greeted each other, he noticed that I carried a steel helmet, which he himself still lacked.

"We can't get those things for love or money," he protested. "Why on earth do they issue them to you chaps?"

"But," I said reproachfully, "I might have to go out in a blitz." He blinked, and said: "How perfectly horrid for you."

He was a gunner in an anti-aircraft battery.

His own marriage soon afterwards, to a girl called Meryl Wardle, on whom he had been concentrating ever since he returned to Nottingham, took place when I had just joined the Navy, and was totally dedicated to the task of learning to salute.

But I saw the wedding photographs; everyone looked very cheerful, and Denys' sergeant's stripes were well to the fore. By the time we met again, he had risen another important peg; the single pip on his shoulder proclaimed him a Second Lieutenant, and it was the A.A. job which had brought him to Liverpool, in charge of a battery which was part of the port defenses. I was part of the port itself, as was my father, and we were very glad to have him there.

When *Campanula* was in harbour, he used to come over to Gateacre on a large and brutal-looking khaki motor-cycle which made mine look like a half-starved chihuahua, and there, while Eileen cooked the dinner and Meryl helped her, we relaxed, and compared our brave deeds, and, the present being so uncomfortable and the future so doubtful, talked mostly of the past.

It seemed then more likely that I would be killed before he

was; and once, when we said goodbye on my sailing day, he used a foolish phrase: "Don't forget to sell your body dearly!" to acknowledge the fact. This was the closest we had ever been to each other, after the brotherly fights and feuds of the past; and it came at the most welcome moment of our joint lives.

I suppose he could picture me on the bridge of *Campanula,* when the darkness was suddenly split by flames; and I could certainly picture him on his frosty gunsite—the up-turned face, the eyes watching the sky, the ears straining, and at his side the pointed fingers of the gun-barrels, also probing a black roof which might at any moment let loose the hurtling splinters of war.

I once said that this waiting for the heavens to fall couldn't be much of a job. He answered: "Oh, I don't know. It's better than a poke in the eye with a burnt stick."

I decided that he must have been mixing with Australians.

There we all were, anyway, united in this hazard; the surgeon (the real surgeon), the sailor, and the gunner, all doing our best for King and Country and above all for Liverpool. But were we winning? It was, as we got deeper into 1941, very hard to tell. As the spy had protested in the Adelphi bar, how was I to know? How was anyone?

Certainly there were nuggets of good news. The pongoes, as we called them, were always bashing away in North Africa, where the desert war continued in a strange ebb-and-flow which kept enthusiasts for sticking pins into maps phenomenally busy. We had captured a sort of joke-town called Sidi Barrani, and another called Bardia on the Libyan-Egyptian border; we had gone on to capture (or was it recapture?) a town called Tobruk, a much-disputed prize which General Wavell had now wrested from Marshal Graziani, with a surrendered garrison of a hundred thousand Italian prisoners.

We had won a spectacular naval victory near Cape Matapan, off the southern tip of Greece, where Admiral A. B. Cunningham, in command of three warships which were actually veterans of the Battle of Jutland (1916), the *Warspite, Valiant,* and *Barham,* had stalked, cornered, and demolished a luckless Italian force of thirteen ships, including four ten-thousand-ton cruisers and three destroyers.

It was, we were presently told, the first use of radar in gunnery. But would small escort-ships ever get this weapon? Think of the difference it would make in station-keeping, in convoy, in spotting surfaced U-boats. . . . It was rumoured that one or two of our destroyers had already been blessed. Would corvettes ever get it?

"*Corvettes?*" our captain pronounced, in scornful dismissal. "We're sucking on the hind tit!"

But however we were placed at the udder of invention, we were at least getting some substantial nourishment from elsewhere. America was now sending us enormous amounts of war materiel, under the all-embracing title of Lend-Lease; and there was tremendous pressure within the United States to see that the stuff arrived safely, instead of being sunk or blown up on its journey across the Atlantic.

Henry Stimson, their Secretary of War, had declared: "The American Navy must safeguard our arms shipments to England. We cannot permit these sinkings"; and, by a generous interpretation of the word "neutrality," they were already operating Neutrality Patrols two thousand miles out into the Atlantic, which was more than halfway over. Presently they were escorting their convoys all the way to Iceland, at which point we took over; and one of the first friends we met, and talked to, in this exchange system was a U.S. destroyer called the *Reuben James,* which was itself the first U.S. warship to be torpedoed on this generous mission.

While a gifted namesake, Myra Hess the pianist, was initiating the National Gallery lunch-time concerts, one of the prime, intimate blessings of the war, Rudolf Hess, Hitler's own Deputy Führer, took off on a strange flying mission which, starting at Augsburg near Munich, ended when he bailed out in southern Scotland.

On arrival, he said that he was on his way to visit the Duke of Hamilton, "who would conduct him to King George," with a view to arranging a peace settlement. The Nazis, more factual, said that he was suffering from hallucinations and had been forbidden to fly. On balance, this very odd escapade was one to us.

Another one to us, much more certain, was the death of

Lieutenant-Commander Gunther Prien, probably Germany's top U-boat commander. In October 1939 he had brought off the most spectacular and daring *coup* of the war, by penetrating the intricate system of defense-nets and guard-ships at Scapa Flow, negotiating the sunken wrecks and the vicious rip-tides of that part of the world, and sinking the battleship *Royal Oak,* with the loss of 833 men.

At anchor inside Scapa Flow, *Royal Oak* had been a sitting duck. But only a brave and skillful man could have got such a prize within his sights, fired four torpedoes at it, stopped to reload, and fired three more. Prien, in U.47, had now been sunk by our own comrade, the destroyer *Wolverine.*

Then there was news which was good and bad mixed. We sank the German battleship *Bismarck,* brand-new and hugely powerful (forty-five thousand tons), after a tremendous sea chase which spanned the Atlantic from the north-west corner of Iceland to the latitude of Brittany. But it cost us another of our own prized warriors, the twenty-five-year-old battleship *Hood,* very early in the action.

Then there was one of the biggest surprises of the war, at least to simple sailors: the cancellation of that cynical pact of eternal friendship between Germany and Russia, by the most effective means available—a massive German attack across an eighteen-hundred-mile front which advanced like a swift steel arrow to within eighty miles of Moscow. It was nice to see our enemies falling out so decisively. But was this good news, or bad?

Then there was what had to be classed as the really bad news, without benefit of happy ending. There seemed to be an awful lot of this, as 1941 unrolled; the April figure of 106 ships lost at sea set the tone for all sorts of other places as well.

While the North African campaign swung to and fro, events in another nearby battle-area, Greece, were only swinging one way, and that was smack in our face. Greece was being steadily overrun by the Germans, and we with it; already we were fighting a rear-guard action, described on 30 April in an ominous phrase as "a fight to the last inch in Greece." In fact, we evacuated our forces two days later.

We then retreated a hundred miles south-east to Crete; and from *there,* less than a month later, after a twelve-day, very heavy attack by German parachute troops, we also withdrew, with a mere handful (fifteen thousand) of our surviving soldiers.

Yet even the Greek and the Cretan and very soon the North African bad news had its single bright side: the proof that we had friends. At this desperate hour, they had all come flooding in to help us, sometimes across half the span of the world—Australian and New Zealand fighting soldiers, South African and Rhodesian airmen, the Royal Indian Navy, and cheerful Canadian sailors sculling to and fro in their own corvettes, built on the shores of the St. Lawrence River.

They were to fight for us on every ocean, in every navigable sky, on every battlefield from Burma to Normandy. Already they were there when they were wanted, not waiting for a plaintive hail; and they had a solid, heart-warming, two-year start on the Americans, who, in the end, scooped the prestige pool.

I belonged to a party which had consistently derided the whole imperial concept, from the plumed helmets to the white man's burden of sweat, and I had done my fair share of making fun of this improbable structure myself. By now, I was sure that I had been wrong.

It was an emotional conversion, under all the pressures of a hard-fought war, but perhaps the Commonwealth, as it was presently to be labelled, was an emotional concept itself. In cold logic, it did not exist at all, except as a pattern of trading preferences; and these were bargains between merchants rather than ties between friends.

Yet the ties were there, strong as a New Year handshake, at this moment of history: ties of blood, of like thinking, of loyalty to "our" idea rather than to "theirs"—theirs being the German, which if it succeeded could bring the curtain down for the longest night of our lives. We needed help, and the help came, not with the sound of dragging feet—nor of dragging chains either—but with a guileless readiness only to be forgotten by the very priests of ingratitude.

Not even those prudent squirrels at the Ministry of Information could fudge or obscure the news about German air-raids, since their bombs were now cascading about our ears with almost continuous loud explosions, and such things got about. This was the beginning of the "Baedeker Raids," so nicknamed from the old German guidebook founded by Karl Baedeker in 1839, which set out the prime architectural treasures for the tourist to concentrate on.

Baedeker's highest praise was: "Not to be missed." Now our tourists were keen-eyed young men in Heinkels and Dorniers and Messerschmidts who, their lofty guidebooks in hand, made the very most of their visits. They hardly missed a thing.

Apart from the obvious, worthwhile ports like Liverpool and Plymouth and Southampton and the Pool of London, there had in fact been a curious concentration of spite upon cathedral cities: Bath, Canterbury, and Norwich were among them. The list of these Baedeker targets in London itself was formidable, by any standard.

They hit Buckingham Palace. They hit the House of Commons, destroying St. Stephen's Hall and damaging the Members' Lobby roof. They demolished our treasured Queen's Hall, where Sir Henry Wood and the Proms had taught me all I knew and loved in music. They bombed Westminster Abbey, St. James's Palace, the London Museum, Lambeth Palace, the Old Bailey, St. Clement Dane's Church, and, spreading their religious favours impartially, the headquarters of the Salvation Army in Victoria Street.

They scored a gruesome hit on the Café de Paris, the glittering night-spot near Leicester Square, so smart and expensive that I had only been there half a dozen times, by courtesy of Cambridge friends or later patrons who picked up the bill. The single bomb went through the roof and fell smack on to the bandstand, killing almost all the orchestra in mid-tune and a large number of people circling the packed dance floor.

The first thing which the rescue squads and the firemen saw, as their torches poked through the gloom and the smoke and the bloody pit which had lately been the most chic cellar in London, was a frieze of other shadowy men, night-creatures who had scuttled within as soon as the echoes ceased, crouching over any dead or wounded woman, any *soignée* corpse they could find, and ripping off its necklace, or earrings, or brooch: rifling its handbag, scooping up its loose change.

It was not the first air-raid looting I had heard of, but for some reason it seemed the worst.

Another sad air-raid casualty was the premises of my new publishers, Cassell's, who had chanced their arm on my first full-length (250,000-word), worthwhile novel, *This Is the Schoolroom*.* This had taken me nearly two years to write, and had been scheduled for publication four days after war broke out, on 7 September 1939, when no one was giving much thought to books or to anything else not directly geared to war.

Though they had held it over until October, it still sank without trace, and had earned, by the war's end, in England and America, £164 4s. 7d.

Now Cassell's themselves had almost been sunk without trace. In 1940 their Watford warehouse, containing two million books, had been gutted; now it was the turn of their cherished headquarters, La Belle Sauvage, at the foot of Ludgate Hill and rather too near St. Paul's Cathedral. Here they lost all their records, as well as priceless manuscripts and archives incorporating the *memorabilia* of such writers as Charles Dickens, Robert Louis Stevenson, Oscar Wilde, Thomas Hardy, W. E. Henley, and James Barrie.

The sad fact—as related to me by Desmond Flower, then a soldier but later, after his father Sir Newman Flower retired, the chairman of this phoenix-rising firm—was that Cassell's itself was not even directly hit. Other buildings in La Belle Sauvage were; scourging fires started all round them; since the faithful Thames was at low tide, the firemen could not get any water for their hoses; and the whole precious corner went up like a torch.

Other bombs even scored a hit on the august, venerable British Broadcasting Corporation. They demolished, among other things, a popular weapon of entertainment called the B.B.C. Theatre Organ; giving us, at least, one of the more superior jokes of the war: "The last thing played on the B.B.C. Theatre Organ was the hose."

But in the main it was an exhausting and terrifying ordeal, for half the nation at least; hardly to be relieved by promises of retaliation on Berlin, nor by such brief tonics as that cheerful Adelphi wave from Mr. Churchill, nor the brave words with which he concluded one of his matchless evening broadcasts:

---

* *This Is the Schoolroom* (Cassell, 1939; Alfred Knopf, Inc., 1940; Pan Books, 1960).

And not by eastern windows only,
When daylight comes, comes in the light;
In front the sun climbs slow, how slowly,
But westward, look, the land is bright.

The reference was, of course, to America, which one day, it was
hoped, would match her armaments with men and get us out of
this hole. But for me the words rang another sort of bell, and
when I looked them up, it was my old friend Arthur Hugh
Clough again, the Liverpool poet whose plaque on the wall of
No. 9 Rodney Street was still unmatched by one on the wall of
No. 11, where I was born myself.

Yet the first four lines of that poem, remembered from school,
had been:

Say not the struggle naught availeth,
The labour and the wounds are vain,
The enemy faints not, nor faileth,
And as things have been, things remain.

and these I found much more depressing, because of the doubts
they raised. Who could, with real confidence, say *not* to the suspicion of futility, at such a moment? Who could really prophesy
that the enemy would suddenly start to faint and fail—and if so,
why?

It sometimes seemed that the labour and the wounds *were*
going to be in vain; that we had started a job which we could
not finish, and that the price of trying would bankrupt us, in
blood and treasure, long before that westward sky brightened
into daylight.

As if to point up this morbid doubt, Liverpool, early in May
and three days after the Churchill broadcast, suffered the most
ferocious punishment of its life, from a week-long series of raids
which altered its pattern and perhaps its spirit forever.

I recorded it in my notebook, day by day, as it all happened,
because *Campanula* was in harbour, in the heart of the docks,
throughout that fearful week.

Liverpool, the hub of the Western Approaches command, was
a target well worth hitting. There were never less than a hundred
ships in harbour, loading and unloading; plus their tugs, and the

oil-storage tanks, and eleven miles of docks with their cranes and ammunition barges and ship-repair yards and warehouses and dock-gates and the whole network of rail-linkage which bound it to the rest of England. Worth hitting, it was now hit, with relentless accuracy, for eight nights on end.

The sustained, continuous bombing started huge fires, laid waste acres of the town, and killed hundreds of people. The fires, indeed, were one of the principal features; at dusk, each evening, there were always one or two of them still burning from the previous night's onslaught, serving as a pointer to the heart of the city from a hundred miles away.

Waiting on board in the middle of the dock area, the main target, we cursed those betraying fires, though without much conviction. We were for it, anyway; there was not much wrong with German air navigation, if they could hit us so hard in the total blackout of Day One.

In fact the docks often fared better than the main part of the town, and especially the crowded slum areas of Bootle and Wallasey, on either side of the river; but where the corvettes were berthed, three abreast along the quayside of Albert Dock, it was certainly bad enough. One night the bonded warehouse alongside us was set ablaze, and we had to land a fire-party to help put it out, expecting all the time that the whole flaming structure, glowing scarlet like a runaway oven, would crash down on to the upper deck.

Since corvettes weren't built for that sort of thing, we always warped ourselves out into the middle of the dock after that; it gave us, at least, an additional twenty yards' margin of safety.

The waiting, each evening, in the absolute certainty that the raids would go on for at least another night, was the finest exercise in patience, nervous control, and the avoidance of heroics, I had ever had; it also kept the sweat-glands in admirable trim. We were all nervous, and we all knew it; this was not our proper element at all: we should have been hundreds of miles out at sea, on one of those nice safe convoys. Sitting in the wardroom with a row of monster whiskies and sodas standing at ease in front of us, we did not bother to keep up even a token conversation.

It was always a relief, though a queasy one, when the sirens sounded, and we could leave the wardroom, pick up a steel helmet from the rack in the lobby, and go out on to the upper deck to man our modest guns, assemble our futile babyish sand-buckets, and tend the fire hoses. Action was the only cure for the acute nervous tension which had been gradually tightening since mid-day.

Each night had the same crude pattern: after the warning, a pause, and then the far-off guns, the near ones, the whistle and crash of falling bombs, the noise of buildings in dissolution, and men and women in pain, and the ring of fires which gave us, to-wards midnight, a daylight horizon all round the dark compass.

As we waited on the upper deck, wondering sometimes where the last bomb of an approaching stick of five was destined to fall, hearing the steel splinters clatter and clang on nearby ships or on *Campanula* herself, watching the sky with the rapt attention which was our twentieth-century substitute for star-gazing, I thought of Denys, somewhere out on the perimeter defenses, and hoped that he was wide-awake and that his shooting would be up to standard. Even if he discouraged *one* enemy plane out of the swarm above us, it bettered our chance of survival, and we could go off to sea again, and be torpedoed.

Campanula herself came nearest to dissolution from a huge land-mine which, floating down by parachute and silhouetted im-pressively against this bombers' moon, fell into the dock-basin with a gentle splash about twenty yards astern of us. Not knowing what sort of activity could touch this sneaky weapon off—it might be noise, electrical interference, temperature change, a certain pattern of vibration, or the simple lapse of time—we closed down everything we had, from the bilge pumps to the radio set, and, moving on tiptoe and talking in whispers, pulled ourselves out of the neighbourhood with our own strong arms. The mine went off next morning, killing nine men on a barge and blowing away a substantial section of the nearest building.

The Germans dropped a lot of those delayed-action land-mines; after the worst raid, on 6 May, they kept going off all the next morning, as if to assure us that we were not forgotten. I lost count at thirty-three. It was on that morning that I drove through the city on my way to Gateacre, to see if Eileen was all right.

There was no public transport, even if there had been negoti-able streets on which to ply; but I had the Frances-Barnett, the only means by which I could have traversed the torn, rubble-strewn acres of the city. As I made my way up from the docks, forced into a dozen slow detours, it was impossible not to feel the poignant contrast between being alive on a lovely May morning, and moving through the newly ruined streets of my birth-place, where billowing black smoke fouled the air, and smuts and wood-ash and charred paper, drifting on the wind, bore the reek of destruction across the whole county.

Poor Liverpool. . . . The Overhead Railway (nicknamed the Dockers' Umbrella), directly hit at James Street station, had collapsed into the street below, in a tangle of wood and metal, stone and trailing high-tension wires. From the docks up to Lime Street and Bold Street, great fires were still burning, their smoke filming the sun with an orange pall; other buildings lay sprawled in the roadway, surrounded by their familiar wartime ant-armies —the rescue workers digging and shoring, the ambulances waiting, the firemen sorting out their tangled hoses, the onlookers lining the curb in dull attendance on disaster.

James Street, Castle Street, it was all the same: buildings seared and scarred by flame, heaps of rubble which had yesterday been shops and offices: sagging overhead wires, a litter of splintered glass, crumbling brick, and torn woodwork defiling every street. A gaping front window in a tobacconist's bore a brave scrawled notice: "YES WE ARE BLASTED WELL OPEN!"

The whole of one side of Lord Street had been destroyed; farther up, near the damaged Adelphi Hotel,* two big stores were shattered and in flames. The streets which I had known so well as a boy, the walks which Felicity and Denys and I had taken, were now in confused ruin; here and there, even in this familiar and loved town, I did not know where I was, so complete was the obliteration.

---

* Jim Harmsworth had dined at the Adelphi one night earlier in the week, when the hotel itself was near-missed, a man killed by a freak blast on the fourth floor, and all the lights in the restaurant put out. That was the end of dinner, of service, and apparently of diners as well. Jim went back next morning, like a good citizen, to pay his bill. The restaurant manager, against a tawdry background of shattered glass and boarded windows, shook his head. "Compliments of the hotel, sir. No one else in the whole restaurant bothered to pay."

I remembered the iron safety curtain which used to be lowered ("By command of the Lord Chamberlain") between the acts at the Playhouse Theatre. It had borne an inscription which had become curiously memorable: "For Thine Especial Safety. Hamlet, Act 1, Sc. 2." Liverpool could have done with that curtain, between such acts as these.

At some street intersections there were soldiers on point-duty, directing the traffic and shepherding the wandering, aimless crowds. The fact gave rise, later, to the foolish slander that Liverpool had been so demoralized by its ordeal that soldiers had been drafted in to keep order and prevent "mutiny." This was nonsense of a wicked kind, shaming a proud record; the truth was that so many ghoulish fools had driven into town to see the fun that troops were called on to help the police with traffic control.

Eileen was all right; we had been equally, and unnecessarily, anxious. (Yet bombs, dropped a little early, could miss docks, and hit villages seven miles away; dropped a little late, they could reverse the process and disqualify the breadwinner.) But our own village now bore a disconcerting and sometimes pathetic air; thronging the sleepy lanes, brushing past the first dusty buds of spring, were bombed-out families from the slums of Bootle and dockland Liverpool, brought out by bus and lorry and Good Samaritan car and dumped upon us, for both sides to make what they could of their total upheaval.

The refugees went from door to door, lugging suitcases and parcels, with staring, grey-faced children in tow; they were hungry, and very tired, and as desperate to go to the lavatory as I had ever been in the heyday of my denial, but they were also strangely undismayed by the violent uprooting. There was no anger and no bitterness, though these would come later; at the moment it was just the air-raids, just bloody Hitler—there'd be another dose that night, for certain, but with luck, out here in the country, they would miss it.

We did what we could, like everyone else; the school was opened and turned into a makeshift dormitory; the police-station, for once in its life, was crammed to the roof. And tea, the only available balm for history's malice, flowed in rivers, as hot and sweet and comforting as the revenge we might one day enjoy.

On my way back into town I called at my father's office in the Medical Institute, which had been shaken by a near-miss and lacked some windows and a lot of plaster from its ceiling. In the center of this dusty discomfort, my father was completing the grim balance-sheet of last night's raid. He looked very tired; in fact he looked nearly seventy, for the first time in our joint lives. He had had no proper sleep, and no meals that were not snatched off a desk-corner, for several days and nights.

I learned later that one of his minor problems, a footnote to his profit-and-loss account, was that a bomb, with grisly precision, had hit a warehouse containing his reserve stock of coffins—all two thousand of them.

As I came in he looked up and asked: "Ship all right?" and when I answered that it was, he said: "Denys just rang up." Then he bid me goodbye again, with the kind of brisk authority which still came very easily.

Campanula went down river at last, in the dusk of the eighth day, and we were damned glad to be going with her. At anchor near the Bar Light Vessel, waiting for our convoy, we had a grand-stand view of the last heavy raid on the port. Now at last one could feel detached, like a prompter in the wings, with a word-perfect cast, watching from the shadows the progress of the play, enjoying—without having to suffer—the full benefits of stage light-ing.

Occasionally a turning German aircraft roared over our heads, shaping up for another run over the target; but all one's attention was for the noise and the astonishing display of fireworks ashore —star-shells, flares floating down like mellow Christmas candles, tracer-bullets from ships, the pin-point flicker of the barrage, the crash of bombs, and the great gouts of flame which followed them.

It was sickening, it was awful. But there was always the ignoble thought—even with my father, my wife, and my brother still there, somewhere under this fiery canopy—which was the identi-cal, ignoble thought of my quarterdeck burials. The dead were lying over *there*. I was still standing *here*.

3.

We were transferred to the Clyde Escort Force—same job, with a different starting gate—early in the summer, which meant goodbye

to Liverpool and all our cherished contacts ashore, and hallo to a
city which, for a dozen reasons, I held in less esteem.

The Clyde had engraved some sour memories for me already.
It was here that *Campanula* had been born, up an oily creek at
Fleming and Ferguson's yard in Renfrew, attended by the ear-
splitting midwifery, the iron uproar of hammering, punching,
drilling and riveting which went to make a ship.

It was here that, ordered by my draft-chit to report to Admiral
Superintending Contract-Built Ships, I solemnized my marriage
to the Royal Navy by knocking on the door of a dockside hut
labelled, ambiguously, "NAVAL OFFICERS KEEP OUT." The
notice had been posted by our first First Lieutenant, an Australian
who was to demonstrate, before he left us, a high-grade talent
which could have supplied the text for a most salable book, short-
titled *The Hundred Best Ways of Being an Objectionable, Uncouth, Workshy, Snarling Sod.*

It was here that our captain sized me up, wearing the expression I had once seen on the face of a referee just before he disqualified *both* boxers for not trying. It was here that I had saluted
Colours at sunset for the very first time, and hoped, against all
belief, that the Navy could meet even halfway my enormous pride
and pleasure in belonging to it, and my hope of achievement in
the future.

The best thing about that part of the world was the approach
to it, particularly after the strife and stress of our job outside.
The Firth of Clyde was and is one of the fairest sea-gateways in
the world; from the moment we rounded the Mull of Kintyre,
chugged past the strange gaunt cone of Ailsa Craig, and set course
northwards for Holy Island, and Garroch Head, and the Great
and Little Cumbraes, and the blue-grey hills of Rothesay and
Hunter's Quay, we were on peaceful passage past a most marvellous coastline, which the sun could turn into a golden riot of
bracken and heather, and the clouds to a misty nobility, with lowering patches of black shadow racing across green sheep-pastures.

Coming up the Mersey River, however much one welcomed the
landfall, was like plodding up a dirty alleyway leading to the back
entrance of an iron-works. Coming up the Clyde was like beginning a sweet-water holiday.

But soon, alas, that fair approach petered out, and we were

back in the alleyway again, with muddy shoes and, usually, a clammy wet raincoat as well.

Our home port was now Greenock. Farther down the coast was another town, Gourock, of the same drab, mean quality, though it had a hotel, the Bay, held in high esteem by rollicking sailors and presided over by a lady whose universal nickname, Two-Ton Tessie, was never a subject of dispute. Such were the delights which awaited us ashore.

But *Campanula* was hardly ever alongside, in any case. The corvette and destroyer anchorage was about a mile off-shore, at the Tail-of-the-Bank, and here we lay in isolation, swinging to our anchor cable, served by supply and liberty boats which, being converted herring drifters built like wooden tanks and crewed by stalwart Scots fishermen who liked to signal their arrival with a good solid thump, were a constant menace to paintwork and plating.

Downstream from us was the vast pool of convoy shipping which was there one night, gone next morning, and replenished with scarcely a half-day's delay as the traffic ebbed and flowed. Among them—another touch of quality—were two French liners now soberly camouflaged for their job of troop-carrying: the graceful *Pasteur,* which had a flaring bow like a very rich man's yacht of the vintage of 1900, and an old friend, the *Colombie,* on whose maiden voyage I had sailed from Havre to Bordeaux, *en route* for a hot solo walk over the Pyrenees in happy, innocent 1936.

Between us lay a day-and-night reminder of how irretrievably that innocence had been lost.

This was a wreck-buoy, painted green, flashing green every five seconds—green for the colour of grisly death. It marked the grave of an ill-starred French destroyer, whose mast and funnel still showed above water, whose crew still lay imprisoned within. Her story had been one of the brief, early horrors of the war: an explosion on board had been followed by a fire, and the ship quickly became one vast incandescent torch, fled by a few leaping men, before the sea surged in and snuffed it out forever.

Now she lay there, as our nearest neighbour, a rusty, weed-washed charnel house; and many times, as we came up river at dusk, looking for our anchorage, and drew near to the green winking eye, I could not help projecting my mind beneath the surface of the water, and trying to picture the details of the horror below, and what it was our anchor saw as it plunged down and came to muddy rest.

Sometimes the feeling persisted long after we had swung and settled down. "You are alive," the green eye accused me, every five seconds. "We are dead, very dead. We are charred, swollen, abandoned. There are scores of us down here, within a few hundred feet of you."

At a certain level of tiredness or despair, one could imagine without too much fantasy that Death, waiting for us outside, had left this pale green calling-card, appropriately French, *pour rappeler*.

It was said, by someone who had met a diver ashore, a diver who claimed to have inspected the wreck for the prospects of salvage, that out of one of the portholes there still wallowed and lolled the head and shoulders of a skeleton, trapped forever in the frenzied act of escape.

Twenty miles away there lay in wait for us a trap of a different sort: the grimy maw of Scotland's pride and joy, the city of Glasgow.

Thus, between convoys, such was my choice of relaxation ashore; Glasgow's brawling crudity (though, to be fair, there was one excellent restaurant with the good old Scottish name of *La Malmaison*): Greenock's pubs or cinemas, and Gourock's Two-Ton Tessie, all to be prefaced by a bracing trip ashore on the open deck of a herring drifter.

I found that, soon, I always stayed on board *Campanula* when we were in harbour, volunteering to take over Officer-of-the-day like some toadying Boy Scout. Robbed of those delicious quiet evenings at Gateacre, it seemed better to swing round the buoy off the Tail-of-the-Bank, and to opt, like any other deprived pensioner, for the wireless.

The war took us on three more summer convoys (though the North Atlantic had not yet been notified that it was summer), and then came a real treat: a refit, and the six weeks' lay-off that went with it. Better even than that, we were to go into dry-dock in Liverpool; and best of all, I was now the heir to the latest of a wonderful line of inventions, which, starting with the motor-car, and building up via the airplane, the telephone, the radio, the talkies, television, and the contraceptive diaphragm, had now topped off the process with the finest blessing a sailor could hope for—a radar set.

It was to work wonders for us, that precious radar. It made station-keeping at close quarters a safe and exact science. It found lost convoys, and wandering escorts, and headlands hidden in the murk of a Hebridean summer day. It could pick up channel buoys as we went down river in fog; and ship's boats whose survivors might otherwise have been left to die; and rain-squalls just over the horizon which, an hour later, would blot out everything except the vague grey hump which was our own windlass; and off-shore fishing-boats careless of their riding-lights.

Best of all, it could find surfaced U-boats and, with the help of an ingenious plotting device, betray their plans. Though radar would never supplant seamanship and skill and watchful common sense, yet it aided them all so enormously that we were left wondering how we had ever survived two years of convoy-escort without it.

But before we could be equipped with this paragon, and benefit also from certain other alterations and improvements, we had to survive those six weeks in a Liverpool dry-dock.

The executive order for this was "H.M.S. *Campanula* will basin at 0800 hours" (what on earth had happened to the English language while we were in Scotland?). In due course we basined; the vast groaning gates swung shut behind us, divorcing us from the sea; finger-flipping men in bowler hats spread-eagled us dead-center on our enseamed bed as the water-level dropped, and enormous oily balks of timber shored us up, to preserve what was left of our poise.

With the ship dripping dry, we were presently able to walk down and inspect the prime collection of marine life clinging to our hull—waving green weeds, crusty barnacles, torpid sea-snails, tiny crabs, and the doomed wriggling shrimps which were the most unwilling of all the gifts from the sea; and then *Campanula*, the orphan of many a storm, began to lose the name of action.

Since two out of the three watches had gone on leave, and I was left in sole charge of the wardroom, the ship would have been something of an echoing iron cage in any case; with the boilers blown down (no heating) and the humming generators silent for the first time in half a year, she seemed somewhat spooky as well. When, preparing for evening rounds, I walked out on to the shadowy quarterdeck which had seen so much mortuary service in recent months, I could not help feeling that we must surely have collected quite a lot of poor drowned ghosts already.

Campanula quickly grew derelict, and cold, and uncomfortable; the assistant cook's meals were so terrible that I knew he must be pining for his peacetime job in the pickle factory; the necessity of using the dockside lavatory instead of our own was an awkward nuisance, with undertones of squalor.

At night, the steady drip of water into the great stone grave below did nothing to lull me into easy sleep. After-dinner drinking did not help either, though I gave it a good try.

But each morning the ship came alive again, in a way I grew to dislike even more than the night's loneliness. From 8 A.M. onwards we were invaded by an army of major and minor technicians concerned with our refit: riveters, welders, joiners, plumbers, painters, electricians, carpenters, caulkers: boiler scalers, funnel sweeps, plain crash-and-bangers, tea-maker's mates. . . . They trooped on board in a snuffling, untidy, foot-dragging, shambling throng, and took over the ship; and the ship, lately so disciplined, so taut, so keyed up to its job, began to suffer from it.

Each day *Campanula* became a dirtier shambles; soon she was no longer a ship-of-war in working trim, but a kind of run-down factory hard hit by the depression, and only waiting for the rats to take over. All the decks which we had kept scoured and scrubbed since the day we commissioned became a barnyard of cigarette ends, cartons, crates, wood-shavings, oily rags, slices of metal, strips of welding, bits of wire: bottles, cans, half-eaten sandwiches, and gobs of prime Liverpool sputum.

At first it made me angry, and then sad, and then resigned. The sight of a filthy raincoat dangling from a gun-barrel had, on Day One, seemed scandalous and insulting. Presently it became a natural part of the infected scene, an item of our squalid camouflage. And common sense told me that a major refit must inevitably turn the place upside down, and propriety with it.

But there was another aspect of the invasion where anger did not ebb away, nor give place to common sense. Most of these people "concerned with our refit" were hardly concerned at all. They were not working very hard. Some of them, as far as I could judge, were not working at all. The first time I came on a school of card-players snugged down in the captain's sea-cabin at ten o'clock in the morning, I was furious, and showed it. I remained furious on all later occasions, but I was officially told not to be, and above all not to "interfere."

There might be a strike. . . . It seemed to me entirely grotesque that the strike-weapon, or the threat of it, could still be used in war, but it was so, and we were instructed to live with it.

Yet it remained wildly, disgustingly unfair that, of two men fighting the same war for the same stake of survival, one of them could enjoy home life, and high-grade pay, and still refuse outright to work unless he was given more, while the other, conscripted at a wretched wage-level, put into a blue suit, and sent far from home and headlong into danger, could have been shot out of hand if he tried the same tactic.

Our able seamen, working like galley slaves in sub-human conditions, got their keep and four shillings a day. An eighteen-year-old fitter's mate ashore who kicked up a row about his "conditions of employment" was found to be earning thirteen pounds a week. These contrasting oddments multiplied as time went on.

In a debate on "voluntary absenteeism" in the war factories (we were even disinfecting the language, in the interests of national solidarity), this habitual Monday morning truancy was blamed on "the application of income tax to the incomes of manual workers."

Mr. Ernest Bevin, the Minister of Labour and National Service, when accused in the House of Commons of having initiated a "Slacker's Charter" by introducing legislation which forbade certain workers being sacked for any malpractice short of sabotage, fought back stoutly on their behalf. In July, a member of the Boilermakers' and Iron and Steel Shipbuilders' Society (there must have been a whole gang of them on board at that very moment) had been fined three pounds by his union's board of discipline for working too hard.

At certain factories suffering from persistent mechanical breakdown, there was said to be a light-hearted variant of one of our patriotic slogans: "Give us the job and we will finish the tools."

My own reaction to this discrepancy between dream and event

reached a certain personal peak of disgust when one of these visiting potentates, tilting up his welder's mask with an agile thumb, offered me "all the petrol I liked" for my motor-cycle, without the formality of coupons.

For me, as for all other sailors, a petrol coupon was not a grubby slip of paper; it was a man, an actual mother's son with frying hair, swimming away from a burning tanker and failing to make it. It was a life. God damn it, it was *my* life! I felt bound to tell him, sniffily, that I was all right for petrol.

After that, I stopped being angry, though I could still be surprised; I stopped thinking that I must be in the wrong job, and knew, sanctimoniously and proudly, that I was in the right one. Yet watching all this going on—or not going on; seeing it at first hand, observing these privileged idlers spinning out their day's quota and fouling up the whole ship in the process, I had my first, my very first suspicion, instantly suppressed for reasons of loyalty and political conviction, that my dead certainty about socialism was not going to prove as certain as all that.

There was a faint misgiving here, a tiny doubt no bigger than a man's hand of cards slapped down on *Campanula*'s chart-table, that, given lots of money, life-long security, and guaranteed social protection, people *perhaps* would come to lean on their spades a little longer than was necessary, in the course of their arduous daily toil.

It was to return later.

"H.M.S. *Campanula* will unbasin at 1400 hours" was the wording of our release order; and H.M.S. *Campanula* duly unbasined. But the melancholy word enshrined a cleansing process which a sailor could only welcome; after the six weeks' ministration of our dockyard maties, the sea at last came to our rescue, and sluiced away the grime of foreign hands, and baptized us under the honest name of ship again.

I leaned over the quarterdeck guardrail and watched as the dry-dock crew began to run the bath-water. The incoming tide sucked and swirled round the balks of timber which had been cradling us for so many days; on its way it picked up a horrid chaplet of wood and rubbish and filth, topped by a grimy slick of coal-dust and oil, as the level rose and climbed step by step up the side of the dock. The gangs of men in waders, stationed far below us, collecting the shores and wedges as they floated free, soon began to retreat in a widening circle, leaving us to our own element.

Presently the good salty Mersey water was climbing up our own side, lapping the fresh paint higher and higher with successive happy tide-marks. One by one our props lurched free, and drifted off, and were retrieved with eighteen-foot boathooks by men now reaching out from the edge of the dock.

There was a long hopeful pause, while the whole basin swirled and filled; then the last timber floated sluggishly up and away, and became the last prize for the shore-gang; with a maidenly tremor, not too convincing, and a small stagger to celebrate her liberty, *Campanula* was released; and thus, on the next tide, we returned to our war.

4.

I had thought that the punishing March convoy was likely to be the worst of that war. But I was wrong, and was smartly proved so, as soon as we had spring-cleaned the ship and rejoined the Liverpool Escort Force; we now embarked on the most horrible voyage of all, made especially foul by the fair weather which blessed us throughout the trip.

This time our run was south to Gibraltar, to calm blue seas and hot sunshine, and to the longest gauntlet of murder we were ever likely to encounter.

As with the March beating, there is no temptation to fight this one again, particularly as we lost it so brutally; but there were such contrasts, astonishing and appalling, in that convoy that memory remained infected forever, and can stand an airing, if only for pity's sake.

We were routed far westwards, in a great arc which started from our usual North Channel exit and curved out for hundreds of miles into the Atlantic, so as to take us out of bomber range of the French coast. The weather, as the smoky hills of western Ireland faded astern, and we made the latitude of the Bay of

Biscay, grew peerless: the sort of "sunshine cruise" conditions which, even in the mid-Thirties, the advertisements had no trouble in selling at a guinea a day.

We were all in good heart, after the long lay-off. We liked our newly furbished ship; we had the radar to fiddle with; above all, there was this canopy of sky and carpet of calm sea which, after the snuffling gloom of Liverpool, seemed far out on the profit side of paradise. There was a new, sensual pleasure in that southward journey which seemed to take the whole ship away from the war and into the simple warming joys of being alive and afloat.

We passed whales, and basking sharks, and once a lone turtle, paddling manfully westwards towards its first and only landfall—Florida, four thousand miles away. Flying fish were reported; in the dog watches the hands sun-bathed, displaying shameful tattoos and snow-white legs; naked stokers, laid out like half-cooked bullocks on the after-deck, listened to the mouth organ before they told the organist to pack it in, and dozed off again.

On my twelve-to-four afternoon watch, nothing happened, and nothing was wonderful. The water slid past under our keel; station-keeping and zigzag were both as simple as marshalling a toy flotilla on a pond; the convoy kept its shape like the flock of good sheep they were, sheep who trusted their good shepherd; *Campanula*'s mast rocked to and fro across the blue, as gently as a frond of seaweed, through a tiny five-degree arc of movement.

All I had to do was to maintain the zigzag pattern by the clock; to answer "Very good" as the look-outs changed at the half-hour, and the helmsman was relieved; to keep up the deck-log (our course and speed); and translate the weather pattern into the required officialese: "Wind light, variable: Sea smooth: Cloud nil: Corrected barometric pressure in millibars, 1002."

Sometimes the Coxswain, totally unemployed in such a benevolent world, came up to the bridge to gossip with me. He would begin with a formal salute, continue with a confederate grin, and, invariably, fire off one of his awful jokes: "Did you hear about the sultan's ninth wife, sir?"

"No, Coxswain, I don't think I did."

"She just got the hang of it."

"Coxswain. . . ."

But in fact I welcomed the variation; I thought it was going to be: "She had it pretty soft," or "She got it twice weakly."

Sometimes there would be a signalman washing out his flags and pennants in a bucket of suds at the back of the bridge, and the Coxswain could never resist a comment.

"Eh, Bunts!" "Bunts" was short for "bunting-tosser": the Coxswain pronounced it "Boonts." Either way, it sounded agreeably rude. "Eh, Bunts! You're making a proper snake's honeymoon of that lot!" Then he would turn back to me. "You don't know whether to laugh or cry, do you? How are we going on, sir?"

"All right. Pretty slow."

"Slow all right." He looked across at our drifting convoy, and astern at our gently furrowing wake. "Six knots and a Chinaman, I'd say."

This was a new one to me. "What on earth does that mean?"

"Old sailing ship yarn." He was always glad when I asked a question, because he always knew the answer. "Like, there was this Chinaman streaming the log to find out how fast the ship was going. He dropped it over the side, and the line ran out too strong for him, and jerked him overboard. Never saw his little yellow botty again. The captain says to the mate: 'How fast are we going?' and the mate says: 'Six knots and a Chinaman.' "

The joke, totally good-humoured, totally heartless, seemed just right for our own secure voyage.

At night, in my middle watch, I was alone above a sleeping ship. On the open bridge, in the calm darkness, one could hear everything: the thresh of a propeller from the nearest merchantman, the ripple and thrust of our own bow-wave. Sometimes there was even the beat of a seabird's wings, unseen, flailing the water as it fled our advance; sometimes we moved through a bath of phosphorescence, and that bow-wave could actually be seen streaming away into the darkness on either side, joining the rippling pattern of the other bow-waves of all the ships in company, which each had this faint luminous line from stem to stern along her waterline.

Sometimes porpoises played at being submarines in this phosphorescent world, darting towards the ship's side at right angles, passing underneath our keel in a swirling glow—a glow always good enough for a missed heartbeat, until the April Fool torpedo proved its innocence by circling swiftly and doing it all again.

The sixth dawn came, on this magic voyage; the luck seemed good, the life wonderful. Dawn was never quite included in my middle watch, even at high summer; but I always stayed on, at the back of the bridge, to watch and wait for it, until at fifteen or twenty minutes past four o'clock the longed-for miracle happened. The change was always swift: at one moment the sea was silvery, the sky black, the stars brilliant, and then, when one next looked round, the colours had all turned pale grey—the grey which was the day's first signal.

Campanula's outline took shape with swift decision, along her whole length; the men on the bridge became faces and figures instead of shadows or voices unseen. The duty steward climbed the bridge ladder, to forage for the plates and cups of the middle watch's picnic. It was the best hour of the twenty-four. We were all still alive, and safe, and one hundred sixty-eight miles nearer harbour; the barometer was rock-steady, and the sun on its way— and then, even as I turned to go below, one of the new look-outs sang out "Sound of aircraft, sir!" and within a second or so I had got it myself, and the sick fear that went with it—the steady hateful drone, somewhere out on the pale fringes of the dawn, which meant that we had alien company.

Some finger, prompt and itchy on the trigger, was already pressing the alarm bell, and *Campanula,* lately so sleepily content, jumped into urgent action. My place of duty, instead of snug between the blankets, was now the anti-aircraft gun-turret aft, where there was newly installed a four-barrelled 0.5-inch pompom, nicknamed a Chicago Typewriter. (A Chicago Piano had eight barrels.)

The gun's crew of five was there almost as soon as I was: five young men, steel-helmeted, their faces puffy with sleep, the white tops of their sea-boot stockings standing out in the faint light of dawn. We closed up round the gun, and tilted its multiple snout skywards, and waited: watching, listening to the snarling anonymous intruder, peering about as the gaining light gave us more to peer at, for a full hour; and then there was a sharp call on the bridge voice-pipe—"Aircraft, red four-five!"—and we all

swung round, to find, far away on the port beam, the author of our
harassment.

It was not a true enemy, but a spy—yet the worst spy we could
wish to see: one of the Focke-Wulf long-range reconnaissance
planes, circling round and round the convoy, far out of range
even of a destroyer's guns.

We had been discovered, and beyond doubt reported; and
before long the cutting edge of war sliced our brief paradise to
bloody rags. The last warning for action was signalled to us, in a
disgusting way, that same afternoon: the sighting of some fresh
human excrement on the surface of the water, where no honest
ship had travelled for many a long day. U-boats. . . . As dusk
fell, violence began to split our whole universe.

We lost fourteen merchant ships in the next five days: fourteen
of our small stock of twenty-one—a percentage so appalling that
the cold print seemed almost worse than the sights and sounds of
action. We lost four tankers, and that was "I can give you all
the petrol you like" in full colour. We lost a small cargo-liner
called the *Aguila,* which had on board the first draft of Wrens
going out to Gibraltar. We lost the rescue-tug which, the previous
night, had picked up the last four or five surviving girls.

We lost a Norwegian destroyer, full of orphaned exiles far
from home. We lost one of our own cherished sisters, a corvette-
in-arms for more than a year, H.M.S. *Zinnia.*

Zinnia was commanded by a tall, friendly, capable man called
Cuthbertson, whom, as an occasional visitor to our wardroom, I
liked very much, if only by reason of contrast; and when I saw
her go up in one quick stab of flame, far out on the wing of the
convoy, and knew it could only be her, I was saddened and sickened far beyond any ignoble thought that at least it was only them,
and not us. What a waste, what a waste. . . . The extent of that
waste was made apparent next morning, when as soon as we
could be spared we were sent back to pick up the bits.

There were only fifteen men alive: Cuthbertson himself (picked
up by another ship), and fourteen wretched members of his crew
of ninety, and corpses a-plenty. I was in charge of the scrambling
nets aft; it was my pride and privilege to yank from the water
half-a-dozen shipmates of this admired man, this oily, half-dead

master mariner—as I found him to be when he came on board at
Gibraltar.

He had nothing much to say then except thank you: what man
could have had anything to say, who had just lost seventy-five of
his crew and a corvette which, turning under full helm, was hit
below the boiler-room and broke in half while those left alive on
the upper deck were still shocked and staring? I could only tell
him that I had looked after his stunned survivors, and buried his
dead: those rows of sailors like ourselves, their badges proclaiming
their faithful service, their wide-open eyes attesting their last
surprise.

Cuthbertson may have forgotten all this quite soon, but, mov-
ingly, his mother never did. She must have been, even then,
quite an old lady; but when my own son was born she sent a
message of congratulation, and for years afterwards, punctually
on his birthday, a card arrived, for me as much as for him, sending her best wishes, still saying thank you.

Lieutenant-Commander Cuthbertson occurred later—I made
him occur later—when, as with the corvette *Coreopsis,* the past
drew together in one extraordinary flight of fantasy. But on that
day in Gibraltar, he was only a shrunken hostage from the sea,
one of the witnesses to the last act of this rotten play when, with
the tatters of our convoy—our seven remaining ships—we had
beaten our retreat.

Faced with reports of "U-boats joining," and old and new
enemies still waiting astride our route to Gibraltar, we fled the
scene. We took what was left of our flock, and led them up the
River Tagus towards Lisbon, within the safe neutral prudent
waters of Portugal—as bitter an act of surrender as could ever
come our way. Then—only a clutch of escorts in line abreast,
not a convoy any more—we made all speed for Gibraltar, past
Cape St. Vincent and other honoured names, to tell our wretched
story.

The last entry I made in the deck-log, on my last middle watch,
was: "Cape Trafalgar bearing due east, twenty miles." We were
thus crossing the very shoals where lay all the iron shot of 1805,
and the bones of the French 74 *Redoutable,* from whose cross-
trees a sharp-shooter had taken aim on an admiral's emblazoned
coat; where Nelson, dying, yet hearing with a sailor's faithful ear

the surf growling under *Victory*'s lee, had given his last recorded order: "Anchor, Hardy! Do you *anchor!*"

But that had been *Victory*, victory.

We were barely past the Straits of Gibraltar, with Spain on the port hand, Morocco on the starboard, the scorched smell of Africa in between, and a distant view of the Rock to lure us homewards, when we were told to turn round again and start a two-day "anti-submarine sweep" through the waters of our defeat: perhaps to teach us the virtues of discipline and fortitude, or to recall a long-ago signal: "England confides that every man will do his duty," or to drive home the disgrace of still being afloat.

We felt we knew enough of all these things already.

It must be admitted that most of us were a little cracked, in all senses, by the time we were finally released: by the time our last landfall, the lighthouse on Europa Point, blinked and gave in to the sun, and we made harbour. It had all gone on too long; we had been nearly a week at action stations, missing meals, missing sleep, with nothing to show in return save a shameful tally of lost ships climbing past the sixty percent mark.

Indeed, we had done nothing more martial than to kill, with a depth-charge, some diving seabirds which, with wings outstretched, bowed to us, flat upon the water, as we passed. Yet Gibraltar proved a healing balm, in a way I would never have thought possible.

There was literally nothing to worry about here, except keeping a look-out for Italian midget submarines which were rumoured to be trying to break into the harbour. There was nothing much to do, especially since the official mail had not caught up with me, and could not do so. The sun shone all the time; we wore the Navy's tropical kit—white bush-jackets and shorts, white stockings and shoes—which was itself a tonic, though white shorts topped by a bushy black beard must really have looked very odd.

With Jim Harmsworth for agreeable company, I swam in what truly seemed a rich man's playground, Rosia Bay, not quite shadowed by the Rock, in the warm Mediterranean water which really could caress an exhausted body. We travelled round the town by gharry, a light, springy, slightly crazy four-wheeled cab topped by a linen awning. There was no black-out. We took our *apéritif*—Tio Pepe sherry—on a balcony overlooking Main Street, crammed with the eddying to-and-fro of the evening parade. We dined *à l'espagnole* off onion soup and *paella* and dripping melon and roughish Algerian wine, while at our back the bristling honey-combed fortress of the Rock stood guard, and seemed by its very name to restore our honour.

Gradually the war faded from this blessed scene. We could not quite forget *Zinnia,* but we began to forget all the rest. We could even recall, with laughter instead of embarrassment, an answer which our captain had sent to another corvette whose signal he had not understood. It had been: "Snow again. I don't catch your drift."

Then, we had all felt very ashamed. Now—and certainly by the time we reached the brandy stage, out on that suspended, honey-coloured stone balcony again—we could agree that certain of the minor horrors of war were minor indeed.

Campanula was berthed in the very shadow of *Ark Royal,* the huge towering aircraft-carrier which was the target of two angry air forces, German and Italian, as long as she was in harbour, as well as of U-boat spite whenever she put to sea. It must have been strange to serve in such a notorious "hunted ship," but it seemed that her crew were inclined to relish their notoriety, as an extra source of pride.

They used to listen to Radio Hamburg, and especially to William Joyce (hanged for treason, 1946) who, like John Amery (hanged for treason, 1946), earned his luxury brand of daily bread by making regular broadcasts urging his British compatriots to give up the fight before it was too late. William Joyce, whose curious, fake upper-class accent had earned him the nickname of Lord Haw-Haw, specialized in announcing bad news about our convoys; in a rasping raven croak, instantly recognizable from the moment he said "Chairmany calling," he took such sour and savage delight in our losses that he positively rolled the tonnage-figures off his tongue.

When he mouthed the phrase "Gross registered tons" he could actually make it sound lustful, as if part of a perverted appetite for dead and dying ships.

Latterly he had taken to asking, over and over again, in a menacing snarl: "Where is the *Ark Royal?*" and in the *Ark Royal*'s messdecks they took an answering delight in roaring back: "HERE!"

In fact, William Joyce must have known very well where the *Ark Royal* was; or, if he did not, some little man just down the corridor could certainly have told him. For we knew all the time that Gibraltar was totally open to the spying eyes of the enemy; across the bay in Algeciras, five short miles away, the complacent Spaniards, our coward foes, had allowed German agents in the guise of diplomats to set up batteries of high-powered telescopes which kept a round-the-clock surveillance of all shipping entering or leaving the harbour.

The Spaniards prayed devoutly for our defeat and, as far as they dared, worked for it. We knew that we had no friends at all in this part of the world, save for Fortress Malta down the street. Here the Rock was everything, and fortunately it was more than enough.

The war—the real war—did come back to us for one poisonous half-day, when the cruiser *Manchester* docked to discharge her cargo. Her cargo was human, or, by then, something less; they were the week-old, oil-and-water-marinated corpses of thirty-eight of her crew, trapped below decks when she was hit by a torpedo, and necessarily left to their wallowing, sealed-up grave until she could make harbour.

We were losing too many sailors.

5.

We were losing too many everything.

The Americans, stung to action by that "day of infamy" at Pearl Harbor, joined us at last. But apart from that turn of fortune, 1941 closed with a cataract of bad news: unbelievably bad, crowning a disastrous year. It came thudding down, in successive blows which tumbled all our hopes and seemed to be tumbling all the world as well. Things were all over the place in North Africa. Malta was being first strangled and then crucified. The whole of the Far East was going up in flames—other people's flames. In November, a single torpedo took the *Ark Royal;* and at last we could tell Lord Haw-Haw where she was—only twenty-five miles from Gibraltar, but forty fathoms down. We lost, in quick succession, seven other big warships.

For sailors, the darkest hour (apart from the 371 Allied merchant ships sunk in three winter months) was the demolishing of two great capital ships, the *Prince of Wales* and the *Repulse,* in one single Japanese air-strike. But this was topped, for all of us, by the loss of Singapore six weeks later, with ninety-five thousand prisoners taken during the brief campaign—the worst capitulation of British arms in British history.

Guns pointing the wrong way! Christ, wouldn't you know it! And now they were calling such antics "battle fatigue." . . . It seemed, unjustly, a typical soldiers' balls-up, only to be expected from what we had come to call, with savage, selfish derision, the Gabardine Swine.*

But as well as blaming the bloody pongoes, we were now looking round for other scapegoats—anyone but ourselves, in fact; and in the process we were beginning to fix the blame, with equal lack of charity, on another identifiable sector of British life, the bloody Conservatives. Our successive misfortunes and retreats now seemed, to a great many people, to be Chamberlain's fault, and before him Baldwin's, and the fault of the droves of beefy company directors, the right-royal fatheads who had passed for Conservative M.P.s in the corrupted Thirties.

They had got us into all this mess. . . . Churchill's massive defeat at the polls in 1945, and everything that followed in its train, was, unfairly, inevitably, being forged now.

Campanula ran eleven convoys that year: two of them awful, two featureless,† and the rest so-so, yawing between bad and not too terrible. But at the end I was still alive—though occasionally astonished by the fact—and home for Christmas!

---

* The R.A.F. were, more affectionately, Intrepid Birdmen. We ourselves were Blue Jobs.
† We missed one with a unique feature of its own. When the Canadian corvette *Chambly* rammed a U-boat, its captain jumped out of his conning-tower and landed on the deck of the corvette, leaving his crew to sort things out for themselves. His rank, appropriate to the very last moment, was Korvetten-Kapitän.

At that season ("That season . . . so hallowed and so gracious . . . wherein our Saviour's birth is celebrated") there was indeed much that was moving, for all sorts of reasons. We still found things to be happy about. My father was less vilely overworked; Denys and Meryl were with us; and an American friend, who could scarcely have imagined what fantastic largesse he was sending our way, slipped me a tinned package-deal consisting of a boned turkey, a segment of sage-and-onion stuffing, and a little tube of cranberry sauce to pour on top. Such riches. . . .

At that season, in the oak-panelled bar of the Black Bull Hotel at Gateacre, I said goodbye to Denys, destined by my guess for a landing in North Africa; and that was the last I saw of my friend and brother. At that season my son Max was, by inference, conceived. But Hong Kong, almost our last bastion in the tormented Far East, fell on Christmas Day; and on the cold morrow I went back to sea.

THIRTY-SIX

1946

LET'S BEAT IT

1.

THOUGH THE FIRST YEAR OF PEACE STARTED with the longest New Year Honours List ever issued, yet gloom hung over us, as thick as the fog itself which, together with ice-bound roads, had affected thirteen thousand square miles of Britain. London was awful, like the rest of the country: a dull drab dreary mess of raincoats and head-scarves, shabby clothes, filthy weather, eternal queueing, balloon-cloth shopping bags, half-empty shops and foul tempers.

Suddenly, it seemed, there wasn't any Britain any more, so brave and enduring and united for six long years. Such generous comradeship had died with victory, or had choked on it. Now there were just a lot of people snapping and snarling at each other, waiting and hoping for what never came, stealing and cheating to try to beat the game—but all in slow motion because, like me, they were all dog-tired.

All I could personally contemplate was the fearful cost of my slice of the war, my own Atlantic corner, which the actuaries had now calculated at three thousand ships sunk, and thirty thousand sailors blown to bits or drowned.

To balance that, 780 U-boats had been sunk. But even this huge total could not restore anything. It could not, for example, restore the summer paradise of Trearddur Bay, where the small tally of our private dead left gaps as wide and deep as the Atlantic itself.

By a coincidence which moved me strongly at the time, I had returned briefly to Trearddur Bay, as a sailor, very near the end of the war, when we had almost won the thing (in the conventional sense) and I had at last begun to think I was safe, and to dream a little of a peaceful future without feeling either guilty or stupid.

At the end of another Gibraltar convoy, we had taken a small clutch of ships into Barry Roads, the last harbour on the left before one got to Cardiff; and then we were routed back to Liverpool, independently, by way of the Welsh coast, and Cardigan Bay, and Anglesey, and therefore by way of Trearddur Bay, the beloved seaside village where I had spent every summer of my life from age zero to age twenty-nine.

There was time to spare, and when we had a good fix on South Stack lighthouse I made a circle into the bay itself, where I had spent uncounted hours sailing, and racing, and fishing, and doing nothing, in the blissful summertimes of the Twenties and Thirties.

I was the boss at last, and I could do this; in fact, if my frigate decided to take a close look at some inshore lobster-pots, that was exactly what she would do, without any comment from anyone. Barring a new-laid minefield (and who would dare to do that to *my* playground?) there was no hazard here that I had not known for more than twenty years.

But though I had been cherishing the idea, and the moment, ever since we had laid a course to cross Caernarvon Bay, it was desperately sad after all. Trearddur Bay—especially Trearddur Bay by moonlight—had too many ghosts. In fact, it had become a ghost itself.

I saw Ravenspoint first, the "big house" where the fabulous Grayson family had lived; its vast luminous façade stood out as sharp as print, dominating and dwarfing our own Hafod next door. From the bridge I stared and stared at the small cottage where we had spent such a magic string of summers, where my brother Denys, heavily veiled, had been brought when he was a few weeks old.

No lights showed; there was just the pale face of the house, and the gash of shadow under the roof of the veranda—no, Mother said it was to be called the *loggia*, and the *loggia* it still was. In front, the garden sloped gracefully down towards the sea. It all looked the same, but of course it could not be; Hafod didn't belong to us any more, we would not go there again, and many of our summer callers would no longer be going anywhere.

We made our slow circle into the arm of the bay. There were a few scattered lights, and once a car with masked headlamps topped the rise of Big Bay Hill; but otherwise we moved through a motionless, mourning silence—our curling bow-wave, and the surf breaking inshore, were the only things that stirred.

There was something important missing, and I was searching for it—and it was the windward racing-mark off Porth Diana, which had been taken up at the end of the last sailing season, and never put down again. When, our circle completed, we passed the Commodore's house, and the tall façade of the Cliff Hotel, there was nothing left of Trearddur Bay except the picnic cliffs of Porth-y-Post, and South Stack lighthouse again.

I had forgotten the sailing-club boat-house, and when I looked for it we were too far off-shore, and I didn't want to go in again. Why should I? Inside it were all our boats, *Clytie* among them, dried out and moldering away as they had been for five years and more. By the time we got back to Trearddur Bay (and that suddenly seemed unlikely) there would be nothing left of them but salty, shabby planking, and turkey-red sails bleached to rotted ribbon.

There would not be much left of some of the owners, either. Too many people had died, between the bright "then" of 1939 and the doubtful "now" of the war's end. Peter Munro, who had taught me to sail: Nigel Wood, who had been my all-powerful crew for years, and had *made* me win races: both Lancaster boys, the Vice-Commodore's sons.

Last of all, there was Denys, who had survived that North African landing with the American First Army, and a year of desert warfare, and had been accidentally and foolishly finished off in a jeep accident. For him, burial in Algiers was the nearest he would get to Trearddur.

There was still time for me to be killed, too. . . . I had the feeling, as we set course to clear the South Stack headland, that whether that happened, as it had happened to Denys and the others, or whether, by some unfair spin of the wheel, I survived this crude gamble, I would not be coming here again, nor would I want to.

But who, in their senses, would want to come back to peace-time London?—that was now the depressing, dominant thought, as one read the morning paper—on any morning, and in any paper—and digested the latest list of things which had gone wrong or, even more discouragingly, were going to stay exactly as they were.

Was this, in fact, *really* the new Britain I had voted for?—the one I had even tried to fashion myself, as a member of Parliament?

I never became an M.P.; in fact, I never got as far as fighting a parliamentary election. But I did try hard, and it must have been a near thing, if simple arithmetic counted for anything in politics.

Though still in the Navy, I was suddenly taken in the spring of 1945 with a lust to enter Parliament. Party politics still meant a great deal to me, though I had hardly given them a constructive thought for five years; except when, as commanding officer, I had to render a monthly report on any evidence of subversive activity on board the vessel under my command—and if that bare statement contravenes the Official Secrets Act, by which I am bound till the day I die, then I apologize.*

But now was the moment to get moving! Peace was on the way. Labour was what I believed in. A really worthwhile job was what I would soon need. . . . I wrote the necessary letter of application, through the accustomed naval channels: starting with the quick-fire word *SUBMITTED,* declaring that I wished to seek political office at the next General Election, asking for permission to indulge in such activities, and expressing my continued humility and obedience towards their Lordships of the Admiralty —which was undoubtedly true.

In accordance with the generous Service custom at that time, I was given this permission without delay, plus all the leave I might need in order to make my bid. But first I had to get myself adopted for a constituency—any constituency; and here I found that I was already late on the scene. Almost every conceivable hole had been filled by the rush of prospective pegs.

When I said that I would take *anything,* I was offered Winchester.

Even that is an exaggeration. I was offered an uncertain stab at Winchester, which had been true-blue Conservative since King Alfred burned the cakes in A.D. 878 (a statue at the bottom of the main street commemorated his reign). For Labour, it could only

---

* A disgruntled stoker, in a letter which he thought would elude censorship, once wrote from a ship which I will not identify to a friend in Scotland: "The officers are a lot of twerps! Roll on the revolution, Jamie!" I let that one go by, the name "Jamie" disarming me.

be the most forlorn of hopes, but I was still, in the contemporary phrase, thrilled to bits. I was going to get into Parliament! . . . I went down on the appointed day, and it was all very exciting, very daunting, very educational, and, at the end, very disappointing. At the time the defeat seemed mortal, and the setback the worst since—well, there was just no yardstick for such an inglorious rout.

I voted Labour, of course, like everyone else—and though that is factually inaccurate, only a massive percentage of "everyone else" could have given Labour 394 seats and an overall majority of 186. It was my mood at the time, and the mood of twelve million other people; domestically, it had been spearheaded, not by the *Daily Herald*, which never managed to spearhead anything sharper than a wet loofah, but by the radical *Daily Mirror*, which for a year had been running a campaign, aimed principally at its women readers, on the simple theme "VOTE FOR HIM!"

"Him" of course was their man overseas: the man linked only by his yearning, disgruntled letters, fed up with the war, still a lance-corporal, mucked about by his twerps of officers, sick of taking orders, footslogging while others rode, loathing all authority, and particularly that authority which had summarily sliced five years off his life, stuck him where he could easily get killed, and still expected to be returned to power as soon as this lot was over.

The Labour victory shifted the entire spectrum of British politics and British attitudes, leftwards, forever; but this was overdue—we had been congealed in our rigid class-aspic for too long. It was also the signal for a decade of dreary "austerity"; in our current fix, that had to happen too, though it earned for the Labour Party, which had to execute the verdict of events, and particularly for Sir Stafford Cripps, President of the Board of Trade and later Chancellor of the Exchequer, a lasting public dislike and also a reputation for a grim, anti-fun, misery-loves-company attitude which stuck forever.

But Stafford Cripps himself was a necessary, an inevitable man. Britain really was broke; our affairs were in a chaotic mess: the idea of "fair shares all round," which in practice meant damned little for anyone, was a matter of hard necessity. If the Conservatives had got in, instead of Labour, they would have had to turn off just as many taps, fix just as many clamps round our necks, and try to keep us just as poor, frugal, and honest as the non-Conformist conscience itself.

Tories might have done it in more style, with rounder phrases, a fruitier voice, and more practice at hectoring the tenants. But done it had to be, and, on balance, Labour were probably the right people to do it. So on that triumphant day of 26 July, when we rolled back the carpet with such a hefty thwack, such a giant stirring of dust, and gave Mr. Attlee—probably the most unlikely successor to Mr. Churchill which even a computer could devise—the helm, I rejoiced, with the majority of my fellow Britons.

I was very sad at not being an M.P., particularly as a lot of friends and contemporaries had turned the trick.

The feeling of being on the outside looking in, and completely excluded from this triumphant turn of events, still rankled after three or four months. There must be *something* I could do to join the march of progress. . . . I ferreted about a bit, in my new home area of Notting Hill, made closer contact with the local Labour Party, got myself chosen as a candidate at the forthcoming Borough Council elections, fought the seat, and won it.

Thus for a dizzy half-year I was Councillor Lieutenant-Commander Monsarrat, North Kensington civic figure, and junior member of two worthwhile committees—welfare and housing. But the Royal Borough of Kensington (North and South were amalgamated for local government purposes) was understandably Conservative; we were very much the minority faction, which might have been exciting if I had not come to the conclusion, before too long, that party politics were hardly relevant at all to civic administration, and that Kensington was being perfectly well run by its solid Tory majority and its titled Mayor.

In fact, local politics were *not* very exciting, and the contrast between being a borough councillor, arguing about rates and rats and rubbish disposal, and being a genuine Member of Parliament, concerned with the very fabric and pattern of Britain, was too great, and too ludicrous.

I began to feel bored with the whole idea; and there was now another area in my life which was also not very exciting, and this, unlike politics, was entirely my own fault.

Eileen and I had, sadly, grown apart during the later war

years, instead of together. The birth of our son had been a significant milestone; indeed, it had been never more significant than at
6 A.M. on 23 September 1942, when the matron of Heswall Nursing Home in Cheshire rang me up and said: "Congratulations,
Lieutenant Monsarrat: you have a daughter!"

I had already dispatched all the necessary telegrams, and was
toying with the name Nicola, before an important correction was
telephoned through.

But after that—I don't know. Perhaps the dissolution had begun
long before. I seemed to be away all the time; leaving Liverpool,
I had been posted back to Greenock, and then to Londonderry;
then *Campanula* was attached to a Canadian escort group, and
I spent more time up the grim creek which was the harbour of
St. John's, Newfoundland, than on our own side of the Atlantic.
It was no longer possible for us to have a house in my home port.

Then I was transferred again, this time to Harwich on the
east coast, and after that, getting my first command was an event
so exciting and important that for a long time it swallowed every
other emotion. The ship and the job were all, leaving no room
for anything but driving hard work and a certain amount of self-
conceit.

The process of division was accelerated by nearly seven months'
absence in America, when I was standing by a newly built frigate
in Providence, Rhode Island—a frigate which, as soon as she could
be made to work, would be my own pride and joy. But she had
been built at lightning speed, together with twenty-three others,
by Henry J. Kaiser; and I was never surprised to learn, not many
years later, that the Henry J. Kaiser car was no bloody good, because the Henry J. Kaiser frigate was no bloody good either.

Mine was called *Perim,* after the tiny island-colony near Aden
(there was another one called *Montserrat,* but they wouldn't give
her to me), and in *Perim* we ran fourteen sea-trials, thirteen of
them resulting in significant damage to our main bearings, before
a little man from Tyneside was flown out, put his stubby finger on
the trouble, and got the program moving again.

Meanwhile, along with my crew of 212 (multiplied by 24, to
cover the crews of all the other sick and rejected ships, which incidentally cost five million dollars each), I was marooned for
months and months on these highly hospitable shores, first in

Boston, then in Providence, and then in New York for a refresher command course in convoy tactics.

Any married man who has spent over six months on the eastern seaboard of the United States during wartime, when it was a patriotic female duty to welcome the fleet aboard, and who still retained his virtue, must have been either queer, or singularly ugly, or a man of so saintly a character that the Navy could have no billet for him in the first place.

I did not behave at all well, in this exotic climate of disengagement, such a long way from the war that we might have been on another planet; the indulgence proved habit-forming, since now, back in London, I was not behaving at all well either. I had no doubt that this was obvious; and it reminded me, with guilt and cheap amusement mixed, of a parallel situation between my own parents, when my father decided, at the age of sixty, that total separation would suit him best, and Mother, announcing the astonishing news, told us: "I knew it all the time! I knew what was happening, as soon as he bought a two-seater! It was so he could go off by himself, without Hollywood [the chauffeur] knowing, without having to keep the Daimler waiting outside. I could see Hollywood smirking, every time your father ordered his own car! He smirked!"

I didn't have a two-seater, nor any other kind of give-away transport; no chauffeur smirked at this master's solemn subterfuges—or suspected subterfuges: the evidence seemed, even then, circumstantial to the point of farce: though my father might indeed have fallen in love, it could have been with a new car, thus anticipating, in 1926, what is now a humdrum liaison.

But part of the present decaying pattern was the fact that Eileen had been staying in the country for a long time, while I camped out in a bedsitting-room in Ennismore Gardens; and that we now lived in guarded domesticity, under a newly bought roof in what I liked to call my constituency, Notting Hill.

I was still, six months after the war's end, in uniform; but already I had been put ashore, and the shore I had landed on was the biggest stone frigate of them all, the Admiralty at the top of Whitehall. I had loathed the idea of shore duty, had resisted it, argued about it, and tried for something better. But there was no doubt that the all-disposing man in Appointments was right.

After five ships, four and a half years of sea time, more than a hundred long and short convoys, I was desperately tired. Tired sailors of thirty-five belonged, in wartime, somewhere else than on the bridge. There were now lots of younger chaps coming along, who deserved their chance and who *wouldn't* make mistakes.

To start with, the Naval Information Department was great fun. I found myself sharing a room with two delightful men, one of whom I had known before the war, the novelist John Moore: the other was an oldish, grey-bearded man of infinite courtesy and consideration, John Scott Hughes, who had been the yachting correspondent of *The Times* since 1934.

I was very glad to meet John Moore again. He was, like myself, a put-ashore sailor, who had survived an exciting term as a pilot in the Fleet Air Arm; a job which had included service in aircraft-carriers and flying, on torpedo missions, those terrifying little aircraft which the Navy called "Stringbags" (I would hate to think what the Fleet Air Arm pilots called them *).

It must be admitted that John Moore had scored an even greater hit, as far as I was concerned, by giving my wartime book, *Three Corvettes,* a marvellous review in the *Observer,* a review so eminently quotable that we were using it on the dust-jacket a quarter-century later. He was a good friend then, and he remained one for the next twenty-three years, when, after dedicating his last book to me, he sadly died.

There we were, anyway, happily and companionably installed in an obscure room which was, to our continuing pleasure, very hard for anyone else to find. We did little official work. Some of us did none at all. We talked, and pondered, and smoked, and jotted things down, and occasionally said "I don't think so" on the telephone, and took hours off for lunch.

---

* Officially these were Swordfish torpedo-bombers, whose top speed of 148 miles per hour made them almost theatrically vulnerable to anything pointed in their direction. It was Swordfish from the *Victorious* and *Ark Royal* which scored the first vital hits on the *Bismarck*. But in a later English Channel action against the battle-cruisers *Scharnhorst* and *Gneisenau,* six of them were flown off and six were shot down. For this brave try, a posthumous Victoria Cross went to Lieutenant-Commander Esmonde, the flight-leader, who had also led the *Bismarck* attack.

John Moore was correcting the proofs of his new book, *Bren-sham Village,* and muttering to himself "It's not right! But it will be!" On Christmas Eve he led us all in chanting his private carol: "Noël! Noël! All book reviewers go to hell!" with a malevolent fervour I was not to appreciate until many years later.

I was scribbling down two different sets of notes; the first for a book about my brother Denys, who seemed to deserve one, if only as an act of piety; and another, highly tentative, for a *possible* novel about the Battle of the Atlantic, which also seemed to merit someone's attention.

John Scott Hughes was drawing up sail-plans for the ideal contender for the America's Cup, and saying: "Of course, all I really want to do is to go back to *The Times.*"

It is worth recording that all these things came true. *Brensham Village* was one of John Moore's bigger successes, after *Portrait of Elmbury;* I did publish, three and six years later respectively, both the books I had been dreaming about; and John Scott Hughes did return as yachting correspondent to *The Times,* and stayed in that agreeable niche for another thirteen years.

But at the time, they both seemed to have a clearer view and a much tighter grip on the future than I had, or was ever likely to; and it was beginning to worry me.

Meanwhile I did what I could, in this climate of sloth, to go on earning my pay, which was now sixty-six pounds a month, without benefit of living free on board ship. I wrote the articles I was asked for: one on "Fine Qualities of the Navy's Little Ships" for the *Imperial Review:* one on "Sea Power in Action" for the *Round Table:* one on the blessings of radar for *The Trident:* and one on "The Royal Navy Fights Japan" for general consumption. I did an occasional B.B.C. broadcast about the deeds of other brave men, in a weekly afternoon feature on the Navy. It was the time of the V1 and the V2, Hitler's last violent effort against a side which was so obviously winning that only a lunatic would go on struggling.

This final try came in the form of a series of bombs and rockets, a short sharp flurry of murder with which the Germans, in desperation, were trying to subdue our civilian population. V stood for *Vergeltung*—retaliation. The V1 was the worst, and the most effective.

This unnerving, soulless, and cruel weapon, aimed almost entirely at Greater London and anyone who might be working or sleeping there, was a pilotless, jet-propelled flying bomb which crossed the Channel at four hundred miles per hour and steered itself towards its huge, sprawling target.

One could hear it coming; presently, when it was somewhere overhead, its engine cut out, there was a silence, and we waited. Then it fell, and the solid ton of explosive in its warhead went off. In its short career the V1 destroyed or damaged three-quarters of a million houses, and killed 6,184 people.

Its companion piece was the V2, a breed of long-range rocket, each weighing twelve tons, which approached in total silence from a peak height of fifty miles. These poisonous arrows killed another 2,700 people before our advancing armies pushed their launching bases out of range.*

But those advancing armies (not pongoes and Yanks any more, but liberation troops, or even simply brave soldiers) were doing all sorts of other things at the same time. Presently, on a day of wild triumph, the war—or at least the German part of it—ended. A long-awaited V-E Day—V for Victory, E for Europe—dawned on 8 May 1945, five years and eleven months from Day One.

The war ended, for me, on a most moving note. All officers above a certain rank in the Naval Information Department had to take their turn as acting "Duty Captain" during the night hours —the proud title meant no more than standing a telephone and signal-watch, as the wakeful link between the outside, land-or-sea world and the people who really did the work, but who preferred, if nothing important was happening, to get some sleep at nights.

I was acting Duty Captain at the Admiralty, charged (on this sub-contracting basis) with Britain's entire naval destiny, on the last night of our war.

* All this last-minute misery and bloodshed was inflicted by courtesy of Wernher von Braun, the German scientist who, as "Technical Director, Liquid Fuel Rocket and Guided Missile Center, Peenemunde," for eight years, masterminded both projects. Since we provided this valuable target practice, Britain does perhaps deserve a tiny Mention in Dispatches, at the very end of the screen credits, for the moon landing (via Saturn rocket) twenty-four years later. This also was by courtesy of Wernher von Braun, now a staunch American citizen.

Even inside the massive building, one could hear the tremendous noise from nearby Trafalgar Square, which, when I had
come on duty at 8 P.M., was already packed with a cheering,
roaring, dancing, swaying crowd: a crowd sampling the magic
taste of the first evening of peace.

I carried the enormous happiness of that moment, the choking
relief, with me into the Admiralty, where everyone else I met was
happy, because, at least from the Atlantic and the Mediterranean,
there would be no more news of U-boats ("Up to nine in your
area"), no more terrible tidings of disaster ("Following six ships
in convoy sunk last night"), no bells tolling across a thousand
miles of the worst widow-maker of them all.

I would have given big money (well, medium-sized money,
suitable to my station) for a celebration drink on this night, but
no such facilities were on tap in our humble area. Instead, I
said "enjoy yourself" to the fortunate man whom I had relieved,
leafed through the last hour's signals, and settled down in the
consequential armchair normally occupied by the Duty Captain.

But by midnight the crescendo of noise and cheering, the
blaring of horns, the fireworks (hoarded for this moment?), the
sounds of amateur music-makers, were very hard to resist. My
telephone had not rung for the past hour. The signal-log was
almost bare. Nothing was happening, because we had won the
war.

On a guilty impulse I deserted my post, and climbed up the
devious stone pathway to the top of Admiralty Arch.

The view from there was marvellous: backwards down the
Mall towards Buckingham Palace, forwards to Trafalgar Square
and the tall honoured pillar with Nelson a-top, a sailor who, at
this particular moment, would have been feeling as joyful and as
proud as anyone within ten square miles of the Admiralty. But
one's first reaction was one of astonishment—not at the crowds,
but at something else.

There were lights! There were lighted windows, unmasked
headlamps, gaping doorways stripped of their black-out screens.
Both Buckingham Palace and the Admiralty Arch itself were
floodlit. There were actual lights, for the first time in nearly six
gloomy years. Apart from victory itself, there could have been
nothing more moving than this simple freedom, this blessing.

I stood there for quite a long time, listening to the crowds, laughing at them and with them; leaning against the parapet which was like the bridge of a ship, except that in front and below me was not the sea, calm or cruel, peaceful or murderous, but an ocean of people with its own surging wave-pattern, its *life*. Then, on a half-turn, I became aware that I was not alone, on top of the Admiralty Arch.

There was someone standing within five yards of me, also staring down at the crowds, and oblivious of close company for the same reason as I had been—because we were both entranced by the magnet of what was going on below. With that perceptible twinge of nervousness which had been built into my life for so many years, I recognized, first the rank and then the man.

The massive display of gold braid told me that he was an admiral, like his brave and lonely brother on top of the column. Then I realized that this was a very superior admiral indeed. I counted one thick band of gold, and *four* thinner ones. He was an Admiral of the Fleet—the highest any sailor could go.

In fact, I suddenly recognized, he was *the* Admiral of the Fleet. The man in my company was the First Sea Lord and Chief of Naval Staff, Admiral Cunningham.

Andrew Browne Cunningham—one remembered the initials, and what they stood for, as one remembered in boyhood the admired labels of great cricketers, jockeys, prefects, even writers. (H. G. Wells was Herbert George; Thackeray was also William Makepeace.) Cunningham had been a legend with us all for years; he was in command at the Battle of Matapan, and Commander-in-Chief of the Mediterranean when, between the onslaught on Malta and the brutal ebb and flow of the North African campaign, it was an ocean which had to be cleansed before we could make any headway at all.

He had done that, and then moved on. In fact, he had probably done more for our side than any other living sailor.

Cunningham, we knew, had joined the Navy at the age of fifteen—in 1898. He had trained in sail. He had been a destroyer-captain at Gallipoli in 1915. But now, in our own inherited war, he had carried this tremendous load for years on end, and all his plans, all his patient, brave, and faithful service had borne fruit. We had won. *He* had won. It must be quite a moment for him.

It was. I watched him surveying the raucous happy crowds. Then he looked up at Nelson. Then he leaned forward, his knuckles planted squarely on the parapet. The movement brought his face into the floodlights shining from below, and I saw, in one bare, glistening fraction of a second, that he was crying.

I returned to duty forthwith.

The duty I returned to had now taken a swift nose-dive. Both John Moore and John Scott Hughes had left, *en route* for the blessings of an assured or at least a planned future; I was now isolated in a new and darker cave, a cellar-room next door to the cafeteria, where I was obviously the Tail-End Charlie of the Department of Naval Information.

There was even less to do than before, and a wise man would have got out; but I was as far as ever from being a wise man, and I clung to office like any other minor limpet.

Sometimes duty called, and I was told to write something, and then summoned upstairs to withstand the scrutiny of the Commander R.N. who now seemed to be charged with my destiny. This humourless fellow, who after all these years was still intent on teaching the R.N.V.R. a thing or two about the Navy, used to keep me stationed in front of his desk for anything up to half an hour, while he leafed through my efforts and digested at his leisure whatever article or broadcast or news-release I had laid before him.

He reminded me of my housemaster at Winchester, another petty tyrant set in authority, another man whose pleasure it had been to nail me upright in this penitential stance while he took his own sweet time over the current inquisition. But now, the tiny edge of rebellion had a little more body to it.

I felt entitled to be angry and mutinous. Here was this fattish, pinkish nonentity, who could keep me standing for twenty-five minutes while he read, frowned over, blue-pencilled, and finally tossed back my draft for a B.B.C. broadcast.

He might, I thought, have asked me to sit down, without any gross violation of naval discipline; there were sumptuous chairs all round the room, no doubt reserved for his superiors. God damn it, I had been at sea for nearly five years; I had been captain of a frigate. . . .

I have no doubt at all, now, that this could well have been an unfair judgment, and that Commander X had probably fought a good hard war before being put ashore, like me, and into a job which he hated as much as I did.

But it was this sort of occasion, imposed by this very man, which decided me against staying on in the Navy, at a moment when there was a real prospect that I would do just that for the rest of my working life.

Various kinds of official bait were being held out. Various promises, which now seem laughable, of interesting and rewarding employment for wartime naval officers who wished to stay on, were going the rounds. It seemed that they still wanted the R.N.V.R., though as it turned out there was to come a time, not many years ahead, when they could not ax their own people quickly enough, and if you, as a regular officer, would kindly leave the Royal Navy well before you were forty, you would be rewarded with a handsome present.

But though I was tempted, because I loved the service and the pride and discipline which went with it, it was not too hard to work out the odds against. As a temporary officer, I might have to revert to lieutenant. The competition for command, in a shrinking Navy, would be fierce. There would be very little sea-time, which was the only kind of time worth spending. Perhaps, once a year, one might be lucky enough to cruise down to Gibraltar, or across to the coral strand of Bermuda, where *Perim* had worked up.

For the rest, it would mean a desk job, and men like this plaguey commander, with all his affectations and false frowns, sitting squarely on my neck for the rest of my career; and, in one's spare time, dancing social minuets with admirals' wives, those formidable brass-bound creatures who could, I already knew, match their husbands, broadside for broadside, on any day of the week; who wore the stripes as other women wore the trousers.

The answer was No; and it was still No, even after a chance re-encounter with a man who had done more for me in the service, and taught me more in a short time, and had left me wiser—had left me, in fact, knowing at long last what the Royal Navy was all about—than any other human being in the whole six years of war.

He had a long label in the Navy List—Lieutenant S. R. Le H.

Lombard-Hobson, R.N.—and he had been captain of my new ship when I finally winkled myself out of *Campanula* and was posted to another corvette, H.M.S. *Guillemot,* as First Lieutenant. He was now a commander, "shopping for a job," as he put it, though the phrase only meant that he was concerned with his next posting in the Navy. I was also shopping for a job. But I had, by then, no such frame of reference.

In fact, what on earth was I going to do now?

I was thirty-six—almost over the hill already. I wasn't going to be a sailor; and by now it seemed that I wasn't going to be a writer either, if the figures were anything to go by. Simple arithmetic was against me, among a formidable array of other things.

In thirteen years I had made £1,647 out of writing eight books. It worked out at £127 a year, a living wage for a starving dog, but not much else. In fact, it worked out at failure. The only theme which had even looked like clicking was the *Corvette* series, and this was now dead forever. I would do the book about Denys because I wanted to; and I *might* try that Battle of the Atlantic idea. But neither of these was likely to keep me alive.

Meanwhile I would need, very shortly, a living wage of my own.

I played with the idea of trying for the B.B.C. but the organization as a whole seemed to have entered a rather precious phase. I needed something more serious, more orderly; after the years of naval discipline, I still wanted an embrace of similar severity and good repute. I could never go back to that pre-war "freedom" which had been wonderful in one's mid-twenties, but seemed sloppy and second-rate when one was shaping up for forty. Also, there was a continuing need to serve. . . . Then I heard about a new thing called UNRRA (the United Nations Relief and Rehabilitation Administration) which was just setting up shop. It was going to help with the reconstruction of a war-torn world. To start with, it was going to the aid of Austria, where there was an outbreak of typhus. Was that the sort of thing?

I discussed it with Eileen, who came back with one of the most perceptive comments she ever made. Though entirely good-humoured and tolerant, her verdict was: "But isn't that just your picture of what Nicholas Monsarrat ought to do after the war?"

I answered, sourly enough, "I suppose so," but I knew that she was right. The idea *was* part of a show-off pattern of "doing good," which though sometimes effective in action was often deeply suspect in motive. I needed something more than to strike ill-paid attitudes of selfless benevolence.

Then an old friend, Morrice James, not for the first nor the last time, came to my rescue.

Morrice had returned from the war as a lieutenant-colonel in the Royal Marines, and was now back at his desk in the Dominions Office. He and I spent a lot of time talking. Though glad to be alive, neither of us was entirely decided on what to do with the extension of life. He was still hankering after something more exciting than spending the next quarter of a century as a slow- or fast-rising civil servant. He talked of writing; in fact, at that moment of time he was a civil servant who wanted to be a writer, while I was a writer who wanted to be something else—even a civil servant.

For relaxation we patronized a theater club of which he was a member, and where probably the best intimate entertainment in London was available: the Players' Theatre, mysteriously situated under one of the arches carrying the suburban traffic from Charing Cross.

After one of these spirited evenings, when we were having a last drink at the slum end of the Café Royal, Morrice said: "We may not be having many more of these, I'm afraid. I'm going to be posted."

"Where to?"

"South Africa."

"Oh." I felt bereaved already. "But what as?"

"Assistant Secretary. On the High Commissioner's staff."

"Who's the High Commissioner?"

"Baring."

I felt I should have known the name and the man, but of course I did not. While I was still considering this brusque turn of events, which would leave me orphaned, without anyone to talk to, Morrice went on: "They're planning to open the first British Information Office there. It will be part of the High Commission, but in Johannesburg instead of Pretoria. It's concerned with British propaganda, really, except that propaganda has be-

come such a tainted word. Let us call it—" I could tell that he
was quoting from some prudent memorandum "—the dissemina-
tion of information about all aspects of the British way of life.
Anyway, they're looking for a director to take charge. Why don't
you try for it?"

"But I don't know enough about it, do I?"

"Oh, I wouldn't say that. You've had a year at the Admiralty.
You've been dealing with the Press and the B.B.C. You can write,
damn it!" He grinned at me over his glass of lager. "I can assure
you, your application would look perfectly adequate on paper."

I had an idea that, as a helpful friend, he might already have
mentioned my name; and this was confirmed, in a roundabout
way, when he said: "Of course, there are one or two other factors.
For example, did you ever actually join the Communist Party?"

I had not known, till then, how sharp his glance could become.

"No," I answered, truthfully. "I nearly did once, as you know.
And I used to sell the *Daily Worker* in Piccadilly."

"Please!" He held up his hand. "Spare me the horrible details.
Then you never actually joined?"

"No. When the time came, I found I didn't believe in it any
more. Spain took care of that. Too much political killing. . . .
The nearest I came to it—" I searched my pre-war archives, "was
to join the Friends of the Soviet Union Sunday Film Society."

"*Potemkin*," said Morrice, whose memory was always excellent.*
"Exactly."

"I think we can overlook the battleship *Potemkin*. And of
course you must have had naval clearance. Well, there it is. If
you like, I'll put your name forward."

The mad idea suddenly took shape. South Africa? Actual *sunshine?* Lots of butter and meat? British propaganda? A responsible
job on the staff of the High Commissioner? A regular salary? Why
ever not?

"I think I'd like that very much."

The keen glance, which might have been more daunting if I

---

* *The Battleship Potemkin*, Sergei Eisenstein's 1925 film about revolution
and the Russian Grand Fleet, was a perennial favourite with progressive audi-
ences, and a masterpiece in its own right.

had not developed one myself, for sea-going use, bore down on me again.

"Naturally you'll have to behave yourself."

"Oh, I think we both will."

I wasn't going to take too much of that daunting glance. For Morrice James himself, an energetic bachelor of thirty with a set of rooms in Albany, this was not a bad moment to move on to South Africa, either.

We had known each other a long time.

After that, things advanced very quickly, giving the lie (for the first and last time, as far as I was concerned) to the idea that the pace of the civil servant was the pace of the world-weary snail, something like six feet for each cup of tea. I was interviewed by a succession of grave men in progressively darker suits. Finally I was interviewed by the Permanent Under-Secretary of State for Dominion Affairs, Sir Eric Machtig, who was in black.

A week later, I received a letter offering me the job of Director of the United Kingdom Information Office, Johannesburg (still to be established). The appointment, in the first instance, was to be for a term of two years; and the salary, *not* subject to an annual increment and *not* carrying a housing allowance, would be £1,250 a year.

It was more than I had ever earned, or was likely to, and nearly double my naval pay.

I talked over the whole thing with Eileen, and found that she was as tempted as I was; it was a big step, but attractive for many reasons, and there was between us, unspoken, the idea that a new country and a new job might give us a fresh start in other directions as well. Against that, there was the feeling, absolutely genuine and valid, that we ought to stay where we were, as loyal British subjects, and sweat it out; if not for the pride and pleasure of sharing national hardship, then for the experience itself.

While we hesitated, a cracking blizzard ("the worst since 1939," just like everything else) hit the entire British Isles; and as if that were not enough, there were fresh warnings of reduced rations, and a news-item from the Ministry of Food not at all calculated to improve the appetite:

"We have a squirrel pie recipe which has not been generally

issued to the public, but is available to applicants. The ingredients are: 1 squirrel, 1 large chopped onion, 1 rasher of bacon, 1 oz. of flour, seasoning, and water. *Instructions:* Wash the squirrel well in salt water, cut in small pieces, roll in flour, place in a pie dish, and bake."

Free cartridges would be supplied by the local pest officer to shoot the squirrel with.

That did it. I sent my letter of acceptance to the Dominions Office, and began a swift round of visits concerned with briefing me for the new job.

"Don't get into any arguments" was the general theme of all this instruction. There were two sets of people in South Africa, English-speaking and Afrikaans-speaking, Briton and Boer (the old phrase was apparently still appropriate); they were almost irreconcilable—always had been, always would be. Monsarrat with his little Information Office wasn't going to alter any of that. But he needn't make it worse. He should talk about what Britain was doing *now*, and was trying to do, and leave it at that.

Above all (and this was added in a voice from which every inflection save that of politeness had been rigorously excluded)— above all, *pas trop de zèle*.

A perceptive fellow, the top expert on South Africa, added that General Smuts (pro-British) was probably on his way out, and would be succeeded by an Afrikaner Nationalist Party government, traditionally dedicated to hating Britain's guts. This might make my job more difficult. But anyway—have a good time.

Suddenly the tempo rose; all the waves curled, and were about to break. We did our packing, and said our goodbyes. As a last gesture in the direction of Socialist brotherhood, I let the Notting Hill house, furnished, to an impecunious Reuter's journalist for four pounds a week—about one-third of the current rate. (No capitalist landlord I.)

I tried, and failed, to sell my naval uniform and bridge-coat ("No market for this sort of stuff"). Instead, I went up to the R.A.F. depot at Uxbridge, and selected my free demob outfit: 1 suit, 1 shirt, 1 tie, 1 pair each of socks, shoes, and braces, 1 pork-pie hat, and (on the way out) 1 packet of Liquorice Allsorts.

Finally I collected my Navy gratuity (£134 for six years' watery slog) and we took off.

2.

We took off in a cargo liner called the *City of Madras,* and finally, after a season of such dreaming indolence as I had never hoped to live again, we rounded smoothly into Table Bay, and the Tavern-of-the-Seas which was Cape Town Harbour; and there, at sunrise, with the wakening town dwarfed by the massive grey backcloth of Table Mountain, and noble smoky-blue hills beyond, and a sparkling green sea behind us, to prove that we had voyaged six thousand miles instead of turning a single page in a picture book, there we came to rest.

It was the end of what was to be my last holiday for two and a half years. But then, I did not know that. All I knew was what I saw and felt, as the mooring hawsers snaked ashore and were secured: the warmth, the sunshine, the bright colours, the excitement, and a view of what a fellow passenger had called the most beautiful country in the world.

At first glance, I saw that this could well be true.

We found a heartening reception committee waiting on the dockside, just the kind one needed when taking the last step down the gangway and the first into a world absolutely new and strange. There was an energetic, bearded young South African called John Bold, who had been the lone Information Officer on the High Commissioner's staff for the past few years; and Ian Maclennan, the First Secretary—the same age as myself, but with an early crop of luxurious grey hair which made me envious; and Patrick Duncan, then the junior member of the High Commission staff.

This was, though we did not know it then, an assembly of very diverse talent. John Bold, who stayed on as a most useful Press Officer in the new organization, finally decided on a more individual career, which was to invent, develop, and popularize one all-embracing native language.

This, destined to be the *lingua franca* for the whole of Southern Africa, he christened Fanagalo. It was a devout dream, but Fanagalo never prospered, and the multitude of tribal languages remains intact.

Ian Maclennan, climbing a lofty ladder, was to be High Commissioner in the Rhodesian Federation and in Ghana, our Ambassador to Ireland, and High Commissioner in New Zealand.

Patrick Duncan, a cheerful young man in spite of a severe and painful limp, the product of some early parental confidence in Christian Science, made his own pathway of honour. Son of a former Governor-General of South Africa, he became disenchanted with the country when it was reshaped under Nationalist rule; he resigned from the public service, and teamed up with various inter-racial and thus outlawed groups; and he went to jail at least once, in a courageous one-man attempt to stem *apartheid,* before he died.

But then, this was just a trio of cheerful young men on the quayside at Cape Town, against a background of market-stalls crammed with marvellous flowers which I had never seen before —cannas, chincherinchees, poinsettias, bougainvillaeas, and tiny sprigs of wild orchid the colour of pale olive stones—with that whopping great monolith of Table Mountain on top of everything.

Meeting them was one hesitant newcomer, wrongly dressed, nervous of authority even one notch above him, and knowing as much about starting up an information office as they did about running a touring ballet company in Peking.

Yet confidence returned, as we were wafted through Customs with a few diplomatic finger-snaps, and then driven in the High Commission car up to the Mount Nelson Hotel, a splendid monument to colonial rule which had survived to become a Cape Town showpiece and a center of old-fashioned opulence. There we settled down, in guilty luxury; forgetting a starving Europe, forgetting our dear ones far away, crouched over their squirrel-pie as the gas pressure faded to nothing; transplanted at a stroke into careless paradise.

After a pre-lunch drink under the trees in the garden, we took our places in a sunny corner of the dining-room, with a matchless view of the slopes leading down to the harbour, and made our selection from the menu. This was a noble document listing some fifteen items, with a footnote: "The limited menu is in accordance with the restrictions imposed by Gov. Reg. 1945." I hoped there would be many more Gov. Regs. like that one.

We feasted off paw-paw, and a new fish-dish called Fried 74, and meat such as we had not tasted for half a decade, and crepes suzettes, and (for me) a cigar, regretfully the smallest they had available, a Corona-Corona for which the going price in London, even if obtainable there, would have been 15s. Here it was 2s. 6d., and here, thank God, I was smoking it.

There was another High Commission man staying in the hotel, a superior character with the memorable name of Hercules Priestman (one took, I thought, a certain chance with such a christening, almost equal in valour and daring to calling one's daughter Venus). Luckily Priestman, who perhaps had been a huge baby, had grown up to be a huge man.

He was sketchily introduced to me as Chief Secretary for B. B. and S. The initials, which stood for the three High Commission Territories of Basutoland, Bechuanaland, and Swaziland, were to prove a load of trouble in the near future.

But on that day they were simply initials, and Hercules Priestman a most engaging companion, though his sense of humour did not always accord with my tender anti-colonial conscience— as when he said, of a formidable woman, an ex-proconsul's wife whose husband had just retired to Basutoland: "Never had the earth been so liberally bedewed with Basuto sweat as when her ladyship started replanning the garden."

Next morning I had my first interview with the boss, High Commissioner Sir Evelyn Baring. The session completed a twenty-four-hour induction as inspiring, hopeful, and reassuring as it could possibly have been.

Baring, son of an earl (Lord Cromer) who had transformed Egypt from a slum into a country at the turn of the century, and the grandson of a marquess, was the first aristocrat of achievement I had ever met, as distinct from the aristocrats of indolence with whom I had wasted so much time at Cambridge, and a couple of aristocrats of tailored incompetence I had met during the war.

He was still under forty-three, and had already carved himself a distinguished career in the Indian Civil Service; he had just completed a term as Governor of Southern Rhodesia, and ahead of him still lay the Governorship of Kenya during the worst of the Mau Mau era, and the chairmanship of the Commonwealth Development Corporation, with £160 million a year to distribute as wisely as possible.

He was tall, he was friendly, he had been at Winchester; and I was an admiring member of his staff for the next five years. He was a wonderful man to work for, while demonstrably working like a demon himself: the first of two High Commissioners (the other was Archibald Nye in Canada) who had what seemed to me the perfect attitude towards the men on the payroll beneath.

This was to teach them, control them, praise them when appropriate, blast their stupid heads off when they made a mistake, *but* —and this was the biggest "but" in this area, widely neglected by other practitioners of authority—always to draw the mantle of personal responsibility over the battlefield, when something had gone wrong.

Baring, agile and energetic in spite of indifferent health, now and then used to climb to the summit of Table Mountain (3,580 feet), in company with the Prime Minister, General Smuts, who at the age of seventy-six regarded Table Mountain as no more than a pleasant, slightly uphill walk. Members of the High Commissioner's staff were always welcome to tag along (Morrice James was one who did so), though my own severe war wound (1940: thrown out of bunk: cracked rib) unfortunately prevented me from volunteering.

But this ascent somehow symbolized for me the section of ladder which now faced me, and the climate of behaviour which my first interview with Evelyn Baring signified. This was a world of strict endeavour, efficiency, good conduct, and the honourable discharge of duty. It was like the Navy, except that now the ranks were vague, and the uniform non-existent. The uniform, in fact, was the civil uniform of service. I wore no other for ten years, and when I lapsed from it, only a selection of glad rags took its place.

Later that day he found time to take me round on a series of visits—and here again the idea was to start me, and the new office, off on the right foot, by giving us his personal seal from the start.

We called on the editors of the two English-language newspapers, the *Cape Times* and the *Argus,* who were cordial in their welcome. We had sessions with the South African Bureau of Information, the Ministry of External Affairs, and the South African Press Association, which under its short title SAPA-Reuter

was the principal export-import agency for all news from this part
of the world, and all news from outside.

We sat in for a dull half-hour at the House of Assembly, now
in mid-session, which, by contrast with the young, new-style fer-
ment now rising at Westminster, seemed incredibly old and tired
and bored. We had reviving drinks at the two clubs, the Civil
Service and the City, of which I was now an honorary member:
clubs so comfortable, leisurely, solid, and important that I knew
I had at last gone up in the world.

Then I went back to the High Commission Office (there was
no doubt that this was a working day), and continued, with the
help of the registry, making my selection of the files which I either
wanted to read on the spot, or take with me when I went up to
Johannesburg.

But there was plenty of time to look about, during the ten days
in Cape Town, and looking about was depressing.

Though this was a handsome city, with some splendid Cape-
Dutch buildings and a magnificent harbour, all guarded by the
bulk of Table Mountain and its attendant Devil's Peak and Lion's
Head: though strange fruits and gorgeous flowers grew like lux-
uriant weeds: though the surrounding coastline, where the Atlantic met the Indian Ocean, was as fair as the Firth of Clyde, with
guaranteed sunshine as the essential bonus: though people were
fantastically hospitable and welcoming, and food and drink as
lavish as at some banquet of all the nations, yet there was poison
in the Cape air.

It was not an undeniable poison, nor a poison beyond argument, nor poison so mortal that it could never be another man's
meat; but it was poison for the man I still was—the compassionate
Socialist with strange and lasting injections of naval discipline,
the mixed-up do-gooder who wanted everybody to be happy, on
the basis (equally mixed up) that we were all God's creatures,
sharing the same huge and bountiful pie, and that if we could not
be generous enough, and wise enough, and nice enough to make
a fair division of such bounty, then we did not deserve the label,
nor the pie either, and would lose the lot on the garbage tip of
history.

The poison was, of course, the colour bar; and though in theory

I knew all about this (it had been Item Number One in my briefing, under the implied heading "None of your business"), yet to
see it put into practice surprised and disgusted me—particularly
as South Africa still marched towards its destiny under the banner of General Jan Christiaan Smuts, one of the prime architects
of the United Nations which, at its inauguration at Lake Success,
had made such valiant declarations of universal brotherhood.

Only later did it occur to me that Smuts had been so busy with
his star billing on the global stage that he had neglected his own
back garden; that while he beamed and bloomed in the heady
sunshine of world acclaim, his own country staggered towards ill-
fortune and a mean, un-Christian, rigid, permanent division into
Have and Have Not.

Within two years, history was to catch up with him, when, in
1948, the Afrikaner Nationalists rode in, spurs a-jingling, whips
poised, to take over the whole restless camp and coin the brand-
new word *Apartheid*.*

They were never to ride out again: not in twenty-two years,
perhaps not in thirty-two, or a hundred and thirty-two, or until
a vast shedding of blood washed all the good and all the bad, all
the love and care and hatred and mean conceit, down the same
drain, which had already served a tormented continent for half
a million years.

But that is a "now" judgment, with all the sad erosion of the
recent past to make it seem valid; then it was "then," in April
of 1946, when all I had to go on were the eyes and ears and the
pursed lips of a new arrival. Then, all these rules were new to me,
and horrid in their implication, and traitorous in their denial of
the last six years.

---

* In 1949. It meant nothing more sinister than "apart-ness." It was first set
down in print in 1950, when the Congress of the Dutch Reformed Church
adopted a resolution calling for "full territorial *apartheid*." It still remains
the most uncompromising and therefore the most honest term for social and
racial discrimination, preferable to all other evasions, glosses, and sneak
short-cuts to segregation.

One would rather hear *apartheid* thus proclaimed, loud and clear, than the
contemptible sneer "Fine old Scottish name!" applied to a Jew, or the slightly
more endearing Liverpool label, "Smoked Irishman," for a Negro. With the
one, you know where you are; with all the others, you know where you are
but you won't admit it.

I had just fought a war—and unless we were all blind-bull idiots, led by the century's most spurious nose-ring, we had *all* fought a war—dedicated to the proposition, happily victorious, that there must be no master-race; that a Jew was an equal man, and a Pole an equal man, and all the other slaves of the Thousand Year *Reich* were equal men.

This *must* mean that a black man was an equal man, with two of everything except where it counted most, where we were once again all equal: that a Cape-Coloured man was just the same: that one could not kill Hitler, and hang his guilty aides, and cleanse the infected air of his dream of race-slavery, and then emerge smiling into the sunlight, to inherit all the loot of violation for which we had just fought him to a standstill.

Yet as soon as one stepped out of the Mount Nelson Hotel, and walked easily downhill through the Gardens towards the High Commission Office, this was what one was supposed to accept, without question.

It came in the form of notices, which were displayed everywhere, even in Cape Town's most quiet retreat, where in the cool shade there was an aviary, and strange trees whose twisted bark followed the turning track of the sun, and an endless succession of warnings: "Europeans Only"—"Non-Europeans Only"—"*Blankes Alleen*," from one end to another of this small Eden.

Down-town it was the same, except that there men and women carried these signs in their eyes as well—or perhaps it was that malady of short sight which I came to know very well, the literal colour blindness which ensured that on the streets and in the shops and at any public gathering, one did not see a black man or a coloured man or any man who did not belong to the white totem.

One looked straight through him; or, shortening the focus, saw him as a dark blur, a grey ghost, a shadow in the path, a near nothing in the white world of everything.

First the brain turned aside, and then the eyes, and then, if necessary, the feet. But this last need scarcely ever happen. Already, in 1946, the coloured man took to the wall, or the edge of the pavement, or the gutter, or the dusty hedgerow, as the white man passed.

On a short train journey down to the beach at nearby Muizenberg, the fact of the separation of man from man was made even plainer.

Here the labels multiplied until they were a permanent frieze of denial; they were on every railway carriage, and every lavatory; on every bench of every station; at every ticket-office, and every shelter, and at every entrance and exit; at every bus-stop outside, and on the wind-blown beach itself, where one did not stray "down there" because that was the coloured section, generously labelled, and They certainly did not stray "up here," because they knew a bloody sight better than to try it on.

Blankes Alleen was the only ticket to have. Anything else was comfortably counterfeit.

I supposed—indeed, I knew—that if one had grown up with it, from blond childhood, it would certainly have been acceptable, like the pox in the Middle Ages, or the later, dirty travesty of democracy which allowed a teacher of the young to tell them that violence was "relevant"—i.e., a permissible way to get what you wanted.

But to an innocent stranger it was a shock, just as sharp as it must have been to a country boy who walked for the first time into the city of fifty years ago, and there read, with astonished, ashamed eyes, the crude notices which commanded him: "Do Not Spit"; "Keep Off the Grass"; "Adjust Your Dress"; "Commit No Nuisance."

Until then, he would have had no thoughts of spitting, or of treading on anything which grew, or of not buttoning up, or of urinating anywhere except behind the nearest, thickest privet hedge in sight.* Now, under the new urban rules, he had to watch his every step, in case he grew careless, or was corrupted by such evil communications.

Of course, the poison in this air *was* one man's meat; it was a lot of men's meat; it was these men's meat, and as neutral visitors we could only watch them enjoying it. It was none of our business, as Ian Maclennan and all the others had been trained to assume automatically on their arrival, whatever their private thoughts, and as they taught their comrades and successors.

---

* "Privet," first noted in 1542, is labelled "origin unknown." I still like to think that the derivation is from *"privatus."*

This was South Africa, and nowhere else; it was *their* country, not ours; we were not there to change it (that chance was long gone, with the wind of change itself, which blew as strongly from the south as it blew from the north). We were only there to observe, to report privately, and to maintain polite and firm contact with an ex-colony which we hoped would not become an ex-Dominion.

That (with a short pause for uncontrollable laughter) was why I was there: to set up our own shop-window, to talk and write about Britain, to preach the virtues of the Commonwealth, but never, except by the mildest implication, to draw any comparison whatsoever.

The journey to Johannesburg, the longest I had ever made on land, was also one of the most fascinating. I had been prepared for the size of the country, but not for its novelty; from the first mile to the last, there was scarcely anything to be seen which I had seen before, scarcely any natural or man-made object of which I could say: "I saw something like that in Spain" (or Hungary, or Fife, or Massachusetts Bay). It was all new, all foreign, and all intensely watchable.

My companions were John Bold, who continued to act as a useful guide and chaperon (he had already rescued me from the solecism of straying into a Non-Whites' lavatory on Cape Town station); and two strangers, two tough young men from the Government Forestry Department on their way to a conference in the capital, Pretoria.*

When talking to each other, they spoke Afrikaans. It sounded basically Dutch, as Yiddish sounds German. It also sounded ugly and slipshod, a kind of guttural baby-talk. I knew, even then,

---

* Pretoria, in the Transvaal, was the administrative capital of South Africa, and Cape Town the legislative capital, where Parliament was convened annually. Twice a year, on the agreed date, a vast migration took place, when train-loads of civil servants, secretaries, and filing-cabinets, plus the entire diplomatic corps (which had to maintain dual establishments), were transferred from one nesting-place to another. The seasonal exchange coincided with the cooler weather awaiting these transients at either end of the country; though the intensive, highly competitive house-hunting which the move imposed took most of the edge off this dividend.

that in spite of the best intentions I would never learn it. But the way they could reel off the mysterious words of Southern Africa—high-veld and low-veld, hinterland and *kraal, wildebeeste, uitspan,* and *aasvogel* *—was an excitement in itself.

There was one local custom I could have done without, on that stirring northward journey, and that was the early-morning cup of coffee, which was compulsory. Promptly at five-thirty, there was a menacing crash at the door; the lights blazed up, and a tray of cups, sloshing over as the train rocked, made a brisk circuit of the assembled company.

When we had swallowed this offering we did our best to settle down again (we had only stopped drinking a fierce brew of brandy called Commando about four hours previously). But hardly had sleep returned when the door crashed open again, the lights repierced the eyeballs, and the tray reappeared. It was the man for the empties.

After that, realizing that South Africa was a young, energetic, early-rising nation, I stayed awake: staring out of the window at the railway embankment which sped past, rising and dipping like water sluicing past a porthole; a view which gradually widened, and receded, and drew away until it reached the skyline of the eastern horizon.

Presently this turned pale, and then began to glow. It was the sunrise, making me free again of a country which seemed to have every variety, from ugly to beautiful, from dull to unbelievable.

We had been climbing, through the great escarpment of the Swartberg Range, all the time since we had left Cape Town; now we were thirty-five hundred feet above sea-level (the exact figures were proclaimed at every wayside station) and travelling through the Great Karroo Desert—which even my patriotic companions dismissed as "miles and miles of bugger all." But the exhausted Karroo was fascinating, nonetheless.

We passed limitless stretches of low scrub, cactus, and stony wasteland; we crossed dry river beds with the bleached bones of animals marking their own last graves. We saw a few sheep grazing ("Average, one to an acre," the tree men volunteered),

---

* Just a vulture.

and a few alert springbok on the horizon; and all round this horizon were the eroded hills, like flat-topped slagheaps, which contained this arid landscape, and seemed to set an absolute limit to it. But of course they did not. This was Africa.

The Karroo, I had once read, was the oldest part of the earth. Within the memory of man it had been fertile; now a brutal drought (no drop of rain for three years), and steady soil erosion, and a parching wind, and the baking sun had all but destroyed it. Even the lone, high-wheeling vultures must be going through a very bad patch.

The few farms, widely spaced out, were of enormous acreage: "As far as a man could ride, from sunrise to sunset, in the old days," John Bold told me, setting out the ground-rules with a romantic gleam in his eye. Each farmstead was surrounded by a private troop of a dozen small windmills, manfully pumping water to sustain some sort of fertility—and to keep alive those lonely sheep which, I already knew, produced mutton and lamb of miraculous succulence.

Sometimes there was no house, nor farm, nor animal, nor man to be seen, as far as the eye could reach. Only a wisp of smoke on the horizon, the kind which used to betray a convoy at sea, but which was here a precious landmark for the traveller, promised that one might find human company at the end of the long day's journey.

The lonely life produced the lonely landscape; and the lonely landscape had a harsh beauty, a pale-yellow, skeletal authority which proclaimed, all the time: whoever first carved out even a bare sustenance in this wilderness, they must have been men; and whoever now lived there were men of the same breed, not likely to surrender, not disposable without a fight of African ferocity.

The wayside stations were strung out along the railway line, with names so varied that the next one could never be foreseen— Worcester, De Doorns, Touws Rivier, Prince Albert Road, Beaufort West, Nelspoort, Three Sisters, De Aar; they were for the most part only halting-places for our train to pick up water.

But I was voyaging all the time towards the High Veld, and the parched yellow was changing to verdant green again. . . . It was irresistible to step down from the train at every opportunity:

to walk, to stare about, to buy grapes or apples or water-melons from an ox-cart manned (the word was inescapable) by some of the biggest women I had even seen.

"Afrikaner women are all big," said one of the Forestry boys, when I commented on these reigning Amazons, squatting tent-like on fecund haunches, like the Albert Memorial with a frilled and faded sunbonnet on top. He did not sound at all displeased. "Lots of kids, eh?"

From these wayside stations, grouped round the huge dripping water-tank which must serve as our life-blood for the next stage of the journey, countless sandy roads as straight as rulers led off into the blue, and disappeared over the far horizon, in hope, or despair, or brave endeavour.

The men and the women who had first trodden them out, the people of the Great Trek—only a hundred years earlier—had never stood still, and never compromised themselves or their hungry faith. At nightfall they had outspanned their oxen from the creaking wagons, and slept within the *laager* like tired giants; at each dawn, they had yoked up again, and set off in search of the dream once more.

Put down in this dry wilderness, they did not sit in sorrow nor lie about in soft stupor, waiting for help. They broke out and away, at a hard right angle to the trodden path, and discovered what was over the farthest hill, and the one beyond that; and when they found exactly what they were seeking—a sheltered green, a spring still running, a bare chance of fruitfulness—there they stopped, and made it their own.

I was already half in love with this whole continent.

Now we were beginning to move through and into the pages of history, some of them having proud links with the past, some unhappy and best forgotten. At dusk we left the vast Cape Province behind, and crossed the Orange River into the Orange Free State, so named a hundred years earlier by those same wandering *Voortrekkers,* whose turning wagon wheels were not to be stopped, even by the Orange River in spate.

But they still had to fight the climate, the Basutos, the British, and the hordes of diamond seekers flocking in from every corner of the world, before their new stake in Africa was confirmed.

This was over the halfway mark of our own trek. Next came

the Modder River, which stood for ancient frontier battles just as memorably as did the Delaware, in that other frontier-country across the Atlantic. Then, when I should have been getting ready to sleep (but who could ever be ready for sleep, on such a journey?), we came to Kimberley.

"Four thousand feet above sea-level," proclaimed the first light falling on the first notice-board. But there were thousands of other lights to mark the thriving town, to remind the traveller of its violent and colourful history, and of the men who had scooped (and were still scooping, though in a more genteel way) diamonds by the million-pounds' worth from Kimberley's peculiar pride and joy, the biggest man-made hole in the world.

It was never a time for sleeping. We crossed the Vaal River in the middle of that night; in the old days, this had been so important, such a decision to make, such a step into the unknown, that anywhere north of that point was called the Transvaal, and still is.

Now we forked right for Johannesburg, instead of left for Mafeking, another ominous name in this ground-plan of history; and at 6:45 A.M. we steamed at last through the frieze of strange-looking sand castles which were in fact very grown-up toys—the mine-dumps, the yellow dross of forty years' frantic boring for gold—and stopped with a shriek and a shudder in Johannesburg itself.

The city was just waking up, and so—lightheaded, sleepless, and enthralled—was I.

3.

I had left Eileen and Max behind in Cape Town with no more sinister motive than the true one—freedom of movement, which would leave me unharassed by the thought of the little woman pining away at home, while the pitiful orphan boy cried out for his daddy before merciful sleep etc.

I now had to become briskly mobile on several fronts at once; an acting bachelor could deal with such short-term pioneering without regard to time-table; and Eileen was better off in Cape Town anyway, where she could await a summons from the frontier-breaking breadwinner from the preferred vantage-point of the Mount Nelson Hotel.

In Johannesburg, I had to find, as the very basis of existence, an office, a secretary, a telephone, a house, and a car; and it had to be done in that order, to justify the new-found status and the lavish salary.

I dived right in, free of all encumbrances, and with a zest—sparked by the sunshine, the thin clear air of six thousand feet, and half a dozen other blessings—such as I had not felt for seven long years; and, like any politician, I could point with pride to the fact that within three days I had collected the nucleus of everything I needed.

In fact, the first U.K. Information Office was already in being—even though it was still only me, John Bold, and the dust on the floor.

But engaging even one good secretary had already proved a problem. By agreement with the South African Government, the High Commissioner's Office could only pay its local staff at the same salary rates as the host government itself, thus preventing too much poaching by richer countries which might be able to advertise unheard-of salaries, and so ruin the market.

My office came under the same arrangement; and the best I could offer a qualified shorthand-typist (they were called "stenos") at that stage was sixteen pounds a month, which was approximately eight to ten pounds under the market rate in ordinary commercial offices outside.

But luckily (there was a lot of luck floating round Johannesburg in May 1946) I found a gem in Miss Pybus, an older woman of great competence and firm character, who said that the salary did not matter, who took me well in hand from the start, and who ran the other office-girls (soon there were six of them) with the kind of motherly authority which reminded me—well, of Mother.

She was to stay with us for nearly seven years—Miss Pybus of U.K.I.O.; though towards the end, she did become slightly disenchanted with the Director. By then I was conducting a torrid love affair with a young woman in Cape Town, involving an exchange of scorching telegrams two or three times a week: telegrams which for some reason always arrived at lunch-time, when

I was out, and had to be read by anyone brave enough to open them, and then lay them, in all their non-official candour, on the Director's desk.

Miss Pybus was always brave enough. But I could not help noticing that her lips, firm even at normal moments, became positively strip-welded as this long-continuing fling progressed.

However, that was in the scarlet future. Now, on Days One, Two, and Three of my endeavours, she was a rock of competence, and I could get on with the rest of my searching, without worrying about stray callers or hot-shot stationery salesmen.

By the second day, from a big selection, I had rented a furnished house in a suburb called Northcliffe, about six miles outside the city. It faced north (in our topsy-turvy continent, that was where the sun was), with a terraced garden and a superb view round three-quarters of the compass towards the Magaliesburg Range and the true high veld. Its rent was twenty-five pounds a month (this was not yet a fashionable place to live); and the wages of the Zulu cook-houseboy were four pounds a month.

Finally, there was the car.

I had already gathered, from cautionary friends, that selling secondhand cars in Johannesburg had now superseded the retail trade in gold bricks, fresh out of the crucible, as a profitable line of endeavour.

But I was one of those who had to have a car at all costs; though "all costs" must not exceed two hundred pounds, which would be everything I had in the world, plus most of next month's salary, plus some savings from my Tropical Clothing Allowance which I was still clinging to.

For the time and the place and the money, it wasn't such a bad car, when I finally found it and wrestled it to my bosom. It was a 1937 Plymouth, 23 horsepower, price two hundred pounds; and certainly there was no lack of competition to acquire it.

I drove nearly two thousand miles by its faked speedometer before the front axle broke, and the Plymouth, subsiding gently onto its sump, slid to a last halt in the heart of Pretoria. But good or bad, it was the first car I had owned for twelve years, and it gave us our first coupon-free spell of simple "driving around" since 1939.

On Day Five, which was a Monday, I engaged an office-cum-messenger boy (the word *boy* did not concern age in South Africa, only racial status) with the charming, the irresistible name of Motorcar B. K. Ratshiko. At midweek, Philip Birkinshaw, who was to be my deputy-director, arrived from England, with gruesome tales of travel by troopship but an undiminished cheerfulness which, in the same circumstances, I could not have matched.

At the weekend, a girl with another euphonious name, Martli Malherbe, a South African who had once worked at the Cabinet Office in London, arrived from those far-off Magaliesburg Hills which I could see from my own mansion, and began to set out her wares as Films Officer.

Now we had to get moving.

But in 1946, the country into which I had thus been pitchforked, with instructions to make friends and influence people, to accept things as they were: *not* to criticize, *not* to argue, *not* to quarrel about anything more important than art or boxing: *not* to strike any attitude save that of a chummy neutrality; yet at the same time to preach the liberal, tolerant, British way of life—this country, and its mainspring the City of Johannesburg, seemed at that crucial point of time and instinct to be the most awful place in the world.

In South Africa, roughly two million whites were playing host to nine million non-whites; to redress the balance, to preserve a decent superiority in such a threatening jungle, the pressure had to be unrelenting. The native population, as well as being generally insulted and ignored, was inexorably clamped and confined into menial jobs.

They were also being pushed farther and farther away from the city centers and into "native townships"—wretched squatters' villages, with one tap to a rutted street, and a bus service so inefficient, overcrowded, and offensive to all the senses that, as the only link between white master and black servant, it also came into the category of permanent insult.

My friend Motorcar Ratshiko, as dependable, honest, and hardworking as anyone I had ever met (quite as good as the Trearddur Bay postman, and better than a thousand Liverpool layabouts)—Motorcar had to join his Orlando bus-queue at 5 A.M. in order to be in the office at eight, when we opened.

Even there, there were things I did not like, but hesitated to check because even this might be interpreted as unwarranted interference by an outsider. Any native, calling with a message or collecting a consignment of films, would always be addressed as "John" by our first receptionist. It was an automatic reaction, like the automatic superiority. A white man had a name, and a welcome. A native boy was John, and "What do you want, John?" his only greeting.

At home, even in our liberal Northcliffe household, Eileen bought meat for us and "boys' meat"—God knows what leaky bundle of chopped gristle and string—for the cook-houseboy, the gardener, and the nursegirl who now made up our modest staff (total cost, £10 15s. a month).

If anyone had asked me what the hell I, a medium-grade civil servant with £30 in the bank, was doing with three permanent servants, who shared two huts and a lavatory consisting of a hole in the ground shaped something like a violin, the only possible answer was: "I'm living in South Africa."

Perhaps this first feeling of guilt was purely, parochially English. It was to disappear, like any other unwanted corpse, with time and corruption. But then it was strong, and so were lots of other feelings, as I surveyed the scene and the temper around me, and found both of them odious.

I had thought Johannesburg itself an absolute nut-house, almost from the moment my train drew into the station with that "shriek and shudder" which was soon to seem so appropriate; and as time went on the verdict only gained in validity. It was a money-mad, raucous, pioneering town, wildly happy when the stock-market was up, dejected beyond belief when it was down; a sixty-year-old mining camp * still flexing its muscles and hacking out a rich living from the baked earth—some of its citizens with picks and shovels, others with honest brains, some with crooked fingers, and all with an avid devotion to the mountain of gold we were sitting on.

My arrival had coincided with a brand-new, fabulously rich gold-strike in the Free State at Odendaalsrust, which I had passed

* Lord Milner, when Governor of the Transvaal, had called it "the university of crime."

on my way north. Even without this, Johannesburg would have had enough fables already, and enough crazy energy to stock the biggest Bedlam in the world; with the Odendaalsrust strike the city took off on a new, dotty extravaganza of rumour, riches overnight, and the ruined hopes of those who had guessed wrong.

There was one curious perversion. In this city of greedy men, there was a virulent anti-Semitism. Oppenheimer was Hoggenheimer; Johannesburg itself was Jewburg. It was the anti-Semitism of a collection of people, themselves as acquisitive as tearing vultures, who feared they might be out-smarted at their own game. If they did win, it was brains. If they lost, it was those bloody Jews again.

Such was this grotesque city, whose interest I had to capture. It was going to be hard. It was hard enough already. A "Victory Parade" through Johannesburg, by South African soldiers who had fought across Africa and up the cruel spine of Italy, was such a flop that even the well-disposed *Rand Daily Mail,* under a cross-heading "Admiring But Silent Spectators," had to admit that "the Johannesburg crowd was the most restrained of all." (They had previously marched through Cape Town, Durban, and Pretoria.)

It was better summed-up by O. C. Troops, an on-the-spot realist, who said: "I have seen more enthusiasm at funeral services."

The enthusiasms were not for anything so vague as memory; they were more sharply focused altogether. Money came first; then a great deal of determined drinking, in which I presently joined, helped by the altitude which was a sovereign cure for hangovers; and then an enormous level of casual fornication—with which, at this, the first prim stage of my lease, I was not connected, even as a knowing spectator.

After that, the major and minor lunacies took over. Where else but in Johannesburg would core-samples be so liberally laced with added precious metal that shares went sky-high before the culprits (trapped by gold-dust in their trouser-turnups) were hauled off to jail?

Where else would window-shopping at night be a pleasure absolutely unknown, since no one with any regard for their safety would walk the streets after dusk? Where else would there be no bottles of liquor on display in any bar or lounge (even in a private club) where women were admitted, since the weaker sex was not allowed to see drinks poured out or corks drawn in public?

Where else, when the ladies had left the gentlemen for coffee after dinner, would a shattering report from the drawing-room be followed by a reassuring: "It's all right, darling—we were just comparing revolvers."

For a writer—even though I had stopped being a writer—all this was irresistible, and I made reams of notes, mostly on Dominions Office stationery which was good, durable stuff of a superior quality. But the sad parts outweighed the mad ones, by far more than that 4½-1 black-white majority; and thus the novel I wrote about it, nineteen years later,* came out sad—sad and angry.

It was clear to me within a few months that I could never love this city nor this country; in spite of all its innocent blessings— the sun, the dry warmth, the champagne altitude of six thousand feet (though my nose did begin to bleed as I climbed the stairs of the *Rand Daily Mail* to call on the editor, Rayner Ellis)—in spite of all this, and a lot of good people who became good friends, I did not want to be exiled for longer than I could help, in a country which seemed to impose an absolute denial of all I had come to believe in, after thirty-six years of trial and error, of chopping and changing; of the reading, writing, and basic arithmetic of man's hoped-for humanity to man.

If I had known that I was to spend the next seven years in Johannesburg, in charge of the same information office, I would have voted against it, firmly and conclusively. But luckily the job itself quickly became so absorbing and so seemingly worthwhile that I could concentrate on that, and give the bleeding heart the most effective tourniquet of all—a conditioned neutrality.

By mid-year U.K.I.O. really was a going concern. We had taken a floor of a new office block, happily named London House; and there we had our reference library, our film library, our photograph library, our poster service, our regular supply of feature articles and trade news, our gramophone-record lending library,

* *The Pillow Fight* (Cassell, and William Sloane Associates, 1965; Pocket Books, 1966; Pan Books, 1967).

our telephone information department, and our link with the British Council and the B.B.C. Transcription Service.

We also had my private pride and joy: the reading room, the only place in the Transvaal (except at the rival U.S. shop up the street) where a Negro could sit down next to a white man, and read *The Times* or the *New Statesman* in peace. Now, it might sound nothing: just the common currency of civil right. Then, I hope and believe, it was a new and crucial blessing for a great many people.

The studious calm which ruled the whole room, from opening time onwards, was all I needed, by way of endorsement.

As a back-up job to this small viable empire, I started running round in various circles; and, over the months, called on every-one of any consequence whom casual contact, or the High Com-missioner's superior hot-line, made available.

Most of them are now only names; sometimes only names on gravestones, with all their energetic lives gone to dust. Then, they were the people to know, and so, putting on the airs appropriate to the Chief of British Information in South Africa, I came to know them: politicians, financiers, social people, drinking people, bedding people, working people; art people, press people, racing people, poker people; stockbrokers, heart-breakers, gold-brickers, born suckers.

In Johannesburg, one need never stop mining such lodes. But in the first year, I could only scratch the crawling surface, with finger-nails manicured to a polite length by protocol, a lingering British reserve, and a salary of £104 a month.

I was now doing regular broadcasts on a Brains Trust type of program called Listener's Forum, though inhibited by the rather large number of topics I could *not* talk about.

I also did some undercover book-reviews for the Johannesburg *Sunday Express,* and began to make a lot of speeches.

For these there was an unlimited range of audience: chambers of commerce, women's clubs, ex-servicemen's organizations, schools, universities, and Rotarians, whose female contingent, sad to relate, called themselves Rotary Anns. Looking down on the bald heads, or the earnest faces, or the blurred after-dinner moons, or the sea of millinery which distinguished those most daunting gatherings, women's luncheon clubs, I dutifully fired off my Set of Variations on a Noble Theme—the theme being Britain, her Manful Past, Energetic Present, and Bright Future.

I believed in this with conviction, even with passion; I believe in it still.

One of my audience, on an early occasion—indeed, a head-table guest, as befitted a solid citizen with diplomatic overtones—was Bill Hamilton, head of the United States Information Office and my opposite number in the current polite tug-of-war for influence —or, as we sometimes phrased it to each other, in moments of enlarged vocabulary and diminished responsibility, the wrestling match for the soul of South Africa.

Hamilton was a robust, charming, immensely capable ball-of-energy; the kind of chap the British ought to have had, as head of *their* information set-up, if the very idea had not been so terribly un-British.

"Nice going," he told me after the speech, when we had adjourned to the underground Goldfields Bar (it was only 3 P.M.) and got stuck into the brandy. "There's nothing I like better than to hear a man with a funny accent whistling in the dark."

At the moment he was having an easier time, professionally, than I was; America seemed to be getting everything right, while most of the things we did were either wrong, or unpopular, or dull. His was now the top nation, beyond any doubt. It was thriving before our envious eyes; and the Marshall Plan for aid to a troubled Europe, the most imaginative and generous effort ever made by any country in the search for a better world, proved that the thriving was not selfish, and that the derided Yankee Dollar could do many other things besides glitter and boast and provoke.

Meanwhile, Britain had imposed bread rationing, for the very first time in her recorded history ("Not even in the darkest days of the submarine war!" Mr. Churchill thundered); there was an allocation of one egg per person per week; the O.B.E. was awarded to the four-foot-high Liverpool comedian, Wee Georgie Wood; an unholy mess began over the stopping by the Royal Navy of wretched immigrant ships trying to get to Palestine; and the rules for people attending Ascot races were thus set out:

Women in the Royal Enclosure are not permitted to bet; nor to smoke; nor to wear pearls [pearls being the only jewellery worn by the women-folk of the Royal party]. Guests should not watch the Royal family too closely. No cameras or sketchbooks may be carried. No divorcées can be admitted.

Bill Hamilton, cutting the item out, sent it across to my office with a scrawled: "Do they let *horses* in?"

For an awkward month, he himself had something not so easy to deal with: the American atom bomb tests in the Bikini Atoll in the Marshall Islands. These had become very unpopular, long before they started; though no one except about fifty Japanese fishermen had ever heard of Bikini Atoll before, it certainly looked a beautiful place, and the idea of blowing it to pieces with those damned bombs, which already seemed destined to be the curse of all our lives, was almost sacrilegious.

I missed Bill very much when, following a ruthless Congressional economy drive, they closed up the U.S. Information Office and sold off every single item in the building—only to re-open it again, about a year later, at enormous expense (the carpet in the reception hall alone cost more than our total annual rent). Bill Hamilton went on to bigger and better things in the State Department, but I can personally guarantee that he was doing all right in Johannesburg.

He had an expression—new at that time, slightly uncouth, explicit—with which he used to close some of our sessions, when even Chiefs of Information had to go back to their offices and sign a few letters: it was "Keep your nose clean." Exiled in South Africa, half in love with it, half revolted by a whole frieze of the most disgusting human violation, I kept my nose clean, occasionally in demanding circumstances, for several months. Then I got into a big row myself.

Foolishly, it had nothing much to do with South Africa. It was Palestine.

As befitted a city where the Jewish community had worked so hard and contributed so much, since the day, sixty years earlier, when the first hopeful peddler had pitched his first tent, Johannesburg had an influential Zionist organization, and was taking a strong interest in what was, and was not, happening in Palestine, the "Jewish Home" which had still to be labelled Israel.

Locally, this was sparked and spearheaded by the Chief Rabbi, Professor L. T. Rabinowitz, who operated under the auspices of the United Zionist Revisionist Party.

Rabbi Rabinowitz, a dedicated, attractive, and ferociously energetic man whom one chance encounter established as an enemy instead of the friend he was later to become, had, or thought he had, a lot to work on, as far as Palestine was concerned. He was dramatically, professionally furious about the whole thing.

He could point to the fact that the entire might of the Royal Navy seemed to have been deployed to intercept and turn back the stream of leaking, broken-down immigrant ships which were currently trying to run the blockade and bring East European Jewish refugees to their only safe harbour.

God knows they had suffered enough already, under murderous persecution first from German, then Polish, then Russian spite. So why could they not be allowed through? (Answer: There was an Anglo-American-Arabian accord which limited the Palestine intake to one hundred thousand per annum, in order to avoid total chaos on the spot. Simple arithmetic could prove that for one incoming Jew, there was likely to be one displaced Arab. Both of them, under this tidal drift of humanity, could starve to death.)

The rest of the dispute was a hideous mixture of charge and counter-charge: the small lie supplanted by the big one, the genuine tear by the crocodile: the honest soldier shot in the back by the honest patriot: the crooked referee lynched by the virtuous crowd. Still saddled with the tail-end of their mandate, the British had to hold the ring.

Against them was ranged the Stern Gang, self-styled "Fighters for the Freedom of Israel," and unlicensed murderers in any language, who once hanged half-a-dozen British soldiers in an orange grove, as sad and sunny a death as could be devised. There was another terrorist organization called IRGUN, which kidnapped five British officers from their club in Tel Aviv; and shot two others in Jerusalem; and then, in the same city, blew up the entire King David Hotel, the British military headquarters, leaving 106 dead (including girls from our Auxiliary Territorial Service).

From our point of view, we *had* to impose a stiff military rule. It was our duty as the appointed custodian. From the Chief Rabbi's, however, the best thing we could do would be to get out, stay out, and let Palestine forge its own destiny. In protest against our continued presence, he had recently discarded all his British military decorations, and sent the lot back to Buckingham Palace. Now he invited me to take part in a public debate on the whole issue.

I might, he said, with a certain menacing honesty which I found difficult to resist, be the only one who would support the British side.

By now, it was thought that I was grown up, and I had a free hand in accepting or declining all such invitations. Perhaps I should have been more wary, in this threatening climate. But some of the things which were being said about us—particularly at an anti-British rally attended by the Mayor of Johannesburg, Mrs. Jessie Macpherson, where we were firmly branded as Fascists, as anti-Semitic tyrants "worse than Hitler"—got under my skin.

The childish business of the Chief Rabbi's medals clinched it. If he thought he had a lot to work on, so did I. I accepted, put on my best suit and a Royal Navy tie, and went down into the arena.

The ferocity of the occasion was a genuine surprise. It developed into a real old-fashioned slanging match; and I might have been playing the bagpipes in a high wind on top of Mount Carmel, for all the progress I made.

All our past efforts were derided or forgotten, up to the moment of "now." Now, it was repeated, we should get out and stay out. We had no business in Palestine, anyway; not even to have our soldiers murdered in the pursuit of liberation. There weren't any arguments on our side. There was only our guilt, our certain humiliation, and our duty to leave the scene in favour of those who were properly entitled to deal with it.

There was one man whom I could talk to, who even paused to listen, on that so-called panel; the rest might have served as fully paid-up members of the Holy Office, conducting a standard inquisition with the faggots noisily piling up in the background.

This was a lawyer called Louis Pincus, a gentle character who was soon to sell up his practice and actually go to Palestine, where he became a member of the Cabinet.

So he was all right: an honest man prepared (as Bill Hamilton would have said) to put his money where his mouth was. The rest of them, safely out of range of the real action, were baying for blood; anyone's blood. Mine was the nearest supply on tap; and mine it was.

At the end I did the best I could, by way of fighting back. After listening to every kind of insult and misrepresentation of the British role in Palestine, with side-swipes at my own effrontery in even daring to answer back, I said that I wanted a couple of minutes of uninterrupted time, to put my point of view. Aided by Louis Pincus, I finally got it.

I then said that we were in Palestine because it was our duty, from which we were not going to run away, however loudly the dogs barked and snapped at our heels. If people were going to call the British names, then they might as well get the names right.

"Fascist" was not a suitable epithet to apply to a nation which had expended enormous efforts and a great many lives in rescuing Jews from a miserable tyranny, and were now in the process of half-starving themselves in order to send food to Middle Europe.

If it had not been for Britain's ultimate challenge to Hitler, there would not now be a Palestine for the Jews to reach, nor any Jews to go there.

The hissing uproar which this provoked was well reflected in the next day's issue of the Zionist newspaper, which carried as slanted an account of my efforts as I had ever read, outside my last school report. I had insulted the entire Jewish community. I had called them dogs. Clearly, out of my own mouth, I was an anti-Semite of the deepest dye. The best thing, the only thing, the British government could do now was to recall me forthwith.

All such mistakes and strokes of misfortune—indeed, all mistakes and misfortunes—are one's own fault; that is the lesson of life, whether one realizes it early, or late, or goes whining to the grave still shrouded in a sense of injustice.

On this occasion I should either have presented my views deep-fried in diplomatic batter; or kept silent; or preferably not been there at all. The silly part was that I was probably the least anti-Semitic person in the whole of Johannesburg.

I had already come to the conclusion that the Jewish community—who actually read books, bought paintings, supported the theater and the symphony orchestra, and gave money to charity with open hands—were the only people who redeemed Johannesburg from its squalor; and I admired and honoured them for it.

Later, when I came to know Harry Oppenheimer—son of the fabulous Sir Ernest, brother of that Frank Oppenheimer who had been a fellow-member of the Lucullus Club at Cambridge—and saw his new mine down at Welkom in the Free State, where he had established unheard-of living conditions for his mine-workers in the face of ferocious opposition from authority; and listened to him as an M.P., and a Cabinet Minister, and the controlling brain of a huge empire of half the world's diamond, gold, and uranium supplies (all this at the same time), I grew more convinced than ever.

His was a blue-print of accomplishment which made nonsense of race or religion; demonstrating just how much one man, with vast inherited wealth, great talent and ability, and an outlook, a code of ethics, which it would be insulting to call Christian, could do with such assets.

But already, without benefit of Harry Oppenheimer or any other particular star to convince me, my feelings were such that the charge of anti-Semitism was baseless. To hell with Rabbi Rabinowitz, I thought, as I read of my misdeeds and awaited the inevitable summons to Pretoria. To hell with such a far-off freedom fighter who could condone murder without a splash of its blood to soil his pious hands.

There were far better Jews, far better citizens, far better men. One had only to seek, and one found them; and I had discovered this already.

4.

The rest of that jumpy year went like the wind, with the office steadily building up to the point when it was taken for granted as part of the scene—though there were some things we simply could not deal with, as when one admirer, complimenting us on our Monthly Diary of Events, wrote: "I would like to receive your Monthly Diary every week in future."

My errors, for the moment, were mainly social, and included one whopping misdemeanour which followed me around for some time. As with every crossroads, big or small, it was only a matter of having said Yes instead of No; but, fresh from the tangle with the Chief Rabbi, I should have had more sense.

There was at that time a murderer in England by the name of George Neville Heath, currently being tried and then hanged for two revoltingly sadistic murders involving women whom he had stripped, bound, stabbed, raped, mutilated, and generally bashed about in the pursuit, presumably, of pleasure. He had been married during the war to a South African girl, and everyone in Johannesburg knew it.

It really was quite a talking point, in a society which had not a great deal to do besides enjoy such light chit-chat. Speculation centered on one intriguing aspect: if George Neville Heath took his pleasures so devoutly, what had it been like to be married to him?

I knew the girl, and her new fiancé, a serious and compassionate young man transparently dedicated to her welfare. At a dance which they bravely attended, they asked me—no, she asked me, while he listened—if people were talking about herself and her late husband. Being in the business of accurate information, I was fool enough to answer: Yes, of course they were. Then, what, she asked, were they saying?

Leaving out certain monstrous expressions of curiosity, I told her that too.

Tears followed, public distress; grim silences; and then a swift withdrawal of patronage which presently left me at an empty table with my innocent and faithful wife, who up till then had been enjoying herself, and with—God damn it—the bill.

"You really *are* a fool!" Eileen said, when I gave her the details. "Why didn't you tell her, No, no one knows anything about it?"

"But she asked me!" I had been taken aback by "fool," which coming from Eileen was extremely rare—perhaps too rare for my own good. "What else could I say? One has to tell the truth."

"Oh, God!"

It could have been a direct salutation, a recognition of a new role, but somehow it didn't sound like it.

Max, son and heir and only child (I seemed to have lost the knack for the moment), was now four: a small, bright, blond boy who had thrived on British rosehip syrup and cod-liver-oil in the past, and was now thriving on South Africa's lavish spread of all other items in the larder. Full of energy but inclined to conserve it, he went everywhere, even to the lavatory, by tricycle.

I could not see much of him, except at weekends. But it was nice to know that my ancient nursery jokes still went down well; that the old riddles ("Why is five o'clock in the morning like a pig's tail?" "Because it's twirly!") were still considered uproarious, and that a brand-new one ("What's the difference between a sick elephant and a dead bee?" "One is a seedy beast, the other a bee deceased" was, after a little explanation, equally successful.

He had a song to sing me, just as I had had one to sing for my father. It was never my first choice, but it was certainly his. It was called "Shoo-Fly Pie and Apple Pan Dowdy."

When Max laughed at a joke, there was always some delighted laughter echoing in the background. This came from Victoria the nursegirl, a loving black shadow who never seemed to be more than ten paces away from him, and was the most devoted attendant he was ever likely to have.

Like all natives—like Adam in the kitchen and Simon in the garden—Victoria was sweetness and gentleness itself with Max, and with any other white child who might be around. Though it was obvious that these privileged children must one day grow up to be privileged tyrants, like all the rest of the white adult world, yet no trace of this foreboding knowledge, this absolute certainty of duress, ever showed in their manner, their voices, their smiles, their infinite patience, as they took care of the rulers-to-be.

Thus it was painful, it was almost disastrous, to note that Max had already picked up, from God knows where, the instinct of lordship over Victoria and the others. He bossed them around, argued with them, ordered Victoria to fetch his toys, or to collect them at the end of the day, plagued her to carry him on her broad back, demanded hand-outs from the kitchen, and, when punished as he had to be for such nonsense, took it out on the victims in any way he could, and always resumed the habit of command.

Where had he got it from? He did not go to school. He would never have learned such arrogance from our own almost morbid solicitude for any native we dealt with. Certainly he played with other children, but they were the children of imports like ourselves, not yet in tune with white South Africa and never likely to be.

Yet in a short half-year he had contracted the disease already. We decided that it must be in the very air—that divine, rare, benevolent air which, for all its seeming purity, carried a horrid contagion as well.

Through a demanding job I could compensate for the shortcomings and imperfections of all around me. Eileen had no such sublimation available, and was much less happy. The freedom to buy a dozen eggs, ten gallons of petrol, a tub of butter, a *sack* of oranges, could not mask the glaring lack of other freedoms, which nagged, or should have nagged, at the conscience and the instinct of decency without giving either of them a moment's rest.

We were both stuck in a cage of demonstrable misery and distress. I could look the other way, for quite a lot of the time. She could not.

But in the world outside, who was happy, towards the end of 1946? One peered about, like a sociologist or a lost sailor, and wondered. Where was the good news?

Not in Britain, under a blight of austerity which would have taken the heart out of a prize lettuce. *Not* in Greece, where a civil war, of brother against brother, was boiling to a crescendo of merciless blood-letting. *Not* in India, split and crucified by religious rioting which left the streets of Calcutta and Bombay littered and reeking with corpses—up to a hundred a day—for the vultures to pick over at their leisure.

Not in nearby Basutoland, where five Basutos, led by the late Paramount Chief's son, were up on a medicine-murder charge (lips, eyebrows, and ears sliced off, to make good strong medicine; then the head wrapped in a cloth and buried under the floor of the hut).

Certainly *not* in the dock at the Nuremberg trials, where after

227 days of evidence and summing-up the death sentence had been passed on thirteen top Nazi war criminals. I felt absolutely hard-hearted about all this; like Nelson confronted by mutineers, I would have hanged the lot on Christmas morning.

Where, indeed, was the good news? *Not,* once more, in South Africa, where a white farmer, having got a black girl pregnant after a brief encounter *under* his parked car, killed her, beheaded her, and then disembowelled her of the tell-tale foetus, which he thought might reveal its pale origin. His wife, equally concerned with social pressures, held the lantern for him to work by.

There were moments when the fullest office day could not drop a curtain anywhere near large enough or thick enough to take care of South Africa. Now and then I knew that if I had been a Negro in Johannesburg, I would have become *anything*—thief, liar, murderer, rapist, revolutionary, medicine killer, political assassin—if it would have improved my lot by half-a-crown a week, or let me get level with even one of my oppressors, whether a tough, head-cuffing policeman, or an indolent white missus.

What, on God's earth, could one do about South Africa?

5.

Being a civil servant with deep though underlying political convictions, I had my answer ready. South Africa, clearly, must be acquired and administered by men of good will; it must be rescued, refashioned, set on the right path, and kept firmly to it.

Thus it was now time for my third invention; after the Automatic Gear Change (1921) and Perpetual Motion (1926) must come South Africa Reconstituted (1946).

Obviously I would have to take the whole place over; or rather *we* would have to take it over—"we" being me and my presidium of the wisest in the land. Over Christmas, I drew up my master plan; and here, in all its naïveté, its good intent, and its inherent bossiness, is the text of that blue-print, forever enshrined in Copy No. 1 (there were no others) in the only SECRET archives which have survived from the past.

Outline of: THE SOUTH AFRICAN PARTNERSHIP
South Africa needs reorganizing, from top to bottom, within

the next ten years: it needs a political, commercial, and ethical spring-cleaning. Already out of date, it is heading for political repression of the worst sort, and ultimate disaster—the fate of ALL police states. To find a cure, seven million natives have somehow to be fitted into the political and social scheme: they cannot be ignored or repressed indefinitely: sooner or later they have to become full and valuable citizens of the Union.

Our aim must be, progressively, to work towards:

(a) A contented labour force, without which this country will grind to a full stop and a consequent blood-bath.

(b) A full black-white partnership, making of this incredibly rich country a model nation and a most successful one.

Our beginning should be on these lines: first and foremost, to raise the standard of living of the Natives: save them from being gypped by Indian traders, European adventurers and opportunists, and their own worst elements: feed them decently and cheaply, clothe them decently and cheaply, give them something to do in their spare time, keep them healthy; and generally make them feel that they are REALLY being looked after by their own natural protectors.

Starting with the four essential provisions—something to eat, something to wear, somewhere to live, and something to do—this is our basic outline of progress:

Establish:

1. Native department stores.
2. Native cinemas.
3. Community centers—meeting-places for natives, comprising a concert hall, rest-room, information and advice bureau, and sports ground.
4. Health centers.
5. Cheap transport to and from their work.
6. Schools.
7. Adult education centers, native training for jobs, native apprenticeship schemes, native trade unions.
8. A first-class native Press.

We must make a start with the first four items on this list, which with seven million customers cannot help being a tremendous financial success. That, of course, isn't going to be the point of it for us, but we need money for power, and especially for Press backing. We should make a start up on the Reef, South Africa's prime problem and plague-spot, where most of the misery and injustice of this continent is concentrated: our first venture should be to establish three of these centers (north-east, north-west, and south of Johannesburg), comprising a department store (two-story, mainly clothes and food, native sales-staff, white supervision until they are educated to take over), a cinema, a meeting-place, and a health center, grouped together into a single entity (say, round a courtyard) which will be trusted, respected, and automatically repaired to by the vast majority of the natives in its district.

Notes on the above—the first nuclear units of the South African Partnership:

(1) DEPARTMENT STORES. Our stores must sell cheap food, cleaning materials, clothes, fuel, radios, and prefabricated houses. (Natives will buy the ready-made parts, assemble them themselves, and pay for them over a period of years. This in itself would solve much of the misery, discomfort, frustration, and violence at present making hell of the Johannesburg locations.) With an enormous turn-over, we need only a marginal profit, and can under-sell anyone else with purely commercial ambitions.

(2) CINEMAS. We must show them the best entertainment films (not out-of-date trash, as at present) and selected educational shorts, with dubbed native language sub-titles if necessary. Later we must commission films with all-black casts: there is no earthly reason why they should not see their own people acting their own stories.

(3) MEETING-PLACES. If you give natives something to do in their spare time—whether it's organized games, sports to watch, art-and-craft classes—it will cure much of the crime-wave overnight. All they need is space, privacy if they wish, and expert and

sympathetic direction. They must also play, sing, and act for themselves: there is unlimited talent. We must also have group-listening to a genuine Third Program, a Bantu one with plenty of audience participation.

(4) HEALTH CENTERS. These are vitally necessary: education and advice on (a) maternity and child welfare, and (b) dietetics, are prime requirements in this field. We must co-operate with the War Memorial Health Foundation, whose head man, Paul Anning,* has all the right ideas on this subject. As a sideline, the Health Centers could train and turn out really good nursegirls.

If this start in Johannesburg is a success, progress and development in the rest of the country will follow naturally: immense political power will result, and in the end we can dictate our own policy. The forces behind us, financial and political, are prodigious: they only need controlling and canalizing on the true lines of progress. The main point is this: we are NOT in it for money. To start with, we need to borrow about £600,000, cheaply, using in the first instance the bait of a stable native population, which clearly pays its own dividend. A man such as Harry Oppenheimer with (a) mining interests demanding a contented labour force and (b) a social conscience seeking an outlet, might be persuaded to finance the whole thing at nominal interest. With no burden of debt to be serviced expensively, and no thirst for inflated profit, we can defeat any purely commercial competitor; and while we are establishing ourselves we will have the political backing (for a variety of reasons which do not matter) of the strongest forces in this country and (important) the approval of Great Britain. In the end we can reorganize TOTALLY the whole political and social life of South Africa, and make it the most influential, socially-minded, and worthwhile country in the world.

It is idle to pretend that natives are now deserving of full

---

* I had the privilege and the good fortune to succeed him as chairman five years later.

partnership with Europeans: they are not within a hundred years of it. But they MUST be set on the right lines, instead of being frustrated or ignored; and above all they must be made to feel that the white man is prepared to back their development with complete honesty and unselfishness.

On its present course, South Africa could destroy itself within a generation; on the basis of an eventual full black-white co-operation, it can be invincible.

N.M. Christmas 1946

Greatly daring, taking an enormous chance with all sorts of hazards, I showed this manifesto to a few South African friends. The reaction was mixed, to say the least; perhaps it was that first sentence, which took too much of their friendship for granted, and was a shade on the arrogant side also.

But I believed in it; and I believed deeply in the idea of a partnership in Africa. Certainly one should make the Negro a full citizen. But why throw out the white man, the forerunner, the contributory brain, at the same time? There was room in Africa for both, and a crying need for them too.

A sketchy attempt at such a policy of partnership was tried, seven years later, in the Rhodesian Federation: tried, and abandoned after ten years as impossible, or futile, or Not Wanted on This Voyage. But that Christmas of 1946, when I mapped out the first timorous beginnings, all was real, and true, and of good repute, as far as it concerned me.

Perhaps it was the last year, the last moment, free of corruption: the last season of innocence, of other-love, of belief.

FORTY-ONE

1951

THE BOOK THAT LOST ITS HEAD

1.

FOR THE FIRST TIME, though happily not for the last, I was waiting for a divorce.

Eileen had gone back to England in 1948, when my contract as director of the Information Office came to an end, and I was asked to renew it for another two years. I wanted to stay on, very much; Eileen did not; it was a mutual acknowledgment that the end of this road had been reached, that she did not like the compromise of values which living in South Africa entailed, whereas I had come to accept them, and even to enjoy them.

There had also been a further complication, only just over the domestic horizon: the beginning of the Cape Town love affair which turned at least three lives upside-down, and continued to do so for another twenty years. Now, three years later, I still had the same prized job; I still wanted to marry the girl; and I was still waiting for things to sort themselves out—waiting in nervous, almost tremulous indecision, for two very good reasons.

The first was that Directors of Information didn't get divorced, any more than ambassadors or bishops or candidates for the U.S. presidency; this was a sensitive area of propriety, diplomatic, fully lime-lit on an old-fashioned apron stage. The second was that the girl herself, tired of waiting, or of me, or of the way I had turned her own life upside-down, had taken off again, and immured herself in Cape Town.

For more than a wretched year, no telephone calls reached their target, no letters were answered, no appeal got further than the blank wall of denial. So, even if the divorce came through, I would still face two questions which had the power to destroy: would the Commonwealth Relations Office stand for it, and would the girl be there to make sense of victory?

Thus deserted, thus miserable and alone, thus taking ferocious advantage of Johannesburg's counter-attractions, I had written a book.

It was that Battle of the Atlantic novel which I had been dreaming about, ever since the war ended. Five years of living that war, three years of thinking about it, two years of writing it, had at last produced the result, for whatever it was worth.

It had been written alone, every single night after the long office day, after the current girl had gone, after the whisky had blurred the edge of tiredness and the sad mourning for the girl who wasn't there: after stillness had fallen on the house and the city, and silence and peace and solitude were all guaranteed. Now I had finished it, and sent it off to Cassell's in London and Alfred Knopf in New York.

It was two hundred thousand words long. There was not a paragraph in it which had not been written and rewritten four or even five times. Into it had gone more alcohol, sweat, semen, hopeless misery, sad music, and grinding determination than anything in my life before. It was my twelfth book, and I had been writing for eighteen years. Now I was waiting to hear if it was any good.

But I was waiting in circumstances which, give or take a few heart-aches, headaches, aches of high-strung conscience and low-slung genitals, suited me down to the ground. For now I really liked Johannesburg, and I didn't want to live anywhere else in the world.

I had a flat in Parkview, just north of the city, part of an elegant house owned by Leon Levson, a talented and highly fashionable portrait photographer, whose wife Freda Troup had written a very worthwhile book about the trials, miseries, near-triumphs and near-misses of the Rev. Michael Scott.*

With the flat went a well-cultivated garden (cultivated by Leon, not by me), a handsome view down a valley, and all the benefits of a cul-de-sac where no traffic could pass, disturbed only by the occasional plodding slurring feet of natives using the short-cut up and down the hillside; natives whom the curfew, or fear of those pass-hungry policemen, drove off into limbo very early in the evening.

* *In Face of Fear* (Faber & Faber, 1950).

With the flat went my ancient and faithful houseboy, whose name, White, adorned one of the blackest Africans in the whole of the Transvaal; whose footfalls were like thunder, whose cooking was so-so—roast beef on Sunday, roast veal on Wednesday, roast lamb on Friday, with mounds of roast potatoes on top and all around, and tinned fruit salad enticingly labelled "KOO" to follow *—and whose patient loyalty was something to marvel at.

To help me on life's journey, which had become a wild mixture of sad solitude, miserable jealousy, laughter, self-indulgence, and the most exhilarating sexual marathon ever likely to come my way, I had alcohol, which (in the true tradition of Johannesburg) was beginning to have great charm by day, and becoming a necessary drug at night; and I had music, blessed music to comfort the dark hours.

Taste had not altered nor progressed much here, except to include César Franck; the Mozart piano concertos were still a staple joy, the Brahms Clarinet Concerto and the Double Concerto were prime favourites, and opera a pleasure yet to come. But I had one sad song, gloriously sung by Kathleen Ferrier, which suited the times so exactly that it did heavy duty for many months: the *Orpheus and Eurydice* gem, "What is life to me without thee?"

The second line of that song was "What is left when thou art gone?"; and what was left to me when she was gone was the remarkably robust life of this city, catering generously for all the appetites, and all the moods save tenderness and compassion. Johannesburg was a male town; my off-duty life was now based on poker, racing, boxing (spectator only), cracking 100 miles per hour in the 2½-liter Riley which had now succeeded my 1½-liter ladies' model, and a little minor gambling on the stock exchange, where the gold-share market was currently enjoying a prime fit of the staggers.

Racing was the Saturday sport, and I went every week; the guaranteed sun and the extremely good amenities out at Turffontein made it a tonic occasion, even though I hardly prised a cent out of the bookies. This was particularly true when I worked up to owning a half-share in two four-year-old race-horses, and dutifully

* Not for years did I discover that this was short for Kooperativ.

paid their feed-bills, and watched them run, and said "Bad luck" to the trainer afterwards.

They were ungenerous crocodiles both; one was called Noted Fox, the other True Measure. God knows what Noted Fox was noted for; it certainly was *not* for winning races, which it never did in its life; and the true measure of True Measure was that it was no earthly good on the race-course either, and, once off it, might well have originated the phrase "Eating like a horse."

But what of it? I owned race-horses! Practically a string of them, like Lord Derby or the Aga Khan! I had my own colours! I could stand in the middle of the paddock, and talk to my trainer and my jockey, and look as if I could tell a forelock from a fetlock! Marvellous!

Johannesburg was a big boxing town as well, with two fistic idols (and they were actually called that, at least in print); one was a heavyweight from Bloemfontein named Johnny Ralph, the other a Lebanese lad from Cape Town, Vic Toweel. Johnny Ralph, the South African champion, was doing all right until he was unwisely matched against two ironclad British bruisers in quick succession, Freddie Mills and Bruce Woodcock; after which he virtually stopped doing anything.

Vic Toweel, extraordinarily quick and strong, had a better run and stayed at the top for a long time. All these fights were refereed by my tailor, Mr. William Corner, whose curious spare-time hobby this was. Whenever I called in to see him after a fight, he used to say: "I think I took their measure correctly"—a pretty good tailor's joke.

But poker was the greatest pleasure of all; the taste I had developed for it at Cambridge, and lost in the serious-minded Thirties, had returned again, stronger than ever. We had virtually the same poker-school all the time I was in South Africa, seven years altogether; it was strictly captained by Johnny Whitehouse, who worked at the Central News Agency and had one of those moustaches one occasionally sees in cartoons denigrating the British Raj.

For our weekly ritual we wore dinner-jackets, started punctually at 8 P.M. and played until 1 A.M., were fined five shillings a time for bad language, kept strict accounts, and enjoyed ourselves thoroughly every Saturday night. Our trades ranged from stockbroker,

Lloyd's agent, gambler, business executive, and newspaperman all the way down to information director. But we were all united in our one devotion, to what we fondly called the Green Baize.

We played "straight" poker, with none of those horrid American and Canadian variations of seven-card-stud and high-low and half the pack wild. Play was not high—certainly not by Johannesburg standards. I once won £126 (four kings against four jacks), and once lost £70.

Over the seven years, I was £84 down altogether, in approximately three hundred games, which meant that the majority of the other six were probably better players than I was, and also that this cherished pastime—the best in the world for skill, luck, deception, intuition, patience, observation of one's fellow human beings, and all the perils of poor judgment and bad guesswork— that this paragon of games was not wildly expensive.

However, it was habit-forming, in more ways than one; hallowed catch-phrases were coined, and persisted to the end. Even in the seventh year, Johnny Whitehouse still gently stroked the broad black ribbon of his monocle when deep in thought; and Bob Crisp was still saying "I've got the biggest pair in Africa," when laying down his two aces.

Soli Ornstein, my wild Balkan friend, still commanded: "Open your legs!" when he meant "Show your hand," and Jack Hyman, a stockbroker who had married the widow of dam-buster V.C. Guy Gibson, still said: "I must go to the office" when he needed time to think.

Whenever I was holding good cards (this I was told, but naturally not until the end) I always put on a special expression of disgust which would not have deceived a drunken child of five.

There was one other Johannesburg ritual, for our pleasure and occasional profit; and that was a five-times-a-week lunch-time session at the Waverley Hotel.

They were just lunches—long, lazy, talkative, greedy, geared to gambling, sex, and idle gossip; they suited us, and Johannesburg, and the golden times in which we lived, and if that was a measure of our idleness, greed, proneness to gossip, and sexual preoccupation, then I would not argue about it for a moment, nor want to change it either.

The Waverley was a small hotel with good food and service,

and a semi-secret, semi-legal back bar presided over by Nick the Greek (in Johannesburg, all Greeks were called Nick, as all natives were called John); and there we gathered punctually at twelve-thirty each weekday, to down an average of six drinks (four on Monday, eight on Friday), and then—slightly weaving, pronouncing our final decision on who was going to win the big race or the big fight, the medium murder-trial or the small divorce—we sat down to lunch.

After that, gambling took over, as it took over almost everything in Johannesburg, from a game of golf to that heads-or-tails juggling with paternity known as Catholic Roulette.

This time the game was called Queen Bee, and it sometimes needed a full hour and a half to complete, with suitable pauses for eating. It was based in its turn on the game of Matches, where one guessed how many matches the other man had in his closed hand, added one's own, and declared the result; a game which, elevated from the nursery where it must have started, could reach extraordinary peaks of ferocity, skill, and inspired guesswork.

Queen Bee was in two parts. First everyone played each other, to determine the first-stage winner, the Queen Bee himself; and then the Queen Bee played each member of the party in turn, for the total price of the lunch. Thus, no one could lose more than that price; but if the Queen was in form he could win all the way round the table.

Lunch for six or seven people cost about five pounds; and so, on a really triumphant day, the winner might take home something like thirty pounds, plus a free lunch, plus the infuriating grin of smugness and superiority to which he was entitled.

The care with which I have described this ludicrous pastime illustrates the importance which it had for us. Lunch was no fun at all without Queen Bee; and to it we brought, every day, all the rapt attention and the ruthless greed of children at a party—in fact, the very spirit of Johannesburg.

After-lunch was my favourite time of the day, except for the one which would assuredly come later, in a city which had emerged as an undoubted favourite. The shadows were lengthening, the caverns of the street growing cooler as the western side was thrown into shade. But the scene was never less than lively, the spirit restless, the mood a challenge to hope and vigour and survival.

The first edition of the *Star* was being snapped up at the street-corners, where people who looked as though they didn't have a penny in the world thumbed through the noon stock-market prices, the race-results from England and Australia, the sweep-stake draws, the rare investment opportunities, the ten-roomed houses for sale in select northern suburbs.

But most of the faces were black. There were women selling lemons and pears and limes and pawpaws; women with sleeping babies strapped to their backs; women in gaudy clothes, the elite from the native brothels. The black men were office-messengers like Motorcar Ratshiko, grimy mineboys trudging in convoy to and from the railway station, herded by a native policeman with a polished, lethal knobkerrie swinging from his wrist; legless beggars squirming on the pavements, loafers, possible pickpockets.

Shabby, gentle old clergymen from the Bush Baptist League looked sideways as they passed the knots of young *skelms,* patently on the alert for the unlocked car, the suitcase forgotten on the back seat, the handbag hanging open, the chattering American tourists who were fair game for anyone.

From the groups playing dice at the street-corners came an occasional pungent drift of *dagga* smoke—the homegrown marijuana which gave courage, or brief happiness, or enough resignation to endure this iron jungle. I did not mind that, either.

On the sunny side of any street, the colours were still bright and glaring; in the shade, we walked in a cool early twilight. When we said goodbye, at one street-corner for Bob Foley and at another for Soli Ornstein, who always said: "Walk one more corner! I have schemes, big schemes!" we were all three on our way to an honest afternoon's work, since Johannesburg was a working town, a pressure-hive of diligence as well as all the rest.

But soon would come the idle hours, and then (speaking only for myself) I would be home again: At Home, in fact (though I dispensed with the old-style engraved invitation), in my own little hive, to whoever had been mutually laid on for the evening.

I was now a bachelor, a Johannesburg bachelor. We did not sit about twiddling our thumbs. In fact we hardly sat about at all.

Something in the altitude, or something in the lordly, beyond-all-censure men, or something in the over-leisured women, had made South Africa, like Kenya, wonderful screwing country; and everyone knew it, and took advantage of it, and made of this hot-house a place of cool yet avid misbehaviour.

Like the cynical Quebec election slogan which I was soon to encounter: "Vote early! Vote often!" there was in Johannesburg an impolite sexual version of this command, which gave to all connoisseurs the freedom of the city, and the urge to prove that our civic motto, *Fortiter et Recte*—Strong and Upright—was no idle boast.

I joined the club, with the same quiet determination, the same preference for private action over public discussion, which was later to emerge as one of the most crucial marks of the generation gap. My own slogan was simple. If I could not have the one I wanted, then I would have all the rest.

Outrageous fact calls, not for gamey reminiscence but for detached prose. It is worth a try.

What was available for this flourish of swordsmanship had all the marvellous, beckoning variety of a really good delicatessen. There were other men's wives, though such shop-lifting could be dangerous. Lovers often came to a sticky end in Johannesburg. My favourite restaurateur had half his head blown off by a jealous husband with a good aim, a shotgun, and a clear view down the drive.

On the other hand, husbands could also provide wonderful insurance. Many of them did not give a damn what was going on, as long as there wasn't too much noise. They were busy enough themselves, wandering the same sort of track. Yet they held the title-deeds, so one could not get stuck with the suddenly vacant mansion. Short of saying: "I'll have a spare latch-key cut," they could not have been more co-operative.

There were other men's sisters, but this posed no problem. When they said: "I'd like to see Martha settled," they usually meant "Settled for next week." There was nothing worse than a sisterly shrew in the house. There were other men's daughters; but the younger generation were such skillful liars that Daddy scarcely had a moment's worry.

Then there were what one could only call (borrowing from the world of popular music) the Old Standards. These were mature ladies, trained in Cape Town convoy work during the war, but still active and willing, seemingly embalmed in rejuvenating fluid.

Sometimes a glimpse of steel-grey pubic hair would serve to date them, as accurately as any other relic. Such energetic hags were two a penny, and, like pennies, quickly spent.

One or two of them shared with older writers a highly critical view of newcomers. "*This* is the proper way to do it," they used to tell me, demonstrating some positive circus-act of applied gymnastics. "Don't you *know?*"

But one had to work through the list. It was like being presented at court, in the old days of social protocol. There could be no such thing as a debutante who had not passed all these hallowed portals.

There was one very finicky lady who asked: "But haven't you a *spare* room? I always think that's nicer, don't you?" Another, a precipitate volunteer, reminisced: "Do you remember how one always made straight for the sleeping-car as soon as the train left Victoria? One didn't want to waste any time!"

Then there were girls, just girls. Girls who came tripping to my lair with shining eyes, to admire the eiderdown and then the ceiling. Girls who took me to their own nest, and said: "I'm sorry it's so narrow." Girls who preferred the open air, to match their legs. Girls with a mother or a husband on the alert, who were only available at lunch-time, and thus imposed the strain of conflicting loyalties. Between Queen Bee and this private hive, who could really choose?

There was one girl who was very beautiful, and knew it. Once the imminence of seduction (to misuse an honest word) had been established, she stripped like an athlete who hears the first bell, and stood in front of me—stark naked, supple as snakeskin, formed for love as an apple is formed for peeling, a sheath for a sword.

"Flawless," she said, turning towards the flattering, caressing lamplight. The dark would have been light enough, but I could not complain, nor disagree. She *was* marvellous: glowing in the bedside light, creamy dark like the last peach of the harvest, promising warm ecstasy at the first bite, and the next, and the next.

Yet "flawless" had been for me to say, not for her. In a way it had been a command, not an invitation. She was in charge of this invasion; she would give the time as well as the place. She was also too critical altogether.

Her last lover had been French; she could not forget this, nor let me escape comparison. *"Mon amour!"* she said as she prepared to clinch the deal, composing those truly gorgeous limbs for a carefully calculated orgasm—and I felt like the male spider, good enough for the working web, soon to be eaten.

"Mon amour!" . . . I was only from Liverpool, and I knew I would not last.

There was a girl with a husband, a garden balcony, and a watchboy who might also have been trained in French farce. I had to park my car down the road, tell the watchboy to watch it, climb the balcony as if all the Montagues and Capulets in hell were after me, and climb down again before the husband came back from his Chamber of Commerce meeting. It was nice work, but too athletic for my age-group.

There was an Afrikaner girl, rarely beautiful, recently widowed, who always wore black stockings, the mark of mourning among her compatriots. She would never take them off; though this doubtless stemmed from feelings of delicacy, the lickerish effect was unimpaired.

There was a curious, almost unexplained girl with a dead-white face and slightly mad eyes. It was like making love in the House of Dracula. There was another girl who was appropriately shacked up at Hotpoint House; this was only a block of flats built round an electrical showroom, but (perhaps for the very first time) the medium was the message. There was a newspaper girl, agile as quicksilver, always eager for that late extra. There was a mother and daughter duet, not at all harmonious.

There was very nearly a queue. Among them must be numbered, in the interests of statistical accuracy, the girl who changed her mind—not on a single coy occasion, but three times in succession. At one moment she would be poised on the diving-board; at the next, she was leaving the pool in a flurry of protest. It really was a case of now you see it, now you don't.

"I should have warned you about her," a confederate friend told me. "I thought everyone knew."

"But *why?*" I was feeling more deprived than any off-white orphan in the land. "Damn it, she said yes!" Or had it been maybe? "And you know how she dances."

"She always dances like that. Once she said to me: 'Darling, they're playing *our* tune!' And you know what it was?—'Stone

Cold Dead in the Market'! I can tell you, I gave up years ago."

If my friend had given up, that was indeed a definitive verdict. "You mean she's a virgin? Even with all that come-on stuff?"

"That's part of the fun. Perhaps it's *the* fun. Power without responsibility." He must have read Rudyard Kipling on harlots. Or perhaps cousin Stanley Baldwin on Lord Beaverbrook. "Actually Jack Hyman put it better, as usual. He said: 'She twirls your nuts, and bolts.' "

But that was a rare bird indeed. Almost without exception, this was a season which Marcel Proust had labelled for me already, twenty years earlier in the wet and pallid wastes of Nottingham, as *A l'Ombre des Jeunes Filles en Fleurs.*

I never improved on that record, nor did I want to; there was only the craving need for it, then the pleasure of notching it up and forgetting about it. *Palmam qui meruit ferat,* as my old schoolmaster-friend Mr. Sutton used to say, when talking of the Winchester examination: Let him who deserves it, bear the palm.

I bore my palm right until the end, right into the private solitude which I could count on, which I had to have; right into the refrigerator. . . . For months and years on end, after such exertions, I had climbed out of my bed, or her bed, or any old bed I had happened on, and regained my solitary lair, and poured out a whopping whisky and soda.

Then I settled down at the typewriter again, to rewrite page 100 or page 300 or page 579 of *The Cruel Sea.*

Now I was waiting to hear. Presently, clear and persistent noises in the wings indicated that I had, incredibly, written a best-seller.

It was incredible because, apart from this last forlorn try, I really had given up writing as a bad job—or as a good job which I just couldn't do. The last book, *My Brother Denys,* had been the usual flop; it had made £366 in three years; I could do better at poker (that wasn't exactly true either, but the line of thought seemed clear).

I had a good job already, which I loved. The killing sweat of being a writer, the animal spark of creation which had been living and writhing somewhere within my gut for at least twenty years, were leading me nowhere. Better to give up, better to fold my spare pair of hands and let the real ones fashion whatever career lay in front of me.

I *could* be head of the C.R.O. Information Service (I was now their senior overseas director). I *could* even be a High Commissioner, somewhere where it didn't matter, if the present trend of treating information personnel as Gentlemen instead of Players continued.

But that writhing spark, or whatever it was, had lived just long enough for two hundred thousand words of narrative to emerge in one piece, one shape, one entity, one compact book. Suddenly, of this book—my very last hostage to enemy fortune—Desmond Flower, chairman of Cassell's, wrote:

"I have just finished the manuscript of *The Cruel Sea*. It is a wonderful book, one of the finest ever to come into the Cassell list, and you are a great writer."

Few letters like that ever come an author's way; none had come mine, and the morning I read that letter was the brightest and happiest I could remember, for a very long time. I stepped as lightly as the dry warm air all round me; I ate through the office work with twice the appetite of yesterday; I drank uncounted extra martinis; *I won at Queen Bee.*

Soli Ornstein, perceptive as a gypsy, asked: "What is it with you, Nicolai?" and when I told him, with bursting pride, he said: *"Fabelhaft!"*—one of the many words which this generous man used to indicate his pleasure in another's good fortune.

But there was more to come, much more to come. . . . Cassell's advance royalty, I learned a fortnight later, was to be an unprecedented £275. From across the Atlantic, Alfred Knopf also indicated his satisfaction, in the guarded terms appropriate to a pillar of the publishing establishment who had introduced Thomas Mann and André Gide to the other half of a waiting world. Knopf's advance would be £430!

The snowball—a very rare thing in South Africa, and even rarer in my own life—gathered speed and size. A fantastic cable from London told me that *The Cruel Sea* was to be a Book Society Choice. The Book Society! I could remember the very first Book Society Choice being unwrapped by my mother, a founder member, in 1929. It had been *The Love of the Foolish Angel,* by

Helen Beauclerk. If only *The Cruel Sea* could do half as well as *The Love of the Foolish Angel.**

Hardly had I taken in that cable than there was another from Alfred Knopf in New York. The book was to be a Book-of-the-Month Club choice in America. Then it had been bought by the *Atlantic Monthly*—a stupendous accolade. Then it was to be serialized (for fourteen weeks!) in the *Sunday Chronicle*. Then it was an *Evening Standard* Book-of-the-Month in London.

There was one film approach, then a second, then a third (from Ealing Studios). The South African Argus Company (Johannesburg *Star*, Cape *Argus*) also wanted to serialize it. Finally *Reader's Digest* made an unheard-of offer (unheard-of by me) for their million-by-million readership of Condensed Books.

All this avalanche of good news came winging, swinging, toppling down on me, four months before the book was to be published.

For that reason alone, all this avalanche, in so short a span, hardly seemed real at all. I wasn't a writer; that question had been settled, in progressive sad stages, via eleven unread books and eighteen years of literary endeavour and literary nothing. Only *this* world was real: the United Kingdom Information Office in Johannesburg, shortly to be expanded to include Cape Town.

This was my real creation. The fly-by-night progress of *The Cruel Sea*, before it had even seen the public light of day, could only be a kind of phantom pregnancy, beyond all credence, suspect from the first surprise swelling.

I had my baby already, and the little bastard was really a-growing.

It was, to say the least, an interesting time to be conducting British propaganda in South Africa. Our ally General Smuts was dead; he had been decently mourned at a state funeral in Pretoria, and then consigned to oblivion within a few months.

The United Party was out—out of office, out of power, out of juice altogether; and the Nationalists, with a secure majority,

* Thirty-nine years after that first Book Society nomination, a novel of mine called *Richer Than All His Tribe* was their last "Choice," before the Society died its sad death.

were beginning also an anti-British rampage which was to reach
its peak ten years later, when they took their country out of the
Commonwealth forever.

The new Prime Minister was Dr. D. F. Malan, who by a rare
coincidence came from the same tiny *dorp,* Riebeeck West in
the old Cape Colony, as his predecessor Smuts himself. Daniel
Malan was an austere character; indeed, his moral rectitude was
a by-word throughout the land. It had been well summed up by
a nice dead-pan caption to a photograph of him and his family,
at the time he took over the premiership: "Dr. D. F. Malan, the
new Prime Minister," it said, "with his wife and children. Dr.
Malan is noted for his strict code of behaviour. He does not drink.
He does not smoke. The children are adopted."

Many of his followers were the same—tough, humourless, dedicated; and one of the things they were *all* dedicated to was a
South Africa run by Afrikaners for Afrikaners, with the English-
speaking section relegated to the very back-alleys of power. The
Engelsman could work, but he was not going to manage or control. Britain was not going to manage or control, either.

In this vastly changed climate, the U.K. Information Office did
its best to present Britain as a fair, broad-minded, well-conducted,
co-operative friend.

Our output of every kind of material—news, photographs, and
films about British politics, fashions, trade, inventions, finance,
theater, cinema, art, music, cars, ships, anything under the pale
sun—had been stepped up until it was a steady spate.

I made a weekly excursion to Pretoria, to discuss and settle
any problems with Evelyn Baring, still the High Commissioner,
and his new Deputy, who under the slightly daunting name of
Horace Algernon Fraser Rumbold concealed both a prodigious
industry and an unfailing kindness and helpfulness towards me,
my office, my prudent and imprudent efforts, and my occasional
lapses.

(I *still* could not master the office estimates. And I could not
help feeling guilty when I faced these admirable men. They
were so nice to me. They behaved so well themselves. We were
all walking a tightrope of protocol in which reputation, manifest
integrity, were paramount. What was going to happen when the
divorce story broke?)

I also made my technical contribution to Baring's occasional dispatches on the state of things in South Africa; dispatches which, addressed to the Secretary of State, ended on a note of charming courtesy: "I am, My dear Sir, With every truth and regard, Your most obedient servant."

We had been given more money for putting on exhibitions and film shows, and for importing visitors—lecturers, concert performers, occasional actors. I had even been given a little more money myself—a rise in salary, and a rent allowance—following a visit from a charming old gentleman called Sir William Clarke, head of the Clarke Commission, which was touring overseas posts to see how we were getting on financially.

It was important to make the point that we were not getting on at all well. Dressed in our oldest clothes, borrowing broken-down cars for transport, serving frugal meals on cracked plates, bringing sandwiches to work—we went through all the motions of an abject poverty quite unsuitable to British representation abroad.

Sir William, a wise man, could not have been deceived on the scale we hoped for, nor perhaps deceived at all. But the results, for me at least, had been a combined salary-jump to the dizzy height of £2,200 a year.

The most interesting visitor that year was Mr. Patrick Gordon Walker, Secretary of State for Commonwealth Relations, who came out to pick up the bits and trim the edges of the Seretse Khama affair.

I had campaigned with him a year earlier in Bechuanaland, in those strange and occasionally baffling goings-on which culminated in Seretse's banishment for five years. From that time on, he was a man I never ceased to admire.

Chief Seretse Khama was a public relations headache of the first order. He was a rather fat, self-indulgent young man of twenty-seven who was the Paramount Chief-Designate of the Bamangwato tribe, the most powerful in Bechuanaland; educated in South Africa and at Balliol College, Oxford, he was due to return to Bechuanaland to pick up his inheritance. Just before he came back, he married a white girl, Ruth Williams.

The marriage occasioned some scandal among his fellow-countrymen, who did not like their future chief straying from the racial-purity fold; it precipitated an uproar in South Africa, where the opposition to a mixed marriage, though different in kind, was certainly a great deal more ferocious and vocal.

One had to look at the map, as Baring was to say later. South Africa was a next-door neighbour, with plenty of leverage; much of Bechuanaland's prosperity, and all her communications, depended on a smooth working relationship. But Bechuanaland, as a High Commission Territory, was our baby, and we did not want any outside interference in a family row.

However, the problem was there, the crisis undeniable. The tribes (eight in number, all beginning with the letter B, all posing problems of pronunciation—Bakgatla, Bakwena, Bangwakatse, Bamalete, Bamangwato, Barolong, Batawana, and Batlowka) were fundamentally split on the marriage question; South Africa was making ugly faces just over the wall; we had to decide whether, in all the circumstances, Seretse would make an acceptable chief. British Government opinion was hardening towards the decision that he would not.

We dived right in; Sir Evelyn Baring in the van, Patrick Gordon Walker later paying two visits to try to patch things up; and Monsarrat trailing along behind, to deal as best he could with the regiment of pressmen from all over the world who flocked in to watch the fun.

We ran into trouble straight away. A great tribal *kgotla,* or gathering, called by Baring at Serowe, the "Native capital," was totally boycotted; not a man turned up, not a dog barked, as I waited at one end of the police telephone link to advise the High Commissioner whether it was worth coming down.

Obviously it was not, and I had to tell him so. Then I walked out, across the dusty deserted *kgotla* ground, towards the crowd of pressmen and photographers waiting under a tree.

They were obviously enjoying our discomfiture; indeed, some of them had done a certain amount to bring it about, by a persistent policy of deriding every effort and every move we made, and flattering the malcontents and dissidents who had been drawn towards this murky brew.

One of them, Noel Monks of the *Daily Mail,* in search of a story—any story—which might embarrass us, had already provoked a first-class fake incident by taking Seretse into a "Whites Only" bar, demanding a drink, and waiting for the resulting scene to reach its natural peak.

I was thus in a bad temper, for a variety of reasons; and the white uniform, white helmet, medals, and sword which I had donned for the great occasion seemed ridiculous. They were also very hot. I then made my second big public relations boob.

I was met by a rapid quick-fire of questions, the kind I had become used to during the last few days. But this time they seemed to have an extra edge to them, and I was fresh from our undisguisable defeat.

"What's happening?" asked the friendliest of the newsmen, who was working for *The Times* and had a grasp, somewhat rare, of what was involved in this tangle. "Is the meeting going ahead?"

"No. It's cancelled."

"Why?"

"Well, obviously—because no one turned up."

"Why not?"

"There's a boycott. You know the situation. The tribe is split."

"If the tribe is split, why didn't some of them turn up?"

"They were—discouraged."

"You mean, kept away?"

"Yes."

Pencils were now very busy. "Who by?"

"People who wanted the *kgotla* to be a flop."

"But what people?"

"I can't give you their names. We don't know for certain. But there is a section of the Bamangwato who were determined that no one should attend the *kgotla*."

"How did they keep them away? Did they use force?"

"They threatened to use force." There was abundant evidence of this from the police.

"Have you got any proof of that?"

"We have police reports."

"What's going to happen now?"

"The High Commissioner will hold a press conference at twelve o'clock."

"Is he going to announce a change of policy?"

"I don't know. I shouldn't think so."

"Is he angry about this?"

"He doesn't get angry. Of course he's disappointed. He wanted to tell as many people as possible what the situation is. Now they won't know, or they'll get the wrong story."

There was some additional sniping on this topic. Finally: "Can we hear some more about the people who are supposed to have used force to stop the *kgotla*? You say you don't know their names. What *do* you know about them? What kind of people are they?"

"A sort of strong-arm gang. Some of them aren't much better than thugs."

That did it. I had been provoked into using a much too quotable word which, though absolutely accurate, looked very unpretty in print. It reached the headlines. It certainly reached the Commonwealth Relations Office, which fired off a remarkably prompt telegram suggesting that Monsarrat should "refrain from further comment."

To my enormous relief, Sir Evelyn Baring came to my rescue, with equal swiftness. An answering telegram, drafted by Arthur Clark, the Chief Secretary, and approved by the High Commissioner, said that I had been doing my best in trying circumstances, that I had been of great help during the past difficult week, and that I enjoyed the High Commissioner's full confidence.

God bless all honest men. . . . Baring was going through a tortuously difficult time himself; the boycott of the *kgotla* was, in its context, an atrocious personal insult; my "thug" remark could only have served to complicate the issue for him, when he had more than enough troubles already.

It was in fact a stupid lapse in self-control. Yet he found time to back me up, when many a lesser man might have tossed me to the Whitehall wolves.

An irredeemable I.O.U. was involved there.

That of course was not the end of the Seretse Khama affair; in fact it was the beginning of a long-drawn-out series of skirmishes in which the British Government, faced by a barrage of hostility from almost the entire world's press, held firmly to their belief that there could be better men than Seretse, with his white wife, carefree habits, and tendency to indolence (he had trouble with his Bar examinations—in fact, he was beginning to sound more and more like me) to rule a divided and restless nation.

That tenacity of purpose belonged to Patrick Gordon Walker,

with a rebellious House of Commons forever on his back. The day-to-day campaigning fell on Sir Evelyn Baring's enduring shoulders. Coping with the press was still my job, and, with all its rough edges and smooth betrayals, I would not have had any other.

On one of his visits, Patrick Gordon Walker also convened a *kgotla,* and this time, after laborious groundwork and some careful sounding of opinion, it turned out a success. There had been a very slow movement of support towards our side, and Mr. Gordon Walker made an excellent impression. At the end there was a formal presentation. Six of the Serowe headmen appeared, bearing between them the most magnificent lion-skin any of us was ever likely to see.

A gasp, and then an excited murmur, went round the *kgotla* ground as the gift was displayed. It really was a matchless trophy— hugely beautiful, tawny-yellow, its shape and its markings perfect. It must have been at least ten feet long; fearful when alive, it was still good for an awed shudder now.

Patrick Gordon Walker beamed as he accepted it. Then he prepared to make his speech of thanks.

The Bamangwato, to whom the lion was royal, may have had some vague idea that the skin was destined, if not for the palace of the King of England, then at least for some noble council chamber in the heart of the Commonwealth Relations Office. But Mr. Gordon Walker had no such delusions.

"On behalf of myself *and my wife—*" he began.

I had very little doubt where that lion-skin was going to finish up.

After a long and wearing tug-of-war, both in Bechuanaland itself, and in the House of Commons, where Mr. Gordon Walker held his ground in an acrimonious series of debates, the final decision was taken. Seretse was to be banished from the chieftainship, and from the Bamangwato Reserve, for five years.

I was the "conducting officer," detailed to see him and his wife safely off the premises.

They could not fly from Johannesburg, which was the obvious take-off point; the Nationalist Government would not have this race-shame horror on their sacred soil at any price. The only way to make the transfer was by a Royal Air Force plane from Bechuanaland to Livingstone in Northern Rhodesia, where no such nonsense ruled.

From there they could catch the BOAC flying-boat to London. BOAC had no funny rules either.

The operation, which was now my responsibility, was not without drama. A well-disposed pressman, the *Star* correspondent from Johannesburg, passed on to me "for what it was worth" the information that there were strong rumours of a kidnap plot, to prevent Seretse leaving.

The airfield, which was a single strip of brown earth trodden flat by that most efficient instrument, the human foot, was to be invaded. A car would be standing by. Seretse would be seized, by force if necessary, and then driven off into hiding.

Well, it was possible. . . . Fearing to use an open telephone line, I spent half the night coding up a message with this dramatic tip-off. It was—it had to be—taken seriously.

Early next morning the little airstrip was surrounded and patrolled by all the policemen we could drum up. No one—not the most loving relative, the most respected tribesman, the most enthusiastic flag-waving child—was allowed past the boundary. The aircraft itself was ringed by R.A.F. guards.

We took off without incident, and headed northwards for Livingstone. After the sad farewells, both Seretse and Ruth Khama were glum, as I would have been myself. I walked forward to the tiny cockpit, and had a look at the chart. It showed that, with a very small alteration of course, we could fly directly over Serowe, the capital, and Seretse's own birthplace.

I went back and asked him if he would like that. The answer was yes, and we spent ten minutes circling the vast spread of mud huts, maize patches, herds of cattle, and dusty tracks before getting back on course again, and steering for the swirling cloud of spray, a thousand feet high, which marked the point where the Zambezi River thundered over the Victoria Falls.

At Livingstone the Khamas were taken over by the District Commissioner, while I was quartered in the local hotel. My unequivocal orders were to see that they caught the flying-boat at eight o'clock next morning.

The last-minute delays, after all that had gone before, were somewhat trying. The flying-boat (which only flew once a week) was prompt to the minute; Seretse was not. When I called in the car to pick him up, he was just sitting down to breakfast.

I think he liked his breakfast; he was certainly enjoying this one, and it was not to be hurried. I could not really blame him; he had me by the tail anyway, and my impatience as he worked his way through the mealie porridge, the eggs and bacon, the soft rolls with chunky marmalade, the cup after cup of coffee, must have been laughable—especially as it was the last laugh he was going to enjoy in this part of the world, for a very long time.

By courtesy of our faithful ally, BOAC, I managed to hold the flying-boat until the last crumb was disposed of, and there was no egg left on anyone's face. Then Seretse caught his plane.

I telegraphed Arthur Clark, in our agreed code: "EXIT." Then I had *my* breakfast.

It hardly needs to be added that Seretse returned to his country at the end of the banishment period: first as a private citizen, then as a councillor, then as Prime Minister, and finally, in 1966, as Sir Seretse Khama, Knight Commander of the Most Excellent Order of the British Empire, and first President of Bechuanaland, now the independent Republic of Botswana.

Then the dam burst, and *The Cruel Sea* flooded over.

2.

Who remembers the old best-sellers?—not as an item in a library catalogue, or even as a brand-name after nearly twenty years, but with the sharp appetite and the wild, explosive excitement of publication day itself? Who wants to? Well, the author wants to, and no one is going to stop him.

The Cruel Sea was scheduled for publication on 6 August in New York, and 31 August in London, and in view of what had happened to the book already both Alfred Knopf and Cassell's had invited me to come over and enjoy the fun. I had months of leave due to me, having served in South Africa for five straight years, and the idea was very attractive. But there was a little question of money.

At the moment I hadn't any. Keeping two homes going, as well as other excesses, had brought me very low.

Even with the air-fares paid, I would need all sorts of expendable cash on a free-ranging trip like this. For some reason, some vestigial trace of the author's awe of his publisher, I didn't like to ask for a further hand-out before more royalties were due.

After thinking about it I wrote to my bank, told them that I had a successful book in the works (it had been widely publicized in South Africa already), and asked if they could possibly let me overdraw to the extent of five hundred pounds.

Bank managers may believe in civil servants, whose salary-checks they know down to the last penny. But this one obviously didn't believe in writers. The answer was a firm no. There could be no overdraft without satisfactory security, or a guarantor. In passing, they drew attention to a debit of three pounds in the account already.

Mortified, I took my intimate problem to Soli Ornstein. I realized that, what with one thing and another (both of them horses), he hadn't any money either. But he did know about banks and guarantees and credits (none better) and he might be able to advise.

"You *pampoen!*" he said, on an immediate note of friendship and support. "You don't *write* for an overdraft! You go and see the man!"

"But I don't know the man."

"Then you should." He sounded distinctly bad-tempered, as if no one could possibly be so stupid after five years of his close company. "Have you any securities to give them? Any shares?"

"No, not yet. But damn it—the book's bound to earn at least ten thousand pounds! The Book-of-the-Month Club alone—"

He cut short this childish dialogue. "Would you like me to guarantee your overdraft?"

"But Soli, how *can* you?"

"I know the man, and he knows me."

I got my five hundred pounds the same afternoon. I also got yet another item to add to the long tally of things I didn't understand, and never would. The idea that Soli Ornstein . . . Ah well.

There was now another new invention to add to my lengthening list, the pure-jet engine; and it was in the brand-new, highly publicized, much admired Comet One that I flew to London on the first leg of my journey.

This was my introduction to long-range flight; the prestige aircraft, in which so much hope was placed, seemed the very last word in luxury and sophistication; and to fly, as we did at one point of that magical night, eight miles high above the black Sahara Desert, and then to see a blood-red moon rising *below* the plane, was like a foretaste of all the other kinds of magic which must be just over the horizon.

I only had a few hours in London before winging on my way; long enough to hear that things at Cassell's were positively steaming (their first print of sixty thousand copies would barely cover the subscription orders from booksellers), and to see the giant coloured posters announcing that only in the *Sunday Chronicle* serial, just started, could one get a preview of that sensational new novel ("The Scoop of a Generation—Most Moving Story Since *All Quiet on the Western Front*") *The Cruel Sea*.

With this swift glimpse of good fortune to come, never dreamed of in all my modest philosophy, I took off for New York.

Once again I was enshrined in luxury. BOAC had just started their "Monarch Service" to and from the United States, and were falling over themselves to make it outshine all competitors. That was the theory, at least, and most of it came true. But headwinds and foul weather spoiled our schedule, and we were seventeen hours between London and New York, stopping off in Iceland for fuel and a change of crew. In those seventeen hours I ate, in swift series, dinner, supper, breakfast (Iceland), breakfast (airborne again), and a "light repast" (canapés, cold salmon, and champagne) before landing.

Stewards had hovered over me with bottles throughout the voyage. There were times when I felt more like taking a sleigh-ride on the silver trolley than sitting in my "full-length reclining chaise longue." By the time we arrived at New York, I was in a high old state of happy benevolence, with strong undercurrents of exhilaration and alcohol—in fact, in a mood exactly suited to this marvellous city.

I knew it, and had been strongly attracted to it, already, though in a minor wartime key; roosting in a single slot of a room, on

British naval pay, at the Barbizon Plaza Hotel was not quite the same thing as being installed at the real Plaza, in a huge, delightfully old-fashioned suite, as comfortable as superb service could make it, with a wonderful view northwards across the whole of Central Park.

Obviously the life of Riley had begun. I could not really believe in any of it, but one did not have to believe in order to enjoy. I had my suite at the Plaza. I had a book which seemed all set for a thunderous success. I had an agent and a publisher, both of whom were obviously going all out for the book and for me. I had two photographers to meet me at the airport.

Though it could not possibly last, it would certainly last out the week.

My agent was Willis Wing, who handled such consequential clients as Somerset Maugham, Nevil Shute, Robert Graves, and Erle Stanley Gardner, and who was later to be president of all the literary agents in America. He had an office, the kind of cramped, almost excessively modest office which only men of undoubted prestige could afford, appropriately sited on top of the Morgan Guaranty Trust Company's bank on Fifth Avenue; and there I went, after a second light lunch fully in keeping with the style of living I had suddenly been born to.

We had not seen each other for nearly seven years, when he had sold two of the *Corvette* books to Lippincott's, and there had been precious little in subsequent books to encourage him to waste time and effort on a rather shadowy British writer. But he had stuck to me, and I to him; and he was still the same rock of a man —in energy, in physical strength (in spite of the crutches which had borne him for many years), in integrity, in his absolute sureness of touch in anything concerned with his job.

He also had an undoubted charm which made instant friends, and must have cost many publishers instant sums of extra money.

Now, after the minimal greetings, he jumped straight in, according to custom.

"It's a fine book," he said, "but I've told you that already. Luckily lots of people hereabouts think the same way. Knopf has done a first print of 35,000, but they reckon that will go in about three weeks, so there's a reprinting on the way. I hear the *Times* Book Review is giving it the front page. The Book-of-the-Month is doing 180,000. *Reader's Digest*—well, they never give out any figures, but I guess that should be worth about seventeen thousand dollars later on. I've got eight serials lined up in local newspapers, here and in Canada, as well as the *Atlantic*. So—" he spread his hands across the desk, and gave his alarmingly attractive grin, "—this thing is really moving, and just for once it's something that deserves to. Incidentally, do you want any money now?"

"It's always nice to have," I said, with British reserve.

"How much—a thousand dollars?"

So much for my credit in *America*. "That'll be fine."

"There'll be a big check coming from Knopf at the end of the month." He glanced down at the scribbling-pad in front of him. "$24,640, to be exact. And of course there'll be a lot more later on."

I swallowed. It was no good trying to be blasé about this. $24,640 was nearly £9,000. "That's fantastic," I said. "I can hardly believe it."

"It's wonderful what you can get used to. . . . Now, about the program. The Book-of-the-Month is giving you a lunch. So is *The New York Times*. So is Alfred, of course. I guess you'd better see the Knopf office next. In fact I made a date for you there at four o'clock. They've set up all the interviews and the TV and the radio. I think they've got Harvey Breit of the *Times* waiting already. They want you to go to Boston, too—they sell a lot of books in Boston. And of course the *Atlantic* people are there, all ready to pounce."

"Pounce?" I had memories of a wartime indiscretion in Boston, when I had got rather drunk at a dinner party given by Edward Weeks, the editor of the *Atlantic Monthly,* and had treated the company to my closely argued lecture on geo-politics, forecasting two giant land-masses, Russia and America, which would carve up the post-war world, leaving Britain a tiny nothing in the middle. It had been a forecast absolutely correct, but currently treasonable in terms of the British war effort—and too long, anyway.

Willis Wing noticed my expression, and as usual could pinpoint its origin. "Don't you fret. All is forgiven. They're giving

the serial a terrific play. And Ted Weeks doesn't like *stuffy* Eng-
lishmen, in any case."

"God knows I wasn't stuffy."

"So I hear. . . . Now, how do you want this money? Or shall
I send you a check to the Plaza?"

Next stop, the Knopf offices on Madison Avenue, where vulgar
commerce was excluded from publishing altogether, and money
never mentioned except in terms of artistic acceptance, which
might lead to a certain number of books being sold—or rather,
absorbed by the reading public on terms agreeable to both sides.

Alfred Knopf, long the General Montgomery of the publishing
world, was well on his way to becoming the Charles de Gaulle.
Tall, distinguished, urbane, and beautifully mannered, he had
at the same time such a lofty disdain of the rat-race indulged in
by the lower orders of publishing, that one could scarcely believe
that his firm published lots of books and made lots of money
out of them.

They did both; and when I met him in his office his guarded
references to the "favourable reception" now being accorded to
The Cruel Sea showed that this latest venture—not a typical
Knopf book at all, a slice of straight story-telling rather than a
work of art—was being handled with the skill and drive which
were, somewhere well out of sight, always at the heart of this
remarkable firm.

They had made a beautiful production of the book—Alfred
was *the* typography expert, and all his Borzoi books were a delight
to see and to handle. I did not like the jacket at all, which showed
a sort of *Boy's Own Paper* version of a corvette at sea, gaily decked
out with signal flags, turning its back on some ships in trouble
on the horizon. But that was the only flaw; otherwise the book,
the prospects, and my own reception were alike uniformly encouraging.

It had been established quite early on that I was very fond of
cigars, and he produced from a massive cabinet in his office a
rare specimen, a Montecristo about as long as a very long pencil.
When I commented on its excellence, he answered: "It has been
maturing for four years. That's the very minimum, don't you
agree?"

At the end of our session, he glanced at his watch and said:

"I had planned to select some more cigars this afternoon. Won't you come along?"

I liked "select," which was not at all the same thing as buying. We strolled sedately up-town to Dunhill's on Fifth Avenue, took the tiny lift to the Cigar Humidor, and entered the very temple of this particular worship.

It was a small room lined from floor to ceiling with tiers of cedar cupboards, each labelled with the name of the tenant. Some of the greatest names in politics, the arts, the financial world, and show business were among this formidable array. Did Bennett Cerf really care so much about cigars? Did Alfred Lunt? Did someone called Vanderbilt? Apparently they did, and so did Alfred Knopf.

Deeply impressed, I watched while four boxes of Belindas were carefully handed down from his private retreat, examined, approved, and put on one side for dispatch. I bought some *Romeo y Julieta*s myself, of a quality suitable for customers who, though not permanent lessees, yet had taste enough to patronize this establishment.

Outside on Fifth Avenue again, Alfred Knopf sighed. "So much for pleasure. . . . Apart from our lunch for you, I shall see you at Purchase at the end of the week. . . . Some of the first reviews should be out tomorrow."

"I'm keeping my fingers crossed," I told him.

Alfred looked as though he did not approve of that sort of thing at all. "They would be very foolish not to praise your excellent book."

I went back to the Plaza, where four preliminary interviews for radio and television had been arranged for the early evening, in great good humour. I really must have one of those cedar lockers at Dunhill's. . . . Awaiting me in my suite were some flowers from the management, two bottles of marvellous Bourbon whiskey from Harold Strauss, chief editor at Knopf, an invitation to enjoy the delights of Sardi's, and Willis Wing's hand-delivered check for one thousand dollars.

Writing suddenly seemed a very agreeable profession indeed.

It continued to be so. The reviews which now began to flood in were astonishing, both in quantity and in what they said about the book.

We had our front page in *The New York Times* Book Review *
and another in the Chicago *Sunday Tribune*. We had three columns in the New York *Herald Tribune,* and three more in the
San Francisco Chronicle.

We had a man in Milwaukee calling it "soaring and vivid,"
another in San Francisco who labelled it "the finest volume on
war afloat ever written," and a girl in Washington (Mary Mc-
Grory) proclaiming it "one of the finest chronicles of action at sea
to come out of this, or any other war."

We had sixty reviews in the first rush, many of them syndicated
ten or fifteen times. We had one absolute stinker, and this, un-
happily, in my very favourite magazine, the *New Yorker.*

One had to make a choice between Clifton Fadiman: "Who
touches this book touches men deep in desperate enterprises,"
and that nameless *New Yorker* scribe's verdict: "A dismal tale
by a dull writer."

One had to make a choice. I certainly made mine.

The book had already climbed into the best-seller list (it was
to be Number Three in its third week), though I could see that
the competition ahead was going to be fierce. The top incumbents at the moment were *The Caine Mutiny, From Here to
Eternity,* and *The Kon-Tiki Expedition,* and two real star-qual-
ity jobs, Salinger's *The Catcher in the Rye* and Rachel Carson's
magnificent *The Sea Around Us.*

Meanwhile, I was manfully working my way through the
nine-day program set up by Knopf's. Into that short space were
crammed six broadcasts and two television appearances.

Television was absolutely new to me; I had only seen it once
before, in the embryo version of 1936; South Africa had hardly
heard of it; and the idea of my actually appearing on it was remote as the moon. . . . The highlight, as far as I was concerned,
was the Dave Garroway "Today" show, for which I rose at 5 A.M.,
presented myself for rehearsal and make-up at six, went on the

---

* It was a good review ("A fascinating story, and a compelling one,") but not
all that good. It was written by W. J. Lederer, an ex-U.S. naval officer; a fact
which prompted Alfred Knopf to publish a counter-advertisement headed
"Isn't there a critic in the house?" and to wonder out loud whether the *Times*
would have assigned Dante's *Inferno* to Billy Sunday for review. Billy Sunday (1862-1935) was an early model Billy Graham.

air at seven o'clock—and eight o'clock, and nine, in repeat performances which grew progressively more unreal.

It was no more than that run-of-the-mill, routine event, the
celebrity interview program, which has now become common-
place, even passé. But Dave Garroway, a charming host (even at
6 A.M.) who had obviously read the book, had a taste for variety,
and I was only one of three star performers in a most curious Hall
of Fame.

The other two were Mrs. Eleanor Roosevelt, who spoke passionately and at machine-gun speed about human rights, and
a talented though sullen chimpanzee called J. Fred Muggs, a
nation-wide favourite which opened *its* performance by taking
a brisk side-swipe at my friendly, outstretched hand.

"You shouldn't have done that," said the trainer (owner?
partner? cousin?) afterwards. "Fred is *very* highly strung."

As with the old joke about the concert pianist ("What do you
think of his execution?" "I'm in favour of it"), I could have
wished that to be literally true.

Thus, between Mrs. Roosevelt on human rights, J. Fred Muggs
all over the studio, and salvo after salvo of advertising breaks, I
did my best to plug a book about British sailors at war. I had
an early-morning hangover. The coffee, unexpectedly, was terrible. The old-style lights were positively grilling.

After our third and last performance, Dave Garroway said:
"It has been a real privilege to meet you." But even he was
sweating, and his orange make-up was cracking like a dried-out
mud lake, beneath which mysterious forces bubbled and stirred
inexorably.

The realization that, while he survived—and must even have
enjoyed—jumping through this hoop five days a week for fifty
weeks of the year, I was an exhausted clown after three hours of
it, gave me an early hint that writing, and only writing, was the
reputable way of life for writers.

All else—particularly all the rubbishy "television personality"
cult—was either show-off, or squandering of precious time, or
admission of failure.

It remained a permanent conviction ever afterwards.

Then I made that trip to Boston, another city I liked very
much. I had already spent quite a long time there during the

war, waiting for the American-built frigate which was so bashful about putting to sea.

This time it was a quick, crowded visit. Calls on bookshops, where, for once in my life, a man could come forward and say: "It's really selling!" and look as though he meant it. Autographing a toppling stack of books already sold. A celebration lunch with Ted Weeks and Charlie Morton of the *Atlantic Monthly*, and being diplomatic about their hideous cover, which showed the author of *The Cruel Sea* with liquid brown eyes and a ship going up in flames by way of a halo (but then, they had once been diplomatic about *me*).

A party given by Alice Dixon Bond, doyenne of literary editors in this area, an old friend who had been kind enough, in her review, to couple the book as "enduring literature" with *War and Peace* (no arguments from me, though certain interior doubts); a party at which a very old lady with patrician features and an immense flowered hat had assured me: "Now I *really* know how to escort a convoy."

A short night at the Ritz-Carlton Hotel (where else, where else?), an early-morning plane caught with the help of loyal, sustaining friends, and I was shovelled back into New York, ready for the second round. Now it was mainly social. There was a lunch-party for twelve given by Alfred Knopf, at which I was seated next to a columnist from the *New Yorker,* who talked affably of everything to do with the written word except the merits and demerits of *The Cruel Sea*.

I decided that I could be just as affable, with an upper lip as stiff as that poisonous *New Yorker* review.

There was a smaller lunch given by the Selection Committee of the Book-of-the-Month Club, which, seeing that they were in the process of making my fortune, posed no problems of any kind except moderation.

Then, best of all, with the greatest sense of occasion for me, was a lunch given in the board-room of *The New York Times,* attended by all the top brass of the editorial staff, publisher Arthur Sulzberger and editor Lester Markel among them. It was another moment when, like my first meeting with Sir Evelyn Baring, I felt I had at last come up in the world.

Sitting, eating, talking, listening, in the very heart of the world's best newspaper, was an undoubted treat which I remembered ever afterwards. There was also a surprise at the end; when the table was cleared, the cigars alight, the brandy comfortably at hand, a sudden silence fell, and Arthur Sulzberger said: "We'd like to hear from you about South Africa."

Feeling nervous, I made the point, first, that I was a civil servant in a diplomatic post, and must talk off the record; and then felt immediately ashamed of the warning—these were not the kind of men who would betray anything except betrayal itself. Then I did my best.

The questions which followed showed me that, even after five years' residence in the territory, much travelling, much covert observation, and free access to all the men who were doing things and all the other men who were trying to stop them, I was often only a bare half-step ahead of what *The New York Times* knew already.

It was a sobering and a reassuring discovery.

Now there was only one more day and night left of my American dream. Spurred on by intensive Johannesburg training, I made it a mixture of the sacred and the profane.

There could be no doubt about the first: Sunday lunch with Alfred Knopf out at Purchase, the setting for his country house about twenty-five miles north of New York, was like a highly enjoyable extension of Divine Service. Once outside the city, Alfred, like many New Yorkers, shed the urban life as if it were unwanted make-up; but it seemed that he only did so in order to assume another disguise, another brand of *maquillage—Caresse Paysanne* instead of *Vie Soignée*.

In this luxurious charade, he did not wear English tweeds—the sun was far too hot. But the English tweeds seemed to be there, nonetheless: part of a phantom, rather endearing country-gentlemanship which affected even the way he walked and talked. Alfred cutting a rose for a button-hole, and Alfred cutting a book critic down to size, were two almost violently different people.

The ease of the transformation was not the least impressive part of it.

I could not complain; I would not have dreamed of doing so. As an urban publisher he, like the Book-of-the-Month Club, had been strenuously concentrating on my interests for many months past; now, as a weekend host, he gave me one of the best lunches I ever enjoyed, conjured up by a food and wine *expertise* without parallel in this part of the world.

It was topped off by one of those exquisite Belinda cigars which I had seen at the very moment of its resurrection from his private mausoleum—and all in surroundings which one could not fault, for comfort and taste and the kind of easy magnificence which had vanished from England with the death of Edward VII.

All made out of books, I thought, in a small moment of assessment, as I sat on a sun-drenched patio, in a chair which might have flattered Cleopatra's reclining limbs, and surrendered to the last stages of all these varied delights. If I could ever do half as well . . . If I could ever do a quarter as well, after another twenty years . . . It was a pity this place had to be called Purchase. . . . Inheritance, perhaps? . . . Accolade?

"I think you will like this liqueur," Alfred said, at the appropriate moment. It was my introduction to *Marc de Bourgoyne,* of which I had never heard, nor tasted its rough, jolting, savage splendour until that day in August 1951. I had thus wasted forty-one years and five months.

In all this indulgence we had been skillfully supported by our hostess, Blanche Knopf. I had been told that the lady was formidable, and report had not erred. Clockwork precision was always at work here; one could not escape the feeling that, for her, entertaining was an intellectual exercise, like skimming the cream from a manuscript, like translating bad French into good English, like making a double-acrostic come out exactly right, like the music of Bach which must have a concise beginning, an ordained middle, and a scrupulously tailored end.

In fact, with life as with art, the pattern was all, the pattern was sacred, and this included Sunday Lunch.

But if the result was this lunch we had so much enjoyed, who could quarrel with the recipe? Certainly not I, who had found this small, supercharged creature alternately stimulating, daunting, and deeply impressive. She was the vice-president of A. A. Knopf, Inc., and a perceptive and watchful hostess at the same time. She was in total command of all her surroundings. Indeed, I could only detect one small weakness, and it was blessedly female.

She was the only human being I ever met who, as a Chevalier of the Légion d'Honneur (as well as a Cavaliera do Ordem Nacional do Curziero do Sul, doubtless a Brazilian cavalry version), had the red-and-white ribbon of the former order seemingly attached to her entire wardrobe. I had noticed it on a town suit earlier in the week. Now, at lunch, it had been sewn onto her cardigan.

Blanche was *not* the sort of woman whom one could ask about her nightwear.

Back now to New York, where at last I had an unequivocal date. It had been gently simmering for a week, since I had always had something more important to do than enjoy love from a stranger —at least, more important from A. A. Knopf, Incorporated's point of view. But we both knew it was all fixed, if we could just get round to it.

One-night stands are probably the best version of the stringless love-affair, as long as the rules are set out beforehand: no prologue, no epilogue, just the significant bit in the middle with a blank margin on either side. She was Jewish, blonde, laughing, alive. She was also a candid prospect. "Have you got your eye on me?" she had asked, earlier in the week. There could only be one answer; it had become obvious already. "Well, when you can just quit being the Great British Author . . ." I quit on Sunday night.

We had twelve hours at the most. First we wandered the town a little, window-shopping down one side of Fifth Avenue and up the other. Saks beckoned us, and Cartier's, and a shop selling freakish male fashions, and then Doubleday's Bookshop, where a superb display of the book was topped by Leon Levson's suave photograph of the author.

"You look older already," she said.

"A year older."

"Better slow down . . ." She put her head on one side, appraising the photograph under the bright lights within. "He made you look rather Jewish, too."

"Perhaps he could foresee the future."

"That isn't the future." She sighed, and laughed almost at the same moment. "That was a hungry sigh, in case you're nervous."

"Then we eat."

We dined at a pitch-dark, elegant retreat called the Barberry Room, and drank champagne, and held hands, and hoped that all the other couples were lovers too, poised on the edge of happiness. Then, at the end, we became practical.

"We could go back to the suite," I said. "But I don't know what the Plaza rules are."

"The Plaza rules are the same as everybody else's rules. Don't do it in our hotel. Please go somewhere else. Otherwise we might *just* knock on your door." But she was alive and alert, beneath all the softness and the compliant glances. "I positively refuse to worry about a thing like that. You come back with me."

All lovers should wake, just once, on a tenth floor high above the East River; and look down on a metropolitan dawn, and watch the tugs and the barges and the police boats threading their way upstream until they were lost in a mist pearly grey at the edges; and then turn to another window, with a view downtown across the whole spread of Manhattan Island; and hear the traffic begin to growl, and decide regretfully that it was time to move, and leave a sleeping girl in a memorable bed.

Innocent once more, light-headed for many good reasons, I walked all the way south, from 100-and-something street to the chaste portals of the Plaza, fifty lonely blocks away. Normally I should have been knifed or robbed five times over on so foolish a journey, but this was my fortunate sunrise, as it had been my fortunate night.

No one at the Plaza seemed at all put out that my bed had not been slept in. Probably they preferred it that way.

At mid-morning I made a last call on the Knopf office, and talked to Harold Strauss and to some salesmen, and heard only good news. Then I had a farewell lunch with Willis Wing at the University Club on the corner of Fifty-fourth Street and Fifth Avenue, a club so solid, so monumental, so well-conducted, so secure, that it could have put the Athenaeum to shame.

We talked no more of copies sold and royalties to come (that had all been disposed of), but only of politics, and music, and the future, and a possible novel about Africa, and the shadows under my eyes ("Hope we haven't been working you too hard"), and the way the world was going to hell and the way that people could, might, *must* somehow do something to stop it.

The *decrescendo* was just right, the sign-off perfect. Half-dead, and exquisitely alive, I said goodbye to Willis in the hot turmoil of Fifth Avenue, taxied out to Idlewild, and caught the 1630 plane back to London.

Though there were still three weeks to go before British publication, the snowball which had never stopped a-rolling was now gathering real speed. Details of the New York reception had preceded me; indeed, I had already had three trans-Atlantic telephone calls from newspapers, inquiring at enormous expense (it seemed that newspapers could invent more ways of wasting money than the people who ran the Groundnut Scheme in East Africa) what it felt like to be successful.

By a stratagem which must take up a great deal of radio-traffic time, and could legitimately infuriate the normal traveller, all other passengers were held back until, first off the New York plane, I had made a carefully posed appearance in the doorway, waved to imaginary adorers, and descended the steps ("Not too fast!") towards the waiting photographers.

Then I was borne into town, by courtesy of the Daimler Hire Company, and intensively interviewed on the way by a reporter from the *Sunday Chronicle*, which seemed to have established a lien on my arrival.

They certainly had a vested interest, as was explained to me a couple of hours later when I called on Cassell's, and talked to one of their directors, Bryen Gentry, already a long-term friend.

"The orders are still rolling in," he told me. "In fact, we're more likely to run out of paper than anything else. The *Chronicle* serial is giving us a marvellous run-up to publication. Just what we want. It hasn't done their circulation any harm, either."

"But shouldn't that affect the book sales?"

"Normally it might. But this thing isn't normal. We're up to eighty-four thousand copies already, and I've got a feeling that it's only the beginning." He smiled at me. "I've been reading your cuttings. What's it like to be so successful?"

"I wish you could think of a really good answer to that one."

"Is it true there are nine translations fixed up?"

"Something like that."

"Christ, you're not getting blasé already, are you?" He looked down at some papers on his desk; everyone now had papers on their desk when they talked to me. "We've got a hell of a program mapped out for you, but it can't start for another ten days. Why don't you take a holiday?"

"This is all a holiday."

"It doesn't look like it. How was New York?"

"Wonderful. A little bit of everything."

"That's what it looks like. . . . But seriously, it wouldn't be a bad idea to drop out of sight till the fun starts. Visit relatives or something. How *are* the relatives?"

I knew what he was talking about. "Just the same."

"Is it going to be all right?"

"I think so."

"I've been worrying a little about that. I mean, a divorce in the middle of all this—"

The line between publicity and public relations suddenly emerged, sharp and clear. "There won't be one. It's still hanging fire."

"Good. . . . You take a holiday," Bryen said again. "But get back here on the twenty-fifth. That's D-day, as far as we're concerned, and you're on 'In Town Tonight.' "

By one of those coincidences which either sweeten or poison life, according to the outcome, the promise of a holiday, a dropout-of-sight, now landed smack on the floor in front of me. I learned that, if I really wanted it, I could have another date— a real date, *the* date—there and then, in Rome.

I really wanted it. I wanted it so much that there was never the remotest question of anything save instant compliance. For pride's sake, I might have said no; but there was no pride here, only love, the other mortal sin.

It was to cost me, in the end, about a quarter of a million pounds.

In those less sophisticated times, it was easier to move quickly; though the impudent nonsense, the tyranny, of "travel restrictions" had already been dreamed up, by people who did not want to go abroad themselves, or had the Ministerial privilege of unlimited junketing, yet the allowance was a comfortable one hundred pounds, and, for anyone coming from South Africa, two hundred pounds.

Within half a day, I had hired a Jaguar (for speed rather than elegance); driven down to Lympne on the south coast, hopped across the Channel in a twenty-minute wave-top arc, by a shuddering plane in which the cars travelled first-class and the drivers sat on a wooden bench in the tail section; landed at Le Touquet, cleared customs, bought lots of francs, and begun to burn up the road towards Paris and the south.

In preparation for the basic one-thousand-mile dash, across all France and most of Italy, which had already provoked a giant mood of exhilaration, I slept that night in Paris and then got on the road bright and early, aiming to break the journey at Avignon on the banks of the Rhône. The first day took me swiftly through the very heart of France: Dijon for the spirit of wine, Lyons for the power-house of heavy industry, the Route Napoléon for the sheer pleasure of travel.

Avignon, ruined bridge and all, was mysteriously beautiful; in the quiet dusk, the ancient ramparts and the castle which had sheltered a dynasty of Popes more than six centuries ago, carried even a flashy Jag driver back into the noble past. But that bridge had a foreboding air, all the same; it started with such huge confidence, so beautifully, so bravely, as if the very stones were proud to lie one on another, and then ended nowhere, thrust out into limbo and imprisoned there forever.

I should have read the lesson right, or listened to *Sur le Pont d'Avignon* for the mourning beneath the melody. But I wasn't reading anything that night except the *Guide Michelin*, the menu, the wine-list, and the arrows pointing to the marvellous future; nor listening to any tune except a singing heart.

Day Two was a harassing one. There were Cannes, Nice, and Monte Carlo to be negotiated, with all the rich folks in their whopping great chariots, all the lumbering lorries which proclaimed their ownership of the road by driving slap down the middle of it.

There was the Grande Corniche, a-swarm with those maniac drivers in Fiats and Ferraris and Alfa Romeos, charging past or through all the opposition, one foot on the accelerator, one hand on the horn, one burning glance for all other mortals, one ruthless ambition. I did not compete. I wanted to reach Rome more than anything else in the world; but I also wanted, very much, to stay in that world, and live.

After that, the journey tailed off into sunlit pleasure, and a necklace of towns like a small history lesson: Genoa, the handsome sea-port whence Columbus sailed, on his way to discover Fifth Avenue for me: Pisa (once round the Leaning Tower and away, away!); Leghorn where Nelson refitted a battered ship but could not save a battered eye, and at last the Seven Hills of Rome.

Two days flat. . . . I was proud of myself as I made a final traffic arabesque and drew up outside the Hotel Excelsior on the Via Veneto; proud, tired, and silly with happiness.

We were not in this city, the world's most beautiful, for reasons of piety; but Rome and piety went hand in hand, like another generation of lovers which had outlived everything except gentleness, and peace, and tranquil meditation.

Whatever one might do within the polished, un-Roman shell of the Excelsior Hotel, the hallowed stones outside guaranteed pardon for it, forgave all straying pilgrims their sins, and guided their feet to God. Since I seemed to have lowered all other guards, even this instinctive one did not matter any more. The most determined infidel—Jew, Moslem, accursed Turk, circumcisèd dog—could here be taken by the throat, could here believe.

We wandered Rome, like children, like lovers, like penitents. Love was in the very air, clinging to the warm stone: love of God, love of man and woman, love of the unassailable past and the enchanted present, love of love.

Love even of proud priests, the elite who should have been humble; of thronging nuns, gabbling and gawking like any other women's club outing; love of the fetid slums of Trastevere, the elegant fountains of Rome, the cascading Spanish Steps, the holy magic of St. Peter's Square, where love of Bernini could almost supplant the official target.

We even wandered through the Colosseum by moonlight, gliding in and out of the shadows like a myriad other ghosts, or the scores of pick-pockets, robbers, sexual stalkers, mean assassins who also haunted hereabouts. Once again, we should have been knifed or robbed, but innocence protected us, even in this temple of much blood, of Christian flesh mauled by real lions, of the cruelty and splendour and concerted wickedness which must cling to these ancient, evil walls.

Just so did love cling to the sheltered humility of the Vatican, and forgivable pride to the statues of the great emperors, good or bad; the vanished, ever-present ghosts of Nero and Caligula, Claudius and Hadrian, Constantine, Tiberius, Trajan, Augustus: and the Latin text-book man who was here only a neighbourhood celebrity, Caius Julius Caesar.

Popes could be called Pius; Popes could be called Clement; Popes could be called Leo, Urban, Benedict, Felix, Deusdedit, Innocent, and Celestine. They could even be called Nicholas the Great. They all lived in these parts. The wolf still suckled Romulus and Remus, the darling twins who had founded all this wonder. One could get purely drunk on the gentle turmoil of history: the stirring past, the barbarian rape, the quiet, holy, heart-embracing present.

All lovers, we agreed, should be lovers in Rome; and whatever outlandish breasts had kept Romulus and Remus alive, eight hundred years before Christ, Rome in A.D. 1951, the Year of Everything, had brought matters up to date: under the banner with the strange device—Excelsior! Excelsior! (four-star hotel)—Romulus and Remus, in drowsy afternoon siesta or under the acute spur of night, tumbled the wolf from its brazen pedestal, and suckled love itself, and were heavenly twins again.

Obviously one could be drunk all the time, without a sip, without a swallow. Yet vulpine teat, flowing Tiber, fountain of Rome, hot and cold holy water—they were all there, and we must have sipped and swallowed without noticing: still believing like innocents, like popes innocent, like damned fools, that we did not need another man, woman, or dog in the world to help us.

Presently we realized that we must watch the calendar, and obey it.

I had driven down, like a lusty Roman charioteer, in forty-eight hours; now we returned as tourists, spreading the journey over a full week, choosing our stopping-places by the clock, the speedometer, and our own indolence.

A day in Florence, with respectful calls on Mantua and Verona, was succeeded by two at San Vigilio, a minute fishing-village on the shores of Lake Garda, where the sunlight and the water matched each other for warmth and gentleness, and the tame trout beneath the balcony were fat from bread-crumbs and tossed chicken bones.

Then came a determined Alpine dash across most of Switzerland; then Dijon again, Paris again, and London at last; London, where there now waited for me a happy, headlong plunge into another kind of turmoil; a turmoil not Roman, not geared to the bloody past, not in the least historical except for us, the only people who mattered, and especially for me—emperor, pope, clown, bond-slave and bonded lover, and Liverpool boy made good.

My faithful and energetic agent, Christine Campbell Thomson, who had been furiously busy throughout all this—negotiating translations from Norway to Japan, serials from Gibraltar to New Zealand, and a film deal with Ealing Studios which was coming swiftly to the boil—had still found time to rent a flat for us, on an open-sided mews, with a reassuring view of Brompton Oratory pointing the way, like St. Peter's itself, to a heaven still available for sinners.

There we settled down, in under-cover domesticity, and there, as a first shot in the campaign, Kenneth Tynan came to interview me.

Tynan was then an innocuous and even agreeable young man, nervous, stuttery, blinking when directly addressed (which could not have been very often). He was earning a little extra bread by writing "profiles" for the *Evening Standard;* the ripe savour of a later personality, the rumble and squeak of his portable lavatory wall, were not yet in the public domain.

He wrote a flattering piece—"The man who has leaped to fame with one book"; talked of its "cruel nobility"; and signed off, after comments on my former pacifism which drew total agreement from me, with: "He is that rare and disquieting creature, a sincere, intelligent, and civilized human being who is at his best in mortal combat."

The last six words of this I thought true, and sad for what they said about the mean shortcomings of our world, but not basically dishonourable; lucky was the country which, pitch-forked into war, could count on its amateurs to turn professional, to be warriors for the working day and then, when all was over, go back to the minor chores of citizenship again.

I was less enamoured of the few side-swipes which Tynan felt bound to include: "Rather a weak mouth, pursed generally round a cigar. . . . A gardening sort of man, you would say, with the deep judicious appraising voice of a cricket commentator. . . . From the neck up he looks saturnine, from the neck down, baggy."

Weak mouth? Gardening? Cricket? *Baggy?* . . . Even my best friends had never told me. My father was particularly indignant. "Who's this fellow Tinnan?" he demanded. "I can assure him, he's talking through his hat! If he knew the trouble I had to get you anywhere *near* the garden!" And the number of callers who rang up and asked to speak to Baggy was wounding indeed.

But the real start of this gorgeous circus was the launching party—almost literally a launching party—given by Cassell's. This consisted of a nice boozy trip down the Thames to the Pool of London and back again in the good ship *Abercorn* (detached from her normal sight-seeing, day-tripping role), with a cargo of newsmen, booksellers, envious publishers, a few human beings, and the biggest floating bar which ever shoved off from Westminster Pier in the shadow of the House of Commons.

Mullally and Warner were the press agents involved in this brave voyage. They had been hired by Cassell's, in a display of enterprise almost unheard of in publishing circles at that time, to put the book and its unknown author on the map, and to keep them both there until natural momentum had taken over from initial energy.

Frederick Mullally was the man, complete with beard; Suzanne Warner was the girl—and one of the most ravishing, rarely beautiful red-heads I had ever seen in my life. They had a consequential office in Hay Hill, just off Berkeley Square, and they did a very good job indeed.

The man who actually shepherded me around was David Davidson. He was a small, bald, forceful man, highly skilled in his somewhat dubious profession. He seemed to know everybody who could be of the slightest importance to me at this crucial moment of time. He fixed interviews, fixed broadcasts, fixed meals and drinks and transport, and also fixed me with a watchful eye at parties, never relaxing his gaze for a moment.

He was essentially a realist, as he made clear very soon after our first meeting.

"People are already asking about that dedication in the book. You'd better tell me what it's all about. We don't want any surprises."

I cut a few corners, as, with David Davidson, it was very easy to do. "We're hoping to get married."

"Not too soon, though?"

"No."

"But that's the girl I met in the flat?"

"Yes. Should I say anything about it?"

"Christ, no! Just leave it blank. Who knows about this, anyway?"

"My publishers. My agent. A couple of people in Johannesburg. That's all." But how could I be sure? And how could I tell Davidson that my real worry was not about the book at all, but about the High Commissioner's Office in faraway Pretoria? "Do you think anybody else knows?"

"Maybe. They will damn soon, anyway. Did you *have* to put in that dedication?"

"Yes."

"Oh well . . . What about your wife? Will she—" His right hand, which was expressive, described a flurry of widening circles in the air.

"No."

There we left it; in fact, there we left it forever. It was, to me, truly remarkable that not a word was ever printed about the estranged wife, the deserted child, and the next candidate cosily installed in Ennismore Gardens Mews, though by the time I left London the whole situation must have been transparently clear, and the topic tailor-made for comment.

It was possibly the most striking compliment that *The Cruel Sea* ever earned. No one wanted to spoil it.

London was now in the thick of the Festival of Britain, our first post-war effort—seemingly forlorn, actually an undoubted success—to inject a bit of spirit into our lagging self-esteem by sprucing things up, slapping on a few layers of paint, hoisting a lot of flags, and putting on a show which would persuade visitors and natives alike that nationally speaking we were not quite dead.

My festival meant the window displays all over town, not only in the bookshops but in stores like Selfridge's, Harrods, the Army and Navy, Barker's: window displays which centered round a life-belt (by courtesy of the Royal National Lifeboat Institution), and pyramids of the book itself, distinguished by a plain, unadorned, instantly recognizable jacket featuring a marine painting of a rolling sea.

It was, ironically, a German picture, which had hung in Sir Newman Flower's study for many years. Now it had changed sides, or at least become neutral, like the Atlantic itself.

My festival was the acres of reviews which were now beginning to pour in, reviews which would have warmed the heart of a dying Christmas cracker riddle-writer. I took as my personal text the one from Compton Mackenzie (Compton Mackenzie!): "In this book can be heard the surge and thunder of the Odyssey."

It was certainly the proudest tribute of my life: it had to be offset by a sniffy verdict from Liverpool, my own home town, where the *Post,* after dwelling on "cheapening episodes" and "woeful" shortcomings, said that a really good book about the Battle of the Atlantic was still to be written.

My festival was a very funny song included in a revue called *Intimacy at 8:30* at the Criterion Theatre. It was entitled "Business in Great Waters," written by David Climie, and sung by a trio of duffle-coated naval officers, whose attitude of stiff-upper-lip correctness alternated (according to the stage directions) "with a kind of asinine jocularity."

The middle verse is enough to give its immediate flavour:

We're three rollicking literary sailors!
Writing of the things that sailors do.
While patrolling our Dependencies some psychopathic
   tendencies
Were shown by certain independent members of my crew.
I said, "Go on and mutiny—I don't care what you do to me—
It's what I need for Chapter Three."
I can't forget the fateful day a Channel port we took;
I hoisted up a signal as we sailed around the Hook—
"England expects this day that every man will write a book"—
A book about the Cruel, Cruel Sea!

I must go down to the sea again,
To the lonely days and the nights;
And all I ask is a small advance
And the *John Bull* serial rights!

My festival was Cassell's, having sold every book in the building in the first five days, now running out of printings one and two (120,000 copies) before the autumn leaves had begun to fall. Edwin Harper, then their able publicity manager, put it to me, man-to-man: "I'm afraid we've got troubles."

It was the first time I had heard the word for months. *"Troubles?"*

"Paper! We've run out of paper! We might even run out of ink! We can't print it fast enough! We're printing another forty thousand in Australia. That won't last till Christmas!"

Though this particular log-jam, studded with Edwin's exclamation marks, eased in early October, as his *Bookseller* advertisement showed,* it continued to be one of the world's happiest headaches for the best part of two more years. I bore it—we all bore it—as best we could. In the meantime, there were a number of other worries, real ones, concerned not with paper and ink but with people.

I had three and a half other preoccupations during the six weeks in England: divorce, my son, my father, and the future of the job.

Eileen, I found, had done nothing about a divorce, though it was three years since she had left South Africa and two since I had asked for what I then called, without irony, "my freedom." There was really no reason, from her point of view, why she should have taken action; the ethics of the betrayed wife could never be clearly defined, cut-and-dried, hard-and-fast, nor even in accordance with local custom.

They were determined always by individual circumstance, with the million variations to which men and women in this fix were both entitled.

Thus she had decided to wait and see; a perfectly reasonable tactic, but, for me, the worst possible answer to my own dilemma. *She* could wait and see. *I* could wait and see. The third party was

* See illustration.

not going to do either, and that was the one I was worried about.

I put on the pressure as best I could, though to do so in the present circumstances made me feel even more than normally guilty. Success deserved to be shared, if only by reason of a shared past. But a conviction of guilt was not going to stop me; it had never stopped anyone or anything once they were set on course, whether a thief, a blackmailer, a mad dog, or a runaway horse.

Presently she agreed—she really agreed—that our position was not retrievable, and that the time had come for dissolution.* With that out of the way, we were able to travel down and take a joint look at our offspring, now at school in Oxford.

This really was a separate operation, without strings. Children do not save a tottering marriage; in fact they are more likely to ruin it forever. At the lower level, it is the noise and the nappies a man longs to be quit of, just as much as the nagging voice, the slattern's housekeeping, the woman he has grown sick of, long before little Charlene came along to complicate things. At the higher, the child is just something else to be rid of, another item in the clean break.

Both such levels are ignoble. But the idea that tiny fingers can curl round an errant heart and make it better again is a soap-opera dream, just as the idea of a double bed as the answer to all marital discord is the dream of the celibate priest. A man lured into this supposed cure for a quarrel is left with a resentment more fierce, a loathing more terrible, than if he and his wife had slept at opposite ends of a warehouse.

All he knows is that he has been swindled again; the glorious, healing balm of sexual intercourse has turned out to be the same old push-pull mechanical contrivance; the burden round the neck remains, and Christ! there might be another snotty kid to add to it.

Thus Max, last seen when he was six, now a sprightly nine, did not unite two lonely hearts. But for both of us he was still a beloved feature of the human race; and for me a surprise—the kind of surprise felt by children themselves when the gift-doll came to life on Christmas morning.

* We were divorced about a year later: my own adultery being proved, and discretion exercised in her favour. The action was heard before His Honour Judge Leon, better known to the world as the writer Henry Cecil (*Brothers in Law, Alibi for a Judge, Settled Out of Court*).

It walked! It talked! It could say Mama—and, if kicked hard enough on its little rump, Papa as well! It was almost human. . . . Max was now at a prep school called Summer Fields, and we went down to see him on Sports Day—a sports day in which he did not seem to be in the least involved.

"I forgot to put my name on the board," he told me, as wide-eyed as I had been myself, thirty years earlier, when I had told *my* father transparent lies about my own lack of success. I supposed that he had been eliminated in the preliminaries, several days before we arrived on the scene. It did not matter.

I was giving rather more attention to some other aspects of his future. He had been entered for Winchester (at least, I thought he had been entered, having filled in all the regulation forms on the stroke of eight years old), though the decision had been a hard one.

If Winchester were currently anything like it had been in the Twenties, then I would as soon have sold him to the nearest glue-factory. But my contemporaries who now had sons there assured me that it was not. Beating was out—or at least, the enthusiastic, nightly lust for it which had so inspired the prefects of my time was no longer fashionable. Politics were more liberal. Boys were sometimes even known by their Christian names, without shame.

My grateful admiration for a true classical education had grown with the years. Snobbery tipped the scale. I put his name down for my old house, and hoped for the best. His school reports were encouraging enough; certainly not as daunting as one which, a generation later, attracted my attention.

The subject was five years old, and the verdict: "Peter is not really mature."

The third family call was on my father, now in his eightieth year. Mother had died four years earlier, in 1947: a sad death, alone and undiscovered, during a brutally cold blizzard which had isolated her small cottage for several days. He had then, at the age of seventy-five, and to the accompaniment of cheers from me, married an "old flame" (the language was his), and he now lived with my step-mother in a Cotswold village near Woolstone, which needs further identification as being near Faringdon.

The village lay in the shadow of a hill, into which was carved a most attractive, beautifully stylized, galloping "white horse"—

the famous Uffington White Horse, in fact, which had certainly been in existence prior to 1084 and was traditionally ascribed to Alfred the Great, who thus commemorated a battle won in A.D. 871.

My father's cottage could not claim this antiquity, but it could certainly claim enough of it—upwards of five hundred years, with all the authentic drafts, discomforts, head-denting beams, and tortuous stone stairs to match.

I am sure that he loved it, and must have found my reluctance to negotiate rope banisters, worn stone steps, whistling winds and icy temperatures in order to go to the bathroom, effete and unworthy. But it was good to see him so happy, so preoccupied over the reception of his latest book, with its unlikely title *Human Desires and Their Fulfilment,* and so well cared for by a loving companion.

There was one thing, and one thing alone, which I did not like about my father's changed and happy circumstances. He had already found it necessary to excise the past, and to rewrite it. For very many years his entry in *Who's Who* had recorded, accurately and perhaps proudly, his marriage in 1898 to "Marguerite, d. of Sir John Turney, Kt."

Now all detail had suddenly been expunged, and a marriage-tie of forty-nine years had been shrivelled down to: *"m.;* one s. one d.; *m.* 1947, Marie, widow of etc."

Such maimèd rites. . . . I did not think, and do not think, that a work of honest reference should thus become garbled, for any reason whatsoever.

Finally, of all the things which lay outside the turmoil of Topic A, there was the big question: whether to stay, or not to stay, in what I still regarded as my real job, the Information Service. Suddenly and obviously, it became important.

I had been offered Establishment, that formidable word which meant that one was assimilated into the permanent civil service, with certain perks such as an annual salary increment, a tiny chance in the Honours List lottery, and a foot on the ladder leading to a modest pension, instead of being part of the help hired in the yard outside. Someone had decided, at long last, that information work was worth doing, and information personnel worth incorporating in the machine.

I agreed with this; and certainly I loved the job, and the feeling which went with it of being, in however minor a degree, inside instead of outside the corridors: the satisfaction of reading the political telegrams, knowing what was going on, and understanding why certain things were being done one way instead of another.

It had always been exciting, in that respect; there was even an instance of this now, while I was in London, when Patrick Gordon Walker, who had to make a further statement and answer some questions about the future of Seretse Khama and Bechuanaland, asked that I should be included in the small back-up team from the Commonwealth Relations Office which attended him in the House.

We sat in a little box, just to the right of the Speaker's chair, and listened, and (as far as I was concerned) hugely enjoyed the feeling of consequence.

I still had some of the same feeling next morning, when I went for my "Establishment" interview.

This was a friendly occasion; I supposed that the High Commissioner had given me the required backing, for which I was very grateful; but I had the impression that the selection board was rather skeptical about me. Did I (I was asked, in different ways, at least three times) *really* want to stay on, now that . . . The "now that" was never exactly defined, but it was sufficiently obvious.

When I said that I was certainly serious about staying, there was some talk about my future, which was likely to lie in Canada, or India, or both—the two information posts which were at the top of the heap.

I raised a gentle query about jobs outside the information circle—ordinary C.R.O. appointments, in fact, which might take one up the ordinary ladder of promotion towards reputable positions *en poste*. The answer was non-committal, in a way which told me that the matter, or at least the theory of it, must be under discussion.

I thought of mentioning John Buchan, who had survived being a writer to become Governor-General of Canada. Then I thought better of it. After all, John Buchan had been a *real* writer.

For I was still deeply skeptical myself, on the opposite side of the fence. The book was a fluke to me, an enormous fluke. I seemed to have been reinstated as a writer again, but how long would that last? Certainly I had lots of ideas for books—fifteen, at least—but I had had lots of ideas before all this, and look what had happened to that early crop.

An idea took shape as I left the C.R.O., bowed (in spirit only, since there were policemen about) to the doorway of No. 10 Downing Street, where my modest hero Mr. Attlee was still installed, and set course along the fringe of St. James's Park. I had been in the job for five years, and I did like it. C.R.O. had always been nice to me. Opposite the Horse Guards Parade, I took an oath to stay on for another five years at least, and then to think again. That would see me through until 1956.

Topic A returned, swiftly enough, with a Savoy lunch given by Sir Michael Balcon and the completion of the film deal with Ealing Studios.

Everything about the film of *The Cruel Sea* was tremendously exciting, from the early, tentative interviews with Charles Frend, who directed it, and Eric Ambler, who fashioned its distinguished script, to the first night at the Leicester Square Theatre, twenty months later in March of 1953, and the subsequent queues which had to wind twice round the block before they could start to pour their money into the till.

I would not have been able to come to London for the premiere without bending the rules about overseas leave out of all reasonable shape, except for a fortunate turn of events. Late in 1952, the promised divorce had come through, and I had promptly remarried, my second wife being a Cape Town journalist whom her fellow gossip-columnists, loath to miss a good chance of myth-spinning, had labelled "The Cruel She." It was a good moment, a very good moment indeed, to leave South Africa, and I was transferred with equal promptness to Canada.

I still had six weeks' leave to come. Our route could only lie through London. We sailed back in the *Athlone Castle,* broke our journey at Claridge's, and dived head-first into the fun.

Fun there certainly was; it was even more exciting, from the nervous author's point of view, than that first night at Daly's Theatre, seventeen years earlier, when *The Visitor* had exploded

on the theatrical scene like a cottonwool bomb and, in spite of
Greer Garson's best efforts, fizzled away to nothing in three weeks.
Then, I could hardly believe any of it, but now, the omens seemed
set and the strong tide running for a rip-roaring success.

There were to be two premieres in London, a preliminary run
for the press and the corps of booksellers who were still keeping
Cassell's busier than they had been twenty months earlier, and
the real first night, which had been captured as a charity event
by the King George's Fund for Sailors, and for which all 1,750
seats had long been sold out. It was at the press show that I had
my first sight of the film.

It was very moving indeed. I thought that Charles Frend and
all the rest had done a wonderful job, and it was fascinating to
see what they had made of the book, and to note how new minds,
working on what was now, to me, old material, had come up with
all sorts of fresh discoveries, which brought the book to life in a
way which could still surprise me.

The journey from one medium to another involved a real,
vivid transformation, and I would never be too proud to acknowl-
edge it.

However, I could have done without one such new mind, too
inventive for me altogether, which saw in the relationship between captain and first lieutenant a strong homosexual tie. "The
film," we were told, "deals skillfully with this aspect, which in the
book was sadly repressed or ignored, perhaps unconsciously, perhaps naïvely."

Well, thank you, sir. One never knows what sailors can get up
to, particularly when one is writing about them.

I had been very lucky in the cast. Jack Hawkins, the captain
and the star (about as homosexual as a hard-boiled egg with its
shell intact), might have been made for the part. Stanley Baker as
the bastard first lieutenant, Donald Sinden, and Denholm Elliott
were all just right.

Moira Lister scored instantly in a tiny part as a bitchy actress
wife, waiting for the coast to clear. "Have a nice trip, darling,"
she said to her wretched husband, due to go out on a murderous
convoy, as brightly as if he were off to New York on a sales spree.
It made one groan for all the betrayed sailors who ever went back,
sick at heart, to sea. The rough-weather photography was superb.

Virginia McKenna, as a loving Wren, was rather less satisfactory. "She seemed to be making love in the Service manner," I said to a reporter afterwards, and then asked him to scratch out the remark, which he obligingly did. But if her cool performance established the point that love and war did not mix, because war must have the priority, then that was all right with me.

It was clear that they had all combined to give me a writer's dream—a film which, far from whoring up the book, had cherished, illuminated, and even honoured it. We waited for the premiere with tremendous appetite. *All* five Sea Lords would be there, and most of the Board of Admiralty. The Duke of Edinburgh would be the star guest, and we would be presented to him afterwards.

There was only one shadow which threatened us. Queen Mary, that marvellous old stalwart, now eighty-five, was very ill. If she died, much of the prestige of the occasion would have to be abandoned.

It was. Sir Michael Balcon gave a party out at Ealing, two nights before the premiere, for the people who had worked so hard and to such good effect. We were having a high old time when the fatal news was announced.

Queen Mary had died peacefully in her sleep. There would be court mourning for a month. The Duke of Edinburgh would have to cancel all his engagements. That included us.

It was a sad blow, for many reasons. But making every allowance for the natural disappointment of those who had set their hearts on building this into a very big event, to crown all their hard work, I was appalled to hear one of my fellow-guests break the silence with: "Oh God! Why did the old girl have to do it *now?*"

Pop-eyed at the best of times, he was positively bursting with rage. As a sentimental monarchist, I had to answer back, and we quarrelled briskly. I was just as disappointed as anyone in the studio, but if someone like Queen Mary had to die, at the age of eighty-five, after a lifetime of service, it should not be to such an epitaph.

Before long the party melted away—there was a great deal of replanning to be done. Then I was privately taken to task for my stuffy attitude.

I could only answer that if anyone didn't like my stuffy attitude, they could stuffy it uppy. Ah, those days of wine and roses. Ah, early signs, broad hints, of multiple strife to come. Ah wilderness, and ah, my head.

Yet in spite of this subdued atmosphere, and the downgrading of what should have been a great occasion (I was very sad myself not to meet the Duke of Edinburgh, a much respected man who would know at first hand what *The Cruel Sea* was all about), the premiere was quite an evening. In fact despite the tantrums of one lady and the death of another, it was terrific.

With two wives, one son, one father (aged eighty-one), one step-mother, one sister, King Hussein of Jordan in a horrid little pin-stripe suit, Jack Hawkins, Lord Winterton, Jim Harmsworth, and eight ex-shipmates from *Campanula, Guillemot, Shearwater,* and *Perim,* the assorted company nearby had its complications.

But the film, most moving in itself, received the kind of absorbed attention—a true participation by everyone watching and listening—which at the end left me almost shaking with emotions long buried, long forgotten.

I knew then what it meant to feel drained—and there was only one cure for a drained man. We gave a party afterwards at the slightly haunted Café de Paris, where the bomb had fallen and the orchestra, the dancers, the waiters, and Ken Snake-hips Johnson fell with it.

That night, some smaller bombs fell on me, as the corks popped and triumph was prophesied. Though I patched it up with the man who had made the Queen Mary remark, I had a secondary row with his wife who, being American, thought my accent was the funniest thing since George III. My own wife, in sultry mood, was giving the general impression that marriages should only last about three months.

But by then I didn't give a damn. By God, that book still lived! . . . And it was marvellous to meet, for the first time, so many beaming admirals.

I was to see that film fourteen times altogether, in various parts of the world, before I decided that an occasional glimpse on late-night TV would be enough in the future. A week after London, we returned briefly to Johannesburg for another very considerable charity bash (Colosseum, 2,200-seat sell-out). This was followed by a premiere in Ottawa, attended by Mr. Lester Pearson, another in Toronto with a multitude of sea-cadets, and a third in Montreal, where I inspected a naval guard-of-honour bare-headed and wearing a dinner-jacket. It cannot be done in any sort of style.

In New York the film broke the house records at the Fine Arts Theatre, and I was honoured to sit between Oscar Hammerstein and the banjo-eyed comedian Fred Allen. In Washington the occasion was stage-managed by Paul Gore-Booth, later to be head of our Foreign Office (and after that a Life Peer) but then my opposite number as director of British Information Services in America —in fact, little better than a humble, card-carrying information officer.

So it could be done, I thought later, as I watched his sky-rocketing career. But perhaps it could only be done by Paul Gore-Booth.

In Washington my next-door neighbour was Senator Estes Kefauver. He had recently been photographed wearing a Davy Crockett coonskin cap, and the spectacle had become a popular subject with cartoonists. When I brought it into the conversation, I had the impression that it was no longer his favourite topic, if it ever had been.*

There was one other curious tailpiece to this comet-ride across and across the film world. Some time in 1956 it was decided to rename a pub in Hampstead "The Cruel Sea" (it had previously been called "The Nag's Head," which made for quite a change of scene), and Jack Hawkins and I went up to open it.

Neither of us had declared a pub open before, though we might have closed one or two in our time; and when the moment arrived to do so, I could think of no more suitable phrase than the executive naval command: "Sink everything in sight!"

The occasion was then happily swamped by large numbers of opportunist sailors who, having heard rumours of free beer all round, flocked in from far and wide and converged upon the bar.

The free-beer concession had to be withdrawn after an hour.

Back in my proper space-time pattern of 1951, with no notion of the real scale of what was to come, I was already sufficiently stunned. What was happening to me was what every writer prays

---

* It was still pursuing him, bushy brush and all, when he went down to defeat as Mr. Adlai Stevenson's running-mate in the 1956 presidential election.

for, whether he will admit it or not: whether he keeps on trying, in face of all the odds, or gives up and becomes a critic or a television person; and that is, to do his very best with a book, and then to see it take off vertically into the clouds.

What makes tens of thousands of people suddenly decide that they want to read one particular book, and no other, and that they won't be happy until they have bought it and taken it home, is a mystery which has baffled publishers, beyond despair and into bankruptcy, since books were first printed and bound and launched into the market-place.

It does not baffle writers in the same way, since (unless they are harlots or computer-boys) they will always write exactly what they want to, and take a chance on success, or failure, or a drawn game.

I had written exactly what I wanted to, and was already stupefied by the result.

But I knew, even then, that an enormous amount of luck had been involved. Nothing had happened to me in the war which had not happened to a hundred thousand other sailors. But it had meshed in with every other factor in my life so far—including the basic one of being born in 1910, so that by the time I was called on to fight I was young enough to have the energy for war, and old enough—just old enough—not to be destroyed by it.

I had already learned my trade as a writer. I had not been killed, nor maimed, nor driven mad, nor brutalized. When I got out, I had a marvellous story to tell: the same as everyone else's story, but still so tremendous that it was a privilege to be given the chance.

Finally I had got there first with my version, and at the very moment when, for absolutely no reason at all except that mysterious tides of impulse, choice, taste, and will *do* move to and fro, as chartless and astonishing as the governing moon itself, thousands of people (presently to be millions) decided that they were ready to think about the war at sea again, and to read a book about it.

The book about it they all wanted to read was mine. The tide itself was mine. It could never happen again, in such a conjunction of fortune, if I lived to be a hundred and the world turned back and I beat the Spanish Armada. It was a once-in-a-lifetime miracle. . . . On which sobering thought—and I certainly needed

one—I closed the *prima donna* account in London and flew back
to Johannesburg and my proper job.

Soli Ornstein met us at Palmietfontein Airport. When I heard
him call out "Nicolai!" in tempestuous greeting across the customs barrier, and then: "I rise my hat!" I knew that I was home.

3.

It was indeed home, but with a vast difference. In our reversed
seasons, when winter was July and Christmas meant eating ritual
turkey and plum pudding in the only oven-hot month of the year,
a golden spring was now under way, with a golden summer to
follow.

I had been enjoying South Africa before. Now, the most beautiful country in the world had become the most beautiful place
to live in—which was something quite different, and violently
arguable if one still had a taste for argument.

But somewhere on the way, somewhere steering south, somewhere in the swift ascent from humble pie to upper crust, I had
lost the will to fly into a passion about the frail rights of man and
the wrongs of stony privilege—except in theory, blessed theory,
which need not cost a penny-piece in performance.

The still-soft conscience did not preclude the hardened attitude,
whether in bed or out of it. One could deride "Let them eat cake"
while still drawing comfort from all that bread in the bank.

Johannesburg had seemed masculine before, with female twang-
ing noises from the world's most subtle instrument only audible
after dark. Now it was all feminine, and elegant, and luxurious,
and proud. The spare hawk became the homing dove, coming in
to rest on golden-slippered claws—the prettiest, most pliant metal
on the market. The domestic cushion grew tassels, the hard pillow
was gentled to a soft, downy whisper. The fat cat sat on the mat.
The dream was cream.

Well, damn all the words for corruption. Bless them, and damn
them.

"Domestic" was the new keynote. Though there were signs of
legal stirring in London, the promised divorce was still only a

promise. Yet in some not too baffling way, I had become a more respectable prospect, a better bet. We therefore settled down together, in scandalous circumstances which, at the Johannesburg level of social acceptance, were no scandal at all.

Our rented nest was a large house in Illovo, north of the city; a house which, with four acres of garden, a swimming pool, seven servants, and a Cadillac in the drive, put me *just* in the ranks of the upper classes hereabouts.

There was no doubt that I had come up in the world, and though a book had done it, it was not literary esteem which had thus jacked me up. It was the twin thrusts of sudden, wall-to-wall money, which was well thought of in Johannesburg, and the social level of those who, when all the smoke had cleared, would constitute the body of my in-laws.

This was a typical South African family of the old school, with connections in mining, racing, finance, alcoholism, slimming pills, energy tablets, lesbianism, uproarious divorce, and, as far as my future father-in-law was concerned, the award of a gold medal at the Olympic Games of 1936, personally presented by Hermann Goering to the chairman of the South African Jockey Club.

It says much for my state of mind that I found all this deeply flattering.

Social life now centered on Sunday lunch, a notable fixture at which the crested club blazer vied with the Paisley silk neckerchief and the reversed-calf pale-green brothel-creepers as acceptable male decor, and on the rather more formal dinner party— ours and other people's.

It would be wrong to think of English-speaking South Africans, then or now, as a bunch of expatriate hicks with tons of money and the taste of newly rich Midlanders or Yorkshiremen or popstars or film whores. In this world, largely above race and above politics, there was considerable sophistication and style.

The best entertaining, outside London or Paris or Rome or Washington, was certainly to be found, as standard practice, within the five square miles of this brand-new contender. It was often hard to keep up. It was also a great pleasure to try.

Thus, when we sat down to dinner under soft candle-light, with a view across the tiled patio to a moonlit garden with the tiny gleam of the watchboys' brazier marking one corner (naturally, we had our own small police force); when we sat down to dinner, with a white-uniformed, white-gloved, scarlet-sashed servant to each two or three guests, and sampled the first mouthful of the shrimps in avocado or the *caviare au blinis,* the mood of "I'm all right, Jack," took on, at least, a superior gloss.

Hands up, those who have travelled from Johannesburg to Cape Town via Alfa Romeo, Battle Class destroyer, bosun's chair, aircraft carrier, and admiral's barge. What, everybody? Ah, but at the age of almost forty-two? Well done, that man!

That man was myself; otherwise I would not be making such a production of it. But there was another character involved in Stage One of this excursion, a polo-playing darling of society called Tommy Charles, one of the few really smooth, really well-tailored, really amusing playboys yet thrown up by twentieth-century Johannesburg.

For twenty years T. Charles has always owed me, in theory at least, the sum of ninety pounds, the result of a very simple gambling operation known as "cutting through the pack" at five pounds a card on a mixed-up occasion when I thought we were playing seriously and he (it later appeared) did not. But the debt, if debt it was, has long ago been forgiven, if only for what followed.

I was due to go down to Simonstown, the British naval base about twenty miles south of Cape Town, to meet Admiral Packer, the recently arrived Commander-in-Chief, South Atlantic. Tommy wanted to try out his new car, an open, two-seater, pale ivory, really beautiful Alfa Romeo which had just been run in. One thing led to another. The result was a wild ride together, of 930 miles against the clock, when we thought we would try to break the unofficial road record between Johannesburg and Cape Town.

We were shooting at something like fourteen hours, an average of more than 65 miles per hour, and I had to be extremely careful about it. Tommy was the playboy type, and habitually did things like this; I was a civil servant, and did not. Society might be indulgent to him if caught; but the High Commissioner would rightly take the dimmest possible view if one of his staff was copped for careering down South Africa at anything up to our top speed of 140 miles per hour.

There would be no question of pleading diplomatic immunity. Fines for speeding were graduated at something like two pounds for every mile over the official limit of sixty. After that, I would find myself on a different kind of carpet—one that really mattered.

However, some spare money and a superior love-affair, soon (I hoped) to be up-graded into a superior marriage, had given me the necessary willful confidence. I said yes to everything, which included splitting the fines, whichever one of us was the official culprit.

We started at first light, while the suburban exits were still free of traffic, and drove in two-hour tricks. Most of the way lay along clear stretches of first-class road, with only one major town, Bloemfontein, to slow us up, hardly any other cars to worry about, and (I must emphasize) no one to kill.

We had to stop in Bloemfontein for petrol, and an admiring crowd gathered round the car. With its high-gloss ivory paintwork, scarlet upholstery, and bonnet about as long as a tennis court, it certainly caught the eye. One of the local sophisticates peered down at the radiator, proudly emblazoned with "Alfa Romeo—Milano," and gave his verdict: "Jolly good cars, these Milanos!"

Even at that late date, there was still one unpaved section to be negotiated, a two-hundred-mile ordeal of ochre mud, packed down into a country-style byway but often viciously corrugated. Once a month the "grader"—a kind of sharp-bladed bulldozer with a parasol on top to protect the patient driver—travelled down one side of it and up the other, scraping off the top ripples and smoothing out the surface.

This must have been the twenty-ninth day of that particular month; parts of the road were like the entrance to Dover Harbour on a bad morning, with the ruffled shirt of the sea running against us, as ferocious and tough as any old iron.

The only way to avoid being shaken to bits was to rev up and float across the waves: to press on regardless, as Tommy Charles, who had been in the Air Force, still phrased it. (I reminded him of another item, dredged up from his wartime handbook: "We were stooging around at nought feet," and he countered with "There was I, surrounded by balloons.") In our present earthy situation, one pressed on regardless until the car began to skate sideways,

and then pulled back a bit. Tommy (perhaps it was his polo training) knew the trick, and was much better at it than I was.

But it was all very beautiful—even that parched, waterless Karroo Desert prostrate under the burning heat: very beautiful, and
exciting, and largely uneventful. We simply kept going, reeling
off the miles with real, thirsty appetite, exchanging one horizon
for the next, one arc of clear sunlight for another even more
alluring. At one point on a long empty stretch Tommy, who had
been dozing, woke up and glanced at the speedometer. It was
registering 190.

"Steady on, dear boy," he said, in mild reproof.

"It's all right. It's only kilometers."

I knew that arithmetic was not his strong point.

We kept up a very good average, better than sixty miles per hour,
for hour after hour, including the necessary stops, those corru-
gated-iron stretches, and a road-gang which, intent on repairing a
washed-out bridge, were having a lot of fun with their red and
green flags. Obviously they preferred the pace of Africa to the
pace of Alfa Romeo.

We raced a train, and waved to its driver, and left it chuffing
away in the distance like a toy abandoned on an enormous, forgotten nursery floor. There was one dead-straight stretch of 15
miles, tenantless, inviting a flat-out surge of speed. Once we did
127 miles in one hundred minutes.

But towards the end of the journey we were fatally slowed
down by a convoy of army lorries crawling up the long, steep,
curling road which climbed to nearly five thousand feet to cross
the Swartberg Range, and with that we lost our chance of a record
run. By then, we knew it could not be done—not on that day,
anyway.

It was 16¼ hours before we were sliding down into the long
shadows of Table Mountain; and against that magnificent drop-
curtain I said goodbye to Tommy Charles ("Let's try it again on
the way back!") and took off for Simonstown and more sedate
company.

Their Lordships of the Admiralty, back in the brave old days
of 1814, had certainly known how to look after the Commander-
in-Chief of the South Atlantic Station; Vice-Admiral Sir Herbert
and Lady Packer, the current heirs of this largesse, lived in very

432   BREAKING IN, BREAKING OUT

considerable style, and their Admiralty House, Simonstown, was an elegant palace, a white Stone Frigate which really deserved the name, and from which one could survey the naval dockyard below with an appropriate sense of ownership and pride.

Lying off the harbour there was now quite an array of British naval strength, currently in South African waters on a showing-the-flag visit which came as a pleasure but no surprise, since I had put out a press-release about it a couple of days earlier.

There were two imposing aircraft carriers, *Theseus* and *Vengeance,* and four brand-new Battle Class destroyers, looking about twice the size, and twice as lethal, as any destroyer that had ever come my way in that ancient, long-ago war of 1939-1945.

But at the moment my preoccupation was social rather than maritime. Lunch with the Commander-in-Chief had, for me, such prestige, such immediate glamour, that I became a dutiful junior officer again with my very first step through the solid portals of Admiralty House.

The amateur who never made the grade, summoned into the presence of the professional who undoubtedly had, could only worry about the correct manipulation of knives and forks, and a light, deferential touch on the conversational ball.

Though I was also there on a private errand of inquiry, I doubted already if this would ever come to anything. There could be few ex-R.N.V.R. officers who would care to ask a Vice-Admiral, across his own lunch-table: "Did you, or did you not, check with the Admiralty to see if I had been lying about my wartime naval career?"

Yet, having still a few naval friends left in conveniently sensitive places, I knew that this was true. I knew also that my modest claims had been endorsed as "Substantially correct" (what bloody impudence! They were *absolutely* correct, down to the last humble syllable); and I wondered if the subject would come up for an airing in lunch-time conversation.

It did so, at one point, and it was brought to light by my hostess, Lady Packer, when she turned to me and said, with that sweetly poisonous innocence which only women swathed in gold braid could get away with, that all this *Cruel Sea* publicity had been awfully good for the Navy. I really must have made the very *most* of my time in the Admiralty Information Department.

I could tell by the confederate smiles and glances from the staff officers among the other guests that they knew what this was all about, and that the C.-in-C.'s wife was judged to have struck home with her first broadside.

Yet Lady Packer was not really like that at all. Nor was the Navy. This was a curious peacetime backlash to the old days, when *they* were the only pros, and *we* were the rats and mice of the service. But there was something here even more curious, and perhaps more disgusting: the fact that, faced with a real Admiral, of formidable presence, at the head of the table, and a ring of watchful sycophants round him, I was once more submissive, still saluting all over.

I returned my hostess an evasive answer. Not even that. I simply agreed. But at the same time I was very glad indeed that I had not stayed on in the Navy.

Perhaps, also, this reluctance to engage had something to do with Lady Packer herself who, though she had to go through the traditional motions, and might even be enjoying them, was not in fact the bullying old battle-ax which her role normally demanded. She was *soignée,* and lively, and unexpectedly warm. She was also a writer—the salt of the earth as well as the salt of the sea.*

Never mind, I thought, relapsing into the unco-operative silence which was the nearest I would ever come to mutiny, even in face of such privileged insolence. Never mind: I had been captain of a frigate when these little tight-arsed courtiers were still wetting their beds. . . . Afterwards I went down to the harbour to look at the ships; and there, the first man I met was a tall, rake-thin commander just stepping ashore from his gleaming motorboat, handled alongside like a jet-propelled cork.

The commander, I saw at the second astonished glance, was one sailor who did *not* think of me as the perennial tit marked "Press" on the wardroom wall. It was my old captain from *Guillemot,* Sam Lombard-Hobson.

* As Joy Packer, she had already published *Pack and Follow* and *Grey Mistress,* with lots of fiction still to come.

He was now, it seemed, the captain of *Jutland,* one of those whopping great destroyers attendant on the carriers. He was also, thank God, still a firm friend.

"Come round to Cape Town with us," he said immediately, when the first surprised greetings (though sailors were never really surprised at such turns of fate) were over. "We're acting as close escort to *Vengeance.* You can stand the middle watch." He went even further. "You can have bacon and banana fritters for breakfast!"

"Good God!"

But I was in the mood to say yes. Who, after 930 miles in the Alfa, and some snide comments from an Admiral's lady, could say no to the promise of sea time again, in a destroyer like *Jutland* or *Agincourt* lying just across the bay? However, I had my own time-table, like any other conscientious wage-slave.

"When are you due in Cape Town?"

"At six o'clock tomorrow morning. We sail at midnight to-night. Well, *we're* not due in Cape Town. The carriers are, but we're coming back here for night exercises. This old boy is very hot." "This old boy" was Admiral Packer, at whose table I had been drooping so despondently, twenty minutes earlier. "But we can transfer you to *Vengeance,* just off Cape Town."

"How? By helicopter? I've never been in one."

"Well—*no.* That would cost rather too much money." He sighed. "This is *peacetime.* Do you realize that these days we're not even allowed to ring full ahead without giving our reasons in writing? In triplicate? No, we'll *transfer* you. We'll rig a bosun's chair and a couple of pulleys, and haul you across. Block-and-tackle job—about fifty sailors at each end." There was now such a gleam in his eye that this could well have been something he had wanted to do ever since 1942. "It'll be like oiling at sea. But at twenty knots. And it'll be a very good exercise for my first lieutenant. He's never done it before."

The prospect was irresistible, for all sorts of reasons.

I was delighted to see Sam again; naturally he had a superb ship, run as every destroyer should be; and although our night's voyage was only fifty miles, with what he called some fiddling about in the middle (changing from one screening pattern to

another, on the curt order "Execute!"), it was the best night which
had come my way for a long time. Even as a passenger, I was
proud to be one of *Jutland*'s ship's company.

We dined in some state in the wardroom, with an assembly
of sixteen officers, many of whom, like policemen, seemed to
have hardly finished with their schooldays. Sam and I revelled in
utterly boring reminiscence. But there was, I thought, a surprised,
even respectful interest round the table when I told them of my
very first night as their captain's first lieutenant; how we had
stalked and sunk a German E-boat off Lowestoft: how spirited
and swift an action it had been—there was I, in fact, surrounded
by tracer bullets as I stood on the quarterdeck: and how one of
those tracers had surged out of the darkness and whistled between
my legs—the nearest I had ever been to utter character-assassina-
tion.

Perhaps it was just as well that such re-encounters did not
happen too often; otherwise, one would be stuck in an incurable,
lifetime groove of reminiscence, with one's listeners (what listeners?) equally stuck, suspended there forever like yawns in aspic.

At midnight, after the customary short nap allowed to middle-
watchers, I went up to the bridge to enjoy our passage at close
quarters.

It was a velvet night, an African night; as we moved out of
False Bay in line ahead, dipping our fore-foot into the last few
miles of the Indian Ocean before it merged into the broad South
Atlantic, that burned smell of Africa wafting across from the
Cape Flats was all round us, just as it once had been at the far
other end of this colossal continent, in the Straits of Gibraltar
between Tarifa and Tangier.

We set course southwards for the true Cape of Good Hope,
with the carrier *Vengeance* as huge as Africa itself against the
yellow moon.

Even after half an hour on *Jutland*'s bridge, I was very glad
I was only a passenger. She would have been too much for me
altogether. The bridge and the two decks below it were crammed
with complex electronic equipment I would never understand;
within a short spell of ten years, the gadgetry involved in running
a ship like this had gone beyond bafflement into total mystery.

The best training any modern R.N. captain could have would have been a degree in applied science, and after that, lots of reading and plenty of luck.

Sam Lombard-Hobson himself confirmed one aspect of this, when he handed his ship over to the Officer-of-the-watch as soon as we were clear of complications, and stayed to gossip, leaning on the wing of the bridge.

"The trouble is, I'm hardly ever up here," he said. "We never get any fresh air. We hardly even see the sea. If there's anything at all interesting going on, the captain has to be down in the plotting room—it's armour-plated all round—watching a lot of knobs and dials, talking into the intercom. You'll see when we start those screening maneuvers. There won't be any real ships round me. Just a lot of damn fluorescent blobs on the plot."

"She's still a wonderful ship," I said.

"Oh yes. But I'd rather smell the sea." He nodded towards the vast blur which was *Vengeance*. The night was so still that we could hear the thresh of her bow-wave. "I'd rather see her up-moon, and *know* I was in station. It isn't any fun, the new way. When we're at action stations, there's just one sub-lieutenant left up here. He's to tell me if it's raining. Do you remember—"

Thus the night, with a calm sea stretching back to India, and forward to Cape Horn, and south to Antarctica, with a mug of cocoa as thick as prep-school porridge when the breeze turned cold. Thus our slow gentle passage round the southern Horn of Africa, and up towards the great iron magnet of Table Mountain. Thus the dawn off Three Anchor Bay. But then it was my turn for all that fun and fresh air, which the captain never had.

I stood on the fo'c'sle-head surrounded by interested spectators, all seeming to wear the kind of expression one sees when the dare-devil high-wire act—"One hundred feet above the arena!—NO safety net!"—is announced with a roll of muffled drums, and watched as we surged alongside *Vengeance*.

A heaving-line went across, and then the first wire, and then a complicated festoon of other wires, which gradually took shape like the top half of a spider's web. I hoped it would prove the strongest spider's web in the world. During long convoys, we used to send fuel pipes across to our supply tanker with this sort of rig. But *people?*

Then, when all was ready, I stepped into a kind of waist-high canvas bucket, wearing a life-jacket, carrying my little briefcase. Between the two ships, keeping pace side by side, the water foamed and boiled; it was twenty feet below *Jutland*'s deck, then receding to a forty-foot drop at the other end.

If I had not known that Commander Lombard-Hobson was running this lot, I would have been worried. As it was, it all happened so quickly that I had no time to be scared until I was safe at the other end.

Half the ship's company was now tailing on to various ropes, taking the strain as the bosun's chair rose and fell. I began to move—out from the safety of the deck, into the empty air and a void of swirling water below. Sam, using the loud-hailer from the bridge, called out: "Good luck, Number One!"—one of the stranger goodbyes of my life. Then the heaving and hauling started, and I sped across.

The chair sagged horribly, to within ten feet of the surface, in the middle; a hundred jokes about the cruel sea came to mind as the surging water seemed to be licking at my feet; then I rose up and up in a great curving loop and into a square black hole in the middle of the mountain. The support of the bosun's chair fell away like dropping trousers (rather too appropriate an analogy) and I stepped out onto a blessedly solid iron deck, to be greeted by a midshipman who saluted and said: "Sir, my father met you in the war."

After that it was something of an anti-climax. Carriers were too big to be interesting; if one wanted to live like that, a large second-class hotel was better. But breakfast was superior, if fritter-less; Table Bay ennobled by a streaky sunrise was as magnificent as ever; and if one had to make a short swift journey from a ship at anchor to the safety of dry land, then an Admiral's barge with its stylized boat-hook ballet at either end was *the* way to travel.

I was happy in love, happy indeed, as who could fail to be when securely installed with a rarely beautiful girl who could also speak, if not with the tongue of angels, then at least with the voice of close command and the barb of wit.

I was also getting away with murder, always a pleasing accomplishment: our nest, even in Johannesburg, had some notoriety, and just down the road in Pretoria was the High Commissioner's Office—not blind, not deaf, not at all inclined to be careless about things like this.

By now I had told them about the coming divorce, but the other subject was never raised—which was astonishing, since I was now "established" and really subject to the whip. Perhaps it was thought that next time round I would settle down into the cosy domesticity—but legal, please—which was the only acceptable norm. Perhaps I was being allowed to be half a civil servant— one wife, two children, one dog, one car—and half a writer— rogue, vagabond, adulterer, swine. Perhaps—I could not even guess.

Meanwhile, and certainly, I was as faithful as any civil servant who wore his marital blinkers from dawn till dusk and dawn again. Normally, the sudden avalanche of money would have meant, at least, that I would be looking round for a better class of woman, and getting it. Now, when it had happened, there was no such ambition. I knew that I was bound forever, or until something awful happened. *La Belle Dame sans Merci* had me in thrall.

It might have been a puzzle what to write next, and God knows there was plenty of advice, from interested, disinterested, and plainly malevolent bystanders, to whom the spectacle of a "best-selling author," that abominably lucky fellow who could not possibly have more than one book in his head, falling flat on his face with its successor, would be a private and public delight.

But I had made up my mind already; this was *my* country, right or wrong, and no bright boy-critic with his little quill dipped in vinegar would ever discourage me. I had a conviction that I was going to be slaughtered anyway, whatever I wrote; the philosophy of "Build them up, let them stand, tear them down" was as deeply ingrained in literature as it was in the construction business.

If I stayed with the sea, I would be "repeating the formula"; if I tried something different, then I should have stayed with the sea, which was all I was fit for.

In any case I did not want to be typed as a sea-writer, like C. S. Forester or even Conrad; *Son of the Cruel Sea* might have been wildly profitable, but it would also have been an ignoble exercise in cashing-in. I had all sorts of other ideas. The only thing to do was to write exactly what I wanted, and take the consequences, whether it meant another explosion or a dull thud; a collective back-slap, or a dubious shaking of the head, or a lethal shot of poison in the cup.

I had one idea in particular which appealed to me. Helen Keller, the blind, deaf-and-dumb, near-genius of communication, had recently toured South Africa, on a fund-raising expedition which was as moving as it was successful.

On a certain savage morning, reading about her triumphant progress, I was struck with the thought of how awful it would be, how vile, how unbelievably corrupt, if Helen Keller or someone like her were in fact a crook, or was being exploited by crooks; if she was not blind at all, nor deaf, nor dumb, but simply a consummate actress, manipulated by criminal conspirators for their own ends.

The idea of course was as far from the true Helen Keller story as it could possibly be. But it was now my story, the one I wanted to write. To celebrate conception, I invested in a new typewriter, giving the old one—a veteran of thirteen years, bought in the honest old days of 1938 when typewriters were built to last, like cars or light-bulbs—to one of the waiters at the Waverley Hotel.

He said endearingly: "You write a book—now I write a book!" and we both settled down to it. Mine was published two years later, in 1953, as *The Story of Esther Costello*.*

Most curiously, it was banned in South Africa, at the instance of a bloody-minded old clergyman who had been instrumental in bringing Helen Keller to the country on her fund-raising tour. He now chose to believe that the book referred to her, and promptly went into action. By way of a first shot, he wrote me a furious letter which contained the strange phrase: "If, during Miss Helen Keller's visit, you did notice anything unusual, I am sure there is an innocent explanation."

I was absolutely sure already. But when I told him so, and added that in fact I had never met, heard, nor seen Miss Keller, even at a distance, he called me, with Christian resolution, a liar.

* Cassell and Alfred Knopf, 1953; Pocket Books, 1955; Corgi Books, 1956; Romulus and Columbia Pictures, 1957; Pan Books, 1966.

In the shadow of Christmas 1951 we made a radio version of *The Cruel Sea* for Springbok Radio, the commercial step-child of the South African Broadcasting Corporation, and it was the hardest piece of sustained work which had come my way for a long time.

A girl on the Johannesburg *Star* named Margot Bryant—in unlikely fact, the Women's Editor—produced the script, and a very good one too; I did the narration myself—introduction, linking material in the middle, and the sad or exciting bits at the end; and we taped twenty-six half-hour episodes in twenty-nine days, rehearsal, sound effects, two hundred speaking parts, and all. We finished with a gasp of triumph on Christmas Eve.

Taped is the wrong word to use, and that was part of the trouble; for some reason connected with the durability of the material, it could not be taped, but had to be cut directly onto a master record. For some *other* reason, whenever we made any sort of mistake, we had to go back to the beginning again. Apparently there was no way of keeping in the good part, and picking up again in the middle.

If anyone fluffed his lines on the twenty-sixth minute of the recording—as I did on one ghastly occasion in Episode 22, by which time we were all getting thoroughly snappish and exhausted—then Cedric Messina, our talented, infinitely patient producer, said "I'm sorry, chaps," and we all went back again to the introductory music, the seagulls, the asdic pings, and the sound of salt water smashing down onto an iron deck, which marked our fade-in.

In the shadow of Christmas I read one absolutely superb novel, *The Case of Mr. Crump* by Ludwig Lewisohn, an account of a horrific, murderous marriage which did indeed end in murder. In the shadow of Christmas, I bought myself a small but sensational car, a two-seater coupé Jaguar XK 120, of palest green like shimmering emeralds, which superseded all other cars in my adoration.

Naturally we gave a reception for it, on a rather special Sunday morning. Twelve strong men hefted it up and carried it across flower beds, round trees, and onto the lawn in front of the *stoep*, where, with an orchid Scotch-taped to its radiator, it made a glamorous show-piece.

Diamonds and rubies completed the rest of the Christmas shopping.

On New Year's Eve we attended the Party of the Year, a recurrent fancy-dress festival given by a generous man called Eric Gallo. Before very long, I decided, *I* would be giving the party of the year.

Still in the shadow of the new year, I cast the accounts for the sensational old one.

In the first five months of its wild life, the book had sold close to half a million copies (eighty thousand in America, where it had notched up fifteen printings and twenty-two weeks in the bestseller list, though perennially second to *The Caine Mutiny;* a huge chunk from the Book-of-the-Month Club; and past the two hundred thousand mark from Cassell's, where the poor struggling fellows still could not print it fast enough).

The sixteenth translation had just been sold to faraway Iceland, though I was still looking and lusting for an Afrikaans version. I asked poet Uys Krige if he would like to undertake this. The answer was no. I offered him a flat one thousand pounds for the job. The answer was still no. (Proud poets are the best.) Then a bi-lingual Nationalist M.P. who must be anonymous volunteered to take on the assignment, if the action could be transferred to the South Atlantic, with "lots of good Afrikaner names," and based on Cape Town instead of Liverpool. The answer was no.*

I was informed that I would be awarded the Heinemann Prize for Literature, with a Fellowship of the Royal Society of Literature to add to the accolade.

My account book, now a firm second-favourite in the library, showed that I had made fifteen thousand pounds that year—for me, an unheard-of total. It was to jump to fifty-eight thousand pounds in 1952, but by that time it was only money.

* This had a parallel in an early German offer to publish, if "tendentious" references to U-boats were deleted. I did not fancy quite such a slim volume as this.

FORTY-SIX

1956

THE YEAR OF THE STUPID OX

1.

THERE IS AT LEAST ONE SIZEABLE CHUNK OF HOLY WRIT which any alert sub-editor, looking for circulation, would have excised with quick, flashing strokes of his blue pencil. It is the "Begat" bit, which starts: "And Cush begat Nimrod": and continues thus for 9 chapters, 397 verses, and 1,125 named characters.

I was reminded of this generative marathon by a letter from Mr. F. B. Wickwire, of the legal firm of MacInnes, Wilson, and Hallett (Halifax, Nova Scotia, six partners). Mr. Wickwire is the latest, though probably not the last, in my own Begat Series, which started in the long, long ago with Mr. Duncan Mactavish, Q.C., of Gowling, Mactavish, Osborne, and Henderson (Ottawa, fifteen partners).

Mr. Wickwire, heir to a formidable line of succession, which has been keeping me under inexorable scrutiny and well-tempered pressure for the past thirteen years, recently begat me a letter.

In it, after a reminder, in the customary sharp terms, of some unpaid alimony (the previous nine years' total payment of $177,230 had still proved insufficient to ward off penury), I was requested, in spite of my "desire to be remembered by posterity," to leave out any reference to my second wife in the next volume of my autobiography.

Ah, posterity . . . It will not be easy. Already posterity seems to be crying out for the facts, more stridently even than that spectral legal firm—Gold, Frankincense, and More!—which still looms as the eternal last enemy, the last Begat. But I will try. Indeed, I try now.

Yet that injunction of 1967, being odd and impudent, would have found itself thoroughly at home with 1956, which must now be down-graded to the realm of chaos: to the *chiaroscuro*—the light and shade—of true lunacy, of a string of scenes lit by flashes of foolish revealing glare, and then darkened again by the drop-curtain of bad judgment, bad behaviour, bad hopes, and bad luck.

Nineteen fifty-six must be branded, also, with the conviction that no one I have ever known, nor read about, nor imagined, ever gave or took his half-share in such squalor of spirit, such waste of work and love, such murderous abrasion of one person by another, such a sad longing for peace, or such a clownish butchery of achievement, as was to bring me to the pole-ax in the Year of the Stupid Ox.

On New Year's morning I woke up in the Royal Victoria Hospital in Montreal, and it was pure, unalloyed bliss.

I could safely claim to be a little ill. I had bronchitis, or—to stretch a point—bronchial pneumonia, or pneumonitis, or a persistent hacking cough which, if used carelessly, could tear a trifle at the lungs.

Laying the groundwork of my duplicity at an appropriate moment, Christmas Eve, I had hacked away like Camille, like Mimi in *La Bohème,* like Robert Louis Stevenson, like Chopin under the baleful gaze of George Sand.

But in fact the symptoms were genuine enough, or excuse enough, for not venturing outside into the ten-degrees-below-zero weather, which now ruled two thousand miles of eastern Canada, from St. John's, Newfoundland, to the shores of Lake Superior. They were good enough for the fateful jargon word, *Hospitalization.* They were good enough for my confederate doctor.

When I had demonstrated to him, on ample evidence, that I had an important book to finish and that I would never finish it at home, he had dispatched me to Montreal for a "complete check-up," which in Canada could mean anything from a loaf in bed to the terminal diagnosis of cancer of the rectum.

I would be staying there for three weeks, my medical adviser assured me, or even a little longer if a little longer would suit my peculiar, slightly pathetic circumstances. After that I had better recuperate, preferably in the Caribbean.

It was true that they had drained my sinuses, a painful and rather disgusting operation, and assembled a small library of X-ray photographs, and committed some rude acts with a barium enema. But then they left me alone. Everyone left me alone. The cracking cold outside, the crisp, glistening snow slopes below the hospital walls, the bare frozen trees through which one could see all the way down to Montreal harbour itself (the very road was called *Côte des Neiges*) were all deeply attractive, especially if viewed through double-glazed windows, buttressed by seventy degrees of steam heat and a permanent "No Visitors" sign affixed to the door of my room.

Thus warmed and protected, in glorious isolation, in blessed, tranquil peace, waking and sleeping only with my typewriter, I finished, at a miraculously fast clip, the last fifteen thousand words of an 840-page manuscript called *The Tribe That Lost Its Head*.

The book, after three years' sweat, was already four months overdue, and this was the only way left to me; and if I had to lie and simulate and insist and plead, and cough up half my lungs in tune with high C, in order to carve a path towards it, then that was the only way also.

Thus did the poison of deceit infect the new year, from its first tender moment. Thus, with an easy, triumphant mind, did I think less than nothing of such subterfuges. Thus did I close the book at last, and the typewriter, and uncurl my toes, and declare that I was ready to leave.

On a happily appointed day, Angus, butler and mainstay of our household, flew down from Ottawa to bring me some different clothes and to pack for me. I distributed half-a-dozen books to half-a-dozen angelic nurses. A hired Cadillac waited upon the halting invalid at the hospital front door. Down-town, I cashed a check for five thousand dollars and drove to Dorval Airport, pausing on the way to inspect summer's apple-of-my-eye, the Dragon yacht *Valhalla,* now tarpaulined under two feet of snow at the Royal St. Lawrence Yacht Club.

Then I slid swiftly southwards, first to New York on literary business and then to Barbados, for the pleasure, the gigantic relief, of idleness in the sun.

The new, hard-won manuscript flew with me, to be delivered to my new, hard-won publisher, Thayer Hobson of Morrow's.

Splendid elements of farce had attended a recent break with Alfred Knopf.

It had started three years earlier with the book I had been determined to write, as a successor to *The Cruel Sea,* for no other reason than that I thought it was a good story, and I felt like doing it: the slightly ill-fated, murderously reviewed, highly enjoyable (for me) novel, *The Story of Esther Costello.*

Alfred Knopf had disliked *Esther Costello* on sight, very heartily indeed, and the fact had been communicated to me, together with some fatherly advice which did not at all suit a supremely buoyant mood. I decided that I did not want another father-figure in my life, on Madison Avenue or anywhere else. My own father, God bless him, was still alive at eighty-one. Alfred was only sixty. And, come hell or high water, *Esther* was going to be my next book, whoever was its publisher. I made that point as strongly as I could.

Proofs and the usual pre-publication drill went ahead, without further comment. Then someone in the Knopf office was fool enough to submit the book to Helen Keller, presumably to find out if she had any objections to it.

No one told me a word about this ridiculous tactic, which clearly betrayed nervousness and thus gave half the game away before we even started, and I was furious when I heard of it. Sabotage! . . . I was still furious when Helen Keller replied, sensibly and accurately, that the book seemed to have nothing whatever to do with her.

Esther Costello, as written, was then published by Knopf, with such a muted fanfare, such minimal enthusiasm, that it might have been an anonymous pamphlet on the merits of bi-metallism, or that volume which once won a *New Statesman* competition as the title least likely to attract: *How To Ride a Tricycle.*

The Knopf production flopped dismally; a pair of lead waterwings would have been air-borne by comparison. It flopped critically, which I had been expecting, and financially, which I had not. It sold, in America, a net total of eleven thousand copies, which in the context of its predecessor was less than peanuts—it was the very *shells* of peanuts, trodden down into the cinema floor.

It was also, in a wider context, a gross reversal of the form. *Esther* did very well in England. It had sold twelve translations. It was going to be filmed. What had happened to it in America? And why?

Hell hath no fury like an author thus fouled-up. If Knopf's didn't believe in the book, they shouldn't have published it. If they did believe, they should have gone to town on it. I felt betrayed, like any decked-out bride left at the church door. But there was another, more weighty item. This bride was pregnant as well.

Already I had another book in the works, a winner, a darling child, and I was absolutely determined that Knopf's would never get their slack hands on it. Damn it, they didn't deserve *The Tribe!* It was much too precious for such prudent mice as these.

The fact that Alfred was possibly right, and myself probably wrong, about *Esther Costello,* only made my resolve the more implacable.

Yet there was a snag here, a familiar snag, a snag with hammer and tongs, teeth and clause. Knopf's still had an option on my next book. They still had the cast-iron right, under contract, to publish the next work of fiction after *Esther Costello.* Even if we were grappling each other by the throat, the right remained.

Balked, bewildered, and still adamant, I took my problem, as usual, to Willis Wing.

As befitted a man whose integrity was always apparent, even across four hundred miles of New York telephone line, Willis was judicious, unruffled, and supremely fair.

When I told him (as he had guessed already) that I wanted to change publishers, and went on to explain why, he swung me back to the right point of departure.

"How's *The Tribe* coming along?"

"Oh, very well." This was far from true. There were already days, many days, when I did not think the book would ever be finished. But that didn't affect what I had in mind. "I'm about halfway through."

"Still?" But he did not waste time on further comment. "When will it be ready, then?"

"Well—probably by the Christmas after this one."

"Christmas *1955?* That's more than a year ahead. You could still change your mind about all this."

"No."

"Don't forget, Alfred did do very well for you with *The Cruel Sea.*"

"I know that." It was something which could never be in doubt. "But he didn't do so well with *Esther,* did he?" Across the humming wires, I could almost *see* Willis' expression, which told me that *Esther Costello* was not *The Cruel Sea,* nor had I meant it to be, and we both recognized the fact. "It's no good, Willis. I know all the arguments. But I don't want him to have the next one."

"Very well." He became an agent again, instead of a wary critic. "It's your decision. . . . Let's go on to stage two."

Stage Two, presently put into operation, was to make a formal request to Knopf's that they should drop their option on my next book, and that our contract should then be cancelled, without my having to submit a new manuscript. Not surprisingly, not even unfairly, this was turned down flat.

Stage Three was an exploratory visit to Ottawa by an entirely new character, Thayer Hobson, chairman and boss of William Morrow and its fellow company William Sloane Associates.

Morrow's was the firm I had already picked, tentatively, after some wide-ranging advice from Willis Wing, as my next publisher. They had a good list. More important, it was my sort of list, with a solid basis of books which sold well, and were not thought to be too awful on that account: of authors who were popular, yet not despised because of it. Among these were Laurens van der Post, Nevil Shute, Ernest Gann, St. John Ervine, Laurie Lee, and (for bulk supplies) Erle Stanley Gardner. Morrow's would suit me fine.

They were also "very nice people," Willis assured me. Certainly the man who now turned up in Ottawa was a very nice man indeed.

Thayer Hobson was then fifty-seven: a tall spare wiry transplant from Colorado Springs, obviously capable, an undoubted charmer who, like Willis himself, could combine this with the tough fiber needed to make effective headway in the iron jungle of New York City.

He was a marrying man, as I was; his second wife later married Alger Hiss; and his third essay had been with Laura Z. Hobson, the novelist whose *Gentleman's Agreement* gave an almost definitive account of anti-Semitism in North America, from its polite social exclusion to the grosser aspects of the snide, Jew-baiting sneer: a story which, translated into a film with Gregory Peck, had doubled its impact as an interior view of racial obscenity.

Thayer's approach to me, a possible new author for his stable, was correct yet perceptive. He was not poaching. He admired Alfred Knopf very much—and he had never yet met a man in the publishing world who did not. But he had heard from Willis Wing that I wanted to make a change, and I would not be the first nor the ten-thousandth author who felt that way and wanted to do something about it.

But when, over a companionable drink at the Rideau Club, with a view of the nearby Parliament Building to remind us of the eternal force of law, we came to "doing something about it," the basic snag was in the forefront of both our minds. It was that unbreakable option.

We walked round this time and time again, like fellow-gardeners wondering whether a certain tree would live or die —or could be made to live, or made to die.

But in the event, there was only one suggestion which had any substance at all. I had to write for a living. I could not stop writing, and sulk. Alfred Knopf had a firm clinch on the next manuscript. Therefore . . .

"You'll just have to write another book," Thayer Hobson said finally. "Before *The Tribe* is ready to be published. It needn't be too wonderful. Just a book. Eighty thousand words, or whatever it is. But it will be the option book. Alfred can publish it, or not publish it, whichever he likes. Either way, that completes your contract, and then you're free to offer *The Tribe* anywhere you choose."

"But I can't possibly write another book!" I objected, scandalized for all sorts of reasons. "I'm having the damnedest time with this one as it is. I can't break off now. Anyway I haven't got a suitable idea for another one."

"There are lots of ideas," said Thayer. "I can always give you an *idea*."

"But how do I write it?"

"Take a month off."

I looked at him across my glass. He was quite serious. "I don't write books in a month. You wouldn't want an author who could."

"I want an author," he said. "You. I'll let you have whatever help I can."

"I still don't think it's possible." The idea of putting aside *The Tribe*, which really was giving me tremendous trouble al-

ready, and writing another whole novel, however lightweight, was
so appalling that I could hardly bear to consider it. It was also an
immoral project, when measured by the scale of virtues still per-
sisting. Whatever the pressures, if contracts had to be cancelled
it should be by more fragrant methods than these. "We'll just
have to think of something else."

"I don't believe there is anything else."

There we had to leave it. His visit, though highly enjoyable,
ended in stalemate. It was only brought to a precipitate boil again
by Stage Four, the fearful saga of the sailing of the liner *Queen
Mary,* from New York's Pier 90, on 26 January 1955.

By then I was due for some leave again, having served two
straight years in Canada, and this time we were destined for a
return visit to Johannesburg, via London, to show off our first-
born son and half of our second to a possibly doting South African
grandfather. It meant a break in writing, but I was used to that,
and so was everyone who now relied on me for a deadline.

To make the first leg of the journey, a suite—*the* suite, £870
for four and a half days—on board a giant Cunarder romping
across the Atlantic from New York to Southampton seemed just
the thing for a thriving author. Together with a nurse, a child,
a fur-lined carry-cot, and a baffling array of other luggage, we flew
down to New York, and moved into the Pierre Hotel for the
forty-eight hours before sailing.

I called round to see Willis Wing on the day of our arrival, but
only in the late afternoon. It would have been better, far better,
if I had done so immediately.

Apart from the subject of changing publishers, which was a
continuing cliff-hanger constantly in doubt until the next installment, I only had one minor query for him: just a little one, a
baby, a throwaway line at the end of a long conversation about
money, and royalties, and film prospects, and his family, and mine,
and snow in New York, and the merits of the Pierre Hotel as
against the Plaza, or the St. Regis, or the Algonquin, which I had
never tried.

"What does it mean," I asked him, "in the sailing instructions,
when it says I have to have a tax-clearance certificate before I can
go on board?"

Naturally, he knew the answer. "That's one of our funnier national customs," he said. "Like painting the Fifth Avenue traffic lines green on St. Patrick's Day. Like you always have crumpet for tea." Willis, I was glad to note, still had certain areas of innocence. "If you leave the States by air, it doesn't matter to anyone. You're just a tourist. But if you go by boat, that could be forever. You could be skipping the country. So they want to be sure all your taxes are paid up. So anyone who sails needs that particular piece of paper."

"I hope that doesn't mean me." But I was not really serious; such solid British burghers as myself could hardly be touched by this vulgarity. Indeed, I was not serious at all until Willis said: "I think it applies to everyone going on board who earns money in America. But don't you worry. Go down and see them tomorrow. They'll dig out your last tax return, and then give you clearance."

This was slightly mysterious. "But I haven't got any tax returns to dig out. Not in America. I've never lived here."

"All the same . . ." Willis was giving me rather an odd look. "Haven't you been putting them in every year?"

"No. Why should I? You deducted the thirty percent flat rate all the time I was in South Africa. Now I pay U.K. taxes wherever I am, because I'm a diplomat."

He shook his head. "You still have to put in a return here, if it's above a certain figure. At least, that's my understanding." He swung round in his agile executive office chair, and took a small tubby book from a shelf behind it. Then he leafed through it, and stopped, and read.

"Here it is," he said after a moment. "Tax-paying made easy. . . . Any alien—that's you—earning more than $15,400 here—don't know why they picked on that figure—has to put in a U.S. tax return anyway. Then, unless there's a tax treaty between the two countries, he probably has to pay a little more than the thirty percent." He looked up. "Didn't your tax people in England tell you about this?"

"No." My tax person in England had been ill, and sometimes did not answer letters for four months, and he was not quite such a universal overseer as I could have wished. "Anyway, there *is* a tax treaty between America and Canada, and Canada and England. I pay full British taxes, for my sins. I've been doing it for years. It's all understood."

"All the same, you still have to put in—" He stopped suddenly. "How about South Africa? There was no tax treaty while you were there. That was why I had to deduct at source."'

"But you did deduct the full thirty percent, all the time."

"That was just the basic rate. I think you'll find that you owe rather more than that. Quite apart from not putting in the returns."

A slight prickling feeling about my scalp began to make itself felt. We had been having such fun, and there was going to be so much more, in the *Queen Mary*, and in London, and in Johannesburg, and in London again, and now all this blasted rubbish. . . . The extra tax—if there *was* any extra tax—didn't matter much. But the sailing permit—

I said, a little desperately: "I can't possibly deal with all this in two days! Less than two days." I looked at my watch; it was of honest gold, bought in South Africa, the country we were talking about. "Less than thirty-nine hours, in fact."

"I think you'll find—" There was that cautionary phrase again— "that they won't let you sail until you've taken care of everything."

"Oh, well." It all sounded horribly complicated, but I was still a respectable person, after all, as well as a dedicated tax-payer all the way round the globe. "I'll go and see them. Tell them I'll pay up in full—*if* I owe them anything—as soon as I get back."

"I don't think our tax people—" Willis stopped again. "It's my belief you'd better see John McCabe right away."

He was one hundred percent right.

John McCabe was Willis' talented tax-accountant, and I had met him earlier, in circumstances which lacked crisis altogether. He was now near retirement; a tall thin old man (as I would have phrased it until I reached his age), grey-haired, slightly stooping, with a very sharp eye and—most unusual for anyone in his grim occupation—a sense of humour as well.

He seemed to know more tax jokes, and to tell them better, than anyone I had met. It was just as well. In the next twenty-four hours, I certainly needed tax jokes.

He asked me a lot of questions, in a gentle voice which disguised its perceptive probe. He looked closely at the royalty accounts which I had brought across from Willis Wing. He did a little figuring, while I listened to the growling down-town traffic outside his office (it was on Liberty Street, which I tried to think of as a good omen) and waited.

Finally, he was ready. "On the face of it, you are delinquent," John McCabe told me, and I could only think: Fancy being delinquent tax-wise as well. All his jargon was very catching, and now it had caught me. He tapped lightly on the half-page of figures in front of him.

"Nineteen fifty-two is the year they're going to hit you on. They can be nasty to you for not having put in any returns, but not too nasty, because most of the time you didn't owe any taxes, and it was only a formality." He smiled. "And of course you were just a simple Britisher. . . . But 1952 is something else, and there's a little bit of 1953 involved as well. In 1952 you paid your statutory thirty percent, deducted at source, but you should have made full returns and paid quite a bit more."

"How much?"

"As near as I can figure it, twenty-three thousand dollars."

"O.K." It was an appalling amount of money, but it wasn't the end of the world. Certainly I would pay them twenty-three thousand dollars, but I couldn't possibly pay it before I sailed, early the day after tomorrow. "If I agree to all this, and promise to pay when I come back, can you get me a tax-clearance certificate?"

He was a wise old man, much wiser than I was, or perhaps would ever be. He knew the odds; I just made the mistakes. He thought for a moment, put down his pencil, and said: "No. I don't think so."

The scalp began to prickle again, in good earnest. "But I *have* to sail!" I almost wailed—and it was true enough. There was a vast amount laid on, in a carefully planned three-months' sequence. The *Queen Mary* trip itself was a long-promised treat. Then there was a whole time-table of meetings and television things in London, the film premiere of *The Ship That Died of Shame,* a booked flight to South Africa, all sorts of arrangements there, and then back to London and back to New York and back to Ottawa, in time to obey a strictly-ordained calendar of leave.

"First things first," said John McCabe soothingly. "Let's say that they agree to our provisional figure of twenty-three thousand dollars. Have you the money?"

"Yes. But it's tied up in gold shares in South Africa. It would need at least three or four weeks to sell up and get the money back here."

"How much could you raise now?"

"Oh—nothing. About a thousand dollars. Travelling money."

His face creased into its first frown, itself enough to daunt the least delinquent tax-payer in New York City. "I guess we'd better go and see them. It's too late now. But early tomorrow morning. As soon as they open. And I think I should warn you—these people have heard everything. They can be *very* tough."

It was my introduction to a wilder day than I would ever care to live again.

The Alien Income Tax Section on Lexington Avenue was a foreboding sort of place, particularly at eight-thirty in the morning: a vast room, astringently clean as conscience itself, full of little steel desks ranged in long rows, like toy soldiers. Behind each desk sat an income tax inspector; in front of each desk was an empty chair, constantly replenished from the cloudy tank of tax-payers who waited on penitent benches at the side.

A steady murmur—of woe? of pleading? of iron insistence?— already filled the air.

Could they all be delinquents? It seemed likely, at that hour, in the mood of anxiety which had steadily been building up since dawn. When John McCabe, my only serviceable escort, my frail Rock of Gibraltar, ushered me in, sat me down on one of the side benches, and began a rangy scouting of this huge cavern of delinquency, I was ready to concede defeat.

I was ready to concede anything, as long as I could go on board the *Queen Mary*, one single sunrise from today.

I noticed that even he, a character of unchallengeable probity, was nervous. Perhaps nervous was the wrong word, unless one could say that Nelson at Trafalgar, Wellington at Quatre Bras, or a fighter pilot taking off from Biggin Hill in the late summer of 1940, were all nervous.

"Keyed up" was probably a better phrase: warily alert for the dangers, the pitfalls, the chances of disaster. This was his testing time. It was his own familiar battleground. Yet perhaps the ground was weak? Perhaps this was a day of misfortune, the stars in a conjunction adverse? Perhaps the case was undeserving, perhaps I was not such a hot ally after all.

Waiting, I wanted to be anywhere but where I was. I wished I had not dined so extensively at the Pavillon the night before, in a mood of such careless indifference to fate that I had invited the entire company to join us on board the *Queen Mary,* for a champagne party at sailing time.

I wished that I did not feel that I really belonged in this room, and would belong there forever, part of the cast of the Alien Income Tax Section, the longest-running, grubbiest puppet-show on Lexington Avenue.

John McCabe returned. His shoulders still stooped, but he was looking a tiny bit brighter. "There's one I know here," he told me. "A lady. She'll see us next."

Presently we were beckoned forward. I sat down in the confessional chair, and faced the opposition. John McCabe sat by my side, on another chair filched from the next desk. The opposition, as he had told me, was a lady.

That's not a lady, I thought, already flippant in adversity. That's a U.S. Government tax inspector wearing a skirt.

I rather liked Miss or Mrs. Tax Inspector, in spite of a formidable air of competence. She was about forty: slim, blonde, not bad-looking at all. It may have been that she rather liked me; I was in the same category of the human animal in its middle years. But the stars were against us from the start. We could not declare our love. I could only declare my income, and she her judgment on it.

We told her our tale. The tale was honest enough, yet inexorably damned by fact. It seemed that I did owe them—the United States Government—this lady here—the rough sum of twenty-three thousand dollars. It was not altogether my fault, except that stupidity was always one's fault. Yet my fault remained at twenty-three thousand dollars, due on that day, with further penalties for delinquency yet to be assessed.

"But I'm booked to sail tomorrow morning," I told her, trying on a little British charm. "If I *promise* to pay as soon as I can make the arrangements, can't I have the tax clearance, on that basis?"

I might as well have been playing a broken flute in a boiler factory. Effete British charm, suspect from the start, came up against sturdy Yankee grit, wilted like sweet violets, and sank like the expendable rubbish it was.

Sure I could have my tax clearance, and catch my boat. They didn't want to be unreasonable. At this stage, they weren't going to argue about a thousand dollars here or there. Just as soon as I paid up the provisional assessment, in cash, the certificate would be mine.

"My client," said John McCabe, a watchful spectator in much of this, "is not in a position to make an immediate cash settlement. But he does have to catch the *Queen Mary* tomorrow. He has gold shares in South Africa, more than enough to cover this. But it will take a little time to realize them. My client also has diplomatic status. He would never consider for a moment—"

It was all wrong, and I knew it; it did not need a mirthless smile from across the table to tell me so. I could read the signs. I could even make up the interior dialogue for myself.

This lady did not have to catch anything so exotic as the *Queen Mary*. Perhaps she never would. In the meantime, perhaps I never would. Diplomatic status? It sounded like part of a familiar swindle. And gold shares? *They* sounded more and more like gold bricks, every time they were mentioned.

The expected verdict was handed down. She was sorry—and perhaps she really was sorry, in a theoretical sort of way. She could afford to be. The figures were there. They were the figures we had presented, the figures she was ready to accept. They showed that I owed the United States Government twenty-three thousand dollars in back taxes. I could only board the *Queen Mary* if I paid up. In barrel-head cash. Before sailing time. It was just too bad, but she had no discretion.

She had everything else, as I realized when, the very shredded wheat of a delinquent tax-payer, I emerged into the pale light of Lexington Avenue.

"I was afraid of this," said John McCabe, sadly. "I think I told you, they can be very tough."

Now I was on my own.

The situation was beginning to be appalling. I was far from home, on a cold and frosty New York morning. I was twenty-three thousand dollars short, with twenty-three hours to get hold of it. Peanuts! announced the man on the corner stall, as I flagged down a taxi to take me back to the Pierre. But he was dead wrong. It was now ten o'clock, and somehow we had to be on board, with our tax-clearance certificates, minus twenty-three thousand of those peanuts, by nine next morning.

At ten-fifteen, back at the Pierre, sipping some scalding onion soup for which I had formed a brief, breakfast-time attachment, I put through a call to the Bank of Montreal in Ottawa. Thank God for the Bell Telephone Company, I thought, as the call came through in less than a minute. They were on my side. If only everyone else would prove as efficient, as friendly, and as productive.

My bank manager, John Hobson, was his usual cheerful self. How was the weather? How was New York? How was that cute youngster? And the *Queen Mary?* All set?

"Well, no," I had to tell him. "There's been a snag, John. I need some help." I explained all about the unpaid taxes and the sailing permit, conscious that twenty-three thousand dollars sounded an awful lot of money, even to an ever-friendly Canadian bank manager: conscious also of a sizeable overdraft already, an overdraft which must have flicked into his agile mind as soon as he heard my voice.

"Twenty-three thousand?" John Hobson, in accordance with his rank, had a good cautionary tone, and he used it now. "Of course I'd be only too glad to help. That's what a bank is for. Isn't that the truth? But what's the exact position with the gold shares? Who has the actual scrip?"

"The Standard Bank in Johannesburg."

"M'm. That makes it a little difficult. Of course we would always extend your loan, against securities like that. But they would have to be deposited here."

"There isn't time for that. Look, can't you stretch a point? The shares are in South Africa. You know they'll get to you as soon as I can arrange it. But I need the tax money *now*. Today."

Already he was regretful. He was also firm, as he had every

right to be. "Stretching a point" was not bank-speech. It was loose writer's talk, liable to close scrutiny from every angle. "I'd have to take a thing like that higher up. It would need a meeting. There's also the exchange control aspect. It would mean two or three days, at the least."

"But John, can you *try?*"

The answer was prompt enough. "I'll call you back in fifteen minutes." He was a good friend. He was also a highly competent professional banker. It was impossible to judge which would win.

By the time I had finished the onion soup, John Hobson was on the line again. His answer was definitive, and absolutely correct. Personally he would like to help me. So would the bank. For a valued client like myself. . . . But even for a valued client like myself, the banking norms must be preserved.

My share certificates would have to be in their possession, and, rather more important, in negotiable form. A dollar loan against South African sterling, though perfectly feasible, was not something which could be arranged at such short notice. He was awfully sorry.

I could tell that he was. Huge banks such as his could be caught in just the same squeeze as tiny customers with their shirt tails hanging out of their trousers. Meanwhile, time was romping on. I said goodbye, and turned to the next idea on my list.

I put through a call to Johannesburg, at four dollars a minute, after doing a small mathematical wrestling-match with the time-factor. Eleven o'clock in New York was five P.M. in South Africa —or was it six? It was six, but the man I wanted was traced to his home. Once more, good old Bell Tel! . . . I made up my mind—I swore devoutly—to leave them something in my will.

The Johannesburg bank was prepared to be helpful, just like Ottawa. Certainly they could send me the share scrip, within three days, though in its present form it was not freely negotiable. Certainly, as an alternative, the shares could be sold on the Johannesburg stock exchange, and—since they had originally been bought with American dollars—the bank could send me the proceeds. But that would take time. The Exchange Control people worked slowly and carefully. Say—a fortnight?

I didn't have a fortnight. Could they not cable me an irrevocable credit of twenty-three thousand dollars, against the security of the shares, and then sell them?

Certainly they could do that, also. (Everyone was wonderfully reasonable that morning.) But a cable transfer of dollars, even in such favorable circumstances, still needed Exchange Control permission. The bank could not possibly move without it. They would have to apply formally. Once again, it would take a little time. They could probably put it through in—say, four days?

Four days was, for me, the same as four months—no good. I said another goodbye, across nine thousand miles. Now it was eleven-thirty. I paid a promised courtesy call on British Information Services. Their elegant office on the sixtieth floor of Rockefeller Center gave the climber a superb view to the south and west.

Within this sector lay the piers of the Hudson River. Within one of these piers, clear to the naked eye, lay the *Queen Mary*, waiting to sail. The red-and-black Cunard funnels were an immediate focus.

"I envy you," said the man.

It was noon. I telephoned Willis Wing. There was only one thing for it. I must ask Alfred Knopf for an advance, against my future books. This would mean—it could only mean—that his options would be extended indefinitely. It could not be helped. Though the money would be repaid within a month, the options would remain, stretching far into the future. That would be the price of accommodation—and, for any quick taker, an unusual bargain.

Willis, asked for his opinion, approved the plan only as a very last resort. I said that this was now what it was. The squeeze was on. I was going to catch the *Queen Mary* if I had to mortgage another lifetime. "I'll call you back," he said, businesslike as ever.

He called me back. The answer from Knopf was an astonishing no. It was astonishing because, even as a restive author, I was surely a minimal risk to him. Short of war, or earthquake, or my untimely death (readily insurable), what in hell could go wrong? "He doesn't want to think in terms of twenty-three thousand dollars," Willis answered.

It was late lunch-time. I had now been thinking in terms of twenty-three thousand dollars since the world's first chicken was plucked. Over a snatched smoked-salmon sandwich in the Pierre suite ("Don't look so harassed," I was told: "there's a man coming from Hammacher Schlemmer") I evolved a wild scheme. The innocent, tax-free parties could go on ahead in the *Queen Mary,* while I slipped back to Ottawa, untraceable, and then flew on to London. It was not actually illegal. Only if I left the States by ship was I forced to pay those back taxes on the nail. I could easily have changed my mind. . . .

But (some second thoughts here) it would spoil everything! There went my £870 suite, blown sky-high! And it could also be made to look and sound extremely odd. I had visions of being stopped at the Canadian border, haled back to New York, and manacled in the dock an as income tax fugitive.

"British Dip Skips Tax Probe"—I could see it all. Reluctantly I dropped the idea onto the Pierre carpet, and, with it, ran out of ideas altogether.

The phone rang (I really must send some flowers to the switchboard girl below). It was Willis Wing with a foot-of-the-scaffold reprieve. "Thayer Hobson was just on the line," he told me. "He's heard something. God knows how. But he says, can he help?"

Thus, between that late smoked-salmon sandwich, the tea-time hour which I no longer observed, and the bottle of champagne which I presently opened, Thayer Hobson of Morrow's—on the off-chance that he might one day be my publisher—sent across a cashier's certified check for twenty-three thousand dollars.

There were only two enclosures. One was an acknowledgment of debt to his firm, to be signed "in case you fall overboard." The other was a scribbled note: "We'll take care of the details later. Have fun."

At five P.M. John McCabe and I hurried down to the Alien Income Tax Section of Upper Manhattan. Now it was a different man we had to see, the man who actually took the money. But he knew the sordid story, and he was not at all impressed: not even by a cashier's check for all those thousands of dollars, obtained by an Alien Delinquent at seven hours' notice.

For him, it was only routine. People always had funny ideas about income tax. In the end, they got over them. Today, like any other day, the tax-whip had cracked, and here was the cur with its check between its legs.

In exchange for all this excruciating turmoil, compressed into a miserable harassment of time, I received a small slip of paper. It was my Certificate of Compliance, certifying that "N. Monsarret" (Christ, they even spelled my name wrong!) had satisfied Section 146(e) and (f) of the United States Internal Revenue Code.

There was another for my wife, who had no such problems, and a third for Nurse Katie Nicolson. The child Marc (at seven months) was O.K.

The plural of sequel is *sequelae*. There were a couple of memorable *sequelae* to this affair, one ludicrous, one astonishing: one as early as next morning, and one delayed for three months.

Next morning, we drove down to Pier 90, with bag and baggage, and went through the slow channelled drill which would take us on board the *Queen Mary*. I felt drained of all excitement, and of every other emotion except the exquisite relief of having won through. The colossal black hull of the ship, shapely as sculpture in motion, towered above us. It towered above everything, as if to mark our triumph, with a brave array of flags to salute it.

I came to the last hurdle of all—Customs and Immigration Control, just short of a covered passageway labelled "First Class Gangway—Up." I presented all the considerable array of documentation which had now accumulated: the passports, the tickets, the company's boarding-passes, the health certificates, the baggage vouchers, the cabin identification. They were all examined, and approved, and sometimes stamped. I kept my prize, my twenty-three-thousand-dollar jail-delivery notice, until the last.

Then I put the Certificate of Compliance (Income Tax) down on the counter.

The man, a friendly fellow in a blue peaked cap, glanced at it. "That's the next window," he said, and turned. I could see that he was looking at a blank space. "Joe!" he called, and waited. Then he shrugged his shoulders. "I guess he's not here this morning," he said. "Why don't you folks just go on ahead?"

After that, it was impossible not to enjoy the voyage.

Thayer Hobson was now in London, and we met. "Not a bad little place you've got here, not bad at all," was his comment on

Suite 418–19 at Claridge's, thus proving, what I had long suspected, that American understatement was just as effective, and phoney, as the British brand. Still sulfurously angry with Alfred Knopf, I told Thayer that I was going to take his advice, and produce that contract-breaking book, though it would mean stopping work on *The Tribe* and somehow sucking some ideas for another story from a well-worn thumb.

"It just so happens," Thayer said, "that I have a pretty good idea for a book. I've had it for years. It's a thriller. It might actually make quite an exciting film. If you want to work on it, you can have it."

"What's it about?"

"International crooks. Beautiful girls. Mysterious castles in the South of France. Mistaken identity. Near-rape. Clean-cut young American boys galloping to the rescue. There's one scene where—" He checked himself. We were in Claridge's. "Let me send you a synopsis of the story-line. I've always thought that something worthwhile *could* be made out of it. Anyway, there's a book there."

He did send me a very full synopsis, and to my surprise I liked it. It had, as he had said, an exciting swing to it. It would certainly do for me.

The book was written at an absurd speed, to shorten the interruption to the other one; eight thousand words a day for about ten days was the ruling rate, practically the speed of speech, a rate never reached before and never attempted since. It was rough and ready; I could not be proud of it; but buried beneath the easy flow there was, as Thayer had said, the germ of a good idea.

It emerged, like one of those old, speeded-up films of a chrysalis turning into a butterfly, as *Castle Garac;* and as *Castle Garac* it was promptly retyped and delivered to Alfred Knopf Inc.

It was rough, *but* ready. For good or ill, it was the option book. Still in the same rebellious mood, I put a price-tag on it of twenty-three thousand dollars, the amount which, at a crucial moment, had been denied to me earlier: a twenty-three-thousand-dollar advance royalty, and *no* future options of any kind. I was absolutely certain that it would be rejected out of hand.

After a pause, Alfred Knopf countered with an astounding cable (I was in London again). *He liked the book.* A contract for it was on its way to Willis Wing. He would pay the huge advance on signature, and publish it in the fall. And—*and*—the Literary Guild had just bought it for thirty thousand dollars. And—*and* Pocket Books would shortly be following suit, for a sum still under negotiation. Kindest regards.

As Thayer Hobson, who was entitled to take a paternal interest in all this, wrote to me later: "It's like dropping something heavy, and it floats up to the ceiling and starts singing. It's like somebody walking on his hands, eating with his feet, and putting the food you know where."

I didn't try to improve on that.

So here I was, almost exactly a year later, with an eight-pound manuscript, *The Tribe That Lost Its Head,* in my hand, a sense of achievement such as must always have come to any Christian who managed to strangle the lion, and a certain aura of invalid *faiblesse*. I was *en route* for Barbados, where, with great care, taking it very easy indeed, I might just recover a shattered health.

Meanwhile it was a celebration, with all the top brass of William Morrow Incorporated to assist me: Thayer Hobson himself, and a charming man, rather like a young Thayer with hair, named Sam Lawrence, and John Willey, their chief editor. We lunched at a French restaurant, now defunct, called the Chambord, a restaurant set in such a sleazy area of East Side New York that its elegance, and presently its cooking, came as almost a bigger shock than the saga of *Castle Garac*.

I gave them their manuscript. Their eyes gleamed. I said I would like *bouillabaisse* for lunch—no more, no less—and when it came, with a lobster on the side and generous ladlefuls of a saffron liquid to replenish it, *my* eyes gleamed. We drank a superior *rosé,* slightly tart, full of body, full of sunshine, served to us by a mountainous *sommelier* dressed as a *sommelier* should be—blue smock, buckled leather belt, silver chain of office, little tasting cup, and all.

Even the serried copper saucepans gleamed, winking down on a quartet of merry literary gents who felt at almost sinful ease with each other, and with all the world.

At half-past three, perceptibly rocking, we stood on Third Avenue outside the Chambord. Third Avenue, run-down, rimed with slushy snow, and ripe for the breakers, looked like a sunny corner of the South of France.

"What now?" Thayer asked me. He had the manuscript in an iron grip under his arm. "Can we do anything for you? Would you like to see the office?"

"On my way back would be better. I've got to do a little shopping. After that I should really get some sleep. My plane leaves in the middle of the night."

"What time?"

"The bawdy hand of the dial stands upon the prick of—about six A.M."

"O.K. What is it you want to buy?"

"Madras cotton Bermuda shorts."

"Oh, God!" This was John Willey, a sartorial purist.

"And a bow-and-arrow."

"Abercrombie and Fitch," Sam Lawrence advised promptly. "They stock everything."

Even at that moment, I was just sober enough to wonder what on earth they really thought of me. This was an English novelist? . . . But they had *The Tribe,* and I had the beginning of a marvellous, exhilarating freedom.

It was eleven o'clock, on a night as soft as velvet when we picked up the glow of Bridgetown Harbour, and the thread of lights along the shore-line. I took the last permitted tot of rum at the airline's expense; and then we dropped down from our high heaven, and came to rest in the warm, embracing air of Barbados.

Miami and the rest of the forsaken world were twelve hours astern of me, twelve hours back into limbo. Even though the pace had already slowed miraculously, they could never catch up with me now. Blessed retreat was mine, and solitude, and the most instant love-affair with a few square miles of good earth that I had ever known.

It was a first visit, and the good earth had been chosen for me, in a fortunate hour, by that same doctor-ally who wanted to see me live a little longer, in command of certain essential faculties. (Translation: "You'd better get away before you go nuts.") Even the hotel itself had been thus chosen, in the knowledge that I had lately developed an odd, embarrassing terror of heights, and that anywhere I lived must be small, and protected, and on no account more than four stories high.

The final prescription was a modest private hotel called Bagshot House, on the west coast of the island, where a fault in the coral-rock surface had produced, x million years earlier, a slight coastal depression presently to be christened St. Lawrence Gap.

When I woke on my first sunrise, and padded out onto a balcony a reassuring twenty feet above a most beautiful, tranquil-as-heaven, azure lagoon, it was to a world of the most blissful innocence and peace.

It was five o'clock in the morning, a time to treasure, a time to make one's own. I wandered down, through just-stirring corridors; patted the yawning dog, saluted the night-watchman, trod softly upon rush mats the colour of pale sunlight; and found myself on the beach, my toes in the warm Caribbean, my head already in cloudy happiness.

The beach formed the inner margin of a small blue lagoon, perfectly shaped, beyond price: the kind one saw in the advertisements, and read about in lying travel supplements, and never found—and I had found it, and it had found me. Its containing edge, three hundred feet away, was a half-circle of coral reef, across which the turning tide was just beginning to thrust—but only gently, as if to say, without insistence, that the sea still had its right of way, even through such a haven as this.

It was bound, by a compact with the moon and the stars, to assert it, twice a day. But then it would retreat again, without staking a claim, without stealing; and that was another compact, another firm promise, on which all beleaguered men could rely.

Soon I was paddling, in and out of the rising tide, and the wavelets as small and neat as pleated silk; wandering like a dog which must explore every single thing in the world; leaving smudged footprints on golden wet sand, just as at Trearddur Bay, and only forty smudged years later. But Trearddur Bay, with all its blessings, could never have shown riches like these.

It had never had delicate double-winged shells (they were called Auroras, I found later: named after the dawn, and as good as the dawn on any morning) in colours ranging from Chinese yellow to royal purple. It had never had six-inch-long flying fish stranded at the edge of the tide-mark, small gasping orphans which a small boy could, and a grown man did, help back into their saviour element.

It had never had a morning air as soft as this, and a sea green-blue like a poor man's emeralds, and ancient drift-wood which might have haunted this Caribbean strand since the first coral pushed up, an inch at a time, a foot in a hundred years, and found the air and light it had always known must be just above the surface of the sea.

It had never had coral itself, pink and grey and mottled brown; coral shaped like skulls, like the branches of trees, like fronded leaves, like the lips of women and the private parts of men.

It had never had a man, an ancient Barbadian in a terrible hat, standing waist-deep in the blue water, twirling and casting a weighted net. Twenty times he poised, and swung, and threw; twenty times the net whirled through the air, and plunged and settled in a perfect circle. Then he whipped it in, hand over hand, and examined it, hand over hand, and put whatever small trophies he had gained into the dripping sack tied across his shoulders.

As he waded ashore, I waded towards him. He smiled, but did not speak. His world was patience, toil, cunning, and fish, not indolent white tourists. But on the beach, he opened the sack—perhaps for me, perhaps for his own proper pride.

His catch was a hundred tiny fingerlings, silver like minnows, gleaming like drops of water, black-backed like baby sharks: the smallest fry of the sea, and his very own.

"What are they?" I asked.

His creased, wizened face came round. It was curiously aloof; the old fisherman, half-naked in faded, threadbare, drenched blue jeans, was still a private man. He was as strong as his own woven net; the sinews in the spare body might have lasted seventy years, but they were as good as mine. Better—they had been put to this testing use, and would be tested again, on the next tide, and the one after that.

Under the drooping tattered hat, he could have been anyone: anyone old and wise: anyone from Moses to Captain Ahab, from Chaka the Terrible to Uncle Tom.

"What was that?" he asked.

I pointed. "What are they?"

"They're fish, man!"

Silly question.

Dreamily I reached the far end of the beach, where an outcrop of rock met the curved arm of the reef. Dreamily I stood and stared, while the land-crabs, which had been scuttling away as I approached, now stood and stared themselves. The hotel, a full mile away, was only a pink dot in the distance, under an arch of sentinel palm trees bending towards the lagoon.

Presently I began to wander back again, through the warm blue water, with the sun already hot on my shoulders. Once a crabby young crab nipped at my ankle. He was welcome to it—and as I jumped I uncovered a marvellous new shell, a pale yellow helmet conch unmarked by time, still flawless after ten thousand tides had rolled it slowly landwards.

From the hotel balcony somebody waved, and I waved back. It was my hostess, Eileen Robinson, slim, attractive, cool in a flowered cotton dress. She had met me at the airport and, at midnight, reopened the bar, the kitchens, everything.

Now she offered me breakfast on my balcony—"Or would you like a rum snap first?"

I had learned already, and appreciated, that rum did not count as a drink in this benevolent corner of the world.

"I'll take both," I told her. "What's for breakfast?"

"Paw-paw. Fried dolphin. Flying fish. Corned beef hash, if you like."

Already I had found all I was looking for.

Life, tranquil life, centered on that blue lagoon. Every morning, when I woke, it was to one of those dawns which only a very clever painter, and no photographer in the world, could ever catch: lucid as water itself, fresh as young virginity, soft as the feathers on the wings of sleep.

One woke to this pale, yellow-green light with quick pleasure: instantly aware of all one's blessings, and clear-headed in spite of yesterday. As in Johannesburg, the sovereign cure for a hangover was the immaculate air itself.

The new day beckoned; one must be ready for it; ready for anything, and—best of all—ready for nothing again. The lagoon below my balcony was the shrine of all this innocent joy.

I spent hours there, sometimes exploring the tide-mark, sometimes wading out to the coral reef. Anything I saw, anything I found, whether it was the bleached feathered skeleton of a sea-bird, as dry as its sanded grave, as dead as Icarus, or a fronded sea-anemone, still beautiful, still living, still urgent for a promised harvest, was part of the same dream of home and life.

I would plod a slow, meandering, barefoot course, or bend to look at new treasures (the reef was alive!—alive all the time, with all the magic of creation), or stare seawards towards the deep water, where the sails of the fishing fleet dipped and swung and stood taut against the north-east Trades. Sometimes I fished myself, with my sophisticated, totally ineffective bow-and-arrow: opposing the whole might of Abercrombie and Fitch against the barracuda which, slim as pencils, agile as electric eels, patrolled up and down the reef.

Once the arrow sliced through the only vacant half-inch between two of these prizes; never did it strike home. But this still seemed the least important thing in the world, even when set against secret ambitions to wade back to the hotel with some great gleaming trophy from the sea, and invite the natives to feast. Happily I returned to standing and staring, savouring the only real prizes, the ocean brine and the hot, life-giving sun.

It was in the very air, this climate of disengagement. It was in the tide, washing across the reef like an invader, yet due to disappear in six hours and twelve minutes exactly. I found that I could watch a single wave—watch it swell, watch it break, watch it retreat, watch it die—and think how stupid, how futile, how tiny was all human endeavour. Such thoughts would never produce a book, but by God! they made contented men!

It was in these moments of trance, in this rum-soaked, sun-blessed, sea-circled paradise, that there was a temptation to contract-out forever; to cast off and sail—by island schooner, by dugout canoe, by outrigger catamaran, by raft—anyhow and anywhere, as long as it was far enough away; to let the awful argumentative world go by; to disappear without trace—and then, if man, stupid man, had to write instead of live, to come back five years later with the best book ever written about the tidal influences of the Humboldt Current: with a skin the colour of rubbed mahogany, and nothing to say to the inquisitive except: "It was heaven."

At noon I would wander back to the hotel—now my home, my shell, as everything on the reef except the questing barracuda seemed to have a shell of sorts—and taste the delights of Inside Soup and whatever else was available for the beach-combing lay-about who had found this submerged, dark-green, urgeless level of contentment. Then I would sleep, fathoms deep, under drugs innocent and insidious at the same time: rum, food, sun, the caress of the sea, the denial of all the built-up world, and of the demanding clock which was the sun itself.

Eileen Robinson, who knew my mood exactly, as she had to know the mood of any other twelve-dollar-a-day tyrant, "ran inter-ference" for me, as we phrased it in Canadian football circles. She knew that, basically, I was still under that blessed "No Visitors" embargo. Sometimes she went a little far, though with the best intentions in all Barbados.

"There were some Canadians here this afternoon," she said once. "They wanted to see you, but I sent them away."

"Who were they? Did you get their names?"

"Mr. Massey, I think it was. Rather a nice old man."

It was just the Governor-General of Canada.

At night soft rain fell obligingly, washing all clean again. At night one slept like the infant Jesus, blameless, guileless, sinless, destined for heaven because it had been set down long ago, in sacred, cool, unarguable print. I would live! If I kept very still, and broke no laws, and traded no insults, and tried to do abso-lutely nothing except float in and out with the tide, I would live.

I had come to Barbados, so my doctor told me, to "unwind." It was another jargon word, like *hospitalization,* like a "fun" party, like love. Sometimes I thought: unwind from what? But I knew very well. In darker moments, I knew absolutely, down to the last half-inch of the very stinking root of knowledge.

Who can tell how oft he offendeth? Usually one had a damned good idea, and was either sad about it, or proud of such accom-plishment. In the present case, I was never more than baffled.

Women are tender plants, like wire wool: soft to a firm hand, harsh to a giving surface, treacherous, surprising, perverse: be-yond forecast or concise estimate. I lived—*we* lived—in a world of violence and gentleness mixed, like the best or the worst of Indian curries, where sweet chutney, or bland coconut, warred with a fierce, breath-stopping, bitter infusion from hell's own kitchen.

It was a His and Hers world of Dexedrine and Equanil, love and hate, gin and Campari, exhilaration and deadly boredom, admiration and smirking mockery; plenty of both, plenty of all, *enough* of everything to choke an elephant, poison a saint, strike the observer dumb.

Sweet reconciliation could, in a moment, give way to wary neutrality, to fear, to plain cowardice. "Anything for a quiet life" grew positive toadstools of poltroonery, successive crops of Late Flowering Funk. I had such a fearful amount to lose.

I could lay solemn claim to being the only man in the Province of Quebec whose forehead had been grazed by a box of fifty Dunhill's No. 1 *Romeo y Julieta* which, having cannoned off his troubled brow, then shattered the neon tube in a brand-new twenty-four-inch television set.

I was certainly the only man who did nothing about it. But I could also lay solemn claim to storing up, within a furious brain, all the exact, gruesome details of this encounter.

I could not forget. No one else seemed to remember.

It was all my fault? I had come to Barbados to do a little thinking, as well as indulge a little self-pity, a little resentful rage against heaven. But Christ stone the crows, I was an *angel*! It was all my fault? Perhaps, perhaps. Books came before wives—was that a betrayal? Two children in eleven months—had that been too ardent, too selfish, too silly for words?

My esteemed grocer, Monsieur Vaillant, had been very concerned about this. But only on my account—this was Quebec. "You will exhaust yourself," he told me. "These things affect a man's strength. You must take great care." But he could add a little Gallic wit—Quebec Gallic. "However, there are compensations. In this province, when you have had ten children, you get one free."

Ten children? I did not want ten children. Sometimes I wanted none; usually I wanted the two incumbents, the two darling tenants, plus peace—PEACE, in capital letters, in blood if need be, in solemn compact anyway. These were still early days. We had only been married three years. But already I could be in despair, in a mood of rueful retreat, in humble surrender if surrender would only be accepted.

I would wag my tail: I would offer my tail on a golden dish marked "DOG." I would *eat* my tail.

I wanted to love, and I wanted to write. But I could no longer add the two things up. I could only subtract them, one from another, taking turn-about to name the loser, like an idiot child with a grown-up puzzle, in nonsensical, degrading, fatuous nonarithmetic.

The law of diminishing returns was not only for woodenheaded, baffled economists. It was for husbands. Already there were days and weeks when I expected nothing, and the man who expected nothing gave nothing.

Why should he? Why get your head shot off when you could cash a check and duck out of sight, out of mind, out of life? The storm-signals, like the shout of "Wolf!," grew meaningless. The cries of rage lost their impact. The noisy weeping became laughable.

But I could not go to hospital every time I had to finish a book.

Yet I *had* finished the book, against odds which often seemed insurmountable; now, a stretcher-case with only my little bow-and-arrow for defense, I was recovering. It was all part of the same wildly theatrical farce. The farce grew more convincing, more pleasurable anyway, when the verdicts on *The Tribe* reached me. Thayer Hobson sent a heartening cable, Desmond Flower of Cassell's a letter at least as encouraging as the one which had signalled *The Cruel Sea*.

Yet—had all life come down to that single, cautious, mousy word?—*yet* the happy issue only reminded me of another pressing problem. There was a firm of money-lenders in Ottawa called Household Finance. I had no dealings with them; I only registered their impassioned pleas on the radio ("Bills getting you down? H.F.C. is waiting for you!"). But the two key words could still strike home to a timid heart.

I had problems of my own, in the realm of Household Finance, and they then seemed, in my blind and blissful innocence, the biggest problems imaginable. The till, forever replenished, was forever empty.

I read Thayer's cable, and Desmond's letter, on a sunlit balcony. I drank to the future gratefully. It sounded as though *The Tribe* would be published with all available panache, and would make a lot of money. But one success could only breed another. It had to, because one success had already disappeared down a gilded drain.

The Tribe would come and go, like the other one. The squirrel's cage would still be there, turning and turning like that blasted "Wheel of Fortune" song. I was forty-six already, to my shame and regret. Would I still be in the excremental soup when I was fifty-six? *Sixty-six?*

To this problem, and its peculiar setting, I presently returned.

2.

It was, and is, a large house, the house where I was bound. Across the river from Ottawa, and therefore in the Province of Quebec by a technical half-mile, it had been built by a construction engineer for his own enjoyment, in 1931, when high-quality materials were cheap and bread-line labour was cheapest of all; and sold to me by one of the sharper real-estate operators of our time, Shann Sherwood.

Mr. Sherwood's starting price was ninety thousand dollars; mine was seventy-five thousand dollars. After a prolonged minuet, where fancy footwork alternated with cries of pain and appeals for justice, mercy, and a reasonable attitude, we settled for eighty-two thousand dollars. It could be called a kind of victory; he had come down eight thousand, I had only come up seven thousand dollars. Plus a little bit more.

"*Not* included in the sale price," Mr. Sherwood wrote promptly, when the preliminary contract was signed, "are the two cords of firewood stacked in the basement. These are best quality trimmed logs. Rather than put you to the trouble of having them carted away" (now watch that, watch that, Mr. Sherwood! It's not my trouble, it's *your* trouble) "I suggest a token price of twenty dollars."

I paid the token price of twenty dollars, thus making the final figure leap to a deplorable $82,020. Though the logs kept at least one room warm for one winter, I still felt outwitted.*

The house, solid as Gibraltar, built of grey stone, oak panelled inside, with well-proportioned rooms (all eighteen of them), was called, to no one's surprise, Stone House. It was set, surrounded by huge elms, in sixteen acres, with a view down to the Ottawa River and the far-off Peace Tower of Parliament across an un-broken eight-acre lawn—and, for students of time-and-motion, it takes a writer, working turn-about with a gardener (old, but sparked by some good Indian blood, and called, naturally, Dinty Moore), a day and a half to mow and trim eight acres of prime greensward to the satisfaction of both.

I adored that house, which really was handsome inside and out, and though I presently grew to loathe it, and threw it back to the winds—for that profitable $105,000, *minus the carpet under-felt*—in two years and four months, the early honeymoon was memorable.

Stone House, when seen in a certain light which was the one I chose to see it in, seemed to be a bargain: an ex-white-elephant (empty for four years) which suddenly suited an unexpected owner. If I wanted a monument (and even then I could acknowl-edge the motive) then this was it.

It cost a fortune to buy, a fortune ($58,000) to furnish, and a fortune ($2,000 a month) to run. It even cost $3,350 to paint (double the estimate, but after I had been encouraged to argue about this, it turned out that all sorts of tricky refinements had been added, and I had to back down, with an embarrassed grin and a check for the full amount), and $1,080 a year to heat.

Servants were a problem, but only the finding of them; paying for our small regular army (butler, cook, nurse, two maids, a gardener, a girl who sewed all the time, an odd-job man, basically a plumber, who later fell out of a tree, a man to plow the snow and another to lop and prune the elms)—this was mere routine, a writer's little chore, like sharpening his pencil every week.

* Such marginal losses always inflict disproportionate wounds. When the time came to sell, the buyer, Mrs. Jules Loeb, insisted that the underfelt of the main staircase carpet (approximate cost, $150) *must* be included in the pur-chase price of $105,000. Otherwise, there would be no sale. Outwitted again, I could only surrender.

So was having a secretary, Mrs. Macdonell, my most stalwart ally, who among a lot of other things kept the accounts and, being married to a Royal Canadian Mounted Police sergeant, was a paragon of discreet non-comment. So, I suppose, was the £750 which it cost to import one of my sisters-in-law from South Africa; and if she stayed with us for seven months, who but a mean old bastard would even notice the fact?

"Well, it'll cost you!" was the recurrent, cautionary phrase used by people invited to do something, or to sell something, or to change something, or to repair something. "Well, it'll cost you," said the man who came to see what could be done about stripping off the jungle-strong ivy creeper and poisoning its roots (and indeed, it did cost thirty dollars).

Everything cost me, where Stone House was concerned. All the grotesque figures should have been alarming, but they never were. I loved the house, like the life, and as long as I could keep on writing, there should always be enough coming in to cope with the bath-water flow running out.

It cost a fourth fortune to enjoy the place.

I had come back from Barbados to celebrate my birthday, with a carefully planned dinner for eighteen. We just happened to have eighteen Crown Derby soup bowls, big plates, little plates, tiny plates, salad plates, butter dishes, and coffee cups; plus the necessary finger-bowls, cocktail glasses, sherry glasses, champagne glasses, liqueur glasses, tumblers, table mats, and ash-trays; plus the vital fish knives, fish forks, other knives, other forks, big spoons, little spoons, snail tongs, cheese scoops; plus enough salted peanuts and fried onion rings to start things off, and enough coffee-sugar crystals, brandy, Cointreau, Curaçao, Tia Maria, Grand Marnier, white *crème de menthe, Marc de Bourgogne,* whisky, Carlsberg lager, and orange juice to round out a modestly hospitable dinner party.

Add: guest towels, Kleenex, cigarettes, cigars, after-dinner mints, flowers, Alka-Seltzer, and monogrammed match-boxes.

N.B. Had I remembered to tell Angus to tell Dinty to switch on the arc lights in the parking area, and to have the Land-Rover ready in case anyone got stuck in the snow?

Answer: No. Sometimes, fantastically, unbelievably in this world of yes, the answer was no. But it was a superior evening, my forty-sixth, nonetheless.

Among the birthday presents brought by the slightly captive guests were a Visitors' Book from the darling old American ambassador, Douglas Stuart, a Chopin record from Lou Rasminsky, Governor of the Bank of Canada, a bottle-opener from Doug Abbott, lately Minister of Defence and now a Supreme Court judge; another bottle-opener, mink-handled, from George Drew, the Leader of the Opposition, a bottle of beautiful Bourbon whiskey from Giff Scull, the American naval attaché, and a three-record version of *La Forza del Destino* from crony and Q.C. Bernard Alexandor—a record which, coming from La Scala, Milan, with Maria Callas as Leonora, and Richard Tucker and Nicola Rossi-Lemeni to complement her rapturous voice, was soon to convert me to opera in general, as the supreme expression of music, and to Verdi in particular as the composer of all composers.

It was a good party, as usual; and, as usual, it was based on a strange, complicated, and vilely expensive operation. The extraordinary fact about it, and about all such parties, was that in terms of dollars to spend on them we had none at all.

I drew my modest salary as Chief of U.K. Information; and a grudging Treasury, before they changed the rules,* allowed me to keep, out of my dollar earnings, nine hundred dollars a year—rather less than the monthly wage-bill for the staff.

Everything else which went to make such an evening, in such a house, from the champagne and its silver cooler to the tall ivory candles on the table (*and* the table), had to be imported from England and paid for in sterling.

The juggling act was entirely legal. It certainly aided the export drive. But it really was the most farcical exercise I had ever undergone since I was taught how to make Molotov cocktails at H.M.S. *King Alfred* in 1940.

I have already quoted a phrase in *Venus and Adonis,* which long ago used to make my imagination smoke a bit: where Venus falls down backwards, and Adonis (who always sounded rather coy, if

* Without telling me. Certain things one finds out too late in life; and too late in life it transpired that this ruling was "out of date," and that I should have been advised that I could retain the lot.

not queer) accidentally falls on top of her, and it says: "Now is she in the very lists of love, Her champion mounted for the hot encounter."

The very lists of love, in my case, were something else again. They came from Lawn and Alder, Gordon and Gotch, Fortnums, the Army and Navy Stores, Harrods, Peter Jones, Cox and Kings, and Saccone and Speed, and many another august firm accustomed to exporting the best of everything to our far-flung empire.

In the garden, the noble lawn outside my study window was a delicious focus for a wandering eye. Across the drive, under the elms, the swimming pool waited for its first spring filling. In the garage, the Land-Rover (sometimes the only weapon which could get me to the office through winter snow) was ready for me; so was the horrid blue Chevrolet; so was the marvellous, run-of-the-mill Rolls-Royce, a grey Silver Cloud bought to replace the Continental Bentley which had been a disappointment.

Rolls-Royce, I found, included a wonderful dead-pan directive in their manual for the new owner. *"Running In:* You should not exceed 90 m.p.h. for the first 500 miles."

In my panelled study, the great log fire kept me warm while I thought about the next book, and did not find much of an answer. In the immaculate drawing-room, the William and Mary veneered walnut spice-cabinet (now accommodating bottles instead) gleamed its welcome. In the sunroom, the wrought-iron furniture from Hammacher Schlemmer was more elegant and comfortable than any overstuffed alternative.

In the kitchen, Mrs. Evans was busy on the roast duck. In the pantry, Angus was polishing the silver. On a distant flower-bed, Dinty Moore was tending the first brave tulips. In the nursery, just over my head, subdued thuds through the solid ceiling indicated that brother was at odds with brother—or was helping him to do something novel and awful: it was difficult to tell.

The phone rang. It was Willis Wing from New York. *The Tribe,* which was being read "on the coast" (meaning that province of the United States centered on Los Angeles), might possibly be sold as a film to Philip Yordan, who had made such a good job of *The Caine Mutiny.*

At the club, I had overheard someone say: "That guy lives like a pig with its ass in butter." Could it be me?

In the nursery . . . I now had two sons. Indeed, I had three, though Max, the original model, already fourteen, was not in evidence, except when he flew across from London during the holidays.

His two half-brothers, aged three and aged two, all my pretty chickens in the Canadian coop, were in charge of Katie Ann Nicolson, nurse.

There are not many human beings of whom one can say: This one is as God intended, warm, generous, kind, hard-working, and efficient. Katie Nicolson came to Stone House by happy chance, selected after a simple exchange of letters before the computer-age fouled things up for good. Born, bred, and raised in the farthest Highlands, trained in Edinburgh, she was a little smiling Scots girl for whom young children had some magic attraction.

It seemed to be entirely mutual. From the first meeting, the small nursery grew large in contentment, and even, now and again, in good behaviour.

In Max's case, I had never been there when I wanted to be, and never enjoyed his small years except in sessions just as small. Now I staked my claim, as a matter of daily routine. At noon I would stop work, or stop fooling around with a slow-thinking typewriter, and say: "I'll take them now, Katie," and shovel the small load into my study.

The seven-foot steel desk had two reliable pull-out shelves, one on either side of the center space. A child was planted on each, and sat there, within reach of a guardian arm. (If I could be scared of any fifth floor, perhaps they could be worried about a drop of twenty-nine inches.) We then pursued an ordained pattern of social intercourse.

"First we'll have a little think," I said. For a couple of minutes they would stare at me, as bright as buttons. Already they knew what a think was; it was smiling silence. Then: "Now both of you tell me a story, one at a time." They were rather short stories, particularly Anthony's, whose command of English was unripe. Occasionally he would produce a string of unrelated syllables, whereupon the two of them would burst into roars of laughter, and I knew that Anthony must have made a very good remark indeed.

"Now I'll finish my drink," and I did so, while they giggled at the theatrical slurping noises which were, I suppose, rather bad for nursery discipline. "Now we'll go for a walk," was the one after that, and the walk was always down the long slope of green lawn, to Aylmer Road and its quick-moving traffic at the bottom.

The two dogs followed us, one making heavy weather of it, the other prancing like a miniature heraldic lion in motion. One was an old, crotchety Sealyham, shortly to disgrace itself with two snarling snaps at the human race, the second of which missed Anthony's eye by less than an inch and left what looked like a life-long scar. After a flurry of blood, shock, dashes to the hospital, and rabies injections which were themselves a considerable hazard, the Sealyham, his grey hairs dishonoured, was asked to leave.

The other dog was mine: a small, sprightly, utterly neurotic French poodle called Noblesse Oblige, which could be very good company when in the mood, and a real little creep when it was not. It survived two years, and then disappeared; run over on the Aylmer Road, it was tossed into the nearest snow-drift, where it was discovered, three months later, on a sad spring morning.

On the return journey, I would say, like my father: "I've got a bone in my leg," and climb the last slope at a sorry limp. Then it was: "Now we'll go for a little drive," and at that point, stern discipline took over. This was *my* Rolls, not their rocking-horse.

"*Don't* jump about. *Don't* touch the door handles. *Don't* put your feet on the seats." These were of finest, pale-yellow ox-hide, and smelled, for more than three years, as fresh and exciting as the new-born car itself. We drove along the Aylmer Road, giving way, like anyone else with a grain of sense in his head, to the dashing Quebec drivers, as far as a high-class hunting and riding stables, known to the ribald, though not to my sheltered children, as the Horses' Astor. Then back to the Country Club, for *one* ice-cream, or Coke, or some other wild, fizzy, pre-lunch stimulant.

Then it was home again, and discipline again, which might perhaps last for the next five minutes. "*Both* wash your hands. *Both* eat all your lunch. *Both* do exactly as Katie tells you. Otherwise—" the language was already coarsening, "there'll be one *hell* of a row!"

Sometimes I said: "Otherwise you will make me very sad," and they would look at me as if their little hearts were ready to crack.

I had time to play father, because I was on retirement leave from my job.

By now I had been in the Information Service for very nearly the second five-year term which I had contracted for, privately, on that summer morning in London in 1951; and the strain was beginning to tell, possibly on both sides.

Certainly this had nothing to do with the current High Commissioner in Canada, to whose staff I was attached as "Counsellor (Information)"—Lieutenant-General Sir Archibald Nye. The enormous luck which had given me Sir Evelyn Baring as boss in South Africa had flowered again; the new overlord was another paragon of important virtues. But though there was remarkable similarity between the two men—both public servants whose energy and devotion went far beyond their duty, and perhaps beyond our deserts—yet there was remarkable contrast also.

Baring, the aristocrat in action, had descended from above. Archibald Nye had rammed a pathway upwards, with astonishing success.

He was a regimental sergeant-major's son, educated at a school for the sons of N.C.O.s, and he started a long climb as a dog-soldier, a 1914 private with a rifle on his shoulder and a ferocious war to fight. He ended his military career, twenty-seven years later, as Vice-Chief of the Imperial General Staff, for a term of years which had never been more crucial for Britain: 1941–46.

He then rounded out all this with an impressive string of peace-time jobs—Governor of Madras, High Commissioner to India, and now to Canada. He was fifty-eight when I met him, sixty-one when I said goodbye.

Like Baring, he was a great man to work for; and, again like Baring, one of the few teetotallers who, as company, was ever worth a damn. The High Commission house was called Earnscliffe, beautifully sited on the banks of the Ottawa River: a handsome old country place which had once been the home of Canada's very first Prime Minister, Sir John A. Macdonald. To be invited there, to make up the numbers or plug a gap at a formal dinner-party, was not an office chore. It was always wholly enjoyable.

Diplomatic Ottawa was a good deal more formal and patterned than anything I needed to cope with in Johannesburg. The list of things one had to do on arrival, and the directives for our later behaviour, covered twenty-two foolscap pages, and ranged in subject from curtseying (*not* to a Provincial Lieutenant-Governor) to the proper manipulation of visiting cards (bring five hundred with you, as a starter): from where to seat Her Excellency's Lady-in-Waiting at a dinner party (she ranked as the wife of a Deputy Minister) to how to get hold of an Esso credit card.

The Ottawa Information Office could only be called "Fair," like unsatisfactory conduct in the Navy, and the accommodation —a converted bowling alley overlooking the Colonial Coach Lines main bus station—was not impressive. There was a first-class man, Donald Kerr, as my deputy director: an Australian who worked with rare, tremendous appetite and who, in the coming expansion program, was to prove himself a tower of strength.

But expansion was certainly the first thing I thought of, as soon as I looked the place over: one such office, and a staff of twenty-four, was hardly adequate for a country of seventeen million people and nearly four million square miles.

I was still enjoying the job very much, and the new country was one I had always wanted to see. Sir Archibald Nye believed strongly in the information arm of his High Commission. But belief was not one hundred percent firm among my other colleagues: not in information, not in me.

At the outset I was told that I was not to make any speeches or broadcasts, for at least six months, until I "knew what to say." I had known what to say for the last seven years in South Africa, a far trickier country, and the restriction was irksome. However, I had to turn down a round hundred of such invitations, without any valid explanation, and that made me feel a fool as well.

As time went on, it began to appear that I couldn't really be trusted in other spheres.

Writing a best-seller, and thereby making large sums of money in the process, was not the best pathway to advancement in the civil service. I was now earning quite a superior salary, measured by the standards of the past; when the rent allowance and the local cost-of-living differential were added, it came to £4,140 a year.

But there were also reports from time to time in the press that my earnings outside the service, as a writer, must be something like ten times that amount. The fact could not have been endearing, though it need not have become an occasion of guilt.

A simple calculation showed that whatever I wrote, by way of official memorandum or draft dispatch, was delivered practically free, while anything I produced for outside consumption earned about ten shillings a word. The contrast must have seemed irresistible. Before long my official prose, which went first to the Deputy High Commissioner, began to have a progressively rough time at Earnscliffe.

The blue pencil came to the fore, and hung poised over each paragraph. What might serve well enough for popular fiction would *not* pass scrutiny here. "Poor construction, Monsarrat," was a phrase used on at least one occasion. "Too many adjectives. (Verbiage.) This is far too long. (Develop.) This surely needs expansion." And sometimes: "I suggest you do it again."

Not the chief editor of Cassell's, not even Alfred Knopf, would have essayed such slaughter.

There was, occasionally, some arbitrary editorship indeed. Once, when I was bringing up to date a survey of the senior members of the Press Gallery, and removed a man who had been dead for a year, he was reinstated.

It had its funny side, but it was deeply depressing nonetheless. I was beginning to think that I would never really prosper in the service, never get the sort of job I wanted; never even be a Deputy High Commissioner, with a little blue pencil in my little grey fist. The social differences between information personnel and those on the other side of the green baize door were still marked. We might be useful; but we still lived and died in the warrant officers' mess.

I could foresee a five-year term in Canada, and probably another five in India. By then I would be fifty-three, and would sweat out my last seven years at the Commonwealth Relations Office in Whitehall, reorganizing their film-strip filing system.

The willing horse so easily became the silly ass. Perhaps, with the best of motives and the worst of common sense, I had already stayed in the service too long.

But my resignation, in the end, was triggered off by a very un-likely man, in a most unusual way.

It came during the last week of that 1955 trip to South Africa, which began in the Alien Income Tax Section of Upper Man-hattan and finished up at my father-in-law's house in Plettenberg Bay, on the south coast of the Cape Province between Port Eliza-beth and Cape Town.

This was a gem of a place, set back in the sandhills within sight of the beach and the sea: within sight of the old whaling station which had been the original reason for Plettenberg Bay's exist-ence, and within sight of the hotel, which naturally belonged to my friend Soli Ornstein.

We were very content there, showing off the infant Marc to cooing Afrikaner neighbours, voyaging about in a motorized surf-boat, and eating all the fish I caught (our staple diet, meat). But by the end I, at least, was not at all content.

The crack in the blue sky came in the form of an express letter from the British High Commission in Cape Town.

This was polite, as usual, and concise, but somewhat ominous. The Commonwealth Relations Office had been in touch with them. There had been a report in a London newspaper of an interview, in which I was quoted as saying that I was about to publish a novel about race relations in South Africa.

C.R.O. was naturally concerned about this, in view of my recent term of office in that country, and felt that they should have more details on what might become a sensitive, or even a controversial matter. In short, what was this all about?

I had, of course, a perfectly good answer to this, and I made it promptly. The man in London had got it wrong, I assured the High Commissioner's office. My novel, which would not be out for at least a year, was not about South Africa—I would never have considered such a project. It was about Africa generally—African problems, African solutions, African hopes for the future.

It was set in an invented country—a mythical island, in fact—which did not bear the slightest resemblance to South Africa. South Africa indeed was scarcely mentioned, and her peculiar race-situation not all all. The book, if it took any particular stand-point, was in praise of British colonial history and administration.

It was a detailed answer, because in all the circumstances I felt

that they, and the Commonwealth Relations Office, were entitled
to it. The reaction was speedy, and scarcely expected. In view of
the information I had given, I was told, it would be best if I came
to Cape Town as soon as possible, to discuss the matter with our
newly arrived High Commissioner.

This was a discomforting turn, for a special reason. The new
High Commissioner was Sir Percivale Liesching, who had been
the Permanent Under-Secretary at the Commonwealth Relations
Office and was now taking up his last job—a job of immense im-
portance, in the light of the fading British connection with South
Africa—before his retirement.

I was lucky enough to know him well, from various calls while
in London, to admire him without qualification, and to know also
that his reputation as an immensely capable administrator was
founded on solid fact, and not on any artificial aids to career-
building.

He was the third in my gallery of three public servants who
deserved all their medals twice over.

It was therefore all the more worrying to have to face him on a
matter like this. I could not help feeling, also, that he had plenty
of more important things to occupy his time.

The meeting was in two parts, and grew progressively more disturbing. Sir Percivale, an iron-grey man with a formidable chin,
gave me a drink, as he had always done before. Then he began
to ask a lot of questions, prefaced by a brief recapitulation of the
ground-rules.

I was a permanent civil servant, subject to the general proviso
that while I was in the service I would not write, for publication,
anything which made any reference, or bore any relation, to the
work I was doing or the country where I was *en poste*. On retirement, I would still be subject to the Official Secrets Act, so far as
it involved any confidential material acquired in the course of
my duties.

I was aware of this?

Yes.

So. . . . The cross-examination started, and it was, as might
have been expected, a very good one.

This book of mine. He had read my letter, and he was sure that
it had cleared up a lot of questions, as far as London was con-

cerned. But there were still some further points on which he, and they, would like assurance. This mythical country of mine. It might not be South Africa. Personally he was sure that it was not. But could it be *supposed* that it was South Africa, with consequent possibilities of embarrassment? Secondly . . .

Tenthly and finally: Would I be submitting the book to the Commonwealth Relations Office before I published it?

This was a crucial point, and it had to be faced. I felt bound to answer: No, I had not thought of submitting it, because the book did not concern either my job, or C.R.O. In similar circumstances, I had never submitted *The Cruel Sea* to the Admiralty, because I knew very well that there was nothing objectionable in it, from the security point of view, even though it was assuredly based on "knowledge acquired during service in the Royal Navy."

Sir Percivale Liesching, bless him, could pounce very swiftly, and he did so now.

The Cruel Sea, he reminded me, had been published after the war, and at least five years after I ceased to be a naval officer. This book about *Africa* (he could smile quickly, as well as pounce) would be published while I was still a member of the Commonwealth Relations Office, and it would follow a very recent appointment to that particular part of the world. In the circumstances, C.R.O. would certainly feel happier . . .

All right, I told him. I *would* submit it, if I were still in the public service.

I was being pressured, and I knew it, and he knew it: courtesy, consideration, measured language still carried their cutting edge. That was possibly—probably—the whole point of our meeting. But I was scarcely prepared for the second stage of the interview. Liesching pressed his bell, and asked a senior member of his staff to come in.

This was someone whom I knew only from inter-office correspondence. It was clear that he did not know me, except as a potential nuisance; it was enough that he knew the reason for the summons. It was even more clear that the session had now become formal, and disciplinary, and that he was to be the witness to it. Suddenly, I did not like this at all.

My attention, Liesching said, when the third man was seated, was drawn to the Official Secrets Act. It was also drawn to my undertaking not to use any material of a confidential nature obtained in the course of my employment. While I was so employed, he must advise me that any book I wrote, even remotely connected with any material I might have acquired during this employment, should be submitted to the Commonwealth Relations Office before publication. It would be better if I sent them a synopsis of my new novel, as soon as possible.

Our witness made unobtrusive notes—the most obtrusive notes of all.

I was by now rather angry, and angry with a good man, for the first time in the whole of my official life. Sir Percivale Liesching was entirely in the right: he was only doing his duty, with his customary thoroughness and honesty. If London was worried, it was up to him to convey the fact to me, beyond any argument, or any later dispute.

I could never admire him less, because of such a confrontation. I even believed, and certainly hoped, that it was not much to his taste. But the anger, the stinging wound, remained.

It was the presence of the witness, doubtless by C.R.O. directive, which got me on the raw. The implications were obvious, and enraging. *Two* people could now swear—if it came to swearing —that I had been duly warned of my dangerous course. Should I even try to twist out of it . . .

Wouldn't those niggling bastards ever trust me? Still furious, I drove back along the winding Garden Route from Cape Town to Plettenberg Bay: three hundred miles of sunlit, and then moonlit, coastal landscape, over hill and dale, across small mountains, past rolling beaches—one of the most magical drives still available to man.

Eleven miles from home, I had a puncture. Eleven miles, out of three hundred—why couldn't my silly old father-in-law, with all those bloody servants, have his tires checked? I walked those last eleven miles, under a moon, and then the stars. There had been rumours of a wild cat, a real wild cat, a mountain lion or puma (or cougar: *Felis Concolor,* anyway) loose in the area.

There was a herd of elephants there already, wandering the Knysna Forest. Every time the roadside grass stirred, or a twig snapped, I braced myself for blood and trampling, claw marks and death.

They would only match what I felt had happened to me in Cape Town.

At some point during that eleven-mile plod, which finished at 2 A.M., I made up my mind. For a whole gallery of reasons, it was obvious that I could not be a civil servant and a writer at the same time. Even if it had not been, by a fantastic margin, the more profitable task, writing was the job for me.

Next morning, fortified by sunshine and Cape brandy, I sent to Sir Percivale Liesching, without the smallest shrinkage of respect, my letter of resignation, and repeated it to Archie Nye, with the same undiminished personal regard.

It could take effect, I said, at any time convenient to them within the next year—my last bow towards duty, discipline, and the pride and pleasure I had always felt, even in such confined employment.

In reply, Liesching sent back one of the nicest letters I had ever received from anyone. Its general purpose was to say how sorry he would be if our recent interview had impelled me to resignation. It had been his duty, etc. . . . I had done valuable work in the Information Service, and it was good to hear that I would not be leaving immediately.

One of the funnier, or sadder, aspects of all this was something which Sir Percivale Liesching did not then know (though I took good care to tell him about it later): that he himself figured prominently in *The Tribe*, as the model or prototype for Sir Hubert Godbold, the Permanent Under-Secretary of my "Scheduled Territories Office," and the only wholly admirable character in the book.

As it turned out, I stayed on for another full year, and I tried to make it a good one. With stalwart help from Sir Archibald Nye, I was able to complete the expansion job on our information service in Canada; in fact I rammed it home up to the hilt, where it still stands—my only monument, but a better one than that stone house on the hill could ever be.

It was Nye himself who had shown me the way, about a year earlier. He came to lunch one day, when we were both temporary bachelors, with wives either visiting relatives in England or addressing women's clubs in far-off Prince Edward Island.

While we walked to and fro under the trees afterwards, he remarked that on the west coast of Canada, where he had just been on a speaking tour, no one except a few newspaper editors who were on our mailing list had ever heard of the U.K. Information Office.

I said that this, though mortifying, was more than likely. Vancouver, for example, was over twenty-five hundred miles from Ottawa—and Vancouver didn't like Ottawa, anyway. There was no reason why they should know that we existed. Unless we were operating on the spot, they never would.

"Exactly!" He had a way of tossing his head up when he wanted to emphasize a point, and he did so now. "So we should be there."

"Yes." After lunch, in my own house, I didn't say "sir."

"And some other places too?"

"Two or three, anyway."

"Right!" He rubbed his hands together, as if he could smell from afar off a battlefield at least as crucial as Alamein or Tobruk. "What I would like you to do," he said, "is to let me have a plan. The ideal information service, to cover the whole of Canada. With all the details—offices and costs and everything."

"It would be very expensive," I told him. I had been playing round with the idea for some months, and the figures, when set against our perennial, atrocious, dreary dollar situation, were awful.

"Excellent!"

It was an unusual word to hear from a civil servant, but he was an unusual civil servant. I believed the man, and therefore the word, and I went to work.

I knew exactly what I wanted to do: to improve on that inadequate, one-office, Ottawa set-up, which simply could not cover the ground. We needed to be *there*—and "there" meant having an office, and a man, and a staff, and a visible presence, in all the major population centers, from the Atlantic to the Pacific.

It was an important idea because, as far as I could judge, the Canada-British link seemed to be fading gently away, like that South African one—though here it was not politics, nor principles, but lack of contact. The miserable wet hand of the Treasury, intent on their penny-pinching travel restrictions (a hopeless handicap to put upon a country trying to sell itself and its wares), dictated that the only Britons whom Canadians ever saw were a few civil servants, the resident mice, and after that, travelling businessmen trying to eke out a handful of dollars as they went their humble rounds.

The monarchy was a faraway charade; even the Commonwealth tie, in which I believed passionately, seemed to be coming unstuck, for lack of a simple, common interchange. All the time there was an enormous, unflagging, relentless pull from the United States, just over the border, hammered home by newspaper, magazine, film, radio, television, and book.

We had to fight the belief that anything efficient, anything worthwhile, whether a car, a TV set, an aircraft, a travelling salesman, a theatrical company, a breeding bull, or a political idea, had to come from America.

There was work to be done—and the British Information Service could at least try to do it. Being cautious, I produced two plans for our expansion; one modest, and therefore cheaper, the plan I thought the Treasury *might* buy, and a second one, far-out, costing the earth compared with our little Ottawa budget.

In the latter, the true ideal, I planned a chain of five information offices, covering the whole vast country: linked by teleprinter, linked with our Trade Commissioners on the spot, linked to Britain by firm, really efficient ties of communication.

It involved a British information "presence" in Quebec, Montreal, Ottawa, Toronto, and Vancouver, with side-contacts to Winnipeg and Edmonton. It was detailed, down to the last square foot of office carpet. It would cost—and I was almost ashamed to set down in cold print the final noughts in the total budget.

When Archie Nye presently came back from a working leave in London ("I had to see the old boy," he said, and the old boy could only be Sir Winston Churchill, now nearing retirement, with whom he was on the best of terms) he called me up and told me that it was all organized, and that I could go ahead. He was almost off-hand—as off-hand as a Lieutenant-General could ever be.

"But which one, sir?" I had to ask. I was going to be very pleased anyway. "Plan A?"

"Plan B."

My normal expletive would have been inappropriate; Nye was

a lapsed Catholic, with (as was often the case) a far more tender conscience towards blasphemy than many another upright citizen. I could only say: "Good heavens!"

"Winston also said," Nye continued, " 'Tell him it was a fine book.' "

I could have slain any dragon that day.

I spent the last nine months of my employment putting together the bricks and mortar of this grand design. Donald Kerr did nearly all the spade-work, travelling to and fro, working like the Canadian beaver itself; making contacts, leasing premises, engaging staff, settling squabbles ("How can I work in *Taronna?*" a girl in the registry asked, as if a move from Ottawa to Toronto, all of 240 miles, was a matter of desperate, last-ditch emigration), sorting out problems which, at first insoluble, melted like thin snow under an imported Australian sun.

When I retired, and he succeeded me as the heir to this new empire, the promotion was so thoroughly deserved that I could not be sad for anything lost, nor envious of anything gained, for more than the customary period of court mourning.

Of course, there were one or two things I missed, and missed for all time. One was the sense of service which had been mine for sixteen years, ever since I was measured for my cherished blue suit in 1940. It was a large slice of a working life, but there were moments when it seemed that such a slice could never be too large; that it ought to go on forever, or at least for the regulation forty years, without complaint and without any thought of making a change for the better.

Anyone could be rich. The reputable thing was to be devoted to duty, and honourably poor.

Another gap was the gap in awareness. As soon as I resigned, I felt out of things immediately; I had been reading telegrams and dispatches and memoranda, some of them highly confidential, ever since I joined the Information Service, and when that source was cut off, when one was no longer "in the know," even in the most limited sense, one felt downgraded. Now all the facts, all the interpretations, had to come from those damned newspapers.

A lot of officially acquired knowledge could never be used, nor even mentioned outside a closed door. But it had always been satisfying to hear it and to have it; to know the real reasons why a certain thing was being done one way instead of another; to be given a glimpse, through a slightly parted curtain, of the orderly, sensible, skillful, and continuing world of diplomacy.

Policy always had a reason behind it, sometimes unstated, often unmentionable until long afterwards. Now I would never know, except by guesswork, why the necessary manipulation of my life, and of tens of millions of other lives, was being so oddly con-ducted. I would never know anything except what I read in the Toronto *Telegram,* and the *Daily Express,* and *Newsweek.* It was a fearsome thought. From now I could only be Yours truly, Frankly Disgusted.

I missed, very much, the chance of meeting important and gifted people which even a minor diplomatic post had given me. At Earnscliffe, for example, I had met the Mountbattens, and Prime Minister Nehru of India, and Prime Minister St. Laurent of Canada, and Duncan Sandys, and Alan Lennox-Boyd, and Field-Marshals Montgomery and Templer, and Lord Swinton, and possibly thirty ambassadors, from the American to the Rus-sian, from Iceland to Indonesia. There was a certain snobbery in-volved in this mixed bag, but it was the snobbery of achievement, and it would never disappear while I was alive to observe and to admire.

There would never be another electric occasion like Sir Win-ston Churchill's last press conference in Canada, in 1954.

He was very frail when he arrived from Washington; he was by then eighty years old, he had barely recovered from his recent stroke, and he was to resign from public life within a year. I think we all knew that Canada would never see him again, nor the world either, before very long, and the atmosphere was charged with emotion on both sides.

I shared the top table with this great man, and Sir Anthony Eden, and Sir Archibald Nye, and it was my job to put the ques-tions to him—written questions, by his choice, which had been sent to me by the assembled correspondents.

Churchill was in wonderful form, from the very beginning, and as sharp at eighty as any two other men at forty each. He arrived late, having been delayed at a Canadian cabinet meeting; but by a curious coincidence, the clock which was a prominent feature of the conference room had stopped at exactly eleven o'clock, the time he was due.

He noticed this immediately, and he began, in that great growling voice which was still strong, though now a little quavering at the edges: "I was about to apologize for keeping you waiting, but—" he looked up at the clock, and all our eyes followed, "I see that, with rare delicacy—"

The rest was lost in laughter, and from then on the fun and the spectacle started. I spoke, he answered; and to be thus involved, even as a verbal postman, was a proud and memorable privilege. A friend in the Canadian Broadcasting Corporation later gave me a recording of the entire proceedings, and it is a treasure which I have taken good care will never be lost.

There was one small, behind-the-scenes diversion which I knew about. In the course of routine inquiries about his accommodation in Ottawa, the High Commissioner had asked what the Prime Minister would prefer to drink during his visit. The answer came back smartly, almost with the pop of a cork: "Rhine wine at luncheon, champagne at dinner, and brandy at all other times."

That was the kind of thing I was going to miss.

I left the service on 20 April 1956, ten years to the day since I had first landed at Cape Town. For a hundred different reasons, we had decided to stay on in Canada. Though it was funny to be free, this was a marvellous country to be free in.

3.

This summer of 1956 I was free of the office, free of the clock, free of everything. Part of that freedom was the first love of all, sailing.

When presenting me and my crew with three of the six available trophies at the end of the 1955 racing season, the Commodore of the Royal St. Lawrence Yacht Club remarked: "It used to be said that the three most useless objects in a sailing-boat were an umbrella, a cow, and a naval officer. You can't be sure of anything these days, can you?"

I could welcome the laughter, having (I thought) earned it, and the silver cups that went with it, the hard way. But now it was 1956, when the boat, ten years old, seemed suddenly to have grown much older than that, and slower than she should be, like a bride become a drudge; and, like the bride, we were not doing so well, in any department.

Except on one rare, delicious occasion, which confounded the bookies and was widely written off as a fluke, the Dragon yacht *Valhalla* spent the season well down among the rats and mice of the racing fleet.

It didn't make any difference. In sailing, nothing mattered except doing it and enjoying it. It was the one realm where the Olympic motto, now reduced to a bad-tempered joke, or a plain lie: "What counts is not the winning, but the taking part," was really, undeniably true.

The Royal St. Lawrence Yacht Club, which was sixty-eight years old that season, had a spectacular position on the shores of Lac St. Louis at Dorval, about ten miles west of Montreal; its manicured lawns and treed slopes stretched down from the highway to the edge of the lake, which was really a widening of the main St. Lawrence channel over on the far side.

It still had its original buildings, turreted, massively timbered, deliciously old-fashioned; inside, the walls were lined with yellowing photographs of old yachts, famous in their day, the outstanding winners of fifty and sixty years ago, and with scale models of their hulls, including the contenders for the Seawanhaka Cup, a trophy which the club held against all American challengers for eight years in succession at the turn of the century.

Now the main buildings were getting shabby, flaking off, running down, and gently falling to bits; there was also an undeniable element of fire hazard. Already vast plans were a-foot for rebuilding the whole place, to make it the foremost sailing club in North America. As a member of the Development Committee, I shared the current doubts as to whether we could ever raise the $450,000 necessary for this vast project. But we did.

Every Saturday morning, at the prime of the day, I would set out from Ottawa to drive the 112 miles down to Dorval. A good average time for this weekly swoop was two hours; once, in a hurry, I did it in one hour and forty minutes, only to be hauled up by the Quebec police, in the last mile, for driving at thirty-five miles per hour in a thirty-miles-per-hour zone, escorted to the police station, and delayed there till well past the starting-gun. (Fine: twenty dollars.)

It was on these trips that I completed, twice a year, a small nerve-testing chore, just to keep my hand in and to show that I still had the spark (and the childish urge to prove it): which was to push the Rolls past the one-hundred-miles-per-hour mark and hold it there for a mile. There *was* one long deserted stretch of Route 2 where this was safe, and not abnormally anti-social.

At the R.S.L. I raced twice on Saturday, morning and after-noon; and spent the night in my rented room in the fire-trap of the "dormitory house"; and raced again on Sunday morning be-fore speeding back to Ottawa. Saturday night passed agreeably in sitting on the balcony of the men's club house.

From that superior vantage-point we watched the dusk falling, the late sailors drifting back into harbour on the tail-end of the breeze, and the St. Lawrence channel lights come winking one by one out of the calm darkness; and discussed without rancour what had gone wrong on the last tack (or the first tack, or any other tack which had put us out of the running and into the ruck of tenth place out of fourteen); and getting quietly stoned in the process.

It was a male world, for my age group at least, and I relished it without regret or second thought. Racing was, as always, ex-citing, tiring, usually disappointing; sailing itself was still the most wonderful kind of movement in the world, and a silent, lazy, sunlit glide up-river to the great locks at Beauharnois, or through to our neighbour lake, Lake of Two Mountains, was a blessing not to be matched by any glittering achievement, nor to be spoiled by any fiasco on the racing-circuit.

Those evenings afterwards were such a respite, such a release from care, such a relief from the idiot jungle of writing, not writing, signing checks, paying bills, quarrelling, apologizing, and warding off real or imagined blows, that I came to count on them, as other men come to count on the prospect of parole after a solid span of years in the clink.

I was a member of the Royal St. Lawrence for thirteen years, and disqualified from membership in sad and foolish circumstances, like a small nagging nightmare tacked on to the end of a happy dream.* But that year, it was still unqualified bliss.

I had been talked into buying a Dragon by an old-time sailing enthusiast, Mr. R. C. Stevenson, a past commodore of the Royal St. Lawrence, a superb, tireless, and foxy helmsman, and a man dedicated, in and out of season, to building up the club fleet. He came into my Ottawa office, soon after I arrived, and suggested that I should join his club, buy a boat, and race it at Montreal, without any further delay.

Perhaps, he allowed, it was too late this year. But what about the next one? And as for a boat—well, Dragons were good boats. He had one himself. The club had seven of them already. How about making it eight?

R. C. Stevenson was then nearly seventy, with the kind of wild enthusiasm I had had when I was thirteen. I temporized, being already wary of people who tried to sell me things, or persuade me to buy them from other people, whether they were vintage cars (say, a 1927 Hispano-Suiza with the only known example of an electric gear-box) or a vintage Frans Hals portrait, a portrait so like "The Laughing Cavalier" that there were many people who were prepared to swear that it must be the original. Now it was a Dragon yacht. To begin with, how much did Dragons cost?

"About six thousand dollars," Mr. Stevenson answered promptly. "Then there's the freight, and a bit of customs duty as well. Then you have to truck it down to the club." My expression must have been less than enthusiastic, because he went on: "But why not start with a second-hand boat? Just to get the feel of it?"

"How much would that be?" I was sorry to sound such a miserable, tight-wadded young bastard, but six thousand dollars was nearly three months' living expenses.

* When I left Canada I was immediately involved, like any other sterling area transplant, in exchange control complications which made it very difficult to settle any dollar debts promptly. For a year I owed the club a twenty-dollar overseas membership fee. Presently I was able to settle this, and my next year's subscription as well; by then, however, their patience exhausted after constant reminders which admittedly I had allowed to pile up, they had thrown me out. But darn it, I had *given* them my $250 building debenture when I left!

He produced, from a bulging briefcase, a copy of the *Yachting World,* and slapped it down on my desk, folded open at a certain page. "There's one here for six hundred pounds. I guess that would be about eighteen hundred dollars. She sounds good. Champion of the Solent for three years."

"I used to write for the *Yachting World,*" I told him, still temporizing. "In fact they took my very first article, back in 1934."

He beamed. "Is that so? Well, now . . ." and I realized that I should never have brought the point up, even as a delaying measure. In some way it seemed to make me one of the family already. "Would you like to write them, or shall I?"

Valhalla was shipped out that winter, and dipped her keel in the frigid waters of Lac St. Louis the following April. Like all Dragons, she was a superbly graceful racing machine, with a thirty-foot black hull shaped like the underside of a dolphin, and just as lively and swift. But there was a whole range of fresh skills to be learned before I could make her work.

The set of her sails, for example, depended on a careful, almost mathematical tuning of the mast, which was something altogether new to me, and somehow decadent, like a velvet smoking-jacket of which the shoulders must be brushed one way and the sleeves another. Yet it quickly became apparent, after trial and error, that unless all *Valhalla*'s standing rigging was precisely set up to allow a forty-foot mast to taper off into a pliant curve, rather like an immensely tall bamboo shoot which only leans against the wind, then we might as well lower the sails and row home.

Being a racing machine, she was almost entirely useless for anything else. People did sometimes use Dragons for overnight cruising, living on sandwiches, sleeping on the floor-boards, and relying on a bucket for all else; but with a cabin-top allowing only four feet of headroom at the most, one had to be enthusiastic indeed to put it to the test—or else to have extra-maritime motives.

"There's plenty of headroom in a Dragon," maintained a noted club Romeo who had just got engaged, "as long as you're lying down."

My motives were different, and with my devoted crew of Reg Gillman and Andy Starke I did my best to crown them with success. But the Dragon class was sprouting swiftly; there were now fourteen of us; the competition had grown hot, the protest flags flew to and fro like writs in the very spring of alimony; and *Valhalla*, in 1956, had to try very hard to rise above double figures in the list of those finishing the course.

There was another hazard that year, which God knows was the same for all of us, but less of an embarrassment to hardened skippers who, like Reg Stevenson himself, knew Lac St. Louis as intimately as the back of their horny hands. This was the building of the St. Lawrence Seaway, now nearing completion, which had lowered the level of the lake by two or three feet, and brought near to the surface rocks and shoals we scarcely knew had been there.

I had seen over this vast project, which probed two thousand miles into the very heart of the continent, the year before, and marvelled at its man-made lakes scooped out of the solid earth, and false islands suddenly imposed, and fresh channels cut through virgin land, and villages submerged and other villages transported bodily to higher ground, and the great chain of new locks which were going to change the whole pattern of this ancient waterway for the next million years.

It was a staggering rearrangement of nature, which had taken years to plan and then to carve out; now at last the bath-water was filling up, and in the process small expendable items like lakeside cottages woke to find themselves a hundred yards from the nearest trickle of water, and sailing clubs suddenly ran out of usable space in which to hold their races.

As a consequence, everyone except the most crafty kept running aground, sometimes with a soft squelching noise as if one had steered nose-first into a nursery blancmange, sometimes with a jarring, spine-cracking thud which, when one limped back to harbour to have the boat hauled out, was found to have removed sizeable slices of lead from our shapely keel.

Dragons, built like rocks themselves, with the loving care which no moulded synthetic hull would ever call for, were tough enough. *Valhalla*, before my time, had won wild cross-Channel races in horrible steep seas and the kind of forcible winds which had wrecked the Spanish Armada. But she did draw three feet eleven inches, like all the rest, and when the rocks now stuck up to within two feet of the surface, we became paper Dragons, and the torture was indeed Chinese.

To begin with—and this had been my first thought, when I was being conned into buying a boat—I had rather scoffed at lake sailing. It was all right, one supposed, for fair-weather mariners, who liked smooth surfaces and a picnic atmosphere, but could it ever match handling an open fourteen-footer in the open Irish Sea, which was the way I had been brought up? It did, and I found the fact out very quickly.

There was one race, a long thirty-mile slog for the Mirage Trophy, the pride of a rival yacht club, which was sailed in the very worst weather I had ever faced in a small boat. Storms could build up and pounce very quickly on Lac St. Louis; and halfway through this race I looked up from some close calculation of the next mark to see, bearing down on us from the head of the lake, a genuine "line-squall"—a villainous purple mass of cloud, straight as a ruler, and underneath it a wall of creamy water building up into a horrid turmoil.

We were leading the field at the time: we might even win—it was one of those rare, blessed days—and I hated to do anything to spoil our chances. We had the ordinary, unreefed mainsail set, and a big Genoa jib, and as the wind freshened we began to move like a train. But perhaps it would be better if—

Then it hit us, and the next thing I said was: "Get your life-jackets on!"

It came down on us like a real blow, like a wicked fist. We were hammered flat, in one awful instant of time, and I thought we were gone; and there the boat stayed, for nearly ten minutes. The jib was ripped and torn to shreds—which was just as well: if it had held, we would have gone under foot by foot, and sunk like a stone.

As it was, the angle of the deck was murderous, and the waves were now pouring in, in a steady cataract. I had to keep some tension on the mainsail; if I let it run out, it would have been in the water, and would fill, and over we would go.

We lay there, absolutely powerless, nearly done, while the wind screamed and bashed at us as if we were its last enemy on the lake.

Somehow we had to get the mainsail down. This meant no

more than letting go a single ratchet; but that was below decks, at the foot of the mast, only to be reached by crawling through two feet of water, with the boat still pinned down at its fearful angle.

I could not do it: I had the tiller to control, a tiller nearly wrenching my arm out of its socket, and I was hanging on to the main sheet as well. Reg Gillman could not do it; he was working like a crazy dog at the pump. That left Andy Starke, whose normal job was to handle the headsails; now, with the jib gone, he was crouched under the cabin top, sheltering from the tearing wind and the waves slapping over us. I had to shout at him twice: "Let go the main halyard!" before he understood what I wanted.

He was young, and strong, and admirably brave. First he took off his glasses, and tucked them inside his life-jacket. Then he crawled down into the little cabin below decks, his back tight up against the cabin top.

The wind dealt us one last, extra, smashing blow while he was still imprisoned below. Then there was an enormous bang which could be felt throughout the boat, and the mainsail, which for once did not jam in its tracks, slid down with a screech, and we came slowly upright.

Andy, our saviour, reappeared, grinning. He put on his glasses again. Then he clawed his way forward, along the sluicing deck, and let go the anchor: a small miniature of courage, and pure gold, even from the rear view.

We stayed where we were for another fifteen minutes, pumping out, getting the tangle straight again, catching our breath after the astonishment of reprieve. If she had gone over in that howling wilderness it would have been a short swim in hell for us, and after that the Lachine Rapids, waiting for us downstream. We still could not see more than ten yards in any direction, so thick was the flying scud. Then the storm ripped away to leeward, and the blue sky came out, as innocent as a harlot on holiday.

Now it could be seen that the next mark was only half a mile to windward, and there wasn't another boat in sight. By God, by God, it was still possible. . . . We took down the rags of the Genoa job, and hoisted a mouldy old substitute in its place; then we hauled up the anchor, got under way, made our mark, turned for home and, while the rest of the battered fleet was still sorting itself out, won that race by a comfortable mile.

I was stiff and sore for a week afterwards. It cost us a nylon Genoa, a mainsail so warped and stretched that it could never be used again, and several moments of terror. All we got in return was a beer-mug each, of disputable pewter, labelled "Pointe Claire Yacht Club: Mirage Trophy." But when really in need of reassurance, I used to drink out of that beer-mug. And never again did I think of lake sailing as something for an idle summer afternoon, with parasols fluttering on the foredeck.

This year, by contrast, we limped through a sad season. New boats were coming along all the time, and, as had happened at Trearddur Bay, twenty-five years earlier, the new boats, light and dry, with sails flat as boards and all sorts of novel gadgets to work them, could out-point and out-sail the old stagers, every time.

Fresh stars emerged; and even if they were forty-year-old doctors like Sandy MacDonald, who was later to represent us in the Olympic Games, rather than fourteen-year-old younger brothers like Denys, the new wave, and its swift success, had the power to wound and to discourage.

Towards the end of the season, I decided that a brand-new Dragon was the only answer, and I ordered one from Camper and Nicolson in Gosport. She was to be called *Shearwater,* I decided, after my long-ago first corvette command, and she would incorporate, among a lot of other refinements, my third and last invention, after the variable gear and perpetual motion: the double-ended, reversible, instant-clip-on spinnaker-boom—and this time it worked!

It was a little too technical to be explained in terms of family reading, but good enough to be adopted as a standard item thereafter.

Camper and Nicolson (who, I learned years afterwards, went by the horrid sobriquet of "Cami-Knicks" among a certain class of yachtsman) were to make an outstanding job of *Shearwater;* and I must admit that in placing this order I had my eye on the 1960 Olympics at Naples, though that was a deep dark secret which luckily I confided to no one except my crew. But no sooner had the contract for her been signed than *Valhalla,* as if to put me to shame for my disloyalty, won a race on which, against all the odds, I had set my heart.

This was the Windmill Point Shield, an admired trophy which

we had won, with all sorts of luck, in 1955. I would have dearly loved to retain it for the second year in succession, but I did not really give ten cents for our chances. We had not won a single race that season, nor ever looked like doing so. I had already kissed the Windmill Point Shield goodbye, halfway between Ottawa and Dorval. But I still longed for it.

The wind that afternoon was light, very fluky, hard to forecast; one had to go and look for it, or guess where it would come from, *if* it came from anywhere, and then be ready for it—which boiled down to being in one particular stretch of Lac St. Louis, and pointing the right way, when everyone else was somewhere quite different, and stern-first towards the winning post. That, by a glorious chance, was exactly what happened.

Half an hour after the start, every other boat in the fleet was playing around inshore, tacking to and fro among the tall trees at the edge of the lake, which for some mysterious reason often seemed able to conjure up a breeze of their own. I decided that if we were going to be thrashed, then we might as well be thrashed real good, as Dr. Billy Graham would have said.

I set our course slap up the middle of the lake, against the main current, never changing tacks, never deviating from a distant mark on the shore-line ahead, under which lay our turning-buoy.

We were entirely alone. The boats inshore were tacking to and fro like mad bees, tearing each other to ribbons. All the Dragon stars—Reg Stevenson, Sandy MacDonald, Archie Cameron, Gerry Letourneau—were there. *But they were not making any more progress than we were.* We sailed placidly on up the main channel; no one bothered us; it was a private world, good enough for hopeless amateurs, of gently rippling water, of sails just filled enough to keep us on course, of a little bubbling wake which meant that we were moving, and always in the right direction.

Presently, far ahead of us, the surface of the lake ruffled, and changed colour, from pale blue to dark. It was the wind—our wind, the one I had been looking for, and only ours. No one else was placed to gain any benefit from it. I knew then that we were going to win, and an hour later we did.

Sometimes *Valhalla,* when I had her properly balanced, moved like a dream, slicing through the water as if she were skating on gentle ice. She did so now. Gathering speed, we romped away into the blue, still completely on our own; and by the time the breeze reached the shore-gang, we could not be caught. With a creaming wake we rounded Windmill Point, three hundred yards ahead of all pursuit, and made for the finishing line; and Max, spending his summer holidays in Canada, was on the committee boat to see us get the gun.

Not even the drenching rain which presently blotted out the lake, and everything on it, could spoil that moment.

"Well done!" said my friend Reg Stevenson later. He never grudged any man anything. "But you had no right to win, you know. All the *reliable* breeze was inshore. It always is. You didn't even try to cover us! By all the rules of racing . . ." He was shaking his head, but smiling at the same time; there was a funny side to this, and after a lifetime's fanatical competition he could still see it very easily. "I don't know why you want to bother with a new boat," he concluded. "On her day, *Valhalla* can't be beaten."

"But it's only one day, out of about five months."

"We'll take darned good care of that!"

But there was something else that summer, and every summer in Canada, which had the true precedence: which was to sailing as a subtle burgundy is to a lively champagne. This was the Shakespeare Festival season down at Stratford, Ontario, a miraculous act of faith now entering its fourth triumphant term. I had just been elected to its Board of Governors, and I was as pleased and proud about that as when, in the unlikely year of 1953, I wrote that this was a project which had the brightest future of anything of its kind in Canada, and wrote, as well, the modest check which made me a Founding Patron.

It had started, like buying *Valhalla*, with a man coming into my office with an idea to sell. He was announced as Mr. Tom Patterson of Stratford, Ontario. I had never heard of Tom Patterson, nor of Stratford, Ontario, either. But at the end of an hour, I knew almost everything about both.

Tom Patterson was a small, diffident, bald young man with a gleam in his eye and a mission. Such visitors were not always welcome at the United Kingdom Information Office. I had, in the past, already wasted acres of prime time listening to single-minded fellow-visionaries trying to enlist my support for epic poetry readings in caves, for a season of British Morris Dancing, for the planting of groves of oaks in memory of Trafalgar.

But Tom Patterson was of a different quality altogether. After ten minutes, I realized that his project, crazy as it was, had a certain wild validity. Less than an hour later, I was a whole-hearted supporter.

Patterson was an ex-journalist who, during some war service in Italy and elsewhere, had the luck to see a lot of theater and opera—a happy dividend, more readily available to soldiers than, for example, to sailors. When he came back to his home town of Stratford he decided—just like that, with a snap of the fingers and perhaps a couple of drinks—that Stratford, even the wrong Stratford, was going to live up to its honoured name. Whether it knew it or not, it was going to build a really great theater, of international quality, dedicated to the plays of Shakespeare.

Stratford, at that time, was a rural town of eighteen thousand people, as plain and prosperous as its surrounding countryside. It served farmers, it made a little furniture and children's foot-wear, it housed its citizens comfortably; it had an extra employment bonus in the shape of a Canadian National Railways repair shop. Apart from that, it was an absolutely typical Canadian community, unsullied by any extravagant notions of culture. There had been no theater there for half a century.

This was the material Tom Patterson had to work on, and in the course of our talk I learned just how far he had got, and at what sort of pace.

First he had taken his lunatic idea to the local council, and told them all about it. Somehow he must have caught them off balance, which was a talent he was able to bring to perfection during the next five years. But even so, they did not go wild.

They voted him the sum of $125, and asked him to examine the prospects and to report back. It seemed probable that the stake, though less than princely, was $125 more than most of the city fathers thought those prospects were worth.

The measure of the man was that, on this frugal basis, he engineered a trip to England, and enlisted the support of Tyrone Guthrie. It must have been an interesting contrast in style; Guthrie, as well as being a talented and sought-after director, was six-foot-four and of somewhat imperious resolution. But presently he wrote back: "I have never before felt so convinced of the obvious practical value of anything I've been asked to be connected with," and he promptly corralled Tanya Moiseiwitsch, Irene Worth, and Alec Guinness to join him in the enterprise.

"Of course I will do the decor and the costumes," said Tanya Moiseiwitsch. "Of course I will come and act," said Irene Worth. "Of course I will play Richard the Third in the opening performance," said Alec Guinness.

"But have you collected any more money?" I asked Tom at this point.

"No, not really," he answered. "But Massey thinks it's a marvellous idea. And we've ordered a tent, and Tanya has already designed the stage."

"You'd better come and have lunch."

There were other things besides Shakespeare and Stratford which could make his eyes gleam. "Lead on! I'm certainly hungry!"

He was indeed to meet prolonged financial troubles before the curtain went up at Stratford; hunger must have seemed the keynote, during all that mangled period when he and the handful of other enthusiasts were walking a tightrope, beneath which yawned a cavern of indifference and spite. No one really believed in the damned thing; or rather, they believed in it in theory, and did nothing to help it in practice. There was a time when the whole undertaking, losing momentum, limped and tottered from crisis to crisis.

It became known that money was only trickling in, and as the word spread (shortage of funds was, in Canada, a worse contagion than the plague) many people involved in the project began to demand cash on the nail. There wasn't any cash; only hope, and the ludicrous dream itself. At one point, construction work on the theater stopped entirely; even a few weeks before the opening, there was a chance that the Stratford Festival would have to be written off altogether.

Its critics and detractors, hard at work on an easy target, came very near to destroying it completely. Then, just in time, the tide turned.

There was really no reason for this, except that people such as Tyrone Guthrie, and others who had never wavered in their support, and Tom Patterson himself, all kept plugging away as if it were beyond question that the promised opening night would take place as advertised, and anyone who thought differently was not fully informed.

Contractors who had seemed cagey and suspicious suddenly turned liberal. The financial appeal, particularly in hard-headed Toronto, began to prosper; and Stratford itself, unaccountably catching fire, subscribed a heart-warming $3.75 for every man, woman, and child within the city limits. Out of a working budget of $150,000, generous Stratford put up nearly half.

There was absolutely no reason for this either, except a sort of constructive civic contrariness. People were saying this thing was going to be a flop? Well, we'll show them. . . . It was all the more astonishing because the local paper, the Stratford *Beacon-Herald,* the only newspaper which most of the inhabitants read, and which should have been as habit-forming as a medical prescription, was vehemently anti-Festival from the start, and had persisted in this almost until curtain time.

For me, and for countless others, there had never been anything like the opening night, in a whole lifetime of theater-going it turned out to be a marvellous banquet for every conceivable palate, whether delicate or strong, jaded or innocent.

Part of the enormous excitement of the occasion was the background knowledge, common to almost everyone in the theater, of the whole chain of crises, all the damnable headaches, which had for so long been conspiring to prevent the first night ever taking place.

These had been overcome, one after the other, by faith and energy and a persistent, dedicated will to win. It had been a very near thing, down to the last few days. But now, here were the trumpets sounding to prove victory, and to acclaim it, and to put Mr. Faintheart and Mr. Envy and Mr. Sneerwell to shame.

A gun went off, a Shakespearean cannon, much too close, making us all jump. Then there was a doom-like note on a bell, and then, under a single diffused spotlight, Alec Guinness appeared on the balcony high above the stage.

Only it was not Alec Guinness at all; it was Richard the Third, in the brave scarlet finery which mocked the pitiable man within. I was not sure what I had been expecting to see, except that it should have been a vaguely familiar face: the reality, the man on the balcony, was a complete stranger, and a figure from a bad dream as well.

He was dwarfish and repellent; a humped shoulder was balanced by a drooping eye; under the red cap, the face shone with a malignant glow; beneath the rusty cloak, a leg dragged, as if unwilling to follow so misshapen a body. But, with all this, the man was a king, noble and hideous at the same time; and when he spoke, the fact was confirmed.

There is indeed such a thing as the "thrilling voice" of fiction, and now we heard it. It flooded the theater with the first words of the Stratford Festival, absolutely prophetic of all that was to come:

> Now is the winter of our discontent
> Made glorious summer by this sun of York.

The play was on.

It was an outstanding evening, one of the best I ever remembered. Everything helped it: great acting, splendid decoration of a quality never seen before, and a universal sense of relief and gratitude that, after all, this astonishing venture had come to full flower. It carried the whole audience with it. The tumult of applause at the end, Stratford's first standing ovation, saluted two things: a wonderful presentation, and a wonderful act of faith.

The range of that faith had been as strange and rare as its quality. The man who delayed sending in his bill for pouring the concrete foundations had shared it with Alec Guinness, who, in Coronation year, might reasonably have been expected to preside over some safe and sumptuous hit in London's West End. This, also, was part of what we were applauding. The echoes never really died away.

I had offered to write a three-article account of that Stratford opening for the *Ottawa Citizen,* as a small gift to God and Tom Patterson, and I signed off my contribution with a couple of paragraphs which it is a treat (of an obvious, I-told-you-so brand) to record:

> There is absolutely no reason why this Stratford Festival should not gather momentum, year by year, until in good time it becomes a going concern without any outside aid.

Something new has been added to the Canadian theatrical scene: something new, something worthwhile, something stunning in its enterprise. It is there for all to enjoy. You may readily and willingly travel miles to attend it. To go to Stratford today is more than a duty—it is a pleasure.

As an earnest of this, that first season of two plays was presently extended from five weeks to six, and sold a phenomenal ninety-eight percent of all the available seats.

Going to the theater is normally a simple and even cold-blooded routine: you buy the tickets, arrive on time, plant yourself in the right seat, sit back, and say: "Now, show me." Going down to Stratford, in 1956, was still a pious pilgrimage; it had been so wonderful in the past three years, and to make the journey again was an avowal of trust that it would be wonderful this time also.

The occasion had now become more professional, and certainly more social. It could not be spoiled by either.

It involved a drive of three hundred and fifty miles, and as usual we took it slowly; it was something to be enjoyed, to be spun out: a picnic with all the signs set fair, an act of piety which would, for a change, earn a positive reward. There was another, twentieth-century reason why the journey should not be hurried. At this point of summer, the Canadian roads, like the woods in the shooting season, were full of sporting idiots.

An Ontario farmer, plagued by stock losses, used to paint the word *COW* on the side of all his cows, as soon as autumn came round and the guns began to roar. On the same basis, one might never get to Stratford at all, unless one crept there like a mouse in a car defensively labelled "CAR."

In any case, how did one want to arrive there, for the first of two nights of theatrical delight? Sweating like a pig? Shaking like a bed-spring? Prematurely drained, like a miscued lover? No one in his senses would thus betray his union. Yet it *was* something of a Canadian habit, to run all the way there, to enjoy a panting rest while the plays were on, and to run all the way back.

We had an Ottawa friend who habitually drove those three hundred and fifty miles in half a day, after an early morning visit to his broker's office; arrived at Stratford at 6 P.M. and checked into his hotel; and then, fortified by a cold shower, a fried-egg sandwich, and five dry martinis, went straight to the theater.

It was a horrid thought that a poet of four centuries ago, and a hundred talented people toiling like dedicated beavers for the past four months, had worked to give this man this owl-eyed moment.

The last thirty miles of the Stratford journey were in odd contrast with what was to come. The road ran straight, through a level and featureless countryside. This was wholesome farming land, well-kept, orderly, prosperous, and dull: one of those pockets of Canada settled by one particular brand of newcomer, and never to lose its original *marque*. Here the settlement had been German, and devoutly thorough, and ploddingly industrious.

From Kitchener (which had been called Berlin until 1914, when the label grew embarrassing), the signposts read like a catalogue inscribed by some homesick exile from the beloved fatherland: New Hamburg, Baden, Guelph, Brunner, Breslau, Mannheim, Wallenstein, Heidelberg. One began to wonder whether it was part of the plot to prove that Shakespeare had been German after all: a towering monument to Teutonic genius which no English country bumpkin could ever have matched.

But then nature, history, and propaganda relented. Suddenly we were back in England, back to the Warwickshire poacher turned actor, back to Ann Hathaway and the second-best bed. The next signpost said Tavistock, and the next village was called Shakespeare. After that, the next and last town was Stratford, through which the River Avon, though pronounced "Avvon," meandered with historic accuracy and was patrolled by authentic swans.

We stayed at a motel, the Imperial, one of the rash of motels which had sprung up as soon as the Festival was seen to be a civic as well as an artistic sure-thing. It was run by a family, and a man, with a name as anonymous as that of some of his clients, Smith.

David Smith had already become a good friend, and his establishment was a model of what one hoped to find at the end of such a journey.

The official party before the opening had started in a small way, at the beginning of the first season, as a matter of courtesy on the part of the Festival Governors, in order to greet their supporters, give the evening some kind of a starting-point, and also to eke out the town's meager eating and drinking facilities. It had then been a drink-and-a-snack show, for which the church-going wives of Stratford had baked and brewed and cut and spread all the preceding day: a modest prelude to the real point of the evening, and modestly priced at two dollars.

Now it had grown until it had changed its nature entirely; the early simple ritual was now buried under an avalanche of compulsive sociality. Tickets for it had soared to six dollars per person and, in the case of some of the guests, it looked as though this intensive spree was the high point of their evening. They shovelled down mounds of food; they dived into the drink as if they would not reach another oasis for a hundred miles or more; in one way or another, they were clearly determined to get their six dollars' worth, or bust. Or both. It was like an orphans' picnic, with the orphans big, glossy, and unsupervised.

The whole atmosphere was a cross between a Buckingham Palace Garden Party after royalty had left, and an Australian bar five minutes before closing time. It was the worst prelude to the evening's entertainment which could possibly be devised, and within a few years had to be abandoned—or rather, transferred to *after* the performance instead of before. But tonight, it was still in full flower, and the sad frown on Tom Patterson's face as he contemplated the prospect was a charitable understatement.

And yet, and yet . . . Stratford, and all the evening before us, was still unspoilable. It began to knit together again with another prelude to our delight, the best that the Festival provided: something which always put me in mind of that exquisite work of Delius which he called *A Walk to the Paradise Garden*. This was the traditional stroll along the bank of the River Avon, on the way to the theater. It was the happiest part of the pilgrimage, and the last moment of calm before the true engagement.

The scene, to paraphrase Polonius, was nocturnal-pastoral. The long stretch of green sloping riverside park had somehow been preserved against building encroachment, against the demands of parking space, against all civic greed and expediency; and it might have been preserved for this moment. The weeping willow trees bent low over the water, the river glowed in the dusk, and along the opposite bank the lights were coming on one by one. The family picnic parties were packing up, and Stratford's circling swans were arching their necks as they reached for their dividend of the scraps.

A group of nuns sitting at a wooden table sedately brushed the crumbs from their habits, and gave devout thanks before rising. (But how did nuns organize an outing such as this? Did one of them, a managerial type, go round from cell to cell, asking "Girls! Who's for Stratford?" Did the Mother Superior nominate the party? Did they forfeit the treat if they were naughty? How naughty?) Car doors slammed one by one as the occupants joined the moving throng; caught in a slow swirling tide, we advanced up the hill towards the brightly lit theater, completing our climb to Parnassus.

At the top, we had to make our way through another kind of audience, ticketless but not at all concerned on that account: the lesser citizens of Stratford, sitting on the railings, standing at the curbside, watching and enjoying this outlandish invasion from another world. I sometimes wondered what they thought of us, and whether this free show was, for them, as compelling as the one we were going to see.

We might have been just as funny, for example, as the bumbling rustics in *A Midsummer Night's Dream* when viewed by sophisticated courtiers. We might not be funny at all, but simply odd, like any other kind of interloper.

Once inside the glaring foyer, all was high-class intercourse; it was the last chance for people who were so inclined to make a significant entrance, before the real actors took over. They did not let it go to waste. Dear friends who had not seen each other since the previous evening screamed their greetings across the intervening space. Toronto tycoons assumed the grand manner of patrons of the arts. Affectation took over from simplicity, and mink from both.

But soon, within the auditorium, it was awe which began to supplant everything else. The very sight of the stage—Tanya Moiseiwitsch's stark and simple apron platform, ready to be put to a thousand uses—was enough to make all amateur performances seem foolish. We settled down as quickly as we could, while the last seat-hopping extrovert gave his last loud salute to a friend, and waited, in taut expectation.

The same fanfare of trumpets sounded as in other years. The same ear-splitting cannon startled us, and the same toll of the bell gave a gentler signal. Then the lights gained strength, and brightened, and the somber stage came alive, with people, with flaring colours, with music and voice: with—

> O for a Muse of fire that would ascend
> The brightest heaven of invention,
> A kingdom for a stage, princes to act,
> And monarchs to behold the swelling scene

and in an instant we had it all before us, in the glittering magic of *Henry V*.

It was very good indeed that year. Christopher Plummer made a noble, eloquent, and potent king, in splendid contrast with the foppish French courtiers, the first contingent of Quebec actors to decorate our stage; though his later courtship scene with Ginette Letondal * as Katharine showed him delightfully unmanned.

The boastful, mincing Dauphin was duly cut down to size when a courtier proclaimed: "He longs to eat the English!" and the unimpressed Constable of France answered dryly: "I think he will eat all he kills." Agincourt was won, the cowards at home condemned, the dead mourned, and victory proclaimed with streaming banners.

It was proclaimed again the next night, when Douglas Campbell stopped being Douglas Campbell, or anything else, and gave us a Falstaff so gross, so rumbustious, so sad, so funny, and so satisfying that it seemed to make the proverb forever true—that inside every fat old man was a slim young stripling yearning to escape, and that this could endure for sixty years, and still be as urgent at the end as at the beginning.

It chanced to be windy that night, and we were reminded of the drawbacks of staging a play in a tent theater, however robust it might be. The actors had to compete for much of the time with

* Another Quebec import of sparkling talent, and a sad suicide shortly afterwards.

the rattle and thud of slatting canvas. Often the whole tent creaked and laboured, like a ship under too much sail.

During a lull, two other hazards made themselves plain: the sound of police sirens wailing down the wind (Now what was it *this* time? we wondered, like any other scandalized citizens), and then a long-drawn-out train whistle, sounding so near, seeming so imperative, that it brought the play to an uneasy stop, and compelled laughter when laughter was not appropriate.

But we had our own remedy for this last interruption. At the sound, almost every occupant of the stalls turned and stared at Mr. Donald Gordon, the president of Canadian National Railways, the man unfairly held to be responsible for this rude intrusion. He bore our gaze stoically; tough enough to survive the yearly prying onslaught of a Parliamentary committee of inquiry, which was dedicated to proving that C.N.R. was the worst-run outfit on the continent, he was certainly able to cope with this small by-product of consumer resistance.

But it was a fact that in all succeeding years, trains entering or leaving Stratford station did so in decorous silence.

Nineteen fifty-six was, in any case, the last year when the Festival tent, which had served us so manfully for four seasons, made its own peculiar contribution to the drama. When it was struck, at the end of the run, it was struck forever, and the new, permanent theater took its place. We (this was the royal "we" of the Board of Governors) passed the final plans and the accounts for this at a committee meeting that same week.

The project was going to be very expensive, like the new Royal St. Lawrence Yacht Club. Our first guess at the overall cost had been $984,000; now we signed for $1½ million; and this was to grow to $2¼ million before the whole thing was completed (including a hefty $400,000 for a vast, essential air-conditioning plant).

But it was promptly paid for by the customers; it stood as an enduring monument to an incredible idea; and it was in fact as handsome, efficient, and manageable as any theater-building could hope to be.

Now, fifteen years afterwards, it attracts playgoers from all over the world; and its quality earns a dependable one million dollars in ticket sales every year—which, as with an author's royalties, is a measure, not of money but of generous and contented people, who return again and again to enjoy its offerings.

Once, when I had a little spare money, or thought I had, we took over an entire local hotel and gave a mid-season party for the cast and the backstage wizards. It was to pay tribute, return thanks, for an outstanding production of *Twelfth Night* by a home-coming Tyrone Guthrie: one of the best evenings ever to be recalled, with Siobhan McKenna a handsome and graceful Viola, and Christopher Plummer, once again, playing Sir Andrew Ague-cheek as a tremulous old club drunk, and at one point falling headlong through a trapdoor, like a gangling sack of potatoes, to give the Festival its loudest, longest laugh of all.

There was also Bruno Gerussi, a small, bouncy, rubbery young man with (off-stage) a ripe Chicago-gangster accent, who contrib-uted a striking performance as the Clown Feste. It was impos-sible not to be achingly moved by the closing scene of this play, when Feste, to crown a happy ending, led the company in succes-sive choruses of "The Wind and the Rain."

Bruno, God bless him, could not sing a note, in any musical sense; he might have saluted Rex Harrison as Caruso. But he gave us pure music that night—they all did—and it was this that I wanted to celebrate.

The party was something of a riot, though the rioters behaved very well, within a theatrical framework. They were fed till the kitchens gaped (hungry actors were as traditional as hungry writers) and sluiced till all the wells ran dry. In return, and without too much coaxing from the host, they sang for their supper.

They sang—for me, for us, for a hushed, spell-bound hotel-full of Festival friends—their song from the end of *Twelfth Night,* with Bruno Gerussi leading, and the rest joining in one by one. I have never forgotten, nor ever will, the eye-pricking moment as the last chorus of that song softly died away, the song which has always left an echo down the enchanted corridors of time:

> A great while ago the world begun,
> With hey, ho, the wind and the rain;
> But that's all one, our play is done,
> And we'll strive to please you every day.

4.

Already it was better to keep moving, instead of sitting at home in the cushioned well-deck of a stone frigate and pretending that "We'll strive to please you every day" was anything but an addled joke. That summer, in addition to all the rest, we drove across to St. Andrew's, New Brunswick, to see David Walker (*Geordie, Harry Black*), a hermit-novelist whose other label had once been "Comptroller to the Viceroy of India."

We also paid homage to Sir James Dunn, a legendary Canadian steel tycoon, and his wife Christy (who later married Lord Beaverbrook), and his stunning Salvador Dali painting, *Christ on the Sea Shore,* to admit which an entire wall of his house had been removed and then replaced.

We drove down the coast of Maine, wolfing "shore dinners" of broiled lobster and steamed clams and cracked crab by the way, to visit Willis Wing in his summer retreat at Boothbay Harbor; and then on to Fisher's Island, on Long Island Sound, where Thayer Hobson and his family were installed for the season in an area of controlled immigration so prestigious that one had to state the make of one's car before being allowed to rent a house.

"Do bring the Rolls," Thayer had written. "It'll look good outside the back door." He was right. "God damn it!" said one of our dinner hosts during the course of our stay, when the weather turned sweltering and the humidity almost unbearable. "We left the air-conditioned Cadillacs at home!" The Texas plural was beyond reproach.

We missed the New York premiere of *The Ship That Died of Shame,* for some stupid reason which must be filed away with all the other stupid reasons why certain people, counted on to be at Point X on Day Y, are inevitably at Point Y on Day Z, and blissfully, shamefully unaware of the gaffe.

But now, at last, it was time for me to be a writer again: to be serious, to call a halt to all the hopped-up nonsense—or, if that was itself too silly an idea, with the merry-go-round still whirling and spinning, then at least to bob up above the tossing tide of painted animals, swinish noise, and shout: "I am here! This is me! The well-known writer! Remember?"

The next stake in my future, which was still very important to me, was now coming up for assessment, and I had wagered, among other things, a considerable expense of spirit on the outcome.

What I had tried to do, with *The Tribe That Lost Its Head,* was what all writers try to do when they fall in love with an idea and want to marry it. They treat it with respect, and cherishing care, and an almighty fear of something going wrong with it. Borrowing from *Othello* ("Speak of them as they are. Nothing extenuate, nor set down aught in malice"), they aim to tell *all* the truth, lay bare *all* the lies, and exhibit every last vestige of hope.

Having lived a long time in a troubled place, I wanted to write its story faithfully and accurately: to explain what might have gone wrong, and what could be right, and above all, what was likely to happen next.

But my troubled place was all Africa; and into a single book I had to put all the problems, perplexities, and ambitions of a whole huge continent at a moment of turmoil.

To this purpose I invented a small country, the island of Pharamaul,* and tried to make it a microcosm of that continent. I peopled it with everyone I had met, or observed, or heard about, during my seven years' African journeying: injected a sudden crisis, and let the thing rip.

Thus my small country was Colonial Africa, to start with—something already vanishing below the rim of history; then Africa waking from its sleep and stretching its muscles; then Africa on the verge of independent, viable life, and choosing a reputable pathway towards it—a moment which no longer exists, either, though it might come again, and in some cases must.

There were two themes which were very important to me: firstly, that in spite of the trend already becoming modish, there was a place for the white man in Africa, a job for him to do, and a dividend in which, as one of the advance guard, he was entitled to share; and secondly, that Britain's colonial past was nothing to be ashamed of, and in many cases had introduced, for the very first time, the pattern of tolerable life itself.

Neither of these ideas was fashionable, even then, which was another reason why they were important.

* Derivation: *Pharos,* a lighthouse, and *Maula,* the tribal name of the inhabitants.

I made the colonial point by portraying most of the civil servants, past and present, as hard-working and devoted, with nothing
but a medal, a dried-out body and spirit, and a derisory pension
to show for it at the end; and added a few ninnies and incom-
petents to balance the account. The progress from pastoral slum
to modest urban prosperity, with hope as the unique bequest, was
there for all to see.

I described, from half-a-dozen grim aspects of real life, the
African dangers now looming: the appetite for cruelty, the taste
for major and minor racketry, the hazards of too quick a freedom,
and the readiness to revert to authoritarian rule, tribal tyranny,
as an easy way out of all dilemmas.

Much of Africa, the book maintained, was far from ready for
emancipation; in spite of all the screams, it was better for the
"colonial power" to leave too late rather than too soon. If it was
a choice of remaining perhaps one more generation, or betraying
all the past and watching it swill down the drain, then honour
bound us to stay put and ride out the storm.

In 1956, that was still a fair hope.

There were indications already that the book would be banned
in South Africa, for reasons a little hard to assess, except that the
idea of a black-white partnership was always unacceptable, and a
black-white rape scene near the end gave partnership even more
of a bad name. However, the Minister of the Interior would not
have to publish his reasons, and there could be no appeal against
such a verdict. Otherwise, all the omens were good.

Already the mysterious undercurrent was at work, the ground-
swell of advance comment which made a book sell—or sometimes
killed it stone dead. The trade papers kept on mentioning it;
individual booksellers already knew all about "the new Monsarrat," like the new Alistair McMouse or the new Hammond Egges.

Cassell's first print would be one hundred thousand copies, and
there were other marks of confidence which made up a satisfying
sum—the kind of sum I now saluted, in common with the Bank
of Montreal, Barclays in London and Barbados, and the Morgan
Guaranty Trust in New York. On the eve of publication, it went
like this:

Cassell advance	£3,600
Morrow advance	5,360
Reader's Digest (U.K.)	1,500
John Bull serial	3,150

Translation rights in Norway, Sweden, Holland, Germany, and France brought this part of the total to £16,000. On top of that, it had been sold to the American *Reader's Digest* for $80,000, of which my share would be another £14,300. It would also be a Book-of-the-Month Club alternate selection in America, if anyone there "chose to read a work of fiction" instead of *This Hallowed Ground,* by Bruce Catton.

They would be fools, I thought, if they did not.

Of course, it could never do as well as *The Cruel Sea,* that child prodigy which no other offspring, legal or bastard, would ever catch up. By now, this had sold over three million copies, and, translated into nineteen languages, from Estonian to Portuguese,* had in five years earned the respectable sum of £166,000 (it looked even more respectable in dollars, $465,000). It was still selling, world-wide, a comforting 100,000 copies a year.

But five years at this sort of rate had been much too fast for income-tax comfort, and the book had been the object of punitive slashing by the Inland Revenue. As a diplomat, subject to U.K. taxation, I could take no avoiding action; I just had to sit there and sweat off the pounds. It was better not to think about it, though there were moments of non-Socialist frustration, even of reactionary rage. I loved my fellow men, but not to the extent of about eighty-five percent of my income.

It had fathered, by proxy, a racehorse called The Cruel Sea (by Seven Seas out of Heidi) which had not done nearly as well as the book (seven wins out of forty-eight races and eight years of hoof-prints). It had been translated into the sign hanging outside that pub in Hampstead. Half-a-dozen yachts had been registered under the name of *Compass Rose* (they were to include, two years later, one of my own, a twin-engined Chris-Craft motorcruiser which finally signalled the abyss between sailor and driver).

---

* And in Polish, under the catchy title of *Okrutne Morze, Tom I & II* (translated by Maria Boduszynska-Borowikowa), and the banner of Wydawnictwo Ministerstwa Obrony Narodowej.

Two people, both of whom I had actively loathed, got a lot of mileage out of claiming to be the originals of my two most reputable characters. A confidence-man in Australia pretended to be the author, and did very profitably until he began to masquerade as "an English nobleman" as well. That of course was more serious, and he went to jail.

A bishop newly destined for a far-northern diocese, and thus able to sign himself, charmingly, "Donald the Arctic" (his predecessor had been "Archibald the Arctic"), was understood to have murmured, on learning of his appointment: "A cruel see indeed."

The title, in fact, had become a brand-name, and I welcomed the idea. Others in the same circumstances did not. I knew that J. B. Priestley, for example, particularly disliked strangers saying to him "Oh yes, *The Good Companions*," when he had written so many other books and plays of which he was entitled to be proud.

But that admirable first huge best-seller did put him plumb in the middle of the map, at a time when he was scarcely known outside literary London, and its echoes must have done a great deal to keep him there for the succeeding forty years.

It seemed ungrateful to neglect, if not disown, one's early offspring, just because the ones that came after were also tall, beautiful, and intelligent, with the added allurement of youth.

The Tribe, I realized already, would never match my own first explosion. But it ought to do a lot better than *Esther Costello* (currently being filmed), and I had tried hard to make it deserve this.

Most important of all, it was *writing,* not fooling around as a semi-celebrity with a diarrhea of O.K. jargon and a smooth mike-side manner. It was the best I could do at the age of forty-six. It was two and a half years' work, and had come out at 538 pages and 250,000 words. It was deadly serious, and lovingly compiled; and the effort to produce it—sometimes as grim and killing as a desert crawl, sometimes as pleasurable as playing the piano all day—had been so utterly private and absorbed that it had erased totally the outside world.

Just as *The Cruel Sea* had been written in warm dry Johannesburg, six thousand feet above sea-level and about as far from it as possible, so *The Tribe* had been written in cold sub-zero Canada, where the only steamy jungle was the House of Commons. Happy in my clam-shell, I had scarcely noticed either.

Now the job was selling it, which could also be killing, and also fun. Now it was time to keep two important appointments, in London and New York, in order to find out, in these twin tough market-places, if the second hard try was any good.

We sailed from Montreal in the *Empress of Scotland,* under Captain J. P. Dobson, at the end of August. I had grown very fond of Dobbie (who among other things had done three years as a wartime commodore of convoys) during previous voyages: he had the liner-captain's talent, highly developed, for being as expert at social navigation (mealtime and dance floor) as he was on the bridge.

All the same, we excused ourselves from sitting at his table, on the ground that (a) I might be working, and therefore late for meals, which was not permissible, and (b) Max was sailing back with us, and might even eat with us now and again.

These were both lies, as Dobbie, a realist, knew. But as a friend he was quite ready to accept them. The fact was that the captain's table was a trap, to be avoided by all voyagers who wanted to choose their company, their daily routine, and above all their wine. Otherwise one could get stuck, for the entire duration of the voyage, with some of the dullest drips who ever put to sea.

There was sure to be a titled couple, proud as show-dogs, acid as lemon rind, empty as old balloons. There was sure to be a lone drunk woman who had a brother or an uncle on the board of directors. There was sure to be a non-stop M.P. with a pet subject (communism, wheat prices, fluoridization, the scourge of campus sex), or a soldier with a howitzer nose and camouflaged eyes, or a Toronto businessman who had made so much money out of metal window frames or plastic cups that he could not be excluded, or a minor diplomat and his major wife, returning to obscurity in farthest Europe.

Above all, there was certain to be one of the vice-presidents on the Canadian sales-and-service side of General Motors, and his wife, of whom all that could be said was that she was the wife of one of the vice-presidents on the Canadian sales-and-service side of General Motors, and had a mink stole, a jangle of jewellery, a face like a Chev radiator, a mouth like a horseshoe with the luck running out, and a conversational style like a show-off parrot, to prove it.

These were the people with whom one could be trapped, for eight days and nights; who gave unavoidable cocktail parties twice a day, and for whom one had to give cocktail parties equally unavoidable; and who dictated, at mealtimes, a deplorable pattern of non-hospitality.

If one wanted champagne at lunch (I was the only one who ever did, until I mentioned it, whereupon everyone clapped their hands), one had to buy it for ten thirsty customers. Next day one received, in return, a glass and a half of sweet Chablis to drink with roast pheasant or rack of lamb.

These were the beautiful people in the ads. . . . Feeling a swine, as usual, I decided that this was Dobbie's bad luck, not mine. We excused ourselves, and ate in selfish state at a banquette for six, and watched the high-ups munching flaming crepes suzettes in wobbling paper hats.

The Atlantic voyage was a great pleasure, and a necessary prelude: smooth as silk, luxurious as a very good hotel, in a ship just the right size which took just the right number of days for such a crossing. We landed at Liverpool on 3 September; a man from Canadian Pacific took care of the baggage and the customs; a man from Claridge's met the boat-train at Euston, and a man from Daimler Hire Company did all the rest. We drove sedately down-town from grimy Euston to immaculate Brook Street, and dived right in.

After that, it was like *The Cruel Sea* all over again, only now I was blasé, and spoiled, and believed that I had earned everything that came my way: everything good, that was—the rest must be the work of envious enemies, of tiny corrupt minds, of bad luck or bad faith. But I kept notes on London and New York, because I had a feeling that it might not happen again for a long time.

Perhaps notes were all it was worth. Reflecting life, they were scrappy and disjointed: hectic and happy, embarrassing, angry, ridiculous, dull and accurate. Sour notes, discordant notes, notes as pure as choir-boys before their little pennies dropped, as magical as music under a night sky, they went like this:

CLARIDGE'S again, thank God: the best hotel in the world, and who argues?

THE MARVELLOUS MATURITY OF LONDON: I would rather be dead in this town than preening my feathers in heaven. The maturity is there, in every theater, opera, play, concert: every whiff of stinking air in Regent Street: every walk down Bond Street to Asprey's: every time you say "Send it round to Claridge's," and Claridge's shell out four hundred pounds C.O.D. and put it on the bill: every time you loiter at Speakers' Corner and hear the Irish and the expatriate blacks and the Communist League of South Stepney kicking the hell out of the British fascist constitution, with a policeman standing by, half-asleep: every time you see one of those fornicating tourists taunting the sentries outside Buckingham Palace or the Horse Guards: every time you sit in the Lobby of the House of Commons, and watch the self-important, show-off roundabout of M.P.s, and know that it works: every time a drunken beggar says "Give us ten bob for a cup of tea," or a girl on a street-corner croaks: "How about it, handsome —I'm very French" (and I'm about as handsome as Ernie Bevin, and she as French as jellied eels): every time a bus queue waits and waits and waits, with never a cross word: every time . . . You hardly need to write about it. You breathe it, swallow it, love it.

"TRIBE" PROMOTION AND PROSPECTS. Edwin Harper has done a slap-up job on the book: sent out one thousand bound-proof copies to booksellers, plus a funny-looking poster apparently made out of reinforced sandpaper, to remind them that Africa is sandy. (Smart, eh?) Hence that whopping advance order. Thirty-three interviews altogether. Did "In Town Tonight" (now on TV) and B.B.C. "Brains Trust," ditto. *Tribe* reprinting already, a couple of days before publication. But just been banned in South Africa—for which I am in mourning for more than a ten-thousand sale. All sorts of people there I wanted to read it. Now it will never get past some creep in the Customs.

REVIEWS. Mostly excellent, including two winners in the *Sunday Times* and the *Times Lit. Supp.* By God, I believe I'm going up in the world! As usual, the good ones exhilarate and the bad ones amuse (Dept. of Defense Mechanism, Quill Pen Division). Some real claw-marks from the *Liverpool Post*, etched in purest critspeak by the same man as snapped his fangs at *The Cruel Sea,* and wrote it off as a smelly old kipper. Acid must be habit-forming.

Another bashing from the *Daily Mail:* "A remarkably high level of gratuitous indecency." (Actually that's rather hard to achieve.) Worst one of all from Nancy Spain, friend of the family and a true artist with the ice-pick. In *Daily Express,* headed "OH DEAR, IT'S *HIS* HEAD HE'S LOST." Drop dead, Spain.*

SOLD 125,000 copies in the first three weeks, and celebrated with a round of visits, an eight-hundred-mile swing round the shires. To Max at school: to Camper and Nicolson at Gosport to see the new Dragon now half-built: to H.M.S. *Victory* across the bay, to pay my respects: to Brixham in Devon to see the replica of the *Mayflower,* nearly finished (I volunteered for the voyage to Plymouth, Massachusetts, but I don't think they want any other writers except skipper Alan Villiers): to Plymouth, our Plymouth, to see the helpful City Librarian, Best-Harris, and collect photostats of some old Armada prints: then back and up to John Moore's at Little Heating—politely called Kemerton Lodge, near Tewkesbury.

Then back to Woolstone to see my father, now eighty-four and blooming: then up to Nottingham to sister Felicity, and her five chattering children, and her ice-cold house. (My bedroom was forty-five degrees in the early A.M.! In Canada it is forbidden to keep dogs at this temperature.) Finally went racing at Newmarket: lost eighty-four pounds.

SAW *The Caine Mutiny,* and talked to Lloyd Nolan (Captain Queeg) afterwards. Splendid performance in every respect. But thank God the U.S. Navy was not really like that at all.

WE ARE THE TARGETS OF THIEVES AND BEGGARS. Interior decorators pile in, likewise portrait painters, bust-sculptors, people who get an (undeclared) ten percent cut on jewellery and clothes sold to us: begging letters enough to make you weep until you start to smell the drains instead.

Men with sure-fire goldmines, men with inventions, men with

---

* She did so, literally, before my very eyes, on Aintree race-course eight years later: crashing in a light plane in the middle of the course, just before the Grand National. I have never again used the expression "Drop dead."

the secret of the Spanish Prisoner's Treasure (heavens, even *I* know about that one!).

Man in Australia who stole substantial sections of *The Cruel Sea,* incorporated them in one of his own paperbacks, and was threatened with prosecution, sent me weepy letter: not his fault, he had been hard-pressed for time. Publisher also sent me weepy letter, with strong flavour of crocodile; could he sell off the rest of the edition if he paid me "a small royalty"? Answer: No. Destroy books. Pay one hundred pounds to the Royal National Life Boat Institution. And *don't try it again.*

Would I like to buy Hitler's Mercedes? Would I like the late Lord Z's steam yacht, a floating palace, A.1 at Lloyd's in 1924? Would I join party of men of sympathetic tastes, chartering airplane to fly to secluded retreat on Island of Rhodes? Would I care to be included in new universal *Who's Who,* Men of Global Distinction, now being actively compiled in Liechtenstein? Subscription only twenty-five pounds, with my name embossed in genuine gold leaf on the cover.

Best of all, the man with the Rembrandt. He was a big bulging man with a very brisk line of talk. "A portrait, I suppose you'd call it. Twelve thousand pounds. Of course I haven't got it here, it's under heavy guard, but I've brought the photograph to show." He unrolled a tattered print. It looked more like a Gainsborough. "Of course it's a genuine Rembrandt!" the man said. "Look at the photograph! It's been certified!" "What?—the portrait has been certified?" "No, no, no—the *photograph*'s been certified." He read out an inscription on the back: " 'This is certified as a true photograph of the portrait attributed to Rembrandt.' There you are! Can't do better than that, can you?"

I said I didn't really want a Rembrandt. "Well, what *do* you want?" It was clear that I must want something, staying at Claridge's, all that stuff in the newspapers. He thought, briefly. "Tell you what. All these new countries—they're all starting up their own airlines, right? Well, I've got, I mean, I can *put my hands on,* a lot of surplus R.A.F. flying boats. They'd do for a start, wouldn't they? Twelve of them. In South Rhodesia. They've been impounded, but *you* can get round that. I read in the paper, you're a diplomat. There's no engines, of course." "Of course." "But I can always get you *engines.*"

I had to say no again. Undaunted: "Didn't I read in the paper, your wife collects old paperweights?" I said that it must be someone else's wife. "Well, maybe. But if you *want* paperweights—"

It seemed a shame not to buy. Not to buy from him, anyway; we bought from everyone else. Bought three minks from Calman Links—and that's a very expensive rhyme.

FILM MEN John and James Woolf ("The Wolves," as Christine called them, perhaps unfairly, though they did get *Esther Costello* for five thousand pounds) gave me succulent lunch at Les Ambassadeurs, then produced Rolls-Royce and chauffeur to take me down to Shepperton (or Pinewood or Elstree: these British film studios are a little blurred) to watch *Esther* being filmed. Talked to American director David Miller, then to Rossano Brazzi and Joan Crawford, the two stars involved.

Rossano Brazzi a small, very good-looking, *soigné,* perfectly barbered and tailored man who could make anyone else (such as a writer, even when dressed by Strickland's of Savile Row, Hawes and Curtis, and Sulka) look and feel like a country boy in his first whip-cord suit. But reminded me of Ivor Novello—the myth of masculine appeal rather than the fact. Married to enormous, delightful wife, Lydia, whose cooking later proved exquisite and whose manner was often pure Wagnerian soprano crossed with doting mother. Would clasp her hands, and intone: "Ross-*ah*-no! Your feet have become wet! You will *die* in this climate!" Then build up his strength with seven different kinds of *pasta.* But he just right as handsome swine of the old school.

Joan Crawford was something else again. Her descent on England had been the subject of usual snide newspaper comment: "Arrived with 28 suitcases, 48 film costumes, one trunk of suits, one trunk of furs, and a millionaire husband." She was just as I had pictured: tough, professional, as sweet as molasses if she was enjoying herself, brutally indifferent if not. I think she had the old-style Hollywood view of writers as something between errand-boys and resident drunks. But she was excellent in the short scene I watched being filmed: she had to cry, and when the moment came the tears flowed readily and almost genuinely, like Niagara switched on to meet a tourist deadline.

I complimented her afterwards. "I can cry any time!" she declared, looking at me as if I had charged her with arrant incompetence. "All I have to do is hit myself twice—*here!*" She gave herself a slap and a jab, somewhere between her sculptured bosom and her invisible navel. Immediately, large tears rolled down her cheeks. "I'm a pro," she said.

Esther ought to be a good film; has the necessary aura of competence, prestige, and lots of money. By contrast Ealing Studios just folded as a separate entity, without a murmur except from sad orphans such as Charles Frend who will be homeless. In future Ealing will be under the thumb of M.G.M., will share distribution with them. In practice, they are dead. One gathers that Michael Balcon will be found floating the right way up.

Going out to dine with Lydia and Rossano, had a slight car crash at Hyde Park Corner; a Green Line bus plowed into our stationary back, giving everyone what is called "the whiplash effect." Had to cancel visit to Cheltenham Festival, and the chance to mingle with such elite as (wait for it) Compton Mackenzie, John Betjeman, Richard Gordon, C. Day Lewis, Edith Sitwell, Colin Wilson, Sir Arthur Bryant, and Ludovic Kennedy. I never meet anybody!

On our dinner arrival, very late, Lydia Brazzi distraught, but in her best style. "Ross-*ah*-no! They are wounded! Come quickly!"

Stuck in Bond Street in the sort of traffic jam which made a taxi the most expensive residential unit in the world, I was loudly hailed by an elegant pedestrian who was out-walking us. It was Moura Lympany, one of the children's godmothers. "Nicholas!" she shouted. "Darling, I'm having a baby!" Before I could answer, the traffic and the stalled taxi ground forwards. "Bad luck, sir," said the driver.

FED UP with endless feuding and screaming (What do you have to do to win a medal? What do you do to avoid firing-squad at dawn? How do you make sure of dawn anyway? Prisoner was shot for his own protection), took off for Liverpool and Trearddur Bay. (Diagnosed as "return to womb." Could be. I say, porter! What's my womb number?) Away for four days, copped in Chester for parking all night outside the Grosvenor Hotel. No fun, but no fun anyway.

SERETSE KHAMA allowed back to Bechuanaland as "private citizen." Well done, that man!—and good luck to him.

PENGUIN published that other book with considerable flapping of wings. First print of 250,000—and, from them, their first-ever illustrated cover.

PEOPLE & PARTIES & POKER. London finished up with a swing; there would never be another bash quite like this one (though, after a breathing-space of eight days at sea and four in Canada, there was still the New York circuit to come). Johnny Metcalf gave farewell party at his elegant shack on Charles Street; then Moira Lister; then Cassell board-room lunch; then Eric Ambler at Pelham Crescent, next door to admired actor Emlyn Williams.

Delicious chance meeting here with never-met heroine of twenty-three years ago. Was talking with handsome-looking woman of about forty; suddenly realized who she was—ballet dancer Baronova, last seen as a chubbyish girl of seventeen or eighteen, one of glamorous trio of "little girls" (Baronova, Riabouchinska, and Toumanova), the darlings of Ballets Russes de Monte Carlo of 1933. Could hear far-off, haunting echoes of *Les Sylphides* and *Présages* all the time we were talking—which was more than an enchanted hour.

Then poker, the last of seven games, in a setting suitable to this most civilized of pastimes: play from eight till ten, a cold supper in the best tradition of Claridge's kitchens, and then on till 1 A.M. I finished about even—i.e., didn't lose more than one hundred pounds on the series.

Cassell's gave me, by way of a farewell present, a beautiful silver statuette of a galleon under full sail, but with a female firmly planted at the helm. Once again, could be.

Claridge's bill, £1,853 for six and a half weeks. Of all creditors, they are the most welcome. Sailed *Empress of Scotland*, 19 October, Dobbie again, and George Formby as a stimulating fellow-voyager. We thought he should finish ship's concert with "He Played His Ukulele as the Ship Went Down," but Beryl, prudent wife-manager, thought not.

New York went at shutter-like speed: now you see it, now you don't, now you don't want to, now you are cursing fate for snatching something away before it has been fully savoured. A rush job to get away from Ottawa, where eight weeks' mail had piled up, the whole water-pump system had broken down (entailing $1,035 worth of rude components such as brass nipples, female adaptors, male elbows, flexible ball sockets, and aircocks), and the Bank of Montreal was quietly steaming on top of a towering overdraft.

On the way south (total mileage, 452) broke the journey at Utica on the edge of the New York Thruway (sorry, that's how they spell it). Note: if you arrive at a motel in a Rolls, the price of a room jumps from ten dollars to eighteen dollars. Next morning, a peerless drive down a half-section of the best road in the world: 240 miles of six-lane motorway, superbly engineered so as *not* to be boring: with carefully calculated slopes and long curves, beautiful fall colours on cunning display, the Hudson River as companion, and the Catskill Mountains as the last backdrop. (The whole highway stretches from the Pennsylvania border, south of Buffalo, to New York, 496 miles without a stop-light, a crossroads, or a check of any sort.) The "lane discipline" was impressive; so were the cops who jumped on any offenders.

Some of this is old Indian country, with funny names as labels for the sophisticated "service areas": Oneida, Indian Castle, Mohawk, Iroquois, Chittenango, Seneca, Canojoharie. A steady seventy miles per hour turned this leg of the trip into a four-hour journey, and the score at the end for the use of this paragon, $4.10.

Stayed at the St. Regis instead of the Pierre, which had not got the *precise* choice of suite available. But they put us on the sixteenth floor, which meant it was my turn to be choosy, and we transferred to much lower down: I simply could not stand the height, and at the first dawn had to lock myself in the bathroom so as not to jump out of the window. Don't know what's happening in this area of nerves. Domestically, they have been christened "the vapours," but by Christ they are real.

Found that the Morrow boys had promoted the book to such good effect that it was in the best-seller list three days before publication: booksellers jumping the gun, illegal but enjoyable, involving forty-six thousand copies and a third printing already. (With that flying start, it reached Number One at a useful moment, nine days before Christmas, was then knocked out by juicy newcomer *Peyton Place*, but stayed somewhere in the tabernacle for twenty-one weeks.)

Front-page reviews in *The New York Times* Book Review and

the *Chicago Sunday Tribune* (what odd items make an author's eyes shine). A real stinker, as usual, in the *New Yorker,* from their lop-sided little ball of venom who won't get a plug from me, beginning with a superior twitter: "Those who have suspected for some time that Mr. Nicholas Monsarrat fluked his literary reputation by writing *The Cruel Sea . . .* may feel confirmed in their suspicions by his new offering." But many of the other reviews rewarmed our shrivelled cockles, particularly in the advertising department.

Eleven interviews and broadcasts, but this time no TV at all; perhaps they've gone off the boil as far as writers peddling their own books are concerned. Recorded for Doubleday Book Concert, "Luncheon at Sardi's," and "Breakfast with Tex and Jinx" (she the beautiful ex-film star Jinx Falkenburg). Funny way to make a living, on both sides. Party for booksellers, party by P.E.N. Club, party in Boston, lunch-party in Philadelphia given by the *Saturday Evening Post* (where I actually heard someone say: "Let's run up the flag and see who salutes").

At the end of lunch, silence fell, and the boss, in a short speech of welcome, asked me if I had anything in mind which might suit their magazine. Off the cuff, I suggested an article, a global survey of American unpopularity, and how it could possibly be reconciled with America's supremely generous record in foreign aid. Round the table, about twenty-two pairs of eyes were watching, not me but the head man. Felt that if he smiled, everyone else would smile, say "Sensational!" "Oh boy!" "Sounds just great!" He did not smile; no one saluted my little flag; after weighty silence the man said: "I had in mind something in the fiction field."

Willis Wing told me funny story on the train going back, one of the canon of Sam Goldwyn apocrypha. At a script conference, it was found that the name of the hero had not yet been settled. Someone said: "Let's go for something plain. Let's call him Joe." "No, no!" said Goldwyn. "Every Tom, Dick, and Harry is called Joe!"

Party down at United Nations given by old South African External Affairs chum, "Pot" Steward. Still called "Pot." How do you learn to say "Please call me Pot" in fifty languages? Best thing about the U.N. is that spectacular East River view. Then

the building. Then the people. A thousand self-important, inflated nothings still add up to zero.

But technically, not a good time to be selling books in New
York, or anywhere else on the continent. They were in the throes
of their election (Eisenhower *v.* Stevenson) and until 7 November
hadn't much time for anything else. After 7 November, still arguing about what went wrong or, for the slight majority, what went
right. And the big Suez Canal row was on, all this time: a shattering point of debate and preoccupation, with everyone taking
sides and all of them seemingly anti-British. Even the cab-drivers
wouldn't talk to the British while the worst was going on. Self
relentlessly pro-Israel, anti-Arab, and feel likely to remain so forever.

For a change of scene, gorgeous party given by Drue and Jack
Heinz. She sent me guest-list beforehand ("But don't change your
mind!") on very superior dark-blue notepaper from which I learned
that the Heinz family motto is *Veritatis et Aequitatis Tenax*
(roughly, Stick to truth and fair play). Her list started strongly,
and so continued:

> Greta Garbo
> Vera Zorina
> The John Roosevelts
> The David and John Rockefellers
> Sir Pierson and Lady Dixon
> Budd Schulberg
> The Jack Warners of Warner Bros.
> Santha Rama Rau
> The Oscar Hammersteins
> The Harvey Firestones
> The Gimbels
> Etc.

Couldn't swear to meeting any of these prestigious people
except Etc. and Budd Schulberg, since the principal party gim-
mick was pink champagne flowing lavishly from a series of beautiful—well, they looked like glass tea urns as designed by someone
like Fabergé, strategically placed round the apartment. Schulberg
a disappointment: a little top-heavy with vast success, though his
Scott Fitzgerald play, based on novel *The Disenchanted,* which
we had just seen, was enough to turn anyone's head. But did enjoy

session with Alistair Cooke, witty and charming man whose radio reports from America I've listened to for nearly twenty years, and before that, when he was B.B.C. film critic in the early Thirties. He gloomy over Suez—about the only guest who was.

By contrast, the final Morrow party something of a shambles. Good start: Thayer Hobson greeted me with: "Well, what's it like to be an avuncular, patronizing bore?" and when I queried this, though politely, as became the guest of honour, he explained: "I just read a *rather* unfavourable review in the *Sydney Morning Herald.*" "Didn't they say anything good?" "Oh, sure!" Thayer pulled a slip of paper from his pocket. " 'A gorgeous hunk of novel'—how about that?" "You better go on." " 'Five hundred and thirty-eight pages of muscular prose, rippling with self-as-surance, swollen with athletic vigour, and invincibly wooden-headed.' Would you like a drink?" "I believe I would."

But the general style of the evening, staged at the Waldorf, grew cramped. Isabelle arrived in spirited mood, and by God she had competition. Halfway through, discovered I had become a lone bachelor. When? How? Where? Sped back to the St. Regis. Only witness the doorman, who reported: "The lady said 'Grand Central Station.' " You can get to a hell of a lot of places from Grand Central.

5.

What was right, and what was wrong? It was time to plot the graph.

The account book showed that I had earned £236,000 since all the flurry started five years earlier. Where was it? It had certainly gone: on taxes, on living, on showing off. The era of constructive penury involved in subsisting on my dollar salary and ordering everything else from England had now passed away; I had been told, officially, that I was free to spend my royalties, from whatever source, as and how I wished, and the result was that I now had an overdraft of ninety-one thousand dollars. A lot of it was tied up in the house; a lot was not.

I had signed over eight hundred checks that year: two a day, fifteen a week, sixty-seven a month—whichever way one looked at it, it was a powerful, sustained effort of writing.

"Total: $9,562.89," Mrs. Macdonell noted at the end of one month, and added a cautionary note: "To this should be added: Interest on bank overdraft." I knew well enough what that meant: another six hundred dollars.

Then there were taxes, taxes, taxes. There was a time when I had built up thirty thousand pounds in Tax Reserve Certificates, ready for the bite; the bite had already swallowed it whole, and was still hungry for more. Towards the end of this year, there had been added an enormous extra complication; a big income tax dispute, not between me and anyone else, but between Canada and the United Kingdom, with me in the middle, facing both ways with a stupid smile and no effective answer.

The engagement could be set out briefly, though its ramifications and its consequential miseries were to prove endless, for the next fifteen years and beyond. After I had been in Canada for three years, paying all my taxes, as a diplomat whose constructive residence was always England, to the United Kingdom, I was suddenly informed that only my diplomatic salary should have been subject to U.K. taxation; all the rest, the Canadian Department of National Revenue now claimed, should have been paid to Canada. What was I going to do about that?

All I could do was to stand quietly to one side while the point was argued. It was, after all, a dispute between governments and their departments: God knows I had paid the taxes promptly enough, and if I had paid them into the wrong till, then that could surely be remedied.

Indeed, that was how it happened; the U.K. Government surrendered the point gracefully, and refunded most of my payments, and I was then newly assessed in Canada. The Canadians then slapped my innocent face with a penalty for three years' "tax delinquency"—i.e., non-payment to *them,* whatever else I had done with the money—for forty-five thousand dollars.

In spite of the best efforts of Cooper Brothers, my new allies, this unjust decision stood, and indeed still stands. It was futile to argue that I had already paid the taxes to the U.K., and that they had accepted them, while later agreeing that they were not so entitled; futile to argue that I was not "delinquent" in any moral sense, since I had always paid up as ordered, and could not know that I had been paying the wrong man.

The *fact* was that I had failed to put in a Canadian tax return for three years. There was, it seemed, "no discretion."

Down on the enormous bill, just for staying alive, went another forty-five thousand dollars; and down, in a private diary of despair, went the conviction that now I would never really catch up.

Just for once, it was not my fault! But try realizing a little ready cash on *that* conviction.

What was wrong continued with niggling little things, as annoying as acne when one has done nothing to deserve it. After the pump troubles came the tree troubles; an army of "tree surgeons" had to descend upon Stone House, to lop, prune, cut down, bolster up, and generally nurse back to health many of our beautiful elms and maples, which had looked so stalwart when I bought the place and were now, it seemed, a sad and sickly grove of invalids.

Then came heating troubles, to coincide with winter; the massive boiler in the basement, which warmed the entire house and the garage, and drank a thousand dollars' worth of prime fuel oil a year, suddenly developed such a fearful fit of the staggers that most of it had to be ripped out and replaced.

Outside, in the garden, while burning off some under-brush, Dinty Moore and I between us managed to set fire to a stand of fir-trees quite near the house. They went up in flames, like quick-burning torches: menacing for one sweating afternoon, irreplaceable thereafter.

What was wrong continued and ended with the darkening domestic scene. While the wounds were still raw, I roughed out a long, well-documented piece about this era of destruction, with an acid content suitable to a writer who could no longer write what he hoped to, even in his own barred corner of the zoo: who had done his best, and beaten his brains out in the process, and felt there was blame to be shared as well as shouldered. One might as well keep the dust off the typewriter keys, somehow, anyhow. But I scrapped it.

Compassion for the once-loved person, gratitude for the always-loved past, warred with furious rage that so much had been tossed down the drain; and compassion won—as it should, if one was ever to reach heaven, or even to stay alive until, in due course, one was dead meat instead of live spirit. It would not have won in the crucifying season of 1956.

Life then was a giant sleeping-pill, an over-stimulant, a stomach pump, a mess: a yearning for the tender past, and a bleak mourning for the present which was being eaten, drunk, misted over, fouled up, hacked to pieces, and thrown away. Life was Equanil for me, the mild essential tranquillizer, on the prescription for which my doctor had written: "Take two as necessary when flying." How many when crawling, doctor? He did not have to tell me.

Life was a near-resident psychiatrist, and a range of funny, bitter jokes about his ministrations, and a whole new gallery of Catholic onlookers to people the clinic: "Father Figure won't like it. Mother Fixation is not at all pleased. Brother Libido may have to leave." Life was a Swedish masseur, twice a week, to bash us both about. We did not need a Swedish masseur, either.

Life was violence, and spells of warm happiness, and the sniping crackle of rifle-fire again. Life was a house full of nurses, a departing cook, a couple of children enthralled, as all children should be, with recurrent dramatic change. Life was snapping dogs, and snapping people.

Life was war and peace, treachery and confederate delight. Life was *"Balls!"* to end a dinner-party argument—and the dinner-party as well.

Life was savage battling, truce-lines passionately sworn to, swift betrayal, white flags presently spattered by so much flying filth that not all the multitudinous seas could make them usable·again.

Life was a spectral voice from a balcony above, sliding down like sleet into the moonlight: "You want a divorce? You'll have to be a ——— good provider!"

I was a fairly good provider—everybody, however inept or wretched, can do *something*—but at this pace it would not last very long. I could not write in this turmoil; I felt I had shot my bolt with *The Tribe,* and in fact I wrote nothing except twelve short stories in the next four years. I knew already that this was going to happen, like a man, sick but sensible, who acknowledges in the most private part of his mind: "This is more than an occasional bad turn. Aspirin is not enough. Spring may not come again. I have cancer."

Having this cancer, the only thing to do was to shrink down very small, to count the blessings instead of all the rest, and to contemplate, with the humble, penitent eye of poverty-in-riches, what was right.

What was right seemed a very small tally, and so entirely self-centered that it lacked any pretensions to maturity. But it would have to do.

I could read other people's novels, and, living in a world devoted to lists, I compiled a list of these also, and solemnly, slowly set out to walk again with the men and women who in the past had been admired companions. That autumn and winter, I assembled and began to read:

> Death of a Hero and All Men Are Enemies: Richard Alding-
> ton.
> Invitation to the Waltz and The Weather in the Streets:
> Rosamund Lehmann.
> Europa and Europa in Limbo: Robert Briffault.
> Number One: John Dos Passos.
> A Farewell to Arms: Ernest Hemingway.
> Babbitt and Elmer Gantry: Sinclair Lewis.
> Wasteland: Jo Sinclair.
> Growth of the Soil: Knut Hamsun.
> The Razor's Edge: Somerset Maugham.
> The Edwardians: V. Sackville-West.
> The Thinking Reed: Rebecca West.
> Brideshead Revisited and A Handful of Dust: Evelyn Waugh.
> The Grapes of Wrath: John Steinbeck.

They were not all great; perhaps they were not all good; but they were the ones which had taken the imagination when their stars first rose, and, rising again, they brought solid comfort from a more generous past. It was curious how some of them went in pairs. Would there come a time when people would re-read my books in pairs? Not at this rate.

I could listen to music, and the music I wanted to hear had turned profoundly sad; it seemed that the hurt within could only be matched by another man telling me his troubles, and making them so moving, so desolate, that one ache assuaged another. There was a secondary sadness here: the fact that I could not write music myself. Often it seemed the only language, the universal tongue, and the most beautiful. There could be no dialogue to match the second movement of the *Kreutzer* Sonata, no terrors like the fearful Witches' Sabbath nightmares of Berlioz in *Symphonie Fantastique*.

But now it was time for the lamenting piano and the guitar, the voices of bereavement. My two "perfect" symphonies, the Mozart G Minor and the Brahms No. 1, remained in their jackets, guests not invited to this wake. They were not sad enough. They still spoke of hope.

I could play with the two little boys, and reassure them, and myself. I could mow the lawn, and find in this repetitious chore, continuing hour after hour, another sort of music, another small accomplishment.

I could collect the letters of Admiral Lord Nelson.

By now I had fifty-two of these, assembled with reverent care over the last few years, with the help of C. R. Sawyer's in London; and if it was not the finest private collection in the world, I liked to think that it was. Usually they came on the market in ones and twos, though sometimes there was a substantial clear-out at auction, and Sawyer's went into action on my behalf.

One happy day we bought fourteen of them at Sotheby's, for a total of £1,172, and they included a rare prize, as sad as I could hope to find in the most evil hour—one of the first letters written by Nelson with his left hand, in crabbed despair, when his right had been shattered and with it, he feared, his whole future.

There was one written to Lieutenant-General John Graves Simcoe, the first Lieutenant-Governor of Upper Canada; dated 1803, it was on black-edged notepaper, Nelson being, with the utmost delicacy, in mourning for Sir William Hamilton. There were several written between 1800 and 1803 to Sir Alexander Ball, Governor of Malta after the French were ousted and the Maltese opted for British rule.

There were three from Carlisle Bay in Barbados ("Barbarous Island") when he was the twenty-six-year-old captain of the frigate

Boreas; and one to Lady Hamilton ("My dearest Emma. . . . Be assured that I am, etc. Nelson and Bronte").

There was the "Plan of Attack" for Trafalgar, to be circulated to his captains, that "band of brothers" who loved this man as much as I now did myself; and, to crown the collection, two written in the cabin of H.M.S. *Victory* on 9 and 10 October 1805—eleven days before Trafalgar: the first to Vice-Admiral Collingwood ("My dear Coll.") and the second to Captain Black-wood of the *Euryalus,* in command of the look-out frigates off Cadiz.

To read, and to touch gently, these letters, revived the fiercest of pride and admiration. In particular, it was wonderful to note how that pitiful left-hand scrawl formed gradually into something firm and free again—like the birth of a new and even braver man. Reading them, I felt at one with the "band of brothers," the captains of ships-of-the-line with such ringing names as *Royal Sovereign, Agamemnon, Tonnant, Bellerophon, Revenge, Téméraire,* and *Dreadnought,* in their hero-worship and their boundless respect.

I spent, with the same sort of pride, nearly five thousand pounds on these my fifty-two jewels. They were all sold, in a sudden alimony squeeze, a few years later, for two thousand pounds; and that was a defiling day indeed.

If I could not write, I could at least plan what I hoped to write; and what I had in mind now was the longest novel ever written about the sea and about sailors; covering nearly four hundred years of maritime venture, from the Spanish Armada in 1588 to the completion of the St. Lawrence Seaway—the farthest foray (2,250 miles) ever made by ships into the heart of a continent—in 1958.

I wanted to tell the story—the whole story—of what sailors had done to open up the known world: by charting its oceans, by fighting, by commerce, by the great voyages of exploration and plunder.

The book would have ships, from Spanish galleon to nuclear-powered tanker; and men, from Drake to Captain Cook, from Nelson to Samuel Cunard, from Pepys to Thor Heyerdahl; and stories, from Henry Hudson's voyage in 1610 to the China Clippers of 1840, from the *Chesapeake* versus the *Shannon* to the

Ark Royal versus U.81; from the "Black-birding" slavers of 1807 to Samuel Plimsoll and his cattle-ships; from the pirates of Port Royal to the last stewards' strike at Southampton.

I also had a "motto" for the whole work, from *The Tempest:* "He has suffered a sea-change, Into something rich and strange"; and a recurrent theme: "He who commands the Sea commands the Situation" (Themistocles, admiral of the Athenian Fleet, 480 B.C.); and I had a title. One day I would write it: all six hundred thousand words of it.*

Marcel Proust's *Remembrance of Things Past* was 1,307,000 words long; Tolstoy's *War and Peace* a mere 490,000. Somewhere in between. . . .

All this play-acting, minuscule endeavour, and fiddling about could always be brought up short—between the third and the fourth whisky and soda, the fifth and sixth cigar, Chopin's Opus 55, No. 1 in F Minor and No. 2 in E Flat—by the fact of non-achievement. Apart from certain dreams of happiness which had been stifled by a sackcloth pillow, other ambitions, formulated long ago in the spring of hope, and latterly swift to rise, were now fading out of sight. It was once more a case of now you see it, now you don't, and now I didn't see it.

Long ago I had made a list, another list, which was beginning to look as silly as a fat Lord Mayor stripped down to his mildewed chain of office and a grubby pair of shorts. It was becoming embarrassing to contemplate it, though very good for the soul to recognize and then to scrub out the ones which could never happen now.

1.   To ride the winner of the Grand National.
2.   To win the America's Cup (J Class).
3.   To be a Member of Parliament.
4.   To write a world-wide best-seller.
5.   To be invited to join the Athenaeum Club.
6.   To get a knighthood.

---

* Four years later, I promised Cassell's that it would be the one after *The Nylon Pirates* (1960). After nine other books, I re-promised them, as recently as May 1970, that it would be the one after the one after this.

7. To win the Nobel Prize for Literature.
8. To receive the Order of Merit.

These were all honourable goals: "A man's reach," said Robert Browning, "should exceed his grasp, Or what's a heaven for?"; but embarrassing was now the word. . . . "Time is the dog that barks us all to hell," and already, so early that it was ridiculous and shameful, time was running out.

Christmas. . . . The white stuff was here again, as certain Canadians phrased it, fearing, like superstitious Africans, to name the name of their enemy. Overnight, the snow had fallen in a soft cataract; now it stretched down from my study window to the Aylmer Road, in a broad sloping carpet, gleaming white, shining under the pale sun, reflecting ten million tiny crystals. It would be there till next spring.

We drove across the U.S. border, and thirty miles beyond to Plattsburg on Lake Champlain, to pick up a basset-hound puppy which had been marooned at a railway depot on its way up from Connecticut. When we found it, it was small, immensely mournful, incontinent, and ravenous. Chekhov seemed the only name for it.

We sent out five hundred Christmas cards, the list being confined to our very dearest friends.

The main Christmas present was a new Plymouth, a long, not bad-looking car with far too much horsepower, painted in a young-at-heart shade technically known as Gulf Stream Blue. Driving it home, I became aware that it was overheating dramatically; presently smoke, and then flames, began to pour out from the radiator grille. I swept blindly into the nearest garage, where the young man at the pumps, not at all put out, threw open the hood and doused the fire with a bucket of sand. A loose fuel connection, spraying petrol onto hot metal, was the culprit.

"So that's the new Plymouth," the young man said.

I hoped that, both as a car and a present, it would last a little longer than all this suggested.

"How was Christmas, Scrooge-wise?" someone at the club asked me. It was not bad, not bad at all. The Spirit of Christmas Past must have taken a hand, with the slam and tinkle of the cash-register to mute the clanking chains. God bless us all, said Tiny Tool.

New Year. . . . Suddenly the house was *not* full of nurses, masseurs, psychiatrists, and thunder-faced servants. Instead, all was sweetness, and light, and even love, and we were giving the party of the year on New Year's Eve.

Earlier, Mrs. Macdonell had made out the final three lists of 1956: 120 first-choice guests, 45 spares as possible replacements, and an *aide-memoire* for the boss as the bits fell into place:

Address List	Completed
Invitation cards	Delivered
Invitations sent out	O.K.
Notices for driveway	Delivered
Piano	O.K. From Lawrence Freiman
Public address system	O.K. From Don Cruikshank
Band	O.K. Champ Champagne plus quintet. Contract with Musicians' Union signed
Flood-lighting for parking area	Jerry plus electrician
Snow-plow, parking area	Dinty
Erect bandstand	Dinty
Police	1 on gate, 1 motor-cycle patrolman will check periodically
Beds for band	Ordered
Champagne	Checked
Barmen	3. Double wages for N.Y. Eve agreed
Carpets lifted	10 A.M. Dec. 30
Additional glassware	Hired. We pay insurance
Coat-hangers	200 on loan from Canadian Legion
Ice	8 × 50-lb blocks, due 5 P.M. 31.12.

After that it was easy. The fancy dress ordained was "Old Film Characters," and old film characters arrived by the cartload. There were three Keystone Cops (among them Jack Heinz, who flew in from Pittsburgh), and two hideous versions of Harpo Marx, and one of Groucho, chomping on *my* cigars. Israel Ambassador Michael Comay and Lawrence Freiman, Ottawa's Mr. Selfridge and the town's most civilizing influence as well, both came as Sheiks of Araby; Yousuf Karsh was a sad-eyed Jackie Coogan.

The sight of my bank manager, Ted Royce, as the evil Dr. Fu Manchu was daunting; so was a certain Quebec intellectual (anyone in this province who could dial a seven-digit phone number was a Quebec intellectual) as Charlie Chaplin. But we had George Arliss with a kiss-curl, Theda Bara with an asp in her navel, Laurel and Hardy, a stone-faced Buster Keaton, and a Fugitive from a Chain Gang, to comfort us.

There were a few Mack Sennett bathing belles. But most of the women seemed to have taken a wild stab at Pola Negri.

The band began its eight-hour stint. Ottawa's only Bad Girl, and very welcome on that account, made her entrance, wearing the sort of Circassian slave outfit favoured by film starlets *en route* for the casting-couch. She looked very fetching, and I complimented her.

"It's my *après*-screw," she said.

The band played on. Dinner was served. A gate-crasher, son of a U.S. diplomat, was thrown out; having pruned the guest-list till the bones showed through, I was not in the mood for immunity. At midnight the two children were brought down by Katie. Sleepy-eyed, puzzled, and then entranced, they made the rounds, Marc under his own steam, Anthony in the arms of god-mother Moura Lympany.

"Isn't it bad for them?" a Spock-minded matron inquired.

"Oh, I hope so."

The band played on. There were only four drunks, and they could have been forecast from the form-book. People began to leave at three. Some people never left. At dawn the motor-cycle cop, making his last rounds, drove into an illuminated Christmas tree and fused all the lights. At 8 A.M. band-leader Champ Champagne laid aside his melodious, tireless, sweet-as-molasses clarinet and asked: "Can I help you with that hair dye?"

My jet-black hair, glossy and lacquered, was still unimpaired, appropriate to the oldest living juvenile lead in the business.

Breakfast was served, and the last of the Louis Roederer (the last that I was going to provide, anyway). Champ Champagne still toiled away at my scalp, with soap and water, petrol, melted butter, and a nail-brush. It became clear that he would never succeed, and that I must remain a raven-haired beauty, well on into 1957.

Early-rising Jack Heinz, nursing a wine-glassful of chilled to-mato-juice ("Oh God!" I had to tell him; "It's *local!*"), said: "That was quite a thrash. You know, I *like* Canada!"

Late-rising Drue Heinz, wandering down later, more beautiful than any woman had a right to be at such an hour, said: "Darling —your hair!"

Champ Champagne, still the most dedicated man of this or any other crusade, said: "What say we try that stuff they put on locks?"

Thus, on New Year's morning, in a positive soup of symbolism, staking my claim to be the only rate-payer on the north side of the Aylmer Road who had to miss the Governor-General's New Year *Levée* because, even with the help of a Negro band-leader, he could not get the black dye out of his hair, I rested my case.

In spite of imperial elevation, I knew that it had only been a breathing-space, a dividend for which the fugitive cashier would later be held accountable. It would last as long as the blessed bubbles, and no longer. I knew also that Lord Byron, club foot, incest, brooding genius and all, still had it right:

> "He seems
> To have seen better days, as who has not
> Who has seen yesterday."